The Sniffy Way!

Here's what makes Sniffy, the Virtual Rat™ such a valuable addition to any learning and behavior class.

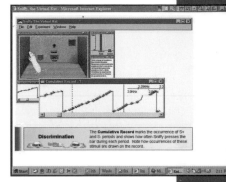

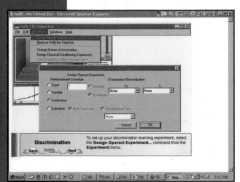

"For a typical undergraduate learning class, Sniffy has got to be much easier to use than live rats… If the aim to allow students to see certain training paradigms and principles in action, Sniffy Pro does a great job! And no muss, no fuss.

In addition to a mid-term and final, I give quizzes in class and homework. In the past, homework has consisted of reading a research article and answering questions on method and concepts. When I used Sniffy, it was as homework assignments (several Sniffy exercises per assignment).

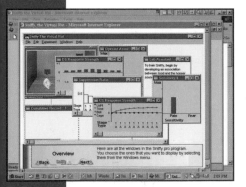

The students ran Sniffy on their own home computers or in one of the various computer labs on campus. Most worked on their own computers.

Student response to Sniffy was great. They really felt it helped them understand the lecture material. In the past, students would get hung up on inhibitory classical conditioning, so I made sure that those exercises were assigned. There seemed to be a much better understanding as a result."

Ingrid B. Johanson
Florida Atlantic University

Test Drive Sniffy on the Web at:
http://psychology.wadsworth.com/sniffy/

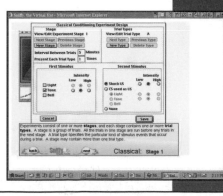

www.wadsworth.com

wadsworth.com is the World Wide Web site for Wadsworth and is your direct source to dozens of online resources.

At *wadsworth.com* you can find out about supplements, demonstration software, and student resources. You can also send email to many of our authors and preview new publications and exciting new technologies.

wadsworth.com
Changing the way the world learns®

FIFTH EDITION

Learning & Behavior

Paul Chance

THOMSON

™

WADSWORTH

Australia • Canada • Mexico • Singapore • Spain • United Kingdom • United States

THOMSON

WADSWORTH

Psychology Editor: *Marianne Taflinger*
Assistant Editor: *Dan Moneypenny*
Editorial Assistant: *Nicole Root*
Technology Project Manager: *Darin Derstine*
Marketing Manager: *Kathleen Morgan*
Marketing Assistant: *Laurel Anderson*
Advertising Project Manager:
  Samantha Cabaluna
Project Manager, Editorial Production:
  Paula Berman

Print/Media Buyer: *Kris Waller*
Permissions Editor: *Stephanie Keough-Hedges*
Production Service and Compositor:
  Scratchgravel Publishing Services
Copy Editor: *Patterson Lamb*
Illustrator: *Diane Chance*
Cover Designer: *Vernon T. Boes*
Cover Image: *Gail Mooney/Masterfile*
Text and Cover Printer: *Phoenix Color Corp*

Printed in the United States of America

3   4   5   6   7   06   05   04

For more information about our products, contact us at:

**Thomson Learning Academic
Resource Center**
1-800-423-0563

For permission to use material from this text, contact us by:

Phone: 1-800-730-2214
Fax: 1-800-730-2215
Web: http://www.thomsonrights.com

Library of Congress Control Number:
  2002107154

ISBN 0-534-59868-4

Wadsworth/Thomson Learning
10 Davis Drive
Belmont, CA 94002-3098
USA

Asia
Thomson Learning
5 Shenton Way #01-01
UIC Building
Singapore 068808

Australia
Nelson Thomson Learning
102 Dodds Street
South Melbourne, Victoria 3205
Australia

Canada
Nelson Thomson Learning
1120 Birchmount Road
Toronto, Ontario M1K 5G4
Canada

Europe/Middle East/Africa
Thomson Learning
High Holborn House
50/51 Bedford Row
London WC1R 4LR
United Kingdom

Latin America
Thomson Learning
Seneca, 53
Colonia Polanco
11560 Mexico D.F.
Mexico

Spain
Paraninfo Thomson Learning
Calle/Magallanes, 25
28015 Madrid, Spain

For Arno H. Luker

Contents

CHAPTER 3   Pavlovian Conditioning   66

CHAPTER 4   Pavlovian Applications   *105*

CHAPTER 5   Operant Reinforcement   *133*

CHAPTER 8   Vicarious Learning   *264*

CHAPTER 9 **Generalization, Discrimination, and Stimulus Control** *302*

CHAPTER 10 **Schedules of Reinforcement**   *346*

CHAPTER 11 **Forgetting**   *388*

CHAPTER 12 The Limits of Learning 425

Preface

When I submitted the manuscript for this edition of *Learning and Behavior* to Marianne Taflinger, my long-time editor at Wadsworth, she expressed surprise at my enthusiasm for the project after so many years. Actually, I am more enthusiastic about the subject of learning and behavior now than I was almost 25 years ago when I began writing the first edition. One reason for this is the steady stream of exciting advances in the field. Another reason, however, is the feedback I've had from users of *Learning and Behavior.* The comments of instructors and students have convinced me that many students will embrace a scientific approach to behavior if it is presented in clear language. And if we can change the way students think about behavior, then we can move toward a society that deals with behavior problems in a more scientific, and more civilized, manner. I have found this very motivating.

The theme of the fifth edition, as in previous editions, is that learning is a biological mechanism that aids survival. The pedagogical features that marked the previous edition have been retained and, I hope, improved. From the very beginning one of my goals has been to write a text that would not merely "cover" the course content but would also help students learn it. I see the textbook as an instructional tool, not a reference work. Toward this end I have attempted to:

- write in simple, straightforward language that makes the ideas easy to understand
- provide lots of examples and applications to make concepts "real" to the student
- emphasize core concepts rather than details. (It is easy for instructors and textbook authors to forget how daunting the learning course is to students.)
- include challenging review questions to stimulate discussions both in class and in the dorms. (Some instructors have said that a few questions are too difficult for undergraduates, but I believe it is a good idea to give students hard problems now and then.)

- emphasize the application of scientific method to questions about behavior
- provide queries throughout each chapter (with answers at the end of the chapter) that help students monitor their understanding and recall
- include practice quizzes that help students review and assess their mastery of each chapter
- recommend additional reading material that students will find stimulating and, in general, not too far over their heads
- provide figures that simply and clearly illustrate facts and concepts
- include analyses of "higher" forms of behavior (such as insightful problem solving, creativity, and the bizarre behavior of some psychiatric patients) of special interest to students

Key Changes in This Edition

I have had a lot of feedback from instructors and students about the fourth edition of *Learning and Behavior*, and as a result, I've made a number of changes, including:

- Updated content. New studies and topics (such as the therapeutic use of noncontingent reinforcement) have been added. Updating is reflected in the fact that many references now have publication dates between 1999 and 2002.
- Brief reviews now appear at the end of each major chapter section. (These replace the chapter summaries of the previous edition.)
- Footnotes have been added. Most deal with historical or methodological details. Some instructors may hold students responsible for all notes; others may draw attention to only a few. Some students may find the notes interesting enough to read even when they are not assigned.
- There are numerous changes in illustrative material: There are many more figures; nearly all figures that were based on hypothetical data have been replaced with figures based on research; complex figures have been simplified; and some line drawings have been added.
- More queries have been added. Queries have been very popular with students, who use them as a way of monitoring their comprehension and recall. Because of this, most queries are now of the "fill-in-the-blank" type. Query answers appear at the end of each chapter.
- The treatment of heredity has been revised to reflect current thinking about the plasticity of genes.

- Additional space is devoted to the logic of scientific analysis, particularly the importance of avoiding circular thinking in explaining behavior.
- The view of learning as an evolutionary mechanism, a prominent feature of previous editions, receives even greater attention in this edition.
- It is explicitly argued that behavior is important in and of itself, not merely as a measure of physiological or cognitive events that may be occurring inside the organism.
- Most of the "mini essays" of the fourth edition have been boxed and moved from the chapter ends to relevant points in the chapters. Others have been moved to the instructor's manual for photocopying and distribution to students as handouts.
- In general, the word *response* is now used only to refer to reflex acts, such as salivating; otherwise the word *behavior* is favored. This is a minor change, but it may help students avoid acquiring the mistaken view that learning researchers reduce all of behavior to reflexes and "S-R" connections.

Acknowledgments

Each new edition of a text is the result of efforts by many people; the present edition is no exception. Many instructors offered information or comments. My sincere thanks go to Henry D. Schlinger, UCLA; Robert Epstein, San Diego State University; Edward K. Morris, University of Kansas; Susan Schneider, West Virginia University; James T. Todd, Eastern Michigan University; Brady Phelps, South Dakota State University; and Susan G. Friedman, Utah State University.

As always, I owe a very special debt to Carl Cheney of Utah State University and to Jerry Venn of Mary Baldwin College, for useful suggestions and moral support. It is with great sadness that I report that Jerry Venn, a friend as well as a constant source of support in my efforts to reach students, died suddenly as this book was going to press. Jerry's input and support over the years were invaluable, the more so because I knew that Jerry always put students first. His students knew that too, and I am sure they will miss him as much as I will.

A special thanks also to Diane Chance, who prepared most of the figures in this edition. I am grateful to Paul Jensen, a student at Utah State University, for valuable library research.

Many students took the time to write to me about the previous edition. I regret that I cannot list all of their names here, but I can assure them that whenever possible I have attempted to incorporate their suggestions in this edition. (Alas, I am unable to include color illustrations, as so many students suggested; I am told it would greatly increase the book's price.)

I am also very grateful to reviewers who critiqued the manuscript for this edition and offered many useful comments. They include Frederick Banato, Saint Peter's College; Barbara Basden, California State University, Fresno; John Caruso, The University of Massachusetts, Dartmouth; Bettye Elmore, Humboldt State University; Nancy Karlin, University of Northern Colorado; Jacquelyne Malon, Tennessee State University; Matthew Normand, Florida State University; Amy Odum, University of New Hampshire; Mark Reilly, Arizona State University; Heffrey Stowell, Eastern Illinois University; Margaret Thomas, University of Central Florida; and Lynne Trench, Birmingham-Southern College.

I hope and believe that this fifth edition is the best so far. If it is, much of the credit goes to those mentioned above; if not, you can lay the blame at my feet. Either way, I hope to hear from you so that I can make notes for improving the next edition. You can write to me at Wadsworth Publishing, 511 Forest Lodge Road, Pacific Grove, CA 93950-9968, or e-mail me at pbchance@aol.com.

Paul Chance
Senior Fellow, Cambridge Center for Behavioral Studies

Introduction: Learning to Change

1

Change is the only constant.

Lucretius

hange, said the Roman philosopher Lucretius 2,000 years ago, is the only constant. Yet we tend to regard change as an aberration, a brief disruption in a normally constant world. When a great volcano erupts, as Mount St. Helens in Washington did in 1980, knocking over thousands of trees and covering the earth for miles around with a blanket of volcanic ash, we think how strange it is that nature should misbehave so. It is, we tell ourselves, a momentary lapse, a kind of geological tantrum; soon our old planet will regain its composure, its sameness.

But the truth is that our short tenure on earth deludes us into seeing sameness. In the course of an individual human's lifetime, volcanic eruptions, earthquakes, and the like are rare, but in the life of the earth, they are the very stuff of existence. Our time here is too brief to see continents crash together and tear apart, mountains rise and fall, vast deserts replace oceans; too brief to see thousands of animal and plant species come and go, like the ever-changing, varicolored crystalline shapes of a kaleidoscope.

Change is not the exception to the rule, then, but the rule itself. Throughout nature, the struggle to prevail is a struggle against change: Food supplies dwindle, prey animals become faster, predators become more formidable, new diseases appear. Some changes, such as the movement of continents, take place over eons; others, such as the advance of glaciers, take thousands of years; still others, such as the rise and fall of the sun or the appearance and disappearance of hungry predators, occur daily. The one constant is change. Any individual or species must be able to cope with change if it is to survive. But how? By what mechanisms can we and other organisms deal with such a fickle world?

Natural Selection

In *On the Origin of Species*, published in 1859, the English naturalist Charles Darwin proposed that species adapt to changes in their world. There is, he argued, tremendous variation among the members of any given species. Some of these variations are well suited to current conditions; others are not. Individuals with favorable variations are more likely to survive and reproduce, so succeeding generations are more

The Face of Change

Stability, if it exists at all, is rare, whereas change is seen everywhere, once we look for it. Perhaps the most obvious changes in the human world are technological. A hundred years ago, most people got around in horse-drawn carriages, scoffed at the idea that people would one day fly, and laughed aloud at talk of space flight. Several decades later, many of those same people could have driven to an airport in a car, taken a jet to Cape Canaveral, and watched as a spaceship rocketed toward the first moon landing. Changes in medical technology have been equally impressive: Polio, a disease that paralyzed thousands for life, is now prevented with vaccine; antibiotics routinely bring speedy recovery from diseases that once killed; and smallpox, which menaced humankind throughout its history, has been eradicated.

Change is not synonymous with progress, however. The automobile, along with all its benefits, brought with it smog, urban decay, congestion, and thousands of traffic deaths a year. The airplane that carries vacationers to far-off lands may bring them back infected with deadly viruses. Improved health care has led to an aging population and this has contributed to sky-high medical costs.

The rate at which different aspects of our world change varies. In a matter of seconds, storm winds may bring an ancient oak tree thundering to the ground, rip a house apart, or knock out electric power to a million people. In a matter of weeks, a vacant lot may be turned into a playground, a municipal park, or a parking area. In a few months, farmland may be converted into a suburban development. And while you have been reading this chapter, several species of plants and animals, some not yet identified by the scientific community, may have become extinct.

Sometimes the pace of change is far slower. The face you saw reflected in your mirror this morning probably appeared no different from the face you saw the day before—or a week or a month ago. Yet we know that the face that stares back at us from the glass is not the same, cannot be the same, as it was 10 minutes ago. The proof is in your photo album: Look at a photograph taken of yourself 5 or 10 years ago and you see clear differences between the face in the snapshot and the face in your mirror. If you lived in a world without mirrors for a year and then saw your reflection, you might be stunned by the change. After an interval of 10 years without seeing yourself, you might not at first recognize the person peering from the mirror. Even something as basic as our own face changes from moment to moment. The next time you look at yourself in the mirror, you will see the face of change.

likely to show helpful characteristics. Thus, features that contribute to survival are "selected" by the environment, a process Darwin called **natural selection**.[1] Evolution (adaptive changes in species over time) is therefore the inevitable product of variation and natural selection.

Although Darwin did not understand the genetic basis of variation (the work of Gregor Mendel did not become widely known until about 1900), he knew from direct observation that variation within a species was common.[2] He also knew that selective breeding of farm animals with a specific variation often resulted in offspring with that characteristic. And he knew that breeding individuals with a given characteristic would, over several generations, result in a high proportion of animals with that characteristic.

Query: Species change through natural _____ .

Darwin went beyond the animal breeders, however, by proposing that this same sort of selection process takes place throughout nature. A characteristic such as the thickness of a mammal's fur varies widely among the members of its species. If the climate turns gradually colder, those individuals with thicker coats will have an advantage over those with thinner coats, so they will live longer and produce more thick-coated offspring. With each succeeding generation, there will be proportionally more animals with thick coats.

Evolution does not require the involvement of any intelligent agent; we need not, for example, imagine God as animal husbandry expert.[3] The slow-witted and the slow afoot are culled by natural predators that are smarter or faster. Those that are not suited to a change in climate or a change in the food supply perish. The environment "selects" desirable characteristics and spurns undesirable ones.

What is desirable is not, however, an absolute. The thick fur that helped a species survive increasingly cold winters becomes a handicap when the winters turn mild or when the search for food leads successive generations into warmer regions. Under these circumstances, those individuals with thinner coats are more likely to survive and pass on their genes. A characteristic is "good" only insofar as it contributes to the con-

---

[1]Terms that appear in **boldface** are defined in the Glossary at the end of the book.

[2]According to David Buss (2000), Mendel sent Darwin papers on his research, but Darwin either did not read them or did not appreciate their relevance to evolution.

[3]It does not follow, however, that Darwin expelled God from the universe, or even from biology. Evolution implies that changes in species and the appearance of new species can be accounted for by means of variation and natural selection; this is not in the least at odds with the existence of God. For more on this, see Stephen Jay Gould's (1999) *Rocks of Ages* and M. Wertheim's (1999) article, "The Odd Couple."

Figure 1-1 *Order out of disorder. The pebbles on a beach are arranged in an orderly fashion by gravity and the action of the waves. See text for explanation.*

tinuation of the species. The sickle-shaped red blood cells commonly found in the indigenous people of Africa can cause a devastating form of anemia. However, they also provide resistance to malaria, a disease that is common to the continent.

It is often difficult for people to see how natural selection can do its work without intelligent direction. But intelligent direction isn't required. Richard Dawkins (1986), in a book called *The Blind Watchmaker*, offers this analogy:

> If you walk up and down a pebbly beach, you will notice that the pebbles are not arranged at random. The smaller pebbles typically tend to be found in segregated zones running along the length of the beach, the larger ones in different zones or stripes. The pebbles have been sorted, arranged, selected. (p. 43; see Figure 1-1)

What has sorted, arranged and selected the stones, Dawkins notes, is the mechanical, unthinking force of the waves. Big stones and small stones are affected differently by the waves, so they end up in different places. Order evolves from disorder without intelligent intervention (see Dawkins, 1995a, 1995b).

The pebbly beach provides a convenient metaphor for natural selection, but it is not proof that natural selection actually changes species. In recent years, however, evolutionary biologists have brought evolution into the laboratory. In one study (reported in Weiner, 1994), researchers raised fruit flies in total darkness. Normally, reproduction in these flies begins with a courtship dance that ends in mating. In a totally dark environment, a courtship dance—which has to be seen to be effective—is of limited value. After 14 generations in the altered environment, a new form of mating ritual had evolved. Instead of dancing for the females, the males moved about in the dark until they found a female and copulated with her. The females, in turn, made no effort to escape the male's advances. In just 14 generations, a new form of mating behavior had evolved in response to a change in the environment.

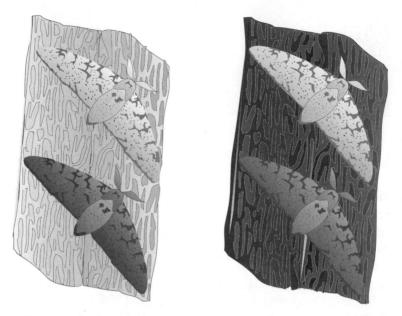

Figure 1-2 *Natural selection in action. Prior to 1850, the gray Peppered Moth was hard to detect against the light trees on which it rested. After that, the industrial revolution darkened the trees, and within a few decades the once-rare black variety became dominant.*

Other research has allowed us to see natural selection at work outside the laboratory. Research on the Peppered Moth (*Biston betularia*), one of the many large moths found on the British Isles, provides an example. The Peppered Moth feeds at night and rests during the day on the trunks and limbs of trees. Its survival depends in large part on its ability to escape detection by the birds that find it an appetizing food. At one time, nearly all of these moths were a mottled light gray color, closely resembling the lichen-covered trees on which they rested. A rare black variation of the moth, first observed in 1848, stood out against this background like coal against snow, making it highly vulnerable. But when pollutants in certain industrial areas killed the lichen and darkened the bark of trees, the light-colored moths increasingly fell prey to birds, whereas the dark moths tended to survive and reproduce (see Figure 1-2). An examination of Peppered Moth collections revealed that in forests near industrial centers, where pollution was common, the black moths had increased in number and the light-colored variety had declined. In some areas, 90% of the moths were of the once-rare black variety (Kettlewell, 1959).*

*Science writer Judith Hooper (2002) casts suspicion on Kettlewell's work, but biologist Bruce Grant (2002) accuses Hooper of character assassination and notes that Kettlewell's conclusions are supported by several independent studies. He writes that "the case for natural selection in the evolution of melanism in peppered moths is actually much stronger today than it was during Kettlewell's time" (p. 941).

It seems likely that the same sort of process that affects the coloration of the Peppered Moth also affects the skin color of humans living in different climates. A natural substance in the skin, melanin, screens out the sun's rays. The more melanin, the darker the skin and the more sunlight is screened out. The people of Scandinavia and Northern Europe, where there is relatively little sunlight, are characteristically fair-skinned, a trait that allows them to absorb the sunlight they need to produce vitamin D. People who live near the equator, where there is an abundance of sunlight, are characteristically dark-skinned, a trait that protects them against the hazards of too much sun. The human species acquires the coloration that survival in a given environment requires.

The work of Peter and Rosemary Grant (reported in Weiner, 1994) provides another demonstration of natural selection at work. The Grants studied finches on one of the Galapagos Islands. They found that only two species of the finches they observed ate the seeds of a plant called the caltrop. The seeds are encased in a hard, spiny shell, and getting at them is difficult. In studying the differences between finches that ate the seeds and those that did not, the Grants discovered that very small differences in the birds' beaks were critical. A bird with a beak 11 millimeters long could crack the shell of a caltrop seed pod; one with a beak 10.5 millimeters could not. In times of severe drought, when practically the only food available is the seed of the caltrop, a difference of half a millimeter may mean the difference between living and dying. The Grants found that the average beak size increased during drought as birds with smaller beaks died off. The big-beaked survivors produced offspring that had beaks 4% to 5% longer than those of birds that had been around before the drought.

When the rains finally returned to the Galapagos Islands, the supply of seeds shifted and the larger seeds became harder to find. Now the shoe was on the other foot, or beak as it were, and the smaller-beaked birds had the advantage. "What a trifling difference," Darwin wrote, "must often determine which shall survive, and which perish!" (quoted in Weiner, 1994, p. 65).

Natural selection accounts for most of the differences within a species from one geographic region to another and from one time to another. However, adaptation is also affected by abrupt changes in genes. These **mutations**, as they are called, can be caused by exposure to radiation and certain chemicals, and perhaps by viral infections. Mutations can occur in any of the body's cells, but when they occur in the genes of reproductive cells (sperm or ova), the mutation is passed on to the next generation.

Offspring with mutated genes may or may not display a new characteristic, just as a person who carries the gene for blue eyes may or may not have blue eyes. But the mutated gene will be passed on, seen or not, to future generations.

Most mutations produce changes that are not helpful to survival. Many of these changes are simply of no consequence, one way or the other. People who, as a result of a mutation, have alligator green or navy blue eyes may experience some ostracism, but their chances of surviving and reproducing are probably not strongly affected. Other mutations put the individual at risk. Mutations can result in two-headed snakes, for example. Since two heads are not, in fact, better than one, such animals seldom live long enough to reproduce their kind. Thus, harmful mutations are "selected out."

Query: An abrupt change in a gene is called a _____ .

Those that occur in _____ cells may be transmitted

to offspring.

On rare occasions, mutations result in adaptive changes. A mutation might, for instance, provide an animal with a new horn shape that proves useful in defense, or it might provide resistance against certain diseases. When mutations are useful, they can mean rapid changes in the characteristics of a species because the offspring of individuals carrying the gene are more likely to survive and reproduce than those that lack it.

Natural selection would be of limited importance to the study of behavior if it applied only to physical characteristics such as eye color, fur thickness, and susceptibility to disease, but behavior is also influenced by genes, and is subject to natural selection. As the environment changes, those individuals that behave in adaptive ways are favored. Variations in behavior and the process of natural selection produce a repertoire of partly innate, adaptive behaviors that include reflexes, fixed action patterns, and general behavior traits.

Reflexes

A **reflex** is a relationship between a specific event and a simple response to that event. Reflexes are either present at birth or appear at predictable stages in development. Most reflexes are found in virtually all members of a species and are part of the adaptive equipment of the organism. All animals, from protozoa to college professors, have reflexes.[4]

Many reflexes serve to protect the organism from injury. The amoeba is an irregularly shaped, one-celled animal that travels by extending a

---

[4]Some things that look like innate reflexes may, in fact, be learned. Paul Rozin (in Bales, 1984) notes that before age 2, children will put virtually anything into their mouths, but he has found that very few adults will eat fudge that has been molded to resemble dog droppings. Evidently this aversion is acquired.

part of its perimeter forward and then pulling the rest along after. When the amoeba encounters a noxious substance, it immediately withdraws from it; this reflex minimizes the harmful effects of the substance. Larger animals do much the same thing when they withdraw a limb from a painful object. The professor who picks up a very hot skillet will immediately release it and withdraw the injured hand. Other protective reflexes in humans include the eyeblink, in which the eye closes when any object approaches it; the pupillary reflex, in which the iris contracts or relaxes in response to changes in light; the sneeze, by which irritants such as dust and pollen are expelled from the nose and lungs; and the vomit reflex, which removes toxic substances from the stomach in an efficient, if indelicate, manner.[5]

Query: A reflex is a _____ between a specific

_____ and a simple _____ .

Other reflexes are important in food consumption. When an amoeba encounters some edible object, such as a dead bacterium, it immediately responds to the object by engulfing it and making a meal of it. Humans have a number of such consummatory reflexes: Touch a baby's face and she will turn toward what touched her; this rooting reflex is useful in finding the mother's nipple. When the nipple touches the baby's lips, this evokes the sucking reflex, which brings milk into the baby's mouth. Food in the mouth elicits the salivary reflex, the flow of saliva that begins the process of digestion. The presence of saliva and food in the mouth triggers swallowing. Swallowing triggers peristalsis, the rhythmic motion of the lining of the esophagus that carries food to the stomach. Thus, the simple act of eating is, in large measure, a chain of reflexes.[6]

We tend not to notice reflexes until they fail to function properly. This can happen as a result of an allergic reaction to medication or as the result of injury or disease. Reflex failure is seen in people who have consumed excessive amounts of alcohol or other drugs that depress the central nervous system. Death from alcoholic intoxication can occur, for example, when the alcohol interferes with the respiratory reflex (inhaling

---

[5]Recent research suggests that blushing, which seems an utterly useless reflex, may protect us from injury by appeasing others we have offended (Keltner & Anderson, 2000).

[6]This discussion of reflexes focuses on those that contribute to survival, but not all reflexes are helpful. Some people have life-threatening allergic reactions to certain foods, such as peanuts. In some people, epileptic seizures can be triggered by flickering lights, a loud noise, a certain type of music, or a particular odor. Reflexes, like other behaviors with a strong genetic component, will vary in frequency throughout a species. Those that contribute to survival will appear more frequently in succeeding generations; those that hinder survival literally "die out."

and exhaling) or when the intoxicated person vomits inadequately and chokes to death on the vomit (a fact that ought to make people think twice about binge drinking). Fortunately, most of us are blissfully unaware that we even have reflexes until, once in a great while, one of them malfunctions.

Reflexes are highly stereotypic; that is, they are remarkably invariant in form, frequency, strength, and time of appearance during development. This is not to say, however, that they do not vary at all. The rooting reflex, for example, may first appear in one infant at the age of seven days but may not show up in a second infant for another week. There is also some variation in the form a reflex takes. A tap below the knee may produce a barely detectable patellar reflex in one person, whereas in another the same light blow may result in a kick that looks like an attempt to make a field goal.

Eliciting a reflex response can increase the intensity or probability of the response to stimuli. This is called **sensitization**. Consider the startle reflex, the tendency to jump at a sudden, loud noise. If you jump when you hear a balloon burst nearby, you are then more likely to jump if you hear another noise, such as the sound of a dropped book hitting the floor. Even a relatively soft noise, one that would ordinarily not make you jump, may do so. The loud sound of the bursting balloon sensitizes you to other noises.

Vincent Dethier and his colleagues (1965) performed experiments on sensitization in the blowfly. The blowfly is endowed with hairs around its mouth that are responsive to various substances. If one of these hairs is touched with a bit of water, a thirsty fly will extend its proboscis, a trunk-like organ through which it feeds, and drink. Dethier and his coworkers gave the blowflies plenty of water, so that touching a mouth hair with water would not result in proboscis extension. Then the researchers touched a mouth hair with sugar water, causing the feeding response. Once again the researchers touched the mouth hairs with plain water. This time, the feeding response did occur. Exposure to sugar water sensitized the flies to plain water.

Sensitization may play a role in drug addiction. Animals given addictive drugs over a period of time are later more sensitive to their effects. In one experiment, Kelly Powell and Stephen Holtzman (2001) gave rats morphine for one to four days and then tested their reaction to the drug after a period of abstinence. The rats showed an increased response to morphine (i.e., sensitization) for up to three months after their last dose. (See also Pontieri et al., 2001.)

Repeatedly evoking a given reflex response will result in a reduction in the intensity or probability of the response. This phenomenon is

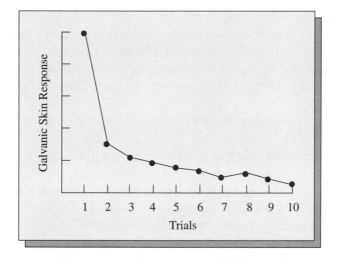

Figure 1-3 *Habituation. Exposure to a novel stimulus produces a change in the electrical conductivity of the skin (the Galvanic Skin Response, or GSR). Repeated exposure to the stimulus results in progressively weaker GSRs. (Hypothetical data.)*

known as **habituation**. Seth Sharpless and Herbert Jasper (1956) noted the effects of loud noises on cats by recording their brain waves on an electroencephalograph (EEG). The EEG showed marked arousal at first, but the reaction declined steadily with each repetition of a given sound, until the noise had hardly any effect.

Wagner Bridger (1961) studied habituation in infants and found that when babies first heard a noise, they responded with an increase in heart rate. With repetition of the noise at regular intervals, however, the change in heart rate became less and less pronounced until, in some cases, the noise had no measurable effect at all.

Habituation has even been demonstrated in the human fetus. A stimulus to the mother's abdomen during the last three months of pregnancy will produce movement in the fetus. If the stimulus is applied repeatedly in a regular way, the fetal response becomes steadily weaker (Leader, 1995).[7] When the course of habituation is plotted on a graph, it usually reveals a fairly smooth, decelerating curve (see Figure 1-3).

Although habituation is a relatively simple phenomenon, it is not so simple as this discussion implies. Repeated exposure to a loud sound will

---

[7]Slow fetal habituation tends to be associated with difficult pregnancy (Hepper, 1995), and there is some evidence that the rate at which a fetus habituates is correlated with intellectual development after birth and so might one day be used to identify prenatal medical problems (Madison et al., 1986).

produce habituation of the startle reflex, but the degree of habituation and the rate at which it occurs depend on the loudness of the sound, variations in the quality of the sound, the number of times the sound occurs in a minute, the time interval between repeated exposures to the sound, and other variables. (For more on this, see Thompson, 2000.)[8]

Query: Sensitization involves a/an _____ in the

probability or intensity of a reflex response; habituation involves

a/an _____ in its probability or intensity.

Although reflexes are more complex and variable than most people imagine, they nevertheless represent the simplest and most uniform kind of behavior. Fixed action patterns are more complex and variable.

Fixed Action Patterns

A **fixed action pattern (FAP)** is a largely inherited series of interrelated acts. Fixed action patterns resemble reflexes in that they have a strong genetic basis; display relatively little variability from individual to individual, or from day to day in the same individual; and often are reliably elicited by a particular kind of event.[9] They differ from reflexes in that they involve the entire organism rather than a few muscles or glands; are more complex, often consisting of long series of reflex-like acts; and are more variable, though still rather stereotypic. Fixed action patterns used to be called *instincts*, but this term has fallen out of favor, partly because it came to refer to any more or less automatic behavior (as in, "Martha instinctively slammed on the brakes").

Some fixed action patterns protect the animal from predators. When confronted by a threatening dog, the house cat arches its back, hisses, growls, and flicks its tail. These acts make the cat appear larger and more formidable than it really is and may therefore serve to put off an attacker. The opossum responds quite differently to predators: It plays dead. Some of the opossum's predators eat only animals they themselves have killed; others will cover a dead animal they find and return to eat it later, so a "dead" opossum has a good chance of surviving.

---

[8]As Thompson (2000) points out, sensitization and habituation may be simple forms of learning.

[9]Because there is some variation even in these relatively fixed behaviors, some authorities now prefer the term *modal action patterns*. Modal means most frequent or typical.

Query: Fixed action patterns differ from reflexes in that FAPs

involve the _____ organism and are more

_____ and _____ .

Other fixed action patterns provide protection against the elements. Geese and many other birds migrate to warmer climes in the fall. When geese migrate, they typically fly in flocks in "V" formation. It has been suggested that this practice allows all but the lead bird to benefit from reduced wind resistance thanks to the bird flying point. The lead bird drops back after a time and another bird takes its place, so that the burden of flying into the greatest wind resistance is spread throughout the flock. The theory is that the "V" formation reduces the amount of energy required for flying and thereby increases each bird's chances of reaching its destination (Ruppell, 1975).

Some fixed action patterns are useful in procuring food. Pigs root for worms, larvae, and truffles beneath the ground; some spiders build webs with which to capture their prey; and woodpeckers tap holes in tree bark to get at the insects that live there.

Many fixed action patterns involve courtship and mating. The male western grebe, a water bird, attracts a mate by running on the water; the male bighorn sheep wins a partner by bashing its head against that of its rival; when the female chimpanzee is capable of conceiving, she approaches an adult male and presents her swollen and inflamed genitals, thereby initiating the mating act. In most animals, courtship and mating are highly stereotypic, with little variation from one individual to another.

Fixed action patterns also govern the care and rearing of the young. After mating, the female of a certain species of wasp builds a nest, places a paralyzed spider in it, lays an egg on top of the spider, closes the nest, and goes on its way, leaving the young wasp to fend for itself after it has hatched and eaten its first meal. The newborn of many higher species of animals require more nurturing, for which task their parents are genetically equipped. Birds work slavishly to feed their hungry young. An exception is the brown-headed cowbird, which cares for its young by depositing its eggs in the nests of other birds, often tricking an unsuspecting sparrow or wren into making a heroic effort to feed a youngster twice its own size.

We saw that reflexes are reliably elicited by specific kinds of events. Fixed action patterns are also initiated by certain events, called **releasers** (or **releasing stimuli**). For instance, the male rat ordinarily will mate only with females that are in estrus (i.e., in heat). The estrus female produces odorous chemicals, called pheromones, that act as releasers for sexual behavior in the male. In the absence of these pheromones, the male will not usually attempt to mate. Similarly, a nesting graylag goose responds to an egg that has rolled out of the nest by "stretching the neck towards it, bringing the bill behind the egg and with careful balancing movements rolling it back into the nest" (Tinbergen, 1951, p. 84). A ball, an oval stone, or almost any more or less egg-shaped object near the nest will release this fixed action pattern.

The stickleback fish provides another example of a fixed action pattern. The male responds aggressively to other males of its species, but this response is triggered by the red coloration on the male abdomen. It turns out that an object that has this color pattern will be threatened or attacked, even if it doesn't resemble a stickleback, whereas objects that lack the color pattern will not be attacked even if they otherwise do resemble a male stickleback (see Figure 1-4). Dawkins (1995b) reports that a stickleback even "threatened" a mail van that had some red paint.[10]

Query: The color red is a _____ for aggression in the

male stickleback.

Because of their complexity and their utility, many fixed action patterns appear to be thoughtful acts. In fact, they are probably no more thoughtful than is the behavior of a person who responds to a rap on the knee by jerking his leg. An illustration of the unthinking nature of fixed action patterns is provided by the tropical army ant. Entire colonies of these ants charge across the forests in what appears to be a highly organized, intelligently directed campaign. In fact, the ants are merely following a chemical trail laid down by the ants ahead of them. T. C. Schneirla (1944) demonstrated that on a flat surface, such as a road, where no obstacles direct the course of the march, the lead ants tend to move toward the ants beside them. The column then turns in on itself, and the ants soon march round and round in a circle. This is not very intelligent behavior.

Various people (e.g., Carr, 1967; Dawkins, 1995a; Skinner, 1966) have suggested that fixed action patterns may be selected by gradual changes in the environment. Consider, for example, salmon that migrate up-

---

[10] This behavior of the stickleback makes us smile because it is so extraordinarily inappropriate. But the behavior appears stupid only because we are looking at the animal outside its natural habitat: Mail vans are not normally part of the stickleback's environment.

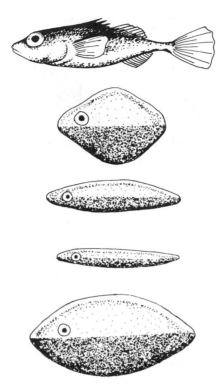

Figure 1-4   *Fighting instinct in the stickleback. A realistic looking model without a red belly (top) elicited fewer attacks than unrealistic looking models with red bellies. (After* The Study of Instinct *[Figure 20, p. 28], by N. Tinbergen, 1951, Oxford, England: Clarendon Press.)*

stream to breed. This act often requires the fish to ascend steep cliffs and swim against rushing currents. At one time, returning to the breeding area might have constituted a relatively easy swim up a gently rising stream. As geological changes gradually increased the steepness of the slope, those fish with the ability to make the trip bred successfully and reproduced their kind, whereas those not up to the challenge failed to reproduce. As geological changes continued to increase the difficulty of the task, the process of natural selection produced salmon capable of mastering it (see Figure 1-5). Other complex fixed action patterns (such as migration and mating rituals) may have been molded by the environment in much the same way.

Are there any fixed action patterns in human beings? It is hard to say. Darwin (1874) wrote of the social instincts (including "the love of praise and fear of blame") and of the instincts of self-preservation, lust, and vengeance, among others. Several decades ago, textbooks still listed dozens of

Figure 1-5   *Evolution of adaptive behavior. As mountains are formed, the slope of a stream bed rises. Those fish that can make their way to the spawning area reproduce, and the others are eliminated from the gene pool.*

human instincts, including the sex instinct, the social instinct, the maternal instinct, and the territorial instinct (see, for example, McDougall, 1908). But the list of human instincts has grown shorter over the years.

Many researchers today maintain that there are no fixed action patterns in human beings, that those previously attributed to people lack the monotonous character of web spinning in spiders and nest building in birds. People, like chimpanzees, approach prospective sexual partners from time to time, but among humans the method of approach varies tremendously from culture to culture, from individual to individual, and even within the same individual from time to time. Humans have invented marriage, dating services, prostitution, singles bars, personals columns, and all sorts of rules and customs for defining how, when, where, and with whom sexual acts may be performed. The complexity and variability of mating rituals among humans is a far cry from the stereotypic mating behavior of most other animals.

The same sort of case can be made against the so-called maternal instinct. True, many women do desire to have children and to protect and nurture them, as do many men. But there is tremendous variation in how mothers perform these tasks. In some societies, young children are fondled and held constantly, and their slightest need is met immediately; in others, children are left largely to their own resources. Moreover, women in Western societies increasingly delay or forgo altogether the traditional maternal role. True fixed action patterns are not so readily discarded.

Some authors make a case for the incest taboo as a fixed action pattern in humans. E. O. Wilson (1978) argues that people have an innate aversion to mating with members of their own family.[11] In support of

---

[11]Wilson (1984) also suggests another human fixed action pattern: biophilia, "the innately emotional affiliation of human beings to other living organisms." Whether this qualifies as a true FAP is doubtful, however.

this, he cites research showing that children reared in Israeli kibbutzim (large, family-like communal groups) almost never marry within the kibbutz (Shepher, 1971).

But even this "instinct" is suspect. Sigmund Freud (1913) pointed out that if there really were a natural aversion to incest, there would be no need for an incest taboo. The taboo, he argued, was a cultural invention designed to avoid problems caused by incest. Further doubt about Wilson's view is raised by studies showing that incestuous behavior is much more common than had been thought (see, for example, Russell, 1986; Watriss, 1982). If the aversion to incest were a true instinct, incestuous acts would be rare.

There are, then, few if any fixed action patterns in humans. The role of genetics in complex behavior is, however, seen in humans in the form of general behavior traits.

General Behavior Traits

Over the past few decades, a great deal of research has been done on the role of genes in determining general behavioral tendencies, or what I will refer to here as **general behavior traits**.[12] These include activity level, aggression, introversion, anxiety, hoarding (of food, for example), and sexual practices, among others. These behavior traits are strongly influenced by genes.

Some behavior traits were once classified as instincts, but they differ from fixed action patterns in important ways. As noted previously, fixed action patterns are elicited by fairly specific kinds of environmental events, called releasers. The gaping mouth of a fledgling induces the parent bird to provide food; a closed mouth does not have this effect. Behavior traits, on the other hand, occur in a wide variety of situations. For instance, under certain circumstances, **aversives** (i.e., those things an organism strives to avoid; they are commonly described as painful, noxious, or unpleasant) will reliably produce aggressive behavior in many animals, including people (Berkowitz, 1983; Ulrich & Azrin, 1962).[13] But the term *aversive*[14] covers a lot of territory: It can include, among other things, an electric shock, a pin prick, a spray of cold water, or an air temperature above, say, 80 degrees. All can increase the likelihood of

---

[12]I have adopted this term in place of inherited behavior traits to avoid the implication that the behavior is solely the result of genetics. No behavior is solely the result of genetics—or of environment (Moore, 2001).

[13]People are, of course, animals. The distinction between animals and people is made here and elsewhere to avoid the impression that we are concerned only with the so-called "lower" species. In fact, our primary concern in this text is with human learning.

[14]Please note that the term is *aversive*, not *adversive*.

aggressive behavior. Fixed action patterns are not released by so many different kinds of events.

Another difference between fixed action patterns and behavior traits concerns the plasticity of the behavior. Compare the fixed action pattern of the web-spinning spider with the aggressiveness of a shocked rat. Each web-spinning spider spins a web with a specific pattern, and it goes about the task with a remarkable sameness, like someone living a recurrent dream. Moreover, the web-spinning of one spider is remarkably like that of other members of the same species (Savory, 1974). But the rat that attacks its neighbor goes about it in a far less stereotypic manner; further, there may be considerable difference between the attack of one rat and that of another.

Query: An event an organism tends to avoid is called an

_____.

Behavior traits are more variable than fixed action patterns, but there is no doubt that heredity plays a role in their appearance. Selective breeding can, for example, produce strains of animals differing in fearfulness (Hall, 1937, 1951; see Figure 1-6), aggressiveness (Fuller & Scott, 1954), activeness (Rundquist, 1933), and addiction proneness (Nichols & Hsiao, 1967; see Figure 1-7).

Research on the reproductive habits of certain snakes offers evidence of the way in which natural selection shapes behavioral tendencies (Madsen et al., 1992). Researchers in Sweden compared female adders (a kind of poisonous snake) that had had several sexual partners with those that had not. They found that the more promiscuous snakes produced more offspring than the others. It turned out that some male snakes were better at fertilizing the female's eggs, perhaps because they had more active sperm. Female snakes that had more partners therefore had a better chance of copulating with the more effective males. To the extent that the tendency to copulate with several partners is inherited, these snakes will pass on this behavior to their young.[15]

If a particular behavior trait is selected by the environment over many generations, there can be profound changes in the species. In a continuing study that began some 40 years ago, researchers selectively bred foxes solely on the basis of general behavioral characteristics (Trut,

---

[15]There is evidence that philandering is common in both males and females throughout much of the animal kingdom, including humans. See *The Myth of Monogamy* (Barash & Lipton, 2001).

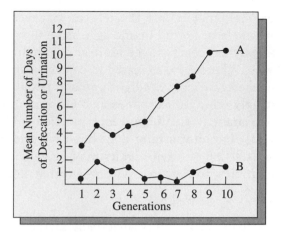

Figure 1-6 *Fearfulness and heredity. Rats were placed in an open enclosure. The most fearful (A), as measured by urination and defecation, were bred with each other, as were the least fearful (B). The results of 10 generations are shown. (Compiled from data in Hall, 1951.)*

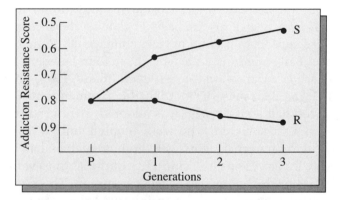

Figure 1-7 *Addiction and heredity. There is no instinct for addiction, but heredity plays a role in its development. From an unselected population of rats (P), rats susceptible (S) or resistant (R) to morphine addiction were interbred for three generations. Susceptible rats became increasingly susceptible to addiction, while resistant rats became increasingly resistant. (From "Addiction Liability of Albino Rats: Breeding for Quantitative Differences in Morphine Drinking" by J. R. Nichols and S. Hsiao, 1967,* Science, 157, *pp. 561–563. Copyright © 1967 by the American Association for the Advancement of Science. Reprinted with permission.)*

1999). The researchers mated only those foxes that were most dog-like in behavior—that is, least fearful of and aggressive toward people. After several generations, the foxes behaved more and more like dogs, and less and less like foxes. Whereas foxes reared in captivity are normally very wary of people, these animals readily approach people and lick their hands. Interestingly enough, the foxes also became more dog-like in their physical appearance, with floppy ears, mottled color patterns, and upturned tails, all characteristic of dogs but very uncharacteristic of foxes. This suggests that behavior traits may be genetically linked to physical characteristics, so that an environment that selects one feature also produces another.[16]

Query: The fox-breeding study selectively mated foxes on the

basis of _____ .

Studies of identical twins separated soon after birth suggest a role for heredity in many human behavior traits. (Farber, 1981; Lykken et al., 1992). Although reared apart, twins may have similar career interests; wear the same styles of clothes; and enjoy the same kinds of art, music, entertainment, hobbies, and so on. Although some similarity among individuals may be expected on the basis of chance, the similarity among identical twins appears to go well beyond coincidence (Bouchard, 1997).

J. Michael Bailey and his colleagues have found evidence of genetic influence in sexual orientation (see Bailey & Pillard, 1995). In one study, Bailey and Deana Beneshay (1993) identified women who were homosexual and who had a sister who was adopted, a fraternal twin, or an identical twin. Of the sisters who were adopted, only 6% were homosexual; 16% of the fraternal twins were homosexual; and 48% of identical twins were lesbian. Thus, the similarity of the siblings varied directly with the degree to which they had genes in common. This study does not demonstrate that homosexuality is an inherited characteristic. (For one thing, 52% of identical twins were *not* homosexual.) But it does suggest that genetics plays a role in sexual preference, a point supported by other research (see, for example, Eysenck, 1976).

Numerous studies have suggested that genes play an important role in some troublesome human behaviors. For example, people are more likely to suffer from manic-depression if they have an identical twin who suffers

---

[16]An implication of the fox selective breeding study is that the transformation of the wolf into the dog may have taken our primitive ancestors far less time than had been thought.

from the disease than they are if they have a fraternal twin who suffers from it (Bertelsen et al., 1977; but also see Torrey & Knable, 2002). Other research suggests a genetic link in anxiety disorders (Kendler et al., 1992), schizophrenia (Gottesman et al., 1987), and even reading disorders (Holquin-Acosta, 1997). Other researchers have found evidence that criminality may be influenced indirectly by genes (Raine & Dunkin, 1990; Rutter, 1997).

Such problem behaviors would seem to be harmful to both the individual and the species and therefore likely to be "selected out," but behavior that is problematic at one time may be helpful at another. Violent tendencies may be useful during war, for instance. Even certain forms of mental illness may have had survival value at one time. Consider agoraphobia, the fear of open spaces. In prehistoric times, those members of a group who held back while the others left the relative safety of a wooded area to enter an open meadow may have been less likely to fall prey to predators hidden in the grass. This idea is open to criticism (Schlinger, 1996), but genes do appear to play a role in maladaptive behavior.

Similarly, although people do not have a "social instinct," most do have a strong tendency toward affiliating with other people. True hermits are rare, if not nonexistent. A sense of group membership seems to be an inevitable consequence of this trait. Certain hunter-gatherer tribal groups refer to themselves by a word that in their language means merely "human being." The implication is that members of other tribes are something other than human beings. Members of sophisticated Western societies have by no means outgrown this tendency (Bandura, 1973; Keen, 1986).

It is easy to see how behavior traits may be products of natural selection. Rabbits are not well equipped for fighting, so the more combative among them are apt to be short-lived. The rabbit that flees the fox may escape, whereas the rabbit that stands and fights is unlikely to mate again. The same evolutionary forces no doubt have had their influence on human behavior: Individuals who preferred isolation to the security of the group, for example, may have been more likely to become some predator's meal. Even today, hikers in bear country are well advised to travel in groups (see Van Tighem, 2001).

Thanks to genetic variation and natural selection, then, adaptive forms of behavior (reflexes, fixed action patterns, and general behavior traits) evolve. As the environment changes, new adaptive forms of behavior appear in the species and old forms of behavior that are no longer adaptive disappear. The environment selects what is needed for the species to survive. Natural selection is a marvelous mechanism for producing behaviors suited to a changing environment, but it has its limits.

The Limits of Natural Selection

The chief problem with natural selection as a way of coping with change is that it is slow. Natural selection does not produce helpful changes in individuals now living; it merely gives a reproductive advantage to those individuals that happen to inherit favorable characteristics.

The evolution of adaptive characteristics is measured not in hours or days, then, but in generations. Natural selection is therefore of limited value in coping with abrupt changes. If the average winter temperature in a particular region were to fall one degree each century for a thousand years, the bears in the area might develop heavier coats and thicker layers of fat. But if that 10-degree fall in temperature should occur over a decade, the bears might well disappear.

Query: The chief problem with natural selection is that it is

_____ .

The sudden appearance of a new predator may also prove disastrous. Tijs Goldschmidt (1996) reports that a fishery officer introduced the Nile perch into Africa's Lake Victoria in the 1950s. The perch have prospered since then, feeding on the indigenous fish in the lake. One of these species, the small furu fish that once were abundant, has suffered. In less than half a century, this one change in the furu's environment has driven it to the verge of extinction. Natural selection was too slow to enable the furu to meet the challenge of the Nile perch.

Another example is provided by the passenger pigeon. These North American birds, which closely resembled their cousin the mourning dove, once flew in flocks so large that they blocked the sun and turned day into twilight. Although they once numbered in the millions, natural selection was no help to the passenger pigeon against the shotgun and unregulated hunting, and the last passenger pigeon died in 1914.

The human species is not immune to such risks. The Ebola virus has no effective treatment, almost inevitably ends in a horrible death, and is highly contagious. The disease originated in and is currently limited to Africa. But this is the age of the jet plane and tourism, not to mention international terrorism, so there is every reason to believe that the Ebola virus will threaten people in every continent during this century. Natural selection is unlikely to work fast enough to produce immunity to such a highly infectious and deadly disease.[17]

Another limitation of natural selection is that it is of no value whatever in helping living individuals cope with change. As a consequence, evolutionary change is always "behind the times." Individuals are not born with particular characteristics because those characteristics will help them survive, but because they helped that individual's *ancestors* survive. As the environment changes, what was for one generation a very favorable characteristic may become irrelevant or even injurious for another.

Query: Natural selection helps the _____ to

adapt to change, not the living _____ .

Lee Cronk (1992) provides several examples of this phenomenon in a delightful article called "Old Dogs, Old Tricks." "Behavioral and physical adaptations that seem to make no sense in an organism's current environment," Cronk writes, "can be traced to the legacy of an earlier, different environment in which those traits were favored" (p. 13). He cites the example of the rabbit that dodges back and forth when pursued by foxes, bobcats, and coyotes. This practice is still helpful in eluding these predators, but it is less effective when the rabbit finds itself on a highway "pursued" by a truck. Similarly, Cronk notes, armadillos befuddled approaching predators for thousands of years by springing into the air. Once again, however, this behavior is not adaptive on modern highways. As Cronk puts it, "Leap two feet high in front of a Buick, and you're buzzard bait" (p. 13).

B. F. Skinner (1983b) has pointed out that human beings also can become hostages to their genetic history. He notes that humans evolved in a world in which salt and sugar were not readily available. Those individuals who had a natural preference for these foods were more likely to get the sodium and the calories needed for survival. We have, as a consequence, evolved into a species with strong preferences for both salty and sweet foods. But our world has changed. In industrial societies, salt and sugar are abundant, and many of us consume too much of them, endangering our health in the process.

---

[17]The same might be said of smallpox. Although it no longer occurs naturally anywhere in the world, samples of the virus exist in laboratories and might be used to spread disease in an international conflict. Our ability to survive threats such as the Ebola and smallpox viruses depends on scientific method, which may be thought of as a highly effective set of procedures for solving problems.

Similarly, a strong appetite for sexual contact favored the survival of our species for thousands of years. Throughout most of human history, diseases killed most children before they reached reproductive maturity; others died in early adulthood from starvation, childbearing, or the routine hazards of an untamed world. Consequently, those individuals with strong sexual appetites were valuable to the species. But in the last 200 years, advances in medicine, sanitation, and food production have so greatly reduced the mortality rate of our young that we no longer need to be so virile for our species to survive. Yet we retain our antiquated sexual appetite, with the result that we have overpopulated the planet.

REVIEW Charles Darwin's theory of evolution holds that genetic adaptation depends on variation and natural selection. A given characteristic varies within a species, and those variations that are adaptive are selected because they contribute to the survival of individuals with that characteristic. Mutations can be passed on to progeny, thereby affecting evolution. Genetically influenced characteristics include physical attributes, such as size and weight, and certain kinds of behavior: reflexes, fixed action patterns, and general behavior traits. The evolution of adaptive forms of behavior plays an important role in the survival of a species, but evolution is a slow process that does nothing to aid the individual organism faced with a new challenge. A mechanism by which the individual organism may adapt to change is learning.

Learning: Evolved Modifiability

Learning is a change in behavior due to experience.[18] The ability to learn is itself the product of natural selection. Indeed, learning may be thought of as the crowning achievement of evolution. It is an evolved mechanism for coping with the challenges of a changing environment.

Learning is a different sort of mechanism from the inherited behaviors that we have been considering. Learning does not give the species the tendency to behave a certain way in a particular situation; rather, it gives the individual the tendency to *modify* its behavior to suit a situation. It is an evolved modifiability.

Learning takes up where reflexes, fixed action patterns, and general behavior traits leave off. It enables the organism to adapt to situations for which its largely innate behavior is inadequate. Consider, for example,

---

[18]We will examine this definition in more detail in the next chapter.

how animals come to avoid eating poisonous foods. To some extent, poisonous foods may be avoided because of an inherited tendency to avoid certain odors or tastes. But these innate preferences are not perfect: Some items that taste bad are nutritious; some that taste good are deadly. How then does an animal or a person survive this danger? The answer is by learning to avoid eating the harmful items. A rat that becomes ill after eating a grain with a particular taste is likely to avoid eating that grain again. We do exactly the same thing when we avoid eating foods that "don't agree" with us.

Poisonous foods are not the only hazards, of course, and learning plays an important role in protecting humans and other creatures from dangers such as fire, storms, famine, and natural predators. There is evidence that learning may even play an important role in fighting off diseases. Some research suggests, for example, that learning experiences can modify the behavior of the body's immune system (Ader & Cohen, 1975; Bovbjerg et al., 1990).

But learning is not merely a defense mechanism. Especially among the higher species (i.e., the better learners), learning is a means of fulfilling both the needs of survival and of achieving "the good life." An intriguing study by anthropologist Shirley Strum (1987) shows how success among baboons may depend on learned strategies. Strum studied a troop of baboons in Kenya. She noted, as others had before her, that the highest-ranking males were the most aggressive. These animals took what they wanted, be it sexual favors or food; low-ranking males were passive. This is just as the British poet, Lord Tennyson, would have it: "Nature, red in tooth and claw." But Strum began taking careful note of which animals actually benefited most from life in the troop. It wasn't, she discovered, the aggressive, dominant males that had the greatest success with females or got the best food; it was the lowest-ranking, least aggressive ones. She found, for instance, that only one out of four successful attempts to mate with females involved aggression. The less aggressive animals used a kinder, gentler approach to getting what they wanted, and it worked.

Strum found that the most aggressive males were generally newcomers; the least aggressive were long-term members of the troop. She speculates that when males first join a troop they are very aggressive, but with time they learn to use other, more effective techniques. "Real power," writes Strum, "resided with those who were 'wise' rather than those who were 'strong'" (p. 151).

Learning also provides the power to modify the physical environment. This is most clearly evident in the case of humans, whose extraordinary learning ability has enabled them to reshape the world. They are, as one writer puts it, "the only animals living in a world almost entirely of their own making. They cocoon themselves in synthetic materials, create their own daylight, breathe climate-controlled air, transform their food by cooking and chemistry and spend much of their time sending and responding to electronic messages" (Marschall, 1992, p. 52). None of these changes are the direct result of inherited behavior; all are products of learning. Such observations induce many people to wonder which is more important in determining human (and animal) success: heredity or learning.

Query: Learning ability evolved because it had

_____ value.

REVIEW Learning is a change in behavior due to experience. It is a biological mechanism for coping with change, and, like other biological features of animals, the product of evolution. Through learning, an organism can cope with changes in the environment for which its innate behavior is inadequate.

Nature and Nurture

One of the longest-running arguments in the study of behavior concerns the roles of nature and nurture. The argument usually focuses on whether behavior is inherited or learned.[19] Do we, as individuals, behave a certain way because we were "born that way," or do we behave that way because our environment "taught" us to behave that way?

The debate is evidenced in aphorisms people use every day, often without thinking about their larger significance. Is it true, for instance, that "blood will tell," or is it more accurate to say that "as the twig is bent, so the tree is inclined"? Are leaders born, or are they made? Can a person "turn over a new leaf," or is the leopard stuck with its spots?

Of course, no one denies that learning is important, at least in higher animals, and no one completely ignores the role of heredity. B. F. Skinner is often called an "extreme environmentalist," yet his earliest research interest was in biology, and throughout his career he wrote of the role of biology in behavior. In one passage, he writes that "behavior requires a behaving organism which is the product of a genetic process. Gross dif-

---

[19] Nurture incorporates more than learning. An injury, for example, often affects behavior.

The Superior Animal

Humans spend an amazing amount of time trying to prove their superiority over other species. Part of this effort has been devoted to finding some uniquely human characteristic, some quality that sets our species apart from lower organisms. We used to say, for example, that homo sapiens was the only animal that reasoned, but studies of animal learning raised serious doubts about that. We said that we were the only creature to make and use tools, but then we discovered that chimpanzees make and use tools all the time. We said that humans were the only animals capable of learning language, but then we taught apes and porpoises to communicate.

One by one, the characteristics that we have held to be uniquely human have been found in other species. The ultimate futility of this endeavor was pointed out by the British philosopher Bertrand Russell: "Organic life, we are told, has developed gradually from the protozoan to the philosopher; and this development, we are assured, is indubitably an advance. Unfortunately, it is the philosopher, not the protozoan, who gives us this assurance" (quoted in Durant, 1926/1927, p. 523).

Perhaps the only uniquely human characteristic is this: So far as we know, we are the only creature that spends time trying to prove its superiority over other creatures. The rest of the animal kingdom treats the matter with indifference.

ferences in the behavior of different species show that the genetic constitution . . . is important" (1953, p. 26). Similarly, biologists such as E. O. Wilson who emphasize hereditary factors in behavior are often labeled "biological determinists," yet they acknowledge that experience plays an important role as well.

Nevertheless, for centuries people have lined up on one side or the other of the nature-nurture debate, arguing that one or the other, heredity or learning, is the more important determinant of behavior.

The trouble with the nature-nurture debate is that it creates an artificial division between the contributions of heredity and experience. The debate wrongly implies that the answer must be one or the other (Kuo, 1967; Midgley, 1987). In fact, nature and nurture are inextricably interwoven in a kind of Gordian knot. The two strands cannot be separated.[20]

---

[20] Someone has said that asking, "Which is more important in determining behavior, heredity or environment?" is like asking, "Which is more important in determining the area of a rectangle, width or length?"

Consider the question, Are humans naturally aggressive? Wilson (1978) reports that among the !Kung San, an aboriginal people of Africa, violence against their fellows was almost unknown. But Wilson points out that several decades earlier, when the population density among these people was greater and when there was less governmental control over their behavior, their per capita murder rate rivaled that of America's most dangerous cities.

Wilson (1978) adds that the Semai of Malaya also have demonstrated the capacity for both gentleness and violence. Murder is unknown among these people; they do not even have a word in their language for the concept. Yet when the British colonial government trained Semai men to fight against Communist guerrillas in the 1950s, the Semai became fierce warriors. One anthropologist wrote that "they seem to have been swept up in a sort of insanity which they call 'blood drunkenness'" (Dentan, quoted in Wilson, 1978, p. 100). Wilson concludes from such evidence that "the more violent forms of human aggression are not the manifestations of inborn drives . . . [but are] based on the interaction of genetic potential and learning" (Wilson, 1978, p. 105).

Experiments with animals support this view. Zing Yang Kuo (1930) of China reared kittens under different conditions.[21] Some grew up with their mothers and had the opportunity to see them kill rats. Others grew up away from their mothers and never saw rats killed. When the kittens had matured, Kuo put them together with rats. He found that 86% of the cats that had been reared with their mothers killed rats, but only 45% of the others did. Thus, even something as basic as killing "natural" prey is influenced by experience.

What is true of aggression is true of other kinds of behavior. Harry and Margaret Harlow (1962a, 1962b) reared infant monkeys in isolation to see how their development would be affected. They found, among other things, that these monkeys became sexually incompetent adults. When given the opportunity to mate with a normally reared monkey, they sometimes showed an interest, but were at a loss as to how to proceed. Isolation had evidently deprived them of learning experiences important to normal sexual functioning.

> **Query:**   Kuo's experiment showed that whether cats killed rats
>
> depended on whether they saw _____.

---

[21]Here and there I mention the nationalities of researchers in order to show that learning research is done around the world. I do not do it all the time because it might get tiresome for the reader, and because nationality is not always easily determined.

Again, the same phenomenon may be seen in humans. The mistaken ideas that children and some uneducated adults have about sex and reproduction make it clear that learning is very important in the development of human sexual behavior, but human sexuality is not entirely the product of learning. Numerous studies have suggested that heredity may play an important part, for instance, in determining the frequency of adult sexual activity, the number of sexual partners a person has in a lifetime, and even the kinds of sexual practices an individual finds acceptable (Eysenck, 1976). As in the case of aggressive behavior, sexual behavior is not entirely a matter of "doing what comes naturally"; it is the product of both heredity and learning.

Child-rearing practices follow a similar pattern. In their studies of monkeys, the Harlows (1962a, 1962b) found that when female monkeys reared in isolation had offspring, they later became poor mothers. They seldom petted or fondled their young, and even neglected to nurse them. There are no comparable studies of humans reared in isolation, of course, but studies do show that many child abusers were neglected or abused themselves as children (Widom, 1989; Wiehe, 1992). Innate tendencies are clearly insufficient to account for human parenting behavior.

Deviant behaviors are the products of the interaction of heredity and learning. Selective breeding can produce successively more deviant offspring, but certain kinds of experience can also produce a "nervous breakdown" in otherwise healthy animals (Pavlov, 1927; Masserman, 1943). The Harlows (1962a, 1962b) found that their isolated monkeys, though genetically normal, grew up to be "neurotic" adults: chronically fearful and socially inept.

A similar picture emerges from a study of deviant behavior in humans. There is evidence that humans can inherit a tendency toward anxiety, bizarre thinking, and other forms of abnormal behavior (Carter, 1933; Pedersen et al., 1988). Experience, however, also plays an important role in aberrant behavior. Henry P. David and his colleagues (1988) report, for example, that unwanted children are more likely than others to show signs of maladjustment, which suggests that early learning experiences play an important role in adult adjustment.

The ability to learn is itself the product of both heredity and experience. Numerous studies have shown that genes play a role in determining differences in learning ability, but many other studies have shown that learning experiences are also important. Animal studies beginning in the 1960s demonstrated that laboratory animals reared in complex environments develop larger brains and learn faster than animals reared in simpler environments (e.g., Rosenzweig et al., 1968). Similar experiments are not possible with humans, of course, but studies of naturally occurring differences in environment yield similar results. For instance, Betty Hart and Todd Risley (1995; for a summary see Chance, 1997) did a longitudinal study of the verbal environment provided by parents with different educational backgrounds. They found huge differences in the amount and kinds of verbal exchanges between parents and their infant children. Those children whose parents talked to them a lot (providing lengthy explanations and lots of positive feedback, for example) scored higher on intelligence and vocabulary tests several years later than those children whose parents were more reticent. The differences held even when race and socioeconomic level were held constant.

It is clear, then, that while we are biological organisms, we are also environmental organisms. Heredity is a very important influence on behavior, but the notion that genes *cause* behavior is now, according to geneticists themselves, thoroughly discredited (Morange, 2001). All forms of behavior reflect a blending of nature and nurture. Heredity and learning are merely different aspects of the same process, the effort to cope with life's one constant—change.

REVIEW   The argument over the relative importance of heredity and learning in determining behavior tends to obscure the underlying fact that both genetics and learning typically contribute to the survival of the individual and the species. They are merely different ways of adapting to change.

RECOMMENDED READING

1. Gould, S. J. (2002). *The structure of evolutionary theory.* Cambridge, MA: Harvard University Press.

   "Mr. Evolution" describes the current status of evolutionary theory.

2. Keynes, R. (2002). *Darwin, his daughter, and human evolution.* New York: Penguin/Putnam.

   A personal look at Darwin during the years after the *Beagle* voyage.

3. Mayr, E. (2000, July). Darwin's influence on modern thought. *Scientific American*, 79–83.

   This article by one of the leading figures in evolution was included in *The Best American Science Writing 2001*.

4. Morange, Michel (2001). *The misunderstood gene.* Cambridge, MA: Harvard University Press.

   Morange maintains that "the concept of the gene that is used both by

the general public and by many scientists is completely outmoded."
See especially the chapter on genes affecting behavior.

5. Trut, L. N. (1999, March/April). Early canid domestication: The farm-fox experiment. *American Scientist, 87,* 160–169.

A 40-year experiment in which researchers bred farm foxes selected for "tamability." The result has been a dramatic change in both the behavior and appearance of foxes.

REVIEW QUESTIONS

Note: Many of the questions that appear here (and in subsequent chapters) cannot be answered merely by searching through the chapter and copying a line or two from the text. To answer the questions properly, you may have to apply information in the text in imaginative ways.

1. Define the following terms. Give an example or illustration of each that is *not* taken from the text.

aversive	mutation
fixed action pattern	natural selection
general behavior trait	reflex
habituation	releaser
learning	sensitization

2. What is the mechanism by which species change as their environments change?

3. Are humans still evolving? Explain.

4. Why has the field mouse not evolved into an animal as large and ferocious as the grizzly bear?

5. In what sense is natural selection the product of experience?

6. In what sense is learning the product of natural selection?

7. How are reflexes and fixed action patterns like the ROM (read-only memory) of a computer?

8. Invent a new reflex, one that would be helpful to humans.

9. One learning specialist (Rachlin, 1976) refers to fixed action patterns as complex reflexes. Do you like this idea? Explain.

10. Who said change is the only constant, and what did he mean?

11. Why is natural selection "behind the times"?

12. During wars, some soldiers sacrifice themselves to save their comrades. Some behavior scientists believe such altruistic behavior is

the product of natural selection. How can this be, when the altruistic act ends the person's opportunities for reproduction?

13. How are reflexes, fixed action patterns, and general behavior traits alike? How do they differ?

14. How would the length of a species' life span affect its chances of adapting to change through natural selection? Hint: Consider fruit flies in the dark.

15. A person is asked to blink his eyes and does so. Is this a reflex act? Explain.

16. Why are most mutations unhelpful?

17. In an unchanging world, would an organism with appropriate innate behavior need to learn?

18. Under what circumstances might learning be *non*adaptive?

19. Captive animals behave very differently from animals in the wild. In which circumstance is their true nature revealed? Where should one look to see true human nature?

20. People sometimes suggest that one thing that separates humans from other animals is the tendency of people to believe in God. Is this distinction valid? If so, is the belief in God innate?

PRACTICE QUIZ

1. Learning is a _____ in _____ due to _____ .

2. The human fondness for sugar and _____ illustrates that behavior that has survival value at one time may be harmful at another time.

3. The sight of a chick with an open mouth reliably results in an adult bird providing food. The chick's open mouth is an example of a _____ .

4. Evolution is the product of _____ and _____ .

5. A reflex is a _____ between a specific _____ and a simple response.

6. In *The Blind Watchmaker*, Richard Dawkins suggests that the arrangement of _____ on a _____

demonstrates how order can come out of disorder without intelligent intervention.

7. _____ is a reduction in the intensity or probability of a response due to repeated exposure to a stimulus that elicits that response.

8. Peter and Rosemary Grant demonstrated natural selection in finches on the Galapagos Islands. They found that during _____ , finches with larger beaks survived and reproduced, while those with smaller beaks died off.

9. The chief limitation of natural selection as a mechanism for coping with change is that it is _____ .

10. An aversive event is one that is _____ .

QUERY ANSWERS

Page 4. Species change through natural *selection.*

Page 8. An abrupt change in a gene is called a *mutation.* Those that occur in *reproductive/germ* cells may be transmitted to offspring.

Page 9. A reflex is a *relation/relationship* between a specific *event/ stimulus* and a simple *behavior/response.*

Page 12. Sensitization involves an *increase* in the probability or intensity of a reflex response; habituation involves a *decrease* in its probability or intensity.

Page 13. Fixed action patterns differ from reflexes in that FAPs involve the *whole/entire* organism and are more *complex* and *variable.*

Page 14. The color red is a *releaser* for aggression in the male stickleback.

Page 18. An event an organism tends to avoid is called an *aversive.*

Page 20. The fox-breeding study selectively mated foxes on the basis of *behavior.*

Page 22 The chief problem with natural selection is that it is *slow.*

Page 23. Natural selection helps the *species* to adapt to change, not the living *individual.*

Page 26. Learning ability evolved because it had *survival* value.

Page 28. Kuo's experiment showed that whether cats killed rats depended on whether they saw *their mothers kill rats.*

The Study of Learning and Behavior

My business is to teach my aspirations to conform themselves to fact, not to try and make facts harmonize with my aspirations. . . Sit down before fact as a little child, be prepared to give up every preconceived notion, follow humbly wherever and to whatever abysses nature leads, or you shall learn nothing.

T. H. Huxley

People have always been interested in learning.[1] Poets, educators, and philosophers have admired learning, sung its praises, and wondered at its power. But learning has been the subject of *scientific* analysis for only about a hundred years.

What does scientific analysis mean when it comes to learning? Answers to this question vary, but many researchers now take a natural science approach to the study of learning. The natural sciences use a variety of techniques to understand their respective fields. The tools of the physicist are not the same as those of the biologist. However, there are certain common elements in their work. One of these is an emphasis on physical events.

The ancient Greeks may have "explained" the behavior of falling bodies by theorizing that the object feels a need to return to its natural place, the earth, but the modern physicist's explanation has to do with the relative masses of the object and of earth and of the distance separating them. In the past, natural philosophers may have interpreted a plant's tendency to turn toward the sun as an act of will by the plant, but the modern botanist explains the phenomenon by pointing to physical changes in the plant produced by sunlight. In the natural sciences, explaining a phenomenon means identifying the physical events that produce it.

This approach has proved tremendously effective, not only in improving our understanding of the natural world but also in producing practical solutions to problems. Yet we have been slow to apply the same approach to behavior. We routinely say, for example, that a man slams a door because he feels angry or that a rat presses a lever because it knows lever pressing produces food.

---

[1]Learning is a major topic in the field of psychology. John B. Watson called it the "great problem in all human psychology" (1910; quoted in Lattal, 2001, p. 351) and it has largely dominated experimental psychology, at least in the United States.

Such "explanations" are troublesome, not so much because the events referred to cannot be publicly observed, but because the explanations they provide are circular. In a circular explanation, the evidence for the explanation is the very thing that is being explained: Why did the man slam the door? Because he was angry. How do we know he was angry? *Because he slammed the door.* Why does the rat press the lever? Because it knows lever pressing produces food. How do we know the rat knows this? *Because it presses the lever.* In science, this simply will not do!

This is not to say that thoughts and feelings do not exist or are unimportant. It may well be that a man who slams a door is angry, but his anger doesn't explain his behavior. For if we blame the door slamming on anger, we must then ask, "Why is he angry?" Similarly, a rat may know that pressing a lever produces food, but why does the rat know this? These questions bring us back again to physical events. To explain behavior, we must identify the physical events that reliably produce it.

Because the natural science approach to behavior is very foreign to many students, this chapter is devoted to its application to the study of learning. We may as well begin with the definition of our subject.[2]

Learning Defined

You saw in the previous chapter that learning is defined as a change in behavior due to experience.[3] But this definition is deceptively simple; to truly understand it, we must examine it with some care.

Learning Means Change

Consider, for example, the word *change*. Why should learning be said to be a *change* in behavior? Why not say, for example, that learning is the acquisition of behavior?

The word *change* is preferred over *acquisition* because learning does not always involve acquiring something (at least, not in the usual sense), but it does always involve some sort of change. Consider this example: Domesticated hens have a tendency to establish a pecking order, or rank.

---

[2] There is a school of thought, popular in university social science departments and in colleges of education, that says the scientific method that has served the world so well for 400 years is now outmoded, that science is just a debate about an unknowable reality. This philosophy, called Constructivism (Cobb, 2000), is sometimes attributed to Thomas Kuhn in his book, *The Structure of Scientific Revolutions.* Interestingly, Kuhn himself rejected this interpretation of his work (Dyson, 1999), as do the vast majority of scientists.

[3] Some authorities insist that only *durable* changes qualify as learning, but since there is no consensus about what durable means (a few seconds? a minute? a week? a year?), adding the term does not seem to help. Some psychologists define learning as a change in "cognitive structures" or as the storage of information, but since these concepts are inferred from behavior, they add little to the definition.

When a new bird joins a flock, it fights with the other birds until it establishes its proper position in the hierarchy of feathered society. It will then dominate those birds beneath it in rank and defer to those above it. Although the tendency to establish a pecking order is innate, learning also appears to be involved. Learning in this case means that the bird continues to peck certain birds, but *gives up* pecking others. In this instance, learning seems to mean that something is lost rather than gained.

Similarly, learning among humans sometimes means giving up something: Joan would like to *quit* smoking; Bill wants to *stop* biting his nails; and Mary and Harry would like to quarrel *less*. All of these reductions in behavior, if they occur, are examples of learning, but nothing has been acquired—at least, not in the ordinary sense of that word.

What Changes Is Behavior

What changes when learning occurs is behavior. **Behavior** may be defined as anything an organism does that can be measured (Reber, 1995).[4] Actually, anything an organism does might qualify as behavior, but for scientific analysis we are necessarily limited to behavior that can be measured. In fact, a particular behavior is defined by its measurement (see Defining Operations).[5]

Some people argue that learning should be defined as a change in the nervous system that makes a change in behavior possible. In this view, behavior change is merely a symptom or correlate of learning. There is probably no learning researcher who would deny that learning involves a change in the nervous system. However, there are at least two problems with equating learning with physiological or anatomical changes. One problem is that we don't yet understand what changes take place when learning occurs. No one can point to changes in a rat's brain and say, for example, "This animal can run a maze better today than it did yesterday." Nor can anyone point to features of a person's brain and say, "This person can play the piano." At present, the only reliable measure of learning is a change in behavior.

A second problem with defining learning as neurological change is that it denies the importance of behavior. It is, of course, important to understand how experience changes the nervous system. But even if we were able to say, on the basis of physiological measures, "This rat can

---

[4] The word *organism* refers to both plant and animal life; I use it in this text to refer only to the latter.

[5] English and English (1958) note that one problem in defining behavior is to identify where behavior ends and physiology begins. For example, is the beating of the heart behavior or physiology? What about the firing of a neuron? Both can be modified by experience, but are they behavior?

Defining Operations

For research purposes, behavior must be defined in terms of of its measurement. Because the operation used to measure behavior defines it, this is called an **operational definition**.

In ordinary conversation, we might talk about the way the smell of good food makes our mouths water. To study this phenomenon, however, we must define mouth watering in some precise way. A person's mouth waters when the salivary glands secrete saliva, so we might measure the excretion from these glands by putting cotton balls in either side of a person's mouth. After a time, we would collect these cotton balls and weigh them; this would give us a measure of salivation. Salivation is defined, in this instance, as the number of milligrams of saliva absorbed by cotton balls of a certain size placed at particular points in the mouth for a specified period of time.

Similarly, we may be interested in teaching a pigeon to peck a small disk, but what is a disk peck? If the bird makes a pecking motion in the direction of the disk, is that a disk peck? If it strikes the area near the disk, does that count? What if it touches the disk very lightly with its beak? If three people observed a pigeon and counted disk pecks, we might easily get three different counts. For this reason, researchers typically use a recording apparatus that is activated when a certain amount of pressure is exerted on the disk. If the bird strikes the disk hard enough to activate the recorder, it has disk-pecked; otherwise, it has not.

Notice that our definition of behavior does not require that each performance be the same as the last. A pigeon may peck a disk hundreds of times in the course of an experiment, but that does not mean that every peck is exactly the same. In fact, it is likely that among those hundreds of disk pecks, no two are exactly alike. A given bird may strike a disk a glancing blow from the right, then from the left, then head-on. It may peck the disk with varying amounts of force. It may peck the center of the disk, the top, the bottom, or either side. It may peck while arching its neck or standing on one foot or flapping its wings. Yet each of these variations in behavior counts as a disk-peck if it activates the recording device.

Although salivating and disk pecking are simple acts, behavior can be very complex. In the laboratory, a researcher may train a rat to run a maze. The maze may be quite intricate, and running it may require making correct turns at dozens of choice points. The behavior called "running the maze" consists of performing all of the steps necessary to reach the end of the maze.

Does our definition of behavior mean that feeling and thinking are off limits to scientific analysis? The point is debated, but most learning researchers would probably say that if feeling and thinking can be operationally defined (i.e., defined in terms of measurement), they can be studied.

If we wish to study fear of spiders in people, for example, we may define fear as a rise in heart rate, an increase in the rate of respiration, an increase in the electrical activity of certain muscles, an increase in the electrical conductivity of the skin, a verbal expression of fear, or as some combination of these or other acts in the presence of spiders. Some behavior scientists would say that fear *is* these acts, whereas others would argue that they merely indicate the presence of fear. But even if sweating and breathing faster are not the same thing as feeling afraid, they are reliably found in people who are judged to be afraid and so they make convenient measures of fear.

Thinking is perhaps more challenging than emotion, but the same standard applies. We cannot measure thoughts directly (although to some extent we can measure their neurological correlates), but sometimes thoughts spill over into the public arena, and can be measured. For instance, when students study for an exam or try to solve a difficult problem, they use the same vocal muscles used in speech even though they remain silent. By electronically monitoring their speech apparatus, we can observe these subtle measures of thought. Even a person who is unable to speak can have thoughts monitored if that person is proficient in sign language. Mute people who use sign language in communicating with others think with their fingers (Max, 1935). We can also study thinking to some extent by asking people to "think out loud" as they work toward the solution of a problem (Ericsson & Simon, 1993). Such "protocol analysis," as it is called, is a popular tool among some researchers, particularly cognitive psychologists.

All of the methods for studying thinking mentioned here involve verbal behavior. Many people would probably say that thinking also includes nonverbal activity, such as imagining. (However, see the discussion of thinking in Reese, 2001.) We may be able to define imagining operationally as behaving as though an object were present when, in fact, it is not. For example, I can show you the floor plan of a house and ask you questions about it ("Is the master bedroom at the east end of the house or the west?"), and I can then remove the floor plan and ask questions. The degree to which your answers when the floor plan is absent are as accurate as those given when the plan is present could be considered a measure of imaging. However, this would be disputed by some researchers, who would argue that we are studying verbal behavior—the answers to questions—not imaging.

In any case, operational definitions are key to the scientific analysis of behavior.

run a maze better today," or "This person can play a piano," it would not follow that the study of behavior is useless. The changes in behavior produced by experience are important *in their own right*, and not merely as a way of studying the nervous system. Insofar as learning is concerned, behavior is literally "where it's at."

Query: Behavior is anything an organism does that can be

_____ .

What Changes Behavior Is Experience

Our definition says that learning is due to experience. For our purposes, the term *experience* refers to exposure to events that affect, or are capable of affecting, behavior. Such an event is called a **stimulus**.[6]

Stimuli are *physical* events: They are the changes in air pressure that we call sound, the light waves we call sights, the tactile pressures we call touch. The delicate fragrance of a rose derives from just so many molecules of "rose matter" arising from the flower. Even the gentle caress and softly whispered words of a lover are, in scientific terms, merely physical events. Stimuli often have significance beyond their physical properties (the smell of a rose may remind us of a friend), but it is their physical properties that define them.

Query: A stimulus is an environmental event that is capable of

affecting _____ .

Not all changes in behavior are due to experience, and not all experiences are learning experiences. If a child cannot walk at all at twelve months, but walks well at eighteen months, the change probably has more to do with maturation than with experience. Similarly, a physician may give an emotionally distraught person a tranquilizer, but we do not then say that the patient learned to be calm. A person who is usually very agreeable may, following a head injury, be very argumentative. If this change in behavior can be attributed to the injury, we do not say that

---

[6] Stimuli can include events that take place within a person's body. An abscessed tooth can cause pain, for example. For the most part, however, learning is the product of events in our surroundings. In laboratory research, a single stimulus may be identified for study, but a given stimulus is always part of a complex array of stimuli. A light that comes on in a small chamber may have different effects, for example, from the effects of the same light coming on in a large chamber.

he learned to be quarrelsome. Thus, changes in behavior that are due to aging, injury, drugs, or disease do not qualify as learning.

REVIEW   Learning is a change in behavior due to experience. The word *change* is used because learning does not necessarily involve acquisition. Behavior is anything an organism does that can be measured, and experience means exposure to events that are capable of having a measurable effect on behavior. Such events are called *stimuli*.

Measuring Learning

If learning is a change in behavior, then to measure it we must measure changes in behavior. This can be done in many ways.

A common way of measuring learning is to look for a reduction in *errors*. A rat can be said to have learned to run a maze to the extent that it goes from start to finish without taking a wrong turn. As training progresses, the rat will make fewer and fewer errors (see Figure 2-1). Similarly, a student is said to have learned a spelling list when she can spell all the words without error. One way to measure progress in reading is to record the number of times the student stumbles over a word, with each such stumble counting as one error.

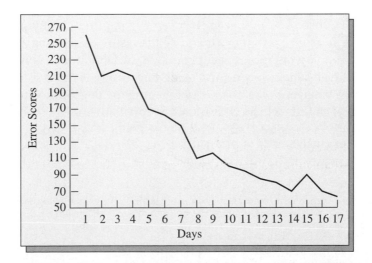

Figure 2-1   *Errors as a measurement of learning. A decline in the number of errors (such as entering the wrong alleys of a maze) is a measure of learning. (Adapted from Tolman and Honzik, 1930.)*

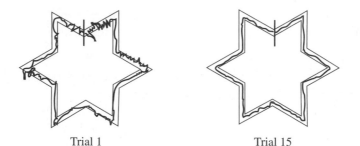

Trial 1   Trial 15

Figure 2-2 *Topography as a measure of learning. A person attempted to trace between the lines of a star while looking at the figure's image in a mirror. On the first trial the participant's performance was shaky and erratic; by trial 15, the performance was much improved. The change in topography is a measure of learning. (Adapted from Kingsley and Garry, 1962, p. 304.)*

Learning may be measured as a change in the *topography* of a behavior, which refers to the form a behavior takes.[7] (You might think of a topographic map, which shows the form of the earth's surface.) Topography may be used as a measure of learning in mirror tracing. The task is to trace a form while looking at its reflection in a mirror. It is harder than it sounds, and at first the pencil line meanders wildly. With practice, however, a person can trace the shape rather neatly (see Figure 2-2). The change in topography is a measure of learning.[8]

We can also measure learning by noting changes in the *intensity* of a behavior. When a laboratory rat learns to press a lever, the resistance of the lever may be increased so that greater force is required to depress it. The increase in pressure exerted by the rat is a measure of learning (see Figure 2-3). The same sort of process occurs outside the laboratory. Having taught a child to sing a song, we can then teach her to sing it more softly. I once impressed my neighbors to no end by teaching my dog, Sunny, to "speak" (bark loudly) and to "whisper" (bark softly) on command.[9]

A change in the *speed* with which a behavior is performed is another measure of learning. The rat that has learned to run a maze reaches the goal faster than an untrained rat (see Figure 2-4). In the same way, a first-

---

[7]There is some overlap in the various measures of learning. For example, in the tracing task illustrated in Figure 2-2, we might count the number of times the pencil marks fall outside the star. If we count each such point as an error, we can measure learning as a reduction in errors rather than a change in topography.

[8]Computers are now being used to track topographical changes in three-dimensional space. For example, the movements of a fish through an aquarium can be tracked (Pear & Chan, 2001).

[9]I received no credit for the dog's performance, however. The dog's skill was attributed to its remarkable intelligence, not to my skill as a teacher. The same thing occurs in classrooms: When a student does well, one rarely hears a parent say, "My, what a good teacher you have."

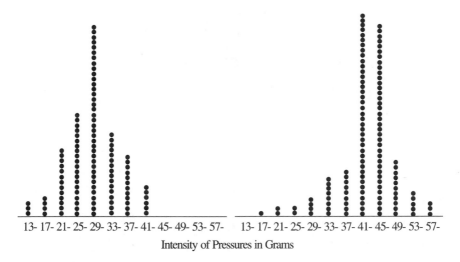

Intensity of Pressures in Grams

Figure 2-3 *Response intensity as a measure of learning. These frequency distributions show variations in the force exerted by a rat in depressing a lever. The left shows the distribution when all lever presses with a force of at least 21 grams produced a food pellet. The right shows the distribution when the requirement was raised to 38 grams. The increase in force exerted is a measure of learning. (After Hull, 1943, p. 305.)*

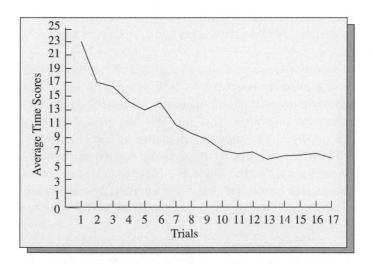

Figure 2-4 *Speed as a measure of learning. The decline in the average time it takes rats to run a maze indicates learning. (Adapted from Tolman and Honzik, 1930.)*

grader takes a long time to recite the alphabet at the beginning of the year but later runs through it with the speed of an auctioneer. Likewise, the beginning typist takes a long time to type a sentence whereas the expert does it quickly. As these examples illustrate, learning often means

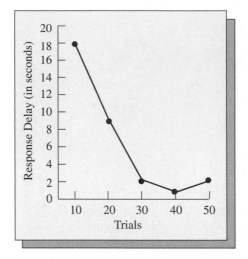

Figure 2-5   *Latency as a measure of learning. There is a long delay before the response (in this case, salivating) appears, but this latency gets shorter with more trials. (Compiled from data in Anrep, 1920.)*

doing something more quickly. It is possible, however, to learn to perform an act more slowly. When children are very hungry, they are inclined to eat quickly; learning good table manners means learning to slow down.

A similar measure of learning is a change in *latency*, the time that passes before a behavior occurs. We will see in the next chapter that a dog can be taught to salivate at the sound of a bell. As the training proceeds, the interval between the bell and the first drop of saliva gets shorter; this change in latency is a measure of learning (see Figure 2-5). Similarly, a student beginning to learn the multiplication table pauses before answering a question such as "How much is 5 times 7?" With practice, the pauses become shorter, and eventually the student responds without hesitation. This decrease in hesitation, or latency, is a measure of learning.

Learning is often measured as a change in the *rate* or *frequency* at which a behavior occurs. These terms refer to the number of occurrences per unit of time. A pigeon may peck a disk at the rate of, say, 5 to 10 times a minute. The experimenter may then attempt to increase or decrease the rate of disk pecking. The resulting change in rate is a measure of learning. Similarly, a person may practice receiving Morse code by telegraph. If the rate of decoding (the number of letters correctly recorded per minute) increases, we say that he has learned (see Figure 2-6). Learn-

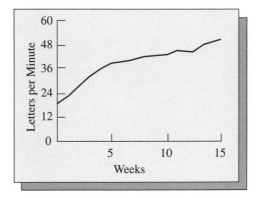

Figure 2-6   *Rate as a measure of learning. Number of Morse code letters correctly received. The increase in rate of decoding is a measure of learning. (Adapted from Bryan and Harter, 1899.)*

ing often means an increase in the rate of behavior, but it can also mean a decrease in rate. A musician may learn to play the notes of a composition more slowly, for example.[10]

Behavior rate has proved to be an especially useful measure of learning, partly because it allows us to see subtle changes in behavior. In laboratory studies, behavior rate is often tallied by means of an electromechanical or electonic **cumulative recorder**. With one such device, every occurrence of the behavior under study is recorded by the movement of an inked pen on a sheet of paper that moves under the pen at a steady pace.[11] So long as the behavior in question did not occur, the pen made a straight line along the length of the paper. When the behavior occurred, the pen moved a short distance at a right angle to the length of the paper (see Figure 2-7A). The higher the rate of behavior, the more pen movements and the steeper the slope of the ink line; the lower the rate, the flatter the line.[12] A given point on the line indicates the total number of occurrences of the behavior to that point, so the graph provides a **cumulative record** (see Figure 2-7B). Today, the cumulative recorder is likely to be gathering dust in a storage room, replaced by computer software such as Med Associates' Med-PC®. The cumulative record produced

---

[10]Note that speed and rate are related, but not identical, measures of learning.

[11]The device described, and pictured in Figure 2-7, was first devised by B. F. Skinner (1938). However, Skinner was not the first to record behavior cumulatively. James Todd (personal communication, December 7, 2001) reports that James A. Slonaker (1912) did so decades earlier.

[12]Since the line indicates the total number of times a behavior has occurred as of a given point in time, it can never fall below the horizontal.

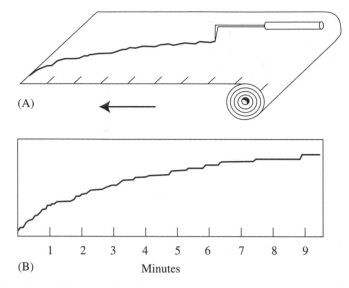

(A)

(B)   Minutes
            1   2   3   4   5   6   7   8   9

Figure 2-7   *Cumulative record and response rate. In a cumulative recorder, an inked pen moves at right angles each time a response occurs (A), thus yielding a cumulative record of behavior (B). A change in the rate of behavior indicates learning.*

by the computer is, however, essentially the same as the one produced by the older electromechanical device.

Query: If the rate of a behavior is increasing, the slope of the

cumulative record _____. A flat record indicates that

the behavior is _____.

The measures of learning discussed here are among the most commonly used in research, but there are others. *Fluency,* for example, is a combination of errors and rate; it is the number correct per minute.[13] For example, a student who calls out the answers to single-digit addition problems (such as 9 + 4, 7 + 3, and 5 + 9) provided by a teacher, may call out 12 answers in one minute. If 10 of those answers are correct, then his fluency measure is 10 correct per minute. If, after instruction or practice, his fluency rate is 22 correct per minute, that provides a clear measure of learning.

---

[13] Cognitive psychologists refer to this as *automaticity.*

REVIEW   Learning can be measured as a change in number of errors, topography, intensity, speed, latency, or rate of behavior. There are other ways of measuring learning as well. The point is that we cannot study learning unless we can measure it in some precise way. But there is more to studying learning than measuring it; there is also the problem of designing research.

Research Designs

Various sources of evidence are available to those who study learning. Each has strengths and weaknesses.

Anecdotal Evidence

Anecdotal evidence consists of first- or secondhand reports of personal experiences. Anecdotes are often identified by phrases such as, "In my experience . . ." and "I've found that. . . ." Sometimes anecdotal evidence takes on the character of common wisdom: "They say that . . ."; "It's common knowledge that . . ."; and "Everybody knows that. . . ."

Unfortunately, what "everybody knows" is not always correct. Bloodletting persisted as a treatment for medical disorders for generations because "everybody knew" that it worked. People can point to anecdotal evidence to support all kinds of principles and practices, but sorting out which anecdotes to believe is often difficult.

Perhaps the best way to demonstrate the trouble with anecdotes is with an anecdote. I once spoke to a psychologist who complained about the school his daughter attended. "You won't believe this," he said, "but they don't teach the kids how to read." He was talking about Whole Language, a method of reading instruction in which students are read to and exposed to books, but aren't taught to decode words by sounding out the phonemes. The assumption is that the students will pick up decoding skills through a kind of osmosis, without any formal instruction. Unfortunately, the psychologist's child, whom I will call Samantha, was *not* learning to read. I asked her father what he did. "We got a how-to book," he said, "and taught her to read."

Now, although Whole Language has been discredited as a way of teaching beginning reading skills (Chall, 1995; Treiman, 2000), this anecdote does not qualify as hard evidence against it: The psychologist may have exaggerated his child's failure to read; the problem may have been due to a poor teacher, an unnoticed illness, or some other variable besides the method of instruction. We simply cannot say *from such anecdotes* that Whole Language is ineffective.

Positive anecdotes are, of course, equally untrustworthy. Let us suppose, for example, that you meet a teacher who is a devoted practitioner of Whole Language. You ask the teacher if the method works. She replies, "Absolutely! I've seen it work. I had one student last year who picked up reading easily without any formal instruction at all. Her name was Samantha. . . ." You see the problem: The teacher who "sees" an instructional method working may be unaware of other important variables, such as instruction in the home.

Despite its limitations, anecdotal evidence is not to be summarily dismissed. Anecdotes can provide useful leads, and they keep us in contact with "popular wisdom" which, after all, is not always wrong. Still, better evidence is required for a science of learning.

Case Studies

We get a slightly better grade of data with the **case study**. Whereas anecdotal evidence consists of casual observations, a case study examines a particular individual in considerable detail.

The case study method is often used in medicine. A patient with a particular disease or symptom may be studied with great care as doctors attempt to understand his illness better. Economists also do case studies. They may study a particular company to find out why it failed or succeeded. Similarly, educational researchers might do a detailed study of a teacher or school that gets particularly good results. And case studies are often used in attempting to understand abnormal behavior, such as delusions.

There are, however, serious problems with case study evidence. One problem is that doing a case study takes a good deal of time. Because of this, generalizations are often based on a very few participants. If those few participants are not representative of the group they represent, conclusions about that group may be in error.

Another problem is that the case study cannot answer certain questions about behavior. We cannot, for example, use the case study to determine whether falling off a ladder is likely to produce a fear of heights. We may interview a person who fell off a ladder and who subsequently developed a fear of heights, but this does not establish that the fall caused the fear. For years, many clinical psychologists and psychiatrists insisted that homosexuality was a neurotic disorder because their homosexual clients were all neurotic. Then, in the 1950s, Evelyn Hooker pointed out that the *heterosexual* clients of clinicians were also neurotic, but no one concluded that heterosexuality was a form of neurosis (see Chance, 1975).

Case study evidence is also flawed in that much of the data obtained comes not by direct observation of the participant's behavior, but from what the participant or other people report about the participant's behavior. Such secondhand reports are notoriously unreliable.

When appropriate, the case study is a step above the anecdote because at least the data are obtained in a fairly systematic way. But a sound science of behavior cannot be built on the sandy soil of the case study. Better control is required.

Query: The chief difference between anecdotal and case study

evidence is that _____.

Descriptive Studies

In a **descriptive study**, the researcher attempts to describe a group by obtaining data from its members—often by conducting interviews or administering questionnaires. To devoted advocates of the case study, the descriptive study seems superficial. But by gathering data from many cases and analyzing the data statistically, the descriptive study reduces the risk that a few unrepresentative participants will distort the findings.

In a typical descriptive study, we might ask people (in interviews or by means of a questionnaire) about their fears and their childhood experiences. We might then compare the childhood experiences of those who have phobias with those who do not. Statistical analysis would then reveal whether there were any reliable differences between the two groups. We might find, for example, that people with phobias are no more likely to have overprotective parents than people without phobias, but are more likely to have had traumatic experiences with the feared item.

Descriptive studies represent a vast improvement over case studies, but they have their limitations. One is that although descriptive studies can suggest hypotheses to explain a phenomenon, they cannot test those hypotheses. We might find that phobia victims are twice as likely as others to describe their parents as overprotective, yet overprotective parenting may not be important in producing phobias. It could be, for example, that overprotective parenting is associated with some other variable, and this other variable is what accounts for the higher incidence of phobias. Even if we replicate a descriptive study and obtain the same findings, we cannot be sure that the findings are a result of the variables we have identified.[14] The only way to do that is to perform an experiment.

---

[14]Unfortunately, people often wrongly conclude from descriptive studies that differences are causes. For more on this, see DeGrandpre (1999).

Experimental Studies

An **experiment** is a study in which a researcher manipulates one or more variables (literally, things that vary) and measures the effects of this manipulation on one or more other variables. The variables the researcher controls are called **independent variables**; those that are allowed to vary freely are called **dependent variables**. In learning experiments, the independent variable is often some sort of experience (an environmental event) and the dependent variable is usually some kind of behavior.

There are many different kinds of experiments, but all fall into one of two types: between-subjects designs and within-subject designs.[15]

In **between-subjects experiments**, the researcher typically identifies two or more groups of participants. (These experiments are also called between-groups or group designs.) The independent variable is then made to differ across these groups. Suppose we wish to study the role of certain experiences on aggressive behavior. We might assign people to one of two groups and expose one of them to the experiences we think will produce aggression. The participants who are exposed to the aggression-inducing experience are called the **experimental group**; those who are not exposed to it are called the **control group**. (The participants need not actually appear in groups; here, the term *group* refers only to assignment to experimental or control conditions.) We next compare the tendency of participants in the two groups to behave in an aggressive manner. If the experimental participants behave more aggressively than the control participants, we conclude that the experiences provided may have been responsible.

Although experiments involving two groups are common, it is quite possible to conduct between-subjects experiments with many groups. In an experiment on aggression, we might have several experimental groups that differ in the number or kind of aggression-inducing experiences to which they are exposed. We would then compare the performance of each group not only with the control group, but with every other experimental group (see Figure 2-8).

The essential element of a between-subjects design is that an independent variable differs across participants. Any differences in the dependent variable are presumed to be the result of differences in their exposure to the independent variable.

This conclusion rests on the assumption that the participants being compared are very similar to one another. It would not do if one group

---

[15]The people or animals whose behavior is studied in experiments used to be referred to as subjects; they are now usually referred to as participants. I use the terms *within-subject* and *between-subjects* designs, however, because those are the terms one finds in the published literature.

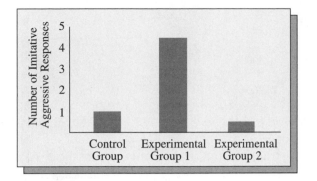

Figure 2-8 *Between-subjects design experiment. Data are compared from different individuals in different conditions. (Compiled from data in Rosenkrans and Hartup, 1967.)*

were appreciably older than the other, for example, because any differences in the results might be due to differences in age rather than to differences in treatment. Likewise, the two groups should not differ in health, sex, or a host of other variables.

Query: The essential element of a between-subjects design is

that the independent variable varies across _____.

To minimize such differences, participants are usually assigned at random to one of the groups. This may be done, for example, by flipping a coin: If the coin comes up heads, the participant goes into the experimental condition; tails, the participant is in the control group. Through such random assignment, any differences among the participants should be distributed more or less equally among the groups. However, with small groups even random assignment leaves open the possibility of differences among the groups, so the more participants in each group, the better. For this reason, between-subjects experiments usually include at least 10 participants in each group.

Another way to reduce pretreatment differences among groups is through matched sampling. In **matched sampling**, participants with identical features are identified. Animals may be matched for age and sex quite easily. Human participants can be matched for these variables, and also for IQ, educational level, and socioeconomic background. Genetic influences can be matched by using identical twins.[16] After participants

---

[16]In the future, it is possible that animals will be cloned for use in studies in order to control for genetic differences.

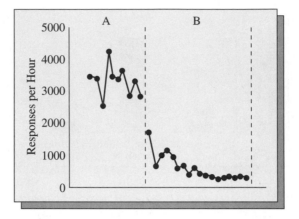

Figure 2-9 *Within-subject design experiment. Data are compared from the same individuals under different conditions (A and B). (Adapted from "The Effect of Contingency upon the Appetitive Conditioning of Free-Operant Behavior," by L. J. Hammond, 1980,* Journal of the Experimental Analysis of Behavior, 34[3], p. 300. *Copyright © 1980 by the Society for the Experimental Analysis of Behavior, Inc. Reprinted by permission.)*

have been matched, usually in pairs, one member of each pair is assigned at random to the experimental group, the other to the control group.

After the results of a between-subjects experiment are in, they are usually submitted to statistical analysis in an attempt to estimate the likelihood that they are due to the independent variable. If they are, the results are said to be "statistically significant."

The alternative to the between-subjects design is the **within-subject experiment** (Sidman, 1960/1988). (These experiments are also called single-case or single-subject designs.) In these experiments, a participant's behavior is observed before the experimental treatment, and then during or after it. The initial period during which a participant's behavior is observed is known as the **baseline period**, because it provides a baseline for comparison. In figures depicting within-subject data, this period is usually labeled "A." The treatment period follows the baseline and is labeled "B." If the A and B periods yield different results (e.g., different latencies or different rates of behavior), this should be apparent in the data graph (see Figure 2-9).

The essential element of a within-subject design is that the independent variable varies within the participants. In other words, each participant is in the experimental "group" and in the control "group" at different times. In learning experiments, this often means that each participant is exposed to a change in the environment and the participant's behavior under these two conditions is compared. Any differ-

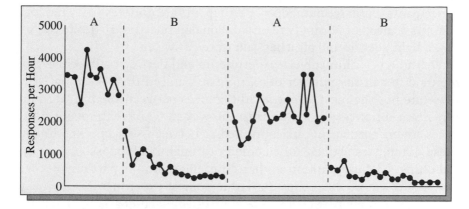

Figure 2-10 *Within-subject design with reversal. A and B conditions can be repeated to verify the effects of the different conditions. (Adapted from "The Effect of Contingency upon the Appetitive Conditioning of Free-Operant Behavior," by L. J. Hammond, 1980,* Journal of the Experimental Analysis of Behavior, 34[3], *p. 300. Copyright © 1980 by the Society for the Experimental Analysis of Behavior, Inc. Reprinted by permission.)*

ences in the dependent variable are presumed to be the result of differences in experiences.

Because the independent variable varies within the same person or animal, concern that the results might be due to differences among participants is greatly reduced. However, it is possible that some extraneous variable coincidental to the experimental manipulation is responsible for the results. An animal could become ill during the experiment, for example. This could give the illusion that the experimental treatment had changed the participant's behavior when, in fact, it had not. To rule out such possibilities, the experimenter may return to the baseline (A) condition in what is known as an **ABA reversal design**. The experimenter may then reinstate the experimental (B) condition again (Figure 2-10). In a sense, the researcher repeats the experiment within the same study.

Query: The essential element of a within-subject design is that

the independent variable varies _____.

Using an ABA reversal design is a little like turning a light switch on and off to see whether it controls a given light. By switching back and forth between A and B conditions, the researcher is able to demonstrate the extent to which a behavior is influenced by the independent variable. The data are all the more convincing if they are replicated with additional participants, but large numbers of participants are unnecessary. Statistical analysis is also not normally required: You don't need statistics to tell you that a light goes on and off when you throw a switch.

Although within-subject experiments and between-subjects experiments differ in the number of participants and in the use of statistics, these are not the most important differences between them. A far more important difference has to do with the way in which extraneous differences among participants are controlled. In between-subjects experiments, these differences are controlled chiefly through random assignment and matching. The assumption is that differences among participants will "even out" across the groups. In within-subject experiments, extraneous differences among participants are controlled by comparing participants against themselves. The assumption is that if the *same* participant is tested under experimental and control conditions, extraneous differences *among* participants are largely irrelevant.

Both between-subjects and within-subject experiments allow us, within limits, to see the effects of independent variables on dependent variables. Not even experimental studies are perfect, however.

Limitations of Experimental Research

The great power of the experiment comes from the control it provides over variables. However, this very control has led to the criticism that experiments create an artificial world from which the researcher derives an artificial view of behavior (Schwartz & Lacey, 1982).

In many learning experiments, the dependent variable is an extremely simple behavior: A rat presses a lever, a pigeon pecks a disk, a person presses a button. The independent variable is also likely to be simple: A light may go on or off, a few grains of food may fall into a tray, a person may receive a nickel or hear the word *correct*. The experiment may also occur in an extremely sterile, artificial environment: a small experimental chamber, for example, or (in the case of human participants) a room with only a table, a chair, and a box with a toggle switch. Some people have a hard time believing that the artificial world of the experiment can tell us anything important about behavior in natural environments.

To some extent the criticism is fair. Experiments do create artificial conditions, and what we find under those artificial conditions may not always correspond with what would occur under more natural conditions. But the control that makes the experiment seem artificial is necessary to isolate the effects of independent variables. Although we are not particularly interested in lever pressing, disk pecking, and button pushing, using such simple acts as our dependent variable allows us to see better the impact of the independent variable. More complicated behavior would be more realistic, but less revealing. This is because understanding lever pressing and disk pecking, per se, is not the researcher's goal; understanding the effect of environment on behavior is. (For more on this point, see Berkowitz and Donnerstein, 1982.)

The artificiality of experiments is largely the result of control. When we create more realistic experiments and study more complicated behavior, we almost inevitably lose control over important variables and produce data that are hard to interpret. One way around the problem is to do two kinds of experiments: laboratory experiments and field experiments.

Laboratory experiments offer the control that allows the researcher to derive clear-cut principles. Field experiments—those done in natural settings—allow the researcher to test laboratory-derived principles in more realistic ways. For instance, we might study learning in the laboratory by having rats run mazes, and then test the principles derived in field experiments of rats foraging in the wild. Or we might test the effects of different lecture rates on student learning in carefully controlled laboratory experiments, and then perform an analogous experiment in a classroom.

Despite their limitations, experiments provide a kind of power that is not available through other means. Consequently, most of the evidence we will consider in the pages that follow will be from experimental research. Much of that research involves animals.[17]

REVIEW Learning may be studied in various ways. Anecdotal and case study evidence are unreliable, though good sources of hypotheses. Descriptive studies can provide useful and reliable information but cannot account for why a phenomenon occurs. Because of these limitations, learning is usually studied by means of experiments; experiments allow us to see the effects of independent variables on dependent variables.

Between-subjects experiments usually involve relatively large numbers of participants assigned to experimental or control groups. The effects of the independent variable are judged by statistical analysis. Extraneous differences between groups may be reduced through random assignment or by matching.

Within-subject experiments involve relatively small numbers of participants. In these experiments, the participant's behavior is observed before and after some manipulation. The effects of the independent variable are judged by noting changes in the participant's behavior. The experiment may be replicated with the same participant in what is called an ABA reversal design.

---

[17]As noted in Chapter 1, I recognize that people are members of the animal kingdom. I follow the everyday convention of speaking of animals *and* people in order to distinguish easily between *homo sapiens* and other critters. I also do it to avoid repeatedly exposing the reader to language such as "human and nonhuman animals."

Animal Research and Human Learning

Most people, including most learning researchers, are far more interested in human behavior than they are in animal behavior. Yet learning research often involves animals. If the goal is to understand *human* learning and behavior, why study rats and pigeons? There are several reasons.

Reasons for Animal Research

Experimental psychologists generally believe that animal research is essential to improving our understanding of human behavior. Richard McCarty (1998) writes that "many of the most important developments in psychology over the past century have been linked to or informed by research with animals" (p. 18). Why are animals so important?

First, animals make it possible to get control over the influence of heredity. Because experimental animals are purchased from research supply companies, their genetic histories are fairly well known. This means that genetic differences from one participant to another, an important source of variability in behavior, can be reduced. We cannot, of course, have breeding programs to produce people with uniform genetic backgrounds. Theoretically, researchers can get control over genetic variability in humans by studying learning in identical twins. But twins are uncommon; relying on them for all research on behavior is impossible.

Second, with animals it is possible to control a participant's learning history. Animals can be housed from birth in environments that are far less variable than their natural environments, thus essentially ruling out the influence of unintended learning experiences. This sort of control cannot be achieved with human participants. Humans, particularly adult humans, come to experiments with highly variable learning histories.

Third, it is possible to do research with animals that, for ethical reasons, cannot be done with people. It might be interesting and useful to know whether a certain kind of experience would make people depressed or induce them to attack their neighbors, but doing such research with people raises serious ethical, not to mention liability, problems.

Despite the obvious advantages of animals as research participants, their use has been criticized. It is appropriate that we consider these objections.

Objections to Animal Research

Perhaps the objection heard most often to animal research is that the results obtained tell us nothing about people. Critics complain, "People are not rats!" or "Just because pigeons behave that way, doesn't mean that *I* behave that way." There is some merit to this criticism: There are important differences in learning and behavior among species. People are not just two-legged rats or flightless pigeons.

Animal researchers are, of course, well aware of the differences among species; indeed, it is through animal experimentation that some of these differences have come to light. One needs to be cautious in generalizing research on one species to another. Experimental research on the effects of smoking on health has been done primarily with rats and mice. These studies provide clear evidence that smoking is hazardous *to rodents*. The assumption is that if there is a relationship between smoking and disease in animals, there will be a similar relationship in people. But that assumption must be bolstered by other evidence, such as that from descriptive studies comparing people who smoke with those who do not. If such data corroborate the findings of animal research (as they do in the case of smoking), then we can have greater confidence in generalizing the animal research to humans.

In the same way, if learning researchers establish that a particular kind of experience affects rat behavior in a particular way, the assumption is that human behavior may be affected in a similar manner. But that assumption must be bolstered by other evidence, such as data from descriptive or experimental studies with humans. In most instances such evidence has corroborated the findings of animal research.

This does not mean, however, that people are no different from other animals. If rats and humans both learn from the same kinds of experiences, this in no way demeans the remarkable achievements of humans. A pigeon can, thanks to the diligent application of learning principles, learn to peck a disk when a sign says "Peck" and to stop when it says "Don't Peck" (Skinner, 1951). This does not reveal human inadequacy, however; rather, it reveals human potential: If rats and pigeons, given the proper experiences, can surprise us with *their* accomplishments, how much greater are the accomplishments of humans likely to be if we provide *them* with appropriate learning experiences? For example, if we can teach pigeons to read, even in a very limited way, surely we ought to be able to teach nearly all children to read in a much more sophisticated way.

A second objection to animal research is that it has no practical value. Unlike the biomedical research that uses animals to determine the health risks of smoking, this argument goes, animal research on behavior merely provides us with facts that only a theoretician could find useful.

It is true that animal research is often aimed at answering basic theoretical questions, but defenders of animal research are quick to argue that many of their findings have had great practical value. Treatments for phobia, depression, self-injurious behavior, dyslexia, hyperactivity, mental retardation, autism, brain damage, Tourette's Syndrome, and numerous other disorders, are directly traceable to animal research. The same principles have been put to good use in other areas, including child rearing (Azerrad & Chance, 2001; Latham, 1994, 1999), education (Hopkins & Conard, 1975; Johnson & Layng, 1992), and business (Daniels, 1994; Redmon & Dickinson, 1990).

The beneficiaries of animal research include animals as well as people. In the past, the training of pets, saddle horses, farm animals, and circus animals relied heavily on aversives.[18] Animal training is now usually done in a far more humane and effective manner than in the past, thanks largely to procedures discovered or perfected through animal research. These same procedures have resulted in improvements in veterinary care and in the quality of life for animals in zoos and similar facilities (Markowitz, 1982; Stewart et al., 2001; also see Chapter 7 of this text).

A third objection to animal research is that it is intrinsically unethical. This "animal rights" view maintains that people have no more right to experiment on rats than rats have to experiment on people. The issue is controversial (Balster et al., 1992; Burdick, 1991; Miller, 1985; Shapiro, 1991a, 1991b) and deserves to be treated seriously.[19]

Ethical problems do arise in the use of animals for research, but these issues also arise when animals are used for other purposes. If it is unethical to use animals for research, is it ethical to eat them? Do people have the right to conscript animals for farm work, such as hauling heavy loads and plowing fields? (In many parts of the world, people and animals alike would starve if such practices were forbidden.) Do equestrians have the right to ride horses and to force them to risk injury by jumping barriers? Hundreds of dogs have spent their lives assisting people who are blind, deaf, or confined to wheelchairs. Do people have the right to require animals to spend their lives this way? Millions of animals (dogs, cats, fish, snakes, frogs, turtles, birds, and many others) are kept as pets; by what right do people keep animals in captivity for their own amusement?[20] Probably most people believe that at least

---

[18] The expression "don't beat a dead horse" comes from the days of horse-powered transportation, when some people beat horses unmercifully, sometimes continuing to beat them even after they had died.

[19] The motives of animal rights activists who break into research labs, "liberating" animals and destroying data and equipment, must, however, be questioned. The released animals are seldom better off. Moreover, thousands of pets suffer at the hands of their owners, and live lobsters in grocery stores all over America await a cruel death; yet animal rights activists seem uninterested in "liberating" these animals.

[20] Some people will say that dogs enjoy human company, but this is true only if they have been socialized by people early in life. Dogs that do not interact with people during their first 12 weeks of life thereafter avoid human company whenever possible (Scott, 1958, 1962). When people socialize dogs, they are taking actions that fundamentally change the nature of the animals.

some of these uses of animals are ethical. If they are, then why is it unethical to use animals in research?

Some people answer that research animals are not as well treated as those that serve humans in other ways. It is true that laboratory animals are sometimes confined to relatively small spaces. On the other hand, they are not beaten, left unfed, subjected to inclement weather or foul living quarters, denied veterinary care, or abandoned—as is often the case with working animals and pets. Conditions for the care of laboratory animals are set by various state and federal laws and by ethical review boards. Indeed, one assumption in interpreting data from animal research is that the animals have received good treatment. It is for this reason that one group of researchers (Balster et al., 1992) writes that "the scientific community goes to great lengths to ensure the welfare of their animals; to do otherwise *is bad scientific method*" (p. 3; emphasis added).

In an effort to prevent unnecessary suffering, the American Psychological Association (1992) and other organizations have established guidelines for the conduct of animal research. These require that certain standards be met in the care and handling of animals. Animals may, for instance, be made to "work" for their food; but the amount of work is typically less than that required of animals in domestic service or living wild. The guidelines also set standards for the use of aversives. If a question can be answered without the use of aversives, they are not to be used. When aversives are deemed necessary, they must be no more severe than is required by the nature of the research. The use of aversives must also be justified by the probable benefits to be gained from the research. Inspections by health departments and humane societies help to ensure that researchers meet these standards.

Some critics maintain that animal research is unethical because it is unnecessary. They argue that computer simulations can replace animals in research: We need no longer run rats through mazes or train pigeons to peck a disk for food, they argue; silicon animals can replace those with fur and feathers.

Computers can be programmed to simulate the behavior of animals in certain situations. A good example of this is *Sniffy the Virtual Rat* (Alloway et al., 2000). This program provides an image of a laboratory rat in an experimental chamber on the computer screen. The simulated rat moves about doing rat-like things: exploring its surroundings, scratching and licking itself, drinking water, eating food it finds in a food tray, and learning to press a lever. Sniffy is a very useful instructional tool, but it is a mistake to think that simulated animals (or people, for that matter) can replace living research participants. We cannot program a computer to simulate the effects of a variable on behavior until we know what those effects are. That is precisely what research attempts to discover.

An illustration may clarify the point. In *The Beak of the Finch*, Jonathan Weiner (1994; see Chapter 1) describes how biologists spent hundreds of hours monitoring the behavior of birds in the Galapagos Islands to determine what effect changes in the environment, such as drought, have on physical characteristics of successive generations of birds. This effort required capturing, banding, and measuring birds as well as observing them through binoculars. The researchers now know a good deal about which birds survive and reproduce under drought conditions and what characteristics their offspring are likely to display. Given this information, it should be possible to write a computer program that would simulate the effects of a drought. But writing such a program would not have been possible *before* the research had been done because no one knew what effects drought would have on the finches.

Although the work with finches involves physical features, the same problem emerges when the questions concern behavior. We cannot hope to write a software program simulating the effects of certain experiences on behavior until we have collected data on those effects.

The point of this discussion is not that there are no valid grounds for objecting to animal research. It is that we should keep in mind that we use animals in a variety of ways for our benefit. Some animals serve by helping the blind find their way, by signaling to a deaf person that a smoke detector is sounding, by pulling a plow through a field, or by providing companionship. Others serve by providing answers to questions about learning and behavior that may improve the lives of both animals and people.

Query: This book reviews many animal experiments, but it is

chiefly about _____ learning and behavior.

REVIEW Both humans and other animals may serve as participants for experiments on learning. Animals make greater control possible, but leave open the possibility that the results do not apply to humans. Often, basic research is done on animals, and the principles derived from this research are tested on humans in applied settings. Animal research raises ethical questions, but so do other common uses of animals.

Learning research is aimed at answering certain key questions. Since the bulk of this book deals with those questions, it may be useful to summarize them here.

Questions About Learning

The study of learning and behavior may be viewed as primarily an effort to answer certain key questions. The remaining chapters introduce these questions and summarize the efforts of researchers to answer them. It may be helpful to review these questions here so that you will better understand the course on which we are set.

1. *What kinds of experiences change behavior?* As you have seen, learning researchers define experience in terms of events in an organism's environment. In the natural environment, these events occur as the result of physical or biological forces; in the laboratory, they are arranged by the researcher. Three kinds of experiences will be dealt with; they are the subjects of Chapters 3 through 8.

2. *How does an experience that changes behavior in one environment affect behavior in other environments?* Suppose a boy learns to ride a bicycle on a paved street; will he then be able to ride the bike on a dirt road? If an animal trainer teaches your dog to heel, will the dog then heel for *you*? We take up these questions in Chapter 9.

3. *What are the effects of the various reinforcement schedules?* Certain events have powerful effects on behavior. The pattern of these events is called a reinforcement schedule. Their distinctive effects on behavior are considered in Chapter 10.

4. *Why do we forget?* Once learning has occurred, it is appropriate to ask under what circumstances the effects of learning will be lost. Chapter 11 attempts to account for forgetting.

5. *What are the limits of learning?* Biology places constraints on learning. These are considered in Chapter 12.

These, then, are the principal questions that fascinate learning researchers. The chapters that follow will attempt to explain why researchers find these questions so absorbing. I hope that in reading these chapters, you will come to share some of the researchers' enthusiasm for finding answers to questions about the adaptive mechanism called learning.

REVIEW The remainder of this book attempts to provide some insight into the answers currently available to certain fundamental questions about learning and behavior. These questions involve the kinds of experiences that produce learning, the circumstances under which learning in one situation carries over to another situation, the effects of different reinforcement schedules, the durability of learned behavior, and the limitations of learning.

Note: If you are typical of students taking a first course in learning, much of the material in this chapter is new to you. Be sure you understand what you have read before going on to the following chapters because an understanding of this material is hereafter assumed. The natural science approach to behavior is very different from the commonsense approach to which most students are accustomed. This new approach will give you a fresh perspective on learning and behavior.

RECOMMENDED READING

1. Bachrach, A. J. (1962). *Psychological research: An introduction.* New York: Random House.

   A highly readable little book on research methods. The author provides an insider's view of behavioral research.

2. Eysenck, H. J. (1965). *Fact and fiction in psychology.* Baltimore, MD: Penguin.

   See especially Chapter 3, "Little Hans or Little Albert?" a comparison of case study and experimental approaches.

3. Monany, V. (2000). *Animal experimentation: A guide to the issues.* New York: Cambridge University Press.

   A discussion of the issues concerning the use of animals in research.

4. Sidman, M. (1960/1988). *Tactics of scientific research.* Boston: Authors Cooperative.

   An in-depth analysis of behavioral research methods, particularly within-subject designs. Not for the fainthearted.

5. Wise, S. M. (2000). *Rattling the cage: Toward legal rights for animals.* NY: Perseus.

   A lawyer sets forth the case for animal rights.

REVIEW QUESTIONS

1. Define the following terms in your own words. Give an example or illustration of each that is not provided in the text.

ABA reversal design	behavior
anecdotal evidence	between-subjects experiment
baseline period	case study

control group   experimental group
cumulative record   independent variable
cumulative recorder   matched sampling
dependent variable   operational definition
descriptive study   stimulus
experiment   within-subject experiment

2. A muscle on your hand twitches involuntarily. Is the muscle twitch behavior, or is it physiology?

3. What are the principal *similarities* between within-subject and between-subjects designs?

4. When would it not be possible to use an ABA design in the study of behavior?

5. We humans see only a small part of the spectrum of light waves. Do light waves that fall outside of our detectable range qualify as stimuli?

6. Give an example of human learning measured as a *decrease* in the intensity of a behavior.

7. How could you quantify the changes in topography associated with learning to speak a foreign language?

8. A researcher studies maze learning in rats by running 50 rats through a maze, one at a time. He does this 10 times. Then he computes the average time for all rats on each run and plots this on a graph. What sort of study is this?

9. Some people dismiss research evidence by saying, "Oh, you can prove anything with research." How would you reply to this comment?

10. Explain how the rate of behavior is reflected on a cumulative record.

11. What is the chief virtue of matched sampling?

12. Give an example of an event that would be a stimulus for one person but not for another.

13. Does the term *toothache* refer to a stimulus or a behavior?

14. What is wrong with defining learning as the acquisition of new behavior?

15. A researcher has 20 rats in a large cage, and he wants to assign them to two groups. He puts the first rat he catches in the experimental group, the second into the control group, and so on. Why is this bad science?

16. You are studying cocaine addiction in rats. An animal rights activist accuses you of animal cruelty. How can you defend your work?

17. You are attempting to discover learning principles by studying the effects of experience on the eyeblink. A friend says that eye blinking is a trivial kind of behavior, not worth studying. Defend your work.

18. A teacher says that learning research relies too much on animal studies and adds, "You can't tell anything about people from research on rats." How could you defend "rat psychology" against this criticism?

19. Some researchers argue that learning is a change in the brain produced by experience. Discuss the virtues and weaknesses of this definition.

20. Why is random assignment of participants unnecessary in experiments with a within-subject design?

PRACTICE QUIZ

1. This book takes the _____ science approach to behavior, the approach that focuses on identifying physical events that affect behavior.

2. One reason that many learning studies use animals is that with animals it is possible to control _____.

3. In an _____ definition, a behavior is defined by the procedure used to measure it.

4. Changes in behavior due directly to the effects of an injury do not qualify as learning. A change in behavior caused by _____ also does not qualify as learning.

5. The kind of experiment that can be likened to turning a light switch on and off is a/an _____ design.

6. _____ design experiments assume that there are no important differences among participants.

7. A change in _____ involves a change in the form a behavior takes.

8. Fluency combines errors and _____.

9. If there is a reduction in the time that passes before a behavior occurs, we say that learning is measured in terms of

_____.

10. The cumulative recorder is used to measure learning as a change in the _____ of behavior.

QUERY ANSWERS

Page 40. Behavior is anything an organism does that can be *measured*.

Page 40. A stimulus is an environmental event that is capable of affecting *behavior*.

Page 46. If the rate of a behavior is increasing, the slope of the cumulative record *rises/goes up*. A flat record indicates that the behavior is *not occurring*.

Page 49. The chief difference between anecdotal and case study evidence is that *anecdotal evidence is based on casual observation whereas case studies examine an individual in detail*.

Page 51. The essential element of a between-subjects design is that the independent variable varies across *participants*.

Page 53. The essential element of a within-subject design is that the independent variable varies *within participants*.

Page 60. This book reviews many animal experiments, but it is chiefly about *human* learning and behavior.

CHAPTER

3

Pavlovian Conditioning

The normal animal must respond not only to stimuli which themselves bring immediate benefit or harm, but also to [those that] only signal the approach of these stimuli; though it is not the sight and sound of the beast of prey which is in itself harmful . . . but its teeth and claws.

Ivan Pavlov

Around the end of the 19th century, a Russian physiologist reached a turning point in his career. He had spent several years doing research on the physiology of digestion, important research that would one day win him a Nobel Prize. But at middle age, still relatively unknown, he wrestled with one of the most difficult decisions of his career: Should he continue his present line of work or take up a new problem, one that might lead nowhere and that some of his colleagues might regard as an unfit subject for a respectable scientist? The safe thing to do, the easy thing to do, would have been to continue the work he had started. But if he had, psychology would have suffered an immeasurable loss, and the chances are that neither you nor I would ever have heard of Ivan Petrovich Pavlov.

Pavlov started his career with research on the circulatory system and then moved on to the physiology of digestion. He developed special surgical procedures that enabled him to study the digestive processes of animals over long periods of time by redirecting an animal's digestive fluids outside the body, where they could be measured. He used this technique to study the salivary glands, stomach, liver, pancreas, and parts of the intestine. In the case of the salivary glands, the procedure was a relatively simple operation. The salivary duct of a dog was detached from its usual place inside the mouth and directed through an incision in the cheek. When the dog salivated, the saliva would flow through the duct and be collected in a small glass tube. With animals prepared in this way, Pavlov could make precise observations of the actions of the glands under various conditions (see Figure 3-1).

One of Pavlov's goals was to understand how the body breaks down food into chemicals that can be absorbed into the blood. This process starts with the salivary reflex: When food is taken into the mouth, it triggers the flow of saliva. The saliva dilutes the food and produces substances that start breaking it down chemically. In a typical experiment

Figure 3-1   *Surgical preparation for studying the salivary reflex. When the dog salivated, the saliva would collect in a glass tube attached to the dog's cheek. This way the strength of the salivary response could be precisely measured.*

on the salivary reflex, Pavlov would bring a dog into the laboratory, put food into its mouth, and observe the result.[1]

Pavlov was fascinated by the adaptability of the glands. He found, for instance, that if he gave a dog dry, hard food, there was a heavy flow of saliva; if he gave the animal watery food, there was very little saliva. And if he put an inedible substance into the dog's mouth, the amount of saliva depended on the amount needed to eject the substance: A marble evoked very little saliva, while sand resulted in a large supply. So the reflex action of the gland depended on the nature of the stimulus. Each time, the gland responded according to the need. "It is as if," said Pavlov, "the glands possessed a 'kind of intelligence'" (quoted in Cuny, 1962, p. 26).

The cleverness of the glands did not end there, however. When an animal had been fed a number of times, it began to salivate *before* anything was put into its mouth. In fact, it might start salivating as soon as it entered the laboratory. Pavlov, like others of his day, assumed that these "psychic secretions" were caused by the thoughts, memories, or wishes of the animal. The ancient Greeks had noticed that merely talking about food often made a person's mouth water. What fascinated Pavlov was that the dogs did not salivate when they were first brought into the laboratory, but only after they had been fed there repeatedly. How could this be? How could experience alter the action of a gland?

This question preoccupied Pavlov to the point of making him shift his attention to psychic reflexes. It was not an easy decision. It was extremely important to Pavlov that he retain his identity as a physiologist.

[1]More often than not it was one of Pavlov's many research assistants, not Pavlov himself, who actually conducted the experiments. Pavlov seems to have run the lab in much the same way Thomas Edison ran his lab in New Jersey.

Ivan Pavlov: An Experimenter from Head to Foot

George Bernard Shaw said he was the biggest fool he knew. H. G. Wells thought he was one of the greatest geniuses of all time. But Ivan Pavlov described himself as "an experimenter from head to foot" (in Wells, 1956).

Of the three characterizations, Pavlov's was probably the most accurate. His discoveries were much more important, and much less commonsensical, than Shaw believed, but they also failed to bring the utopia that Wells anticipated. There is, however, no denying that Pavlov was a brilliant experimenter, a zealot fiercely committed to science.

Pavlov was born in Ryazan, a small peasant village in Russia, in September 1849, a decade before the publication of Darwin's *On the Origin of Species*. His father was a poor priest who had to keep a garden to ensure that his family would eat.

As a boy, Pavlov showed little promise of later greatness. His academic performance was mediocre, and probably few people in his village expected him to become a famous scientist—or a famous anything else, for that matter. He grew up to be slim, agile, athletic, and incredibly energetic, with blue eyes, curly hair, a long beard, and the fire of genius.

As Professor Pavlov, he was sometimes an impatient, stubborn, and eccentric man who waved his hands excitedly when he spoke. If one of his assistants botched an experiment, he might explode in anger; half an hour later, he would have forgotten all about it. But of all the things that one might say about Pavlov, surely the most important is this: He was an experimenter. Nothing was so important, nothing so precious, as his experiments. "Remember," he once wrote, "science requires your whole life. And even if you had two lives they would not be enough. Science demands. . . the utmost effort and supreme passion" (in Cuny, 1962, p. 160).

Pavlov's passion for science stayed with him throughout his long life. Age slowed him, of course, but not the way it slows most of us. Ever the experimenter, he observed the toll that time had taken and noted it with objective interest. On his deathbed, he was the observer, as well as the subject, of a final experiment. As life slowly left him, he described his sensations to a neuropathologist so that these data might be recorded for the benefit of science. Somehow he kept this up almost until the end. One report of Pavlov's death (in Gantt, 1941) relates that in those last moments he slept a bit, then awoke, raised himself on his elbows, and said, "It is time to get up! Help me, I must get dressed!"

The effort was understandable. He had been away from his laboratory, from his science, for nearly six whole days.

If psychic reflexes really were the products of the mind, then they were not a fit subject for a physiologist. On the other hand, if psychic reflexes involved glands, then why should a physiologist not study them? Pavlov argued with himself along these lines, back and forth; finally, he could no longer resist the challenge. He had to understand these psychic reflexes.

Basic Procedures[2]

Pavlov began by observing: "I started to record all the external stimuli falling on the animal at the time its reflex reaction was manifested . . . at the same time recording all changes in the reaction of the animal" (1927, p. 6)[3] At first, the only reaction was the ordinary salivary reflex: When an experimenter put food into a dog's mouth, it salivated. But after a while, the animal would salivate before receiving food. By observing the "external stimuli falling on the animal," Pavlov was able to see what triggered these psychic secretions (see Figure 3-2). He noticed, for instance, that the sight or smell of food would cause the dog to salivate. "Even the vessel from which the food has been given is sufficient . . . and, further, the secretions may be provoked even by the sight of the person who brought the vessel, or by the sound of his footsteps" (p. 13).

There are, Pavlov concluded, two distinct kinds of reflexes. One kind is the largely inborn and usually permanent reflex that is found in virtually all members of a species and that varies little from individual to individual. The dog that salivates when food is put into its mouth manifests this type of reflex. Pavlov called these **unconditional reflexes**, since they occur more or less unconditionally.

The second type of reflex is not present at birth; it must be acquired through experience and is relatively impermanent. Because these psychic reflexes depend on experience, they vary considerably from individual to individual. The dog that salivates to the sound of a particular person's footsteps manifests this type of reflex. Pavlov called these **conditional reflexes**, since they "actually do depend on very many conditions" (p. 25).

Pavlov admitted that other terms would have served as well: Unconditional reflexes might have been referred to as inborn, unlearned, or species reflexes; conditional reflexes could have been called acquired,

---

[2] When learning experiences are provided by an experimenter, they are often referred to as procedures. But keep in mind that these procedures are not just laboratory exercises: They usually mimic, at least in their basic forms, experiences that occur spontaneously in the animal's natural environment.

[3] Unless otherwise noted, all references to Pavlov refer to *Conditioned Reflexes*, first published in English in 1927. A Dover Press reprint is available.

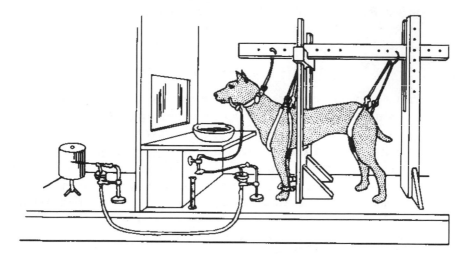

Figure 3-2 *Pavlov's conditioning stand. Once a dog was strapped into a stand as shown, an experimenter could begin testing the effects of various stimuli on the salivary response. Saliva could be collected in a glass tube at the fistula (as shown in Figure 3-1), or it could be directed by a tube to a graduated vial. In addition, a cumulative record of the amount of saliva could be obtained from the movements of a needle on a revolving drum. See Pavlov, 1927, pp. 18–19. (From Yerkes and Morgulis, 1909.)*

learned, or individual reflexes. But the terms *conditional* and *unconditional* caught on and are still used today.[4]

An unconditional reflex consists of an **unconditional stimulus (US)** and the behavior that it evokes, the **unconditional response (UR)**.[5] Meat powder is an unconditional stimulus that reliably evokes the unconditional response of salivation:

$$US \longrightarrow UR$$
$$\text{meat powder} \longrightarrow \text{salivation}$$

A conditional reflex consists of a **conditional stimulus (CS)** and the behavior it reliably evokes, the **conditional response (CR)**. When the sight

---

[4]Most authors and instructors use the terms *conditioned* and *unconditioned*. The words *conditional* and *unconditional* are, however, closer to Pavlov's meaning (Gantt, 1966; Thorndike, 1931/1968), so these terms are used here.

[5]Unconditional stimuli are typically events that are important to the organism's survival. For example, Karin Wallace and Jeffrey Rosen (2000) demonstrated that rats show a strong unconditional fear response to an odorous chemical derived from fox feces. As the authors note, "In the wild, when a rat is attacked by a predator, it is usually . . . too late for defensive maneuvers" (p. 912). Thus the rat that has an innate tendency to freeze or run away when it detects odors associated with its enemies has a better chance of avoiding those enemies.

of a food dish regularly evokes salivation, the food dish is a CS and salivating is a CR:

CS   ⟶ CR
food dish   ⟶ salivation

Pavlov's next question was, How does a neutral stimulus (one that does not naturally evoke a reflex response) come to do so? How, for example, does a food dish become a CS for salivating?

Pavlov had noticed that stimuli associated with food, such as the food dish and the handler who fed the dog, became conditional stimuli for salivating. He began conducting experiments to understand better how this association led to salivating.

Query: Pavlov identified two kinds of reflexes,

_____ and _____.

In some experiments, Pavlov paired food with the sound of a metronome. At first, the ticking had no effect on salivation; but after the sound of the metronome had been repeatedly paired with food, the ticking began to elicit the salivating. Pavlov found that virtually any stimulus could become a conditional stimulus if it were regularly paired with an unconditional stimulus.

An example will illustrate the point. If you were to clap your hands near a dog, it might respond in a number of ways, but salivating is not likely to be one of them. As far as the salivary reflex is concerned, clapping is a neutral stimulus. Now suppose you clapped your hands and immediately put bread crumbs into the dog's mouth:

CS ⟶ US ⟶ UR
clap ⟶ bread ⟶ salivate

If you were to repeat this procedure several times, the dog might begin salivating when you clapped your hands:

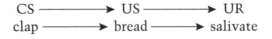

CS ⟶ CR
clap ⟶ salivate

Each pairing of CS and US is one trial, and the procedure is known as **Pavlovian, classical,** or **respondent conditioning.**[6]

---

[6] The term *respondent conditioning* reflects the fact that the behavior is "respondent," i.e., a refexive response to a stimulus. Technically, the stimulus that is paired with the US is not a CS until it is capable of eliciting a CR. However, because it isn't easy to say when the transition from neutral stimulus to CS occurs, it is customary to refer to the stimulus as a CS from its first pairing with a US.

What's What in Pavlovian Conditioning?

Students sometimes have difficulty identifying the components of a conditioning procedure (the CS, US, CR, and UR), especially when given an unfamiliar example of conditioning. The following questions (adapted from Hummel et al., 1991) may help you identify the elements of any conditioning procedure:

1. What reflex response occurs before conditioning?

   _____. This is the UR.

2. What stimulus elicits the UR before conditioning?

   _____. This is the US.

3. What reflex response occurs as a result of conditioning?

   _____. This is the CR.

4. What stimulus elicits the CR?

   _____. This is the CS.

It is important to note two things about Pavlovian conditioning. First, the presentation of the two stimuli is independent of the behavior of the organism; the CS and the US are presented *regardless of what the organism does.* Second, the behavior involved is a reflex response, such as salivating, blinking an eye, sweating, or jumping in response to a loud noise.

It seems clear that the ability to develop conditional reflexes would give any organism a much improved chance of surviving in a changing world. As Pavlov suggested, a deer that reacts with fear to the sight, sound, and odor of a tiger is more likely to live long enough to pass on its genes than one that responds only to the feel of the tiger's teeth in its neck. The same thing is true, of course, for another of the tiger's prey, homo sapiens.

One can never be sure when a tiger or another predator may come along, so Pavlovian conditioning would also be useful if it helped prepare for mating. There is evidence that it does. In male rats, sexual arousal is indicated by an increase in certain hormone levels in the blood. This increase is a reflex response to the presence of odorous chemicals, called pheromones, emitted by sexually receptive female rats. Physiologists J. M. Graham and Claude Desjardins (1980) exposed male rats to the vapors of wintergreen, an odorous chemical, just before exposing them to a sexually receptive female rat. Thus, the researchers paired two odorous stimuli, one of which was a US for the release of hormones. After pairing the two stimuli each day for 14 days, the researchers presented the CS alone. They found that the blood levels of sex-related hormones were now as high when the rats were exposed to wintergreen as they had been when they were exposed to the female rats.

Anything that prepares a male rat for copulation before a receptive female appears may reduce the time required for mating. That, in turn, may reduce the chances of copulation being interrupted by a hungry, not to mention rude, predator. The rat's response to pheromones may have evolved precisely because it has these effects. A rat that can learn to respond to stimuli associated with pheromones may be even better off when it comes to passing on its genes. Whether such conditioning plays a similar role in human reproduction is less clear.

REVIEW Pavlov showed that there are two kinds of reflexes: unconditional and conditional. An unconditional reflex consists of an unconditional stimulus and an unconditional response; a conditional reflex consists of a conditional stimulus and a conditional response. Unconditional reflexes are largely innate; conditional reflexes are acquired. The procedure by which a conditional response is established is called Pavlovian, classical, or respondent conditioning. There are two critical features of Pavlovian conditioning: The CS-US pairing occurs regardless of what the organism does; the behavior involved is a reflex response.

The basic conditioning procedure appears to be important to survival. However, a variation of this procedure greatly extends the importance of conditioning, especially for humans. This variation is called higher-order conditioning.

Higher-Order Conditioning

The basic Pavlovian procedure, as you have seen, consists of pairing a neutral stimulus with an unconditional stimulus. Conditioning can occur, however, without a US. If a neutral stimulus is paired with a well-established CS, the effect is much the same as if the stimulus had been paired with a US. This was demonstrated in Pavlov's laboratory by G. P. Frolov.

Frolov trained a dog to salivate at the sound of a ticking metronome by pairing the metronome and food. When the metronome was well established as a CS for salivating, Frolov paired it with another stimulus, the sight of a black square. He held up the black square and activated the metronome:

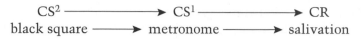

$CS^2 \longrightarrow CS^1 \longrightarrow CR$

black square $\longrightarrow$ metronome $\longrightarrow$ salivation

At first, the dog salivated at the sound of the metronome, but not at the sight of the black square. After several pairings of the two stimuli, however, the dog began salivating when it saw the square. The black square had become a CS for salivating *even though it had never been paired with food:*

$CS \longrightarrow CR$

black square $\longrightarrow$ salivation

The procedure of pairing a neutral stimulus with a well-established CS is called **higher-order conditioning**.

Higher-order conditioning greatly increases the importance of Pavlovian conditioning, because it means that many more stimuli can come to elicit conditional responses. By way of example, we may take the Graham and Desjardins (1980) study described earlier. These researchers demonstrated that a male rat that responds to a sexually receptive female by increasing the level of certain hormones will respond in a similar manner to an odor that has been paired with a receptive female. Thanks to higher-order conditioning, a new stimulus may now become a CS by being paired with the odor, without its ever being paired with a receptive female. It is easy to see how this might give the rat a reproductive advantage in the wild: The rat that responds to a stimulus associated with the odor of a receptive female has an advantage over the rat that responds only to the odor itself.

Higher-order conditioning is probably far more important to human adaptation than to that of rats. Among people, words are particularly likely to become conditional stimuli by being paired with conditional stimuli—including other words. In one classic experiment, Carolyn and Arthur Staats (1957) asked college students to look at nonsense syllables such as *YOF, LAJ,* and *QUG* as they were flashed on a screen. At the same time, the students repeated words spoken by the experimenters. For some students, the experimenters paired the syllable *YOF* with positive words such as *beauty, gift,* and *win,* and the syllable *XEH* with negative words such as *thief, sad,* and *enemy.* For other students, the associations were reversed: *XEH* was paired with positive words, *YOF* with negative ones. (Notice that no US was ever presented.) After this, the students rated each nonsense syllable on a 7-point scale ranging from unpleasant to pleasant. The results indicated that the nonsense syllables came to elicit emotional responses similar to the emotional value of the words with which they had been paired. When a nonsense syllable was regularly associated with pleasant words, it became pleasant; when it was paired with unpleasant words, it became unpleasant. In other words, *YOF* came to elicit good feelings in some students and bad feelings in others, depending on the words with which it was paired. Higher order conditioning appears, then, to play an important role in the emotional meaning of words.

Query: In higher-order conditioning, a neutral stimulus is

paired with a well-established _____ stimulus.

REVIEW   In most conditioning experiments, a neutral stimulus is paired with a US, such as food. In higher-order conditioning, a neutral stimulus is paired with a well-established CS. This procedure is generally less effective in establishing a CR than CS-US pairings, but it is probably very important in the lives of humans. Many of our emotional reactions (our likes, dislikes, fears, and loves, for example) appear to be acquired at least partly through higher-order conditioning.

Pavlovian procedures are very effective in producing conditional responses. Measuring the course of conditioning is, however, more difficult than it might appear.

Measuring Pavlovian Learning

In most studies of Pavlovian conditioning, the CS and US are presented close together. Because the US is by definition capable of evoking the UR, how is it possible to tell when learning has occurred? Suppose, for example, that you sound a tone and then, 2 seconds after the tone stops, you put food into a dog's mouth. How can you tell when the dog is salivating to the tone as well as to the food?

One answer is to note when salivation begins. If the dog begins salivating after the CS begins but *before* the presentation of the US, conditioning has occurred. In this case, the amount of learning can be measured in terms of the latency of the response—the interval between the onset of the CS and the first appearance of saliva. As the number of CS-US pairings increases, the response latency diminishes; the dog may begin salivating even before the tone has stopped sounding.

In some conditioning studies, the interval between CS onset and the appearance of the US is so short that using response latency as a measure of learning is very difficult. One way to test for conditioning in these situations is to use **test trials**.[7] This involves presenting the CS alone (i.e., without the US) every now and then, perhaps on every fifth trial. If the dog salivates even when it gets no food, the salivation is clearly a conditional response to the tone. Sometimes, test trials are presented at random intervals, with the conditional stimulus presented alone perhaps on the third trial, then on the seventh, the twelfth, the thirteenth, the twentieth, and so on (Rescorla, 1967; but see Gormezano, 2000). When test trials are used, the number of CRs in a block of, say, 10 test trials is plotted on a curve. Learning is thus represented as an increase in the frequency of the conditional response.

Another way to measure Pavlovian learning is to measure the intensity or amplitude of the CR. Pavlov found that the first CRs were apt to be very weak—a drop or two of saliva. But with repeated trials, the saliva flow in response to the CS increased rapidly. The increase in the number of drops of saliva is a measure of learning.

One problem in attempting to measure Pavlovian learning is a phenomenon known as **pseudoconditioning** (Grether, 1938). Suppose a nurse coughs just as he gives you a painful injection. When you receive the injection, you wince. Now suppose that after the injection, the nurse coughs again. Very likely you will wince again, just as you did when you received the injection. You might think conditioning has occurred—the cough appears to have become a conditional stimulus for wincing. But you might be mistaken. A strong stimulus, such as a needle jab, can sensitize you to other stimuli so that you react to them more or less as you would react to the strong stimulus. If a nurse jabs you with a needle, you may then wince when he coughs, even if he did not cough before jabbing you. You wince, not because conditioning has occurred, but because the needle jab has sensitized you to other stimuli. (See the discussion of sensitization in Chapter 1.)

Obviously, if a stimulus has not been paired with a US, any effect it produces cannot be a result of conditioning. A problem arises, however, when a stimulus *has* been paired with a strong US. Is the behavior that occurs a conditional response, or is it the result of the earlier exposure to a strong stimulus? The answer can be determined by presenting the CS and US to control group subjects in a random manner so that the stimuli sometimes appear alone and sometimes appear together (Rescorla, 1967; but see also Rescorla, 1972). The performance of these control subjects is then compared with experimental subjects for which the CS and US always (or at least usually) appear together. If subjects in the experimental

---

[7]Test trials are also called *probe trials*.

group perform differently from subjects in the control group, the difference in behavior may be attributed to conditioning.

REVIEW   Various techniques are used to measure the effectiveness of Pavlovian procedures. One method is to continue pairing CS and US and observe whether the reflex response occurs before the presentation of the US. Another technique is to present the CS alone on certain trials and see whether a CR occurs. In testing for learning, it is important to control for the phenomenon of pseudoconditioning, in which a stimulus may elicit a CR even though it has not become an effective CS. The difficulty of measuring Pavlovian learning is one thing that complicates its study; another is that it is sensitive to a number of variables.

Variables Affecting Pavlovian Conditioning

The course of Pavlovian conditioning depends on a number of variables. Perhaps the most important of these is the manner in which the conditional and unconditional stimuli are paired.

Pairing CS and US

Pavlovian conditioning involves the pairing of stimuli. The amount of learning that occurs depends to a large extent on the way stimuli are associated. There are four basic ways of pairing stimuli (see Figure 3-3).

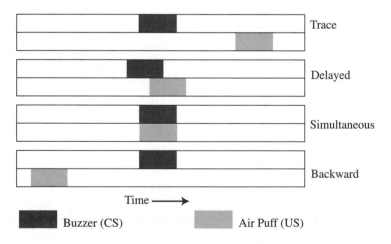

Figure 3-3   *Pairing CS and US. A CS may precede, overlap with, occur simultaneously with, or follow a US. See text for explanation.*

In **trace conditioning**, the CS begins and ends before the US is presented. In the laboratory, trace conditioning may be used to study eyelid conditioning in people. Typically, a buzzer sounds for, say, 5 seconds, and then, perhaps a half second later, a puff of air is blown into the person's eye, causing him to blink. After several such pairings of the buzzer and air, the person blinks at the sound of the buzzer.[8]

Trace conditioning also occurs outside the laboratory: We see the flash of lightning and, an instant later, we hear the crash of thunder; we hear the dog growl and then feel its teeth; the mother sings to her baby before offering the nipple. The identifying feature of trace conditioning is that the CS begins and ends *before* the US appears.

Query: In trace conditioning, the _____ begins

and ends before the _____ appears.

In **delayed conditioning**, the CS and US overlap. That is, the US appears before the CS has disappeared. To apply the delayed procedure to eyelid conditioning, we might sound a buzzer for five seconds and, some time during the last two seconds that the buzzer is sounding, we might send a puff of air into the person's eye.

Like trace conditioning, delayed conditioning often occurs outside the laboratory: We often hear the thunder before the lightning has faded from the sky; the dog may continue to growl even as it bites; the mother may continue to sing softly as she nurses her baby. As in trace conditioning, the CS appears before the US; the difference is that in the delayed procedure the CS and US overlap.

Some researchers distinguish between short-delay and long-delay procedures. The difference refers to the length of time the CS is present before the US appears. In the short-delay procedure, the CS may be present from a few milliseconds (a millisecond is .001 second) to a few seconds before the US appears. For instance, a light may come on a tenth of a second before an electric current is applied to the grid floor of a rat's experimental chamber. In the long-delay procedure, the CS may persist for several seconds or minutes before the US appears. A light may come on and remain on for five minutes before an electric current is applied to the chamber floor.

Initially, short- and long-delay procedures produce similar results: A conditional response begins to appear soon after the CS appears. But in

---

[8]The procedure is called trace conditioning because researchers assumed that the CS left some sort of trace of itself in the brain after it had ended.

the case of long-delay conditioning, the CR latency (the interval between the CS and the CR) gradually increases. Eventually, the CR does not appear until just before the onset of the US. Apparently, what happens in long-delay conditioning is that the CS is not merely the stimulus presented by the experimenter, but the appearance of that stimulus for a given period of time.

Query: In delayed conditioning, the _____ ends

only after the _____ begins.

Both trace and delay procedures are capable of producing conditional responses, and most studies of Pavlovian conditioning involve one of these two procedures. However, two other procedures for pairing CS and US are possible.

In **simultaneous conditioning,** the CS and US coincide exactly. We might, for instance, ring a bell and blow a puff of air into a person's eye at the same moment. Both stimuli begin and end at the same instant. The simultaneous appearance of CS and US also takes place in the natural environment: Thunder and lightning sometimes occur together if the storm is nearby; the dog may snarl and bite at the same instant and stop snarling the moment it releases your leg; the mother may provide the nipple at the very same time she sings to her baby, and she may stop singing the instant she withdraws the nipple.

Simultaneous conditioning is a weak procedure for establishing a conditional response (Bitterman, 1964; Heth, 1976). In fact, if lightning always accompanied thunder but never preceded it, a sudden flash of lightning might not make us flinch in the least.

Finally, it is possible to arrange things so that the CS follows the US, a procedure called **backward conditioning**. For instance, a puff of air directed at a person's eye could be followed by the sound of a buzzer. The US-CS sequence also can occur outside the laboratory, as when a person sits on a splinter and then (having jumped up from the uncomfortable resting spot) sees the offending object.

It is very difficult, if not impossible, to produce a CR with the backward procedure. Pavlov described some of the attempts made at backward conditioning in his laboratory. In one experiment, one of his assistants exposed a dog to the odor of vanilla after putting a mild acid into the dog's mouth. (The acid was a US that elicited salivation.) The assistant presented acid and vanilla, in that order, 427 times, yet the odor of vanilla did not become a CS for salivating. However, when another odor was presented *before* the acid, it became a CS after only 20 pairings. These results are typical of those obtained by others who have attempted backward

Pavlovian Flowchart

Students are often confused by the various methods of pairing conditional and unconditional stimuli. When presented with a new example of conditioning, they may have difficulty deciding whether the procedure used was trace, delayed, simultaneous, or backward. The following flowchart, a modified version of one provided by John Hummel and his colleagues (1991), may help.

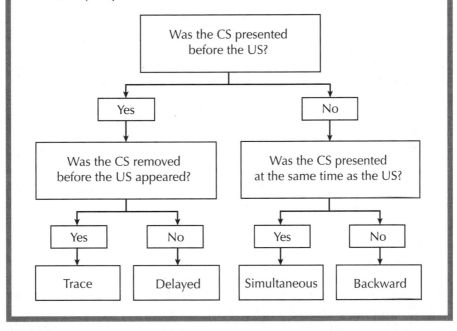

conditioning (Gormezano & Moore, 1969). Some researchers have argued that backward conditioning is sometimes effective in establishing a conditional response (e.g., Keith-Lucas & Guttman, 1975; Spetch et al., 1981), but the procedure is, at best, very inefficient (for reviews, see Hall, 1984; Wilson & Blackledge, 1999).

Because of the ineffectiveness of simultaneous and backward procedures, they are seldom used in studies of Pavlovian conditioning.

CS-US Contingency

A **contingency** is a kind of if-then statement. One event, Y, is contingent on another event, X, to the extent that Y occurs if and only if X occurs.

Various experiments have suggested that the effectiveness of Pavlovian procedures varies with the degree of contingency between CS and US. In one study, Robert Rescorla (1968) exposed rats to a tone followed by a mild shock. Although all the rats received the same number of CS-US pairings, in additional trials the US sometimes appeared alone. In one group, the shock occurred in the absence of the CS in 10% of the additional trials; in a second group, the US appeared alone in 20% of the trials; and in a third group, the US appeared alone in 40% of the trials. The results showed that the amount of learning depended on the degree to which the CS predicted shock. When the CS was nearly always followed by the US, conditioning occurred. When a shock was about as likely to occur in the absence of a CS as in its presence (the 40% group), little or no learning took place.

Rescorla concluded that contingency was essential to Pavlovian learning, but later work raised doubts about this. Some researchers have found evidence of Pavlovian conditioning even when there is *no* contingency between CS and US (Durlach, 1982; see Papini & Bitterman, 1990, and Wasserman, 1989, for discussions of this issue). Nevertheless, we can say that, other things being equal, the rate of Pavlovian conditioning will vary with the degree of CS-US contingency.

In the laboratory, it is a simple matter to ensure rapid learning by creating a high degree of contingency between the CS and US. Pavlov was able to pair a ticking metronome with food so that if the metronome was ticking, the dog always got food, and if it was not ticking, the dog never got food. Outside the laboratory, however, life is more complicated. A stimulus will sometimes be paired with a particular US and other times will appear alone—or, to be more precise, it will appear with *other* stimuli. For example, you may meet someone new and have a short, pleasant exchange on one occasion, but the next meeting may be neutral or unpleasant. This second experience will tend to undermine the positive effects of the first pleasant meeting. The lack of perfect contingency between a CS and a given US (or, as in this example, a well-established CS) not only makes for less than ideal learning conditions but may also account to some extent for the ambivalent reactions we often have toward people or things in our environment, as when we find ourselves saying, "I can't decide whether I like that person or not."

CS-US Contiguity

Contiguity refers to the closeness in time or space between two events. In Pavlovian conditioning, contiguity usually refers to the interval between the CS and US. In trace conditioning, this means the interval between the termination of the CS and the onset of the US; in delayed conditioning, where the two stimuli overlap, it means the interval between the onset of the CS and the onset of the US. In general, the more contiguous the CS and US, the more quickly a CR will appear (Mackintosh, 1974; Wasserman, 1989). However, the simultaneous procedure, with no interval at all, is very ineffective. The optimum interval depends on a number of variables.

One important variable is the kind of response being learned. For instance, in establishing a conditional eyeblink response, the ideal CS-US interval is about one-half second; intervals as long as a minute are unlikely to be effective. It is possible, however, to obtain very good results with long CS-US intervals in studies of taste aversion. Taste aversion conditioning usually consists of pairing a distinctive taste with a substance that induces nausea. Some researchers have produced taste aversions with CS-US intervals of several hours (Revusky & Garcia, 1970; Wallace, 1976; for more on taste aversions, see Chapter 4). Other research shows that the ideal CS-US interval varies with the level of stress (Servatius et al., 2001).

Query: In Pavlovian conditioning, _____

usually refers to the interval between CS and US.

The optimum CS-US interval also varies according to the type of conditioning procedure used, with short intervals generally being less important in delayed conditioning than in trace conditioning. However, even in trace conditioning, extremely short intervals may not work well, as a study by Gregory Kimble (1947) demonstrates. Kimble trained college students to blink in response to a light. The gap between the light and a puff of air to the eye was short, from 1/10 of a second to 4/10 of a second. On every tenth trial, Kimble withheld the US to see whether the students would blink. At the end of the experiment, he compared the response rates and found that the group with the longest CS-US intervals produced conditional responses on 95% of the test trials. Groups with shorter intervals responded less frequently; the shortest intervals produced CRs on an average of only 45% of test trials (see Figure 3-4).

It is difficult to generalize about the role of contiguity in Pavlovian conditioning. Although shorter intervals are generally preferable to longer ones, the ideal interval varies in complex ways from situation to situation. However, the contiguity of CS and US cannot be ignored, because it will affect the success of any given conditioning procedure one way or another.

Stimulus Features

The physical characteristics of the CS and US affect the pace of conditioning. It might seem that given several neutral stimuli, one would serve as a CS as well as another. But although nearly any stimulus can

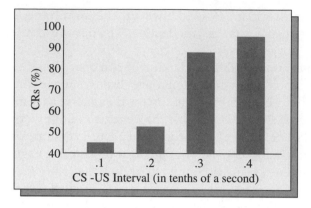

Figure 3-4 *CS-US interval. The average percentage of conditional responses on test trials revealed improved conditioning with longer CS-US intervals up to .4 second. (Compiled from data in Kimble, 1947.)*

become an effective CS, some stimuli serve the purpose far more readily than others.

This is illustrated by experiments in which the CS consists of two or more stimuli (e.g., a red light and a buzzer) presented simultaneously. Such a **compound stimulus** is paired with a US for one or more trials, after which the experimenter tests for conditioning by presenting the compound stimulus and each component of the CS alone.

In one of the first studies of compound stimuli, one of Pavlov's assistants simultaneously presented cold and tactile stimulation to a dog, followed by a few drops of mild acid in the mouth (a US for salivation). Then the experimenter tested the dog with the cold stimulus alone, the tactile stimulus alone, and the compound stimulus. The results revealed that although both the tactile stimulus and the compound stimulus were effective conditional stimuli, the cold stimulus alone was utterly ineffective.

This phenomenon is known as **overshadowing** because, as Pavlov noted, "The effect of one [stimulus] was found very commonly to overshadow the effect of the others almost completely" (p. 141). The overshadowed stimulus does not go entirely unnoticed; it simply does not become an effective CS (Rescorla, 1973).

Perhaps the chief distinguishing characteristic of an effective CS is its intensity: Strong stimuli overshadow weak ones. Leon Kamin (1969) used a compound stimulus consisting of a strong light and a weak tone and found that when he presented each stimulus alone, the light produced a stronger CR than the tone. Other studies demonstrate that a loud noise makes a better CS than a soft noise, that a bright light is more

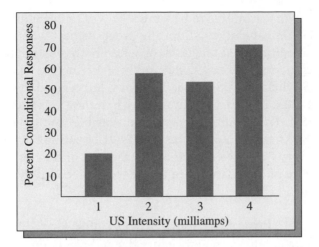

Figure 3-5 *Conditioning and US intensity. Average percentage of CRs on seventh day of training for cats exposed to four levels of shock. Generally, the more intense the US, the more effective the training. (Compiled from data in Polenchar et al., 1984.)*

effective than a soft light, that a strong flavor or odor works better than a mild one, and so on.

The intensity of the US also is very important, with stronger stimuli producing better results, in general, than weaker ones. This was demonstrated by Kenneth Spence (1953) in a study of eyelid conditioning. The US was a puff of air exerting either 1/4 pound of pressure per square inch (psi) or 5 pounds psi. In a 20-trial test period, college students trained with the weak US gave an average of fewer than 6 conditional responses to the CS, whereas those trained with the stronger US gave an average of 13 CRs. In a more recent experiment, Brett Polenchar and his colleagues (1984) used four levels of mild shock (from 1 to 4 milliamps) as the US. They sounded a tone and then delivered a shock to the hind leg of a cat, causing it to flex its leg. The rate of CR acquisition increased with the intensity of the shock (see Figure 3-5).

It is possible, however, for either a CS or a US to be too intense. In eyelid conditioning, a bright light may make a better CS than a dim one, but if the light is very strong, it may be an unconditional stimulus for blinking and will therefore interfere with learning. Likewise, a very weak electric current makes a poor US, but so may a very strong one.

Query: If one part of a compound stimulus fails to become a

CS, _____ has occurred.

The ability of a stimulus to become a CS varies depending on the nature of the US. In general, conditioning proceeds best when both the CS and the US affect internal receptors or when both affect external receptors. In experiments with rats, for example, a distinctive taste is likely to become a CS when the US causes sickness, but a combination of sight and sound is more likely to become a CS when the US is shock (Garcia & Koelling, 1966). This finding seems quite sensible from an evolutionary standpoint: Sickness is likely to be the result of eating tainted food, and such food is likely to have a distinctive taste; painful external stimuli—such as the bite of a predator—are likely to be preceded by a distinctive sight or sound.

Prior Experience with CS and US

The effects of a conditioning procedure depend partly on the organism's previous exposure to the stimuli that will serve as CS and US. Suppose, for example, that a dog hears a bell that is sounded repeatedly but is never paired with food. If an experimenter then begins pairing the bell with food, how will the dog's previous experience with the bell affect learning?

Research shows that it takes longer for the bell to become a CS than it would have had the dog never heard the bell by itself.[9] The appearance of a stimulus in the absence of a US interferes with the subsequent ability of that stimulus to become a CS (see Figure 3-6). This phenomenon is called **latent inhibition** (Lubow & Moore, 1959). Janice McPhee and colleagues (2001) added a 28-day interval between the CS pre-exposure and the conditioning session, and still latent inhibition occurred.

Latent inhibition suggests that novel stimuli (stimuli with which the organism has had little experience) are more likely to become conditional stimuli than are stimuli that have appeared many times in the absence of the US. But what if the novel stimulus is part of a compound stimulus that includes an effective CS? Suppose, for example, that a researcher conducts an experiment on Pavlovian learning in rats, first by repeatedly pairing a tone and electric shock, then by repeatedly pairing a compound stimulus consisting of the tone and a novel stimulus (light) with the shock. What will happen if the researcher now presents the light alone? Leon Kamin (1969) performed this experiment and found that the light did not become a CS. This phenomenon, called **blocking**, resembles overshadowing in that one stimulus interferes with the ability

---

[9]This is a good example of why animals are important in learning research. People are more likely than laboratory animals to have had experiences with a CS or a US that will affect a conditioning procedure in unknown ways.

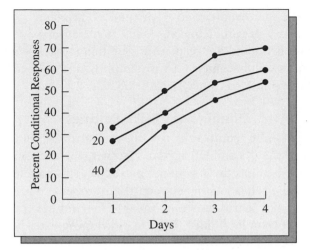

Figure 3-6 *Latent inhibition. Percentage of CRs (leg flexion) in sheep and goats on four days following 0, 20, or 40 pre-exposures to the CS. (From "Latent Inhibition: Effects of Frequency of Nonreinforced Preexposure of the CS," by R. E. Lubow, 1965,* Journal of Comparative and Physiological Psychology, 60, *p. 456, Figure 2. Copyright © 1965 by the American Psychological Association. Reprinted by permission.)*

of another to become a CS. In overshadowing, however, the effect is the result of differences between the stimuli in characteristics such as intensity; in blocking, the effect is due to prior experience with one part of a compound stimulus.[10]

There is another way in which experience with a neutral stimulus can affect later conditioning. Suppose two neutral stimuli, such as a bell and a light, are repeatedly presented together but are not paired with a US. Then one of these stimuli, perhaps the bell, is repeatedly paired with an unconditional stimulus so that it becomes a CS. What effect will this procedure have on the capacity of the light to become a CS? Wilfred Brogden (1939), using dogs as subjects, paired a light and a bell for 2 seconds, 20 times a day for 10 days. Then, for some of the dogs, he repeatedly paired the bell with a mild shock to one of the animal's front legs to elicit a reflex movement. Next, Brogden presented the light to see what would happen. He found that this stimulus often elicited a CR even

---

[10]Blocking is not, however, the inevitable result of pairing an established CS with a novel stimulus. John Batson and Robert Batsell (2000) paired the fragrance of almond and a US that induced nausea, and then paired the odor, now a CS for nausea, and a novel stimulus, a sweet taste, with the US. Based on research on blocking, we might predict that the taste would *not* become a CS for nausea, but it did. In fact, the procedure facilitated conditioning to the taste. The researchers call this surprising phenomenon augmentation (see also Batsell, 2000).

though it had never been paired with the US. Brogden called this phenomenon **sensory preconditioning**. Dogs that had not been exposed to the bell-light pairing did not respond to the light in this way. In general, then, a stimulus will become a CS more rapidly if it has been paired with another stimulus that has since become a CS.

Number of CS-US Pairings

Because conditioning requires the pairing of stimuli, it seems logical that the more often the CS and US appear together, the more likely a conditional response is to occur. In general, nature accepts this logic.

However, the relationship between the number of stimulus pairings and the amount of learning is not linear: The first several pairings are more important than later ones. Thus, conditioning usually follows a decelerating curve (see Figure 3-7).

From a survival standpoint, the curvilinear relationship between CS-US pairings and learning makes excellent sense. If important stimuli are reliably associated, the sooner the organism adapts, the better. If, for instance, the sight of a poisonous snake is associated with a painful bite, it is important that we acquire a healthy fear of the snake right away. Those who require several CS-US pairings for learning in this situation are obviously at a serious disadvantage.

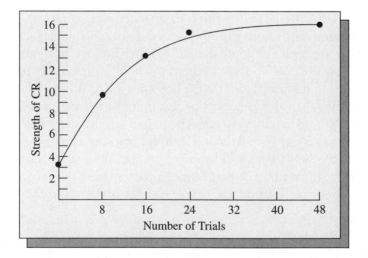

Figure 3-7 *Number of CS-US pairings and conditioning. The more times a shock to the wrist followed a tone, the stronger the response to the tone alone. (After Hull, 1943, from data in Hovland, 1937b.)*

Intertrial Interval

We saw earlier that the CS-US interval was important to learning. Another interval that affects the rate of conditioning is the gap between successive trials. (Recall that each pairing of the CS and US is one trial.) The **intertrial interval** can vary from about a second to several years. Suppose you want to train a dog to salivate when you clap your hands. You decide that you will pair the hand clap with food 10 times. How much time should you allow between each of the 10 trials?

In general, experiments comparing various intertrial intervals find that longer intervals are more effective than shorter ones. Whereas the optimum interval between CS and US is often a second or less, the best intertrial interval may be 20 or 30 seconds or more (see, for example, Prokasy & Whaley, 1963).

Query: Four variables that affect the rate of conditioning are

_____, _____, _____, and

_____.

Other Variables

The variables discussed thus far are perhaps the most important, but many others affect the course of Pavlovian conditioning.

For instance, Harry Braun and Richard Geiselhart (1959) found that the success of a Pavlovian procedure varied as a function of age. These researchers investigated eyelid conditioning in children, young adults, and senior citizens. As Figure 3-8 shows, learning was closely related to age; in fact, the procedure was not effective in establishing a conditional eyeblink in the oldest subjects.[11]

Temperament can also affect conditioning. Pavlov noticed that some dogs are highly excitable whereas others are much more sedate. He found that these differences, which may be largely due to heredity, affect the rate of learning: the more excitable dogs learned faster.

Stress also affects conditioning. Janet Taylor (1951) found that anxious students acquired conditional responses more quickly than those who were more relaxed (see Figure 3-9). More recently, Servatius and colleagues (2001) also found that, in general, stress facilitated Pavlovian learning.

---

[11]Recent research suggests that poor conditioning in elderly people may signal the early stages of dementia (Woodruff-Pak et al., 1996).

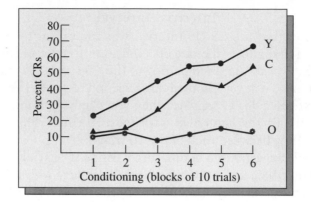

Figure 3-8 *Conditioning and age. Eyelid conditioning for the first 60 trials proceeded more rapidly among children (C) and young adults (Y) than among older adults (O). (After Braun and Geiselhart, 1959.)*

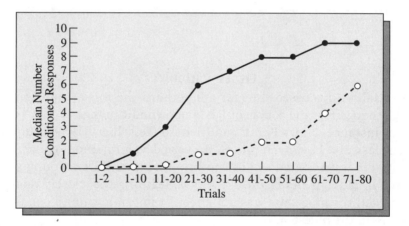

Figure 3-9 *Conditioning and anxiety. Eyelid conditioning proceeded more rapidly among anxious college students (solid line) than among relaxed ones (broken line). (From Taylor, 1951.)*

REVIEW Although Pavlovian conditioning appears to be quite simple, it is complicated by the effects of a number of variables.[12] Chief among these is the manner in which the CS and US are paired; these include

---

[12]Indeed, Pavlovian conditioning is far more complicated than this chapter suggests. By way of example: Recent research shows that a stimulus may, under certain circumstances, serve as a US that establishes two *different* conditional responses simultaneously (Lett et al., 2001). Just thinking about that gives me a headache.

trace, delayed, simultaneous, and backward procedures. The length of the CS-US interval and the degree to which the US is contingent on the CS also affect the rate of learning. Characteristics of the stimuli involved can be important as well. When a compound stimulus is used as CS, for example, one aspect of the stimulus may overshadow another. Prior experience with either the CS or the US can affect learning; exposure to a stimulus before conditioning can cause latent inhibition and blocking. Other important variables include the number of CS-US pairings and the length of intertrial intervals.

Many other variables affect the course of Pavlovian conditioning. Once a conditional response has been well established, however, it tends to be quite durable and may last for many years. This result is not inevitable, however; conditional responses can be extinguished.

Extinction of Conditional Responses

Once a conditional response is established, it can be maintained indefinitely so long as the conditional stimulus is sometimes followed by the unconditional stimulus. If, however, the CS is repeatedly presented without the US, the conditional response will become weaker and weaker. The procedure of repeatedly presenting the CS without the US is called **extinction**. When, as a result of extinction, the CR no longer occurs (or occurs no more than it did prior to conditioning), it is said to have been extinguished.

Pavlov was the first to demonstrate extinction in the laboratory. After training a dog to salivate at the sight of meat powder, he repeatedly presented the food without giving it to the dog. With each presentation, the dog salivated less and less (see Figure 3-10).[13]

A study of eyelid conditioning by E. R. Hilgard and D. G. Marquis (1935) provides another example of Pavlovian extinction. In this study, dogs learned to blink in response to a light. By the fifth day, 3 of the 4 dogs gave conditional responses to the CS over 90% of the time; the 4th dog responded 76% of the time. When the experimenters put the response on extinction, the CR declined steadily, and after 50 extinction trials the response rate had fallen to about 25% for each dog.

At first glance, extinction looks something like forgetting. However, forgetting refers to a deterioration in performance following a period without practice. For example, after a dog has learned to salivate at the

---

[13]A similar pattern emerges when other measures of conditioning are used. For example, in one experiment on extinction, Pavlov saw the CR latency increase from 3 seconds to 13 seconds over 7 trials.

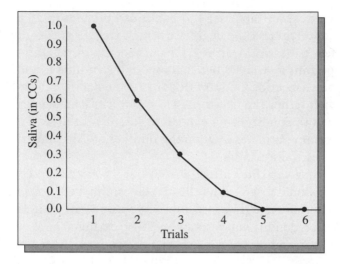

Figure 3-10 *Extinction of a CR. A conditional response will extinguish if the CS (in this case, the sight of food) is repeatedly presented alone. (Compiled from data in Pavlov, 1927.)*

sound of a metronome, we might discontinue training for a day, a week, or a decade, and then test it again with a ticking metronome. If the dog no longer salivates at the sound, we may say that forgetting has occurred. Extinction is a very different procedure: the practice sessions continue, but the sound of the metronome is not paired with food. Thus, extinction can be viewed as a form of conditioning in which the CS is paired with the *absence* of the US. During extinction, Pavlov's dogs could be said to be learning the "not salivating" response (see Figure 3-11).

The extinction curve shown in Figure 3-10, which is fairly typical, suggests that the CR steadily approaches zero and stabilizes at some very low level. This is not quite the case. Pavlov discovered that if, after a response seemed to have been extinguished, he discontinued training for a time and then presented the CS again, the dog was very likely to salivate (see Figure 3-12). This sudden reappearance of a CR after extinction is called **spontaneous recovery**. If Pavlov once again presented the CS alone several times, the CR would rapidly extinguish. But the fact that a CR can reappear following extinction means that to eliminate it, it must be extinguished on at least two occasions.

Although extinction may reduce the frequency of a CR to zero, it does not entirely undo the effects of conditioning. This is evident from Pavlov's observation that an extinguished CR usually can be reestablished far more readily than it was established initially. Mark Bouton and Dale Swartzentruber (1991) reviewed the animal research on extinction

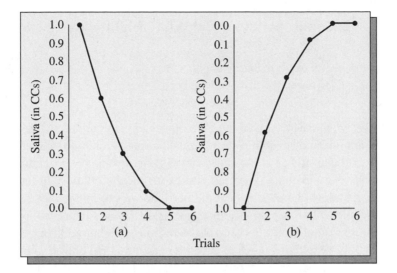

Figure 3-11 *Extinction as learning. The extinction of the salivary response may be plotted as the decrease in the salivary response (a) or as the increase in the "not-salivating response" (b). (Compiled from data in Pavlov, 1927.)*

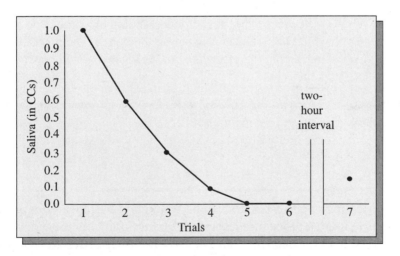

Figure 3-12 *Spontaneous recovery. A conditional response will extinguish if the CS is repeatedly presented alone. Following a rest period, the CR spontaneously reappears. (Compiled from data in Pavlov, 1927.)*

and concluded that extinguished behavior remains sensitive to environmental cues. In other words, events that occurred during training can trigger a CR's reappearance after extinction.

Edwin B. Twitmyer and What Might Have Been

For of all sad words of tongue or pen,
The saddest are these: "It might have been!"
John Greenleaf Whittier

In 1902, when Pavlov was in the early stages of his conditioning research, a young man named Edwin B. Twitmyer made a small, but important, mistake.

A graduate student at the University of Pennsylvania, Twitmyer was doing research on the patellar (knee jerk) reflex for his dissertation. In his experiments, he allowed a pair of small rubber hammers to fall against a person's knee so as to cause the familiar knee jerk reflex. He was interested in the way muscle tension affected the force of the response, so before letting the hammers fall, he would ring a bell to alert the person that the blows were coming. One day Twitmyer unintentionally rang the bell without releasing the hammers. That was the small, important, mistake.

Although the result was a surprise to Twitmyer, you can guess what happened: The subject's feet shot forward as if his knees had been hit with the hammers. Twitmyer was intrigued by this, especially when the subject insisted that the response was as much a surprise to him as it had been to Twitmyer.

Twitmyer followed up this serendipitous finding by conducting new experiments in which he systematically paired the bell and hammer blow and then tried the bell alone. The procedure produced what would now be called conditional responses.

REVIEW   Conditional responses can be weakened by repeatedly presenting the CS alone, a procedure known as extinction. This procedure is often confused with forgetting, but the two are quite different. Following extinction, the CS may elicit the CR again, a phenomenon known as spontaneous recovery.

Despite many experiments conducted over a period of about a hundred years, we still do not thoroughly understand Pavlovian conditioning. A number of experts have, however, attempted to construct theories to account for various Pavlovian phenomena.

Twitmyer thought he was on to something and arranged to talk about his work at the meetings of the American Psychological Association in 1904. At the end of a morning session chaired by William James, the giant of the times, Twitmyer read his paper, *Knee Jerks Without Stimulation of the Patellar Tendon*.

There had been a good deal of discussion following previous papers, so the session was running into the lunch hour. Twitmyer spoke to an audience that hungered less for knowledge than for roast beef. When the young man had completed his remarks, James asked the audience if there were any questions or comments. The audience replied with an awesome—silence. There being no questions, James said, the session is concluded.

Twitmyer was devastated. He had given his Gettysburg Address and considered his effort a failure. He never did another experiment on conditioning. Twitmyer received his degree and went on to do good work in other fields. But what *might* he have done? What if he had pushed on from that first defeat? What if he had published his findings, done additional research, given other talks?

He would not have supplanted Pavlov, who had a small army of assistants doing conditioning experiments. But Pavlov's work was virtually unknown in the United States until 1927. Twitmyer could have become his Western counterpart and one of the most prominent figures in American psychology.

Alas, poor Twitmyer. What *might* have been!

Theories of Conditioning

There is no unified theory of Pavlovian conditioning, no set of propositions that together account for the various findings we have considered thus far. Instead, efforts to construct theories have attempted to answer certain key questions. Some theories, for example, try to determine which of the many factors affecting conditioning is the most crucial. Some theorists believe the contiguity of CS and US is primary (Pavlov, 1927; Papini & Bitterman, 1990); others believe that the degree of contingency between CS and US is paramount (Rescorla, 1968, 1988; Rescorla & Wagner, 1972).

Another theoretical issue that is debated is even more basic than the contiguity-contingency issue. This is the matter of what is learned during conditioning. When a dog salivates at the sound of a bell, learning clearly has taken place, but what exactly has the dog learned? We will consider two answers: stimulus substitution theory and preparatory response theory.

Stimulus Substitution Theory

Pavlov believed that conditioning involved the formation of a new neurological connection between the CS and the US. The US, Pavlov speculated, must stimulate an area of the brain that triggers the reflex response. Stimulation of this neural area must trigger the reflex response. Putting food in a dog's mouth, for example, stimulates the area of the brain that controls salivation. By repeatedly pairing a bell with food, Pavlov said, the bell comes to stimulate, indirectly, the salivation area of the brain. Thus, the CR and UR both result from excitation of the same area of the brain.

"The path of the inborn reflex," wrote Pavlov, "is already completed at birth; but the path of the signalizing reflex [i.e., the CS-US connection] has still to be completed in the higher nervous centers" (p. 25). Pavlov used the telephone as a convenient analogy. "My residence," he wrote, "may be connected directly with the laboratory by a private line, and I may call up the laboratory whenever it pleases me to do so; or on the other hand, a connection may have to be made through the central exchange. But the result in both cases is the same" (p. 25).

It follows from Pavlov's theory that the CR and the UR are one and the same. According to Pavlov, then, conditioning does not involve the acquisition of any new behavior, but rather the tendency to respond in old ways to new stimuli. The CS merely substitutes for the US in evoking the reflex response. This is called **stimulus substitution theory**.

A critical problem with the stimulus substitution theory is that there is evidence that the CR and the UR are *not* always the same. As a rule, the conditional response is weaker than, occurs less reliably than, and appears more slowly than, the UR. These differences are not too troublesome. The CS may simply be said to provide weaker stimulation of the US area of the brain; hence, the CR is weaker than the UR.

But there are often qualitative differences between conditional and unconditional responses. For instance, Karl Zener (1937) trained dogs to salivate and then watched their spontaneous responses to food and to the conditional stimulus. Like Pavlov, Zener found that both the CS and the US elicited salivation, but Zener noticed that the two stimuli also elicited other behavior as well. When the dog received food, it made chewing movements but otherwise remained still; when the CS appeared, the dog became active but did not chew.

An even more serious difficulty for the theory is the finding that the CR is sometimes the *opposite* of the UR (Hilgard, 1936). The unconditional response to electric shock, for example, is an increase in heart rate, whereas a CS that has been paired with shock elicits a *decrease* in heart rate.

Despite these problems, stimulus substitution theory has its defenders. Roelof Eikelboom and Jane Stewart (1982), for example, dispute the notion that the conditional response is sometimes the opposite of the unconditional response. They propose that only when the UR does not involve the central nervous system are the CR and the UR opposites. Nevertheless, stimulus substitution theory is generally out of favor, largely supplanted by preparatory response theory.

Query: According to stimulus substitution theory, the

_____ substitutes for the _____.

Preparatory Response Theory

The discovery of differences between conditional and unconditional responses led gradually to **preparatory response theory**. The idea here is that what is learned during Pavlovian conditioning is a response that prepares the organism for the appearance of the US. Sometimes the response required is nearly identical to the UR. On other occasions, the CR is quite different. In both cases, the CR helps the organism prepare for what is about to happen.

When a dog responds to a bell by salivating, for instance, this behavior prepares the animal for the food that is about to come. By beginning to salivate before food arrives, the dog prepares to digest the food it will receive. In the same way, responding with fear at the sight of a dog that bit us on a previous occasion prepares us to fight or flee the danger.

Shepard Siegel (1983) has suggested that in certain cases, notably those involving addictive drugs, the conditional response prepares for the unconditional stimulus by compensating for the effects of the US. The unconditional response to morphine, for instance, includes decreased sensitivity to pain, but the CR to stimuli associated with morphine is *increased* sensitivity to pain (Siegel, 1975). In this case, the organism prepares for the drug by suppressing the body's response to it.

Conditioning and Awareness

Many students who have read about Pavlovian conditioning will, if asked to explain it, say something like this: "Pavlov rang a bell and then gave a dog food. After doing this several times, the dog associated the bell with food. When the bell rang, the dog knew food was coming and that made it salivate."

This view of conditioning assumes that an awareness of the relationship between CS and US is essential to, and must precede, the appearance of the CR. "After all," the student is likely to say, "why would the dog salivate unless it knew food was coming?"

The awareness view is popular not only with students but with some psychologists (Allen & Janiszewski, 1989). Nevertheless, it faces serious difficulties. For instance, research with human participants has demonstrated that conditioning sometimes occurs without awareness that the CS and US are related. In one study, K. Diven (1937) asked people to take a word-association test. The subjects were presented with certain words and after each one they were to say whatever words came to mind. One of the test words was *barn*; while the subject was responding to this word, he always received a shock. All of the subjects showed a conditional response (the galvanic skin response) to the word *barn*, yet half of them were unable to say what word preceded shock. (See also Papka et al., 1997; Schiffman & Furedy, 1977). If conditioning sometimes occurs without awareness, then awareness cannot be said to be necessary for conditioning.

Another problem for the awareness model arises when simple animals undergo conditioning. Roundworms and flatworms, for example, condition very well, yet it is hard to believe that they have an awareness of the CS-US relationship. Worms do not have brains, in the usual sense of the word, so what are they supposed to have used to recognize, for example, that a light precedes a shock? Worse still for the awareness model, Pavlovian procedures have been used successfully with some one-celled organisms such as the

This means that when people repeatedly take a drug in a particular setting, aspects of the setting may become CSs for reduced responses to the drug. Thus, the preparatory response theory accounts for the phenomenon of drug tolerance. It also predicts that drug tolerance will not occur if drugs are taken in the absence of the conditional stimuli.

This prediction has some empirical support. In one study, L. O. Lightfoot (1980) had male college students drink a substantial amount of

amoeba. It seems absurd to suggest that an amoeba could be aware of a CS-US relationship.

It could be argued that conditioning works differently in humans than in lower organisms: A person must become aware of the CS-US relationship to produce a conditional response; a worm need not. The trouble with this argument is obvious: Why should a more intelligent species be less efficient at learning than a less intelligent species? If an amoeba can learn to respond to a light without being aware that a shock will follow, why can't a person?

Despite these and other problems faced by awareness advocates, the issue is still researched and debated (see, for example, Purkis & Lipp, 2001). The problem is complicated and not easily resolved. However, the rancor with which the awareness issue is debated suggests that it has an importance that transcends Pavlovian conditioning.

The real debate seems to be between a natural science model of behavior, which says that behavior can be accounted for entirely in terms of biological and environmental events, and a model that insists that behavior is the product of an autonomous mind (see, for example, Furedy & Kristjansson, 1996; Shanks & St. Johns, 1994).

Those who believe in the autonomous mind accuse their opponents of treating the person as an "empty organism." But the natural science approach does not suggest that people (or other animals, for that matter) are empty. A person (and perhaps a dog) may become aware at some point that a bell will be followed by food. This awareness may precede *or follow* the appearance of a conditional response. The point is that if awareness occurs, it is, like the CR itself, the result of events in the organism's environment. Awareness of the association between CS and US is evidently not a *cause* of learning, but *part of what is learned.*

beer in a 30-minute period on each of 5 consecutive days. The first four drinking sessions took place in the same location. On the fifth day, some students drank beer in the familiar setting whereas others imbibed in a new place. All the students then took tests of intellectual and perceptual-motor skills after drinking. Those who drank in the familiar setting scored higher on the tests, indicating they were less inebriated, although they had had the same amount of alcohol. Evidently, stimuli previously associated with drinking had muted the effects of the alcohol. The novel setting lacked these CSs, so there was no preparatory CR and the alcohol hit with greater force.

Preparatory response theory may also account for certain cases of sudden death following drug use. Such deaths are commonly attributed to accidental overdose, but sometimes they occur following a dose that, given the person's history of drug use, should not have been fatal (Reed, 1980; Siegel, 1984). Anecdotal evidence suggests that the deaths are sometimes due to the absence of stimuli normally present during drug use. Siegel (1984) asked 10 former heroin addicts who had nearly died following drug use about the circumstances surrounding their close call. In 7 cases, there was something unusual about the near-fatal event. Two addicts had used different injection procedures, two had taken the drug in unusual locations, and so on. A woman who usually required two or more attempts at penetrating a vein nearly died after she injected herself successfully on the first try. Apparently, the unsuccessful attempts had become a CS that evoked a preparatory response. The absence of the CS meant no preparatory CR and a stronger, nearly fatal, reaction to the drug.

Laboratory research with animals supports the anecdotal data. Siegel and his colleagues (1982) gave three groups of rats, some of which had never received heroin before, a strong dose of the drug. The heroin-experienced rats received the test dose either in the same place they had received previous doses or in a novel setting. The results were clear-cut. The dose was lethal for 96% of the inexperienced rats, but for experienced rats mortality depended on where they received the drug: Of those injected in a familiar environment, 32% died; of those injected in a strange environment, 64% died.

These studies are interesting in their own right, but they are also important to an understanding of what is learned during Pavlovian conditioning. When the US is food, the CR is salivation. When the US is an addictive drug, the CR is a reaction that subdues the effects of the drug. In each case, and in many other instances of conditioning, the CR prepares the organism for the US that is about to appear. Such studies support preparatory response theory and demonstrate the adaptive value of Pavlovian conditioning.

REVIEW Pavlov believed that what an organism learned during conditioning was to respond to the CS in the same way as to the US. He believed the CR and UR were the same and that the CS merely substituted for the US, hence the name, stimulus substitution theory. Subsequent research showed that the CR and UR are often quite different, and this led to preparatory response theory, the idea that Pavlovian conditioning involves the formation of a response that prepares the organism for the US.

Many students come away from the study of Pavlovian conditioning convinced that Pavlov taught us little more than how to make dogs slobber at the sound of a bell. In fact, Pavlovian conditioning has proved immensely useful in understanding a wide range of human and animal behavior (Turkkan, 1989). The work of Pavlov and his successors has also led to many practical applications, as you will see in the next chapter.

RECOMMENDED READING

1. Cuny, H. (1962). *Ivan Pavlov: The man and his theories.* (P. Evans, Trans.). New York: Fawcett.

   An excellent review of Pavlov's work, along with a number of selected writings by Pavlov.

2. Hollis, K. L. (1997). Contemporary research on Pavlovian conditioning: A "new" functional analysis. *American Psychologist, 52,* 956–965.

   This review of recent research makes it clear that Pavlovian conditioning is still a very dynamic and important field.

3. Pavlov, I. P. (1906). The scientific investigation of the psychical faculties or processes in the higher animals. *Science, 24,* 613–619.

   This article is perhaps the earliest English language report by Pavlov on his conditioning experiments.

4. Todes, D. P. (1997). From the machine to the ghost within: Pavlov's transition from digestive physiology to conditional reflexes. *American Psychologist, 52,* 947–955.

   Todes describes Pavlov's transition from physiologist to behavior scientist.

5. Windholz, G. (1997). Ivan P. Pavlov: An overview of his life and psychological work. *American Psychologist, 52,* 941–946.

   A brief review of Pavlov's life and work.

REVIEW QUESTIONS

1. Define the following terms:

   backward conditioning   classical conditioning
   blocking   compound stimulus

conditional reflex	preparatory response theory
conditional response	pseudoconditioning
conditional stimulus	sensory preconditioning
contiguity	simultaneous conditioning
contingency	spontaneous recovery
delayed conditioning	stimulus substitution theory
extinction	test trial
higher-order conditioning	trace conditioning
intertrial interval	unconditional reflex
latent inhibition	unconditional response
overshadowing	unconditional stimulus
Pavlovian conditioning	

2. What did Pavlov mean when he said that glands seemed to possess intelligence?

3. One of Pavlov's most important discoveries was that salivation could be attributed to events occurring in the dog's environment. Why is this important?

4. Why do you suppose Pavlovian conditioning is also called *classical* conditioning?

5. Explain the use of test trials in the measurement of Pavlovian learning.

6. Why is pseudoconditioning a problem for researchers?

7. Give an example of higher-order conditioning from your own experience.

8. Give an example of overshadowing.

9. How is overshadowing different from blocking?

10. Why is it a mistake to speak of *simple* Pavlovian conditioning?

11. Explain the differences among trace, delayed, simultaneous, and backward conditioning procedures. Illustrate each procedure with an example not given in the text.

12. If you wanted to establish a conditional eyeblink in response to a light, what procedure (from among trace, delayed, etc.) is least likely to be successful?

13. What is the principal flaw in Pavlov's stimulus substitution theory?

14. In what sense is a CR a preparatory response?

15. How would you determine the optimum intensity of a CS for eyelid conditioning?

16. Peggy Noonan, a political speech writer, reports that soon after she had a baby she returned to the campaign trail. One day she saw something in a crowd and began lactating. What did she see?

17. Some dentists ask their patients to listen to music through headphones while having their teeth worked on. The idea is to help the patient relax, thereby reducing the painfulness of the procedure. Should the patients listen to music they like or music they dislike?

18. Some victims of insomnia sleep better at strange hotels than they do in their own bedroom. Explain why.

19. In 1957, an amateur psychologist named James Vicary flashed imperceptible messages on a screen during showings of the film *Picnic*. The messages were "Hungry? Eat popcorn" and "Drink Coca-Cola." Although Vicary claimed these "subliminal ads" increased sales of popcorn and Coke, research proved him wrong. However, the ads did have the effect of arousing hostility toward Pavlovian conditioning. Was Vicary's amateur experiment really a study of Pavlovian conditioning?

20. How has the discovery of Pavlovian conditioning altered your view of human nature?

PRACTICE QUIZ

1. The conditional response is so named because it depends on many
   _____.

2. In higher-order conditioning, the CS is paired with a well-established _____ stimulus.

3. _____ thought Pavlov was one of the greatest geniuses who ever lived.

4. Pavlovian conditioning usually involves _____ behavior.

5. In Pavlovian conditioning, the appearance of the US is normally _____ on the appearance of the CS.

6. Generally speaking, the shorter the CS-US interval, the _____ (faster/slower) the rate of learning; the shorter the intertrial interval, the _____ (faster/slower) the rate of learning.

7. Braun and Geiselhart found that older subjects acquired conditional responses _____ (more/less) rapidly than younger subjects.

8. Siegel's research on drug effects supports the _____ _____ theory of conditioning.

9. The least effective form of Pavlovian conditioning is probably the _____ procedure.

10. Latent _____ is the result of the CS having appeared alone before conditioning trials.

QUERY ANSWERS

Page 72. Pavlov identified two kinds of reflexes, *unconditional* and *conditional.*

Page 76. In higher-order conditioning, a neutral stimulus is paired with a well-established *conditional* stimulus.

Page 79. In trace conditioning, the *CS* begins and ends before the *US* appears.

Page 80. In delayed conditioning, the *CS* ends only after the *US* begins.

Page 83. In Pavlovian conditioning, *contiguity* usually refers to the interval between CS and US.

Page 85. If one part of a compound stimulus fails to become a CS, *overshadowing* has occurred.

Page 89. Any four of the variables discussed qualify: *how the CS and US are paired; CS-US contingency; CS-US contiguity; stimulus features; prior experience with CS and US; number of CS-US pairings; intertrial interval; age; temperament; emotional state/stress.*

Page 97. According to stimulus substitution theory, the *CS* substitutes for the *US.*

CHAPTER

4

Pavlovian Applications

These are our facts. I do not know what the psychiatrists will say, but we shall see who is right!

Ivan Pavlov

Because Pavlovian conditioning involves simple reflexive behavior, many people dismiss it as unimportant. Pavlov, these people say, provides no insight into human nature except to show us how to make animals drool and twitch. Even some psychologists have said that Pavlovian conditioning is merely of historical interest, a dead subject in the morgue of behavior science.

Nothing could be further from the truth. Although thousands of studies of Pavlovian conditioning have been carried out since Pavlov's day, it remains a rich lode that behavior scientists continue to mine for insights into learning and behavior (Hollis, 1997; Turkkan, 1989). Many of these studies have shed light on the role Pavlovian conditioning plays in the adaptation (and sometimes maladaptation) of people and other organisms to their environments. Pavlovian research has also led to new applications in the treatment of human problems and holds out the promise of still more progress. In this chapter we will take a brief look at the way Pavlovian research has changed our views of six phenomena of particular importance to people: fear, prejudice, advertising, paraphilia, taste aversion, and the functioning of the immune system. We begin with fear.

Fear

The first person to study human emotions systematically was John B. Watson.[1] In Watson's day, fear was commonly thought to be either the result of faulty reasoning or a kind of instinctual reaction (Valentine, 1930). For example, people were assumed to be innately afraid of fire, snakes, and the dark.

The work of Watson and his students changed all that. They found that relatively few stimuli arouse fear or other strong emotional reactions, but objects that are paired with emotion-arousing items will soon come to elicit those emotions as well. We now know that our emotional reactions, including not only fear but love, hate, and disgust, are largely

---

[1]Long before Watson's work, Pavlov studied conditioned fear in dogs.

learned, and they are learned mainly through Pavlovian conditioning. Watson called them **conditioned emotional responses**. His work has vastly improved our understanding and treatment of emotional disorders, particularly the unreasonable fears called phobias.

Phobias are among the most common behavior problems. One survey found, for example, that out of every 1,000 people interviewed, 198 were afraid of their dentist and 390 were afraid of snakes (Agras et al., 1969). (No doubt dentists are comforted to know that they are preferred over snakes.)[2]

Watson and graduate student Rosalie Rayner (Watson & Rayner, 1920; Watson & Watson, 1921) began their study of fear by testing a number of infants to see their reactions to fire, dogs, cats, laboratory rats, and other stimuli then thought to be innately frightening. They found no evidence of innate fear of these objects. They did find, however, that a sudden loud noise is an unconditional stimulus for crying and other fearful reactions.

Next, the researchers attempted to establish a fear reaction through classical conditioning. Their subject was Albert B., a healthy, 11-month-old boy who showed no signs of fearing a white rat, a pigeon, a rabbit, a dog, a monkey, cotton wool, or a burning newspaper. He appeared to be a happy, normal baby who rarely cried. The researchers established that a loud noise was a US for fear. When they struck a steel bar with a hammer behind Albert's head, he would jump suddenly. Using this loud noise as an unconditional stimulus, it took little time to establish a conditional fear response to a white rat. Watson and Rayner presented Albert with the rat, and then one of the experimenters hit the steel bar with a hammer. After a few pairings of this sort, Albert began to cry and show other signs of fear as soon as he saw the rat. He had learned, through Pavlovian conditioning, to fear white rats.

Query: Albert became fearful of the rat because the arrival of

the rat regularly preceded _____.

Other studies have since verified that Pavlovian procedures can establish fears in people. For example, Arne Öhman and colleagues (1976) had college students look at pictures of snakes until they had habituated—that is, until the pictures had no emotional effect as measured by the GSR. Then the researchers paired the pictures with electric shock to

---

[2]Given the fearful reactions many people have to snakes and dentists, it is perhaps not surprising that one sometimes finds an aquarium filled with fish in a dentist's waiting room, but never one with snakes.

Thank You, Albert

The experiment with Little Albert has been harshly criticized on ethical grounds (Harris, 1979), and rightly so. Today, most people find the idea of deliberately causing a phobia in a baby outrageous, and a similar experiment would no longer be considered ethical. We should remember, however, that the ethical standards of Watson's day were quite different.

We should also recognize that Albert's sacrifice completely changed our understanding of phobias and other emotional problems, and immediately suggested effective treatments for them. Mary Cover Jones's use of counterconditioning to treat Peter's fear of rabbits is an example (see text). These treatments, which are based on Pavlovian conditioning, have since relieved the suffering of tens of thousands of people.

Unfortunately, Little Albert was taken away before his phobia could be treated by additional training. If Albert is alive today, he may yet have an unreasonable fear of laboratory rats and other furry white objects. He has, however, contributed in a very important way to the alleviation of human suffering. He showed the way to therapies that have helped thousands of people overcome fears and other debilitating emotional problems. Albert made a contribution in infancy far in excess of anything most of us accomplish in a lifetime. We are indebted to him.

Thank you, Albert, wherever you are.

the hand. There was, of course, a fear response to the shock, and soon the pictures also evoked a response. This CR continued to occur even when the CS once again appeared alone.

We can readily come up with examples of fearful reactions that very likely were established through Pavlovian conditioning. Most people, for example, are made uneasy by visits to the dentist. This is hardly surprising when one considers that dental visits frequently entail some discomfort. The whine of the dentist's drill is all too often accompanied by pain, so the sound of the drill soon arouses anxiety. We may even come to fear anything associated with the painful drill, such as the dentist and the dentist's assistant (Ost & Hugdahl, 1985).

Very likely, the same sort of process accounts for the fear many people experience in a doctor's examining room, the school principal's office, or a mathematics classroom. A person who struggles with a math course, for example, may feel ill at ease in the classroom even when class is not in session.

Watson's work not only improved our understanding of fears but also led to effective treatment procedures. Mary Cover Jones (1924a, 1924b), another of Watson's students, was the first to show that Pavlovian conditioning could help people overcome fears as well as acquire them. Jones's subject was Peter, a 3-year-old with a fear of rabbits.[3] Peter's fear was "home grown," as Watson phrased it, not the result of deliberate conditioning. The experiment with Albert showed how Peter's fear may have been acquired; more important, it suggested how it might be removed.

Jones started by bringing a rabbit in view, but kept it far enough away that it did not disturb Peter as he ate a snack of crackers and milk. In this way, Jones paired a CS for fear (the sight of the rabbit) with a positive US (crackers and milk). The next day, Jones brought the rabbit closer but was careful not to bring it close enough to make the child uneasy. On each succeeding day the experimenter brought the rabbit closer, always pairing it with crackers and milk, until Peter showed no fear even when Jones put the rabbit into his lap. Finally, Peter would eat with one hand and play with the rabbit with the other. This use of Pavlovian procedures to reverse the unwanted effects of conditioning is called **counterconditioning**.

Various forms of counterconditioning have been developed since Jones's work with Peter.[4] Probably the best known of these therapies is systematic desensitization, a procedure in which a phobic person imagines a very weak form of the frightening CS while relaxed (Wolpe, 1973). The most recent variation of counterconditioning involves the technology called virtual reality.

Virtual reality technology creates a highly realistic electronic simulation of an environment. Such highly realistic simulations have been used for years to train pilots, but in recent years the technology has been applied to the treatment of phobias. Barbara Rothbaum and her colleagues (1995) conducted the first controlled experiment using virtual reality to treat a behavior disorder.[5] In their study, people with a fear of heights wore a kind of helmet that provided computer-simulated scenes. While in an office, they experienced walking on foot bridges and outdoor balconies of varying heights and went up a glass elevator that could ascend 50 floors. The treatment involved exposing the subjects to low-level fearful stimuli in the absence of any real danger. When a subject

---

[3] Albert and Peter are famous in behavior science, but they are often confused with one another, even in psychology texts. To keep these two studies straight, think of the story of Peter Rabbit, and you will remember that it was Peter and the *rabbit* and Albert and the *rat*.

[4] Those forms of counterconditioning that pair a disturbing CS with neutral or positive stimuli are often referred to collectively as exposure therapy.

[5] Rothbaum refers to this form of therapy as virtual reality exposure therapy (VRE). See previous note.

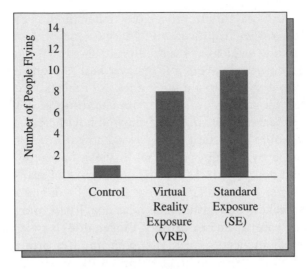

Figure 4-1 *Fear of flying. At the conclusion of the treatment phase all subjects (Ss) had the opportunity to fly on a plane. Of the 15 people in each group, only one control S flew, while 8 and 10 people in the counterconditioning groups (VRE and SE) did. (Compiled from data in* A Controlled Study of Virtual Reality Exposure Therapy for the Fear of Flying, *by B. O. Rothbaum, L. Hodges, S. Smith, J. H. Lee, and L. Price, 2000, paper presented at meeting of the American Psychological Association, Washington, DC, August.)*

felt comfortable walking on a low virtual bridge, he or she would walk on a higher bridge. The result of the procedure was a marked reduction in fear of heights. In fact, most people who completed treatment voluntarily exposed themselves to situations that had once been frightening, though they were not asked to do so.

In another study, Rothbaum and colleagues (2000) applied the same kind of virtual reality therapy to treat a fear of flying, a problem that afflicts about 25 million adults in the United States (Deran & Whitaker, 1980, reported in Rothbaum et al., 2000). In this study, Rothbaum's group compared virtual reality treatment with similar treatment using real airplanes. They found no difference in effectiveness between the two treatments, but people in both treatment groups fared substantially better than those in a no-treatment control group. Treated subjects reported less anxiety about flying and far more of them actually flew after treatment than did those in the control group (see Figure 4-1). By six months following the end of treatment, 93% of those who had received treatment had flown in a plane.

Virtual reality software is available for treating post-traumatic stress disorder in Viet Nam veterans (Rothbaum et al., 2001), fear of public speaking (Anderson et al., 2000), and fear of spiders (Carlin et al., 1997),

What Rats Can Teach Us About Fear

Fear, at least the unreasonable fear called phobia, is one of the curses of humanity. Yet good experimental research on fear in human volunteers is often difficult to do. An animal analog of human fear would be very useful, but where can you find a good, reliable measure of fear in a laboratory animal?

Enter the laboratory rat. If a rat is trained to press a lever at a steady rate and you then give it an electric shock, it will stop pressing the lever momentarily and may even "freeze." The stronger the shock, the more it suppresses the rate of lever pressing.

This is well and good, you say, but what does it have to do with studying learned fears? William Estes and B. F. Skinner (1941) provide an answer. They trained a rat to press a lever for food. When the animal was responding at a steady rate, they periodically sounded a tone; when the tone stopped, the rat received a shock. At first, the tone had no noticeable effect: The rat continued to press the lever at the same rate. But after the tone and shock had been paired several times, the rat decreased its rate of lever pressing when it heard the tone and did not resume its previous rate of activity until after it received the shock. Note that the rat's activity had absolutely no effect on the appearance of the tone or the delivery of the shock, yet the tone clearly reduced lever pressing. This reduction in the rate of ongoing behavior due to exposure to an aversive CS is called **conditioned suppression**.

Conditioned suppression provides a convenient measure of fear. The more lever pressing is suppressed by the conditional stimulus, the greater is the rat's fear. Once fear is defined in this objective manner, it can be studied in a systematic way. We could, for example, study the effects of reducing shock intensity on the level of fear. If there is less conditioned suppression, then weaker shocks induce less fear. Or we could put alcohol in the rat's water, and see whether fearful rats drink more. All sorts of questions about the nature and treatment of fear can be answered with the conditioned suppression procedure.

Conditioned suppression takes on even greater importance once you realize that the phenomenon seems to occur in people as well as in rats. Little Albert, for example, not only cried at the sight of the rat, he also stopped playing with blocks or whatever he happened to be up to at the moment. Charles Ferster and S. A. Culbertson (1982) extrapolate beyond these data to everyday experiences: "The same process," they write, "appears to operate when a person suddenly loses a job or when a close relative dies. One is likely to stop playing sports that one otherwise enjoys, eat less than one customarily does, and be disinclined to talk to people, except about the loss one has just experienced or about one's discomfort" (p. 115).

Sometimes you can learn a lot from a rat.

among other problems. Although virtual reality is definitely "high tech," its use in treating phobias is fundamentally the same therapy Mary Cover Jones used years ago to help Peter overcome a fear of rabbits.[6]

REVIEW   For most people, the word *conditioning* brings to mind a dog salivating at the sound of a bell, but the same procedures that Pavlov made famous have enhanced our understanding of a number of areas of human behavior. Watson demonstrated that human emotions are largely due to conditioning. Conditioned emotional responses include Albert's fear of white rats and the fears many people have of heights, snakes, and other parts of their environment. Conditioning can be used to alleviate many unreasonable fears.

Prejudice

To be prejudiced is, in its most general sense, to prejudge, to judge before one has the relevant facts. The word is most often used, however, to refer to negative views about a person or group; in everyday parlance, to be prejudiced is to hate.

Hate is another of those conditioned emotional responses Watson identified. We seem to learn to hate people and things in much the same way that we learn to fear them. This notion is supported by some brilliant experiments by Arthur and Carolyn Staats. Their basic strategy was to pair a neutral word with one that was presumably a CS for a positive or negative emotional response. In one study (Staats & Staats, 1958), college students watched as ethnic words, such as *German*, *Italian*, and *French*, flashed on a screen. At the same time, the students repeated words spoken by the experimenter. The experimenters paired most of the nationalities with unemotional words such as *chair*, *with*, and *twelve*; they paired the words *Swedish* and *Dutch*, however, with more potent words. For some students, they paired *Dutch* with *gift*, *sacred*, *happy*, and other positive words, while they paired *Swedish* with negative words such as *bitter*, *ugly*, and *failure*. For other students, this procedure was reversed: *Swedish* appeared with pleasant words and *Dutch* with unpleasant ones. Afterward, the students rated each nationality on a scale. These ratings showed that the feelings aroused by the words *Swedish* and *Dutch* depended on the emotional value of the words with which they

---

[6]For more information, go to www.virtuallybetter.com. Some of the people doing research on virtual reality therapy may have a vested interest in the success of the technology, so a degree of skepticism may be warranted.

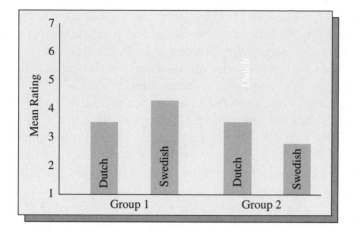

Figure 4-2 *Conditioned prejudice. For subjects in Group 1,* Dutch *was paired with pleasant words, while* Swedish *was paired with unpleasant words. In Group 2, the procedure was reversed. After training, subjects rated the words* Dutch *and* Swedish *from pleasant (1) to unpleasant (7). The ratings reflect the words with which* Dutch *and* Swedish *had been paired. (Compiled from data in Staats and Staats, 1958.)*

had been paired. For example, when the word *Dutch* had appeared with positive words such as *happy* and *sacred*, it got a more positive rating than when it appeared with negative words such as *bitter* and *ugly* (see Figure 4-2).[7]

It seems reasonable to suppose that much of the prejudice directed toward certain ethnic, racial, and religious groups is a result of naturally occurring conditioning resembling the Staats and Staats experiment. Even factually accurate statements, such as, "On September 11, 2001, Muslim extremists highjacked two planes and flew them into the World Trade Center, killing thousands of people," pair emotionally charged words (highjacked, killing) with the words designating a particular group (Muslims) and are likely to affect our feelings toward members of that group. You could argue that the Staatses established certain *words* as conditional stimuli, not the people those words represent. But there is evidence (e.g., Williams, 1966; Williams & Edwards, 1969) that the two are related, that if the word *Arab* is paired with words like *terrorists* and *cowards*, this pairing will affect how we react toward Arabs as well as toward the word *Arab*. Indeed, these words were frequently paired following the violent attacks against the United States by Arab extremists on

---

[7]Please note the similarity of this study with the one described in Chapter 3 in which Staats and Staats paired nonsense syllables, such as YOF, with positive and negative words. You may have thought that study was silly; important research often seems silly—until we see the implications.

September 11, 2001, and it is probably not a coincidence that assaults against Arabs in the United States increased markedly thereafter. Similarly, if the words *Negro, Republican, black, Irish, white,* and *communist* are paired with words that arouse hate, we can expect those words, and the people they represent, to arouse hate as well.[8]

Information is often offered as a cure for prejudice. People hate, it is said, because they are ignorant of the facts; provide them with the facts and their hate will die. But if prejudice is largely the product of conditioning (and the evidence suggests it is), facts alone are unlikely to be an effective antidote for hate. A related tactic is to put the prejudiced person in contact with people in the groups he hates. But this tactic may be weak against a prejudice that is the result of a lifetime of conditioning (Horowitz, 1936).

> **Query:**   Prejudice is an example of a CER, or _____.

Yet we may be able to counter "hate training" with "love training." If the word *Arab* (or *Muslim*) is often paired with negative words, such as *fanatic, cowardly,* and *murderers,* and with other negative stimuli, such as images of Arabs killing innocent people, then hatred for Arabs is likely. If, however, *Arab* is sometimes paired with positive words, such as *charitable, religious,* and *peace-loving,* and with other positive stimuli, such as images of Arabs condemning violence, then the influence of the negative associations will be weakened. Songwriter Oscar Hammerstein reminds us, "You've got to be carefully taught."[9] Conditioning research has shown us that one way to reduce hatred is to teach love.

REVIEW   Prejudice is another kind of conditioned emotional response. Carolyn and Arthur Staats demonstrated that higher-order conditioning could account for the acquisition of likes and dislikes toward ethnic groups, including groups with which we have not had direct contact.

Advertising

Pavlov's laboratory is a long way from Madison Avenue, but advertising agencies are very interested in the emotional reactions people have to objects. They are particularly interested in making objects arouse feelings

---

[8]Children learn to sing, "Sticks and stones will break my bones, but names will never hurt me." But the truth is that calling people names *can* hurt them.
[9]From the movie *South Pacific.*

of fondness, on the reasonable assumption that people are apt to buy things they like.

Advertisements regularly pair products with stimuli that reliably elicit positive emotions. In television commercials, for example, a particular brand of beer will be associated with attractive people having a good time. There will be no mention of alcoholism or fetal damage caused by alcohol consumption, no scenes of fatal car accidents, no photographs of battered women who, after drinking, fell victim to date rape. We see only young, healthy, attractive people drinking beer and having a good time. Or a product may be paired with praise from a celebrity. No doubt some women get goose bumps at the sight of George Clooney. If Clooney waxes eloquent on the value of a particular brand of mouthwash in a TV commercial, some of his fans may get goose bumps when they see that product in the store. Another technique is to pair competing products with items that arouse negative emotions. A competitor's trash bag, for example, may be shown falling apart, leaving garbage all over the kitchen floor.[10]

Do such ads really induce us to like the advertised item? The millions of dollars spent by manufacturers on advertising certainly suggest that they think so, and research suggests that they are right.[11] For instance, Gerald Gorn (1982) conducted an experiment in which college students listened either to a tune from the film *Grease* or to classical Indian music. (Gorn assumed that the students would enjoy the popular American music more than the unfamiliar Eastern variety.) While listening to the music, the students viewed a slide showing either a beige or a blue pen. Later, the students were allowed to have one of the pens. Of those students who had listened to the popular music, 79% chose a pen of the same color they had seen while listening to the music; 70% of those who had listened to the Indian music chose a pen *different* in color from the one they had seen on the slide.[12]

---

[10]The same basic procedures are used to "sell" a political candidate during a campaign. In recent years the emphasis has been on "negative ads," those that pair the candidate's opponent with stimuli that are likely to arouse negative emotions.

[11]The tobacco industry provides a very good illustration of the use of conditioning principles to influence sales. Similarly, names given to some medicines are obviously intended to induce people to feel good about the product. Some pharmaceutical companies now even give names to clinical trials research they sponsor so that they have appealing acronyms, such as MORE (short for, Multiple Outcomes of Raloxifene Evaluation; see Goodman, 2001). Such acronyms are later referred to again and again in scientific meetings and in the literature used to market the product. If MORE or HOPE or CURE is repeatedly paired with a product name, the good feelings that these words engender may influence what doctors recommend and patients use. Not everyone in drug marketing has grasped this concept, however. While browsing Medscape.com, I encountered a drug trial called Trial of Org 10172 in Acute Stroke Treatment, the acronym of which is TOAST.

[12]Note the similarity of this study to those of Staats and Staats earlier in this chapter and in Chapter 3.

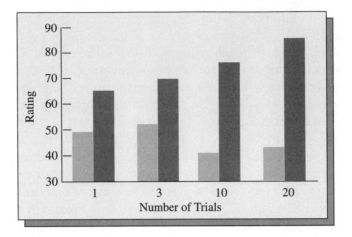

Figure 4-3 *Conditioning and brand appeal. Mean ratings of Brand L toothpaste as a function of number of trials for control group (light bars) and conditioning group (dark bars). Higher ratings indicate more positive feelings. (Compiled from data in Stuart et al., 1987.)*

In another experiment, Elnora Stuart and her colleagues (Stuart et al., 1987) had college students view a number of slides. Some of the slides depicted various fictitious products (e.g., Brand V candy, Brand R cola); others depicted a variety of scenes that were known either to be neutral (e.g., a radar dish, a license plate) or to arouse positive feelings (e.g., a mountain waterfall). For some students (the conditioning group), scenes that aroused good feelings regularly followed Brand L toothpaste; for the other students, the scenes that followed Brand L toothpaste were almost always neutral. The researchers evaluated the students' feelings about Brand L toothpaste with four rating scales at the conclusion of the study. The result was that students in the conditioning group rated Brand L toothpaste more positively than did students in the control group. Moreover, the more times the toothpaste and pleasant scenes appeared together, the more positively the students felt about the product (see Figure 4-3). Students in the conditioning group were also much more likely than controls to indicate a willingness to buy Brand L toothpaste, should it become available.

Similar experiments have not always shown conditioning effects (e.g., Allen & Madden, 1985), but evidence does suggest that ad agencies are correct in believing they can induce people to feel good about, and want, a product by pairing that product with stimuli (pleasant music, attractive people, and the like) that make them feel good (see Grossman & Till, 1998). They are also probably wise to avoid pairing their products

Bite Your Tongue!

Harper's Magazine ("Chickens of the Sea," May 1992), published an excerpt from a training manual used by tour guides at Sea World in Orlando, Florida. The manual warns that "certain words and phrases have negative connotations." It advises guides to avoid these words and offers substitutes:

Suspect Word	*Recommended Word*
sick	ill
hurt	injured
captured	acquired
cage	enclosure
tank	aquarium
kill	eat, prey upon

The negative connotations Sea World is eager to avoid were probably acquired along the lines suggested by Staats and Staats. It seems likely that the word *captured* is more often paired with negative words, such as *kill*, *enslave*, and *torture*: people are captured and killed, captured and enslaved, captured and tortured. The word *acquired*, on the other hand, is often paired with positive words: we acquire wealth, learning, and prestige.

This notion might be tested by asking people to say the first word that comes to mind as each of Sea World's taboo words is read aloud. Chances are the words Sea World wants its guides to avoid will produce more negative responses than the recommended replacements.*

*If you do this experiment, please let me know what you find.

with things that make viewers uncomfortable. Companies routinely pull ads when a TV news program is going to air a graphic segment on a massacre, a topic such as sexual predators, or terrorism. People who see ads for Super Clean Soap while watching a program in which people are tortured do not necessarily think of the torture when they see the soap. But the negative emotional response (disgust or fear, for example) to the torture carries over to things connected with it—including any products or services that may have been advertised just prior to the objectionable scenes.

Query: Advertisers pair their products with items that arouse

_____ .

Of course, the use of conditioning procedures to sell products began long before Pavlov began his studies on salivating dogs. In the 1800s, for example, the manufacturers of a medicine for gonorrhea called their product *Listerine,* thereby pairing it with Joseph Lister, a highly regarded physician of the time (Marschall, 1993). What researchers have contributed is not so much new marketing techniques as a better understanding of the role conditioning plays in consumer behavior.

REVIEW   Advertising can be viewed as the business of creating conditioned emotional responses toward products. One way marketing experts do this is by pairing products they want to sell with items that already arouse positive emotions.

The Paraphilias

Sigmund Freud said that people are "polymorphous perverse," meaning that they can achieve sexual pleasure in a great many ways. Society approves of some of these activities and disapproves of others.[13] Items on the disapproved list are widely considered perverse or unnatural and are called paraphilias.[14] They include voyeurism (viewing a person who is nude or partially clothed or who is engaging in sexual activity), exhibitionism (displaying one's genitals to another person without his or her consent), fetishism (an attraction to certain objects or body parts, such as the feet), transvestism (wearing the clothes of the opposite sex; also called cross-dressing), sadism (inflicting pain on a sexual partner), masochism (being humiliated or hurt by a sexual partner), pedophilia (sexual activity with a prepubescent child), and rape (having intercourse with a person without the person's consent). Various studies, many involving college students, have shown that the paraphilias are more common than many people would like to think. A survey of 60 undergraduate males found, for example, that 2% reported exhibitionistic behavior, 5% had forced someone to have sex, and 42% had participated in voyeuristic activities (Templeman & Stinnett, 1991). Another study found that one in five male college students reported being sexually attracted to children. The paraphilias are uncommon in females (Feierman & Feierman, 2000).

---

[13]What is considered abnormal behavior varies from time to time and from society to society. In the Greece of Plato's day, homosexuality (at least among males) was quite acceptable. By contrast, until a few decades ago the mental health community in the United States considered homosexuality a form of mental illness. Now it is increasingly acceptable.

[14]Paraphilia literally means incorrect love.

Thanks to Freud, many people believe that the tendency to become sexually aroused in unconventional ways is due to mysterious unconscious forces. The masochist's behavior, for example, is said to be driven by a death wish or by a need to suffer degradation and pain as a way of doing penance for Oedipal urges. Although different paraphilias may have different origins, there is no scientific evidence for the Freudian explanations. There is evidence, however, that learning plays a strong role.

Consider masochism, for example. The masochist is sexually aroused by being subjected to painful or degrading experiences. One masochistic man, for example, wrote in his diary, "Debbie spanked me so hard I was burning. My skin was blistered in certain parts. . . . *I need Debbie*" (Pipitone, 1985; emphasis added). How does a person come to experience sexual pleasure when exposed to what are normally aversive events?

Pavlov described an experiment that may offer an answer. In this experiment, Pavlov followed an electric shock with food. Incredibly, the dog soon salivated in response to the shock, just as it might have salivated in response to a bell. In other words, the shock became a CS for salivating. Other dogs learned to salivate in response to other painful stimuli, such as pin pricks. What is even more astonishing is that these stimuli seemed to lose their aversive qualities. Pavlov (1927) wrote that

> not even the tiniest and most subtle objective phenomenon usually
> exhibited by animals under the influence of strong injurious stimuli
> can be observed in these dogs. No appreciable changes in the pulse
> or in the respiration occur in these animals, whereas such changes
> are always most prominent when the noxious stimulus has not
> been converted into [a CS for salivating]. (p. 30)

Pavlov's dogs behaved as if they actually enjoyed what were once painful stimuli! It is possible that masochism has a similar origin. If painful or degrading experiences are repeatedly paired with pleasurable sexual stimulation, the aversive stimuli might themselves become sexually arousing. It is easy to see how analogous experiences might contribute to the development of other unconventional sexual activities.

Query: The repeated pairing of children (or pictures of children) with _____ might result in pedophilia.

Pavlovian conditioning also provides a basis for treatment of paraphilia. One such treatment is called **aversion therapy**. A CS that elicits inappropriate[15] sexual arousal is paired with a US that elicits an unpleasant response (often nausea). When such therapy is effective, the stimuli that once elicited sexual arousal no longer do so and may even elicit feelings of anxiety and discomfort.

A fairly typical example of aversion therapy is provided in a case study reported by N. I. Lavin and colleagues (1961). They used aversion therapy to treat a married man who was sexually aroused by dressing in women's clothing. His interest in cross-dressing began when he was 8 years old; in adolescence, his masturbation always accompanied cross-dressing fantasies. Even after marrying, he continued to seek sexual stimulation by dressing in women's clothing. He sought treatment at age 22 after his wife discovered his idiosyncrasy and urged him to get help. He was also worried that others might discover his secret.

When he asked for help, the therapists began by taking photographs of him in female dress. Next they gave him an emetic drug, and just as it began to make him nauseated, they had him look at the slides of himself in women's clothing. He also heard a tape of himself, recorded earlier, in which he described what the slide showed. The slides and recorded voice were repeatedly paired with nausea. As the training sessions proceeded, cross-dressing had less and less appeal. After 6 days of very intensive treatment, the young man showed no further interest in cross-dressing. A follow-up several years later found no evidence of a recurrence of the problem.

In a variation of this procedure, Barry Maletzky (1980) has the patient imagine that he is about to perform the inappropriate behavior, and then presents him with an extremely unpleasant odor.[16] In one experiment, Maletzky treated 10 exhibitionists in this way. Just as the patient imagined that he was about to expose himself, the therapist held a bottle of a foul-smellng acid under the patient's nose. (The odor was described by patients as a cross between rancid butter and dirty gym socks.) The patient went through these sessions twice a month for an average of about 3 months. The result was a dramatic decline in the incidence of exhibitionism. Not only did the patients report fewer instances of exhibitionistic fantasies and dreams, but claims of improved behavior were corrobo-

---

[15]The question arises, "Who decides what is 'inappropriate'?" Probably in most cases the decision is made by the individual being treated, although this may be under pressure from family, friends, or an employer. Sometimes people are pressured into treatment by the criminal justice system. In any case it is not normally the therapist's decision.

[16]Maletzky (1980) calls the procedure assisted covert sensitization and considers it a variation of Cautela's (1966) covert sensitization. Both procedures, however, may be viewed as variations of aversion therapy.

rated by police reports and field observations. The men also expressed increased self-confidence and esteem. Some of the patients were referred for treatment by legal authorities and may have been in therapy involuntarily; *this made no difference in the results.* A follow-up 12 months after treatment found no occurrences of exhibitionism.

This is not to say that the paraphilias always respond well to treatment. In fact, these problem behaviors tend to be particularly resistant to all forms of treatment, and relapse is common. Pedophilia and rape are especially problematic. Even when treatment is effective, "booster" sessions (periodic re-treatment) are often required to maintain the initial gains. Still, many people can be helped by one form or another of conditioning therapy.

Because aversion therapy involves the use of noxious stimuli, such as emetic drugs and foul-smelling solutions, it is often depicted as an Orwellian abomination. Critics often cite the use of aversion therapy in the film *A Clockwork Orange* as evidence that this is a dangerous and offensive form of treatment. It is important to realize, however, that clients typically volunteer for aversion therapy, often after other treatments have failed. Whether pedophiles and rapists, who seldom volunteer for any form of treatment, should be compelled to undergo aversion therapy is a question for society to debate. Other treatments, based on medical interventions rather than learning, have their own problems.[17]

Some people disapprove of aversion therapy under any conditions on the grounds that if we become accustomed to using it to treat behavior problems, we might gradually embrace it to bring all sorts of unconventional people "into line." Certainly aversion therapy has the potential for abuse; so has morphine, an excellent means of relieving pain. But we do not ordinarily reject effective treatments merely because they *could* be misused.

REVIEW Conditioning can help us understand how various forms of sexual behavior, including those generally considered unhealthy, are established. It also suggests ways of changing some of those behaviors.

---

[17]According to Feierman and Feierman (2000), surgical castration has been effective in treating several paraphilias. It has recidivism rates of only 3% to 5%, far better than aversion therapy. It is very controversial, however, and is rarely used in the United States. The use of drugs to suppress testosterone levels, a procedure called chemical castration, also can be effective in reducing sexual offenses (Cordoba & Chapel, 1983), but ensuring that the offender takes the drug presents problems.

Taste Aversions

Eating is essential to survival; however, it is also dangerous. Some edible substances are quite nutritious; others can kill. It would be very helpful if we had an innate tendency to avoid eating dangerous substances, but for the most part such behavior is learned. But how?

Much of the groundbreaking research on this problem was done by John Garcia and his colleagues. His interest in the topic may have stemmed from a personal experience: When Garcia was 10 years old, he had his first taste of licorice. Several hours later, he came down with the flu. After he recovered, he found he could no longer tolerate licorice (see Nisbett, 1990). Of course, the licorice had nothing to do with making Garcia sick, but he had formed an aversion to licorice all the same.

There was nothing new about this; many people had had similar experiences. The English philosopher John Locke (1690/1975, cited in Garcia, 1981) noted that a person who eats too much honey may later feel ill merely at the mention of the word.[18] What was new about Garcia was that he realized that this common phenomenon deserved study.

In one of his first studies, Garcia and his colleagues (1955) gave rats a choice between ordinary tap water and saccharin-flavored water. The rats preferred the sweet-tasting water. Then Garcia exposed some of the rats to gamma radiation while they drank the sweet-tasting water. (Irradiation is a US for nausea.) These rats later avoided saccharin-flavored water. Moreover, the higher the radiation level the rats were exposed to, the stronger their aversion to sweet water (see Figure 4-4). Presumably, sweet water had become a CS for nausea; in other words, its taste made the animals sick. The rats had acquired a **conditioned taste aversion**.

Query: In the Garcia experiment just described, the CS is

_____ and the US is _____.

Garcia's study differs from Pavlov's work, and from most other research on Pavlovian learning, in two important ways. First, the CS and US were paired only once, whereas most studies of conditioning involve many pairings. Second, the interval between the CS and US was several minutes; in most studies successful conditioning requires an interval of no more than several seconds. The situation was, however, analogous to

---

[18]According to Campos (1984), the Spanish philosopher Juan Luis Vives (identified as Johannes Vives by Campos) wrote about a similar experience with cherries in 1538. Although virtually unknown among psychologists, Vives is considered by some experts to be the father of the field (Padilla, 2000).

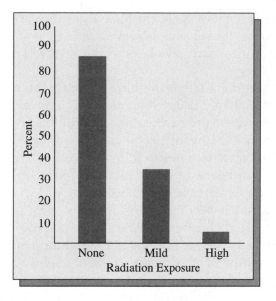

Figure 4-4 *Conditioned taste aversion. Saccharin-flavored water consumed as a percentage of total water consumption. Exposure to radiation while drinking saccharin-flavored water produced an aversion to sweet-tasting water. (Compiled from data in Garcia et al., 1955.)*

Garcia's boyhood experience with licorice: One exposure to licorice followed much later by illness resulted in an aversion to licorice.

Foods that can make an animal ill might also kill it or make it vulnerable to attack or disease, so one-trial learning can mean the difference between life and death. The animal that has a narrow escape and thereafter avoids eating that food is more likely to survive than one that must have 10 or 15 narrow escapes before it learns the lesson. Further, the effects of poisonous foods are often delayed, sometimes for several hours. The animal that acquires an aversion to a toxic food despite such delayed effects has a distinct advantage over an animal that learns only if it becomes ill immediately after eating. Thus, the ability to acquire taste aversions quickly and in spite of long delays between eating and illness would seem to have considerable survival value.

Numerous studies support this view. Lincoln Brower (1971) has studied taste aversion in the blue jay, which feeds on all sorts of insects, including butterflies. In the larval stage, the monarch butterfly sometimes feeds on a kind of milkweed that is harmless to the monarch but renders it poisonous to other animals; it retains its poison in the butterfly stage. Blue jays generally refuse to eat monarch butterflies, but this tendency is not innate. If deprived of food for some time, the blue jay will eat a monarch, and if the insect is not poisonous, the bird will continue eating them. The jay quickly recovers its aversion, however, as soon as it eats a poisonous monarch. Sometimes, such jays later vomit at the sight of a monarch butterfly.

The phenomenon of latent inhibition (see Chapter 3) suggests that we should be more likely to develop aversions to novel foods than to familiar ones. This seems to be the case. Alexandra Logue and her colleagues (1983) found that many people have conditioned taste aversions, most of them traceable to illnesses following eating. But the researchers found that these aversions generally involved foods with which the person had had little experience before becoming ill. An alcoholic whose preferred intoxicant is beer might, for instance, acquire an aversion to whisky, but not beer. Or a person who rarely eats Mexican food might develop an aversion to salsa, but not to the Italian pasta he eats almost daily. Thus, becoming ill after eating a kind of food we have eaten many times before is not likely to result in a taste aversion.

Conditioned taste aversions are sometimes the by-products of certain types of medical treatment. Many forms of cancer are treated with chemotherapy, a therapy that can cause nausea (Burish & Carey, 1986). Chemotherapy patients often develop "anticipatory nausea"—they begin to feel nauseated even before they receive the drug (Morrow & Dobkin, 1988; Redd & Andresen, 1981). Ilene Bernstein (1978) wondered whether such experiences produced conditioned taste aversions. To find out, she studied children undergoing treatment for cancer. She asked the children about their diets and found that those who were undergoing chemotherapy were more likely to report taste aversions than were those not undergoing chemotherapy.

Bernstein thought the chemotherapy might be responsible, so she performed an experiment to find out. She divided the children into three groups, two of which are of particular interest. One group ate a novel-flavored ice cream, a combination of maple and black walnut flavors, before their regular chemotherapy treatment. The second group had ice cream but no chemotherapy. Two to four weeks later, the children were given a choice between eating the maple-walnut ice cream and playing a game. Of those who ate ice cream before chemotherapy, only 21% chose the ice cream; of those who had ice cream but no chemotherapy, 73% chose the dessert.

Such research suggests that chemotherapy may play a role in establishing taste aversions. Because good nutrition is especially important for cancer patients, taste aversions may pose a serious problem for patients undergoing chemotherapy. They may, as the result of Pavlovian conditioning, experience nausea in response to many foods that have been paired with treatments that cause nausea. Thus, the learning that is so

Changing the Coyote's Menu

To some sheep ranchers, the only good coyote is a dead coyote. For many years ranchers have attempted to solve the problem of sheep predation by shooting, trapping, and poisoning coyotes. This approach has major drawbacks. For one thing, it creates a public relations problem. If an outraged public boycotts sheep products, the ranchers lose more than they gain by killing coyotes. Another problem is that killing coyotes increases the population of rabbits and rodents, the coyote's natural prey. Rabbits and rodents compete with lambs for grass, so killing coyotes may ultimately reduce the rancher's productivity. What to do?

Enter Carl Gustavson, a behavior scientist with an interest in wildlife conservation. Gustavson read John Garcia's laboratory research on taste aversion and wondered if the same procedure might be used to give coyotes an aversion to the taste of lamb. Working with Garcia and others, Gustavson (Gustavson et al., 1974) gave hungry coyotes the opportunity to kill and eat a lamb in an enclosed pen, which they readily did.

After this, the researchers gave the coyotes lamb meat, wrapped in lamb hide, that the researchers had laced with lithium chloride, an emetic. The coyotes ate the meat and soon became sick. After one or two of these meals, the coyotes would no longer touch a lamb placed in an enclosed pen. In one case, the coyote sniffed the lamb, vomited, and moved away. When the lamb followed, the coyote growled and snapped at it, but did not attack. The coyotes were tested repeatedly, and although they willingly killed and ate rabbits, they steadfastly refused to attack lambs.

Of course, this procedure does not offer a practical solution to coyote predation: We cannot expect ranchers to capture wild coyotes and feed them tainted lamb meat. But Gustavson and his colleagues conducted field experiments that suggest a more efficient way of making use of taste aversions (Gustavson et al., 1976; Gustavson et al., 1982). The researchers treated sheep carcasses on ranches, hoping that coyotes would find and eat them, become sick, and thereafter avoid killing lambs.

Not all tests of this procedure have been successful, and the Gustavson plan remains controversial. (For more on this, see Forthman & Nicolaus, n.d.; Gustavson & Gustavson, 1985.) But at the very least this work illustrates how basic research can provide new perspectives on real-world problems. Some people may object to Gustavson's research and to the work of Garcia on which it is founded, on the grounds that it is cruel to the animals involved. But it is worth noting that if ranchers are able to use these findings to reduce sheep losses, the beneficiaries will include not only ranchers, but also thousands of coyotes and sheep.

beneficial under ordinary circumstances is a hindrance under these special circumstances. However, an understanding of the role of conditioning in taste aversions may help reduce the problem. It might be wise, for example, for people who are undergoing chemotherapy to eat something with a distinct taste, a food that does not make up an important part of the patient's diet, shortly before each treatment. An aversion to that particular food would develop, but the patient's appetite for other foods might remain intact.

REVIEW   Conditioned taste aversions result from the pairing of distinctive flavors and aversive (especially nausea-inducing) stimuli. Whereas the CS and US must normally appear close together for conditioning to be effective, taste aversions often occur even when the US is delayed for an hour or more. Research in this field has not only helped us understand taste preferences but may also be useful in dealing with certain practical problems, such as improving the diet of cancer patients and reducing sheep predation by coyotes.

Immune Function

The body's efforts to heal injuries, remove toxins, destroy harmful viruses and bacteria, and generally fight to restore good health are collectively referred to as the immune system. Recent research has suggested that the immune system is susceptible to influence (both positive and negative) by Pavlovian procedures.

For the sake of illustration, let us look at an experimental demonstration of the role of conditioning in allergic reactions. An allergic reaction involves the release of histamines by the immune system in response to certain kinds of substances known as allergens. The histamines serve to rid the body of allergens by attacking them at the molecular level and by expelling them from the body by, among other things, sneezing and coughing.

Researchers have long known that allergic reactions are not always due entirely to genetically based reactions to allergens. A hundred years ago, J. MacKinzie (reported in Russell et al., 1984) described the case of a patient who had an allergic reaction when presented with an *artificial* rose.

As a result of such reports, some scientists have wondered whether certain allergic reactions might be partly the result of conditioning. Michael Russell and his colleagues (1984) exposed guinea pigs to the protein BSA so they would be allergic to it. Next, the researchers paired BSA (now a US for an allergic response) with the odor of fish or sulfur. After several pairings, the guinea pigs were tested with the odors alone. The animals reacted with an immediate rise in blood histamine, a sure sign of allergic reaction. The odors had become conditional stimuli that elicited a conditional allergic response. In other words, the animals had become allergic to certain odors through Pavlovian conditioning. Russell suggests that, in the same way, a person who is allergic to a substance may become allergic to things frequently associated with it. Thus, the person who is allergic to tomatoes may break out in hives on eating something that has the taste, smell, or look of tomatoes, even though there are no tomatoes in it. Similarly, a person who is allergic to rose pollen may sneeze at the sight of a rose—even an artificial one.

Conditioned allergic reactions might be assumed to be merely faint imitations of "the real thing," but Russell and his colleagues found that the histamine levels produced in response to conditional stimuli in their experiment were nearly as high as those elicited by BSA. Thus, the person whose sneezing, wheezing, and headache are due to a CS is not necessarily less miserable than the person whose symptoms are caused by exposure to an allergen.

Pavlovian conditioning may one day form part of the armament in the battle against cancer. The same chemotherapy used to combat cancer has also been found to suppress the immune system. This is a very unfortunate side effect because it not only reduces the body's efforts to destroy the cancer but also makes the person vulnerable to other illnesses, particularly infectious diseases.

Pavlovian conditioning suggests that stimuli associated with chemotherapy would, in time, also suppress the immune system, perhaps exacerbating the negative effects of chemotherapy. There is evidence that this is the case. Dana Bovbjerg and her colleagues (1990) found that women receiving chemotherapy for ovarian cancer showed decreased immune functioning when they returned to the hospital for treatment (see Figure 4-5). Apparently, the hospital itself had become a CS for conditioned immunosuppression (i.e., suppression of the immune system). This could mean that, because of conditioning, the treatment that is meant to help patients also hurts them (see also Ader & Cohen, 1975, 1993).

However, such findings also raise the possibility that Pavlovian procedures can be used to *boost* the immune system. If a neutral stimulus can be paired with a drug or procedure that facilitates immune functioning, that stimulus might then become a CS for conditioned immunofacilitation.

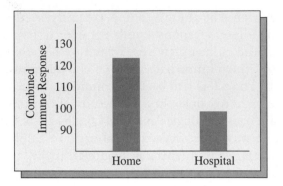

Figure 4-5 *Conditioning and immune response. Combined measures of three immune responses at home and in the hospital where patients had received nausea-inducing chemotherapy. (Compiled from data in Bovbjerg et al., 1990.)*

REVIEW Pavlovian conditioning has provided a new understanding of the immune system. In the past, medical treatment of serious illness tended to ignore the immune system; today, the emphasis is increasingly on facilitating the immune system. Through conditioning, we may one day be able to enhance the immune response to help people fight off diseases such as cancer.

We have seen that Pavlovian conditioning provides insights into phobias, prejudice, advertising, the paraphilias, taste aversion, and immune system functioning.[19] The analysis of these phenomena illustrates how important naturally occurring conditioning is to our daily lives and to the lives of most creatures. "The inborn reflexes by themselves," wrote Pavlov (1927),

> are inadequate to ensure the continued existence of the organism, especially of the more highly organized animals. . . . The complex conditions of everyday existence require a much more detailed and specialized correlation between the animal and its environment than is afforded by the inborn reflexes alone. (p. 16)

---

[19] These applications of Pavlovian conditioning are representative, but there are many others, and more are being explored all the time. It is known, for example, that the rate of conditioning declines with age (see Chapter 3). Diana Woodruff-Pak and colleagues (1996) found that people who learned poorly through conditioning were much more likely than others to develop dementia later. Thus, Pavlovian conditioning may be a useful way of identifying people in the earliest stages of dementia. This may become very important as early stage treatments are developed. Other work suggests that people with autism or obsessive-compulsive disorder condition *more* rapidly, under certain circumstances, than other people (Tracy et al., 1999), so conditioning might be useful in assessing people with these disorders.

Our ability to be modified by the association of stimuli also contributes in important ways to our individuality. Do you, for example, prefer jazz to classical music? Are you more comfortable alone than in large crowds? Does your blood boil when you see Ku Klux Klansmen marching in a parade? Do you feel a shiver up your spine when you hear the national anthem? Does reading *Romeo and Juliet* move you to tears, or put you to sleep? When you hear rap music, do you sway in rhythm with the beat, or do you plug up your ears with cotton? All such reactions, and thousands of others that we think of as embedded in the very fiber of our being, are at least partly attributable to Pavlovian conditioning. Those who dismiss Pavlovian conditioning as a procedure for getting dogs to salivate clearly have a lot to learn.

RECOMMENDED READING

1. Garcia, J. (1981). Tilting at the paper mills of academe. *American Psychologist*, 36(2), 149–158.

   Garcia's findings on conditioning with long CS-US intervals were so at odds with previous research that he had trouble getting other researchers to accept them. Here he discusses his work and shows that even scientists are sometimes slow to embrace new ideas.

2. History of psychology: Pavlov's contribution. (1997; Special section). *American Psychologist*, 52(9), 933–972.

   A special section devoted to Pavlov's work, in celebration of the 100th anniversary of his book, *The Work of the Digestive Glands*. The articles cover not only historical issues but contemporary developments.

3. Ledoux, J. (1996). *The emotional brain*. New York: Touchstone.

   A discussion of the neural mechanisms involved in emotional conditioning.

4. Pavlov, I. P. (1941). *Conditioned reflexes and psychiatry* (W. H. Gantt, Trans.). New York: International Publishers.

   This is volume 2 of *Lectures on Conditioned Reflexes*. In it, Pavlov attempts to apply conditioning principles to the interpretation of neuroses.

5. Wolpe, J. (1973). *The practice of behavior therapy* (2nd ed.). New York: Pergamon Press.

   Provides an excellent look at the therapeutic use of conditioning procedures by one of the world's leading experts.

REVIEW QUESTIONS

1. Define the following terms and provide an example of each:

aversion therapy	conditioned suppression
conditioned emotional response	conditioned taste aversion
	counterconditioning

2. Suppose your doctor advises you to eat liver, which you despise. How might you overcome your aversion to liver?

3. You are the dietitian in charge of cancer patients at a hospital. How might you apply your knowledge of taste aversions to improve the health of your patients?

4. Pavlovian learning usually requires CS-US intervals of no more than a few seconds. Taste aversion conditioning is an exception. Why does this exception exist?

5. A man of about 80 named Albert walks into a psychologist's office asking for help in overcoming an irrational fear of white, furry creatures. What can the psychologist do to help him?

6. How can you increase the likelihood that your child will share your devotion to jazz music?

7. You are in charge of rehabilitating criminals convicted of various hate crimes. Can Pavlovian learning help?

8. What do salivating dogs have to do with masochism?

9. It has been said that people who have amorous encounters under clandestine conditions are sometimes later unable to enjoy amorous experiences under more ordinary conditions. Explain why.

10. What does the work of Staats and Staats lead you to predict about the backgrounds of Ku Klux Klan members?

11. In what sense are psychosomatic illnesses caused by events outside the patient's body?

12. Invent a better term for the disorders known as psychosomatic illnesses.

13. Why is it a mistake to speak of simple Pavlovian conditioning?

14. What sort of procedure (trace, backward, etc.) did Garcia use in his experiments on taste aversion?

15. Why are people more likely to develop aversions to foods they have not often eaten?

16. How is Pavlovian conditioning used to sell beer?

17. What is the essential difference between the way Peter and Albert acquired their fears?

18. What is a euphemism? Why are euphemisms used?

19. Many people hate groups of people with whom they have had no direct experience. How can Pavlovian conditioning account for these emotions?

20. How has reading this chapter altered your view of Pavlovian conditioning?

PRACTICE QUIZ

1. The phenomenon of latent _____ suggests that we are more likely to develop aversions to novel foods than to familiar ones.

2. People used to believe that children were instinctively afraid of fire, animals, and many other things. John Watson and Rosalie _____ found that many such fears were acquired through conditioning.

3. The first person to use counterconditioning to treat a phobia was probably _____.

4. The work of Staats and Staats suggests that prejudice may be partly the result of _____-order conditioning.

5. Dana Bovbjerg and her colleagues found that women receiving chemotherapy in a hospital later showed decreased functioning of their _____ system when they returned to the hospital.

6. Gorn influenced product choice by pairing pens of a certain color with certain kinds of _____.

7. In _____ therapy, a stimulus that elicits an inappropriate response is paired with an aversive stimulus such as shock or an emetic drug.

8. The pairing of a particular food with nausea-inducing stimuli often results in a conditioned _____.

9. Carl Gustavson did research aimed at reducing predation of _____ by coyotes.

10. Masochism may be the result of pairing stimuli that cause
    _____ with those that cause _____.

QUERY ANSWERS

Page 107. Albert became fearful of the rat because the arrival of the rat regularly preceded *a loud noise.*

Page 114. Prejudice is an example of a CER, or *conditioned emotional response.*

Page 117. Advertisers pair their products with items that arouse *positive emotions/positive emotional responses.*

Page 119. The repeated pairing of children (or pictures of children) with *sexual stimulation* might result in pedophilia.

Page 122. In the Garcia experiment just described, the CS is *saccharin* and the US is *radiation.*

CHAPTER

5

Operant Reinforcement

Nothing succeeds like success.

French Proverb

About the same time Pavlov was trying to solve the riddle of the psychic reflex, a young American graduate student named Edward Lee Thorndike was tackling another problem: animal intelligence.

In the late 19th century, most people believed that higher animals learned through reasoning. Anyone who owned a dog or cat could "see" the animal think through a problem and come to a logical conclusion, and stories of the incredible talents of animals abounded. Taken together, these stories painted a picture of animal abilities that made some pets little less than furry Albert Einsteins. Thorndike recognized the impossibility of estimating animal abilities from this sort of anecdotal evidence: "Such testimony is by no means on a par with testimony about the size of a fish or the migration of birds," he wrote, "for here one has to deal not merely with ignorant or inaccurate testimony, but also with prejudiced testimony. Human folk are as a matter of fact eager to find intelligence in animals" (1898, p. 4).[1]

This bias led people to report remarkable feats, but not more ordinary, unintelligent acts. "Dogs get lost hundreds of times and no one ever notices it or sends an account of it to a scientific magazine," wrote Thorndike, "but let one find his way from Brooklyn to Yonkers and the fact immediately becomes a circulating anecdote. Thousands of cats on thousands of occasions sit helplessly yowling, and no one takes thought of it or writes to his friend, the professor; but let one cat claw at the knob of a door supposedly as a signal to be let out, and straightway this cat becomes the representative of the cat-mind in all the books. . . . In short, the anecdotes give really the . . . *supernormal* psychology of animals" (pp. 4–5).

But how could one go about studying the *normal*, or ordinary, psychology of animals? How could one study animal intelligence scientifically? Thorndike's answer was to present an animal with a problem. Then he would give the animal the problem again and see whether its performance improved, test it again, and so on. He would, in other words, study animal intelligence by studying animal learning.

---

[1] Unless otherwise noted, all references to Thorndike are to his 1898 dissertation.

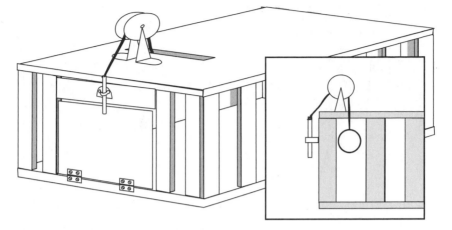

Figure 5-1 *Box A, one of Thorndike's puzzle boxes. Pulling on the loop (see side view, inset), released a bolt and the door fell open. (Drawn from description in Thorndike, 1898, by Diane Chance.)*

In one series of experiments, Thorndike put a chick into a maze. If the chick took the correct route, it found its way to a pen containing food and other chicks. When Thorndike first put a chick into a maze, it tried to jump out of the enclosure and then wandered down one blind alley after another, peeping loudly all the while, until it finally found its way out. With succeeding trials, the chick became more and more efficient; finally, when placed in the maze it would go directly down the appropriate path.

Thorndike's most famous experiments were done with cats. He would place a hungry cat in a "puzzle box" and put food in plain view but out of reach (see Figure 5-1; Chance, 1999).[2] The box had a door that could be opened by some simple act, such as pulling a wire loop or stepping on a treadle. Like the chicks, the cat began by performing a number of ineffective acts. Thorndike wrote that the cat typically

> tries to squeeze through any opening; it claws and bites at the bars or wire; it thrusts its paws out through any opening and claws at everything it reaches; it continues its efforts when it strikes anything loose and shakey; it may claw at things within the box. (p. 13)

---

[2]Thorndike noticed that the cats showed little interest in the food, and seemed mostly interested in getting out of the box. In experiments with dogs, Thorndike found the animals seemed more interested in the food than in getting out of the box. Dog and cat owners will probably find these observations unsurprising.

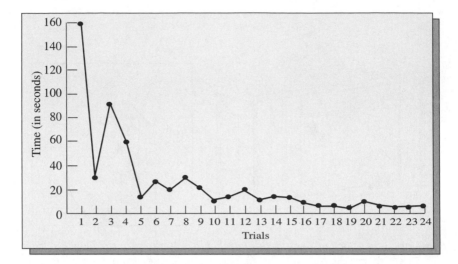

Figure 5-2 *Puzzle Box learning curve. The time cat 12 took to escape from box A (see Figure 5-1) on succeeding trials. (Compiled from data in Thorndike, 1898.)*

Eventually, the cat would pull on the loop or step on the treadle, the door would fall open, and the cat would make its way to freedom and food. When Thorndike returned the cat to the box for another trial, it went through the same sort of activity until it again did what was required to open the door. With each succeeding trial, the animal made fewer ineffective movements until, after many trials, it would immediately pull on the loop or step on the treadle and escape. Thorndike recorded the time it took the animal to escape on each trial and plotted these data on a graph, producing what are probably the first learning curves (see Figure 5-2).[3]

Query: Thorndike studied animal learning as a way of measuring animal _____.

Thorndike concluded that a given behavior typically has one of two kinds of consequences or effects. Thorndike called one kind of consequence a "satisfying state of affairs," the other an "annoying state of affairs." If, for instance, a chick goes down a wrong alley, this behavior is followed by continued hunger and separation from other chicks—an an-

---

[3]Ebbinghaus (1885) created graphs that showed forgetting, but I believe Thorndike's are the first to show learning. It is interesting to note that people today often say, "There's a steep learning curve," to convey the idea that a learning task is difficult. Actually, a steep learning curve shows rapid learning, and therefore indicates an *easy* learning task. To express a difficult task, we should say, "There's a shallow learning curve."

noying state of affairs. If the chick goes down the correct alley, this behavior leads to food and contact with other chicks—a satisfying state of affairs. When a cat tries to squeeze through the bars of its cage, it remains confined and hungry—an annoying consequence; when it pulls at a wire loop, the door opens and it escapes and finds food—a satisfying consequence.

Thorndike (1911) later called this relationship between behavior and its consequences the **law of effect**.[4] The law says that the strength (frequency, durability, etc.) of a behavior depends on the consequences the behavior has had in the past.[5] Another way of saying essentially the same thing is this: Behavior is a function of its consequences.[6]

John Nevin (Mace et al., 1992; Nevin, 1992) has suggested that reinforcement gives behavior something akin to momentum. Just as a heavy ball rolling down a hill is less likely than a light ball to be stopped by an obstruction in its path, behavior that has been reinforced many times is more likely to persist when "obstructed" in some way, as (for example) when one confronts a series of failures.[7]

Thorndike was not, of course, the first person to notice that consequences influence behavior. Philosophers had long debated the role of hedonism, the tendency to seek out pleasure and avoid pain, in behavior. But Thorndike was the first person to show that behavior is systematically strengthened or weakened by its consequences. Prior to Thorndike, learning was thought to be primarily a matter of reasoning; Thorndike shifted our attention from inside the organism to the external environment.

---

[4]Although Thorndike's 1898 dissertation is often cited as the source of the law of effect, in fact the law is never mentioned. Apparently the first appearance of the law in print was in Thorndike's *Animal Intelligence*, a book published in 1911. There he expressed the law of effect this way: "Of several responses made to the same situation, those which are accompanied or closely followed by satisfaction to the animal will, other things being equal, be more firmly connected with the situation, so that, when it recurs, they will be more likely to recur; those which are accompanied or closely followed by discomfort to the animal will, other things being equal, have their connections with that situation weakened, so that, when it recurs, they will be less likely to occur" (p. 244).

[5]A general assumption of behavioral research is that any feature of a behavior may be strengthened by reinforcement, so long as reinforcement can be made contingent on that feature. Amazingly, even the randomicity of behavior can be modified with reinforcement. S. Page and A. Neuringer (1985) provided reinforcers to pigeons for a series of 8 keypecks, but only when the series of keypecks was different from the previous 50 sequences. Under these circumstances, the keypeck patterns became almost truly random.

[6]Our concern is with the way experience changes behavior, not with the changes it produces in the nervous system. However, Thorndike (1911) speculated that reinforcement strengthened bonds or connections between neurons, a view that became known as connectionism. The basic idea is similar to current views in cognitive science called—connectionism (Donahoe, 1999). Nevin (1999) has recently offered evidence supporting Thorndike's theory.

[7]Sportscasters often speak of momentum in athletic competition. Nevin and colleagues (Mace et al., 1992) applied the concept of behavioral momentum to basketball.

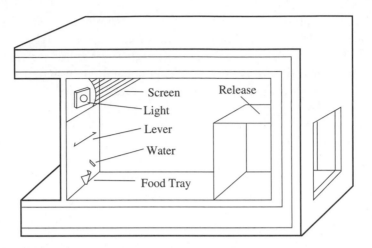

Figure 5-3   *One of Skinner's original experimental boxes, now generally referred to as a Skinner box. One wall has been cut away to show the inside of the box. The food magazine and other apparatus were contained in the space outside the left panel. Each time a rat pressed the lever, it activated the food magazine, which dropped a few pellets of food into the tray.* (From The Behavior of Organisms: An Experimental Analysis *[p. 49], by B. F. Skinner, 1938, New York: Appleton-Century-Crofts. Copyright © 1938, renewed 1966. Reprinted by permission of B. F. Skinner.)*

Building on the foundation laid by Thorndike, B. F. Skinner (1938) began a series of studies in the 1930s that would greatly advance our understanding of learning and behavior. Skinner designed an experimental chamber, now often called a Skinner box, designed so that a food magazine could automatically drop a few pellets of food into a tray (see Figure 5-3).[8] After a rat became accustomed to the noise of the action of the food magazine and readily ate from the tray, Skinner installed a lever; when the rat pressed the lever, food fell into the tray. Under these conditions, the rate of lever pressing increased dramatically (see Figure 5-4).

These procedures, whereby behavior is strengthened or weakened by its consequences, became known as **operant learning** because the behavior can be said to *operate* on the environment. The behavior is typically

---

[8]Clark Hull, a psychologist at Yale University, dubbed the chamber the "Skinner box," and the name quickly caught on and is still heard today. Skinner preferred the term *operant chamber,* but *experimental chamber* may be more accurate since it is used for research on a variety of problems, including Pavlovian conditioning, forgetting, cognition, pharmacology, and medicine. Most of this research is done with pigeons and small rodents, especially rats, but some variations of the chamber are used in studies of primates.

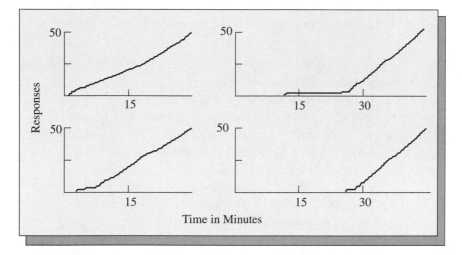

Figure 5-4 *Lever pressing and reinforcement in four rats. The cumulative records above show that when each lever press was followed by food, the rate of pressing increased rapidly. (For help in interpreting these records, see Figure 2-7.) (Adapted from* The Behavior of Organisms: An Experimental Analysis *[p. 68], by B. F. Skinner, 1938, New York: Appleton-Century-Crofts. Copyright © 1938, renewed 1966. Reprinted by permission.)*

instrumental in producing these consequences, so this type of learning is also sometimes called **instrumental learning**.[9]

Operant learning is often referred to as operant conditioning. Unfortunately, the word *conditioning* gives many people the impression that the procedure is analogous to Pavlovian conditioning, in which a stimulus elicits a reflex response. But operant learning is *not* S-R learning; the principal behavior involved is not reflexive and is often complex. In operant learning the organism acts on the environment and changes it, and the change thus produced strengthens or weakens the behavior. Whereas the organism undergoing Pavlovian conditioning may be described as passive, in operant learning the organism is *necessarily* active.

REVIEW The scientific study of operant learning began with the puzzle box experiments of E. L. Thorndike and his formulation of the law of effect. B. F. Skinner built on this foundation with his studies of behavior rate change in rats and pigeons using an experimental chamber.

---

[9]Some researchers (e.g., Gormezano, 2000) make a distinction between operant and instrumental procedures, but in general the terms are used interchangeably.

E. L. Thorndike: What the Occasion Demanded

E. L. Thorndike started life on the 31st of August, 1874, the son of an itinerant Methodist minister. His parents, who were bright and idealistic, ran a tight ship—so tight, in fact, that someone once said of the family, "There is no music in the Thorndikes." Thorndike's biographer, Geraldine Joncich (1968), wrote that there was "a smothering of lightheartedness and carefree gaiety . . . with Victorian culture and fundamentalist religion" (p. 39). This home life produced a boy who was well mannered, industrious, and studious, but also shy, serious, and moderate to excess. Thorndike himself hinted that he lacked spontaneity and humor when he said, "I think I was always grown-up" (in Joncich, 1968, p. 31).

In 1893, the young grown-up went off to Wesleyan University, where he developed an interest in literature. As a graduate student at Harvard, he shifted from English to psychology and took up the problem of animal intelligence. As there was no laboratory space for his subjects, he kept the animals in his room and conducted the experiments there "until the landlady's protests were imperative" (Thorndike, 1936, p. 264). Finally, William James (one of the founders of modern psychology) offered him the use of his cellar, and this became Thorndike's new laboratory. The work in James's basement went well, but Thorndike had little money, and when the offer of a fellowship at Columbia University came along, Thorndike packed up his "two most educated chickens" and moved to New York. It was at Columbia that Thorndike wrote the dissertation on animal intelligence that started him off on a brilliant career.

Toward the end of that career, Thorndike must have thought about these and other events in his life as he prepared a short autobiographical article. In it, he argued that his accomplishments were not the result of any deliberate plan or "inner needs." Instead, he seemed to compare his own behavior with the trial-and-success activity of his experimental animals. "I did," he explained, "what the occasion seemed to demand" (1936, p. 266).

Thorndike's bibliography lists over 500 items, including 78 books. In addition to his work in learning, he made important contributions to educational psychology (a field he practically invented) and to psychological testing. We are lucky indeed that Thorndike had such a demanding environment.

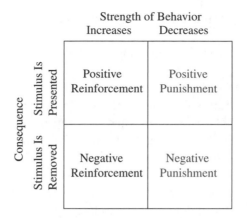

Figure 5-5   *Contingency square. In operant procedures, the strength of a behavior increases or decreases depending on its consequences.*

Basic Procedures

There are four operant procedures (see Figure 5-5). Two strengthen behavior, and two weaken it. In this chapter, we will focus on experiences that strengthen behavior.[10] They are called reinforcement.

Reinforcement is the procedure of providing consequences for a behavior that increase or maintain the strength of that behavior.[11] Charles Catania (1998) pointed out that a procedure must have three characteristics to qualify as reinforcement: First, a behavior must have a consequence. Second, the behavior must increase in strength (e.g., occur more often). Third, the increase in strength must be the result of the consequence.[12]

---

[10]As with Pavlovian conditioning, the procedures identified in the laboratory and used in applied settings are similar to experiences that occur naturally.

[11]Reinforcement is often defined as the procedure of providing consequences for behavior that increase or maintain its rate. The emphasis on frequency or rate is understandable, because one of the things we most want to know about behavior is how likely it is to occur. However, reinforcement has other strengthening effects besides rate increases: It increases the tendency of the behavior to persist after reinforcement is discontinued, the tendency of the behavior to occur despite aversive consequences (e.g., punishment), and the tendency to persist despite the availability of reinforcers for other behaviors. Strength, by the way, is a descriptive, not an explanatory, term. To say that a reinforcer increases the strength of behavior means only that it has certain measureable effects on behavior, such as an increase in frequency or resistance to extinction (Killeen & Hall, 2001). Various attempts have been made to replace the terms *reinforcer* and *reinforcement;* Brown and Hendy (2001), for example, propose *selector* and *selection.*

[12]Notice that the concept of reinforcement does not assume awareness of the relationship between behavior and its consequences. Operant learning sometimes occurs without any sign of awareness of the relation between the behavior modified and its consequences. For example, in one experiment, researchers were able to reinforce the contraction of an individual muscle fiber, yet the human participants were unable to say what they did to produce reinforcement (Laurenti-Lions et al., 1985). As in Pavlovian conditioning (see Chapter 3), however, there are people on both sides of the issue of awareness in operant learning (see Gewirtz, 1997).

Query: To reinforce a behavior is to provide _____

for the behavior that increase its _____.

There are two kinds of reinforcement. In **positive reinforcement**, a behavior is followed by the appearance of, or an increase in the intensity of, a stimulus. This stimulus, called a **positive reinforcer**, is ordinarily something the organism seeks out.

The effect of a positive reinforcer is to strengthen the behavior that precedes it. For instance, if a dog happens to bark and someone then gives it a bit of food, the dog is likely to bark again. In positive reinforcement, the occurrence of a behavior (B) is followed by the appearance of a reinforcing stimulus (S^R):

$$B \longrightarrow S^R$$
$$\text{bark} \longrightarrow \text{receive food}$$

The procedure is not, of course, limited to animals. If you put money into a vending machine, and the machine then gives you candy, you are likely to put money into that machine in the future. The act of putting money into vending machines has been reinforced. Similarly, the saxophone playing of the novice may be reinforced by the notes he produces, even if, to other ears, the result is marvelously unmelodic.

Because the reinforcers used in positive reinforcement are usually things most people consider rewarding (success, praise, recognition, approval, money, special privileges, etc.), positive reinforcement is also sometimes called **reward training**. It is important to remember, however, that something you or I might consider a reward is *not* necessarily a reinforcer.[13] In addition, things that would appear to be aversives have sometimes been positive reinforcers. For example, reprimands, restraint, captivity, and electrical shocks have been found, on occasion, to reinforce behavior.

In **negative reinforcement**, a behavior is strengthened by the removal of, or a decrease in the intensity of, a stimulus. This stimulus, called a **negative reinforcer**, is ordinarily something the organism tries to escape or avoid. For instance, if a dog is caught outdoors in a hailstorm, it may escape being pelted with hailstones by stepping under some sort of canopy. If it does so, it is likely to seek out a canopy the next time hail

---

[13]Skinner (1987) thought it was important to distinguish between rewards and reinforcers: "The strengthening effect is missed when reinforcers are called rewards. *People* are rewarded, but *behavior* is reinforced" (p. 19).

begins to fall. Its behavior will have been reinforced. In negative reinforcement, as in positive reinforcement, a behavior is followed by a reinforcing event:

$$B \longrightarrow S^R$$
step under canopy $\longrightarrow$ escape hailstone pelting

People who are caught in hailstorms also seek shelter under canopies because they, too, have in that way escaped being hit on the head. Similarly, if your neighbor's amateurish saxophone playing is as irritating as fingernails scraped across a blackboard, you may pound on the wall separating your apartments. If the screeching noise then stops, you are apt to pound on the wall the next time a neighbor makes unpleasant noises. Pounding on the wall has been reinforced. Because what reinforces behavior in negative reinforcement is escaping from an aversive stimulus, this procedure is also called **escape training.**

Query: Positive and negative reinforcement have this in

common: Both _____ behavior.

Both positive and negative reinforcement maintain or increase the strength of behavior. The difference is that in positive reinforcement, the reinforcing consequence is the *appearance* of a stimulus, whereas in negative reinforcement the reinforcing consequence is the *removal* of a stimulus. The terms *positive* and *negative* do not describe the nature of the consequence; they merely indicate that something has been *added* (positive reinforcement) or *subtracted* (negative reinforcement).[14]

REVIEW   The term *operant learning* indicates that the organism operates on its environment. Operant procedures that increase the rate of behavior are called reinforcement. There are two types of reinforcement, positive and negative; the chief difference between them has to do with whether a stimulus is presented or removed following a behavior.

---

[14]Negative reinforcement is a particularly troublesome term, because the word *negative* suggests something bad is involved. Even some psychologists are confused by the term. One psychologist wrote that negative reinforcement means that something *good* is taken away. When you encounter such misuse of the term, try to remember that reinforcement strengthens behavior. (Does it seem likely that taking something "good" away would strengthen a behavior?) Because of the confusion it causes, some researchers have suggested doing away with the distinction between positive and negative reinforcement (e.g., Michael, 1975). Nevertheless, the distinction and the terms persist.

B. F. Skinner: The Darwin of Behavior Science

Burrhus Frederic Skinner was born in Susquehanna, Pennsylvania, in 1904. His mother kept house while his father earned a living as a lawyer.

After high school, he went off to Hamilton College in New York where he received a classical education. He continued to enjoy literature, history, music, and the arts throughout his life. After Hamilton, he lived in New York's Greenwich Village for a time and tried to become a novelist. The attempt failed, and after reading the work of Pavlov and Watson, he went to graduate school at Harvard to become a behaviorist.

After Harvard, Skinner began the research that would eventually be published, in 1938, as *The Behavior of Organisms*. His views of behavior offended many, and Skinner was thereafter attacked and misrepresented. It was the misrepresentation that bothered him more. People erroneously and repeatedly said that he denied the existence of thoughts and feelings; that he denied a role for biology in behavior; that he believed people were robotic machines; that he rejected freedom and dignity. What Skinner actually said can scarcely be recognized from the writings of his critics (Morris, 2001; Todd & Morris, 1992).

Even Skinner's critics acknowledge, however, that he made many important contributions to our understanding of behavior. He made changes in the rate of behavior a standard measure of learning; made the individual, rather than the group, the object of experimental study; practically invented the ABA research design; replaced Thorndike's subjective terminology with the more precise language we use today; and suggested ways that a natural science of behavior could be applied to medicine, work, child rearing, education, and

Discrete Trial and Free Operant Procedures

Thorndike and Skinner went about studying operant procedures in different ways. Thorndike used what has since become known as the **discrete trial procedure**. The defining feature of a discrete trial procedure is that the behavior of the participant ends the trial. For example, each time one of Thorndike's cats escaped from a box, that marked the end of the trial. Thorndike had to return the cat to the box to observe the behavior again. In another example of a discrete trial experiment, a researcher puts a rat into the starting box of a maze. When the rat reaches the end of the maze, that ends the trial, and the experimenter returns the rat to the starting point.

other fields. Along the way he won practically every award ever given to a psychologist, including the American Humanist of the Year Award.

In January 1990, Skinner was diagnosed as having leukemia. It was, he said, not a bad way to go. There would not be much suffering, just an increasing vulnerability to infectious diseases, one of which would, sooner or later, carry him off.

On August 10, 1990, at its annual convention, the American Psychological Association awarded Skinner a special citation for a lifetime of outstanding contributions, the first such award ever granted by the association. Skinner was quite frail, but he approached the podium unassisted, and spoke for 15 minutes without notes. His thesis was a familiar one: Psychologists should embrace the natural science approach to behavior.

It was Skinner's last public appearance. He left the auditorium to return to his home where, in his private study, he continued rising early in the morning to write, answer his mail, and greet visitors. Five days later he was admitted to the hospital. On August 19, while in the hospital, he worked on the final draft of an article. The next day he slipped into a coma and died.

It is now more than a hundred years since the death of Charles Darwin, and creationism is still taught in our schools. Yet the basic principles of evolution are understood and taken for granted by most educated people. A hundred years from now traditional ideas about behavior may still prevail, but perhaps the basic principles of behavior will be understood and taken for granted by educated people. If so, much of the credit will have to be given to the Darwin of behavior science, B. F. Skinner.

In discrete trial training, the dependent variable is often the time taken to perform some behavior under study, such as pulling on a loop or reaching a goal box. Other dependent measures sometimes used are the number of errors made (e.g., number of wrong alleys entered on running a maze) and the number of times the participant performed a behavior within a given time limit.

Skinner used a **free operant procedure**. In this approach, the behavior may be repeated any number of times. For instance, in some experiments Skinner placed a rat in an operant chamber equipped with a lever. Pressing the lever might cause a bit of food to fall into a tray, but the rat was free to return to the lever and press it again and again.

Usually the dependent variable in free operant experiments is the number of times a particular behavior, such as pressing a lever or pecking a disk, occurs per minute.

Both discrete trial and free operant procedures are also used in clinical settings (Delprato, 2001). A child who speaks with a lisp, for example, may be asked to imitate a teacher when the teacher says "scissors." The teacher says, "Say *sizz-orrs*," and the client responds, "Thizz-orrth." After this the teacher may provide some consequence, such as, "That's better," or, "No. Try again. *Sizz-orrs*." Each time the client attempts to perform the task, he or she completes one trial.

To treat lisping using a free operant procedure, the therapist might engage the child in conversation while playing a game. The teacher would not ask the child to say words that were difficult to pronounce, such as *scissors*, but whenever the child happened to say such a word correctly the teacher might say, "Oh. You said *scissors* very well."

Query: In the _____ procedure, the behavior

ends the trial.

Clinical research still often involves discrete trial procedures, although free operant procedures are gaining ground. The free operant procedure has certain advantages in applied settings. In particular, most people perceive it as more natural and less intrusive than the discrete trial procedure (Schreibman et al., 1991).

Both discrete trial and free operant procedures are apt to strike students as unnatural and superficial. "What" they often ask, "has a cat in a puzzle box or a rat pressing a lever got to do with why I behave as I do?" Most people have difficulty seeing the relevance of laboratory experiments to their everyday lives, regardless of which experimental procedure is used. But scientific analysis of any phenomenon requires simplification. When Galileo studied gravity, he did it by rolling iron balls down an inclined plane. Only by simplifying the problem in this way could he hope to analyze the effects of variables such as the distance traveled and the height of the starting point. In attempting to identify the cause of a particular cancer, the medical researcher brings the cancer into the laboratory in the form of an animal with the disease or in the form of a preparation of human cancer cells. Only in this way can the researcher manipulate variables and reliably determine their effects.

Laboratory researchers simplify problems so they can identify functional relationships between independent and dependent variables. If the relations so identified are valid, they will enable the researcher to predict and control the phenomenon in future experiments. They will also lead to hypotheses about how real-world problems may be solved. Field experiments that successfully test these hypotheses offer additional corroboration about the laboratory researcher's analysis.

REVIEW Operant researchers distinguish between discrete trial and free operant procedures. In the discrete trial procedure, the performance of the behavior studied ends the trial. In the free operant procedure, the organism is free to perform the behavior any number of times.

Operant and Pavlovian Learning Compared

Operant and Pavlovian procedures are sometimes confused, so it may be useful to point out the differences between them.

The most important difference is that in Pavlovian conditioning one stimulus (the US) is contingent on another stimulus (the CS), whereas in operant learning, a stimulus (the reinforcing or punishing consequence) is contingent on a behavior. Thorndike likened operant learning to the process of natural selection: Useful behaviors "survive," and others "die out."[15]

Pavlovian and operant procedures also usually involve different kinds of behavior. Pavlovian conditioning typically involves "involuntary" (reflexive) behavior, such as the blink of an eye or the secretion of digestive juices; operant learning usually involves "voluntary" behavior, such as the wink of an eye or the purchase of food. The distinction between voluntary and involuntary behavior is somewhat problematic, however. It is sometimes difficult, for example, to distinguish between an involuntary eye blink and a voluntary eye wink. Also, behavior that is normally involuntary, such as vomiting, can sometimes be modified by operant procedures (Wolf et al., 1965).

Theoretically it may be possible to distinguish between the two kinds of behavior on the basis of the biological structures involved. Reflexive behavior involves the autonomic nervous system and smooth

---

[15]Thorndike wrote that a cat in a puzzle box does many different things to escape, and "from among these movements one is selected by success" (p. 14). Skinner (e.g., 1981, 1984) later made much of the idea that reinforcement selects behavior. In fact, he suggested a parallel between the evolution of species through natural selection and the "evolution" of individual behavior through reinforcement. However, the basic idea seems to have originated with Thorndike. Please note that in Thorndike's view it is success that selects behavior, not failure. Thorndike is often said to have studied learning by "trial and error," but he preferred the phrase "trial and success."

muscles and glands; "voluntary" behavior involves the voluntary nervous system and skeletal muscles. In practice, however, this distinction is of limited value.

The situation is further complicated by the fact that the two procedures often occur together (Allan, 1998; Davis & Hurwitz, 1977). Consider the case of Little Albert, discussed in Chapter 4. Albert learned to fear a white rat when the rat was paired with a loud noise. This would appear to be a simple case of Pavlovian conditioning, and so it is. But read Rayner and Watson's laboratory notes about the experiment: "White rat which he had played with for weeks was suddenly taken from the basket (the usual routine) and presented to Albert. He began to reach for rat with left hand. Just as his hand touched the animal the bar was struck immediately behind his head" (quoted in Watson, 1930/1970, p. 160). Note that the loud noise occurred just as Albert *reached for the rat.* Thus, the loud noise followed a behavior. Pavlovian conditioning was involved, because the rat and the noise were paired regardless of what Albert did; but operant learning was also involved, since the loud noise followed reaching for the rat.

> **Query:**   The fact that Albert reached for the rat just before the
>
> loud noise occurred means that _____ learning
>
> was involved.

Similarly, consider the dog trainer who reinforces the appropriate response to various commands, such as *sit, stay, come,* and *fetch.* Each appropriate act is followed by a bit of food. Described in this way, this seems to be a simple case of operant learning. But notice that the commands are sometimes followed by food, and this pairing of stimuli (command and food) is the essence of Pavlovian conditioning. We may expect, therefore, that the dog will not only learn to respond appropriately to the commands but will also come to enjoy hearing the commands and may even salivate when it hears them.

In some instances, Pavlovian and operant procedures are so intertwined that it is hard to say where one begins and the other ends. This is especially evident when negative reinforcement is involved. For example, J. Bruce Overmeier and Martin Seligman (1967) strapped a dog into a harness and presented a tone followed by shock. The shock always followed the tone, and nothing the dog did—jumping about, barking—had any effect on the shock. When the experimenters put the dog into a box divided by a barrier and delivered shock, they found that the dog made no effort to escape; it had learned to be helpless.[16] The initial experience is often described as Pavlovian conditioning: A tone is paired with shock, and neither the tone nor the shock is contingent on the dog's behavior. But another way to look at the experiment is as a punishment procedure in which *all* behavior has the same consequence—shock. Everything the dog did in its attempts to escape shock was punished.

Thus, the distinction between Pavlovian and operant procedures, though appealing, is somewhat arbitrary. It is likely that when one sort of learning occurs, so does the other. (For more on this topic, see Donahoe & Palmer, 1994; Malone, 1990; Pear & Eldridge, 1984; Sheffield, 1965).

REVIEW Students sometimes confuse operant learning with Pavlovian conditioning. In Pavlovian conditioning, two stimuli are paired regardless of what the organism does, whereas in operant learning the appearance of a stimulus follows a particular behavior. In addition, Pavlovian conditioning involves reflexive behavior, whereas operant learning usually involves behavior mediated by skeletal muscles. Though different, Pavlovian and operant experiences often occur together.

Primary and Secondary Reinforcers

There are two kinds of reinforcers: primary and secondary. **Primary reinforcers** are sometimes said to be naturally or innately reinforcing. This is typically true, but it is more accurate to say that primary reinforcers are those that are not dependent on their association with other reinforcers. Besides food and water, examples include sexual stimulation, weak electrical stimulation of certain brain tissues (e.g., the brain's so-called pleasure centers), relief from heat and cold, and certain drugs. Primary reinforcers are powerful, but they are relatively few in number and in advanced societies they probably play a limited role in human learning.

Secondary reinforcers are those that are dependent on their association with other reinforcers. Examples include praise, recognition, smiles, and positive feedback (e.g., "That's correct"). The term *secondary reinforcer* indicates that these reinforcers are secondary to (are derived from) other reinforcers. Ultimately, secondary reinforcers owe their effectiveness directly or indirectly to primary reinforcers.

Because secondary reinforcers acquire their reinforcing power by having been paired with other reinforcers, they are also called **conditioned**

---

[16]Seligman called the phenomenon learned helplessness, and proposed that it could help account for depression in humans. For more on this, see Chapter 7.

reinforcers. An example is provided by Donald Zimmerman (1957), who sounded a buzzer for two seconds before giving water to thirsty rats. After the buzzer and water had been paired in this way several times, Zimmerman put a lever into the rat's chamber. Each time the rat pressed the lever, the buzzer sounded. The rat soon learned to press the lever, even though lever pressing never produced water. The buzzer had become a conditioned reinforcer.

In another study, W. M. Davis and S. G. Smith (1976) paired a buzzer with intravenous injections of morphine. The researchers were then able to use the buzzer as a reinforcer for lever pressing. Not only was the buzzer an effective reinforcer, but its effectiveness was directly related to the amount of morphine with which it had been paired (see also Goldberg et al., 1981). It is easy to see how other secondary reinforcers might acquire their powers in essentially the same way. Food reduces hunger, and because one needs money to buy food, money is regularly associated with food. Thus, money acquires its reinforcing properties by being paired with the things it buys.

Of course, a buzzer that acquired reinforcing power by being paired with another reinforcer will lose its effectiveness if it is never followed by that reinforcer again. But if water sometimes follows Zimmerman's buzzer, the sound will retain its reinforcing quality.

Conditioned reinforcers are generally somewhat weaker than primary reinforcers, but they have certain advantages. For one thing, primary reinforcers lose much of their reinforcing value very quickly. A bit of food is powerfully reinforcing to a hungry person, but it becomes less reinforcing with each bite. The same is true of water, sexual stimulation, and other primary reinforcers. Conditioned reinforcers sometimes become less effective with repeated use, but this occurs much more slowly.

A second advantage of conditioned reinforcers is that it is often much easier to reinforce behavior immediately with them than with primary reinforcers. If you are training a horse to walk with its head held high, you might offer the animal a few grains of oats—a primary reinforcer—each time it does so. But this would require walking to the horse and that would mean a delay in reinforcement. If you repeatedly pair the sound made by a clicker (originally, a small metallic toy called a cricket, but now a device widely used by animal trainers) with oats, you can then reinforce behavior with clicks. The sounds provide immediate reinforcement (Skinner, 1951). If the clicks are at least sometimes followed by food, they will remain reinforcing. Porpoise trainers use a whistle in the same way (Pryor, 1991).

Another advantage of conditioned reinforcers is that they are often less disruptive than primary reinforcers. Eating and drinking take time, and those activities interrupt training. A clicking sound or a word of praise can reinforce behavior without interrupting it.

Conditioned reinforcers also have the advantage that they can be used in many different situations. Food is a very effective reinforcer, but only when the animal or person is hungry. A stimulus that has been paired with food, however, may be reinforcing when the animal or person is hungry, thirsty, or not particularly deprived in any way. Reinforcers that have been paired with many different kinds of reinforcers can be used in a wide variety of situations. Such reinforcers are called **generalized reinforcers**. The most obvious example of a generalized reinforcer may be money.

Although conditioned reinforcers have several advantages over primary reinforcers, they have an important disadvantage: Their effectiveness depends on their association with primary reinforcers. Money, for example, is powerfully reinforcing. In certain situations, it may be more reinforcing than any primary reinforcer. Yet money loses its reinforcing capacity once it is no longer associated with primary reinforcers. Money printed by the Confederate States of America began to lose its value even before the end of the Civil War because it could not be exchanged for food or other reinforcers. Once the war was over, Confederate money became worthless—except as fuel or mattress stuffing. Primary reinforcers are much more resilient: A hungry person will work for food even if the food cannot be exchanged for anything else.

REVIEW   Reinforcers are classified as primary and secondary. Primary reinforcers are largely innate; secondary (or conditioned) reinforcers seem to be acquired through their association with other reinforcers. Stimuli that are effective reinforcers in a wide variety of situations are called generalized reinforcers.

Reinforcement with either primary or secondary reinforcers is a very powerful procedure for increasing the rate of behavior, but how can it account for the appearance of new forms of behavior? Afterall, a behavior can be reinforced only if it occurs! The answer to this riddle is a pair of procedures first described by Skinner: shaping and chaining.

Shaping and Chaining

We saw earlier that if lever pressing results in food falling into a tray, a rat may learn to press a lever. But what if the rat never presses the lever? How could we get it to do so?

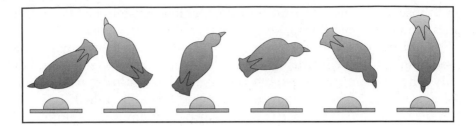

Figure 5-6 *Shaping clockwise turns. As viewed from above, a pigeon is shown at points at which its behavior was reinforced. At first (extreme left figure), any turn to the right produced food. After this, reinforcement required successively closer approximations of a complete circle. The first complete circle appeared after about 15 minutes of shaping. (Figures drawn by Diane Chance from photographs by Paul Chance.)*

One answer is to reinforce any behavior that *resembles* lever pressing. Suppose a hungry rat is sitting in a corner, away from the lever, scratching and grooming. You watch carefully, and when the rat turns its head toward the lever, you press a button that causes a few food pellets to fall into the food tray. This operation causes a sound that has been paired with food many times in the past. As a result, the rat immediately runs to the food tray and eats. After eating, the rat turns away from the lever, wanders a bit, and then turns again toward the lever. You press the button again and the rat immediately runs to the food dish and eats. After a few more reinforcements, the rat is spending its time in the immediate vicinity of the food tray. Now you begin reinforcing any movement toward the lever until the rat is next to it. When the rat touches the lever in any way, you reinforce that. Soon the rat presses the lever, and you provide reinforcement. Now you provide food only when the rat presses the lever, and soon it presses the lever steadily, stopping only to go to the food tray and eat. This training procedure, the reinforcement of successive approximations of a desired behavior, is called **shaping**. Often shaping makes it possible to train behavior in a few minutes that never occurs spontaneously (see Figure 5-6).

Query: Shaping is the reinforcement of successive

_____ of a desired behavior.

The shaping procedure seems so obvious, once it is pointed out, that students sometimes fail to appreciate Skinner's contribution in describing it. It is therefore worth contrasting Skinner's shaping procedure with earlier training methods. Thorndike (1898), for example, describes how he attempted to teach a dog to go to the corner of a large pen:

> I would pound with a stick and say, "Go over to the corner." After an interval (10 seconds for 35 trials, 5 seconds for 60 trials) I would go over to the corner (12 feet off) and drop a piece of meat there. He, of course, followed and secured it. On the 6th, 7th, 16th, 17th, 18th and 19th trials he did perform the act before the 10 seconds were up, then for several times went during the two-minute intervals without regarding the signal, and finally abandoned the habit altogether. (p. 77)

Had Thorndike known about the reinforcement of successive approximations, he very likely would have had the dog going to the corner on command in a few minutes.

Shaping is not restricted to animal behavior. Skinner (1977) describes how he shaped the behavior of his daughter, Deborah, when she was less than a year old. Skinner held Deborah on his lap, and when the room grew dark he turned on a nearby table lamp. Deborah smiled at this, so Skinner decided to see if the light would reinforce her behavior. He turned off the light and waited until Deborah lifted her left hand slightly, then turned the light on and off quickly. She moved her hand again, and Skinner turned the light on and off. Gradually, Skinner required bigger and bigger arm movements for reinforcement until Deborah was moving her arm in a wide arc "to turn on the light" (p. 179).

The shaping procedure can be put to more practical use. A teacher can praise a student's first efforts at printing the alphabet even though the letters are barely recognizable. Once the student can easily make these crude approximations, the teacher can require something better for reinforcement. In this way, the teacher gradually "ups the ante" until the student prints the letters clearly. Similarly, a rehabilitation therapist may place relatively mild demands on a patient at first and congratulate the patient for achieving them. When the patient becomes comfortable with the required task, the therapist can raise the standard slightly.

People often unwittingly shape undesirable behavior in their children.[17] Tantrums, for example, are typically the products of shaping. A tired parent may give in to a child's repeated requests "to shut him up."

---

[17]Shaping is sometimes put to nefarious uses. For example, B. Robinson and L. J. Bradley (1998) note that potential members of a religious cult are exposed to "love bombing," heavy doses of approval and affection. These reinforcers are at first contingent only on being involved with the cult. Later, the affection becomes contingent on complying with minor requests. The requirements for reinforcement are gradually increased until the recruit is obliged to demonstrate complete obedience to the cult leader.

Tips for Shapers

The rate at which shaping proceeds depends primarily on the skill of the trainer. Instructors often have students practice shaping by training a rat to press a lever or a pigeon to peck a disk. There is always a good deal of variability in the rate at which the animals progress. The students usually attribute these differences to the intelligence of the animals. Sooner or later a student whose animal has made no progress will complain, "My rat is too stupid to learn to press a lever!" At this, the instructor often turns the animal over to a student who has already succeeded at the task. Within a few minutes, the "stupid" rat is pounding on the lever like a drummer boy.

You may conclude from this that it is not the *rat* that is stupid, but the student who failed to train it. But in doing so, you are making precisely the same mistake the student made. Learning failures have less to do with the instructor's or trainer's intelligence than they do with his or her skill at shaping (see Todd et al., 1995).

What distinguishes good shapers from poor ones? First, they reinforce small steps. Trainers who get poor results often require too much at once. After reinforcing the rat's turning toward the lever, the poor trainer may wait for the rat to walk over to the lever; the more successful trainer waits only for the rat to take a single step in the direction of the lever.

Second, good trainers provide immediate reinforcement. Poor trainers often hesitate slightly before reinforcing an approximation—often explaining, "I wanted to see if he'd do more." The successful trainer reinforces the instant the desired approximation occurs.

Third, good shapers provide small reinforcers. Shaping laboratory animals usually involves the mechanical delivery of a uniform amount of food, one or

On the next occasion, the parent may resist giving in to the child's usual demands. The child responds by becoming louder or crying. The parent yields to avoid causing a scene. On a subsequent occasion, determined to regain control, the parent may refuse to comply when the child cries or shouts, but gives in when the child produces bugle-like wails. And so it goes: The parent gradually demands more and more outrageous behavior for reinforcement, and the child obliges, eventually engaging in full-fledged tantrums.[18]

---

[18]Ironically, pediatricians and other experts on child rearing often advise parents to take steps that are almost certain to reinforce unwanted behavior, such as crying. For more on this, see Azerrad and Chance (2001).

two food pellets for a rat, a few pieces of grain for a pigeon. However, if food delivery is done by hand, some trainers will give larger amounts of food. This necessarily slows the course of training because the animal takes longer to consume a larger amount of food. Similarly, people attempting to shape behavior in humans sometimes slow learning by providing too much in the way of reinforcers. If you give a child candy or toys to reinforce each approximation, these reinforcers are apt to become the focus of attention. A simple "Well done!" or even "That's better" is usually more effective.

Fourth, good shapers reinforce the best approximation available. The trainer may work out a shaping plan in advance that includes five or ten distinct approximations of lever pressing that are to be reinforced. The poor trainer will stick to that plan no matter what, reinforcing approximation D only after approximations A, B, and C have been reinforced. The more successful trainer will use the plan as nothing more than a rough guide. If the rat skips a few intermediate steps, fine; the good trainer will reinforce any progress toward the goal. If you get lucky, take advantage of it.

Fifth, good trainers back up when necessary. Learning doesn't always progress smoothly. The rat that has been spending a good deal of time near the lever may move away from it and groom or explore other parts of the chamber. At this point, the trainer may need to take a backstep—to reinforce an earlier approximation, such as turning in the direction of the lever. The trainer who is willing to lower the standard when necessary will progress more rapidly than the one who insists on waiting for something better.

Often the parents and other adults attribute tantrums and other annoying behavior to character flaws. "He's so immature!" they may say, or "What a willful child!" The children themselves seldom understand the shaping process any better than their parents and often grow up attributing their misbehavior to immaturity, temperament, or other internal traits, just as their parents had. But the child has merely done what was required for reinforcement.

Some animals seem to use a kind of shaping procedure in the training of their young. Otters, for example, first feed their young on prey that they have already killed. As the pups mature, their parents bring animals that are dying; the young otters find the prey easy to kill. After this, the parents bring injured prey; their young must finish the job in order to eat. Finally, the adults take their young to the hunting area and bring them uninjured prey. Thus, the young otters build on past skills until they master the art of hunting and killing prey on their own.

Shaping goes a long way toward explaining the appearance of new forms of behavior. Such behavior is, in a sense, constructed out of old behavior. But shaping alone is not sufficient to account for all forms of new behavior; to understand them, we must consider chaining.

Women gymnasts compete on something called a balance beam. Basically this competition requires them to walk across a 4-inch-wide beam and, along the way, do somersaults, handstands, back flips, and other impossible stunts without landing on their heads. Competing on the balance beam consists of performing a number of acts in a particular sequence. Such a connected sequence of behavior is called a **behavior chain**.

Among the more ordinary (and less hazardous) behavior chains is making a telephone call: You pick up the receiver, listen for a dial tone, dial a set of numbers, and hold the receiver to your ear. Dining in a restaurant consists of sitting at a table, studying the menu, placing an order with a waiter, eating the meal, paying the bill, and leaving. A good deal of animal behavior consists of partly learned behavior chains. Predators, for example, search for prey, stalk it, pursue it, kill it, and eat it.

Usually the segments of a chain must be completed in a particular order. In using a telephone, if we dial the number before we pick up the receiver, the call will not go through. Similarly, dining out may not go well if we attempt to order a meal before being seated.

Query: What are the parts of the chain known as brushing

one's teeth?

Training an animal or person to perform a behavior chain is called **chaining**. Skinner (1938) trained a rat named Plyny (whether it was Plyny the Elder or Plyny the Younger is unrecorded) to pull a string that released a marble from a rack, pick up the marble with its forepaws, carry it to a tube projecting two inches above the floor of the experimental chamber, lift the marble to the top of the tube, and drop it inside. Each behavior in the chain had to be shaped.

Other researchers and animal trainers have trained laboratory animals to perform even more complex chains. Carl Cheney (personal communication, August 21, 1978) trained a rat to climb a ramp, cross a drawbridge, climb a ladder, walk across a tightrope, climb another ladder, crawl through a tunnel, step into an elevator that carried it back down to

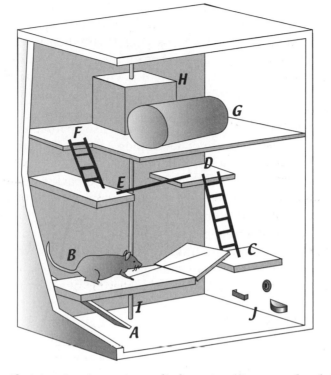

Figure 5-7 *Chaining. Starting at A, rat climbs ramp to B, crosses drawbridge to C, climbs ladder to D, crosses tightrope to E, climbs ladder to F, crawls through tunnel to G, enters elevator at H, descends to I, presses lever at J, and receives food. (Drawn by Diane Chance.)*

its starting point, press a lever, and finally receive a few pellets of food (see Figure 5-7).

The first step in chaining is to break the task down into its component elements, a procedure called **task analysis**. Once the individual links of the chain have been identified, it is possible to reinforce the performance of the links in the correct sequence. There are two basic ways of going about this: forward chaining and backward chaining.

In **forward chaining**, the trainer begins by reinforcing performance of the first link in the chain. This is repeated until the task is performed without hesitation. At this point, the trainer requires performance of the first *two* links, and this short chain is reinforced until it is performed smoothly. Then the trainer requires performance of the first three links, and so on.

If any of the links does not readily occur, the trainer uses shaping to build it. For example, rats do not readily pull on strings or pick up marbles. If you wanted to train a rat to replicate Plyny's performance, you might begin by shaping string pulling, perhaps by providing a bit of food whenever the rat touched the string, then when it bit the string, then when it held the string in its mouth, then when it pulled it. Similarly, in teaching a student to recite a poem (a linguistic chain), you might need to shape the proper pronunciation of a word, or the expression given a particular phrase.

Forward chaining is a logical, commonsense approach, but it is not always the most efficient way of developing a chain. Sometimes the better way is to begin with the *last* link in the chain and work backward toward the first element. This procedure is called **backward chaining**. In Plyny's case, you might first train the rat to drop a marble down a tube. Next you would train the animal to carry the marble to the tube and drop it. When the rat readily performs the last two tasks, you can require performance of the last three links, and so on. As in forward chaining, any behavior that does not occur spontaneously must first be shaped.

Note that in backward chaining, the chain is never *performed* backward. Plyny does not drop a marble down a tube, then carry the marble to the tube, and so on; the parts of the chain are always performed in their proper sequence. Training is backward only in the sense that links in the chain are added from "back to front." So, once a rat has learned to perform the last link in a chain, it then learns to perform the last two links in the chain, then the last three, and so on.

Query: How would you use backward chaining to train a rat to

run a maze?

An interesting thing about chaining is that each link in the chain is reinforced, at least in part, by the opportunity to perform the next step in the chain. Each step in making a cake, for example, is reinforced by access to the next step in the cooking process: Getting the ingredients together is reinforced by being able to mix them; mixing the ingredients is reinforced by being able to put the batter into the cake pans; filling the cake pans is reinforced by being able to put the pans into the oven; putting the pans in the oven is reinforced by seeing the batter rise and turn brown, and so on. Similarly, each link in the predator's chain is reinforced by the subsequent link: Searching for prey is reinforced by the opportunity to stalk it; stalking prey is reinforced by the opportunity to chase it; chasing prey is reinforced by the opportunity to attack it, and so on.

Only the last act in a chain typically produces a reinforcer that is not part of the chain. In the laboratory this is usually a primary reinforcer.

This is sometimes the case outside the laboratory as well: The predator gets to eat the prey it has hunted, stalked, chased, and killed, and we get to eat the cake we labored so long in making. Yet this last, external reinforcer is crucial; without it, the chain is not likely to be performed. Even a well-established chain eventually breaks down if the final link in the chain does not produce a reinforcer.

REVIEW   Shaping is the process of reinforcing successive approximations of a desired behavior. Chaining is the process of reinforcing each of a series of linked behaviors to form a behavior chain.

Operant reinforcement is basically very simple. Nevertheless, its effects depend on the complex interactions of many variables. Next we consider a few of the more important of these variables.

Variables Affecting Reinforcement

Contingency

Where operant learning is concerned, the word *contingency* refers to the degree of correlation between a behavior and its consequence. The rate at which learning occurs varies with the degree to which a behavior is followed by a reinforcer.

Lynn Hammond (1980) performed an experiment reminiscent of Rescorla's (1968) study on contingency in Pavlovian conditioning (see Chapter 3). Hammond manipulated the probability that food would come after a lever press and in its absence. He found that if rats were as likely to get food by not pressing the lever as they were by pressing it, they did not continue to press the lever (see Figure 5-8). A contingency between lever pressing and the reinforcer was essential.

It is easy to see why contingency is important to learning. Learning to touch-type is difficult, even though there is a perfect correlation between the key pressed and the letter that appears on the page or computer monitor. Now imagine learning to type using a keyboard that is defective: Sometimes when you press the letter *a* you get *a*, but sometimes you get *c* or *d* or some other letter. When you press the *c* key, you may get a *c*, but sometimes you get something else. And so on, with each of the 26 letters of the alphabet. Even if you get the appropriate letter 90% of the time (i.e., correct actions are reinforced 9 out of 10 times), learning to touch type is almost certain to take much longer.[19]

---

[19] So far as I know, no such experiment has ever been performed. It would make for a very interesting student project.

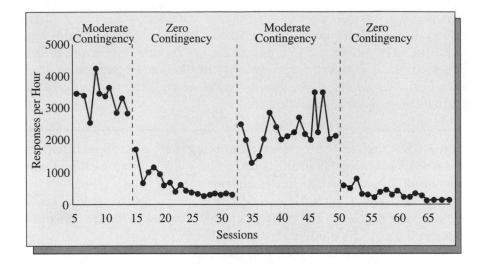

Figure 5-8   *Contingency and reinforcement. The mean response rate of lever pressing for 10 rats when food was contingent and noncontingent. (Adapted from "The Effect of Contingency Upon the Appetitive Conditioning of Free-Operant Behavior," by L. J. Hammond, 1980,* Journal of the Experimental Analysis of Behavior, *34[3], p. 300. Copyright © 1980 by the Society for the Experimental Analysis of Behavior, Inc. Reprinted with permission.)*

Even small reinforcers can be very effective if there is a strong correlation between the behavior and the reinforcer. In fact, numerous small reinforcers, when contingent on a behavior, are generally more effective than a few large ones (Schneider, 1973; Todorov et al., 1984).

Contiguity

The gap between a behavior and its reinforcing consequence has a powerful effect on the rate of operant learning. In general, the shorter this interval is, the faster learning occurs (Dickinson et al., 1992; Hunter, 1913; Schlinger & Blakely, 1994; see Figure 5-9).

A study by Kennon Lattal (1995) will illustrate. Lattal attempted to shape disk pecking in a pigeon, but with the reinforcer delayed automatically for 10 seconds. In other words, when the bird moved toward the disk, Lattal would press a switch controlling the food magazine, but a device would prevent delivery of food for 10 seconds. Lattal spent an hour each day trying to shape disk pecking, but even after 40 days he was unsuccessful. The bird moved back and forth in front of the disk, but never pecked it. When Lattal changed the delay from 10 seconds to only 1 second, he was able to shape disk pecking in about 15 to 20 minutes (Lattal, personal communication, 1996).

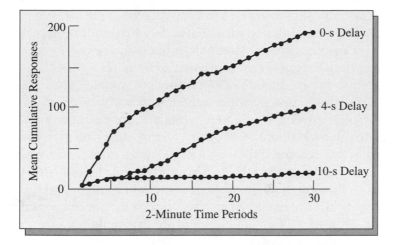

Figure 5-9 *Contiguity and reinforcement. Mean cumulative responses when reinforcement was immediate, delayed 4 seconds, and delayed 10 seconds. (Adapted from "The Effects of Delayed Reinforcement and a Response-Produced Auditory Stimulus on the Acquisition of Operant Behavior in Rats," by H. D. Schlinger, Jr., and E. Blakely, 1994,* The Psychological Record, 44, *p. 396, Figure 1. Copyright © 1994 The Psychological Record. Reprinted with permission.)*

Some studies of contiguity have raised doubts about its importance in learning (e.g., Azzi et al., 1964). Part of the confusion arises because contiguity is sometimes entangled with other variables. Jeffrey Weil (1984) notes, for example, that most studies of delayed reinforcement are confounded by the number of times the behavior is reinforced. To illustrate, let us compare two experiments: In one, lever pressing is reinforced immediately; in the second, pressing is reinforced after a 5-second delay. If we run animals under both conditions for 1 hour, we are likely to find that immediate reinforcement results in faster learning. But a problem arises in interpreting the results because immediate reinforcement means that the behavior is reinforced more often in an hour's time than is the case with delayed reinforcement. Weil dealt with this problem by making the number of reinforcements constant. The results showed that reinforcement delay *did* make a difference: the shorter the interval between behavior and reinforcer, the more rapidly learning occurred.

Query: Weil wanted to separate the effects of _____ of

reinforcement and _____ of reinforcements.

Reviews of the literature on contiguity have found that operant learning varies fairly consistently with contiguity. Susan Schneider (1990), for instance, in an examination of one subset of this literature, found that "no clear exceptions to support for contiguity exist as yet" (p. 247).

One reason that immediate consequences produce better results is that a delay allows time for other behavior to occur. This behavior, and not the appropriate one, is reinforced. Imagine, for example, that you are learning to pilot an oil tanker. Big ships change direction slowly, so there is a delay between turning the ship's wheel and a change in the ship's direction. You may turn the wheel appropriately, but by the time the ship finally responds, you may have taken some other, inappropriate, action. This inappropriate behavior is then reinforced by the desired change in direction. This delay is no doubt one thing that makes learning to steer great ships difficult.

Even though immediate reinforcement clearly produces faster learning, a number of studies have shown that learning *can* occur despite reinforcement delays (Dickinson et al., 1992; Lattal & Gleeson, 1990; Wilkenfield et al., 1992). The effects of delaying reinforcement can be muted if the delay is regularly preceded by a particular stimulus. Henry Schlinger, Jr., and Elbert Blakely (1994) conducted an experiment that compared the effects of signaled and unsignaled delay of reinforcement. They set up a photoelectric beam near the ceiling of an experimental chamber. When a rat broke the beam by rising up on its hind legs, food fell into a dish. For some rats, breaking the beam resulted in immediate food delivery; for others, food came after a 4-second or 10-second delay. For some rats receiving delayed reinforcement, a tone sounded immediately after the rat broke the beam.

As expected, the results showed very clearly the superiority of immediate reinforcement over delayed reinforcement. They also showed that a 4-second delay was less detrimental than a 10-second delay. However, the effects of delay were not so great when the delays were preceded by a tone (see Figure 5-10).

One explanation of the effect of signals is called the marking hypothesis (Lieberman et al., 1979). This is the idea that the signal draws attention to the behavior that preceded it. However, as Schlinger and Blakely point out, this explanation merely "describes the effect and uses the description as the explanation" (1994, p. 405). To explain why signals increase the power of delayed reinforcers, we have to identify the variables that produce the increase. Perhaps the most likely explanation is that the signal became a conditioned reinforcer because it was regularly followed by food. Thus, signaled delayed reinforcement gets better results because

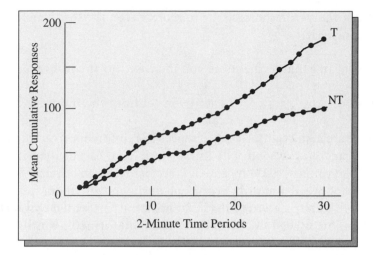

Figure 5-10 *Effects of signaled delayed reinforcement. Mean cumulative reponses when delayed reinforcement was preceded by a tone (T) and when there was no tone (NT). Reinforcement was delayed 4 seconds in each case. (Adapted from "The Effects of Delayed Reinforcement and a Response-Produced Auditory Stimulus on the Acquisition of Operant Behavior in Rats," by H. D. Schlinger, Jr., and E. Blakely, 1994, The Psychological Record, 44, p. 396, Figure 1. Copyright © 1994 The Psychological Record. Reprinted with permission.).*

more reinforcement is involved: the food, and the stimulus that precedes the food. However, the conditioned reinforcement explanation is not above reproach (see Schlinger & Blakely, 1994).

Reinforcer Characteristics

Although small reinforcers given frequently usually produce faster learning than large reinforcers given infrequently, the size of the reinforcer does matter. Other things being equal, a large reinforcer is more effective than a small one (Christopher, 1988; Wolfe, 1936). If you happen to look down while walking along a sidewalk and see a dollar bill, the chances are you will continuc looking in that arca, and may continuc looking down even when you go on your way. But the reinforcing effect is apt to be much stronger if what you see is a $100 bill.

The relation between reinforcer size (sometimes referred to as reinforcer magnitude) and learning is not, however, linear. In training a 100-pound dog, for example, you might get much better results using one gram treats than you would with half gram treats, but there would be little if any difference between a 50-gram treat and a 100-gram treat. In general, the more you increase the reinforcer size, the less benefit you get from the increase.

Query: In general, the more you increase the amount of a

reinforcer, the _____ benefit you get from the increase.

   There are also qualitative differences in reinforcers. You might think that to a rat, food is food, but in fact rats have rather discriminating tastes. R. Simmons (1924) repeatedly ran rats through a maze. Some rats found a bit of bread and milk at the end of the maze; others found a sunflower seed. Rats receiving bread and milk outperformed those that received sunflower seed. M. H. Elliott (1928) performed a similar experiment comparing sunflower seeds with bran mash. Again the group fed sunflower seeds came in second. It would appear that, to the rat, the sunflower seed is a rather inferior food. In other studies, animals and people given a choice between performing a task for either of two reinforcers often show strong preferences (Parsons & Reid, 1990; Simmons, 1924). Identifying preferred reinforcers can improve the effectiveness of a reinforcement procedure in applied settings (Mace et al., 1997).[20]

Task Characteristics

Certain qualities of the behavior being reinforced affect the ease with which it can be strengthened. Obviously, learning to walk a balance beam is easier than learning to walk a tightrope. Less obviously, behavior that depends on smooth muscles and glands is harder to modify through operant procedures than is behavior that depends on skeletal muscles.

   At one time it appeared that reinforcement could increase or decrease the heart rates of rats by 20% (Miller & DiCara, 1967). These astonishing results led people to envision the treatment of medical problems such as high blood pressure and irregular heart beat through reinforcement. Unfortunately, researchers were not always able to replicate the early findings. Neal Miller (1978), one of the early researchers in this field, began to express doubts, and he and collaborator Barry Dworkin (Dworkin & Miller, 1986) finally concluded that "the existence of visceral learning remains unproven" (p. 299). Today the general consensus seems to be that biofeedback can work in certain situations, but (with the exception of treatment

---

[20]You can see food preferences easily at a bird feeder. Make black oil sunflower seeds and striped sunflower seeds available in different feeders, and you will probably find that chickadees and titmice prefer the former. Gray squirrels, in my experience, eat both with equal gusto.

of migraine headaches) the benefits are generally too small to be of practical value (Hugdahl, 1995/2001). Even with the best of reinforcers, then, learning to lower your blood pressure is more difficult than learning to lower your voice.

Deprivation Level

The effectiveness of food, water, and warmth as reinforcers varies with the extent to which an organism has been deprived of food, water, and warmth. For instance, E. C. Tolman and C. H. Honzik (1930) gave rats food on reaching the end of a maze; some rats had been deprived of food, others had not. As Figure 5-11 shows, those that had been deprived showed much better progress than those that had not.

In general, the greater the level of deprivation (e.g., the longer the interval since eating), the more effective the reinforcer (Cotton, 1953; Reynolds & Pavlik, 1960). At least, this is the case with primary reinforcers (such as those just mentioned) that satisfy a physiological need. This implies that such reinforcers will become less effective over the course of training, and this is, in fact, what happens.

Deprivation is less important where secondary reinforcers are concerned. Money is not always less reinforcing for those who are rich than for those who are "money deprived" (college students, for example).

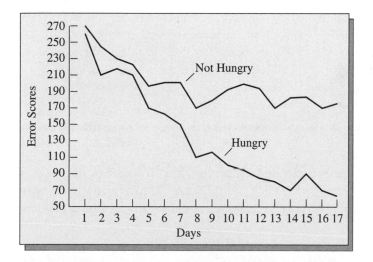

Figure 5-11 *Food deprivation and learning. Rats that had been deprived of food learned to run a maze (at the end of which they found food) more efficiently than rats that had not been deprived of food. (Adapted from Tolman and Honzik, 1930.)*

Octopi Individuality

Peter Dews (1959) discovered that individual differences in learners affect the course of learning, even when the learners are octopi.

Dews wanted to see if lever pulling could be shaped in three octopi, Albert, Bertram, and Charles. Each octopus lived in a tank filled with salt water, with a lever mechanism attached to the tank during training sessions. The basic procedure consisted of shaping lever pulling by providing the octopus with food when it approached the lever, then when it touched it, and finally only when it pulled it.

Learning proceeded by the book with both Albert and Bertram. Charles also learned to pull the lever, but things did not go as smoothly with him. Instead of pulling the lever while floating, Charles anchored several tentacles to the sides of his tank, wrapped the others around the lever, and pulled with great force. He bent the lever a number of times and finally broke it, which led to the unplanned termination of the experiment.

Charles also displayed unusual interest in a light suspended over the water. He repeatedly grasped the light with his tentacles and pulled it toward the water. This, as Dews observed, was incompatible with lever pulling.

Perhaps Charles's most interesting behavior was a tendency to squirt water out of the tank, generally in the direction of the experimenter. Dews reports that Charles "spent much time with eyes above the surface of the water, directing a jet of water at any individual who approached the tank. This behavior interfered materially with the smooth conduct of the experiments, and is, again, clearly incompatible with lever-pulling" (p. 62).

Charles's behavior demonstrates that individual differences exist, even among octopi. The differences may be due to previous learning, heredity, or other factors. Whatever their source, such individual differences play an important role in the course of operant learning.

Similarly, praise can be reinforcing, but it does not necessarily become less reinforcing with each compliment. Deprivation level is important, then, mainly when the reinforcer alters some physiological condition.

Other Variables

The variables just reviewed are among the most important in determining the effectiveness of operant procedures, but other variables also play a part (see Octopi Individuality). Previous learning experiences are particularly important. There is evidence, for example, that much of the difference between fast- and slow-learning school children disappears when both have similar learning histories (Greenwood, 1991). Another important variable is the role of competing contingencies: The effects of reinforcing a behavior will be very different if the behavior also produces punishing consequences or if reinforcers are simultaneously available for other kinds of behavior (Herrnstein, 1970). Reinforcement is far more complicated than is usually supposed by those who incorrectly refer to it as trial-and-error learning.

REVIEW   Reinforcement outcomes depend on a number of variables. These include the degree of contingency, contiguity, reinforcer characteristics, task characteristics, deprivation level, and other variables.

Extinction of Reinforced Behavior

You will recall that in classical conditioning, extinction means repeatedly presenting the CS without the US. Following operant learning, **extinction** means withholding the consequences that reinforce a behavior.

In an early study of extinction, Skinner (1938) trained rats to press a lever and then, after reinforcing about a hundred lever presses, disconnected the feeding mechanism. Everything was as it had been during training, except that now lever pressing no longer produced food. The result, as you might expect, was a gradual decline in the rate of lever pressing (see Figure 5-12).[21]

Although the overall effect of extinction is to reduce the frequency of the behavior, the immediate effect is often an abrupt *increase* in the behavior on extinction. When extinction is used to treat practical behavior problems, this **extinction burst,** as it is called, gives the impression that the procedure has made the problem worse, rather than better. If extinction is continued, however, the extinction burst is typically followed by a steady and fairly rapid decline in the behavior.

Another effect of extinction is an increase in the variability of behavior. That is, the organism "tries something else," often a variation of the previously reinforced behavior. We can make use of this phenomenon during shaping: After repeatedly reinforcing an approximation of the desired behavior, we can withhold reinforcement. This increases the variability of the behavior, which makes it likely that a better approximation of the goal

---

[21]Figure 5-12 shows extinction on a cumulative record. The same data can be presented as number of responses per minute, in which case the data line will resemble that in Figure 3-11.

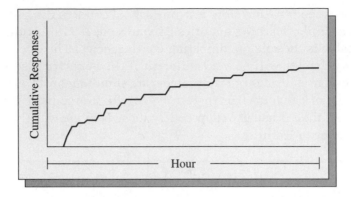

Figure 5-12 *Extinction curve. This cumulative record shows the decrease in response rate of one rat when lever pressing no longer produced food. (Compare Figure 5-4.) (Adapted from* The Behavior of Organisms: An Experimental Analysis *[p. 75], by B. F. Skinner, 1938, New York: Appleton-Century-Crofts. Copyright © 1938, renewed 1966. Reprinted by permission.)*

behavior will appear. When it does, it can be reinforced. This use of extinction during shaping is a delicate procedure, however, because if one waits too long for a better approximation, the behavior may deteriorate.

Extinction also often increases the frequency of emotional behavior, particularly aggression. Rats that have received food for pressing a lever have been known to bite the lever when pressing it no longer produced reinforcement. The aggression will be directed at another animal if one is handy, even though the other animal was in no way responsible for the failure of the reinforcer to arrive (Azrin et al., 1966; Rilling & Caplan, 1973). Research also provides evidence that extinction can produce an increase in aggressive behavior in humans (e.g., Todd et al., 1989). The tendency of extinction to provoke aggressive behavior will be familiar to anyone who has ever kicked a stuck door, slammed down a telephone receiver when a call did not go through, or pounded on a defective vending machine.

One extinction session is often not enough to extinguish behavior. This is often so even when the extinction session lasts for several hours and involves hundreds or even thousands of unreinforced acts. What usually happens is this: The rate of the previously reinforced behavior declines and finally stabilizes at or near its pretraining level. Extinction appears to be complete. If, however, the animal or person is later put back into the training situation, the extinguished behavior occurs again, almost as though it had not been on extinction. You may recall that this reappearance of a previously extinguished behavior also occurs during

Pavlovian extinction and is called spontaneous recovery. The longer the interval between the two extinction sessions, the greater the recovery.

We may witness spontaneous recovery in everyday situations. A person who has made a number of unsuccessful attempts to get food from a defective vending machine may give up, but may try once again when passing by the machine later in the day. This reappearance of the behavior is spontaneous recovery. Likewise, the teacher who finds that he has been reinforcing silly comments from students by smiling when they are made, may put the behavior on extinction by not smiling. The frequency of silly remarks will fall off, but may then reappear unexpectedly. In the absence of reinforcement, behavior that has spontaneously recovered soon drops out again. However, behavior that reappears after extinction often is reinforced. The person who tries the vending machine after numerous failures may find that it now works, and the teacher who has extinguished silly remarks may laugh out loud when one of the students says something foolish.

Another effect of extinction is the reappearance of previously reinforced behavior, a phenomenon called **resurgence** (Epstein, 1983, 1985; Mowrer, 1940). Suppose a pigeon is trained to peck a disk and then this behavior is extinguished. Now suppose some new behavior, such as wing flapping, is reinforced. When the bird is flapping steadily, this behavior is put on extinction. What does the bird do? Wing flapping declines, as expected, but something unexpected also occurs: The bird begins to peck the disk again. As the rate of wing flapping declines, the rate of disk pecking increases (see Figure 5-13).[22]

Resurgence has been observed by many researchers over the past 50 years. Karen Pryor (1991) describes an instance of resurgence in a porpoise. An animal named Hou received reinforcement for performing a behavior learned in the previous training session. If this behavior were not reinforced, Hou would then run through its entire repertoire of previously learned stunts: breaching, porpoising, beaching, and swimming upside down.

The notion of resurgence may help us understand what some clinicians call regression, the tendency to return to more primitive, infantile modes of behavior (Epstein, 1985; Mowrer, 1940). The man who is unable to get his wife to behave as he would like by asking her nicely may resort to having a tantrum, a form of behavior that got good results with his mother when he was a boy. The behavior "asking nicely" is on extinction, and the man reverts to a form of behavior that had been reinforced in similar

---

[22]Figure 5-13 illustrates resurgence with hypothetical data. The only figure I have seen that depicts resurgence with real data is rather more complicated; see Epstein, 1985.

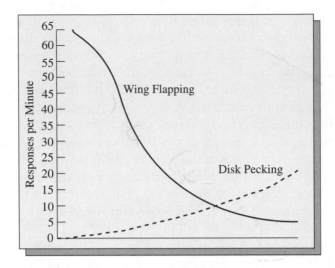

Figure 5-13   *Resurgence. When a response (wing flapping) is put on extinction, a previously reinforced response (disk pecking) reappears. (Hypothetical data.)*

situations in the past. This is not to say that the man thinks, "Well, asking nicely isn't working, so I'll try tantrums; that always worked with Mom." The behavior may very well be unconscious: that is, the person probably cannot specify the learning history that produced it. However, Robert Epstein notes that there is no need to assume, as Freud did, that the behavior that resurges will be more primitive than the behavior it replaces. It need only be a behavior that was once reliably reinforced; it *may* be more primitive than the behavior now on extinction, but it need not be.

If a behavior is kept continuously on extinction, it will continue to decline in frequency. When the behavior no longer occurs, or occurs no more often than it did before training, it is said to have been extinguished. The rate at which extinction occurs depends on a number of factors, including the number of times the behavior was reinforced before extinction (Williams, 1938; see Figure 5-14), the effort the behavior requires (Capehart et al., 1958; see Figure 5-15), and the size of the reinforcer used during training (Reed, 1991).

Extinction and reinforcement are parallel procedures, but they do not have equal effects: One nonreinforcement does not "cancel out" one reinforcement. Skinner (1938) noticed that a single reinforcement might be followed by dozens of unreinforced lever presses. On one occasion he provided one reinforcement, consisting of three food pellets, and the rat then pressed the lever 60 more times even though it received no more food. Thus, behavior is usually acquired rapidly and extinguished slowly (Morse, 1966).

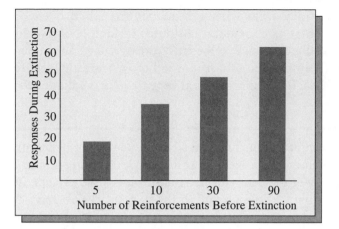

Figure 5-14 *Extinction and number of reinforcements. The average number of responses made during extinction increased with the number of reinforced responses prior to extinction. (Compiled from data in Williams, 1938.)*

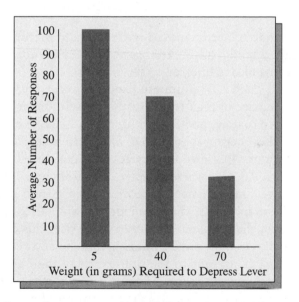

Figure 5-15 *Effort and extinction. The more force required to depress a lever, the fewer responses made during extinction. (Compiled from data in Capehart et al., 1958.)*

Although the *rate* at which a behavior declines during extinction will vary, the eventual result is the same. It is not possible to say, however, that extinction entirely erases the effects of previous reinforcement. Even after performing an act thousands of times without reinforcement, the behavior may occur with a frequency that slightly exceeds its base-line level. There is considerable doubt, in fact, about whether a well-established behavior can ever be truly extinguished, in the sense that it is no more likely to occur than it was before training (see, for example, Razran, 1956). To paraphrase Shakespeare: What's done can n'er be (entirely) undone.

REVIEW   Reinforcement increases the frequency of behavior. Withholding reinforcement, a procedure called extinction, results in a decline in the frequency of the behavior. Extinction has other effects, including the extinction burst and an increase in the variability of behavior. During extinction, other previously effective behaviors may appear, a phenomenon known as resurgence. Following extinction, the extinguished behavior may suddenly reappear; this is called spontaneous recovery.

Theories of Reinforcement

We often hear that "practice makes perfect," as if merely performing a skill repeatedly would lead inevitably to mastery. Thorndike showed, however, that this idea is in error.

Thorndike (1931/1968) conducted several experiments intended to separate the influence of practice from that of reinforcement. In one experiment, he tried to draw a four-inch line with his eyes closed. He drew the line over and over again for a total of 3,000 attempts, yet there was no improvement. On the first day of practice, the lines varied from 4.5 to 6.2 inches; on the last day, they varied from 4.1 to 5.7 inches. The medians for each day also reveal no evidence of learning (see Figure 5-16). In a similar experiment, Thorndike (1927) had students draw a 4-inch line 400 times without feedback; there was no improvement. After this he had the students draw the line 25 more times, but this time he allowed them to open their eyes after each attempt to see the results of their effort; this time there was marked improvement. Thorndike concluded that practice is important only insofar as it provides the opportunity for reinforcement.

But *why* do reinforcers strengthen behavior? Many psychologists have attempted to solve the riddle; here, we will consider the efforts of Hull, Premack, and Timberlake and Allison.

Hull's Drive-Reduction Theory

Clark Hull (1943, 1951, 1952) believed that animals and people behave because of motivational states called **drives**. For him, all behavior is literally driven. An animal deprived of food, for example, is driven to obtain

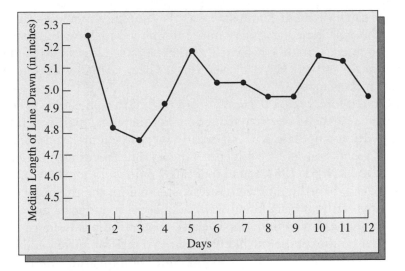

Figure 5-16 *The effect of practice without reinforcement. Attempts to draw a 4-inch line while blindfolded showed little improvement. (Compiled from data in Thorndike, 1931/1968.)*

food. Other drives are associated with deprivation of water, sleep, oxygen, and sexual stimulation. A reinforcer is a stimulus that reduces one or more drives.

Hull's **drive-reduction theory** works reasonably well with primary reinforcers such as food and water because these reinforcers alter a physiological state. But there are many reinforcers that do not seem to reduce physiological needs. Teachers more often reinforce behavior with positive feedback (e.g., "OK," "That's right") and praise than with food and water. Employers are more likely to strengthen desirable employee behavior with bonuses and commendations than with sleep. Yet there is no evidence that feedback, praise, money, and commendations satisfy physiological needs. How, then, can reinforcement be explained in terms of drive reduction? Hull answered this criticism by suggesting that such secondary reinforcers derive their reinforcing powers from, and are therefore dependent on, their association with drive-reducing primary reinforcers.

The distinction between primary and secondary reinforcers is widely accepted today, but Hull's critics were not satisfied that this distinction saved his theory. They pointed out that some reinforcers are hard to classify as primary or secondary. For instance, Einar Siqueland and Clement Delucia (1969) modified a pacifier so that it could be used to control the focus of a pattern on a television screen. When an infant sucked on the pacifier, the image came into focus; when the baby stopped sucking, the image became blurred. The result was that sucking increased; in other words, the appearance of a sharp image reinforced sucking. But why does a focused image reinforce behavior? Is there a physiological drive that focused images satisfy? Have focused images been paired with other reinforcers, such as food?

Even reinforcers that normally seem related to a physiological condition may not depend on drive reduction. For instance, male rats find the opportunity to copulate with a sexually receptive female reinforcing, a fact that seems consistent with Hull's theory. But Frederick Sheffield and his colleagues (1951, 1954) found that rats would work for such an opportunity even when the rats were interrupted before the male ejaculated. Copulation without ejaculation would not seem to reduce a drive, yet it was reinforcing. Is it reinforcing because copulation has been associated with other reinforcers? How likely is that in a rat? Moreover, edible substances such as saccharin that have no nutritional value, and therefore no drive-reducing value, nevertheless are reinforcing.

Because of such problems, most psychologists today find Hull's drive-reduction theory an unsatisfactory explanation of why reinforcers work. There are just too many reinforcers that neither reduce drives nor acquire their reinforcing properties from their association with primary reinforcers. Hull is not without his defenders (see Smith, 1984), but most researchers find other theories of reinforcement more attractive.

Relative Value Theory and the Premack Principle

David Premack (1959, 1965) took an altogether different approach to the problem of reinforcement. Whereas reinforcers are ordinarily viewed as stimuli, Premack noticed that they could be thought of as behavior. Take the case of reinforcing lever pressing with food. The reinforcer is usually said to be the food itself, but it can just as easily be considered the act of eating.

It is clear, said Premack, that in any given situation some kinds of behavior have a greater likelihood of occurrence than others. A rat is typically more likely to eat, given the opportunity to do so, than it is to press a lever. Thus, different kinds of behavior have different values, relative to one another, at any given moment. It is these relative values, said Premack, that determine the reinforcing properties of behavior. This theory, which may be called the **relative value theory**, makes no use of assumed physiological drives. Nor does it depend on the distinction between primary and secondary reinforcers. To determine whether a given activity will reinforce another, we need know only the relative values of the activities.

As a measure of the relative values of two activities, Premack suggested measuring the amount of time a participant engages in both activities, given a choice between them. According to Premack,

> reinforcement involves a *relation*, typically between two responses, one that is being reinforced and another that is responsible for the reinforcement. This leads to the following generalization: Of any two responses, the more probable response will reinforce the less probable one. (1965, p. 132)

This generalization, known as the **Premack principle**, is usually stated somewhat more simply: High probability behavior reinforces low probability behavior.[23]

The Premack principle suggests that if a rat shows a stronger inclination to drink than to run in an exercise wheel, drinking can be used to reinforce running. Premack (1962) tested this idea by conducting an experiment in which he deprived rats of water so that they were inclined to drink, and then made drinking contingent on running: To get a drink, the rats had to run. The result was that the time spent running increased. In other words, drinking reinforced running.

> **Query:** According to the Premack principle, _____
>
> _____ behavior reinforces _____ behavior.

Premack's theory says that it is the *relative* value of activities that determines their reinforcement value. This theory implies that the relationship between drinking and running could be reversed, that running could reinforce drinking if the relative value of running could be made greater than that of drinking. Premack tested this idea by providing rats with free access to water but restricting their access to the exercise wheel. He then made running contingent on drinking: To get to the exercise wheel, the rats had to drink. Under these circumstances, drinking increased. In other words, running reinforced drinking (see Figure 5-17).

In another experiment, Premack (1959) gave first-graders the opportunity to eat candy dispensed from a machine or to play a pinball machine. The children could stick with one activity or alternate between the two. Some children spent more time at the pinball machine; others preferred to eat candy. After identifying these relative values, Premack

---

[23]It might also be stated this way, although some authorities might object: Strong behavior strengthens weak behavior. Keep in mind that "strong" merely means likely to occur, resistant to extinction, and the like. For more on the current status of the Premack principle, see Klatt and Morris (2001).

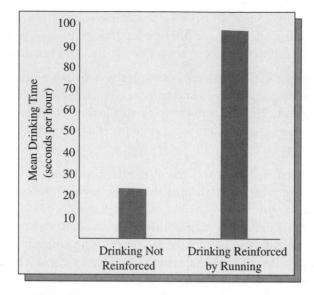

Figure 5-17 *Relative value and reinforcement. Water reinforces running in rats deprived of water, but Premack showed that running reinforces drinking in exercise-deprived rats. (Compiled from data in Premack, 1962.)*

made access to each child's more probable behavior contingent on performance of that child's less probable behavior. For instance, a child who preferred to spend time playing pinball now had to eat candy to get access to the pinball machine. The result was that the less probable behavior increased.

Premack's theory of reinforcement has the advantage of being strictly empirical; no hypothetical concepts, such as drive, are required. An event is reinforcing simply because it provides the opportunity to engage in preferred behavior. The theory is not, however, without its problems. One problem concerns those troublesome secondary reinforcers. As Premack (1965) himself notes, his theory does not explain why the word *yes* (for example) is often reinforcing. Another problem with the theory is that *low* probability behavior will reinforce *high* probability behavior if the participant has been prevented from performing the low probability behavior for some time (Eisenberger et al., 1967; Timberlake, 1980). The latter problem has led some researchers to turn to response deprivation theory.

Response Deprivation Theory

Because of the problems with Premack's relative value theory, William Timberlake and James Allison (1974; Timberlake, 1980) proposed the **response deprivation theory** of reinforcement.[24] The central idea of this

---

[24]It is also called equilibrium theory and response restriction theory.

theory is that behavior becomes reinforcing when the organism is prevented from engaging in it at its normal frequency.

Any behavior that occurs with some frequency has a baseline level. For instance, if a rat is given the opportunity to drink or run in an exercise wheel whenever it likes, it will, over a period of time, establish steady rates for each behavior. Response deprivation theory predicts that if we restrict access to drinking, so that the rate of drinking falls below the baseline level, the rat will engage in behavior that provides access to water. In other words, drinking will be reinforcing. If the rat is allowed to drink freely, but its access to the exercise wheel is restricted so that the rate of running falls below the baseline level, the rat will engage in behavior that provides access to the exercise wheel. In other words, running will be reinforcing.

This all sounds very similar to Premack's relative value theory, and indeed, response deprivation theory is an extension of Premack's work. The difference is that response deprivation theory says that the relative value of one reinforcer to another is not vital; what is vital is the extent to which each behavior occurs below its baseline rate. Put another way, a behavior is reinforcing to the extent that the organism has been prevented from performing that behavior at its normal rate.

Response deprivation theory predicts that the opportunity to engage in any behavior that has fallen below the baseline level will be reinforcing. For instance, suppose a boy normally watches television for three or four hours each evening. This, then, is his baseline rate for this activity. Now suppose something disrupts this pattern of behavior. With television viewing reduced to, say, one hour, he is likely to engage in activities that provide access to television. If carrying out the garbage or performing other household chores earns him a chance to watch television, the frequency of such activities is likely to increase.

Query: According to response deprivation theory, school-

children are eager to go to recess because they have been

deprived of the opportunity to _____.

Response deprivation theory works well enough for many reinforcers, but like the theories of Hull and Premack, it has trouble explaining the reinforcing power of *yes*. Words such as *yes*, *right*, and *correct* can be powerfully reinforcing. Recall that when Thorndike provided such feedback to students attempting to draw a 4-inch line while blindfolded, they improved rapidly (Thorndike, 1927). How are we to fit such findings into response deprivation theory? Still, response deprivation theory provides an intriguing way of looking at the problem of reinforcement.

REVIEW   Many theorists have wondered what it is about reinforcers that makes them reinforcing. Hull proposed the drive-reduction theory, based on the idea that reinforcers reduce a drive caused by physiological deprivation. Premack's relative value theory discards the drive concept and argues that reinforcers are effective because they provide access to preferred kinds of behavior. The response deprivation theory of Timberlake and Allison suggests that reinforcement depends on the discrepancy between the baseline rate of a behavior and the present opportunity to perform the behavior.

The theories of reinforcement considered so far concentrate on positive reinforcement. Some researchers have focused their attention on explaining avoidance, and it is to these theories that we now turn.

Theories of Avoidance

In negative reinforcement, a behavior is strengthened when it is followed by the *removal* of a stimulus. This stimulus is an aversive event—that is, something the animal or person will normally escape or avoid, given the opportunity. Richard Solomon did research on negative reinforcement with shuttle boxes. In one study, Solomon and Lyman Wynne (1953) put a dog in one compartment of a shuttle box. After a time the light in the compartment went off, and 10 seconds later the dog received a shock through the floor. Typically the dog whimpered and moved about in an agitated manner for a time and then jumped over the hurdle to the second compartment. The light in this compartment was on, and there was no shock. Some time later the light went out and, 10 seconds later, the floor would again provide a shock. The dog again escaped the shock by jumping to the other compartment. With each trial the dog endured the shock for a shorter period before jumping. Soon it jumped the instant the shock began. Eventually the dog began jumping when the light went off and thereby avoided shock entirely. After once avoiding shock, most dogs received few additional shocks. As this study illustrates, negative reinforcement often starts out as escape and ends as avoidance. For this reason, negative reinforcement is sometimes referred to as **escape-avoidance learning**.

The same sort of experiment has been repeated many times with rats and other creatures, including (in modified form) humans, and the results are always the same.

The fact that an organism jumps a hurdle when shocked is not particularly puzzling: Escape from an aversive stimulus is reinforcing. But why does the organism perform an act that *avoids* shock? As Murray

Sidman (1989a) noted, "Successful avoidance meant that something—the shock—did not happen, but how could something that did not happen be a reinforcer?" (p. 191). After all, Sidman adds, things are not happening all the time! It seems illogical to say that things that do not happen can explain things that do happen, so explaining avoidance became a major theoretical problem. Two main accounts of avoidance have been offered: two-process theory and one-process theory.

Two-Process Theory

Two-process theory says that two kinds of learning experiences are involved in avoidance learning: Pavlovian and operant (Mowrer, 1947). Consider the dog that learns to jump a hurdle to escape a shock. A light goes off and shortly afterward the dog receives a shock. Soon after that the dog jumps over the hurdle to a shock-free compartment. Escaping shock is negatively reinforcing, so the dog soon jumps the hurdle as soon as the shock begins.

But wait: If the trials continue, the dog begins to jump the hurdle *before* it is shocked. It learns not only to escape shock but also to avoid it. Why? What reinforces jumping when there is no shock to escape?

This is where Pavlovian conditioning comes in. Recall that before the shock begins, a light goes out. Shock is a US for fear. Any stimulus that reliably precedes a US for fear becomes a CS for fear. So, through Pavlovian conditioning, the extinguished light becomes a CS for fear. The dog can escape this aversive stimulus (the dark chamber) by jumping the hurdle, and this is what it does. Thus, jumping *before* receiving a shock is reinforced by escape from the dark compartment.

According to two-process theory, then, there really is no such thing as avoidance, there is only escape: First the dog escapes the shock, and then it escapes the dark chamber.

Query: The two processes in two-process theory are

_____ and _____.

Two-process theory fits all the essential facts. In addition, the theory leads to logical predictions that can be tested. In one experiment, Neal Miller (1948) demonstrated that escape from an aversive situation can reinforce behavior. He put rats into a white compartment and shocked them. They soon learned to jump through a door to a neighboring black compartment where they did not receive shocks. Miller put the rats in the white compartment again, but this time he did *not* shock them. Once again the rats went to the black compartment, even though there

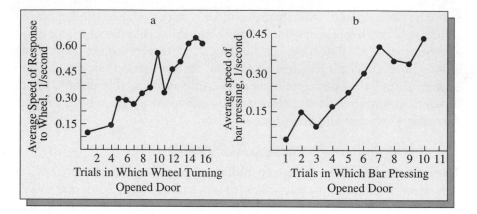

Figure 5-18 *Two-process theory and escape. After a white compartment was paired with shock, a rat learned to turn a wheel (a) and press a lever (b) when these acts enabled it to escape the compartment. (Adapted from Miller, 1948, Figures 2 and 4, pp. 94 and 96.)*

were no shocks to escape. The rats, it seems, were escaping from the white compartment. Miller put the rats into the white compartment again, but this time he closed the door. The rats could escape to the black compartment by turning a wheel that opened the door, and they soon learned to do so even though, once again, there were no shocks in the white compartment (see Figure 5-18a). Miller put the rats into the white compartment and again closed the door, but this time turning the wheel did nothing; to escape to the black compartment, the rats had to press a lever. The rats soon gave up on the wheel and learned to press the lever even though, as before, there were no shocks (see Figure 5-18b). These experiments suggest that pairing the white compartment with shock caused it to affect behavior in much the same way as the shock. Through association with shock, the white compartment had become a CS for fear, and escaping from it was reinforcing.

Unfortunately, not all tests of two-process theory have produced supportive evidence (Herrnstein, 1969). The idea that the avoidance behavior is reinforced by escape from an aversive CS leads logically to the prediction that if the CS were to lose its aversiveness, the avoidance behavior would cease to occur. There is evidence that the signal for shock does lose its aversiveness, yet the avoidance response persists!

Solomon and Wynne (1953; see description above) noticed that the dogs in their study showed considerable evidence of fear of the CS in the early stages of learning, but once they had learned to avoid shock, the CS no longer seemed to trouble them.

Leon Kamin and his colleagues (1963) conducted an experiment to see whether Solomon and Wynne were right. In their experiment, they first trained rats to press a lever for food. Then they trained the animals to escape shock in a shuttle box, with the shock preceded by a tone. Training continued until the rats had made from 1 to 27 consecutive escapes. Then the researchers returned the rats to the original training chamber where they could press a lever for food.

You will recall that an aversive CS will reduce the rate of ongoing behavior, a phenomenon called conditioned suppression (see Chapter 4). Kamin and his co-workers used conditioned suppression as a measure of the aversiveness of the sound that signaled shock. While the rats were in the chamber with the lever, the researchers sounded the tone to see whether it would suppress the rate of lever pressing. They found that the rats that had avoided shock 27 times showed less fear (i.e., conditioned suppression) than those that had avoided shock fewer times. This is consistent with what Solomon and Wynne noticed: Fear of the CS decreases as the animal learns to avoid shock. This finding poses a problem for two-process theory, for if the CS becomes less frightening as avoidance training continues, what reinforces the avoidance behavior?

A related problem for two-process theory has to do with the failure of avoidance behaviors to extinguish. Consider the rat that can avoid shock by jumping a hurdle when a tone sounds. As learning proceeds, the rat receives fewer and fewer shocks until finally it receives no shocks at all. When the rat avoids shocks, the tone and shock are no longer paired. This means that escaping the tone should become progressively less reinforcing. Two process theory therefore leads to the prediction that the avoidance behavior, once learned, will begin to extinguish: The rat will delay longer and longer before jumping the hurdle until it finally receives a shock. Thus, we should see a pattern of deteriorating avoidance behaviors followed by shock and escape. The predicted scenario is not, however, what happens. Instead, the animal steadily performs the avoidance behavior. Indeed, avoidance behaviors are remarkable for their persistence. Even after many trials without receiving a shock, the rat continues to jump the hurdle.

Two-process theory lost still more ground with Murray Sidman's research on what is now known as the **Sidman avoidance procedure** (Sidman, 1953, 1966). In this procedure, the shock is not preceded by a tone or other signal. A rat receives shocks at regular intervals through a grid floor, but it can delay the shocks for 15 seconds by pressing a lever. If it presses the lever again before the end of this delay period, it earns another 15-second delay. Thus, by pressing the lever regularly, the rat can completely avoid shock. The important aspect of the Sidman procedure is that there is no signal (no light going off, no tone sounding) correlated with impending shock.

Sidman found that not much happened at first: the rat received shocks periodically and, between shocks, it explored the chamber. But after several minutes, the rat began to press the lever and delay some shocks, and therefore received fewer shocks each minute. This was bad news for two-process theory because no signal means no aversive stimulus to escape, and escape from an aversive stimulus is what is supposed to reinforce avoidance behavior.

Douglas Anger (1963) proposed that there *is* a signal in the Sidman procedure: time. The shocks, said Anger, occur at regular intervals. The passage of time therefore signals the approach of shock. The animal does not escape the CS in the same way it might by jumping a hurdle, but it is allowed to get "further away" from the shocks—further away in terms of time, not distance.

Anger's proposal raised a new dilemma: How could one rule out the possibility that time became a CS in escape-avoidance situations? Richard Herrnstein and Phillip Hineline (1966) provided an elegant solution to this problem. In their experiment, rats had a choice: If they pressed a lever at a steady rate, they would receive shocks an average of once every 20 seconds; if they did not press the lever, they would receive shocks an average of about once every 7 seconds. Note that these shock intervals are merely averages: A rat might press the lever and get an immediate shock, or it might not press the lever and receive no shock for several seconds. Still, the rat was better off, in the long run, if it pressed the lever. What Herrnstein and Hineline had done was to render time useless as a possible signal for shock. According to two-process theory, no signal means no avoidance behavior, yet 17 of the 18 rats in the Herrnstein and Hineline experiment learned to press the lever and avoid shocks.

The problems with two-process theory have led many researches to embrace one-process theory.

One-Process Theory

One-process theory proposes that avoidance involves only one process: operant learning (Herrnstein, 1969; Sidman, 1962). Both escape and avoidance behaviors are reinforced by a reduction in aversive stimulation. Consider, once again, the dog in a shuttle box. A light goes off, and a few seconds later it receives a shock. Jumping a hurdle is reinforced by the termination of shock. So far, so good. But what is the reinforcer for avoiding shock? Two-process theorists said that the absence of shock could not reinforce behavior: How can something that does *not* happen be a reinforcer? But one-process theory says that something *does* happen: There is a reduction in exposure to shock, and this is reinforcing.

The Herrnstein and Hineline (1966) study described above supports one-process theory, and so do other experiments. But what about the extreme resistance of avoidance behaviors to extinction? Can one-process theory explain this? One-process theory says that the animal that has learned to avoid shocks by jumping a barrier continues to do so because by doing so it continues to avoid shock. If this is the case, one way to get the animal to stop jumping the hurdle would be to prevent it from jumping after you have disconnected the shock apparatus. The animal would try unsuccessfully to jump the hurdle, and—nothing would happen. No shock! After several such trials, when the animal is again free to jump the hurdle, it should decline to do so. And this is just what happens. In fact, the best way to get an animal (or person) to stop performing an unnecessary avoidance behavior is to prevent both the behavior and its aversive consequences from occurring.

One-process theory of avoidance has an elegant simplicity, but it cannot be said to have won the day. In 2001, a prestigious journal devoted a special section to an article making the case for two-factor theory (Dinsmoor, 2001) and to commentaries by other experts. The debate rages on.

REVIEW Avoidance learning has generated its own distinct theories. Two-process theory assumes that both Pavlovian and operant procedures are involved. One-process theory explains avoidance entirely in terms of operant procedures.

We have seen how important reinforcement is in understanding behavior; in the next chapter we turn our attention to punishment.

RECOMMENDED READING

1. Bjork, D. W. (1993). *B. F. Skinner: A life.* New York: Basic Books.

   As much an analysis of operant psychology as it is a biography, this book is both readable and scholarly.

2. Skinner, B. F. (1953). *Science and human behavior.* New York: Free Press.

   A classic theoretical work in operant behavior. See especially Chapters 5 and 6, which bear directly on the subject matter of the present chapter.

3. Skinner, B. F. (1981). Selection by consequences. *Science, 213,* 501–504.

   In this paper, Skinner develops the analogy between reinforcement and evolution first hinted at by Thorndike.

4. Sternberg, R. J. (1984). Operant analysis of problem solving: Answers to questions you probably don't want to ask. *Behavioral and Brain Sciences, 7,* 605.

   A well-known cognitive psychologist takes a look at the role of consequences in problem solving.

5. Thorndike, E. L. (1898). Animal intelligence. *Psychological Review Monographs, 2*(8).

   Although the methodology is primitive by today's standards, this is one of the seminal volumes in learning and, indeed, in all of behavior science.

REVIEW QUESTIONS

1. Define the following terms in your own words:

backward chaining	negative reinforcer
behavior chain	one-process theory
chaining	operant learning
conditioned reinforcer	positive reinforcement
discrete trial procedure	positive reinforcer
drive	Premack principle
drive-reduction theory	primary reinforcer
escape-avoidance learning	reinforcement
escape training	relative value theory
extinction	response deprivation theory
extinction burst	resurgence
forward chaining	reward training
free operant procedure	secondary reinforcer
generalized reinforcer	shaping
instrumental learning	Sidman avoidance procedure
law of effect	task analysis
negative reinforcement	two-process theory

2. Apply Thorndike's reasoning about animal anecdotes to anecdotes about other remarkable phenomena such as telepathy, astrology, and dreams that "predict" the future.

3. Thorndike objected to the term *"trial-and-error" learning.* Why do you suppose he did so?

4. One of Skinner's chief contributions to psychology is said to be the use of behavior rate as a dependent variable. How does this approach differ from Thorndike's studies of chicks running mazes?

5. How was the "Skinner box" an improvement over Thorndike's puzzle boxes?

6. Explain the difference between negative and positive reinforcement.

7. In the "experiment" in which Skinner turned on a light when his baby daughter moved her arm, did Skinner shape Deborah's arm movements or did Deborah shape Skinner's light switching?

8. What is the single most important difference between Pavlovian and operant learning?

9. A worker used to slip away from the plant every afternoon to hunt rabbits. When his employer found out, he gave the man a raise "as an incentive to work harder." What do you think of the employer's action?

10. Does the children's game, Hot and Cold, make use of shaping?

11. How could a Spanish instructor use shaping to teach a student to roll r's?

12. Describe the procedure you would use to train a dog to retrieve the morning newspaper from your front lawn.

13. How is chaining a form of shaping?

14. Some teachers object to the use of shaping and chaining in classroom instruction because the procedures have been used to train animals. How would you defend their use?

15. What is one characteristic that influences the reinforcing power of touch?

16. Why is the Premack principle sometimes called Grandmother's Rule?

17. Design an experiment to determine the optimum amount of food to use in training rats to perform a new behavior. Plot a hypothetical graph of the data you would expect to obtain.

18. What are the problems with the drive-reduction theory of reinforcement?

19. What is the chief difference between Premack's relative value theory and Timberlake and Allison's response deprivation theory?

20. How has your study of operant learning changed your views of human nature?

PRACTICE QUIZ

1. Reinforcement is the process of providing consequences for a behavior that _____ the behavior.

2. Thorndike's early research used a _____ trial procedure, whereas Skinner used a _____ operant procedure.

3. Secondary reinforcers are also called _____ reinforcers.

4. Shaping is the reinforcement of _____ of a desired behavior.

5. The first step in building a behavior chain is to do a _____ analysis.

6. Kennon Lattal found that he could not shape disk pecking in pigeons if the reinforcer was _____ .

7. The reappearance of previously effective behavior during extinction is called _____ .

8. According to David Premack, reinforcement involves a relation between two _____ .

9. According to _____ theory, an activity becomes reinforcing when the organism is prevented from engaging in it at the baseline rate.

10. The two processes of the two-process theory of avoidance are _____ and _____ .

QUERY ANSWERS

Page 136. Thorndike studied animal learning as a way of measuring animal *intelligence*.

Page 142. To reinforce a behavior is to provide *consequences* for the behavior that increase its *strength*.

Page 143. Positive and negative reinforcement have this in common: Both *strengthen* behavior.

Page 146. In the *discrete trial* procedure, the behavior ends the trial.

Page 148. The fact that Albert reached for the rat just before the loud noise occurred means that *operant* learning was involved.

Page 152. Shaping is the reinforcement of successive *approximations* of a desired behavior.

Page 156. Answers will vary. A typical chain might include picking up a toothbrush, dampening the brush under the spigot, putting toothpaste on it, moving the brush against the teeth, rinsing the mouth, rinsing the brush, and returning the brush to its container. Obviously, the chain could be extended considerably. *The Odd Couple*'s Felix Ungar would specify the precise manner in which each tooth is to be brushed.

Page 158. Put food in the goal box (the end of the maze), put the rat just outside the goal box, and release the rat. On the next trial, put the rat farther away from the goal box. Keep backing the rat up in this way until it is starting at the beginning.

Page 161. Weil wanted to separate the effects of *delay* of reinforcement and *number* of reinforcements.

Page 164. In general, the more you increase the amount of a reinforcer, the *less* benefit you get from the increase.

Page 175. According to the Premack principle, *high probability/likely* behavior reinforces *low probability/unlikely* behavior.

Page 177. According to response deprivation theory, schoolchildren are eager to go to recess because they have been deprived of the opportunity to *move about/exercise*.

Page 179. The two processes in two-process theory are *Pavlovian conditioning* and *operant learning*.

CHAPTER

6

Operant Punishment

Fear preserves you by a dread of punishment that never fails.

Machiavelli

Those who are feared, are hated.

Benjamin Franklin

Reinforcement is essential to our survival: We learn to do those things that have, in the past, led to food, water, shelter, reproduction, approval, and safety. But not all behavior has reinforcing consequences. Our survival and happiness also depend on our learning *not* to do things that have, in the past, threatened our well-being.

Most of the injurious events we experience are, to some extent at least, products of our behavior. We get an electric shock from a faulty toaster, but only if we touch the toaster. We hit our thumb with a hammer, but only if we swing the hammer incorrectly. We catch cold, but only if we consort with those who are sick.

Many of the slings and arrows that outrageous fortune throws our way come at the hands of other people. Even small children are sometimes shouted at, insulted, slapped—and much, much worse. A teacher once told me that when she reached out to touch some of her students, they would duck and raise an arm in front of their faces as if to fend off a blow. Apparently, the only time anyone at home ever reached toward these children was to hit them.

Some of those children will fare only slightly better in school than in their homes. The United States Education Department reports that children in American schools were paddled nearly 500,000 times in school year 1993–1994 (reported in Wilgoren, 2001).[1]

Of course, not all human interactions involve one person hurting another. Many parents would not dream of beating a child, and rear their children successfully by relying largely on smiles, praise, and other forms of positive reinforcement. Many teachers totally reject both sarcasm and the paddle, and instead praise good efforts and arrange their lessons so that all students can have some measure of success. Many employers provide recognition, awards, bonuses, raises, and promotions for a job well done. And most of us do not make a habit of beating up people when

---

[1]Surveys show that about 50% of Americans approve the use of corporal punishment in school (Gallup & Elam, 1988).

we disapprove of their behavior. But the use of aversive consequences to suppress unwanted behavior is a very common procedure, and we must come to terms with it.[2]

Basic Procedures

You will recall that the law of effect says behavior is a function of its consequences.[3] The previous chapter focused on reinforcement, the procedure of providing consequences that strengthen behavior. The present chapter will focus on **punishment**, the procedure of providing consequences that reduce the strength of behavior.[4]

Following Charles Catania's (1998; see Chapter 5) observations on reinforcement, we can say that a procedure must have three characteristics to qualify as punishment: First, a behavior must have a consequence. Second, the behavior must decrease in strength (e.g., occur less often). Third, the reduction in strength must be the result of the consequence.

The consequences involved in punishment are often referred to as **punishers**. Typical punishers include reprimands, fines, and physical blows, such as those delivered in a spanking. It is important to remember, however, that punishers (like reinforcers) are defined by their effects on behavior. If an event does not reduce the strength of the behavior it follows, that event is not a punisher and the procedure is not punishment.

There are two kinds of punishment (see Figure 6-1). In one, something is added to the situation. A dog that wanders onto a stranger's porch may, for example, be bitten by the dog that resides there. If the trespassing dog is less likely to visit that porch again, then the behavior has been punished. In this form of punishment, a behavior (B) results in something (S^P) being added to the situation, and this reduces the strength (frequency, persistence, etc.) of that behavior:

$$B \longrightarrow S^P$$
$$\text{step on porch} \longrightarrow \text{receive bite}$$

---

[2]So common is the use of punishment and negative reinforcement that Jack Michael (1991) concludes, pessimistically, "The world runs on fear" (p. 239).

[3]Thorndike's (1911) law of effect says, with respect to punishment, that behaviors "which are accompanied or closely followed by discomfort to the animal will, other things being equal, have their connections with that situation weakened, so that, when it recurs, they will be less likely to occur" (p. 244).

[4]The word *punishment*, as used by behavior scientists, has nothing to do with retribution or justice; it has to do with reducing the strength of a behavior. Because of this difference, the term confuses students and other innocent people. To avoid the confusion, various alternative terms have been suggested for *punisher* and *punishment*; most recently, Brown and Hendy (2001) propose *deselector* and *deselection*, respectively. Thus far, there has not been an outpouring of support for the new jargon.

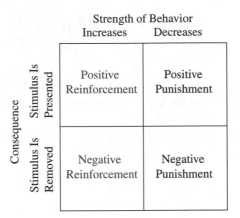

Figure 6-1　*Contingency square. In operant procedures, the strength of a behavior increases or decreases depending on its consequences.*

　　Similarly, if you go for a walk in the park and are mugged, you may be less likely to walk in that park in the future. If so, walking in that park has been punished. This type of punishment is sometimes called **positive punishment** because something (an aversive event) is *added* to the situation.[5]

　　In the second type of punishment, the consequence is that something is *subtracted* from the situation. A dog that is chewing on its master's shoe may come when its master calls. If the shoe is then taken away, the dog may be less inclined to answer its master's call the next time it has a shoe. Taking the shoe away punishes coming when called. In this form of punishment, a behavior results in something being removed from the situation and this reduces the strength of that behavior:

$$B \longrightarrow S^P$$
answer call $\longrightarrow$ shoe is taken away

　　People encounter this sort of punishment when they are made to pay a fine for speeding or when they are docked for damaging merchandise at work. In each case, their behavior results in something being taken away. Parents and teachers use this sort of punishment when they take away privileges, such as eating dessert, watching television, playing a game, or using a computer. This kind of punishment is sometimes called **negative punishment** or **penalty training** (Woods, 1974).

---

[5]Positive punishment necessarily involves aversives.

Aversive Confusion: Positive Punishment and Negative Reinforcement Compared

Positive punishment and negative reinforcement are often confused. This is partly because both procedures involve aversive events such as shocks, spankings, pinches, and criticism.

To reinforce is to strengthen, so any reinforcement procedure, positive or negative, makes behavior more likely to occur. Thus, negative reinforcement means strengthening behavior by *removing* an aversive.

To punish is to weaken behavior, so any punishment procedure, positive or negative, makes behavior less likely to occur. Thus, positive punishment means weakening behavior by *adding* an aversive.

Consider a typical example of negative reinforcement: A rat is in an experimental chamber. The floor of the chamber delivers a mild, constant shock to the rat's feet. If the rat presses a lever, the shock ceases for five seconds. In other words, the consequence of pressing the lever is the *removal* of shock. As a result, the rate of lever pressing *increases*. Lever pressing has been negatively reinforced by the removal of shock.

Now consider a typical example of punishment: A rat is in an experimental chamber. It has previously learned to obtain food by pressing a lever. It goes to the lever and presses it—and receives a brief shock to its feet. It presses the lever again and receives another shock. The consequence of pressing the lever is *delivery* of a shock. As a result, the rate of lever pressing decreases. Lever pressing has been punished by the delivery of shock.

Positive punishment and negative reinforcement are, most people agree, very unfortunate terms because they are confusing. But we are stuck with them for the present. To keep the concepts straight, remember that both use aversives, but one adds them and the other takes them away. The key is to remember that positive means add, and negative means subtract. Then it all adds up.

Query: Positive and negative punishment are similar in that

both _____ a behavior.

The terms *positive* and *negative punishment* are at least as troublesome to students as the terms *positive* and *negative reinforcement*. How can punishment be positive? As in the case of reinforcement, the terms positive and negative refer to the procedure, not the nature of the stimulus involved. If something is added to a situation, we speak of positive punishment; if something is removed, we speak of negative punishment. The two variations of punishment have also been called type 1 and type 2 punishment, respectively.

> **Query:** In positive punishment, something is _____;
>
> in negative punishment, something is _____.

Students typically have a good deal of difficulty keeping the various kinds of operant procedures straight. They are especially likely to confuse positive punishment with negative reinforcement (see Aversive Confusion). Because of these and other problems, some authorities have argued for a revision of the terminology (Kimble, 1993; Michael, 1975). Unfortunately, the terms are embedded in the field and must be learned.

> **Query:** Negative reinforcement _____ the strength
>
> of a behavior; positive punishment _____ it.

REVIEW Punishment in everyday use means retribution, but to learning researchers it means the procedure of providing consequences that reduce the strength of behavior. There are two forms of punishment: positive and negative. In the first, something is added after a behavior; in the second, something is removed.

Variables Affecting Punishment

Punishment, like reinforcement, is basically a simple procedure. However, the effects of the procedure depend on the complex interactions of many variables. Many of the same variables that are important in reinforcement are also important in punishment.

Contingency

Punishment involves making an event contingent on a particular behavior. The degree to which the procedure weakens a behavior (e.g., reduces its frequency) varies with the degree to which a punishing event is correlated with that behavior. If a rat receives a shock each time it

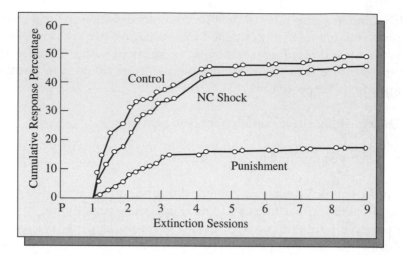

Figure 6-2 *Contingency and punishment. Cumulative record of the median number of responses (as a percentage of responses before punishment) following no shocks (control), noncontingent shocks, and response-contingent shocks (punishment). (Adapted from "Permanent Effects of Punishment During Extinction," by E. E. Boe and R. M. Church, 1967, Journal of Comparative and Physiological Psychology, 63, pp. 486–492. Copyright © 1967 by the American Psychological Association. Reprinted by permission.)*

presses a lever, *but not otherwise,* then there is a clear contingency between lever pressing and shock. If, on the other hand, lever pressing and shock delivery are independent of one another, there is no contingency. The greater the degree of contingency between a behavior and a punishing event, the faster behavior changes.

An experiment by Erling Boe and Russel Church (1967) will illustrate. After first training rats to press a lever for food, Boe and Church put lever pressing on extinction for 20 minutes. During 15 minutes of this period, some rats received shocks occasionally, regardless of what they did; other rats received shocks, but only when they pressed the lever; and the remaining rats (the control group) never received shocks. After this, all the rats underwent an hour-long extinction session each day for the next nine days; none of the rats received shocks during any of these sessions. The result was that the amount of lever pressing during extinction varied with exposure to shock (see Figure 6-2). Rats that had never been shocked showed a gradual decline in the rate of lever pressing, as is expected during extinction. The performance of rats that had received noncontingent shocks was almost identical to that of rats that received no shocks. But rats that had received shocks only when they pressed the lever showed a marked reduction in lever pressing during extinction. Thus, the greater the contingency between a behavior and a punisher, the greater the suppression of the behavior.[6]

Contiguity

The interval between a behavior and a punishing consequence has a powerful effect on the rate of operant learning. The longer the delay the less effective is the procedure.

The importance of contiguity is nicely illustrated in an experiment by David Camp and his colleagues (1967). In this experiment, rats periodically received food for pressing a lever. They also sometimes received shocks for lever pressing. For some rats, the shocks came immediately after pressing the lever; for others, the shocks were delayed by 2 seconds; and for still other rats there was a delay of 30 seconds between lever presses and shock. The researchers measured the effectiveness of shock in terms of a suppression ratio—basically the percentage of the responses that would have been expected without shocks. The results showed that immediate shocks suppressed lever pressing very effectively. When shocks followed lever presses by 2 seconds, they were far less effective in suppressing the behavior; a shock delayed by 30 seconds had even less value (see Figure 6-3).

The importance of contiguity in punishment has also been demonstrated in experiments with people. In one study, Ann Abramowitz and Susan O'Leary (1990) studied the effects of immediate and delayed reprimands on the "off-task" behavior of hyperactive first- and second-graders. (Being off-task means doing things other than the assigned work.) In this study, teachers reprimanded the students either immediately or two minutes after the off-task behavior had begun. Reprimands were effective in suppressing forms of off-task behavior in which the child interacted with another student, but only the immediate reprimands got results; delayed reprimands were useless.

Perhaps delays reduce the effectiveness of punishment because during the delay interval, other behaviors are bound to occur, and these

---

[6]There is evidence that inconsistent punishment can sometimes be effective if the probability of a punishing consequence is made very high and is then *gradually* reduced (Lerman et al., 1997). As a practical matter, however, the rule is this: If you are going to use punishment, make it highly likely that the behavior will result in a punishing consequence.

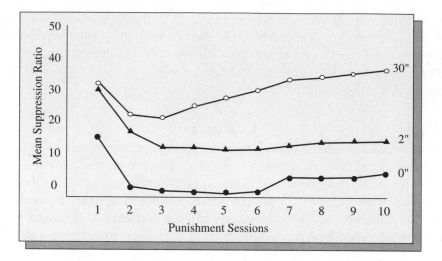

Figure 6-3 *Contiguity and punishment. Average suppression ratios for rats receiving response-contingent shocks that were immediate or delayed 2 or 30 seconds. The lower the suppression ratio, the more effective the procedure. (From "Temporal Relationship Between Response and Punishment," by D. S. Camp, G. A. Raymond, and R. M. Church, 1967,* Journal of Experimental Psychology, *74, Figure 3, p. 119. Copyright © 1967 by the American Psychological Association. Adapted with permission.)*

may be suppressed rather than the intended behavior. Thus, a delayed punisher may suppress the same amount of behavior, but it may suppress several different behaviors slightly. Immediate punishment is more likely to act on the intended behavior. In any case, the rule of thumb is clear: For maximum effect, punish behavior immediately.

Unfortunately, outside the laboratory this rule is known more for its violation than for its observance. A mother on a shopping trip tells her mischievous child, "Just wait 'til we get home." Such threats are normally not very effective because the threatened punishment comes (if at all) long after the offense. Teachers make the same error when they tell a youngster at nine o'clock in the morning that she will have to stay after school at the end of the day—five hours later. It also seems likely that one reason our criminal justice system is ineffective is the delay between the commission of a crime and its eventual punishment. A thief who is caught "red-handed" may be out on bail going about his business (including stealing property) for months before his case comes to trial. Those who would use punishment effectively must find ways of reducing the gap between the deed and the consequence.

Punisher Intensity

The strength of the punisher is an important factor in its effects on behavior. Very mild punishers have little effect. In one early study, for example, B. F. Skinner (1938) trained rats to press a lever for food, and then put the behavior on extinction. During the first 10 minutes of extinction, some rats received a "slap" from the lever each time they pressed it. When Skinner compared the cumulative records of these rats, he found that punishment markedly reduced the rate of lever pressing, but the rate increased quickly once punishment ended. The end result was that punished rats pressed the lever about as often as those that were not punished.

Similarly, Thorndike (1932) presented college students with Spanish words or uncommon English words and asked them to choose a synonym from an array of five alternatives. If they guessed correctly, the experimenter said, "Right;" if incorrectly, the experimenter said, "Wrong." Thorndike then looked at the tendency of students to repeat right and wrong answers. He found that "Right" increased the tendency to repeat an answer, but "Wrong" did not decrease it.

As a result of these and other experiments, Thorndike and Skinner concluded that punishment has little effect and that effect is only temporary. This conclusion proved to be false. The punishers Thorndike and Skinner used were very weak; studies with stronger punishers got much better results.

Several studies have shown a clear relationship between the intensity of a punisher and its effects. This relationship is perhaps best seen in the use of electric shock because the gradations of shock can be controlled precisely. In one experiment, Camp and his colleagues (1967) trained rats to press a lever for food and then periodically punished lever pressing. During the punishment sessions, lever pressing continued to be reinforced. Punishment consisted of very brief shocks that varied in intensity. The result was that the mildest shock had little effect, compared to a no-shock control group, but the strongest shock essentially brought lever pressing to a halt (see Figure 6-4).

Query: Figure 6-4 shows that the more _____

a punisher, the more it _____ the rate of a

behavior.

After reviewing research on this problem, Nathan Azrin and W. C. Holz (1966) concluded, "All studies of the intensity of punishment have

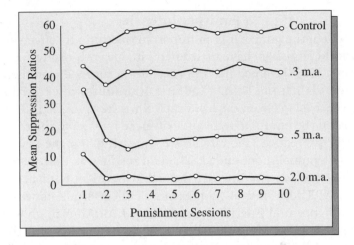

Figure 6-4 *Punisher intensity. Average suppression ratios for rats receiving no shocks (control) or occasional response-contingent shocks of three intensities. The lower the suppression ratio, the more effective the procedure. (From "Temporal Relationship Between Response and Punishment," by D. S. Camp, G. A. Raymond, and R. M. Church, 1967,* Journal of Experimental Psychology, 74, *Figure 1, p. 117. Copyright © 1967 by the American Psychological Association. Adapted with permission.)*

found that the greater the intensity of the punishing stimulus, the greater is the reduction of the punished responses" (p. 396). That conclusion still stands today.[7]

Introductory Level of Punishment

In selecting a level of punishment, one may begin with a strong punisher that is almost certain to suppress the behavior, or one may begin with a weak punisher and gradually increase its intensity until an effective level is found. Azrin and Holz (1966) argue that using an effective level of punishment from the very beginning is extremely important.

The problem in beginning with a weak punisher and gradually increasing its intensity is that the punished behavior will tend to persist during these increases. In the end, a far greater level of punisher may be required to suppress the behavior. Neal Miller (1960) demonstrated this in a study with rats. He first exposed rats to very weak electric shock

---

[7]In the previous chapter, we noted that the amount of reinforcement is generally less important than the frequency of reinforcement. It is generally better to reinforce a behavior 10 times with a small amount of food, for example, than to reinforce the behavior once with a large amount of food. The opposite seems to be true for punishment. Small, frequent doses of punishment may soon have no effect, whereas a single large dose often has a pronounced effect.

when they entered an alley, then gradually increased the intensity of shock. The result was that the rats eventually endured levels of shock that would have suppressed their behavior had such shocks been received at the outset. Similarly, Jules Masserman (1946) found that cats would continue to respond despite strong levels of punishment if the punisher was initially weak and gradually increased. A punisher that might have suppressed a behavior entirely had it been used at the beginning became ineffective when a series of weaker punishers was used first. It follows that if punishment is to be used, one must begin with a punisher that is intense enough to suppress the behavior dramatically.

This point is by no means obvious. It is common practice for parents, teachers, and judges to attempt to punish a behavior with a very mild consequence and then, if the result is not satisfactory, gradually increase the level of punishment. A parent may give a child a stern look at a first offense, reprimand him after a second offense, shout at a third offense, slap him after the fourth offense, and paddle him after the fifth offense. Judges often do essentially the same thing. A person convicted of drunk driving may get off with a warning on the first offense, pay a small fine for a second offense, have his license suspended for a few months for a third offense, and so on. It is as if we were trying to increase the person's tolerance for successively higher levels of punishment. In any case, that is all too often the result.

Reinforcement of the Punished Behavior

In considering punishment, remember that the behavior concerned is maintained by reinforcement. If this were not the case, the behavior would probably not occur, or would occur very infrequently. It follows that the effectiveness of a punishment procedure depends on the frequency, amount, and quality of *reinforcement* the behavior produces.

Consider a pigeon pecking a disk for food. If pecking ceases to produce food, pecking will sooner or later fall off. Similarly, an employee who frequently leaves work early does so because there are more rewarding things to do than stay at work. The success of efforts to punish behavior will depend, then, not just on the punishing consequences the behavior has but also on its reinforcing consequences. Experiments have shown that if behavior produces reinforcement, it may persist despite aversive consequences (Azrin & Holz, 1961; Camp et al., 1967).

In one study, Phil Reed and Toshihiko Yoshino (2001) used a noise to punish lever pressing in rats. When lever pressing was likely to produce food, rats pressed the lever even though doing so also caused a loud noise; when lever pressing did not "pay" so well, even a half-second tone reduced lever pressing.

Abnormal behavior in people frequently persists despite punishment efforts because the behavior produces reinforcers as well as punishers. David Rosenhan (1973) and his students got themselves admitted as patients in psychiatric hospitals and observed what went on there. One thing they noticed was that most of the time staff members ignored normal behavior. Often the only way a patient could get the staff to interact with him at all was by creating a disturbance—shouting, fighting, throwing things. Such behavior usually resulted in harsh treatment. A patient might be wrestled to the floor and put in restraints, for example, or he might be put in isolation. To engage in behavior that produces such unpleasant consequences might seem very bizarre, but it may be that the behavior produced reinforcers (attention) as well as punishers.

Alternative Sources of Reinforcement

A related factor in the effectiveness of a punishment procedure is the availability of alternative ways of obtaining reinforcement. Consider a hungry rat that receives food when it presses a lever. Now suppose we begin shocking the rat when it presses the lever. You can see that if the lever is the rat's only means of obtaining food, it is likely to continue pressing despite the shocks. On the other hand, if the rat has another way of obtaining food, the shocks will likely suppress lever pressing.

In a study by Herman and Azrin (1964), male psychiatric patients continued to perform a behavior that periodically produced reinforcers, even though the behavior also produced a loud, annoying sound. However, when the patients were given an alternative way of obtaining reinforcers (one that did not produce noise), they elected to do that. In other words, punishment completely suppressed the original behavior when there was an alternative means of obtaining reinforcement (see Figure 6-5).

This finding has an obvious implication for the practical use of punishment: When punishing an unwanted behavior, be sure to provide an alternative means of obtaining the reinforcers that maintained the undesirable behavior. For instance, if a child receives adult attention by playing with his food at the dinner table, make sure that he can obtain attention in more acceptable ways.

Deprivation Level

A factor that is closely related to the reinforcement of the punished behavior is the level of deprivation. A rat that receives both shocks and food when it presses a lever may press the lever steadily if it is very hungry; however, the rat may not press the lever at all if it has recently eaten. In one study, Azrin and others (1963) compared the effects of pun-

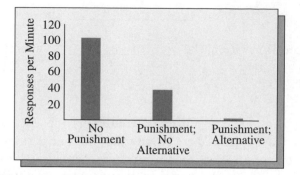

Figure 6-5 *Punishment and alternative source of reinforcement. Average number of responses per minute when the response was periodically reinforced, but never punished; when it was punished but there was no alternative means of obtaining reinforcement; and when it was punished but there was an alternative means of obtaining reinforcement. (Compiled from data in Herman and Azrin, 1964.)*

ishment on disk pecking when birds were under different levels of food deprivation. Punishment had little effect when the birds were very hungry, but it suppressed disk pecking almost completely when the birds were only slightly hungry (see Figure 6-6).

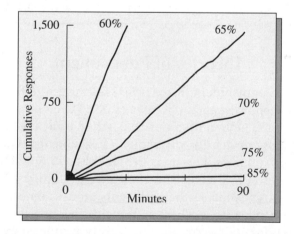

Figure 6-6 *Reinforcer deprivation and effects of punishment. Rate of behavior of bird 76 at various levels of food deprivation. Responses were periodically reinforced with food; every 100th response produced a strong shock. At the lowest level of food deprivation (85% of free-feeding weight), punishment was very effective; at higher levels of deprivation, it was less effective. (From "Fixed-Ratio Punishment," by N. H. Azrin et al., 1963,* Journal of the Experimental Analysis of Behavior, 6[3], *p. 146. Copyright © 1963 by the Society for the Experimental Analysis of Behavior, Inc. Reprinted with permission of the publisher and author.)*

Query: In general, the _____ the level of

reinforcer deprivation, the _____ effective a

punisher is.

Other Variables

The variables just reviewed are among the most important in determining the effectiveness of punishment, but other variables play a role. Qualitative features of the punisher, for example, will influence the effects of a punishment procedure. A high-pitched sound, for instance, may be a more effective punisher than a low-pitched sound. Punishment, like reinforcement, is more complicated than it appears on first inspection.

Query: Name four variables affecting punishment.

REVIEW   Although punishment is basically a simple procedure, it is complicated by the many variables that affect it. These include contingency, contiguity, punisher intensity, the introductory level of punishment, the availability of reinforcement for the punished behavior and for alternative behaviors, and the level of deprivation, among other things.

Theories of Punishment

Early theories of punishment (Estes, 1944; Guthrie, 1960; Skinner, 1953) proposed that response suppression was due to the disruptive effects of aversive stimuli. They pointed out that when a rat is shocked it may jump, then freeze or run hurriedly about. This behavior is clearly incompatible with, say, pressing a lever, so the rate of lever pressing is bound to decline. Skinner (1953) gives the example of a child who giggles in church. If the parent pinches the child, this arouses emotional behavior that is incompatible with giggling, so the giggling stops or declines. The punished behavior, said Skinner, "is merely temporarily suppressed, more or less effectively, by an emotional reaction" (p. 188).

Research on punishment undermined this explanation by producing two key findings: First, as we have seen, the effects of punishment are not as transient as Skinner thought if sufficiently strong aversives are used. Second, punishment has a greater suppressive effect on behavior than does aversive stimulation that is independent of behavior. This last point takes a bit of explaining.

If punishment reduces behavior rates merely because it arouses incompatible behavior, then it should make no difference whether the aversive stimuli used are contingent on behavior. But in fact it makes a great deal of difference. Recall the study by Boe and Church (1967), described earlier, in which some rats received noncontingent shocks. The experimenters also ran a group of rats that received occasional shocks, but in this group the shocks were contingent on lever pressing. Thus, some rats received shocks contingent on lever pressing, others received the same number of shocks independent of their behavior, and a control group received no shocks at all. As noted earlier, the noncontingent shocks did suppress lever pressing, but this effect was nothing compared to that of contingent shocks (see Figure 6-2).

The disruption theory of punishment could not explain this discrepancy between contingent and noncontingent aversives. Today, the two leading theories are the two-process and one-process theories we encountered in considering avoidance learning.

Two-Process Theory

Two-process theory says that punishment involves both Pavlovian and operant procedures (Dinsmoor, 1954, 1955; Mowrer, 1947). The theory is applied to punishment in much the same way it is applied to avoidance (see Chapter 5). If a rat presses a lever and receives a shock, the lever is paired with the shock. Through Pavlovian conditioning, the lever then becomes a CS for the same behavior aroused by the shock, including fear. Put another way, if shock is aversive, then the lever becomes aversive. The rat may escape the lever by moving away from it. Moving away from the lever is reinforced by a reduction of fear. Of course, moving away from the lever necessarily reduces the rate of lever pressing.

Critics of the two-process theory charge that the theory has all the flaws when applied to punishment as it does when explaining avoidance. For instance, the theory predicts that punishment would reduce responding in proportion to its proximity to the punished behavior. A rat that has been shocked when it pressed a lever should be less inclined to press the lever than to touch it, less inclined to touch it than to stand near it, less inclined to stand near it than to approach it, and so on. But this may not be the case.

In one study, R. Mansfield and Howard Rachlin (1970) trained pigeons to peck two disks for food. The birds received food only if they pecked both disks in the proper sequence, first the right disk, then the left. Next the experimenters began shocking the birds each time they pecked the disks in the proper, right-left, sequence. They began with mild shocks and each day increased their intensity. They reasoned that if the two-process theory were correct, at some point the birds would peck the right disk, but not the left. The right disk, being further removed from punishment, would be less aversive than the left and therefore would be more likely to be pecked. It is as if a student were punished for calling out answers instead of waiting to be called on by the teacher. After being punished, he might *start* to call out an answer, and "catch himself." Similarly, the birds might start the key peck sequence, but catch themselves and stop. It turned out, however, that behavior rates on the two keys declined together. If the birds pecked the right disk, they nearly always went on to peck the left. Because of such findings, the two-process theory has lost ground to the one-process theory of punishment.

Query: The two processes of the two-process theory are

_____ and _____ .

One-Process Theory

The one-process theory of punishment is similar to the one-process theory of avoidance (see Chapter 5). It says that only one process, operant learning, is involved. Punishment, this theory argues, weakens behavior in the same manner that reinforcement strengthens it.

The idea goes back to Thorndike (1911), who originally thought that punishment was the mirror image of reinforcement. He later abandoned the idea when he found that mild punishment (such as saying, "wrong" after an answer) did not reduce the likelihood that the behavior would occur (Thorndike, 1932). Other researchers later showed, however, that Thorndike's punishers were just too weak to be effective, and that stronger punishers produced effects parallel to reinforcement (Azrin & Holz, 1966; Premack, 1971; Rachlin & Herrnstein, 1969).

There is other evidence in favor of the one-process theory. As you know, the Premack principle states that high probability behavior reinforces low probability behavior. If the one-process theory is correct, then the opposite of Premack's reinforcement rule should apply to punishment: Low probability behavior should punish high probability behavior (Premack, 1971). This is, in fact, what happens (Mazur, 1975). If, for example, a hungry rat is made to run following eating, it will eat less. The low probability behavior (running) suppresses the high probability behavior (eating). One-process theorists conclude that Thorndike was right in the first place: punishment and reinforcement have essentially symmetrical effects on behavior.

REVIEW   The main attempts to explain how punishment works are two-process theory, which relies on Pavlovian and operant procedures, and one-process theory, which accounts for punishment entirely in terms of operant procedures.

Reinforcement and punishment show a certain symmetry, but this does not mean that they are equally desirable ways of changing behavior. Indeed, punishment leaves much to be desired as an agent of change. It works, but it can also create problems.

Problems with Punishment

One reason that punishment is so widely used is that it is effective—at least in the short run. In other words, we use punishment because doing so is reinforcing. Sometimes the reinforcement is positive, as when a teacher is praised by a principal for "running a tight ship." Sometimes the reinforcement is negative, as when we escape criticism by rebuking our critics.

Punishment is a very powerful procedure. If the punisher regularly follows a behavior and is delivered immediately in sufficient strength from the outset, it typically produces a very rapid and substantial reduction in the punished behavior. If reinforcement of the unwanted behavior is discontinued and an alternative way of providing the same reinforcer is provided, the punished behavior may entirely disappear.

Punishment is also fast; there is no need to continue the practice for days or weeks to determine whether it will work. If a given consequence is going to reduce the frequency of a behavior, it will begin to do so immediately. Proper use of punishment can also produce a permanent suppression of the behavior, which is especially important if the behavior is potentially injurious.

And punishment has beneficial side effects. In a review of studies using shock in the treatment of autistic children, K. L. Lichstein and Laura Schreibman (1976) found that the children became more sociable, more cooperative, more affectionate, more likely to make eye contact, and more likely to smile. They actually seemed happier after their aberrant behavior was suppressed with punishment.

Unfortunately, there are certain potential problems with punishment of which everyone should be aware (Sidman, 1989b). They include escape, aggression, apathy, abuse, and imitation of the punisher.

Escape

A typical (and quite sensible) reaction to punishment is to try to escape it. The child struggles to free himself from the parent who is spanking him; the failing student plays hooky from school; the employee who has botched an assignment "hides out" until the boss has cooled down.

Sometimes it is possible to escape without actually fleeing. In one study, a rat received both food and shock when it pressed a lever (Azrin & Holz, 1966). The shock came through a grid floor, and the rat learned to lie on its back and press the lever while upside down. Presumably the rat's fur insulated it somewhat from the shocks. Murray Sidman (1989b) notes that we humans often escape punishment by "tuning out." We "close our ears," for example, to a spouse, parent, or employer who repeatedly criticizes our work.

We can also escape or avoid punishment by cheating and lying. The student who did not do his homework escapes punishment by copying someone else's work or by saying "The dog ate it." Making excuses, fawning, crying, and showing remorse are other tactics that are often reinforced by escape from or avoidance of punishment.[8] Indeed, one common result of frequent punishment is that people become quite good at these escape tactics.

The "ultimate escape," as Sidman (1989b) terms it, is suicide. Prisoners under torture will sometimes kill themselves to escape the pain. People who live in abusive relationships or who are victims of harassment by government sometimes escape these situations by removing themselves irrevocably from them. Suicide is an extreme measure to take, and better options are almost always available, but it illustrates the efforts to which people will sometimes go to escape or avoid punishment.

Aggression

An alternative to escaping punishment is to attack those who punish. We criticize our critics, disparage those who disparage us, and answer each blow in kind. Aggression is particularly likely when escape is impossible. Like escape, aggression is often an effective way of exerting control over those who punish.

An employee who is routinely badgered on the job or a student who is bullied and humiliated at school may retaliate with aggression. Unfortunately, both kinds of events have become all too common in the United

---

[8]This tendency is readily seen in our judicial system. Judges and juries often award milder penalties when the offender shows "genuine remorse." The message is plain: If you are convicted of an offense, be sure to say you feel terrible about it.

States.[9] Even more common are milder forms of aggression. Employees who are mistreated often steal materials, sabotage products, or deliberately slow production rates. Students who are miserable in school and cannot withdraw may vandalize school property or assault teachers. Religious and ethnic groups attack those who have injured them, and those they attack reply in kind. When terrorists killed thousands of people in the attacks of September 11, 2001, there were calls for retaliation to "get even." In some cases, such as the dispute between Catholics and Protestants in Northern Ireland, the attempt to "get even" goes on for generations.

The aggression is not always directed at the source of injury. If two animals are put into the same chamber and one of them is shocked, the shocked animal will attack its neighbor (Ulrich & Azrin, 1962; Ulrich et al., 1965). This is so even though the other animal had nothing to do with the attacker's pain. Shocked animals will even attack much larger neighbors: A mouse will attack a rat, a rat will attack a cat. If no other animal is available, shocked animals will attack inanimate objects. If no suitable object is available, a rat will work to obtain an object to bite (Azrin et al., 1965).

We can see much the same phenomenon in people. A familiar example suggests the way aggression sometimes "progresses" through a family: A husband strikes his wife, the wife strikes a child, the child strikes a younger sibling, the sibling strikes the family dog. Humans, like animals, will also attack inanimate objects if no living creature is handy: Most of us have thrown an object or slammed a door after being insulted.

People, unlike other animals, often try to make their aggression against innocent parties seem rational. The British philosopher and mathematician Bertrand Russell reports that while a lad in school he saw one of his classmates beating a younger boy. When he reproached the bully, the latter replied, "The Bigs beat on me, so I beat the babies. That's fair." Of course, there is nothing fair about it. The boy has at least recognized, however, that the beating he gives is in some way connected to the beating he receives.

Apathy

A third problem with punishment, particularly when escape and aggression are not possible, is a general suppression of behavior. If aversives are a common consequence of many kinds of behavior, the result may be a

---

[9] When an employee or a student shoots those who have antagonized him or her, people often explain the behavior by saying the person "just snapped." This is another of those useless pseudoexplanations: The precise meaning of "snapped" is never offered, and the only evidence to support it is the very behavior it is supposed to explain.

suppression not only of the punished behavior, but of behavior in general. A kind of malaise, or apathy, is a by-product of situations in which punishment is commonplace. Unless strong positive reinforcers provide a counterweight to punishment, the best thing to do may be nothing.

When Carl Warden and Mercy Aylesworth (1927) punished rats for entering one of two passageways, they found that the rats tended to avoid entering either. Instead, they stayed in the release chamber. We may see a similar phenomenon in the classroom when a teacher regularly ridicules children for asking "stupid" questions. Those children not only become less likely to ask questions, they may be reluctant to answer questions or participate in other classroom activities.

Abuse

Another difficulty with punishment, especially physical punishment, is the potential for abuse by the punisher. The use of corporal punishment in schools has resulted in broken bones, ruptured blood vessels, hematomas, muscle and nerve damage, whiplash, spinal injuries, and even death (Gursky, 1992). Child abuse in the home is often punishment that got out of hand. A parent slaps a child harder than intended and breaks a jaw, boxes the child's ears and breaks an ear drum, shakes a crying baby and causes brain damage. Sometimes parents inadvertently reinforce more and more objectionable behavior (see Chapter 5) and then resort to extreme forms of punishment to suppress it. Parents sometimes begin with a very mild form of punishment and gradually use stronger and stronger consequences. Eventually they may find themselves using forms of punishment that cause bodily injury.

Imitation of the Punisher

Another problem with punishment is the use of punishment by the punished. When parents rely heavily on punishment in rearing their children, for example, the children rely heavily on punishment in dealing with siblings and peers (Bandura & Walters, 1959; Sears et al., 1957). As they become spouse, friend, co-worker, and parent, they use punishment to deal with the troublesome behavior of others. Similarly, the boss who relies on punishment to keep his managers "in line" may find that those managers use similar methods in dealing with their subordinates.

Because of the problems with punishment, its use raises ethical questions. Is it right, for example, to paddle children who misbehave? Questions of this sort are not, of course, scientific questions. The science of behavior can demonstrate that punishment can be used effectively. It can even demonstrate that punishment can alleviate suffering (see Chapter 7). But science cannot tell us whether what *can* be done *should* be done. The use of punishment inevitably proves to be controversial.

Of course, not all forms of punishment are equally troublesome. There is a great deal of difference between hitting a child in the head with your hand and denying the child television viewing privileges. Note also that *when properly used,* punishment can have very beneficial effects. It not only reduces the frequency of the punished behavior but often has positive side effects. Autistic and retarded people who repeatedly injure themselves, for example, often become more outgoing and seem happier after the self-injurious behavior has been suppressed with punishment. After reviewing the literature on this issue, Saul Axelrod (1983) wrote that "the vast majority of studies have reported positive side effects" (p. 8; see also Newsom et al., 1983; Van Houten, 1983). Nevertheless, the potential for problems exists, particularly when physical punishment is involved, and experts seem increasingly inclined to rely on other procedures.

Query: Name five problems with punishment.

REVIEW   Although punishment is often very effective in reducing the frequency of a behavior, it often gives rise to certain problems, including escape, aggression, apathy, abuse, and imitation. Because of these and other problems, it is wise to consider alternatives to punishment.

Alternatives to Punishment

Because of the problems with punishment, clinical researchers have sought alternative ways of modifying troublesome behavior (Lavigna & Donnellan, 1986). The simplest of these is response prevention.

Response Prevention

One alternative to punishment is to prevent the behavior from occurring by altering the environment in some way, a procedure called **response prevention.** Instead of punishing a child for playing with the family's precious china, we might put the china out of reach. A telephone lock may curb a child's tendency to make telephone calls to people on the other side of the globe. Poisons and firearms can be put under lock and key. A child who bites his hands may be made to wear boxing gloves.

Response prevention is often the simplest and fastest means of reducing unwanted behavior, especially in young children. Unfortunately, it has its limitations. The child who bites his hands may be made to wear boxing gloves, but this effectively gives the child a severe disability. (It is impossible to feed oneself or use the bathroom while wearing boxing gloves.) Response prevention techniques that work well with young children do not always work well with teens or adults; they may pick the telephone lock or remove the hinges on the cabinet where drugs or firearms are kept. Moreover, some forms of behavior cannot be prevented by modifying the physical environment. Young children, in an effort to manipulate a parent, will sometimes hold their breath until they turn blue. It is not clear how a parent could change the child's physical environment so as to prevent this from occurring. Because of these limitations of response prevention, other tactics are sometimes necessary. One safe procedure that often works is extinction.

Extinction

We saw in Chapter 5 that withholding all reinforcement for a given behavior will reduce the frequency of that behavior. Using extinction to get rid of unwanted behavior requires first of all identifying the reinforcers that maintain it. For example, adult attention is frequently the reinforcer that maintains misbehavior in children (Azerrad & Chance, 2001; Hart, et al., 1964). Some parents make a big fuss over the child who wets his bed and express concern over the child's health. Similarly, teachers tell wandering students to return to their seats, perhaps lecturing them or explaining why roaming about is wrong. Studies have shown that such attention, though intended to punish behavior, often reinforces it. Research by K. Daniel O'Leary and his colleagues (O'Leary & Becker, 1968–1969; O'Leary et al., 1970) showed, for example, that when school children were reprimanded loudly for misbehaving, their behavior got worse, not better. In other words, loud reprimands, although intended to punish a behavior, actually reinforced it.

Adult attention is not, of course, the only reinforcer that can maintain unwanted behavior. The principle, however, is the same: If the reinforcer maintaining unwanted behavior can be identified and removed, the rate of that behavior will decline. Thus, extinction is sometimes an attractive alternative to punishment. It is not, unfortunately, an ideal alternative in all situations.

One problem with extinction is the extinction burst, an increase in the behavior on extinction. Extinction also often provokes emotional outbursts, especially aggression and angry displays. The rat that normally gets food for pressing a lever may, during extinction, bite the lever or another rat if one is available. The child who is accustomed to getting whatever she wants for breakfast may, when told she has to eat the oatmeal in front of her, cry, scream, or throw the food on the floor. Thus, in the early stages of extinction a problem often gets worse before it gets better. This can lead people to abandon the extinction procedure, at least temporarily. Alternating extinction with reinforcement may actually *increase* the rate of behavior, making the problem worse. In theory, these problems can be avoided by maintaining the extinction procedure: If a behavior is never reinforced, it will disappear. (Rats, people, and other animals do not continue to do what never works.) In practice, however, people often "give in" to escape the obnoxious behavior.

Another problem with extinction is that the unwanted behavior often declines slowly. This is annoying when the behavior involved is tantruming or running around a room; it is dangerous when the behavior may cause serious injury. Sometimes behaviors occur thousands of times during extinction before they reach acceptable levels. If a child is hitting himself in the eyes or stabbing others with pencils, a great deal of harm may be done before the behavior extinguishes.

Extinction is also limited when the reinforcers maintaining troublesome behavior are not under our control. Children may steal to get adult attention, but they may also steal to enjoy the toys, food, and other items they obtain through pilferage. Young students may roam about the room less because it earns them the attention of the teacher than because it gains them the company of a fellow student. A student may make silly remarks not for the fun of annoying the teacher but because of the laughter of his peers. Extinction cannot be used if the relevant reinforcers cannot be withheld.

Query: One problem with extinction is that the behavior often

declines _____.

Where appropriate, extinction is safe and effective, and for these reasons it is a highly desirable alternative to punishment. Unfortunately, there are many situations in which it is inappropriate. In these situations, we may turn to differential reinforcement.

Differential Reinforcement

The frequency of a behavior can often be reduced by using extinction in combination with reinforcement, a procedure called **differential reinforcement**. There are several forms of differential reinforcement.

In one form of differential reinforcement, called **differential reinforcement of low rate (DRL)**, reinforcers are provided for a behavior, but only when it occurs infrequently. For example, suppose a pigeon is pecking a disk one or two times a second. To reduce the rate of pecking, we might provide reinforcement only if a minimum of two seconds passes since the previous disk peck. The fast rate is now on extinction, but reinforcement is available for pecking at a lower rate. We can gradually increase the interval required between disk pecks so that eventually the bird might peck at a steady rate of, say, once every 30 seconds. DRL can be useful in applied settings when the behavior concerned is appropriate but occurs too frequently. Consider, for example, a teenager who is constantly pointing out flaws: "The paint on the house is starting to peel . . . My teachers all stink this term. . . . This spaghetti sauce needs more salt." Identifying problems can be very useful, but a constant grumbling is annoying. DRL might help reduce the frequency of complaints.

Another way to reduce the rate of a behavior is with **DRO,** which stands for **differential reinforcement of zero responding**. In this case, reinforcement is contingent on *not* performing the behavior for a specified period of time. For example, the pigeon that is pecking a disk one or two times a second may receive food only if two seconds pass without pecking. When the pigeon meets this standard consistently, we might require a period of three seconds without pecks, then five seconds, then eight, and so on. (Since the delivery of reinforcement necessarily coincides with some behavior other than the unwanted behavior, the procedure is also called differential reinforcement of other behavior.)

Both DRL and DRO provide reinforcement only if the behavior of interest does not occur for a specified period. The difference is that in DRL the behavior of interest is reinforced at the end of the interval, but in DRO reinforcers are provided only if the behavior does *not* occur. DRL is thus appropriate if the goal is to reduce the rate of the behavior; DRO is appropriate if the goal is to eliminate the behavior entirely.

Another form of differential reinforcement is called **differential reinforcement of incompatible behavior (DRI)**. In DRI, we reinforce a behavior that is incompatible with the unwanted behavior. Moving rapidly is incompatible with moving slowly; smiling is generally incompatible with frowning; standing is incompatible with sitting down. By increasing the rate of a desirable behavior, we automatically reduce the rate of an incompatible undesirable behavior. Take the case of the teacher who has children moving about the room when they should be working at their desks. Sitting at a desk is incompatible with walking about the room; it is impossible to do one if you are doing the other. If a teacher praises or talks to students who are working at their desks, the time students spend at their desks is likely to increase. If so, the time they spend wandering about will necessarily decrease.

It is not always necessary, however, to focus on incompatible behavior. In **differential reinforcement of alternative behavior (DRA)**, the reinforcers that were available for the problem behavior are made contingent on some more desirable behavior.

This approach to reducing troublesome behavior has proven very effective. For instance, Edward Carr and Mark Durand (1985) treated four children who engaged in various kinds of disruptive behavior. They taught the youngsters alternative ways of obtaining reinforcers they were accustomed to obtaining through disruptive acts. Following the brief training period, all four children showed greater than 90% reduction in unacceptable behavior. In another study, D. A. Wilder and colleagues (2001) used DRA to reduce the amount of bizarre speech in a psychotic patient. Whenever the patient spoke sensibly, they paid attention and replied appropriately to his comments; whenever he spoke nonsense, they looked away and were quiet. As a result of this simple procedure, psychotic speech almost ceased, and normal speech nearly doubled. Other studies have yielded similar results (Carr & Kemp, 1989; Carr et al., 1990a, 1990b), making this arguably the most promising alternative to punishment.[10]

> **Query:** In differential reinforcement, unwanted behavior is
>
> placed on _____, and a more desirable behavior
>
> (or rate of behavior) is _____.

One advantage of differential reinforcement is that it focuses attention on strengthening desirable behaviors rather than suppressing undesirable ones (Carr et al., 1990a, 1990b; Goldiamond, 1975b). Keep in mind that differential reinforcement includes putting the unwanted behavior on extinction. Differential reinforcement may be of limited value if the troublesome behavior continues to be reinforced at its usual rate.

Noncontingent Reinforcement

Recent research suggests that unwanted behavior can be weakened with **noncontingent reinforcement (NCR)**—that is, reinforcement delivered without regard to behavior. The basic procedure is to identify the reinforcers that maintain the unwanted behavior, and then to provide those reinforcers on a regular basis regardless of what the person is doing at the

---

[11]Carr (1985, 1988) calls the procedure functional communication training, but it may be viewed as a form of DRA.

time. In other words, what the person used to have to work for (by behaving in ways others consider undesirable), he or she now gets "for free." For example, if a psychiatric patient engages in bizarre behavior because doing so produces attention, providing attention noncontingently may reduce the bizarre behavior. Some studies have shown that this is often just what happens (Carr et al., 2000; Roane et al., 2001; Vollmer et al., 1995). One possible explanation for this result is that the noncontingent reinforcement reduces the reinforcing value of the reinforcers. If the patient can obtain the reinforcers for "free," there is no need to work for them by behaving bizarrely.

Noncontingent reinforcement may be useful in reducing inappropriate behavior in other settings, such as schools and homes. However, it is a procedure that might easily backfire. For example, if the reinforcer is delivered after the troublesome behavior, the problem may become worse. Or, concidental reinforcement of other forms of unwanted behavior could occur, which would replace one problem with another. As a procedure for reducing the frequency of unwanted behavior, noncontingent reinforcement should be used with caution (see Vollmer et al., 1997).

REVIEW   Fortunately, there are effective alternatives to punishment. These include response prevention, extinction, and various forms of differential reinforcement. There may be instances in which punishment must be used, but the world would be a better place if all of us relied less on punishment and more on positive methods of influencing behavior.

RECOMMENDED READING

1. Azrin, N. H., & Holz, W. C. (1966). Punishment. In W. K. Honig (Ed.), *Operant behavior: Areas of research and application* (pp. 213–270). Englewood Cliffs, NJ: Prentice Hall.

   This chapter provides a good overview of punishment and its limitations.

2. Bandura, A., & Walters, R. H. (1959). *Adolescent aggression.* New York: Ronald Press.

   This study found that heavy reliance on punishment by parents was a common factor in the backgrounds of aggressive adolescents.

3. Carey, J. (1987). *Eyewitness to history.* Cambridge, MA: Harvard University Press.

Anyone who thinks that the problems with punishment are obvious should peruse this book for the examples of the horrific use of aversives throughout human history.

4. Sidman, M. (1989). *Coercion and its fallout.* Boston, MA: Authors Cooperative.

   This critique of aversive control, including punishment, is by an expert on the subject.

5. Skinner, B. F. (1953). Punishment. Chapter 12 in *Science and human behavior* (pp.182–193). New York: Free Press.

   Skinner makes his case against punishment.

REVIEW QUESTIONS

1. Define the following terms:

differential reinforcement	penalty training
DRA	positive punishment
DRI	punisher
DRL	punishment
DRO	response prevention
NCR	

2. Why do people rely so much on punishment?

3. Benjamin Franklin said that we hate those whom we fear. Do you think he was right? Explain.

4. What is the key difference between positive and negative punishment?

5. Many people believe that raising the price of cigarettes will reduce smoking. If so, does this constitute punishment?

6. Why is it important to use extinction in conjunction with differential reinforcement?

7. If you were the only person in the world, could you still be punished?

8. What is the key difference between negative reinforcement and punishment?

9. People often say they seek "open, honest relationships." Why are such relationships so rare?

10. What is the key difference between the two-process and one-process theories of punishment?

11. How would you distinguish between punishment and abuse?

12. Why do you suppose it took researchers so long to appreciate the power of punishment?

13. Some psychologists have suggested that people could reduce unwanted behavior in themselves, such as nail biting, by wearing a rubber band around their wrist and snapping it against their skin whenever they perform the unwanted behavior. What do you think of this technique?

14. Five-year-old Mary has misbehaved. Her father spanks her and sends her to her room. Has Mary been punished?

15. How might David Premack define a punisher?

16. Give examples of the side effects you might expect if you used punishment to control the behavior of a spouse or friend.

17. If you were a practicing physician, how would you alter the behavior of an elderly person who frequently comes in with vague, inconsequential symptoms?

18. Suppose you are a pediatric dentist and many of your patients constantly suck their thumbs, a practice that may cause dental problems. What would you do?

19. How could a principal use differential reinforcement to reduce the use of punishment by her teachers?

20. You are preparing guidelines for the use of corporal punishment in a reform school. What one point will you emphasize most?

PRACTICE QUIZ

1. The first formal studies of punishment were probably done by _____ around the turn of the century.

2. Positive punishment and _____ are often mistakenly thought to refer to the same procedure.

3. Murray Sidman, an expert on punishment, wrote a critique of the subject called _____.

4. According to the two-process theory, punishment involves two procedures: _____ and _____.

5. Punishment is more likely to suppress a behavior if the organism has _____ means of obtaining reinforcement.

6. Benjamin Franklin observed that people who are feared are _____.

7. David Camp and his colleagues found that a delay of 30 seconds greatly reduced the effects of contingent shock. They found that even a delay of _____ seconds made shocks less effective.

8. In using punishment, it is best to begin with a punisher that is _____ (slightly stronger/slightly weaker) than the minimum required to suppress the behavior.

9. The fact that an annoying behavior occurs implies that it has _____ consequences.

10. Five problems are associated with punishment. Three of these problems are _____.

QUERY ANSWERS

Page 192. Positive and negative punishment are similar in that both *weaken/suppress/reduce the strength of* a behavior.

Page 193. In positive punishment, something is *added/presented*; in negative punishment, something is *subtracted/removed.*

Page 193. Negative reinforcement *increases* the strength of a behavior; positive punishment *decreases/reduces* it.

Page 197. Figure 6-4 shows that the more *intense* a punisher, the more it *reduces* the rate of a behavior.

Page 202. In general, the *higher/greater* the level of reinforcer deprivation, the *less* effective a punisher is.

Page 202. Any four of the variables covered may be named: contingency, contiguity, punisher intensity, beginning level of punishment, availability of reinforcement for the punished behavior, alternative sources of reinforcement, deprivation level, and qualitative features of the punisher.

Page 204. The two processes of the two-process theory are *Pavlovian conditioning* and *operant learning.*

Page 209. The five problems that can arise with punishment are escape, aggression, apathy, abuse, and imitative use of punishment.

Page 211. One problem with extinction is that the behavior declines *slowly.*

Page 213. In differential reinforcement, unwanted behavior is placed on *extinction,* and a more desirable behavior (or rate of behavior) is *reinforced.*

CHAPTER

7

Operant Applications

IN THIS CHAPTER . . .

The great end of life is not knowledge, but action.

T. H. Huxley

B. F. Skinner often suggested that in operant procedures the environment selects behavior in much the same way that the environment selects species characteristics: An organism behaves in a certain way, and the environment reinforces, punishes, or ignores that behavior. Behavior that is useful, that contributes to survival, endures; behavior that is harmful or useless dies out. In this way, the environment shapes behavior.[1]

Clearly, humans and other animals can and do learn in this way, but does operant learning provide any insight into complex behavior? And does it offer practical solutions to important behavior problems? Because so much of what we have learned about operant procedures has been learned from research with animals, perhaps it is appropriate to begin by considering whether this work has improved the lives of the animals in our care.

Animal Care and Training

Operant procedures are often used to facilitate veterinary care of captive animals, especially those that are large and potentially dangerous or sensitive to the stress of being handled. In the past, such problems were solved with restraints, or aversives, or by anesthetizing the animal. These traditional procedures can be dangerous for both the animal and its caretakers. Positive reinforcement is not only a more humane solution to such problems but is less risky for all concerned.

For instance, animal trainer Gary Wilkes (1994) describes the application of operant procedures to solve a problem with an aggressive elephant. He notes that working with elephants is very dangerous because their size makes it easy for them to do serious harm. Veterinary care of captive elephants includes periodically trimming calluses that build up on their feet. If the calluses are not removed, the animal eventually is unable to walk. An aggressive bull elephant at the San Diego Zoo had not had its calluses trimmed in almost 10 years. Normally the job is done by going into

---

[1] As noted in Chapter 5, Thorndike (1898) was probably the first to observe that reinforcing consequences *select* behavior.

Figure 7-1 *How do you give an elephant a manicure? With shaping. See text for explanation.*

a pen with the elephant and cutting away at the calluses with a sharp tool. Given this animal's history of aggressive behavior, there was probably not a lot of enthusiasm for this idea. Instead, the behavior specialist at the zoo, Gary Priest, had a large steel gate built at one end of an enclosure. The gate had a large hole about the size of an elephant's foot (see Figure 7-1). "Now," writes Wilkes, "all that had to be done was to ask a violent, bull elephant to daintily put his tootsies through a blank wall and let strange little creatures hack away at his feet with knives" (p. 32).

This was accomplished by shaping the desired behavior.[2] Because shaping usually proceeds best with immediate reinforcement, the trainers established a clicking noise, made by a toy called a cricket, as a conditioned reinforcer (Skinner, 1951). They did this by making the clicking sound and then giving the elephant a piece of carrot. When the clicking sound was reinforcing, the trainers used it to reinforce approaching the gate. When the animal approached the gate, a trainer sounded the clicker and tossed the elephant a bit of carrot. When the animal was in front of the gate, the trainers reinforced lifting the left front foot off the ground, then reinforced raising the foot several inches, then moving it toward the hole, and so on. Wilkes writes that "soon the animal would voluntarily walk to the gate and put one foot after another into the mysterious hole. He would hold it there while the keeper trimmed the pads of his feet and groomed the animal's nails" (p. 33). An interesting but not unusual side

---

[2] To review the shaping procedure, see Chapter 5.

Reinforcement Goes to the Dogs

More dogs die each year because of behavior problems than from all diseases combined (reported in Jankowski, 1994). What often happens is that a dog develops a "bad habit" such as constantly barking, scratching at a door, or biting people. When efforts to change this behavior (usually with inappropriately applied aversives) fail, the dog is abandoned or taken to an animal shelter.

Sadly, even those dogs that make it to an animal shelter often face a grim fate because their behavior makes them unappealing. The history of exposure to inappropriately used aversives can produce a dog that behaves in an excessively shy, fearful, or aggressive manner. A dog that cowers in a corner with its tail between its legs and looks away from a visitor is unlikely to find a good home. It is fairly obvious that if such dogs were trained to behave in more attractive ways, fewer of them would be destroyed, but such training has not been available.

But that may be changing. Lauren Beck, the manager of an animal shelter, has used shaping to get dogs to make eye contact with people, to do a trick, and to display good canine manners (see Pryor, 1996). This change in behavior makes the animals far more appealing. When someone comes to the shelter hoping to adopt a dog, a member of the shelter staff points out the dog's virtues and invites the visitor to give the trick command and reinforce the behavior with a clicker. The usual reaction is something like, "This dog is brilliant!"

Of course, the dog is not brilliant. It has simply had good training for a change.

effect of the procedure was that the elephant's temperament changed. He became far less aggressive and seemed to enjoy the training sessions.[3]

Query: The procedure used to modify the elephant's behavior

was _____.

It is probably safe to say that animal trainers today rely far more on positive reinforcement and less on negative reinforcement and punishment than in the past. Animal trainers seldom acknowledge (and may

---

[3]For more on how learning principles have been used to enrich the lives of captive animals, see Hal Markowitz's, *Behavioral Enrichment in the Zoo* (1982).

not be aware of) their debt to learning researchers. Nevertheless, shaping and other operant procedures have filtered down from the research lab to the training ring—to the great benefit of animals and trainers alike.[4]

REVIEW   The use of positive reinforcement, shaping, and chaining is almost taken for granted by professional animal trainers and caretakers today, but 50 years ago trainers relied almost exclusively on negative reinforcement and punishment. Operant procedures provide humane ways of training Seeing Eye dogs and other animals to assist people with handicaps, inducing zoo animals to cooperate with essential veterinary procedures, and getting Fido to fetch the newspaper.

Self-Awareness

To be self-aware is to observe one's own behavior.[5] "I was angry" means "I observed myself behaving in ways commonly identified as anger." A more scrupulous self-observer might say, "I noticed that my voice trembled, my face and neck felt warm, I clenched my teeth, made fists with my hands, felt my heart beat fast, and cursed silently."

When we say "I think I'll quit school," we are really saying, "I have observed myself behaving in ways that suggest I will quit school." Saying "I think I'll quit school" is not, in any fundamental way, different from saying "I think Joe will quit school." The events that lead to either observation will be nearly identical: negative statements about school, failure to attend classes, poor grades, unsuccessful efforts to make friends or join social clubs or athletic teams, and so on. In other words, we make observations about our own behavior that are essentially the same as the observations we make about others. Of course, when we observe ourselves, we can note forms of behavior—such as thoughts—that we cannot readily observe in others.

Query: To be self-aware is to _____.

---

[4]Even today, however, many educated people do not understand the role of learning in establishing or changing troublesome behavior. Michael Fox (1999), a veterinarian and newspaper columnist, writes, for example, "Excessive barking most often means that a dog is lonely, bored, or suffering from separation anxiety. It is a sign that the dog is distressed, so it should not be ignored " (p. G11). Fox is evidently unaware that barking may have reinforcing consequences, such as the occasional attention of a person, perhaps someone who is concerned about the dog's "separation anxiety."

[5]This discussion of self-awareness relies heavily on Skinner's analysis of the subject in *Science and Human Behavior* (1953).

It is easy to see why we observe the behavior of others: Doing so is reinforced. We may notice that Mary is "in a good mood," and our efforts to engage her in conversation on such occasions are followed by pleasant exchanges. Or we may notice that Mary is "in a foul mood," and this allows us to avoid the unpleasant exchanges that are likely to follow certain kinds of behavior, such as attempting to engage her in conversation.

We observe our own behavior for the same reason: Doing so is reinforced. If we are able to detect from our own behavior that we are in the early stages of flu, we may speed our recovery by getting additional rest before the symptoms hit with full force. Similarly, if we notice that we are "in a bad mood," then we may avoid an unpleasant argument by postponing a meeting to discuss wedding plans with our future in-laws. When we observe our behavior carefully, we can better predict what we will do, just as we can predict the behavior of a close friend. Self-awareness allows us to behave more effectively.

It was once thought that such self-knowledge was available only to humans. Two prominent psychologists not so long ago wrote in a psychology textbook that "one of man's unique distinctions, setting him off most sharply from other animals, may be just this extraordinary capacity to look at himself" (Krech & Crutchfield, 1961, p. 202). But recent research has shown that other animals may be capable of at least a rudimentary form of self-awareness.

Gordon Gallup (1970, 1979) was apparently the first to provide experimental evidence of self-awareness in an animal other than humans. In his first study (Gallup, 1970), he exposed chimpanzees to a full-length mirror for several days. Initially, the animals responded to their reflection as if to another animal, but these social behaviors were gradually replaced by self-directed behavior. Increasingly, the animals used the mirrors to groom parts of their bodies they could not otherwise see, to pick food from between their teeth, to look at themselves as they made faces or blew bubbles, and so on. After this, Gallup anesthetized the animals and dabbed them with an odorless red dye on one eyebrow ridge and the upper part of one ear. On recovering from anesthesia, the animals were observed for 30 minutes with the mirror removed and then for 30 minutes with the mirror present.[6] The chimps made almost no effort to touch the dyed parts of their bodies when there was no mirror, but made from four to ten efforts with the mirror present. Sometimes the animals would look in the mirror, touch the dye with their fingers, and then examine their fingers closely. When chimps that had not had

---

[6]Anesthetizing the animals was important, since dabbing them with dye while they were awake could have induced them to touch the affected areas.

experience with mirrors were anesthetized and marked, they did not touch the dyed spots and showed no signs of using the mirror to inspect themselves. Gallup concluded that "insofar as self-recognition of one's mirror image implies a concept of self, these data would seem to qualify as the first experimental demonstration of self-concept in a subhuman form" (p. 87).

Robert Epstein and others (Epstein et al., 1981) found that even the pigeon is capable of showing evidence of self-awareness. These researchers first trained pigeons to peck dots on their own bodies, then to peck a wall after seeing a dot flashed there, and then to peck the wall after seeing the flashing dot reflected in a mirror. After this, the researchers put a blue dot on each bird's breast beneath a bib. The bib prevented the bird from seeing the dot directly, but it could see the dot reflected in a mirror. Each bird was tested first with the mirror covered; none of the animals tried to peck the blue dot. Next, the birds were tested with the mirror uncovered, and each of them soon began pecking at a spot on the bib corresponding to the dot on its breast.

Whether chimpanzees and pigeons really are self-aware in the same sense as humans is a matter for conjecture. These studies demonstrate that animals can become careful observers of their own bodies, but they do not demonstrate that animals observe their own moods and thoughts and other private behavior the way humans do. But the experiments do offer support for the notion that self-awareness "can be accounted for in terms of an environmental history" (Epstein et al., 1981, p. 696). In other words, self-awareness is learned.

Humans learn to observe themselves not so much from mirrors as from other people (Cooley, 1902; Mead, 1934). Skinner (1953) notes that we teach a child to say "that itches," "that tickles," "that hurts," when we observe behavior or events that typically accompany such experiences. For instance, scratching suggests itching, giggling when brushed with a feather suggests tickling, moans and tears suggest pain. By observing and commenting on behavior that suggests certain experiences, we teach the child to observe those private events.

Skinner also notes that we teach children to make comments on and predictions from self-observations. We do this, in part, by asking the child questions: What are you doing? What are you going to do? Why are you doing that? How do you feel? Are you in a good mood? Do you want to play? Are you sleepy?

These and countless other questions direct the child to observe and comment on private experiences—that is, thoughts and feelings. When the observations are accurate, they are likely to be reinforced. At noon, we ask a child if she is hungry, and if she says yes, we provide food. If the

The Shaping of Awareness

Most people think of coma as deep sleep, but in long-term cases, patients often behave as though they are about to wake. They may open their eyes, turn their heads, move a hand. Often, they seem trapped in a fog-like state somewhere between sleep and wakefulness. Operant learning may help some coma victims break through the fog.

Mary Boyle (Boyle & Greer, 1983) worked with 3 people who had been comatose for at least 6 months. Each of the patients made some slight spontaneous movements, such as squinting or moving the head from side to side. Boyle tried to increase the frequency of these acts by reinforcing them with music. First, she asked the patient to make some movement that he or she had been seen to make spontaneously. Then she encouraged the desired act by, for example, moving the patient's head from side to side. After this, she repeatedly asked the patient to make that movement. Each time the patient complied with the request, Boyle played a short selection of the patient's favorite music. Training continued for 2 sessions a day, 7 days a week, for 4 months.

There was nothing new about the idea of playing music for coma victims; what was new was making music *contingent* on the patient's behavior. But coma victims are, by definition, not responsive to their environment. Would the procedure modify their behavior?

Results varied. The patient who had been in coma for the shortest period of time produced the best results: a clear increase in the likelihood of performing an act when asked to do so. Eventually, this patient came out of his coma. Did the reinforcement procedure have anything to do with the patient's recovery? Boyle is cautious, but she thinks the answer is yes.

Perhaps reinforcement of spontaneous behavior will one day be part of the standard treatment for coma. Perhaps successively more wakeful behavior (e.g., opening the eyes, keeping the eyes open for longer periods, tracking moving objects with the eyes, and so on) could be reinforced. In essence, therapy would consist of reinforcing successive approximations of wakefulness. Awareness would be shaped.

child has accurately reported her private state (if she is correct in saying she is hungry), food will reinforce her observation. If the child says she is hungry when she is not, the food may not be reinforcing and may even be aversive if she is forced to eat it. By means of such experiences, the child learns to observe herself carefully.

REVIEW To be self-aware is to observe one's own behavior, including thoughts and feelings. Studies with animals suggest that we learn to observe ourselves, perhaps mainly as a result of consequences provided by others, because doing so has reinforcing consequences.

Self-Control

The term *self-control* refers to the tendency to act in our own best interests. When a person drinks in moderation, turns down a second helping of dessert, studies for a test rather than chatting with friends, or gives up smoking, we say the person has good self-control.

Each of these, and most other self-control situations, involves a choice. The party-goer must choose between drinking a lot now and waking up without a hangover later. The diner must choose between having a second helping of dessert now and being relatively thin later. The student must choose between visiting with friends now and doing well on a test tomorrow. In these examples, the choice is between two attractive outcomes, but this is not always the case. The smoker must choose between going through the pain of withdrawal now or risking the pain of major illness later. Thus, to have self-control means to choose wisely, to choose to do things that are in our best long-term interests.

Laboratory studies of self-control also present choices. A child might be told that she can have a small treat (perhaps a spoonful of ice cream) now, or she can have a large treat (a bowl of ice cream) later. Or a college student might be asked to perform a task and offered an immediate payment of $5, or $20 to be paid in one week. Or a rat may obtain a not very tasty food immediately by pressing one lever, or a much better food later by pressing a different lever. The choices made reflect the complex interaction of the nature of the reinforcers and the amount of delay for each.[7]

Some people show self-control even when there are strong inducements to choose unwisely. Usually those who have good self-control are said to owe it to some inborn quality called willpower, discipline, or strength of character. But such explanations are circular: We say a person rejects dessert because he has willpower, and we say he has willpower because he rejects dessert. Willpower, discipline, and strength of character are merely names we give to behaving sensibly in situations in which people often behave foolishly. The terms do not explain the behavior; they just name it.

---

[7]For a detailed analysis of these variables in self-control, see Howard Rachlin's, *The Science of Self Control* (2000).

Query: Willpower is a circular explanation of behavior because

the evidence for willpower is _____ .

But if this is so, why do some people act in their own best interest while others do not? Why do some people elect to study rather than chat, to go to the dentist rather than to the park? And why can some people who smoke, eat too much, or bite their fingernails break these habits?

The answer has to do, in part, with the use of certain self-control techniques. One such technique has been called *physical restraint*. This means doing something that physically prevents a behavior from occurring. The story of Ulysses and the sirens provides an example: Sailors who attempted to pass by the sirens were drawn onto the rocks by the sirens' song. Ulysses wanted to hear the sirens but he also wanted to avoid disaster, so he had himself tied to the mast, and then ordered his crew to stuff wax into their ears. In this way he prevented his men and himself from being led astray.

You use a more common example of restraint when you clap a hand over your mouth to keep yourself from laughing aloud when laughing would be inappropriate. The expression "bite your tongue" suggests an effective way of preventing ourselves from saying something we might later regret. Similarly, the fingernail biter may wrap his fingertips with adhesive tape to prevent nail biting. People use physical restraint when they lock liquor away in a cupboard and give someone else the key; give their cigarettes to a roommate with instructions to provide them with only three cigarettes a day; or cut up their credit cards to prevent themselves from making purchases beyond their budget.

Another technique is called *distancing*. Most troublesome behaviors are more likely to occur in certain situations than in others. One way to avoid engaging in undesirable behavior is to keep our distance from situations in which that behavior is likely to occur. The boy with a chip on his shoulder may avoid getting into a fight by walking away from his tormentor. The smoker can eat in the nonsmoking section of restaurants and avoid his smoking friends when they are likely to smoke. Some unsuccessful dieters keep a bowl of candy on their desk, insisting that they should be able to resist the temptation. The truth is that one way of resisting temptation is to keep it at a distance.

A similar technique is called *distraction*. At a dinner party, a person who is annoyed by the comments of the person on his left may prevent himself from making an angry outburst by changing the topic of conversation or by starting a conversation with the person on his right. Faced with temptation, we can often distract ourselves by reading a book, watching a film, or participating in sports.

Skinner (1953) identifies a technique he calls *deprivation and satiation.* He suggests that a person who wants to eat lightly at a dinner (perhaps so as not to become preoccupied with eating and neglect conversation with his host) may eat a small meal beforehand, thus partially satiating on food.

Another technique is to *inform others of your goals.* The person who would like to stop smoking or eat more sensibly is more likely to be successful if he makes those intentions public. This is because the people around us inevitably behave in ways that help or hinder our efforts to change. Friends and acquaintances are, for example, important sources of reinforcement. If they know we are trying to lose weight, they may praise our efforts and compliment our appearance as the pounds fall away. If they know we have given up cigarettes, the nonsmokers among them may spend more time with us, and even the smokers may admire our effort.

Involving others in our efforts to change may not sound very much like *self*-control, but self-control requires changing our environment in ways that make the desired behavior more likely to occur. The people with whom we interact on a daily basis are an important part of that environment. By informing them of our goals, we may change *their* behavior in ways that affect *our* behavior for the better.

Another commonly recommended self-control technique is *monitoring behavior.* A person who is annoyed by his tendency to think self-denigrating thoughts may get control of the thoughts merely by tabulating their occurrence. This can be done by carrying a wrist counter such as those golfers use to keep score, or by making hash marks on a three-by-five card. Each day's tally is transferred to a frequency graph. Merely monitoring behavior in this way often results in desired changes in its frequency.

Query: Name three self-control techniques.

These and other self-control techniques are described in a number of sources (e.g., Epstein, 1996; Goldiamond, 1965; Logue, 1998; Martin & Osborne, 1989; Skinner, 1953; Watson & Tharp, 1989). Anyone can adopt them and get better control over his or her own behavior, yet many people do not do so. The use of self-control techniques is itself behavior that is established and maintained by its consequences. In other words, the use of self-control techniques is learned.

We can see this most clearly in research on children. Given a choice between receiving a small prize immediately and a bigger prize later, young children typically opt for the immediate reward whereas older children will wait for the bigger one (Bandura & Mischel, 1965; Ito & Nakamura, 1998). With time, children learn to distract themselves and use other techniques to make better choices (Patterson & Mischel, 1976). Research also shows that instruction in self-control procedures can increase their use. In one study, James Larson and colleagues (1998) found that aggressive adolescent boys could be taught to use self-control techniques to reduce their disruptive behavior. People who do not have good self-control do not lack willpower or character; they lack instruction.

The natural science approach to behavior, with its underlying assumption that all behavior is the product of some combination of environmental and biological variables, sometimes strikes students as a depressing view of human nature. But the study of self-control teaches us that determinism is not the same thing as fatalism (Epstein, 1997). An understanding of the ways that behavior is influenced by events improves our ability to control our own behavior, turning us not into automatons but into autonomous human beings.

REVIEW   Self-control means acting in our own best interests. The tendency to make wise choices varies with the reinforcers available for different behaviors and with the delay in delivery of reinforcers. We say that a person has good self-control when a person chooses wisely even when there are reinforcers for choosing unwisely. People can learn to exert self-control in such situations by practices such as physical restraint, distancing, distracting, and monitoring behavior, among others.

Verbal Behavior

The traditional view of language holds that words are symbols for communicating ideas. Ideas are said to be encoded in the form of words (and word groups) by one person and "sent" to another person in speech or writing. The receiver of the message then decodes the message and thereby achieves understanding. Ideas are in this way, so the theory goes, transferred from head to head.

This ancient approach to language is still the view held by most people. Another approach is, however, possible. It may have had its roots in the early work of Thorndike, but it received its fullest expression in a book by Skinner called *Verbal Behavior* (1957). Skinner's analysis is very complex, and we can do no more here than make a brief survey of its key features. Even a brief survey, however, will reveal a stimulating and promising approach.

Skinner rejected the view that ideas are encoded into words by one person and decoded by another. Instead, he proposed that to understand the nature of the spoken and written word, we must first recognize that they are forms of behavior. Moreover, he proposed that verbal behavior is not essentially different from any other behavior. And, like other behavior, verbal behavior is to be understood in terms of functional relationships between it and environmental events, particularly its consequences. Like the pawing of a cat at a loop and the lever pressing of a rat, verbal behavior is a function of its consequences.

If we want to understand verbal behavior, we must examine the effects of verbal behavior on the environment, particularly the social environment. For it is the social environment, the behavior of other people, that shapes and maintains verbal behavior.

Query: Verbal behavior is governed by the law of

_____.

This begins in infancy. Babies begin making sounds that, while perhaps not random, do not resemble any known language. (Baby vocalization is not called babbling for nothing.) Parents select certain sounds for reinforcement, and the more those sounds resemble words in the parent's language, the more reinforcers the parent provides. When the baby's efforts approximate *Ma-ma* or *Da-da*, all sorts of wonderful things are apt to happen: adults smile, tickle the child, laugh, clap, and so on. Through such shaping, parents teach their children the rudiments of language. After a time, *Ma-ma* no longer results in reinforcement; the child must say *Mommy*. In the same way, *cook* must give way to *cookie* or no treat is forthcoming. Later the child may be required to use complete, grammatically correct sentences, such as "May I have a cookie, please?"

In the normal course of events, we learn to speak because speaking produces reinforcers more reliably than other forms of behavior. Saying "Please pass the sugar" produces sugar more reliably than crying or pointing at the sugar bowl. When the professor says, "Why weren't you in class Monday?" he behaves in a way that is apt to produce various kinds of reinforcers: a satisfactory explanation, perhaps, an amusing story, or an apology. The student may reply, "My aunt died. I had to go to her funeral." The student's comment is apt to produce reinforcing consequences: expressions of sympathy, for example, or the opportunity to make up a missed exam. Of course, verbal behavior need not correspond perfectly with reality in order to produce reinforcement, so the relatives of college students are notoriously susceptible to fatal illnesses, especially during midterm exams.

A good deal of research supports the idea that verbal behavior is strongly influenced by its consequences. For instance, Joel Greenspoon (1955) asked college students to say as many words as they could think of in a given period. The exact instructions were, "What I want you to do is to say all the words that you can think of. Say them individually. Do not use any sentences or phrases. Do not count. Please continue until I say stop. Go ahead" (p. 410). In one condition, the experimenter said, "Mmm-hmm" after each plural noun spoken by the student. In another condition, the experimenter said, "Huh-uh" after each plural noun. Control subjects heard nothing from the experimenter regardless of what they said. The results showed that the frequency of plural nouns varied with the consequences it produced. Reinforcement ("Mmm-hmm") resulted in more plural nouns, compared to the control group, whereas punishment ("Huh-uh") resulted in fewer plural nouns.

The work of Greenspoon clearly showed that verbal behavior is a function of its consequences. Unfortunately, the experiment did not closely resemble the ordinary use of language. Research by William Verplanck (1955) came closer to the mark. In one experiment, Verplanck or a colleague engaged one person at a time in casual conversation under ordinary circumstances. For the first 10 minutes the researcher surreptitiously tallied the number of times the person started a sentence with the words, "I think that," "I believe that," or the like. During the next 10 minutes, the experimenter attempted to reinforce such expressions of opinion by paraphrasing them or expressing agreement. For the final 10-minute period, the experimenter no longer reinforced opinions. The result was that every one of the 23 subjects in the experiment showed a higher rate of opinion statements during the reinforcement period than during periods when reinforcement was unavailable.

Query: In his opinion study, Verplanck used a/an

_____ research design. (See Chapter 2.)

In a second experiment, Verplanck engaged people in conversation for 10 minutes and then introduced a new topic. For the next 10 minutes, some of the subjects received reinforcement for any statement bearing on the suggested topic while the other subjects did not. The results showed that those who did not receive reinforcement dropped the suggested

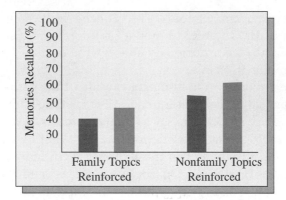

Figure 7-2   *Reinforcement and memories recalled. When mention of family topics produced a mild reinforcer ("uh-huh"), the proportion of family topics increased from the baseline level (dark bar). When "uh-huh" followed nonfamily topics, the proportion of those topics increased. (Compiled from data in Quay, 1959.)*

topic within 2 or 3 minutes, whereas those who received reinforcement talked about almost nothing else for the next 10 minutes. When the experimenter stopped reinforcing discussion of the topic, statements on the topic fell to zero.

Herbert Quay (1959) wondered whether the tendency of psychotherapy patients to talk about family experiences was because of the unique importance of these experiences or whether this tendency might be the result of subtle forms of reinforcement from the therapist. To find out, he asked college students to recall events from their early childhood. With some students, Quay said *uh-huh* whenever he or she recalled a family experience; with other students, he said *uh-huh* whenever the recollection had to do with anything *but* family. *Uh-huh* (like *Mmm-hmm*) is an expression that commonly indicates mild interest, yet when *uh-huh* was contingent on certain kinds of recollections, those kinds of recollections increased (see Figure 7-2). This finding suggests that the tendency of clients to talk about family relationships may have less to do with their importance to the client than with the reactions they get from the therapist.[8]

Of course, it is not merely the current reinforcement contingencies that influence verbal behavior. The speaker comes to his audience after a

---

[8]Not all efforts to reinforce conversational content have been successful (e.g., Madler & Kaplan, 1956; Sullivan & Calvin, 1959). The failures may have been due to reinforcement delay. Small differences in the administration of reinforcement can mean large differences in results. It is well to remember that just because you don't paint like Manet doesn't mean there is something wrong with your brush.

long and complicated history of reinforcement. This history, as well as the listener's reactions, mold his speech. Skinner (1953) notes that when people are asked to call out numbers at random they inevitably produce a nonrandom series of numbers. He suggests that the reason has to do with the history of reinforcement. "Various sequences of numbers are reinforced as we learn to count by ones, twos, threes, or fives, to recite multiplication tables, to give telephone numbers, and so on" (p. 211f).[9]

The importance of reinforcement history in determining verbal behavior can also be seen in word associations. Given the word *black*, far more people will say "white" than would be expected if their replies were simply random answers. It is likely that this has to do with the tendency for the words *black* and *white* to appear together. (For example, "They're as different as black and white"; "It's in the contract in black and white"; "I prefer black and white photos for portraits.") This tendency could be due to the fact that the words commonly occur together, but association may be less important than reinforcement. We receive reinforcement (in the form of smiles, nods, or other signs of understanding) when we say, "Here it is in black and white." We do not receive reinforcement if we say, "Here it is in black and green."

Query: Given the word "up," most people probably say

"down." Why?

Much of our learning involving verbal behavior occurs without our awareness. The studies of Greenspoon, Verplanck, and Quay, for example, offered no evidence that the subjects knew there was a reinforcement contingency in force. Verplanck's subjects were not even aware they were the subjects of an experiment. In fact, Verplanck reports that he described his research to someone in casual conversation and that, while they talked, the person listening to him began systematically reinforcing Verplanck's verbal behavior, with predictable results. Verplanck was completely unaware that his companion had been shaping his verbal behavior!

Many other studies show verbal learning without awareness (Krasner, 1958). Whether verbal learning regularly occurs without awareness is not, however, particularly important. What is important is that much of our verbal behavior is a function of its consequences. The idea

---

[9] It was once believed by some that people were incapable of behaving randomly (Tune, 1964; Wagenaar, 1971). However, Alan Neuringer (1986) has shown that with practice and feedback (i.e., reinforcement), people can learn to generate numbers randomly. Incredibly, their performance sometimes approximates that of random number generators.

Rewarding Lies

Paul Ekman (Ekman & Patterson, 1992), a social psychologist famous for his work on nonverbal communication, reports that 91% of Americans lie routinely. He adds that 86% lie regularly to parents, 75% to friends, and 69% to spouses. Why is lying so popular?

An experiment by Robert Lanza and colleagues (1982) suggests that reinforcement may be involved. The researchers trained pigeons to use symbols to communicate about a color that was hidden from another pigeon. The pigeons learned the task readily enough, but when reporting that the hidden color was red paid off better than reporting the color that was actually hidden, the birds sometimes reported red. In other words, when lying paid better than telling the truth, they lied.

No doubt people sometimes lie because lying has been positively reinforced in the past. Suppose, for example, that a classmate asks, "What did you think of my speech?" It was really rather mediocre, but you lie and say, "I thought it was great!" We may lie in such situations because there are sometimes positive consequences for doing so: The speech maker smiles pleasantly, and may offer to do us some kindness. ("Well, I'm glad you liked it. How are you coming in calculus? Need any help?")

I suspect that most lying, however, has less to do with positive reinforcement than with negative reinforcement. By lying about a classmate's speech, we avoid rejection, criticism, and other unpleasantness. People realize this, of course, and so are apt to implore us to be honest and tell them what we *really* think. "Don't hold back," they tell us, "I can take it." Only sometimes they can't. After begging us to critique a speech honestly, they often rebuke us for having done so. We may then try to escape the unpleasant situation our honesty has created by temporizing our earlier opinion— in other words, by lying.

that what we say and write depends on the effects of our behavior on others may seem, in hindsight, like nothing more than common sense, but it represents a radical departure from the traditional view of language as the transfer of ideas from head to head.

REVIEW   The traditional view of verbal behavior holds that ideas are encoded into language by one person and decoded by another. An analysis in terms of operant learning suggests that verbal behavior is shaped and maintained by its consequences, chiefly its effects on others. Experiments by Thorndike, Greenspoon, Verplanck, and others provided empirical support for this notion.

Insightful Problem Solving

Problem solving is an area that is shrouded in mystery. It is often spoken of in conjunction with references to "the mysteries of mind" and is said to be one of those subjects that defy scientific analysis. Researchers who have approached problem solving from the standpoint of operant learning have given the lie to that view.

A problem is a situation in which reinforcement is available, but the behavior necessary to produce it is not. Often, the necessary behavior is not currently in the organism's repertoire. Consider Thorndike's cats: To get out of the boxes the cats had to do something they had never done before, at least not in that situation. Thorndike noticed that the cats solved the problem by scratching and pawing at things in the box until they happened to trigger the mechanism that opened the cage door. Thorndike said they learned to solve the problem through "trial and accidental success."

> **Query:** A problem is a situation in which _____ is
>
> available, but the behavior necessary to produce it is not.

When people attempt to solve problems, they often try one thing and then another, like Thorndike's cats, until they hit on a solution. But there are said to be times when the solution appears suddenly, in full form, like Athena springing from the head of Zeus. In these instances, problems are said to be solved "by insight."

The best-known experiments on insightful problem solving are those described in *The Mentality of Apes* by the German researcher Wolfgang Kohler (1927/1973). In one of the most famous experiments, Kohler gave a chimpanzee named Sultan two hollow bamboo rods. The end of one bamboo rod could be inserted into the end of the other to make one long rod. Outside Sultan's cage lay a bit of fruit, just far enough from the bars that it could not be reached with either short stick alone. After an hour of unproductive work, Sultan sat down on a box and examined the sticks. His keeper wrote that

> while doing this, it happens that (Sultan) finds himself holding one rod in either hand in such a way that they lie in a straight line; he

> pushes the thinner one a little way into the opening of the thicker,
> jumps up and is already on the run towards the railings . . . and
> begins to draw a banana towards him with the double stick. (p. 127)

Sultan, Kohler said, solved the problem through insight: Sitting there on the box, looking at the two sticks, he had a sudden flash of understanding about the problem. Such insightful problem solving, it was said, could not be accounted for by operant learning, because the correct solution appeared suddenly, without benefit of reinforcement. But did it?

Some years after Kohler's work, Louis Peckstein and Forrest Brown (1939) performed experiments similar to Kohler's and found no evidence of solutions emerging suddenly without benefit of reinforcement. In a replication of Kohler's two-stick problem, for example, they found that it took a chimpanzee 11 trials over a period of 4 days to learn to put two sticks together to retrieve food. Their chimpanzee first learned to retrieve food with a single stick, and then learned to combine two sticks while playing with them. It then *gradually* learned to use the combined sticks to retrieve food.[10]

Other experiments have added doubts about the apparent suddenness of insight into problems. Harry Harlow (1949) provided monkeys with a problem in which a bit of food could be found under one of two lids that varied in some way, such as color, size, or shape. In one series of trials, the prize would always be under the larger lid; in another series, it would always be under the square lid, and so on. Success on the first trial of any series was necessarily a matter of chance; there was no way of telling which lid covered food on the first trial. Success on the second and subsequent trials could be successful if the monkeys selected the same kind of lid that hid food on the first trial. Unfortunately, Harlow's monkeys showed no inclination to behave in this way.

In any given series, Harlow's monkeys would slowly learn to pick the correct lid. Gradually, over many series of learning trials, their learning rate improved (see Figure 7-3). Eventually, they would get the second problem in a new series right about 90% of the time. This change emerged slowly, however, and was clearly the result of the animal's reinforcement history. Harlow repeated the same experiment with children between the ages of two and seven and got the same result: no sudden emergence of insight, but a gradual improvement in performance due, apparently, to the reinforcement of correct choices.[11]

---

[10]Jerome Bruner (1983) wrote, concerning Kohler's experiments, that insight is without benefit of learning. But we now know that insight depends fundamentally on previous learning.

[11]Great scientific insights also may be the end results of years of work. Weiner (1994) notes that Darwin's great insight about evolution evolved slowly over many years.

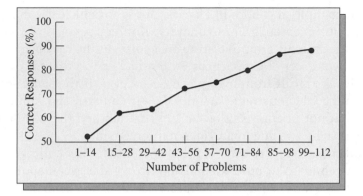

Figure 7-3 *The "evolution" of insight. The percent of correct solutions on trial 2 of a series increased gradually with training. (After Harlow, 1949.)*

Query: Harlow's data show that "insightful" solutions may be

arrived at _____ as a result of a number of

learning experiences.

Nevertheless, people and animals *do* sometimes solve problems suddenly. They may struggle unsuccessfully with a problem for some time, and then abruptly produce a solution. If, however, the sudden appearance of a solution can be shown to be dependent on learning history, the notion that insightful problem solving is fundamentally different from operant learning is seriously challenged.

One of the most frequently cited demonstrations of insightful problem solving is Kohler's suspended fruit problem. In this experiment, Kohler suspended a banana or other piece of fruit from the ceiling of a cage in a corner and placed a large box in the center of the cage. The chimpanzees under study attempted to reach the fruit by jumping, but the fruit was too high. Sultan

soon relinquished this attempt, paced restlessly up and down, suddenly stood still in front of the box, seized it, tipped it hastily straight towards the objective, but began to climb on it at a (horizontal) distance of half a metre, and springing upwards with all his force, tore down the banana. (1927/1973, p. 40)

In such instances of problem solving, the solution's abrupt appearance is said to be an inexplicable "act of mind," not to be accounted for in terms of the reinforcement of previous behavior. The claim is that such insight is different from the gradual selection of correct actions seen, for example, in Thorndike's cats. But is insight really independent of prior reinforcement? Unfortunately, Kohler's records of the experiences of the animals prior to testing are spotty. In the case just cited, it is not clear what sort of experiences Sultan had had in the use of boxes or the retrieval of fruit from high places. However, if the same sort of insight could be demonstrated in animals with a particular reinforcement history, but not in animals that lacked that history, this would suggest that the insight was due to previous reinforcement.

In a brilliant experiment, Robert Epstein and his colleagues (1984) taught pigeons (a) to push a small box toward a green spot that was placed at various points in the chamber and (b) to climb on a box that was already beneath a toy banana and peck the banana. In addition, each bird spent time with the banana until the bird neither jumped nor flew toward the banana. Once this was accomplished, the researchers hung the toy banana from the ceiling out of reach of the pigeon and placed the box elsewhere in the chamber. Note that the researchers did *not* train the bird to push the box toward the banana. In fact, the situation was quite similar to that confronted by Sultan. The bird's behavior was also remarkably like that of the chimp:

> It paced and looked perplexed, stretched toward the banana, glanced back and forth from box to banana and then energetically pushed the box toward it, looking up at it repeatedly as it did so, then stopped just short of it, climbed, and pecked. The solution appeared in about a minute for each of three birds. (Epstein, 1984, p. 48f; see Figure 7-4)

One could, of course, argue that the birds had solved the problem through some mysterious process (e.g., the workings of the avian unconscious); but it is more parsimonious to attribute the solution to the animal's reinforcement history.

Query: Epstein's experiment demonstrates that

insightful problem solving is largely the product of

_____.

Note that in this experiment, the solution appeared suddenly after a period of "contemplation," as is supposed to happen in insightful problem solving. The point is that this "sudden insight" depended on the previous reinforcement of the separate behaviors required for a solution. Birds that had been trained to climb the box and to peck the banana, but

Figure 7-4 *Insight in the pigeon. In A and B the bird looks back and forth from banana to box. In C it pushes the box toward the banana. Then in D it climbs on the box and pecks. (Original photo credit: Dr. Robert Epstein. Reprinted by permission.)*

not to push the box, did not solve the problem. It would appear that achieving insight into a problem depends largely on the reinforcement of behavior related to the problem's solution.[12]

We humans are, of course, far better at solving problems than are other animals, but this does not mean that our reinforcement history is less important. Indeed, our greater success may be largely due to our being more adept at learning from the consequences of our behavior. As Thorndike observed in 1911, "Because he learns fast and learns much, in the animal way, man seems to learn by intuitions of his own" (p. 281).

REVIEW Insight into problems, once thought to be an unfathomable phenomenon, is now understood to be the product of a particular learning history. Experiments suggest that the "sudden" appearance of insightful solutions is not so sudden, and that the appearance depends directly on the organism's history of reinforcement.

[12]For more on Epstein's theory of insight, see Epstein (1999).

Creativity

If insightful problem solving has been shrouded in mystery, it is nothing compared to that surrounding creativity. This realm of behavior is often said to defy scientific analysis. But is creativity really unfathomable?

Let us begin with a definition. Creativity has been defined in many ways, but one feature that is always mentioned is novelty. For a drawing, sculpture, story, invention, dance, idea, or anything else to be judged creative, it must be novel; that is, it must be relatively unlike other drawings, sculptures, stories, inventions, dances, or ideas.

Novelty is seldom sufficient, in and of itself, for a product to be judged worthwhile. A two-year-old child scribbling on the wall with a crayon may produce a composition unlike any the world has ever seen, but it is not likely to be called art. A biologist may theorize that plant life evolved out of animal life. That may be a novel idea, but it may not be embraced by other biologists. However, nothing (regardless of its merits) is judged creative unless it is different from other products of its type. To be creative, then, means above all else to behave in original ways.

Where does original behavior come from? In ancient Greece, people believed that the muses (spirits that specialized in art, music, or literature) visited a person. If one wanted to write poetry, one waited for Erato, the muse of poetry; the poet was merely an instrument for Erato's work. This theory is still expressed occasionally by people in the arts today. A more modern version of the theory moves the muse into the person, usually lodging her in the "unconscious mind."

An analysis of creativity in terms of operant learning looks chiefly to the history of reinforcement. The idea that reinforcement may lead to creativity may seem a logical absurdity. A reinforcer is, by definition, something that strengthens the behavior it follows. But the whole point of creativity is to get *new* forms of behavior, not old behavior. How is it possible to get novel behavior with reinforcement?[13] A porpoise named Malia provides an answer.

Query: The idea of increasing creativity by means of rein-

forcement seems illogical at first because reinforcement

_____.

_____

[13]Many people mistakenly believe that reinforcement *must* suppress creativity since, by definition, it strengthens the behavior that produces reinforcement. This statement is at odds with research on creativity.

In the 1960s, Karen Pryor (1991) was an animal trainer at the Ocean Science Theater in Hawaii. The theater was a kind of aquarium at which people could watch porpoises and other sea animals perform tricks. One day Pryor and the other trainers realized that the show they put on for the public was getting stale. The animals were getting "a little too good, a little too slick, a little too polished" (p. 234). To liven things up a bit, the trainers decided to demonstrate how the animals were trained by waiting for Malia, one of their star performers, to do something and then reinforcing that behavior. The audience would actually see learning take place as the reinforced behavior increased rapidly in frequency. The plan worked extraordinarily well, and the trainers made it a regular part of the show. In the next few days, Malia received reinforcement for all sorts of typical porpoise behavior: tail slapping, swimming upside down, rising out of the water, and so on. After only 14 shows, however, the trainers had a new problem: They were running out of behavior to reinforce.

Malia solved the problem for them. One day Malia "got up a good head of steam, rolled over on her back, stuck her tail in the air, and coasted about 15 feet with her tail out" (p. 236). It was a delightful sight, and everyone, including the trainers, roared with laughter. Malia received a fish and repeated the stunt a dozen times.

Pryor gradually realized that all a trainer had to do to get novel behavior was to reinforce novel behavior. Malia was soon producing novel behaviors on a regular basis; she had learned to be creative.

Pryor (Pryor et al., 1969) repeated the experiment in a more formal fashion with a porpoise named Hou. The new pupil was not as fast a learner as Malia had been, but Hou eventually produced four novel stunts in one training session. After this, Hou "came up with novelty after novelty, sinking head downwards, spitting water at the trainer, jumping upside down" (p. 242). By the 13th training session, Hou had produced a novel behavior in six out of seven consecutive sessions. Note that Pryor did not decide beforehand what Hou should do, nor did she shape creative behavior; she simply reinforced any novel behavior that appeared.

Even some small-brained species can show remarkable creativity if originality is systematically reinforced. Pryor and her group (1969) reinforced novel behavior in pigeons. As a result, some of the birds engaged in such unusual behavior as lying on their backs, standing with both feet on one wing, and hovering two inches above the cage floor.

A number of studies have shown that the same basic technique, reinforcing novel behavior, can increase the creativity of people. In one study, John Glover and A. L. Gary (1976) asked fourth- and fifth-graders to think of uses for various objects such as a can, brick, or pencil. The students worked in teams and earned points by coming up with uses for a particular object. At various times, different kinds of criteria had to be met to earn points. The results showed that reinforcement affected the kinds of behavior produced. When unusual uses earned points, the number of unusual uses rose sharply. For instance, during the baseline period, students asked to come up with uses for a box might suggest variations on the idea that a box is used to store things in (e.g., "hold books in," "hold leaves in," etc.). But when originality earned points, some very unusual uses appeared. Asked for uses of a brick, for example, one student suggested attaching a brick to each foot as a way to develop leg strength. Another, asked to come up with an original use for blackboard erasers, proposed that they could be stuffed into his shirt "to make my shoulders look bigger." Originality and other measures of creativity showed a strong increase as a result of reinforcement for creative ideas.

Kathy Chambers and her colleagues (1977) obtained similar results when they reinforced originality in block building. In this study, one of the experimenters asked first- and second-graders to build things with blocks. Each time a child in the experimental group produced a new form of construction, the experimenter praised him or her. The experimenter watched children in the control group work but made no comment about their constructions. Praise resulted in nearly twice as many different constructional forms being produced by children in the experimental group.

Query: How could an auto manufacturer increase the

creativity of its designers?

Other studies of the effects of reinforcement on creative behavior have produced similar results (Goetz, 1982; Goetz & Baer, 1973; Sloane et al., 1980; Winston & Baker, 1985). Increasing creativity seems to be no great trick; all you need to do is reinforce creative acts whenever they occur.

Despite such evidence, some psychologists have argued that reinforcement (or, more precisely, reward) actually makes people *less* creative (Amabile, 1983; Deci & Ryan, 1985; Hennessey & Amabile, 1988; Lepper, 1998; but see also Eisenberger & Cameron, 1998). Typically they point to studies in which people are promised a reward for performing a task, and their performance is compared to that of other people who were promised nothing. Those offered a reward are generally less creative. In one experiment, for example, Arie Kruglanski and colleagues (1971) asked college students to invent titles for paragraphs and found that those who were promised a reward produced less novel titles than those who weren't. In a similar study, Teresa Amabile (1982) offered children a reward for constructing a collage, and their efforts were less creative than those of children who performed the task without expecting to receive anything.

Why do some studies show that rewards reduce creativity? Probably the answer has to do with the way rewards are used. In studies that get negative results, there is typically no contingency between creative performance and the reward. Essentially a person is told, "Do this task and you'll get a reward." In studies that show increased creativity, reinforcers (or rewards) are contingent on creative behavior.

This is a fundamental difference. Robert Eisenberger and Stephen Armeli (1997) found, for example, that if they rewarded conventional performance on a task, they got more conventional performance, but if they rewarded creative performance, they got more creativity. Other studies have produced similar results (Eisenberger et al., 1998; Eisenberger & Rhoades, 2001; Eisenberger & Selbst, 1994). Increasing creativity seems to be no great trick; all you need to do is reinforce creative acts whenever they occur.

But why are people inclined to be less creative when promised a reward for merely performing a task? Eisenberger and Linda Rhoades (2001) suggest that in our society creativity is not always appreciated. When offered a reward for performing a task, the surest way of pleasing a person and receiving the promised reward is to perform the task in a conventional (i.e., generally approved) way. If there is no reward at stake, one can afford to be more creative.

Suppose, for example, that you were hired to paint a man's house white with blue trim. You could paint not only the shutters blue, but the rain gutters, spouts, windows, and doors. That would be rather creative, but if you wanted to be sure of getting paid, you would probably do the job in a more conventional manner.

The clear implication of creativity research, taken as a whole, is that if you want people to be more creative, you should make reinforcing consequences contingent on *creative* behavior, not merely on the performance of a task. For, as Steven Kerr (1975) pointed out years ago, it is folly to reward A, and expect to get B.

It ought not to surprise us that success (obtaining reinforcers) can increase creativity. Interestingly enough, recent research suggests that *failure* can also increase creativity. It has long been known that when a behavior that has been repeatedly reinforced is put on extinction, there is an increase in the variability of behavior. In other words, when old tactics fail, the organism tries something different. Alan Neuringer and colleagues (2001)) trained rats to get food by performing a complex series of acts. When this behavior no longer worked, the rats tried variations on the previous tactic. Thus, they became more creative. This finding implies that if we want people to be more creative, we might teach them how to solve problems in a certain way and then, when they have mastered the technique, present them with problems that *cannot* be solved in that way. The failure may induce them to come up with new ways of solving the problem. This tactic would have to be used cautiously, however, because failure tends to be punishing; with too much failure, you might see no creative effort, or any effort at all.

REVIEW   Like insightful problem solving, creativity now seems less mysterious than it once did. Instead of attributing the creative act to a muse or some dark, hidden recess of the soul, we can see that creativity is a function of learning. This new understanding brings with it the realization that creativity is not the domain of the chosen few; we can all learn to be creative.

Superstition

In most instances of operant reinforcement, the behavior causes the reinforcer to occur. This raises an interesting question: What is the effect of a reinforcer if its appearance following a behavior is merely coincidental? Suppose, for example, that you put a pigeon into a Skinner box and modified the feeding mechanism so that grain became available every 15 seconds, *regardless* of what the bird happened to be doing at the time. Would the delivery of food in this way affect the pigeon's behavior?

Skinner (1948) actually performed this experiment. He found that out of eight pigeons, six developed some clear-cut behavior: One bird turned in counterclockwise circles, another raised its head toward one of the corners of the cage, one pigeon bobbed its head up and down, two birds swung their heads to and fro, and the sixth pigeon made brushing movements toward the floor, as if trying to peck it. The animals appeared to have learned to perform strange rituals, even though the reinforcer came regardless of whether the birds engaged in the behavior. Skinner called these acts **superstitious behavior** because the birds behaved as if their rituals produced reinforcement, when in fact they did not.

Skinner's explanation of this phenomenon is quite simple. When the first reinforcer arrived, the animal had to be doing *something*. If the bird happened to be bobbing its head up and down (something that pigeons are inclined to do occasionally), then head bobbing was accidentally reinforced. This meant that head bobbing was likely to occur again, which meant it was still more likely to be reinforced, and so on.

Superstitious behavior is not restricted to pigeons. Gregory Wagner and Edward Morris (1987) of the University of Kansas conducted a carefully designed study of superstitious behavior in children. They began by introducing preschool children to a mechanical clown named Bobo that periodically dispensed marbles from its mouth. Bobo spit out marbles at fixed intervals regardless of what the children did. The researchers told the children that "sometimes Bobo will give marbles" and that they should take any marbles Bobo might provide and put them in a box. When they had collected enough marbles, they would be able to trade them for a toy. The researchers worked with one child at a time and, after explaining about the marbles and the toys, left the child alone with Bobo. What Wagner and Morris found was that superstitious behavior emerged in 7 of the 12 children studied. Some children sucked their thumbs, some swung their hips back and forth, some touched Bobo or kissed him on the nose. These and other actions were judged to be superstitious only if the behavior emerged after adventitious (i.e., accidental, coincidental) reinforcement began and occurred with increasing frequency during intervals between reinforcement.

In another study, Alfred Bruner and Samuel Revusky (1961) used adventitious reinforcement to establish superstitious behavior in four high school students. Each student sat in front of four telegraph keys. If the student pressed the right key, a bell would sound and a red light would go on. Each time this happened, the student would earn five cents, which could be collected later. The solution consisted of depressing the third key from the student's left, but this behavior was reinforced only if it occurred after an interval of several seconds. What happened was that the students began pressing the other keys during these periods of nonreinforcement. Eventually, the nonreinforcement period would end, the student would happen to hit key 3 again, and this act would be reinforced. However, the key presses that immediately preceded hitting key 3 were also reinforced, even though they had nothing to do with making the bell sound and the light go on. Eventually, each student worked out a pattern of key presses, such as 1, 2, 3, 4, 1, 2, 3. Interestingly, the experimenters report that none of the students suspected that any part of their behavior was superstitious. The students believed they had discovered the one correct formula for producing reinforcement.

Koichi Ono (1987) of Komazawa University in Tokyo established superstition in university students. The students sat at a table with three levers. At the back of the table was a partition with a signal light and a counter that recorded points earned. Ono simply told the students they were to earn as many points as they could. In fact, nothing the student did had any effect on the accumulation of points. Periodically the light would go on and the counter would register one point—regardless of what the student did.

Most students developed superstitious behaviors. Analysis of the data revealed that each superstitious act began after it happened to be followed by delivery of a point. Most of the superstitions involved pulling the lever in some way, but coincidental reinforcement led one student to develop rather strange behavior having nothing to do with the levers. At one point, this student stopped pulling the lever momentarily and happened to put her right hand on the lever frame. Ono writes:

> This behavior was followed by a point delivery, after which she climbed on the table and put her right hand to the counter. Just as she did so, another point was delivered. Thereafter she began to touch many things in turn, such as the signal light, the screen, a nail on the screen, and the wall. About 10 minutes later, a point was delivered just as she jumped to the floor, and touching was replaced by jumping. After five jumps, a point was delivered when she jumped and touched the ceiling with her slipper in her hand. Jumping to touch the ceiling continued repeatedly and was followed by points until she stopped about 25 minutes into the session, perhaps because of fatigue. (p. 265)

Richard Herrnstein (1966) has argued that superstitious behavior can occur as a kind of by-product of training. He notes that in many instances, a particular feature of a behavior is essential for reinforcement, but other features are not. If the essential feature produces reinforcement, the other features are adventitiously reinforced. He cites handwriting as an example. As students make the various letters of the alphabet, reinforcement is contingent on their producing certain features of the letters. However, there is a good deal of latitude in how the letters may be formed. For example, in making a cursive, lowercase *t*, it is necessary to produce a nearly vertical straight line and to cross that line with a horizontal line. But the vertical line may, in fact, be a loop (like the cursive letter *l*), and it can be short or long; likewise, the horizontal line can be short or long, perfectly horizontal or angled up or down, and it can appear near the top of the vertical line or near the bottom. If essential features are performed in such a way as to gain reinforcement, other nonessential features of handwriting are adventitiously reinforced. The implication is that the wide differences in handwriting, among other idiosyncrasies, are superstitious behavior. Some research supports Herrnstein's hypothesis (see, for example, Leander et al., 1968; Vyse & Heltzer, 1990).

Query: Herrnstein suggests variations in handwriting are due

to _____.

But many human superstitions seem too complex and too widespread to be attributed to adventitious reinforcement alone. Many people sprinkle salt over their shoulders or carry good luck charms. In some societies, people have engaged in rain dances and human sacrifice. Can such practices be attributed to adventitious reinforcement of individual behavior?

Herrnstein (1966) argues that it is unlikely that such behavior is shaped by adventitious reinforcement. However, he proposes that if a person can be induced to perform a superstitious act, it might be maintained by adventitious reinforcement. To test this idea, he trained a pigeon to peck a disk by reinforcing each disk peck that occurred after an 11-second interval. (In other words, the bird received no reinforcement for disk pecks during the interval.) When disk pecking was well established, Herrnstein stopped reinforcing this behavior and began providing food every 11 seconds *regardless* of what the bird did. Note that although the reinforcement contingencies had changed, the animal was expected to show a relatively high frequency of disk pecking, at least initially, because previously the behavior had paid off. Thus, the now ineffectual behavior of disk pecking could easily be adventitiously reinforced. Under these conditions, the rate of disk pecking declined somewhat but did not die out. Apparently, the adventitious reinforcement was sufficient to maintain the behavior. (See also Neuringer, 1970, and Gleeson et al., 1989.)

Herrnstein's experiment suggests that almost any behavior, however complex and improbable, can be maintained through adventitious reinforcement if the organism can be induced to perform it at least once. He notes further that the most common human superstitions arise in a social context. We hear about rabbits' feet, about the dangers of black cats, about Friday the 13th, about spilling salt. Further, we are encouraged to perform superstitious acts. Children, for example, may be required by a parent to throw a bit of salt over one shoulder after spilling salt on the dinner table. A child may be encouraged to carry a rabbit's foot "for luck." Once such behavior is performed, there is the chance that it will be adventitiously reinforced. If a child who carries a rabbit's foot is unhurt in a minor bicycle accident, his or her belief in the protective power of a rabbit's foot may have been greatly strengthened.[14]

---

[14] It is probably not a coincidence that superstitions seem to be particularly common among people engaged in risky work, such as fishermen, athletes, professional gamblers, and stock speculators. In such cases negative reinforcement might be involved as much as positive reinforcement: If you spend a day rock climbing without being hurt, you might attribute it to your "lucky" socks.

Quick! Get Some Mud!

What would you do if, while camping miles from the nearest hospital, you were bitten by a poisonous snake?

There seems to be no end of ideas about how to cure snake bite. Some advocate covering the wound with mud. Others believe the cure is to drink whiskey. Some think the answer is to fast, while others are convinced you need to kill and eat the snake that bit you. Some people believe it's possible to save yourself by casting a spell. Others will scoff at that idea—and urge you to cauterize the wound with a red hot knife.

Why are there so many superstitious cures for snake bite? I believe the answer probably has to do with the fact that the victim is likely to survive no matter what you do. This means, of course, that whatever you do is likely to be reinforced.

It has been reported that when poisonous snakes bite humans, only about half of the victims actually are injected with venom. This means that in half the cases of *poisonous* snake bite, whatever treatment is tried will appear to be helpful. Additionally, many harmless snakes are commonly mistaken for poisonous ones. And even if the snake is poisonous and does inject venom, many victims will survive without any treatment. All of which means that the odds are very good that no matter what steps a person takes to treat snake bite, the person will probably survive—and the treatment applied, however useless, will be reinforced.

You cannot, of course, persuade the person who has "seen it work" that his particular cure is superstitious.[15] So if you are ever out camping with friends and are bitten by a snake, don't be surprised if someone shouts, "Quick! Get some mud!"

Not everyone is happy with the reinforcement theory of superstition. John Staddon and Virginia Simmelhag (1971) and W. Timberlake and G. A. Lucas (1985), for example, have failed to obtain the complex rituals Skinner reported, and suggest that adventitious reinforcement merely increases the rate at which naturally dominant behaviors, such as pecking and wing flapping, occur (see the discussion in Staddon, 2001). Other studies have, however, produced results similar to Skinner's (e.g., Justice

---

[15]For hundreds of years physicians treated all manner of disease, from general malaise to cancer, with "purges" (enemas and laxatives) and bloodletting, although it is likely that these treatments killed far more patients than they helped. The history of medicine shows that physicians have often been slow to give up ineffective treatments, even when experimental evidence showed them to be useless. The physician all too often persists in the superstitious practice, claiming, "I have seen it work!"

& Looney, 1990; Ward, et al. 2002). Moreover, there is the evidence that adventitious reinforcement has produced clearly superstitious behavior in people. Did Koichi Ono's university student jump toward the ceiling because she had a natural tendency to jump?

Is there a way we might protect ourselves from our superstitious inclinations? Indeed there is. It is called scientific method. At its most fundamental level, scientific method means making observations under controlled conditions. Although it is not always practical to apply scientific method to everyday problems in the same rigorous way the researcher does in the laboratory, it is often useful for testing hypotheses in a more informal way. Had Ono's jumping college student tested her point-earning techniques by comparing them with other methods or by doing nothing at all, she might have discovered her error.

Superstitions can be harmful (the inappropriate use of antibiotics, for example, undermines their effectiveness against bacteria), but they are usually fairly innocuous. As Stuart Vyse (1997) points out, Skinner's pigeons risked little by turning in circles or engaging in other superstitious acts. "There is a strong tendency," Vyse writes, "to repeat any response that is coincident with reinforcement. In the long run, this tendency serves the species well: If turning in a circle really does operate the feeder, the bird eats and survives another day; if not, little is lost" (p. 76). Humans also "turn in circles" when this behavior is coincidentally reinforced. Most of the time, little is lost.

REVIEW   When a behavior is coincidentally followed by a reinforcer, that behavior is more likely to be repeated. Repetition of the behavior means that coincidental reinforcement is more likely to occur again. Behavior that is shaped or maintained by coincidental reinforcement is called superstitious. Some researchers question whether coincidental reinforcement can shape new behaviors, and certainly coincidental reinforcement does not, in itself, entirely account for all superstitions. But it seems clear that reinforcement does play a role in superstition.

Learned Helplessness

Some years ago, Martin Seligman and his colleagues (Overmier & Seligman, 1967; Seligman & Maier, 1967) were interested in the effects of Pavlovian fear conditioning on operant escape learning. In their experiments, they strapped a dog into a harness and paired a tone with shock. Next, they put the dog into one side of a shuttle box, sounded the tone, and delivered a shock to the dog's side of the box (see pages 148–149).

Normally, when a dog is put into a shuttle box and shocked, it runs about for a bit and then jumps over the barrier to the shock-free compartment. Each time the dog receives a shock, it escapes over the hurdle more quickly. If shocks are preceded by a tone, the dog learns to jump the hurdle when the tone sounds and thereby avoids shock entirely. (See Chapter 5 for a discussion of avoidance learning.) Seligman and his co-workers were interested in observing what effect the tone would have on escape learning after the tone had been paired with shock. For example, if the tone that sounded were already a CS for fear, might the dog jump the barrier and avoid shock on the very first trial?

What actually happened astonished the researchers and the research community. Seligman (1975) writes that the

> dog's first reactions to shock in the shuttle box were much the same as those of a naive dog: it ran around frantically for about thirty seconds. But then it stopped moving; to our surprise, it lay down and quietly whined. After one minute of this we turned the shock off; the dog had failed to cross the barrier and had not escaped from shock. On the next trial, the dog did it again; at first it struggled a bit and then, after a few seconds, it seemed to give up and to accept the shock passively. On all succeeding trials, the dog failed to escape. (p. 22)

The degree of passivity in these dogs was impressive. Seligman removed the barrier from the shuttle box so that the dog need only walk to the other side, yet the dog remained where it was, passively enduring the shock. Then Seligman got into the safe side of the box and called to the dog; the dog made no effort to move. Then the researchers put salami on the safe side of the box; although the dog had been deprived of food, it continued to lie there enduring shock.

Seligman called this phenomenon **learned helplessness**, since the inescapable shock seemed to teach the dogs to do nothing, to be helpless.[16] Further research demonstrated that it was not the prior exposure to shock, per se, that produced helplessness but the inescapability of the shock. Researchers have demonstrated helplessness repeatedly in other species, including fish (Padilla et al., 1970), rats (Maier et al., 1973), cats (Masserman, 1943), possibly the cockroach (Horridge, 1962), and people (Hiroto, 1974; Hiroto & Seligman, 1974).

Seligman proposed that learned helplessness might help us understand human depression, at least those depressions that are reactions to life

---

[16] Thorndike described the same phenomenon in 1898. He found that cats that repeatedly failed to escape from a box would, when put into that box, make no effort to escape. Notice that the cats developed learned helplessness even though the only aversive was repeated failure. This finding has important implications for teachers and parents.

events. Depression is characterized not only by sadness but by general in-activity. Depressed people often stop going to school or work, spend a great deal of time lounging about or sleeping, and generally become passive. Faced with a problem, they often do nothing about it. Depressed people, like Seligman's dogs, may refuse to take any steps to help themselves. Efforts to prod them into action with supportive statements ("Cheer up! There are other fish in the sea") or advice ("You should leave the jerk if he treats you so meanly") are usually ineffective. Like Seligman's dogs, many depressed people simply endure their pain and do nothing.

If helplessness is learned, can learning experiences prevent helpless-ness? There is some evidence that they can. For instance, Seligman and Steven Maier (1967) gave one group of dogs 10 escape trials in the shuttle box before exposing them to inescapable shock. When they tested these dogs in the shuttle box again, they performed like dogs that had never been shocked.

Other research demonstrates that "immunization training" may produce amazing resilience in the face of adversity. For example, Joseph Volpicelli and others (1983) trained some rats to press levers to escape shock and exposed others to the same amount of inescapable shock. After this the researchers put the rats in a shuttle box. In this study, unlike those described above, shuttling from one side of the box to the other did not allow the rats to escape shock. The reason for this change in procedure was to see whether the animals would continue trying to escape shock even though their efforts did not pay off. The result was that naive rats—those that had had no shocks beforehand—at first jumped readily from compartment to compartment, but their rate of shuttling declined sharply as testing continued. Rats that had been exposed to inescapable shock showed far less inclination to shuttle, and their rate of shuttling declined further with continued testing. Rats that had been able to escape shock by pressing a lever, however, behaved very differently in the shuttle box. These rats shuttled at a constant high rate, showing almost no decline over the course of 200 trials. After once learning to escape shocks, these rats refused to give up!

REVIEW   Learned helplessness has given us a new way to look at the failure of some people (previously dismissed as shiftless, lazy, or irresponsible) to deal effectively with life's challenges. It may also help us understand how the Unsinkable Molly Browns among us become "unsinkable." There is reason to believe that there are things we can do to immunize ourselves, and our children, against helplessness.

Delusions and Hallucinations

People in mental hospitals often have delusions (false beliefs such as "Everyone is out to get me" or "There are little green men inside my stomach") or hallucinations (they might hear voices that say "You're no good" or "You shouldn't have done what you did"). Delusions and hallucinations can and often do have an organic basis: Schizophrenia, syphilis, Alzheimer's disease, traumatic brain injury, and other disorders can induce them. But even when an organic disorder exists, the frequency of delusions, hallucinations, and other forms of bizarre behavior may be a function of reinforcement.

Joe Layng and Paul Andronis (1984) provide the example of a psychiatric patient who complained that her head was falling off. She seemed quite frightened, so a member of the staff sat with her to calm her down. The delusion got worse. A discussion with the patient led to the discovery that she found it very difficult to engage the staff in conversation. Sometimes when she approached them, they responded with obvious annoyance. Her delusional behavior produced the desirable effect (interaction with the staff) without the risk of hostile reactions. In other words, the delusion was reinforced. Once the woman learned how to approach the staff without incurring hostile reactions, the delusion disappeared, and her head remained securely attached.

Layng and Andronis also describe the case of a middle-age man admitted to a locked hospital ward after he tried to pull a pair of clothesline poles out of the ground in his backyard. He shouted that the poles were blasphemous statues of the cross and that Jesus had told him to tear them down. It turned out the man's efforts to involve his wife in his demanding business problems had been unsuccessful; she showed concern only when he behaved strangely. In other words, she inadvertently shaped increasingly pathological behavior until he finally behaved so bizarrely that he was hospitalized. When she learned to show concern for her husband's business problems instead of his bizarre behavior, his symptoms began to subside.

Another example is provided by Brad Alford (1986). He worked with a young schizophrenic patient in a psychiatric hospital. The man was greatly helped by medication but continued to complain that a "haggly old witch" followed him about.

Alford asked the patient to keep a record of his feeling that he was being followed. The patient also indicated the strength of his belief, from 0 (certainty that the belief was just his imagination) to 100 (certainty that there really was a witch). During the treatment phases, Alford reinforced expressions of doubt about the witch. The result was that the patient's reported confidence in the delusion declined (see Figure 7-5).

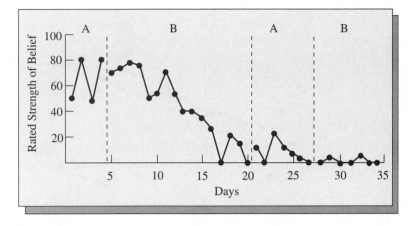

Figure 7-5 *Reinforcement and the strength of a delusion. During treatment (B) phases, expressions of doubt about a "haggly old witch" were reinforced, and the patient's confidence in the belief declined. (From "Behavioral Treatment of Schizophrenic Delusions: A Single-Case Experimental Analysis," by B. A. Alford, 1986,* Behavior Therapy, 17, *pp. 637–644. Copyright © 1986 by the Association for Advancement of Behavior Therapy. Reprinted by permission of the publisher and author.)*

One could argue, of course, that the patient believed in the witch as much as ever and merely learned not to admit it. To test this idea, Alford looked at the medication the patient received before and during the study. He found that the man received one kind of medication, a tranquilizer, only when he seemed agitated. If the patient remained convinced that the witch was real, then tranquilizer consumption should have remained constant. In fact, however, use of tranquilizers declined sharply (see Figure 7-6).

These findings do not mean that psychotic behavior is entirely the product of learning; diseases of the brain, such as schizophrenia, *do* produce bizarre behavior. However, even when behavior arises from an organic disease, the bizarre behavior associated with it may be modified by its consequences.[17]

One objection to the operant analysis of psychotic behavior is that such behavior often occurs even when it is not reinforced. Goldiamond (1975a) describes a woman virtually paralyzed by fear of cockroaches.

---

[17]Objections have been made to certain uses of positive reinforcement with psychiatric patients. For example, in treating lethargic patients, clinicians have made reinforcers contingent on doing things, such as making their bed or cleaning their room. Civil libertarians objected that the patients were being forced to work. So, even though programs of this sort are usually beneficial to patients, litigation has sometimes prevented them from being implemented.

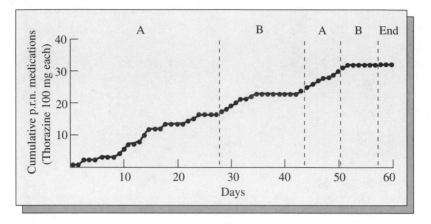

Figure 7-6   *Reinforcement and the strength of a delusion. During treatment (B) phases, when doubts about a witch were reinforced, the patient's consumption of tranquilizers declined. (From "Behavioral Treatment of Schizophrenic Delusions: A Single-Case Experimental Analysis," by B. A. Alford, 1986,* Behavior Therapy, 17, *pp. 637–644. Copyright © 1986 by the Association for Advancement of Behavior Therapy. Reprinted by permission of the publisher and author.)*

She remained in bed, too afraid to move about. Her husband was sympathetic and gave her the attention she had previously been denied. This attention was apparently the reinforcer that maintained her phobic behavior. But there seems to be a problem with this explanation since the woman stayed in bed even when her husband was not around to provide reinforcement. Why?

Goldiamond suggests that the answer is simple. If a person behaves bizarrely only when reinforcement for bizarre behavior is available, people catch on. Reinforcement for bizarre behavior is therefore often contingent not only on the occurrence of the behavior but on the occurrence of the behavior *at times when reinforcement is unavailable.* "In other words," write Layng and Andronis (1984), "the apparent absence of maintaining consequences or the presence of aversive consequences on some occasions, may be requirements that must be met for reinforcement to be available on other occasions" (p. 142). The idea is familiar to every person who, as a child, got out of going to school by feigning illness: As soon as you leap for joy at being allowed to stay home, you get sent to school![18]

---

[18]This helps to explain why many children who are at death's door at 7 A.M. are completely recovered by noon, at which time, coincidentally, there is little likelihood that they will be taken to school.

REVIEW   The traditional approach to delusions and hallucinations assumes that disordered thoughts reflect a disordered inner world. The traditional clinician therefore attempts to understand this private world, often by inviting the patient to describe it in great depth, an ineffective treatment. But an analysis in terms of learning suggests that delusions and hallucinations partly reflect a disordered *environment*. This means that the clinician's task is to understand and modify the patient's surroundings.[19]

Self-Injurious Behavior

One of the most disturbing problems faced by clinicians is self-injurious behavior. Although "normal" children sometimes intentionally injure themselves, serious cases are usually found in those suffering from autism or mental retardation. Some patients repeatedly bite, scratch, or hit themselves, or bang their heads against hard objects. Patients have been known to blind themselves by poking themselves repeatedly in the eye with a finger or fist. Some have chewed off fingers. Repeated biting or scratching can cause scarring and blood poisoning, and head banging can cause retinal detachment and brain damage.

Not so very long ago, self-injurious behavior was dealt with by putting the patient into restraints. This might take the form of a straitjacket or straps that fastened the hands to the sides. Sometimes patients were tied to their bed, spread-eagle, so they could not hurt themselves. This practice is far less common today thanks to the development of effective treatments based on operant learning.

In the 1960s, Ivar Lovaas discovered that punishment could be used to suppress self-injurious behavior (see Chance, 1974, for a summary). In one study, Lovaas and J. Q. Simmons (1969) worked with a boy who hit himself as many as 300 times in a 10-minute period if not restrained. (That is one blow every 2 seconds!) This behavior ended abruptly when the experimenters provided a painful but noninjurious electric shock to the boy's leg when he hit himself. Incredibly, a single shock practically ended the self-injurious behavior. After a total of only *four* contingent shocks, the self-injurious behavior did not recur. An extremely high rate of self-injurious behavior had been stopped with just a few contingent shocks.

---

[19]Many studies have demonstrated that the bizarre behavior of psychotic patients can be modified by changing their environment (see, for example, Ayllon & Haughton, 1962; Haynes & Geddy, 1973).

Query: Once self-injurious behavior was thought to be

due to an unconscious need to suffer, but if that were the

case, the shocks given by Lovaas and Simmons would have

_____ self-injurious acts.

Many other experiments demonstrated that long-standing self-injurious behavior could be ended or greatly reduced in short order with punishment. The aversives used (electric shock administered with a shock stick, a slap on the thigh or buttock with the open hand) were painful, but not injurious. And the ability to end self-injurious behavior meant that other therapeutic efforts could move forward (Lovaas, 1987, 1993). Still, no one liked the idea of shocking or slapping a retarded or psychotic patient, so a good deal of research attention went into developing other procedures for dealing with self-injurious behavior. These efforts were successful, and aversives are now generally used only when other procedures have failed.

The effort to deal with this problem became easier once researchers began to get a clearer idea of why self-injurious behavior occurs. It had been assumed that the behavior was merely a symptom of the underlying organic disorder, but then researchers began to find that the behavior tended to occur more often in certain situations than in others.

Montrose Wolf and his colleagues (1967) noticed that self-injurious behavior in disturbed children seemed to be precipitated by teacher requests. When a teacher asked a self-injurious child to do something, the rate of self-injury went up. When the teacher stopped asking a child to perform the tasks, the frequency of self-injury went down. Some time after this observation, Edward Carr and his colleagues (1976) studied the self-injurious behavior of an 8-year-old boy named Tim. The researchers tallied the number of self-injurious acts that occurred during lessons and compared it with the number that occurred during free play. They found that almost all the self-injurious behavior occurred during the lessons—that is, when demands were being placed on the child (see Figure 7-7).

In other studies, researchers found that self-injury and other forms of bizarre behavior were often negatively reinforced (Carr & Newsom, 1985; Iwata et al., 1994). What happens is that the child finds that he can escape from an aversive situation by behaving in a bizarre or disruptive fashion.[20]

---

[20]As a result of these discoveries, it is an increasingly common practice for therapists to do a "functional assessment" before attempting to treat any serious behavior disorder. A func-

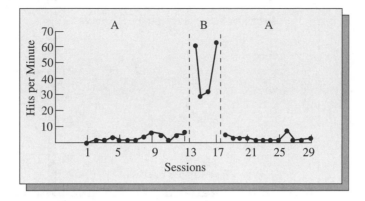

Figure 7-7   *Negative reinforcement of self-injurious behavior. Number of times 8-year-old Tim hit himself each minute during free time (A) and during lessons (B). The data suggest that escape from lessons might have reinforced the behavior. (From "Stimulus Control of Self-Destructive Behavior in a Psychotic Child," by E. G. Carr, D. D. Newsom, and J. A. Binkoff, 1976,* Journal of Abnormal Child Psychology, *4, pp. 139–153 Copyright © 1976 Plenum Publishing Corporation. Reprinted with permission.)*

The discovery that self-injurious behavior is often the result of reinforcement led to new, nonaversive treatment approaches. For instance, Edward Carr and Jack McDowell (1980) treated a case of self-injurious scratching in an otherwise healthy 10-year-old boy. Jim began scratching following exposure to poison oak. The dermatitis cleared up after a few weeks, but Jim continued to scratch for *three years*. When Carr and McDowell finally saw Jim for treatment, his skin was covered with scars and sores and he was the object of ridicule among his peers. The experimenters found that nearly all the scratching occurred at home and seemed to be maintained by parental attention. When Jim's parents saw him scratching, they would often make comments about it ("Jim, stop scratching") or attempt to restrain his hands. To be sure that this attention was acting as a reinforcer, the experimenters had the parents systematically withhold or provide attention for scratching. The results clearly showed that scratching depended on attention (see Figure 7-8).

---

tional assessment consists of observing the behavior under study, usually in a natural setting, to identify naturally occurring events that might be influencing it. Hypotheses are formed, for example, about what events may be reinforcing the behavior, and these are then tested in a controlled way. This typically suggests an effective treatment. Functional assessments are so useful in identifying effective interventions that some therapists now consider it unethical to treat a problem without doing one (Hineline, in Morris et al., 2001). For more on functional assessment, see Horner (1994).

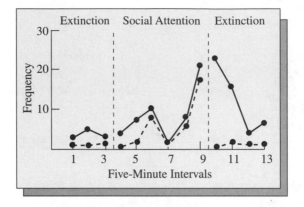

Figure 7-8   *Reinforcement of scratching. Scratching declined when ignored and increased when attended to. Note the high degree of correspondence between the frequency of attention (broken line) and scratching (solid line). (After "Social Control of Self-Injurious Behavior of Organic Etiology," by E. G. Carr and J. J. McDowell, 1980,* Behavior Therapy, *11, pp. 402–409. Copyright © 1980 by the Association for the Advancement of Behavior Therapy. Reprinted by permission of the publisher and author.)*

Jim's scratching might have been treated by having the parents simply ignore scratching entirely—that is, by putting the behavior on extinction. Unfortunately, the scratching so annoyed the boy's parents that they were unable to ignore it for long. Carr and McDowell therefore asked the parents to use punishment in the form of time out: Each time they saw Jim scratch, they were to send him to a small, rather uninteresting room for several minutes. The researchers also recommended reinforcement for not scratching: Jim earned weekly rewards, such as a trip to a museum or a skating rink, by reducing the number of sores on his body. Thus, the researchers combined punishment with positive reinforcement. This treatment resulted in a sharp reduction in the number of sores (see Figure 7-9). By the end of the study, Jim had only two sores, and these were almost completely healed.

Several other procedures have been used to control self-injurious behavior without the use of aversives (Foxx, 2001). Hughes Tarpley and Stephen Schroeder (1979), for example, showed that differential reinforcement of incompatible behavior can reduce self-injurious behavior. In one case, they periodically provided food to an 8-year-old boy if, instead of hitting himself in the face, he played steadily with a ball. Within 40 minutes, the rate of face punching had fallen by over 90%.

Some traditional psychodynamic (e.g., Freudian) therapists claim that any problem behavior eliminated with learning procedures will be replaced by a new problem, an idea called symptom substitution. There

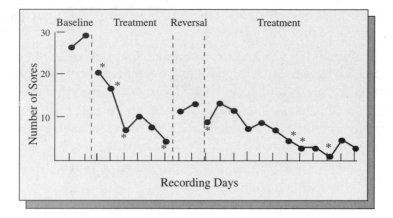

Figure 7-9 *Reducing scratching. Number of body sores recorded over a 9-month period. Treatment consisted of positive reinforcement (indicated by asterisks) for a reduction in sores, and punishment (in the form of time out) for scratching. (After "Social Control of Self-Injurious Behavior of Organic Etiology," by E. G. Carr and J. J. McDowell, 1980, Behavior Therapy, 11, pp. 402–409. Copyright © 1980 by the Association for Advancement of Behavior Therapy. Reprinted by permission of the publisher and author.)*

is little or no scientific support for symptom substitution, and the American Psychiatric Association (1973) dismissed it long ago. (See also, Baker, 1969; Cahoon, 1968; Myers & Thyer, 1994; Yates, 1958). Nevertheless, the myth of symptom substitution persists.

REVIEW Self-injurious behavior can be a very serious, even life-threatening, problem. For many years there were no effective treatments for the worst cases, which typically occurred in mentally retarded or psychotic people. Today, however, it is often treated very successfully, usually without aversives, thanks to procedures based on operant learning.

The topics discussed above do not, of course, exhaust the applications of operant procedures. But they may give some idea of the range of those applications. Clearly, operant research has much to offer humanity, both in our efforts to understand ourselves and in our efforts to create a more humane world.

RECOMMENDED READING

1. Braginsky, B., Braginsky, D., & Ring, K. (1971). *Methods of madness: The mental hospital as a last resort.* New York: Holt, Rinehart & Winston.

The authors describe research showing that psychiatric patients know where the reinforcers are.

2. Goldiamond, I. (1975). A constructional approach to self-control. In A. Schwartz & I. Goldiamond (Eds.), *Social casework: A behavioral approach* (pp. 67–130). New York: Columbia University Press.

   Traditional behavior therapy focused on eliminating inappropriate or troublesome behavior. Goldiamond shifted the focus to constructing new useful behaviors.

3. Latham, G. I. (1994). *The power of positive parenting.* Salt Lake City, UT: Northwest Publishing.

   A supremely practical, humane, down-to-earth guide for parents, solidly based on operant learning principles.

4. Vyse, S. (1997). *Believing in magic: The psychology of superstition.* New York: Oxford University Press.

   Stuart Vyse offers a fascinating review of superstitious behaviors and the attempts to explain them.

5. Wilkes, G. (1994). *A behavior sampler.* North Bend, WA: Sunshine Books.

   If you are thinking of becoming a veterinarian, animal trainer, or zoo director, this book by professional "animal behaviorist" Gary Wilkes will be an eye-opener.

REVIEW QUESTIONS

1. Define the following terms in your own words:

   learned helplessness   superstitious behavior

2. In what sense is the relationship between an organism and its environment reciprocal?

3. How is self-awareness like the awareness we have of others? How is it different?

4. Janet hypothesizes that people who are good at observing others are good at observing themselves. Design a study to test her hypothesis.

5. Does the use of a mirror by Gallup's chimps imply a concept of self?

6. How is an operant analysis of verbal behavior different from the traditional approach to language?

7. Given the role of reinforcement in verbal behavior, what reasons can

you give to explain why some people talk to themselves when alone?

8. In supporting the operant view of verbal behavior, which research described in this chapter is more important: that of Quay or that of Verplanck?

9. Occasionally the solution to a problem comes to a person in a dream. Can you account for this in terms of operant learning?

10. Why is insight not an adequate *explanation* of problem solving?

11. Studies show that students who have difficulty learning higher level skills, such as algebra, often perform poorly at lower level skills. Explain why.

12. You head the product development division of a major corporation. How can you get the people in your division to come up with more ideas for new products?

13. How can a writing instructor get his students to write more creative stories?

14. There is some evidence that very creative people are more inclined toward mental illness. Assuming this is true, how might you account for it in terms of operant learning?

15. Why are so many gamblers inclined to be superstitious?

16. Explain why people within the same family often share the same superstitious beliefs.

17. Could delusions sometimes be a form of superstitious behavior?

18. Suppose a psychiatric patient claims he is Napoleon. How could you determine whether this delusion is under the control of reinforcing consequences?

19. Why have the topics covered in this chapter resisted scientific analysis for so long?

20. What mysteries of human nature not covered in this chapter might succumb to an operant analysis?

PRACTICE QUIZ

1. In animal training, secondary reinforcement may be provided with a toy called a _____.

2. Gordon Gallup provided experimental evidence of awareness in
   _____.

3. Two strategies for achieving self-control are _____
   and _____.

4. The study in which William Verplanck reinforced opinions is an
   example of an _____ or within-subject experiment.

5. The experiment in which pigeons pecked a banana hanging from
   the ceiling demonstrated that insight is the product of the history of
   _____.

6. Gregory Wagner and Edward Morris studied _____
   behavior with the help of a mechanical clown named Bobo.

7. When a behavior is maintained by coincidental reinforcement, that
   behavior is _____.

8. Immunity against learned helplessness may be provided by exposure to aversive stimuli that can be _____.

9. Self-injurious behavior is often maintained by attention and by
   _____.

10. Many therapists now do a _____ assessment before
    attempting to treat a behavior problem.

QUERY ANSWERS

Page 221. The procedure used to modify the elephant's behavior was
shaping.

Page 222. To be self-aware is to *observe one's behavior.*

Page 227. Willpower is a circular explanation of behavior because the
evidence for willpower is *the behavior it is supposed to explain.*

Page 228. Self-control techniques include physical restraint, distancing,
distraction, deprivation and satiation, informing others, and monitoring behavior.

Page 230. Verbal behavior is governed by the law of *effect.*

Page 231. In his opinion study, Verplanck used an *ABA/within-subject/
single case* research design.

Page 233. Using the phrase is often reinforced in Western society: We
say that a wave goes up and down, that excited kids jump up and

down, that yo-yos go up and down, that the stock market goes up and down, and so on.

Page 235. A problem is a situation in which *reinforcement* is available, but the behavior necessary to produce it is not. Note: The problem solver is often physically capable of performing the behavior (recall Thorndike's cats) but does not perform it.

Page 237. Harlow's data show that "insightful" solutions may be arrived at *gradually* as a result of a number of learning experiences.

Page 238. Epstein's experiment demonstrates that insightful problem solving is largely the product of *the organism's learning history/previous learning*.

Page 240. The idea of increasing creativity by means of reinforcement seems illogical at first because reinforcement *increases the strength of old behavior*. (But if we reinforce *creative* behavior, we are likely to get more creative behavior.)

Page 242. The company might try providing bonuses, promotions, or awards to people when they produce creative designs. These actions should reinforce creative behavior.

Page 247. Herrnstein suggests variations in handwriting are due to *adventitious coincidental reinforcement*.

Page 256. Once self-injurious behavior was thought to be due to an unconscious need to suffer, but if that were the case, the shocks given by Lovaas and Simmons would have *reinforced* self-injurious acts.

Vicarious Learning

You can observe a lot by watching.

Yogi Berra

Sometimes the history of science is the story of a steady progression, rather like the climb up a winding staircase. Progress requires effort, and occasionally the scientist is found panting on a landing, but movement is always forward and usually upward. The study of classical conditioning, for example, began with the brilliant experiments of Pavlov and his co-workers and progressed more or less steadily until today our understanding of this phenomenon is fairly sophisticated. The study of operant learning followed a similar course. But sometimes the history of science is more like a roller-coaster ride than the climb up a staircase: One moment we're plummeting toward ruin; the next we seem to be headed for the stars. Vicarious learning is a case in point.

The problem posed by vicarious learning seems simple enough: Can one organism learn by observing the experience of another? The search for an answer to this question began with Thorndike. In Thorndike's day, it was widely believed that animals often learned by observing others. Everyone knew that the house cat watched people opening cabinet doors and then imitated their behavior. Could cats and other animals really learn this way? According to anecdotal evidence, the answer was yes.

Thorndike was not so sure, so he dealt with this belief the same way he had dealt with beliefs about animal intelligence: He submitted it to experimental test. His first subjects were chicks, cats, and dogs. In a typical experiment, Thorndike (1898) put one cat in a puzzle box and another cat in a nearby cage. The first cat had already learned how to escape the box, and the second had only to observe its neighbor to learn the trick. But when Thorndike put this cat into the puzzle box, he found that it did not imitate its more learned fellow. Instead, it went through the same sort of operant learning any other cat went through in learning to solve the problem. No matter how often one cat watched another escape, it seemed to learn nothing.

Query: The basic question posed by vicarious learning is

_____.

Thorndike found there was not the slightest difference between the behavior of cats that had observed a successful model and those that had not. He got similar results with chicks and dogs and concluded that "we should give up imitation as an a priori explanation of any novel intelligent performance" (p. 62). In other words, until someone demonstrates that animals learn by observing others, we ought not to assume that they do.

These experiments on vicarious learning, perhaps the first ever done, were published in 1898 as part of Thorndike's classic treatise on animal intelligence. Shortly thereafter, Thorndike (1901) conducted similar experiments with monkeys, but despite the popular belief that "monkey see, monkey do," Thorndike concluded that "nothing in my experience with these animals . . . favors the hypothesis that they have any general ability to learn to do things from seeing others do them" (p. 42). A few years after this, John B. Watson (1908) performed a similar series of experiments on monkeys with nearly identical results.

These negative findings seem to have had a devastating effect on research on vicarious learning. There was, in fact, almost no experimental investigation of this problem for a generation. Then, in the 1930s, Carl Warden and his colleagues conducted a number of carefully controlled experiments and clearly demonstrated that monkeys can learn by observing others.

Query: How might the lack of research on vicarious learning

have been due itself to vicarious learning?

These studies should have prompted an upswing in research on vicarious learning, but it continued to receive little attention. Then, in the 1960s, research in this area began to take off. Much of the impetus for this change was the research of Albert Bandura and his colleagues and the use of modeling in treating behavior disorders. These studies showed the importance of vicarious learning and spurred interest in the subject. Although research in this area continues to lag behind (Kymissis & Poulson, 1990; Robert, 1990), the subject is no longer ignored (Hirata & Morimura, 2000; Myowa-Yamakoshi & Matsuzawa, 2000).

Basic Procedures

Learning is a change in behavior due to experience. **Vicarious learning** may be defined as a change in behavior due to the experience of observing a model.[1]

---

[1]Vicarious learning is also known as observational learning.

For instance, a dog (the observer) might look on as another dog (the model) is exposed to the pairing of a bell and food. The model, of course, responds to this procedure by learning to salivate at the sound of the bell. If the observer also salivates at the sound of the bell, then we may say that the observer has learned through observation.

A similar procedure can be carried out with an aversive US, such as shock. If a dog is touched by a handler and then receives a shock, we may expect the dog to cringe when its handler reaches toward it. If another dog observes as this training takes place and later cringes when the handler reaches toward it, then we may say that vicarious learning has occurred.

An observer may also learn by observing a model undergo operant training. For instance, a monkey might look on as one of its peers lifts a cup, under which it finds a raisin. If, as a result of this experience, the observer lifts the cup and retrieves the raisin when given the opportunity, then vicarious learning has taken place.

Similarly, an observer may look on as a model's behavior is punished. A monkey might watch as a model reaches for a raisin in a bowl and receives a rap on its knuckles (and no raisin) each time it does so. Unless the model is very hungry, it will probably give up reaching into the bowl. If the observer declines to reach into the bowl when given the opportunity, then vicarious learning has occurred.

> **Query:** Vicarious learning may be defined as _____
>
> _____.

Do such procedures produce changes in behavior? Can people or animals really learn by observing others? The answer is not quite as straightforward as you might think. Let us examine some studies that have attempted to answer these questions.

Vicarious Pavlovian Conditioning

Patricia Barnett and David Benedetti (1960) conducted a study in which a model (a confederate of the experimenter) appeared to receive shocks shortly after a buzzer sounded. The observer, who was never shocked, watched as the model underwent training. Would the procedure result in the buzzer becoming a CS for fear in the observer? The researchers looked for a change in the observer's galvanic skin response (GSR), since the GSR is a measure of emotional arousal. They found that the buzzer did become a CS for fear in observers, even though they had never been shocked.

In a similar study, C. F. Haner and E. R. Whitney (1960) had one person, the model, rest a finger on a device that could produce a shock. Each time a light came on, the model withdrew his finger as if he had received a shock. The observer sat passively by and watched all this but was never in contact with the shock mechanism. As in the Barnett and Benedetti study, the experimenters recorded the observer's galvanic skin response as a measure of fear of the CS. They found that every observer in the experiment did, in fact, acquire a conditional response to the light.

In another experiment, Seymour Berger (1962) took GSR readings of observers as they watched a model undergo conditioning. The model sat at a table and rested a finger on a shock apparatus. Periodically a buzzer sounded, followed closely by the dimming of a light. The study is complicated and involves four different experimental conditions, but we are concerned with two groups in particular. Berger told these participants that the model would periodically receive a shock. For observers in one group, each time the light dimmed, the model quickly withdrew her hand from the apparatus. For observers in the other group, the model never moved.

Berger was interested in seeing whether differences in experimental conditions would affect the development of a conditional response, as measured by GSR, in observers. The result was that observers who saw the buzzer paired with apparent shock showed a strong tendency to react to the buzzer. Those who saw a model who apparently was *not* shocked showed little reaction (see Figure 8-1).

Gullermo Bernal and Seymour Berger (1976) attempted to demonstrate vicarious eyelid conditioning. In this study, observers watched a videotape of a person undergoing classical eyelid conditioning. As the observer watched the pairing of a tone with a puff of air in the model's eye, the experimenters recorded the observer's own tendency to blink. They found that before long the observer acquired a conditional eyeblink response.

Taken together, these studies seem to provide clear evidence of vicarious Pavlovian conditioning. Unfortunately, it is entirely possible that the conditional responses in observers were due to higher-order classical conditioning rather than to vicarious conditioning. Take, for example, the Bernal and Berger experiment just described. How do we know that seeing someone blink is not a CS for blinking? And if it is, then an observer may come to blink in response to a tone simply because the tone is paired with a well-established CS for blinking.

A study by Jerry Venn and Jerry Short (1973) suggests that this may be just what happens. Venn and Short had preschool children watch a film in which a 5-year-old boy responded fearfully to one of two plastic toys. The toys were plastic figures of two cartoon characters, Mickey Mouse and Donald Duck. The film shows a woman offering her son each toy in turn. Each time the mother offers the child Mickey Mouse, he

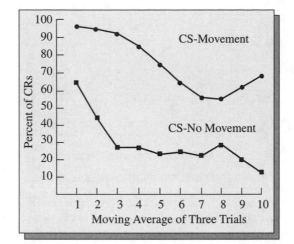

Figure 8-1 *Vicarious Pavlovian conditioning. Percentage of observers giving CRs when the CS was paired with movement (CS-Movement) and when it was not (CS-No Movement). (Adapted from "Conditioning Through Vicarious Instigation," by Seymour Berger, 1962,* Psychological Review, 69, *p. 458. Copyright © 1962 by the American Psychological Association. Reprinted with permission.)*

screams and moves away; each time she offers him Donald Duck, he looks about the room and makes irrelevant comments. Notice that, so far as the *model* is concerned, Mickey Mouse is not paired with an aversive US.

After having preschoolers watch the film, Venn and Short had the children sit at a table with two telegraph keys side by side. Each key had a plastic toy mounted on top of it: Mickey Mouse on one, Donald Duck on the other. There was a signal light over each telegraph key. The children had learned before watching the film that they could earn M&M candies by pressing each telegraph key whenever its signal light was on. After seeing the film, the researchers told the children they could again earn M&Ms by pressing the telegraph keys, but this time the two signal lights would go on at the same time. When the lights were on, the children could press one of the keys, or switch from one to the other. The researchers assumed that if the observers had acquired the model's fear of Mickey Mouse, they would show a preference for the Donald Duck key.

And in fact they did. The children showed no bias for either toy before watching the film, pressing the Mickey Mouse key about as often as the Donald Duck key. But after viewing the film it was a different story; now the children showed a strong preference for the Donald Duck key (see Figure 8-2). Apparently the children had acquired an aversion to the Mickey Mouse toy.

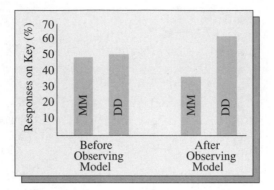

Figure 8-2 *Vicarious or direct fear conditioning? Average percentage of responses on the Mickey Mouse (MM) and Donald Duck (DD) keys before and after observing a model. The model was afraid of a Mickey Mouse toy. (Compiled from data in Venn and Short, 1973.)*

In a second experiment, Venn and Short (1973) had children view a film in which a model demonstrated a particular *liking* for the Mickey Mouse toy, rather than a fear of it. When the observers were then given the opportunity to earn M&Ms by pressing the Mickey Mouse or Donald Duck keys, they showed a strong preference for the Mickey Mouse key.

The important point about these experiments, for our purposes, is that the model did not undergo conditioning as the observer looked on. The observers saw the model presented with the Mickey Mouse toy, and they saw the model's reaction to the toy, but they *never saw the toy paired with a shock or other US.* Thus, the observers cannot be said to have undergone vicarious conditioning. Instead, we must view the change in the observers' behavior as the direct result of the pairing of the Mickey Mouse toy and the reaction of the model. When the researchers paired the toy with a fearful model, the observers developed an aversion for the toy. When the researchers paired the toy with a happy model, the observers developed a preference for the toy. Although observing a model is involved, strictly speaking the study demonstrates classical conditioning, not vicarious conditioning.

This conclusion is supported by research on vicarious conditioning in monkeys by Susan Mineka and Michael Cook (Cook & Mineka, 1990; Mineka & Cook, 1988). In one experiment, Mineka and Cook and their colleagues (Mineka et al., 1984) had six young monkeys that had earlier shown no fear of snakes look on as their wild-reared parents reacted with intense fear to snakes. (Captive monkeys do not have an "instinctive" fear of snakes.) After this experience, five of the six observer monkeys reacted with intense fear of snakes themselves. It took only 8 minutes of seeing one of their parents behave fearfully toward snakes for the observing youngsters to acquire the fear. In another experiment (Cook & Mineka, 1990), monkeys acquired a fear of snakes by watching a videotape of fearful monkeys.

However, in these experiments, as in those by Venn and Short, the model does not undergo conditioning. As far as the model is concerned, the snake is not paired with a fearful stimulus. This means that the learning of the observing monkeys can be accounted for in terms of ordinary conditioning: The snake is paired with the fear response of a model.

It is certainly true that people and some animals acquire conditional responses while observing models undergo conditioning, but it is by no means certain that this is a different procedure from ordinary conditioning. At present, the existence of vicarious Pavlovian conditioning appears to be doubtful at best. Now let us consider the case of vicarious operant learning.

Vicarious Operant Learning

Carl Warden (Warden et al., 1940; Warden & Jackson, 1935) was among the first to demonstrate experimentally that some animals can benefit from the consequences of a model's behavior. Warden began by constructing a special experimental environment with two compartments so that identical problems could be solved in each compartment (see Figure 8-3). He put an observer monkey in one compartment and restrained it so that it could not get to the problem apparatus. Then he put another monkey, the model, in the other compartment. The model had already learned to perform whatever act was necessary to obtain reinforcement.

In one study (Warden & Jackson, 1935), the simplest problem involved pulling a chain that opened a door and revealed a raisin the model could retrieve and eat. After watching the model perform this act five times, the observer got a chance to tackle the same problem in its own chamber. If the observer did not solve the problem within 60 seconds, the experimenters pulled the monkey away from the apparatus and restrained it for about half a minute before letting it have a second trial. The researchers repeated this procedure on the next two days for a total of six trials before going on to the next problem.

The results showed clearly that the observers had benefited substantially from watching the model, often responding correctly on the very first trial. Furthermore, when an animal succeeded, it often did so in far less time than would have been expected had it not watched a model. Forty-seven percent of all the solutions occurred within 10 seconds (almost as fast as the model's performance), and about 75% of the solutions occurred within 30 seconds.

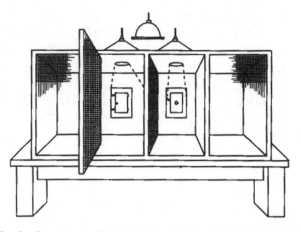

Figure 8-3   *The duplicate cage developed by Warden and used by him and his colleagues to study observational learning. From "Imitative Behavior in the Rhesus Monkey," by C. J. Warden and T. A. Jackson, 1935,* Journal of Genetic Psychology, *46, p. 106. Reprinted by permission of the Helen Dwight Reid Educational Foundation. Published by Heldref Publications.)*

Warden and his co-workers performed other, similar experiments with equally encouraging results. For instance, in one study (Warden et al., 1940), observer monkeys performed correctly on 76% of 144 trials, and about half of the solutions occurred within 10 seconds.

In addition to noting the number of successes, Warden and his colleagues also kept tabs on the nature of their monkeys' failures. In many instances the monkey made the correct response but with too little force to operate the mechanisms; in other instances the monkeys approached the right part of the apparatus but manipulated it in the wrong way. Thus, even when a monkey failed to solve a problem, the topography of its behavior suggested that some learning had occurred.

Following Warden's lead, Marvin Herbert and Charles Harsh (1944) demonstrated vicarious learning in cats. They designed a structure that would allow as many as four cats at a time to watch a model as it worked at one of five problems (see Figure 8-4). In the turntable problem, a circular platform rotated on a bicycle axle (see Figure 8-5). By grasping the black cleats on the turntable, a cat could spin the platform so that a food dish came into its cage. On any given problem, the cat that served as model would have 30 trials while observer cats looked on. Some observers watched all 30 of a model's trials before tackling a problem; others watched only the last 15 trials. By comparing the performances of the observers with those of the models, the experimenters could determine how much vicarious learning had taken place.

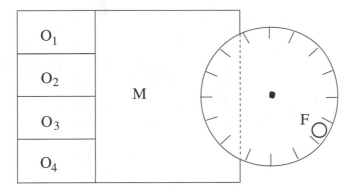

Figure 8-4 *View from above the Herbert and Harsh apparatus with the turntable problem installed. Observers sat in chambers at O_1, O_2, O_3, and O_4 and watched as a model, at M, worked on the problem of getting the food at F. (After Herbert and Harsh, 1944.)*

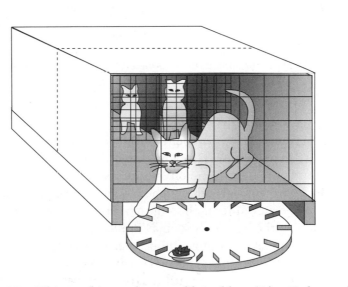

Figure 8-5 *Miss White working at the turntable problem. (After Herbert and Harsh, 1944.)*

The results showed that the observer cats outperformed the models. Moreover, the more observing a cat did, the more it learned (see Figure 8-6). On the turntable problem, for instance, the models took an average of 62 seconds to solve the problem on the first trial. Cats that had observed 15 trials took an average of 57 seconds, and those that had observed 30 trials took an average of only 16 seconds.

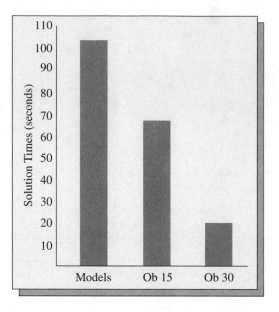

Figure 8-6 *Number of observed reinforcements. Average solution times on first trial of four problems by models and observers. Observers watched models perform on 15 or 30 trials. Data from one problem, failed by 4 observers, are not included. (Compiled from data in Herbert and Harsh, 1944.)*

W. J. Presley and Arthur Riopelle (1959) performed an experiment on vicarious avoidance learning. They put a monkey in one side of a box divided by a hurdle. A light came on and four seconds later the model received a shock through a grid floor. The model could escape the shock by jumping to the other side of the compartment, or it could avoid the shock by jumping the hurdle as soon as the light came on.

During the model's training, an observer monkey got a good view of the model's behavior but never received any shocks. The experimenters continued the model's training until it avoided the shock on 28 out of 30 trials. Then it was the observer's turn. The idea was to see whether the observer would learn to avoid shock more quickly than the model had. The results showed that the observers reached the criterion in considerably fewer trials than the models required. In fact, the researchers noted that the *slowest* learning observer did as well as the fastest learning model.

E. Roy John and his colleagues (1968) performed a similar experiment with cats. In this study, a buzzer sounded for 15 seconds and was followed by a shock through a grid floor. The shock could be avoided if the cat jumped a hurdle when the buzzer sounded. The observer cats received one training trial, and then watched the training of a naive cat and the perfor-

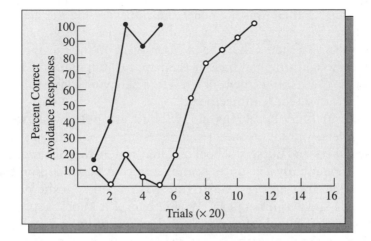

Figure 8-7 *Vicarious avoidance learning. Representative performance of an observer (●) and a naive model (○). (From "Observation Learning in Cats" by E. Roy John, P. Chesler, F. Bartlett, and I. Victor, 1968,* Science, *159, p. 1490, Figure 1. Copyright © 1968 by the American Association for the Advancement of Science. Reprinted by permission.)*

mance of another, well-trained cat. When the naive model avoided the shock on 90% of its trials, the researchers put the observer cat back into the training chamber and trained it until it reached the same criterion required of the model. Five of the six observers reached the criterion level in fewer trials than the naive model required (see Figure 8-7).

Numerous studies have demonstrated vicarious operant learning in children. In one study, Bandura and Fred McDonald (1963) had children listen to stories and judge which of two characters was naughtier. In a typical story, John breaks 15 cups while answering his mother's call to dinner; in another story, Henry breaks one cup while in the act of stealing cookies. In pretesting, the experimenters found that some children tended to make their moral judgments on the basis of the intent of the protagonist; on this *subjective* basis, Henry is naughtier than John because he was stealing. Other children based their decision on the amount of damage done; on this *objective* basis, John is naughtier because he broke more cups. The experiment consisted, in part, in attempting to teach subjective children to use the objective approach. The children were assigned to one of three conditions, two of which are of special interest. In one condition, the child and an adult female model took turns in evaluating stories. The model always used the objective approach to make her judgment, and an experimenter approved these judgments. The experimenter also approved the child's judgments when they reflected the objective approach. In the second condition there was no model, but the experimenter approved the child's choice whenever it was based on the objective method. After this training, the researchers tested the children again on their own to see what influence the training had had on their moral judgments. The results showed that the reinforcement of a model's behavior added substantially to the effects of direct reinforcement.

A study by Mary Rosekrans and Willard Hartup (1967) shows the differential effects of reinforcement and punishment of a model's behavior. The researchers had nursery school children watch an adult model as she played with some toys, at times beating a large inflated doll on the head with a mallet and poking a clay figure with a fork. As she played, the model made such comments as "Wham, bam, I'll knock your head off" and "Punch him, punch him, punch his legs full of holes." In one condition, these aggressive acts were praised by an adult who made remarks such as "Good for you! I guess you really fixed him that time." In another condition, the model's behavior was repeatedly criticized by an adult who said things such as, "Now look what you've done, you've ruined it." After watching the model play and seeing her behavior either praised or criticized, the observer then got a chance to play with the same toys. The results showed that children who saw aggressive behavior reinforced tended to play aggressively, whereas those who saw aggressive behavior punished tended to play more peacefully (see Figure 8-8).[2]

Ellen Levy and her colleagues (1974) studied the effects of model reinforcement and punishment on picture preference. Some of the subjects were children ranging from preschoolers to sixth-graders. The children looked on as a model went through a series of picture pairs, indicating which of each pair she preferred. Each of these choices resulted in approval, disapproval, or a neutral consequence. The observers then went through the picture pairs, indicating their own preferences. The results showed that the children were influenced by the consequences of the model's choices. Children tended to imitate the model when the model's choice won approval and to select the opposite picture when the model's choice was criticized.

Stephen Higgins and his co-workers (1989) found that children would imitate superstitious behavior after watching a videotape of a model engaging in the behavior. The model pressed a doll's nose and received marbles. This behavior was superstitious because pressing the doll's nose

---

[2]One of the reasons society punishes criminals is to reduce the tendency of *other* people to commit the same crime. The story is told of a horse thief who was condemned to the gallows. "I think it very hard," the man complained, "to hang a man for stealing a horse." To this the judge replied, "You are not to be hanged for stealing a horse. You are to be hanged so that others will not steal horses." It is not recorded whether the thief found the judge's comments of any comfort.

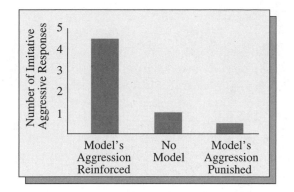

Figure 8-8 *Imitation and the consequences of model's behavior. Average number of imitative aggressive responses by observers who saw a model's aggressive acts reinforced or punished or who saw no model. (Compiled from data in Rosekrans and Hartup, 1967.)*

did not cause the marbles to appear; reinforcement was accidental. The observers repeatedly imitated this behavior even though the marbles they received were not contingent on it.

Of course, vicarious operant learning has been demonstrated in adults as well as in children. In one study, Frederick Kanfer and Albert Marston (1963) had college students sit in an experimental room alone and communicate with the experimenter by way of a microphone and earphones. Each time the experimenter signaled the student, he or she said the first word that came to mind. As the students waited for the signal, they could hear what seemed to be the responses of other students taking their turn. What the students really heard was a prerecorded tape. Over the course of the experiment, the people on the tape responded with more and more human nouns (presumably words such as *boy*, *woman*, and *hero*).

There were four different treatment groups, but two are of special interest: In one group, each time one of the people on the tape responded with a human noun, the experimenter said "good"; in the second group, the observer heard the same taped response but the experimenter made no comment. In neither case did the observer receive any direct reinforcement for saying human nouns. These two groups of students showed the same inclination to say human nouns during the baseline period when no responses were reinforced, and both said more human nouns as they heard others do so. But the students who heard human nouns approved showed a much greater increase in nouns than did those who had not heard nouns approved (see Figure 8-9).

Adult imitation of models is also influenced by the punishment of the model. The failure to punish modeled criminal behavior may be one

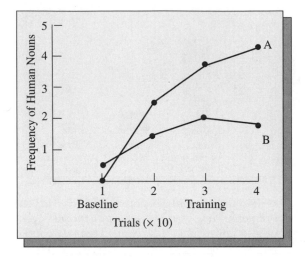

Figure 8-9 *Reinforcement of modeled verbal behavior. Group A heard people praised for saying human nouns; Group B did not. (Adapted from "Human Reinforcement: Vicarious and Direct," by Frederick Kanfer and Albert Marston, 1963,* Journal of Experimental Psychology, 65, *p. 293, Figure 1. Copyright © 1963 by the American Psychological Association. Reprinted by permission.)*

reason for its imitation. If sports fans see athletes behaving aggressively on the playing field without being punished, the fans may also become violent. If there are then no aversive consequences for the violent fans, more fan violence is likely. The failure to punish modeled violence may account, in part, for the riots that sometimes occur at sporting events.[3]

Not all studies of vicarious operant procedures result in learning (see, for example, Austad et al., 1984). But the procedures work well enough in humans and other primates to erase all doubts about the importance of vicarious learning in their adaptation.

REVIEW Vicarious learning has received less attention over the years than Pavlovian and operant procedures, partly because early attempts to show vicarious learning in animals failed. In vicarious procedures, an observer looks on as another animal or person interacts with the environment. There is some doubt about the existence of vicarious Pavlovian conditioning, but there is good evidence that observers can learn operant behavior from models.

---

[3]Fan violence at sporting events is not new. In the year 532 B.C., 30,000 Romans died in riots at chariot races, and there was rioting among fans at gladiatorial contests in ancient Pompeii (Horn, 1985).

Vicarious Learning Versus Imitation

Vicarious learning is sometimes equated with imitation: The observer watches a model perform an act and then the observer does likewise. Monkey see, monkey do. But imitation of a model does not necessarily imply that vicarious learning has occurred, nor does a failure to imitate a model necessarily mean that learning has *not* occurred.

Suppose that two children, Dick and Anne, are individually instructed in the art of making a toy boat out of newspaper. Dick is later seen building such a boat while Anne looks on, and then Anne builds a boat of her own. Anyone watching the children might be tempted to conclude that Anne learned to build a paper boat by watching Dick build one. If we did not know that Anne already knew how to build paper boats, we might make the same mistake. Anne's performance *may* have been somewhat imitative. That is, she might not have built a boat if Dick had not done so. (We cannot say without more information.) But you can see that just because an observer performs an act after a model performs it does not necessarily mean either that the observer is imitating the model or that she has learned from the model.

Similarly, an observer may learn from a model, yet not imitate the model. In fact, imitation may even serve as evidence that vicarious learning did *not* occur. Imagine that Dick and Anne are invited to take a treat from either of two bowls. The blue bowl contains pieces of grandmother's delicious fudge, while the green bowl contains pieces of grandfather's rock-hard taffy, but the children don't know which candy is in which bowl. Dick reaches into the green bowl and gets stuck with the inedible taffy. If Anne now imitates Dick's choice, we might reasonably conclude that she had not learned much from observing him. In this situation, learning from the model implies *not* imitating his behavior. Thus, although vicarious learning and imitation are closely related, they are not synonymous terms.

REVIEW   The terms *vicarious learning* and *imitation* are sometimes used interchangeably, but they do not really refer to the same things. Vicarious learning means a change in behavior due to observing a model, but that may mean doing something very different from what the model does.

Generalized Imitation

In studies of vicarious learning, an observer looks on as a model undergoes training. Typically the model's behavior is reinforced and is imitated by the observer. However, an observer will sometimes imitate a model's behavior even though the behavior is *not* reinforced.

A study by two Italian researchers, Graziano Fiorito and Pietro Scotto (1992), provides an illustration.[4] They trained several octopi to attack either a red or a white ball. The researchers attached a bit of fish to the far side of one ball to reinforce attacks on it. If an animal attacked the other ball, it received an electric shock. Some animals learned to attack the red ball, some the white ball. During the vicarious training phase, an untrained octopus in a tank adjacent to the model observed four trials in which the model attacked either the red or the white ball. During these trials, neither the model nor the observer received any food. Next, the researchers gave the observers five trials during which they could attack either the red or white ball. These animals received neither food nor shocks, regardless of their choices. The results showed a very strong tendency of the observers to imitate the choices of the models. For example, in 150 trials, the animals that observed models attack the red ball did likewise on 129 trials, choosing the white ball only 13 times.

Clearly the observers learned from, and imitated, the model's behavior. But why? Why should an observer imitate a behavior that, so far as the observer can tell, does not have reinforcing consequences?

Donald Baer and J. Sherman (1964) investigated this problem many years ago. They used a puppet to provide social reinforcers for imitative behavior in young children. The puppet modeled four behaviors: mouthing, head nodding, speaking nonsense, and pressing a lever. Whenever the children imitated any of the first three of these behaviors, the puppet provided reinforcement in the form of approving comments. The researchers discovered that as the tendency to imitate these behaviors increased, so did the tendency to imitate the fourth behavior, lever pressing, even though lever pressing did not produce reinforcement. When the researchers stopped reinforcing imitative mouthing, head nodding, and nonsense talking, their frequency declined—and so did the frequency of imitative lever pressing. When the first three imitative behaviors again resulted in praise, they increased—and so did imitative lever pressing. Baer and Sherman concluded that it is not only possible to reinforce the imitation of particular acts, but to reinforce a general *tendency* to imitate. They called this tendency **generalized imitation**.

Numerous studies have replicated Baer and Sherman's findings (see Baer et al., 1967; Baer & Deguchi, 1985). Ivar Lovaas and his colleagues (1966), for example, established generalized imitation in two schizophrenic children. They reinforced accurate imitation of English words and found that as performance improved, accurate imitation of Norwe-

---

[4]As mentioned earlier (note 21, Chapter 1), I mention the nationalities of some researchers in order to remind readers that learning research is not exclusively an American interest.

gian words increased as well, even though imitation of the Norwegian words had never been reinforced.

> **Query:**   Generalized imitation is the tendency to imitate
>
> modeled behavior even when imitation of the behavior is not
>
> _____.

Our tendency to imitate models is the product of experience. We learn to observe and imitate successful models because doing so is reinforced, but we may also learn to observe and imitate models even when their behavior is not reinforced. If you are walking down a city street, and suddenly a crowd of people comes rushing toward you as if they are fleeing space aliens, you are likely to follow their lead even though you have not observed that their running has been reinforced. You are likely to imitate them because imitating others in similar circumstances has paid off in the past. Similarly, teenagers and young adults often imitate the drug abuse of popular models even if the behavior has no discernible positive consequences. The reason may be that imitating popular models often results in becoming more popular.

Our concern in this chapter is with vicarious learning: changes in behavior that result from observing models whose behavior produces reinforcing or punishing consequences. However, it is important to understand that imitation is itself a kind of behavior that can be strengthened or weakened, depending on its consequences. And it is important to keep in mind that people, and some animals, sometimes imitate behavior even when it does not produce important consequences.

REVIEW   Generalized imitation is a descriptive term for the tendency to imitate modeled successful behavior. Studies show that this tendency can be strengthened by reinforcement.

Variables Affecting Vicarious Learning

The variables that are important in Pavlovian and operant procedures seem to affect vicarious learning in a similar manner. Because there is considerable doubt about whether vicarious Pavlovian conditioning occurs, we will restrict ourselves to variables affecting vicarious operant learning.

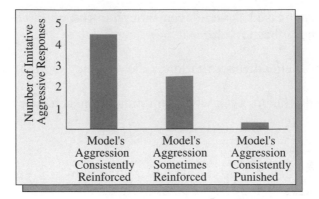

Figure 8-10 *Consistency of model's consequences. Average number of imitative aggressive responses by observers who saw aggressive acts consistently reinforced; sometimes reinforced and sometimes punished; or consistently punished. (Compiled from data in Rosekrans and Hartup, 1967.)*

Consequences of the Model's Behavior

Reinforcement of the model's behavior is clearly important. Consistent reinforcement or punishment of a model's behavior gets better results than inconsistent consequences. In the Rosekrans and Hartup (1967) study described earlier, when a model's aggressive behavior was consistently reinforced, the observer tended to adopt it; when it was consistently punished, the observer tended to avoid making it. There was also a condition, not mentioned earlier, in which children saw a model whose aggressive acts were sometimes rewarded and sometimes punished. Not surprisingly, the tendency of these children to adopt the model's aggressive behavior fell midway between the other two groups (see Figure 8-10).

Consequences of the Observer's Behavior

If observing others pays off, we tend to spend more time observing others. Japanese researchers Satoshi Hirata and Naurki Morimura (2000) noticed this in chimpanzees. They paired chimps and gave them a problem that required using a tool. Once an animal had solved a problem, it never observed its partner's efforts. On the other hand, if a chimp attempted the problem and failed, it then watched as its neighbor struggled with the problem.

The consequences of imitating a model's behavior are also powerful. If a given behavior produces one kind of consequence for a model and a very different kind of consequence for an observer, the latter consequences will eventually win out. For example, if a model is successful at a computer game and clearly enjoys playing it, an observer is likely to give the game a try. If, however, the observer is consistently unsuccessful, she is likely to abandon the game. Similarly, a young man who lacks finesse with women may observe another man as he introduces himself to a woman, interacts with her, and arranges a date. The observer may then approach a woman and attempt to imitate the model's words and gestures. But if his efforts result in a snub rather than a date, the observer may be unlikely to try the model's methods again. Ultimately, people usually do what works for *them*—regardless of whether it worked for a model.

Characteristics of the Model

Numerous studies have demonstrated that human observers tend to learn more from models who are competent, attractive, likable, and prestigious than from models who lack these characteristics. A study by Berger (1971), in which college students participated in what was ostensibly an investigation of extrasensory perception (ESP), will serve as an example. The model was introduced to the observer either as a fellow subject or as an assistant to the experimenter. Later on, those observers who thought they had watched a fellow student showed less evidence of learning than did those who thought they had observed the experimenter's assistant. The model was actually the same person in each case and behaved in the same way, so the difference in the observer's behavior apparently was due to the model's status. Studies of this sort raise an interesting question: Why should model characteristics such as status, attractiveness, competence, and so on have any effect on what an observer learns?

Research by Judith Fisher and Mary Harris (1976) provides a plausible answer. Fisher and Harris approached people in a shopping center or on a college campus and asked them to guess the prices of certain items. An experimenter would appear to approach two subjects simultaneously, but one of the people approached was actually a confederate of the researchers. In one experiment, the model sometimes wore an eye patch. The model would guess at the price of an item and then the observer would make a guess. Later, when the observers tried to remember the answers the model had given, the ones who were generally more accurate were those who had seen the model with an eye patch.

In a second experiment, the researchers manipulated the mood of the model. In one condition, the model smiled and nodded her head as the experimenter asked her questions. In another condition, the model frowned and shook her head. In a third condition, the model behaved in a neutral manner. In other respects, this experiment was similar to the first. The results showed that observers who had witnessed one of the more expressive models recalled her behavior better than did observers

Vicarious Learning and Human Nature

Viki had no memory of her natural parents. After all, she was only a few days old when Keith and Catherine Hayes (1952) adopted her and took her home. The Hayeses reared their adopted daughter with great care and affection. Their devotion paid off, for Viki proved to be extraordinarily precocious. For example, when she was less than a year-and-a-half old, she began to learn, simply by observing her parents, how to dust the furniture and wash dishes. Before she was 2 years old, she would look in the mirror and put on lipstick as she had seen Catherine do.

When Viki was between 2 and 3, her parents, who were psychologists, decided to test her to see just how well she could learn from observing others. They gave her, and some other youngsters of about the same age, a series of problems. For instance, in the Stick and String problem the Hayeses put an object in a wooden box. The object could be retrieved from the box only by hitting a string with a stick. The Hayeses demonstrated the correct solution to the problem and then gave Viki a shot at it.

Overall, Viki did quite well. She solved the Stick and String problem, for instance, after only one demonstration. Some children who worked on that problem required four demonstrations before they could solve it. Viki's performance did more than demonstrate vicarious learning, however. It raised all sorts of questions about human nature. Viki, you see, wasn't like the children with whom she competed on those problems.

Viki was a chimpanzee.

who saw an impassive model. It made no difference whether the model's mood was positive or negative, as long as it was not neutral.

According to Fisher and Harris, these model characteristics (eye patch and moodiness) affected the observer's learning because they attracted the observer's attention. Status, likability, age, sex, competence, and other model characteristics affect vicarious learning because they induce the observer to look at the model. The more attentive an observer is to a model, the more likely he or she is to learn from the model's behavior.

Query: Model characteristics are important because they can

induce the observer to _____.

Model characteristics also have a strong effect on the tendency to imitate. Models who are attractive, powerful, or very popular are much more likely to be imitated than models who are not. Celebrities are especially likely to be imitated. The hairstyles, clothing, language, and social behavior of popular figures in the entertainment field are likely to appear among their fans. Let Britney Spears get a tattoo on her calf or have a ring inserted through her navel, and within a short time calf tattoos and navel rings are a common sight (Stack, 1987, 2000; Wasserman, 1984).

Even fictional celebrities can be influential. Angie, a character in a televised soap opera called *EastEnders* broadcast by the BBC (British Broadcasting Corporation), took a drug overdose to get attention. (Note that the actress playing the part did not take an overdose; the character she played did.) After this, cases of self-poisoning shot up at certain hospitals (Fowler, 1986; see also Stack, 1987, 2000).[5]

Observer's Age

Age is sometimes a factor in vicarious learning. Young monkeys, for example, are more likely to imitate a model than are older monkeys (Adams-Curtiss & Fragaszy, 1995). Similarly, the study by Levy and others (1974) described earlier found that children tended to imitate the picture choices of a model. The results were different with adult observers: The consequences of the model's behavior had no effect on their choices. These findings nicely demonstrate that vicarious procedures may have different effects with different age groups.

Although younger subjects may be more likely to imitate than older subjects, this does not necessarily mean that the youngsters learn more from models. On the contrary, adults generally learn better than children from observation, and older children learn better than younger ones. For example, Brian Coates and Willard Hartup (1969) had young children watch a film in which a model performed various novel acts. The older observers recalled more of the model's behavior than did the younger children. (See also Yando et al., 1978.) Those advanced in years, however, often are slower to benefit from the experiences of others than are the young (Kawamura, 1963).

Observer's Learning History

The ability to learn from a model may also depend on learning experiences prior to viewing a model. A child whose aggressive behavior has been reinforced on numerous occasions is probably more likely to imitate an aggressive model than is a child with a different learning history.

---

[5]Nor is this phenomenon new. The *Sorrows of Young Werther*, by Wolfgang Goethe, describes a depressed young man who commits suicide. The book was extremely popular throughout Europe in the 18th century, and suicide rates went up as the book gained popularity.

The Venus Effect or, How Can I Learn Anything When You Look at Me with Those Big Brown Eyes?

There's no doubt about it: Emotional arousal can have a profound effect on learning. Why this should be so is not always clear, but sometimes the reason is fairly obvious.

Warden and Jackson (1935) trained a monkey to solve a problem and gave other monkeys the opportunity to profit from the model's experience. Several observing monkeys did just that, but some paid little or no attention to the problem or how the model went about solving it. These wayward animals seemed interested in another sort of problem. The researchers noted that animal H, for example, "showed sex interest in [model]; 'presented' to him and ignored the problem; sat at screen near [model]." About another miscreant they wrote simply, "sex excitement marked," and they noted that another "masturbated frequently and ignored the problem."

That the emotional state of the observers put them at a severe disadvantage becomes immediately clear when their performance is compared to that of the less distracted animals (see Figure 8-11).

It may have already occurred to you that monkeys are not the only creatures affected by the Venus Effect. In fact, it seems likely that this phenomenon is at work (in somewhat milder form, to be sure) in high school and college classrooms around the world.

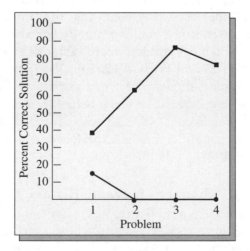

Figure 8-11 *Sexual arousal and vicarious learning. Percentage of subjects solving each problem on first trial. Top line shows performance of observers who attended to the problem; bottom line shows performance of observers who were sexually aroused and attended to other matters. (Compiled from data in Warden and Jackson, 1935.)*

It is difficult to separate age and learning history as independent variables. Perhaps one reason the age of the observer is important is because of differences in the learning histories of older and younger observers. For instance, adults may learn more than children from observing others because the adults have had more practice at it. In any case, the observer's learning history is an important factor in vicarious learning.

Other Variables

Several other variables affect the course of vicarious learning. The emotional state of the learner while observing the model is important. Warden and Jackson (1935) found that emotional arousal could severely interfere with learning (see "The Venus Effect").

Another factor is the complexity of the task being modeled. Complex tasks are not as readily picked up through observation as are simple tasks (Hirakawa & Nakazawa, 1977; Richman & Gholson, 1978).

> **Query:** Two important variables in vicarious learning are
>
> the _____ of the model's behavior and the
>
> _____ of the observer's behavior.

REVIEW   As with Pavlovian and operant learning, the effectiveness of vicarious procedures depends on many variables. Some important variables arc thc consequences of the model's behavior, the consequences of imitating a model's behavior, characteristics of the model (e.g., competent models are more readily imitated than incompetent models), and the observer's age, learning history, and emotional state.

Theories of Vicarious Learning

The two main theories of vicarious learning are the social cognitive theory of Albert Bandura and the reinforcement theory of Neal Miller and John Dollard. Both theories focus on vicarious operant learning and imitation.

Bandura's Social Cognitive Theory

Albert Bandura (1965, 1971a, 1971b, 1971c, 1977, 1986) argues that vicarious learning is accounted for by four processes that occur during or shortly after observation of a model. These processes are attentional, retentional, motor reproductive, and motivational.

Attentional processes have to do with the organism's observing the relevant aspects of the model's behavior and its consequences. Various studies have demonstrated that if the observer does not attend to the model, or attends to irrelevant aspects of the model's behavior, little learning will take place (e.g., Warden & Jackson, 1935). As we saw earlier, a number of variables affect the extent to which an observer attends to the appropriate aspects of a model's behavior.

Once an organism is attending to the relevant aspects of the model's behavior, Bandura reasons, **retentional processes** come into play. These are acts the observer performs to aid recall of the model's behavior. One important retentional process consists of representing the model's behavior in some way, often in words. With the acquisition of language, it is often possible to reduce complex behavior to a few words. A cooking student watching a chef make a soufflé might say to himself, "He *folds* the batter; he doesn't whip it."

Another important retentional activity consists of repeatedly performing the model's behavior, or a verbal representation of that behavior, in some covert way. After seeing a tennis pro demonstrate the perfect backhand, for example, you may covertly imitate that behavior without making any perceptible movement of your arm. Or you might silently repeat some verbal representation of the model's behavior, such as, "Keep the wrist straight."

Query: What sort of process would Bandura say is involved in

answering this query?

Bandura's theory includes other factors that affect the performance of modeled behavior. The observer must have the **motor reproductive processes** required to perform the modeled behavior. A child may watch a circus performer juggle balls in the air, but he is unlikely to imitate the behavior successfully without a good deal of practice. A middle-aged adult may observe a skilled dancer perform a dance move, yet be incapable of performing it.

Bandura also argues that **motivational processes** are important, especially in determining whether a modeled behavior will be imitated. According to Bandura, the observer must have an expectation that an imitated behavior will produce reinforcement; otherwise, he will not perform it.

These four processes can be easily illustrated. Suppose your aunt points to a wall safe and says, "I'm going to open that safe and then lock it again. If you can open it, you can keep whatever you find inside." Your aunt then proceeds to open the safe. She turns the dial clockwise to 20, counterclockwise to 40, clockwise to 20. She pulls down the handle and swings open the door, then immediately closes it.

Now, as you watch your aunt work, you carefully attend to which way she turns the safe dial and the numbers at which she stops. You may also represent her behavior by picturing a little pot-bellied Santa Claus whose measurements are 20–40–20. More likely, however, you repeat to yourself (or perhaps aloud), "Right 20; left 40; right 20."

After Auntie has demonstrated how to open the safe, you may want an opportunity to practice the motor skills necessary for opening it. You might practice on some sort of cardboard model, for example, or you might get an exact duplicate of the safe and practice on it. But whether you will imitate your aunt's behavior, or even attend to it, will depend, according to Bandura, on whether you expect to receive something of value after opening the safe.

Bandura's theory has tremendous intuitive appeal. It seems to capture the experience of vicarious learning as humans know it. Probably because of this, it is very popular. The theory is not, however, without problems.

We might question, for example, the explanatory value of attentional processes. Certainly it is important that the observer attend to the model's behavior. But why does one person attend to a model while another does not? Do they really differ in their "attentional processes," or do they have different learning histories?

We might also question the explanatory value of retentional processes. People do seem to engage in covert practice of observed skills. Yet bats, pigeons, rats, and other animals can learn through observation. Is it realistic to assume that such animals learn through the sort of retentional processes Bandura describes? And if these creatures can learn without sophisticated retentional processes, must we assume that the processes are essential to vicarious learning in humans?

If you know that your aunt is rich, that rich people often keep valuable things in safes, and that safes are often opened by turning a dial this way and that, then you might very well expect that opening the safe will be reinforced. But is it the expectation of reward that explains your behavior or the experiences that led to that expectation?

Because of such problems with Bandura's theory, many researchers prefer the reinforcement theory of Miller and Dollard.

Miller-Dollard Reinforcement Theory

It is possible to treat vicarious learning as merely a variation of operant training. According to this view, first proposed by Neal Miller and John Dollard (1941; see Skinner, 1969, for a similar analysis), the changes in an observer's behavior are due to the consequences of the *observer's* behavior, not those of the model.

Suppose, Miller and Dollard suggest, a boy hears his father returning from work and runs to greet him. Suppose also that the boy's younger brother follows him to the door. If the father greets both boys cheerfully and gives them pieces of candy, what behavior has he reinforced? In the case of the elder boy, the reinforced behavior is the act of running to the door when his father comes home. In the case of the younger boy, the reinforced behavior is the act of imitating his elder brother in going to the door. Put another way, the younger boy learns that going to the door when big brother does pays off.

Miller and Dollard performed a number of experiments that supported their theory. They found, for example, that rats would learn to follow another rat through a maze if such imitative acts were reinforced. They also showed that imitation in children was a function of reinforcement. In one study, children could get candy from a machine if they manipulated the handle the right way. A model used the machine just before the child. In one condition, if the child imitated the model's behavior, the machine provided candy. In another condition, the machine provided candy only if the child did *not* imitate the model. The children learned to imitate the model when imitating paid off, and they learned *not* to imitate the model when not imitating the model paid off (see also Baer & Sherman, 1964; Baer et al., 1967).

Query: According to Miller and Dollard, we imitate successful

models because _____.

Some psychologists have asked why, if an observer receives reinforcement for imitating a model's behavior, imitative acts occur even when the model is no longer present. A boy may see his older brother run to the door, for example, but be prevented from imitating this act. Several minutes later, when the boy is free, he may run for the door even though his older brother is no longer modeling this behavior. This phenomenon seems troublesome at first, but it poses no special problem for Miller and Dollard. We often continue to be influenced by a stimulus that is no longer present. You may, for example, see an ad for a movie on one day and go to the theater the next. The ad is no longer present, yet it still affects your behavior. Stimuli generally have their most powerful effects immediately, but they may continue to affect behavior long after they have disappeared.

A more serious problem with the theory is that imitation often occurs in the absence of reinforcement of the observer's behavior. For instance, the children who learned to imitate a model to get candy from a machine later imitated other models in other situations even though they received no reinforcers for imitating these models. If imitative behavior is the product of reinforcement, why did the children imitate these models?

Such behavior may be examples of generalized imitation, discussed above. We learn not only to imitate a particular behavior by a particular model, but to imitate *other* acts by *other* models. Observers learn to imitate the behavior of successful models and to avoid imitating the behavior of unsuccessful models. They may even learn to imitate unsuccessful models if doing so is reinforced. Thus, when very popular public figures are in traffic accidents because of driving too fast or while intoxicated, some of their admirers follow their lead. The modeled behavior produces injury, fines, or prison terms, so it cannot be considered successful by ordinary standards. But it may also produce public attention and sympathy, and these are often reinforcing consequences.

The Miller-Dollard and Bandura theories are in active contention as explanations of vicarious learning and will probably remain so for some time. Perhaps the real difference between them has to do with different ideas about the nature of scientific explanation. Bandura's theory looks for explanation inside the individual, appealing to cognitive processes to account for learning. The Miller-Dollard theory looks to the situation and the observer's learning history for an explanation. To choose between these two theories is to choose between two different ideas about what constitutes scientific explanation.

Both theories are dated: Neither takes into account recent developments in learning and behavior (see Masia & Chase, 1997, for more on this). But the theories are still of value because they encourage basic and applied research on vicarious learning and imitation.

REVIEW   There are two prominent theories of vicarious learning. Bandura's social cognitive theory argues, in part, that attentional and retentional processes occurring while the observer is observing a model are crucial. The Miller-Dollard theory assumes that vicarious learning is really a form of operant learning; it depends on a history of reinforcement for observational and imitative behavior.

Attempts have been made to examine the role of vicarious learning in various areas. For illustrative purposes, we will consider three areas in which vicarious learning seems to be important: foraging, the impact of television on criminal behavior, and the treatment of phobias.

Applications of Vicarious Learning

Foraging

Surviving means finding food, and anecdotal evidence suggests that vicarious learning plays a role in that quest. One fascinating report involves British songbirds. J. Fisher and R. A. Hinde (1949; Hinde & Fisher, 1972) reported that songbirds made a regular practice of opening milk bottles left on porches. It appeared that a few birds learned the trick on their own and were imitated by other birds. Similarly, Syumzo Kawamura (1963) noticed that a macaque monkey learned to remove sand from sweet potatoes by dipping the potatoes into water, and that others in the troop then did so. Here, it seems, are very clear instances of vicarious learning.[6]

Although evidence of this sort is fascinating, it is of limited scientific value in understanding the role of vicarious learning in food gathering. David Sherry and B. G. Galef (1984) point out, for example, that because many birds are drinking from bottles does not necessarily mean that birds have learned to open bottles by watching others do so. They note that the presence of a bottle opened by one bird would provide the opportunity for many birds to feed without their having learned anything from a model. And, of course, what one bird can learn on its own (i.e., without observing models), other birds can learn on their own. Similarly, the fact that many monkeys wash potatoes does not necessarily mean that they learned to do so by watching others: What one monkey can learn on its own, others can learn on their own.

Such issues can be resolved only through experimental research. Sherry and Galef (1984) captured black-capped chickadees on the campus of the University of Toronto and presented each with a foil-covered plastic cream tub of the sort restaurants serve with coffee. Four of the birds spontaneously pecked through the foil top and fed on the cream. These four birds then served as models for four birds that had not opened the tubs. Each model demonstrated the technique for an observer on five trials. Another four birds received five trials with a sealed tub, but without observing a model. After this, the researchers presented each of the birds with a sealed tub to see what it had learned. They found that birds in the vicarious learning group opened the tubs while the untrained group did not. The researchers concluded that some birds probably do learn to open milk bottles by observing others do so.

In another experiment, Connie Gaudet and M. Brock Fenton (1984) studied vicarious learning in three species of bats. They began by training

---

[6] The monkey episode has been widely reported, but with some embellishments. One claim, for example, was that once a hundred monkeys had mastered the skill, it then spread to other troops miles away. Michael Shermer (1997) notes that such claims are unsupported, and that, in fact, the skill spread slowly and only within the troop.

one member of each species to find a bit of mealworm from a target fastened to a wall. The bats would fly to the target, remove the food, return to their starting point about two yards away, and eat the meal. A bat of the same species was allowed to observe the model up to 20 times a day for five days. (Contrary to popular belief, bats are *not* blind.) There were two control groups. In one, the bats were simply put into the experimental chamber alone; in the other, the bats were individually trained, through reinforcement training, to find the food. The result was that the bats that had observed a model learned to find food faster than those that were trained through operant reinforcement. Bats that were placed in the chamber without benefit of a model or operant training did not find the food.

Some forms of food gathering that may seem innate turn out to be at least partly the result of vicarious learning. You may recall that Zing Yang Kuo (1930) found that whether cats killed rats depended partly on whether they had ever seen their mothers kill rats. Apparently, modeled behavior plays an important part in a cat's diet.

Query: How do you use vicarious learning in your own

"foraging" efforts?

Crime and Television

Bandura (1973) provides a great deal of evidence that criminal behavior is powerfully influenced by the observation of models—and television provides many criminal models. Bandura notes that, thanks to television, both children and adults have unlimited opportunities to learn "the whole gamut of felonious behavior within the comfort of their homes" (p. 101). As Bandura points out, people often put such learning to use: "Children have been apprehended for . . . sniping at strangers with BB guns, for sending threatening letters to teachers and for injurious switchblade fights after witnessing similar performances on television" (p. 101*f*.).

The studies reported in this chapter suggest that people are unlikely to imitate criminal acts unless the model's behavior is reinforced. But television crime often *is* reinforced. Otto Larsen and his co-workers (1968) found that in television programs intended for children, TV characters achieved their goals by violent or illegal acts 56% of the time. Casual observation suggests that this figure would be much higher today. It is little wonder, then, that a link has been found between television viewing and criminal behavior.

Leonard Eron (in DeAngelis, 1992) reports that a longitudinal study found that the more time children spent watching television at age 8, the more likely they were at age 30 to have been convicted of a serious crime and to be aggressive when under the influence of alcohol. This is correlational research, and correlation does not necessarily mean causation; however, experimental research lends strong support to the notion that viewing televised aggression increases aggression in children (see Huesmann & Miller, 1994, for a review).

The best-known studies in this area are those of Albert Bandura and his colleagues. In one famous study (Bandura et al., 1963), nursery school children watched a 5-minute videotape of two men, Rocky and Johnny, interacting in a playroom. In the video, Johnny plays with toy cars, plastic farm animals, and various other appealing toys. Rocky asks Johnny to share the toys, but Johnny refuses. Rocky then hits Johnny several times with a rubber ball, overpowers him when he tries to defend his property, hits him with a baton, and generally gives poor Johnny a rough time. Rocky's aggressive behavior is reinforced, since he ends up having all the fun. The researchers write that

> the final scene shows Johnny seated dejectedly in the corner while Rocky is playing with the toys, serving himself generous helpings of 7-Up and cookies, and riding a large bouncing hobby horse with gusto. As the scene closes, Rocky packs the playthings in a sack and sings a merry tune, "Hi, ho, hi, ho, it's off to play I go," as he departs with the hobby horse under his arm and the bulging sack of loot over his shoulder. A commentator's voice announces that Rocky is the victor. (p. 602)

After watching the videotape, each child went to a playroom that contained a number of toys, including those shown in the film and several others. Each child spent 20 minutes in the room while judges watched through a one-way mirror and noted how often the child hit a Bobo doll (a large, inflated doll) or performed other aggressive acts. The data indicated that children were far more likely to commit aggressive acts if they had seen a model reinforced for the same behavior. The similarity of the children's behavior to that of the model was sometimes striking. At the end of one session, a little girl who had imitated a good deal of Rocky's behavior looked at the experimenter and asked, "Do you have a sack here?" (p. 605).

Query: A child watches a TV show in which a child is spanked for stealing. What two things is the child likely to learn from observing this?

Although the role of television in promoting criminal behavior, particularly violent acts, is still disputed by some, the issue seems to be pretty well settled. A panel of experts, including members of the American Academy of Pediatricians, American Psychological Association, American Academy of Child and Adolescent Psychiatry, and American Medical Association, reviewed more than a thousand studies conducted over a 30-year period on the effects of violence on television and in films on aggressive behavior in children (Wyatt, 2001). The panel concluded that the evidence for a causal connection was "overwhelming."

Therapy for Phobia

Vicarious procedures have been put to good use in treating various behavior problems. One example is phobia (Ost & Hugdahl, 1985; Rachman, 1977).[7]

One technique for helping people overcome phobias is to have them observe models who interact with the feared object without ill effects. Perhaps the first person to use this procedure was Mary Cover Jones (1924b), who called it the "method of social imitation." Seeing a child hold a rabbit without being eaten alive by it seemed to reassure the frightened child that he, too, could hold it without being injured. The only real problem with this procedure is that it sometimes backfires. The bold child who is supposed to serve as model can end up imitating the fearful child who is supposed to be the observer. Jones describes the case of Vincent, a boy who

> showed no fear of the rabbit, even when it was pushed against his hands or face. His only response was to laugh and reach for the rabbit's fur. On the same day he was taken into the pen with Rosey, who cried at the sight of the rabbit. Vincent immediately developed a fear response; in the ordinary playroom situation he would pay no attention to her crying, but in connection with the rabbit, her distress had a marked suggestion value. The fear transferred in this way persisted for over two weeks. (p. 390)

Obviously, this is not what was supposed to happen: the fearful Rosey was supposed to learn from the bold Vincent, not the other way around.

A safer procedure is to have the fearful person view a filmed or video-taped model. Bandura and Frances Menlove (1968) used this technique to help children, aged 3 to 5 years, overcome a fear of dogs. Some of the

---

[7]Another example is exhibitionism. In a form of therapy called vicarious aversive behavior rehearsal (V-ABR), the exhibitionist watches a video of an exhibitionist as he exposes himself to a group of critical people in a clinical setting (Wickramasekera, 1976).

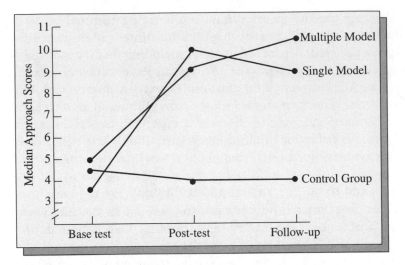

Figure 8-12 *Vicarious extinction of fear. Median approach scores of children in three experimental conditions at three stages in the experiment. (Adapted from "Factors Determining Vicarious Extinction of Avoidance Behavior Through Symbolic Modeling," after Albert Bandura and Frances Menlove, 1968,* Journal of Personality and Social Psychology, 8, *p. 102, Figure 1. Copyright © 1968 by the American Psychological Association. Reprinted with permission.)*

children saw a series of eight films, two per day on every other day. One group saw a fearless 5-year-old boy interact with a cocker spaniel; over the course of the eight films, the model became bolder and bolder in his contacts with the dog. A second group of children saw similar films except that there were several models of varying ages who interacted fearlessly with several dogs of various shapes and sizes. The remaining children saw films of Disneyland and Marineland.

After seeing the films, the children were retested to see whether they were still afraid of dogs. The results clearly showed that those who had been exposed to fearless models had lost much of their former fear (see Figure 8-12). Even when tested a month after the end of training, these children were not afraid to interact with dogs. Children who had not had training (those who had watched films of Disneyland and Marineland) showed no improvement.

Another therapeutic technique that has proved effective combines modeling with traditional counterconditioning (see Chapter 4), a procedure called **participant modeling** (Ritter, 1968). In participant modeling, the observer first watches as the model performs the desired act, then the model guides the observer through the same behavior.

Bandura and others (1969) used participant modeling to help college students overcome their fear of snakes. First, the observer watched through a one-way glass as the model demonstrated that handling a king snake does not have painful consequences: For 15 minutes the model held the snake close to his face, allowed it to crawl over his body, and let the snake wander freely about the room. After this, the model returned the snake to its glass cage and asked the observer to enter the room. Gradually the model guided the observer through a series of interactions with the snake. The model would touch the snake and then have the observer touch it; the model would stroke the snake and have the observer stroke it, and so on. Eventually, most of the observers lost their fear of the snake; they would hold it and allow it to crawl over their bodies or wriggle around the room.

> **Query:** In _____ modeling, a model demon-
>
> strates a behavior and then helps the observer perform it.

It is impossible to say what proportion of human learning is due to direct experience and what proportion is due to observation. We do know, however, that if people suddenly lost their ability to learn by observing others, the effect would be noticeable immediately. Imagine, for example, the difficulties we would encounter if we could not rely on modeling in teaching preschoolers to tie their shoes, first-graders to write, or employees to operate machines. Not only would shaping such behavior be much slower, but in many cases, reliance on operant procedures could be dangerous. As Bandura (1971a) has pointed out, it would be very unwise to ignore vicarious procedures in teaching children to swim, adolescents to drive automobiles, or medical students to perform operations.

This is not to say that Pavlovian and operant procedures are unimportant in the lives of human beings. Both have a good deal to do with our daily activities, but we humans also rely heavily on vicarious learning in our efforts to cope with the changing world around us.

REVIEW The value of vicarious learning in adaptation can be seen in studies of foraging, crime, and phobia treatment, among other areas. Although it now appears that many species can learn from observing models, it is especially important in human adaptation.

RECOMMENDED READING

1. Bandura, A. (1977). *Social learning theory*. Englewood Cliffs, NJ: Prentice-Hall.

   Bandura sets forth his theory of vicarious learning and imitation.

2. Bandura, A., Ross, D., & Ross, S. A. (1963). Vicarious reinforcement and imitative learning. *Journal of Abnormal and Social Psychology*, *67*, 601–607.

   A classic in the area of vicarious learning.

3. Bandura, A., & Walters, R. H. (1963). *Social learning and personality development*. New York: Holt, Rinehart, & Winston.

   An important study of how children are influenced by adult models.

4. Masia, C. C., & Chase, P. N. (1997). Vicarious learning revisited: A contemporary behavior analytic interpretation. *Journal of Behavior Therapy and Experimental Psychiatry*, *28*, 41–51.

   These writers build on the Miller-Dollard theory by incorporating recent developments in behavior science.

5. Miller, N. E., & Dollard, J. (1941). *Social learning and imitation*. New Haven, CT: Yale University Press.

   An operant reinforcement theory of vicarious learning. Includes both human and animal research.

REVIEW QUESTIONS

1. Define the following terms in your own words:

   attentional processes   participant modeling
   generalized imitation   retentional processes
   motivational processes   vicarious learning
   motor reproductive processes

2. Why has vicarious learning received less attention than other forms of learning?

3. If vicarious learning can lead to the widespread use of certain practices, how can one determine whether those practices are innate or learned?

4. Given what you know about vicarious learning, what advice would you give a friend whose children watch 4 to 5 hours of television daily?

5. How could you use vicarious procedures to create a fad on a college campus?

6. How might the value of Bandura's retentional processes be tested experimentally?

7. If you wanted to ensure that an observer would learn from a model, what sort of model would you choose?

8. How would you determine whether snakes can learn through observation?

9. How could you teach a child to tie her shoes *without* using modeling?

10. Studies of vicarious learning of aggression usually involve children. Why?

11. After Marilyn Monroe died, apparently by suicide, several other people took their own lives. Explain these copycat suicides.

12. Why do so many fads get started by rock groups and movie stars?

13. Design an experiment to determine the role of delayed reinforcement of a model's behavior in vicarious learning.

14. How might superstitious behavior be acquired through vicarious experiences?

15. What is the chief difference between the Miller-Dollard theory and Bandura's theory of vicarious learning?

16. According to the Miller-Dollard theory, vicarious learning is merely a form of operant learning. Describe the researchers' reasoning.

17. Design a study to determine whether Kawamura's monkeys really learned to wash potatoes by observing models.

18. Suppose you proved that vicarious learning ability improves markedly as children develop speech. How would Bandura account for this finding? How would Miller and Dollard account for it?

19. How might our view of human nature differ if psychologists had never succeeded in demonstrating vicarious learning in animals?

20. If you could learn in only one way (through Pavlovian, operant, or vicarious procedures), which would you choose?

PRACTICE QUIZ

1. Vicarious learning can be defined as a change in behavior due to the experience of _____.

2. Research suggests that what appears to be vicarious classical conditioning may in fact be a form of _____ conditioning.

3. Susan Mineka studied fear of _____ in
_____.

4. The tendency to imitate models even when the modeled behavior is not reinforced is called _____ imitation.

5. Vicarious learning is affected by characteristics of the model. For example, models are more likely to be imitated when they are
_____.

6. Viki was a _____.

7. Bandura's theory relies on four processes. These include
_____ and _____ processes.

8. The Miller-Dollard theory says that the tendency to observe and imitate models depends on reinforcement of the
_____'s behavior.

9. Zing Yang Kuo found that cats were far more likely to kill rats if they had _____.

10. A form of treatment for phobia that combines modeling with counterconditioning is called _____.

QUERY ANSWERS

Page 265. The basic question posed by vicarious learning is, *Can one organism benefit from the experiences of another?*

Page 266. Early efforts to demonstrate vicarious learning failed. Other researchers observed this and learned that such research did not pay off.

Page 267. Vicarious learning may be defined as *a change in behavior due to the experience of observing a model.*

Page 281. Generalized imitation is the tendency to imitate modeled behavior even when imitation of the behavior is not *reinforced.*

Page 284. Model characteristics are important because they can induce the observer to *observe the model's behavior.*

Page 287. Two important variables in vicarious learning are the *consequences* of the model's behavior and the *consequences* of the observer's behavior.

Page 288. Bandura might say the query involves an attentional process, since it draws attention to certain parts of the text. Or he might say it involves a retentional process, since it might induce behavior that improves recall.

Page 290. According to Miller and Dollard, we imitate successful models because *imitating successful models has had reinforcing consequences in the past.*

Page 293. Answers will vary. However, if you have ever been hungry and followed other people you knew were also hungry, you have used vicarious learning to "forage" for food.

Page 294. The child is likely to learn (a) that you shouldn't steal (or, that if you do steal, you shouldn't get caught), and (b) when you do not like the way people behave, you should hit them. Please note: Whether the creator of the TV show *intends* to teach these two things is irrelevant.

Page 297. In *participant* modeling, a model demonstrates a behavior and then helps the observer perform it.

CHAPTER 9

Generalization, Discrimination, and Stimulus Control

When you've seen one redwood tree, you've seen them all.
                                        Ronald Reagan

Like—but oh! How different!
                                        William Wordsworth

We have discussed three kinds of learning, three kinds of experiences that change behavior. To say that learning is the product of certain kinds of experiences is to say that it arises in certain kinds of situations. Pair a white rat with a frightening noise, and a child will become fearful whenever confronted with that rat; put a cat in a box from which it can escape by pressing a treadle, and it will press the treadle when placed in that box; let a child get candy from a machine by imitating the actions of an adult, and he will imitate that adult in getting candy from that machine.

But learning would be of little value as an adaptive mechanism if it helped us adapt only to precisely the same environment in which learning occurred. We rarely, if ever, find ourselves in precisely the same situation twice, so it is important that what we learn in one situation carries over to new situations. And it does: The child who has learned to fear one white rat fears other white rats and may fear things that resemble white rats; the cat that has learned to escape a box by stepping on a treadle is likely to step on treadles when placed in other boxes; the child who learns to operate one machine by observing an adult's performance then operates similar machines in a similar manner. This tendency for learned behavior to "spread" to situations not involved in training is called *generalization*.

You can see that generalization is of great value. On the other hand, learning would be a handicap if what was learned carried over to situations where it was inappropriate. The child who has learned to fear a white rat is not better off if he fears a black dog as well; the cat that has learned to escape a box by stepping on a treadle is not better off stepping on things in a box with a hook-and-eye latch; the child who imitates an adult's method of operating a candy machine does not do well to apply the same technique to the operation of a telephone. It is often best if behavior learned in one situation does *not* carry over to very different situations. And usually it does not. This tendency to behave differently in different situations is called *discrimination*.

These two phenomena, generalization and discrimination, are the subjects of this chapter. Although treated as two separate phenomena, they are really two sides of the same coin. It is a coin without which we could not survive.

Generalization

Generalization is the tendency for learned behavior to occur in the presence of stimuli that were not present during training.[1] For instance, in Pavlovian conditioning, a dog may learn to salivate to the sound of a tuning fork vibrating at 1,000 cycles per second (cps). After this training, the dog may then be found to salivate to the sound of a tuning fork vibrating at, say, 950 cps to 1,100 cps, even though it was never exposed to these stimuli. The conditional response spreads, or generalizes, to stimuli somewhat different from the CS.

The famous Watson and Rayner (1920) study (see Chapter 4) provides another example of the generalization of a conditional response. You will recall that Little Albert learned to fear a white rat. After establishing this fear, Watson and Rayner tested Albert to see whether other, previously neutral stimuli would also elicit fear. They presented Albert with a rabbit, raw cotton, and a Santa Claus mask. None of these stimuli had been present when the rat was paired with the loud noise, yet Albert was afraid of them. Albert's fear had spread, or generalized, from the white rat to other white, furry objects.

Perhaps the first report of generalization following operant learning came from Thorndike (1898) when he observed that "a cat that has learned to escape from [box] A by clawing has, when put into [box] C or G, a greater tendency to claw at things than it instinctively had at the start" (p. 14). In other words, clawing generalized from box A to boxes C and G.

Thorndike (1898) demonstrated generalization by training animals in one puzzle box and then another. For example, after a dog escaped from box AA (which required pulling on a loop near the door) 26 times, Thorndike put him into box BB, in which the loop was at the back of the box. After 10 trials in this box, the dog escaped as soon as it was put into the box. Thorndike next put the dog into box BB1, which resembled BB except that the loop was considerably higher. Learning proceeded even more quickly in this box. Several days later, Thorndike put the animal into a box resembling BB1, except that a small wooden platform, instead of a loop, dangled from the roof. Although the platform did not in the least re-

---

[1]This is called *stimulus generalization*, to distinguish it from *response generalization*. The latter has to do with the variations in behavior that occur in the presence of a given stimulus. In this text, the term *generalization* refers only to stimulus generalization.

semble the loop, the dog's performance again showed improvement. The more experiences an animal had at escaping from boxes, the more quickly it learned to escape from new boxes.[2]

Those who followed Thorndike studied operant generalization in a more rigorous manner. In a typical experiment, a pigeon might receive food when it pecks a yellow disk. After this training, the bird is given the opportunity to peck the disk, but sometimes the disk is yellow, sometimes a yellowish orange, sometimes dark orange, and sometimes red. Regardless of the color, pecking is no longer reinforced. The experimenter records the number of times the bird pecks each colored disk. The inevitable outcome is that the bird pecks the disk most often when it is the color used during training, but it also pecks the disk when it is other colors (Guttman & Kalish, 1956).

Generalization is not restricted to highly specific behaviors, such as disk pecking. Broader behavioral tendencies also generalize. Robert Eisenberger and his colleagues (Eisenberger, 1992; Eisenberger & Cameron, 1996; Eisenberger et al., 1982) have found, for instance, that rewarding a high level of effort on one task increases the level of effort on other tasks, a phenomenon they call learned industriousness. This means that trying hard may, if reinforced in one situation, generalize to another.

But generalization cannot be taken for granted. D. E. Ducharme and S. W. Holborn (1997) conducted a social skills training program with five hearing impaired preschool children. The training program produced high, stable rates of social interaction in that setting. However, the social skills did *not* generalize well to other teachers, to peers, or to activities different from those used in training. Ducharme and Holborn had to modify their program to include features aimed specifically at increasing generalization.

One way to increase generalization is to provide training in a wide variety of settings. This has implications for education. Many educators assume that once a student understands a principle, such as the Pythagorean Theorem or the refraction of light by water, the student is then able to apply it in any number of situations without additional practice. In fact, even *with* understanding, practice in a variety of situations is usually essential.

Generalization is not always helpful. Sometimes a behavior that is useful in one situation generalizes to situations in which it is not appropriate. Thorndike (1898) noticed, for example, that a cat that had learned

---

[2] Thorndike wrote that "any reaction . . . to totally new phenomena, when first experienced, will be called instinctive" (p. 14). In other words, we react to new situations on the basis of genetic dispositions, not learning. But *are* there any "totally new" situations, or is everything we experience a variation of some other experience?

to escape from a box by pulling on a loop would later paw at the same spot—even though the loop had been removed! In the same way, a college student whose off-color jokes get big laughs in the dormitory may later find that the same jokes are not appreciated at the family dinner table.

C. S. Dweck and N. D. Repucci (1973) showed how generalization can work against a teacher and her students. Teachers first gave students unsolvable problems. Later these teachers gave the students problems that *could* be solved, but the students failed to solve them. Perhaps the tendency to give up generalized from the first situation to the second. This seems to be the case, because when a *different* teacher gave the students solvable problems, they were successful.

Generalization can also make problem behaviors more troublesome than they would be if they did not generalize. For instance, if punching a large inflated doll is reinforced, children later tend to be more aggressive when interacting with their peers (Walters & Brown, 1963). There is a substantial difference between an inflated doll and a child, yet the behavior generalized from one situation to the other.

Generalization Gradients

The fact that a behavior generalizes to stimuli not present during training does not mean that all new stimuli are equally effective in eliciting the behavior. Nor is generalization an arbitrary and unpredictable phenomenon that occurs in some situations and not others. Indeed, generalization is a reliable and orderly phenomenon that has "a pattern and sense" (Guttman, 1963, p. 144).

When stimuli can be arranged in an orderly way along some dimension (such as pitch or hue), from most like the training stimulus to least like it, a clear relation between stimulus similarity and generalization can be seen. This can be demonstrated by training an organism to behave in a particular way in the presence of a stimulus and then presenting several new stimuli of varying degrees of similarity to the training stimulus. The typical finding is that the more similar a novel stimulus is to the training stimulus, the more likely the participant is to behave as though it *were* the training stimulus. When these results are plotted on a curve, they yield a figure called the **generalization gradient**.

Query: A generalization gradient shows the tendency for a

behavior to occur in situations that differ systematically from

_____.

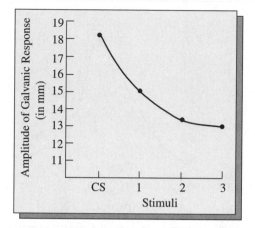

Figure 9-1 *Generalization gradient. Average strength of conditional response (GSR) to the CS, and to other tones of decreasing similarity to the CS (1, 2, 3). (From "The Generalization of Conditioned Responses: 1. The Sensory Generalization of Conditioned Responses with Varying Frequencies of Tone," by Carl Hovland, 1937, Journal of General Psychology, 17, p. 136, Figure 2. Copyright © 1937 by the Journal Press. Reprinted by permission of the Helen Dwight Reid Educational Foundation. Published by Heldref Publications.)*

Carl Hovland (1937a) produced a generalization gradient following Pavlovian conditioning. He began by training college students to respond to a tone. The US was a mild electric shock and the UR was the galvanic skin response, or GSR (a measure of emotional arousal). The CS was a tone of a particular pitch. After 16 pairings of the CS and US, Hovland then presented four different tones, including the CS. The results showed that the CR diminished as the stimuli grew less like the CS. Hovland plotted the data to produce the generalization gradient shown in Figure 9-1.

Another sort of generalization gradient is illustrated in Figure 9-2. This gradient is the product of a classic study by Norman Guttman and Harry Kalish (1956). In their experiment, birds learned to peck a disk of a particular color and later had the opportunity to peck disks of various colors, including the color used in training, for 30 seconds each. Pigeons pecked the disk most frequently when it was the color used during training, but they also pecked the disk when it was other colors. As the generalization gradient reveals, the more closely the disk resembled the training disk, the more often the birds pecked it. If a disk were almost the same color as the training disk, the birds pecked at it almost as much as if it were the training disk; if the disk were a very different color, the pigeons seldom touched it.

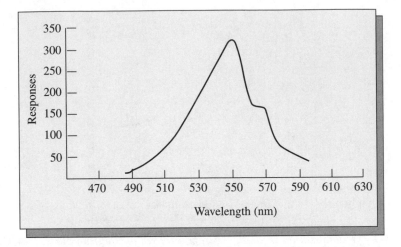

Figure 9-2 *Generalization gradient. When pecking a disk of a particular color (in this case a wavelength of 550 nanometers) had been reinforced, pigeons were likely to peck that disk at a high rate. However, they would also peck disks that were similar to the original disk. (After Guttman and Kalish, 1956.)*

Query: Fire drills are meant to teach appropriate behavior

during a fire, yet people don't always behave during fires as they

do during drills. Why?

The generalization gradients depicted here are typical of those found in learning texts, but it would be a mistake to assume that all generalization gradients are more or less alike. The form of the gradient depends on many variables, including the amount of training, the method of testing for generalization, and the kind of stimuli involved (Honig & Urcuioli, 1981). Nevertheless, there is a systematic relationship between an organism's behavior in the presence of a stimulus and the similarity of that stimulus to stimuli present during training. That systematic relationship is usually based on some physical aspect of the stimuli in question. However, generalization can be based on more abstract features, as studies of semantic generalization make clear.

Semantic Generalization

Most studies of generalization, like those just described, are based on the physical properties of the stimuli involved—color, size, shape, pitch, loudness, and so on. But learned behavior sometimes generalizes on the basis of an abstract feature. This phenomenon is known as **semantic generalization**.

Generalized Therapy

The patient was a 37-year-old woman who stood 5 feet 4 inches and weighed 47 pounds. She looked like a survivor of a Nazi concentration camp, but the emaciation that threatened to kill her was due to self-starvation. She had a mysterious aversion to eating called anorexia.

Arthur Bachrach and his colleagues (1965) took on the task of ending this woman's self-destructive refusal to eat. They used shaping and reinforcement principles to get her to eat more. The strategy worked, and she gained enough weight to be released from the hospital. But what would happen when she went home? Would she go back to starving herself again, or would the effects of the therapy generalize to the new situation?

The problem of generalization is critical for therapists: There is little value in changing behavior in the hospital or clinic if those changes do not carry over to the home and workplace. One way to attack the problem of generalization is to try to alter the natural environment so that appropriate behavior continues to be reinforced at a high rate. Bachrach and his co-workers used this approach. They asked the patient's family to cooperate in various ways. Among other things, they asked the family to avoid reinforcing invalidism, to reinforce maintenance of weight by, for example, complimenting the patient's appearance, and to encourage her to eat with other people under pleasant circumstances.

With reinforcement of appropriate behavior in the home, the behavior might then generalize to other settings. The reinforcement that naturally occurs in these settings would, it was hoped, maintain the desired behavior. The hope seems to have been fulfilled. For instance, the patient attended a social function at which refreshments were served. It had always been the woman's custom to refuse food on such occasions, but she surprised everyone by asking for a doughnut. All eyes were on her as she devoured the snack, and she later admitted that she got considerable pleasure from all the attention.

Generalization is not always established this easily (Holland, 1978; Miller & Sloane, 1976; Wolf et al., 1987). The juvenile delinquent who acquires cooperative social skills in a special rehabilitation center and then returns to a home and community where aggressive, antisocial acts are reinforced and cooperative behavior is punished is apt to revert to old habits. The chain smoker who quits while on a vacation with nonsmokers must return to a world of smoke-filled rooms. The rehabilitated and repentant child abuser returns to a neighborhood filled with naive and easily seduced children. The problem of getting therapeutic gains to generalize to the natural environment is one of the most difficult the therapist faces, but understanding the principles of generalization helps.

Gregory Razran (1939) did what may have been the first study of semantic generalization. Razran had three adults chew gum, lick lollipops, or eat sandwiches to make them salivate. As they ate, they watched the words *style, urn, freeze,* and *surf* flash on a screen. Then Razran presented the words alone and collected saliva in cotton balls that rested under each individual's tongue. Razran weighed the cotton after each testing period to determine the effectiveness of the procedure: The heavier the cotton, the stronger the CR.

After the people had learned to salivate at the sight of the words, Razran showed them words that were either homophones (words with similar sounds, but different meanings, such as *stile, earn, frieze, serf*) or synonyms (*fashion, vase, chill, wave*) of the words used in training. The idea was to determine whether the CR would generalize more to words that had similar sounds or to words that had similar meanings. The results showed that, as expected, the participants salivated in response to the homophones. However, they salivated even more in response to the synonyms. Thus, although there was some generalization based on the sounds of the words, there was even more generalization based on word meanings (see Figure 9-3).

Query: The Razran study involved the kind of training procedure called _____.

Semantic generalization has been demonstrated in a number of other studies. John Lacey and his colleagues (1955), in a study with college students, paired farm words such as *corn* with electric shocks, so that they became conditional stimuli that would elicit an increase in heart rate. Then the researchers presented words that were semantically related (other farm words such as *cow, plow, tractor*) but which had never been paired with shock. They found that these related words also caused hearts to beat faster. Words that were not related to farming did not have this effect.

Studies of semantic generalization demonstrate that, at least among humans, generalization can be based on abstract concepts as well as physical properties. It is easy to see how this phenomenon might be important in human affairs. For example, in the United States during World War II, the word *Japanese* was often paired with unpleasant words such as *dirty, sneaky, cruel,* and *enemy*. The work of Carolyn and Arthur Staats (see Chapter 4) showed that such pairings are likely to result in the word *Japanese* eliciting negative emotional reactions. The work on semantic generalization suggests that such emotional responses

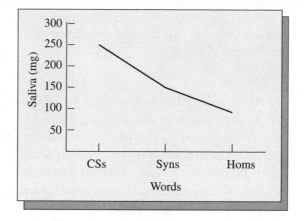

Figure 9-3 *Semantic generalization. Average amount of saliva (in milligrams) secreted in response to words used in training (CSs) and to synonyms (Syns) and homophones (Homs) of those words. (Compiled from data in Razran, 1939.)*

may generalize to other, semantically related words, such as *Oriental* and *Asian.*

It is reasonable to suppose that there might be generalization from words to the people the words represent. During World War II, American citizens of Japanese descent were treated with suspicion and hostility; thousands were imprisoned in concentration camps and their property confiscated, although their only crime was that they resembled the enemy (Robinson, 2001; Smith, 1995). Years later, during a downturn in the American economy, Vincent Chin, an American of Chinese descent, was beaten by two unemployed autoworkers who thought he was Japanese (Roylance, 1986). Following the horrific attacks against the United States by Arab extremists on September 11, 2001, many people of Arab descent living in the United States, some of them American citizens, were assaulted. No doubt in most instances the victim's only crime was *resembling* those who had committed crimes.

Query: Racial prejudice probably involves _____

generalization.

Of course, positive emotions generalize in the same way. When an American president takes an action that is favorable to another country, Americans visiting that country are welcomed and treated kindly, even though they had nothing to do with the president's action. Positive emotions toward the president generalize to other Americans. Thus, semantic generalization appears to play an important role in prejudice and other kinds of emotional behavior.

Generalization Following Extinction and Punishment

Studies of generalization usually involve the tendency of behavior that is reinforced in one situation to spread to another situation. But generalization is not limited to the tendency of *reinforced* behavior to spread; changes in behavior produced by extinction and punishment also spread beyond the training situation.

For example, R. E. P. Youtz (reported in Skinner, 1938) trained rats to press a horizontal lever for food and then put the behavior on extinction. After this, he tested the rats in a chamber with a vertical lever. He found that the effects of the extinction procedure reduced the rats' tendency to press the new lever. Youtz trained other rats to press the vertical lever, then put the behavior on extinction and tested them on the horizontal lever. Again, he found that the effects of extinction spread to the new situation. Overall, the extinction procedure reduced the tendency to perform in a similar situation by 63%.

Another example of the generalization of extinction is provided by Carl Hovland's (1937a) famous study, described earlier. After pairing a tone with shock, Hovland repeatedly presented the tone alone. After this extinction procedure, he measured the conditional response (the GSR) to four tones. He found that the effects of the extinction procedure spread to these tones, with the greatest generalization to those tones that most resembled the one used during extinction.

The suppression of behavior produced by punishment spreads in much the same way as the effects of reinforcement and extinction. For example, Werner Honig and Robert Slivka (1964) trained pigeons to peck disks of various colors. When the birds were pecking all the colors at the same rate, the experimenters began providing brief electric shock on some occasions. They continued reinforcing disk pecks but also punished pecking whenever the disk was a particular color. The tendency to peck the disk when it was that color declined, of course, but so did the tendency to peck when the disk was other colors. The frequency of pecking varied systematically with the similarity of the disk to the punished color. Thus, the effects of punishment formed a generalization gradient like those seen following reinforcement and extinction. Much the same phenomenon has been demonstrated in humans (O'Donnell & Crosbie, 1998).

REVIEW   Generalization is the tendency to behave in situations that are different from the situation in which the behavior was learned. The tendency for behavior to generalize to new situations varies with their similarity to the training situation. This tendency can be depicted with a generalization gradient. Most studies of generalization involve the physical properties of stimuli—sound, color, shape, and so on. But behavior sometimes generalizes on the basis of the meaning of a stimulus, a phenomenon called semantic generalization. The effects of reinforcement generalize, but so do the effects of extinction and punishment.

Discrimination

Discrimination is the tendency for learned behavior to occur in one situation, such as the presence of a red light, but not in other situations, such as the presence of a blue or green light. The organism behaves differently in different situations.[3]

Discrimination and generalization are inversely related: The more discrimination, the less generalization. Generalization gradients therefore also reflect the degree of discrimination. A relatively flat gradient indicates little or no discrimination; a steep gradient indicates considerable discrimination (see Figure 9-4).

We saw earlier that the more a stimulus resembles the training stimulus, the greater will be the degree of generalization. It is therefore clear that the less similar a stimulus is to the training stimulus, the greater will be the degree of discrimination. It is often possible, however, to establish a discrimination between very similar stimuli through discrimination training.

Discrimination Training

Any procedure for establishing a discrimination is called **discrimination training**. In Pavlovian discrimination training, one stimulus (designated **CS+**) is regularly paired with a US, and another stimulus (designated **CS–**) regularly appears without the US. For example, we might put food

---

[3]Discrimination is also a tool of evolution. Amotz and Avishag Zahavi (1999) suggested that an antelope that "stots" (jumps high into the air) when it sees a lion, discourages attack. Thus, predators evolve the ability to discriminate between easy and difficult prey, and the prey animals evolve mechanisms for making use of the predator's discriminatory ability.

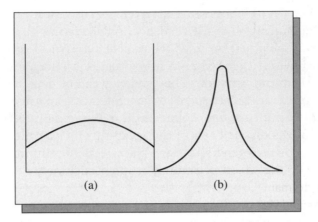

Figure 9-4 *Discrimination and the generalization gradient. A relatively flat gradient (a) indicates little discrimination; a steep gradient (b) indicates considerable discrimination. (Hypothetical data.)*

into a dog's mouth each time a buzzer sounds and give the dog nothing when a bell rings. The result will be that the dog will salivate at the sound of the buzzer (the CS+) but not at the sound of the bell (the CS–). At this point, we say that the dog discriminates between the buzzer and the bell: It behaves differently in the two situations.

Pavlov (1927) conducted many experiments on discrimination training. In one, a dog saw a rotating object. Whenever the object rotated in a clockwise direction, the dog received food; whenever the object rotated in the opposite direction, the dog did not get food. The dog soon discriminated: It salivated at the CS+ (clockwise rotation) but not at the CS– (counterclockwise rotation).

Other experiments yielded similar results. Pavlov's dogs learned to discriminate between different volumes of a particular sound, different pitches of a tone, different geometric forms, and different temperatures. Sometimes the level of discrimination achieved was remarkable. One dog even learned to discriminate between a metronome that ticked at the rate of 100 beats a minute and one that ticked 96 times a minute. Although a good deal of research has been done on Pavlovian discrimination, we will focus on operant discrimination.

In operant discrimination training, one stimulus (designated S+ or S^D, pronounced ess-dee) typically indicates that a behavior will have reinforcing consequences, and another stimulus (S– or S^Δ, pronounced ess-delta) indicates that the behavior will not have reinforcing consequences. S+ and S– are **discriminative stimuli**—i.e., stimuli that are associated

Worlds Apart: Punks and Skinheads

To many people, birds are birds. Sparrows, starlings, finches—they all look alike. The same thing is often said of certain groups of people. Yet members of these groups have no trouble at all distinguishing members of their group from members of other groups. This is well illustrated in an article by Bill Bartlett (1992), who was (and perhaps still is) a member of the variety of humans known as punks.

Punks and skinheads adorn their persons in highly unconventional manners. To many people, they are all one sort of bird, indistinguishable. But punks and skins have no trouble telling themselves apart. Bartlett explains the difference for those of us who have not learned to discriminate between them:

Punks, he says, usually wear spike-studded leather jackets or denims. They also wear T-shirts with the names of punk bands or antigovernment slogans, spiked belts, tight-fitting jeans, and combat boots. Sometimes they have antigovernment slogans tattooed on their arms, and most have pierced noses, lips, or eyebrows.

Skins, on the other hand, wear army flight jackets, Fred Perry or Polo shirts, and suspenders. They also wear jeans or khaki slacks that fit around the ankles. They wear tattoos of the American flag, swastikas, or the letters *SWP* (for "supreme white power").

Skins and punks have very different political views (punks lean toward anarchy, skins toward fascism), so they are not, as a rule, inclined to picnic in the park together. Because of this mutual hostility, it is important that they be able to discriminate between members of the two groups. To other people, discriminating between them is not so important. They are simply "birds of a feather."

with different consequences for behavior.[4] To illustrate: We might arrange an experimental chamber so that a rat receives food each time it presses a lever, but only if a lamp is on. The result will be that when the lamp is on (S^+), the rat presses the lever, and when the lamp is off (S^-) it does not press. At this point, we say that the rat discriminates between

---

[4] Some people reserve the term *discriminative stimulus* for the event that indicates the availability of reinforcement. However, both S^+ and S^- are essential for discrimination to occur, and therefore "each is a discriminative stimulus" (Keller & Schoenfeld, 1950, p. 118). For reasons that have more to do with history than logic, CS+ and CS− are *not* usually referred to as discriminative stimuli, a term that is reserved for the S^+ and S^- of operant discrimination training. Nevertheless, the stimuli serve analogous functions.

the "light on" situation and the "light off" situation: It behaves differently in the two situations.

Other forms of operant discrimination training are possible, some of them much more complicated than this. For example, a behavior may be reinforced when a light is on and punished when it is off. Or, the behavior may produce a large or particularly desirable reinforcer when the light is on, but a smaller or less desirable reinforcer when it is off. Or, two stimuli may indicate different probabilities of reinforcement. Many other arrangements are possible: Every second lever press might produce food when a lamp is on, and every third lever press when a lamp is off. And there are other possibilities. In all cases, however, one stimulus "pays off" better than (is more reinforcing than) another. The stimulus that signals the more reinforcing consequence is designated S^+ (or S^D); the stimulus that signals the less reinforcing consequence is designated S^- (or S^Δ). The essence of discrimination training is the *relative* reinforcement value of the available options: Discrimination occurs when one consequence is more reinforcing than another.[5]

It is amazing what can be accomplished with discrimination training, even in birds and rodents. Pigeons have, for example, learned to discriminate between paintings by Picasso and those of Monet (Watanabe et al., 1995). They not only discriminated between the pictures by Picasso and Monet used during training, but also discriminated between pictures by these artists that *they had never seen before*. More than that, the birds were then able to discriminate between other painters of these two schools.[6] Other researchers found that pigeons could learn to discriminate between the music of Bach and Stravinsky (Porter & Neuringer, 1984). Humans can, of course, learn these and perhaps even more subtle discriminations.

These examples of successful discrimination training are apt to give the impression that learning subtle discriminations is quite easy. But these studies show discrimination training under carefully controlled laboratory conditions. Under more natural conditions learning is apt to proceed more slowly. All of us have had some "training" in discriminating between people who are lying and those who are telling the truth. Yet few of us are good at making these discriminations. Saul Kassin (1997) writes, "In fact, even so-called experts who make such judgments for a

---

[5]Jennifer O'Donnell (2001) has suggested an alternative notation system for discrimination training: S^D, S^{Dp}, and S^Δ to indicate that the behavior will result in reinforcement, punishment, and nonreinforcement, respectively. But if the essential aspect of discrimination is that one option is more reinforcing than another, two symbols (such as S^+ and S^-) would seem to be sufficient.

[6]Interestingly enough, the birds did not discriminate so well when the researchers turned a painting by Monet upside down, but turning a Picasso upside down made no difference. Devotees of modern art will have no difficulty explaining this result.

Lessons from Lepers

In ages past, victims of leprosy were outcasts of society, forced to wander the countryside begging for food. Lepers were required by law to ring a bell as they traveled, to warn others of their approach. The bell served as an S^+ for taking cover—thereby avoiding sight of the lepers and the risk of contamination. Carrying bells may have been reinforced by reducing the leper's risk of being stoned, a common practice among those who came upon lepers. Today, lepers no longer carry bells to warn of their coming, but in a strange way, many of us do practice a kind of "bell ringing" to influence the behavior of those we meet. It's called the T-shirt.

Today, people wear T-shirts decorated with messages that announce their views, their affiliation with certain groups, and their involvement in various activities. A baseball fan's shirt may announce, for example, "I can't help being weird—I'm a Mets fan." The dedicated bird watcher's shirt may read, "I'm for the birds." And the classic music lover's attire may declare, "Bach is Back." Such comments can have the effect of inducing other people to initiate conversations because they indicate that certain kinds of comments will be reinforced. When you encounter someone whose shirt says, "I'm for the birds," you can be fairly confident that any interest you show in bird watching will be positively reinforced by that person.

It is interesting to note, in this regard, that sartorial messages usually appear on the front, not the back, of clothing. This is probably because we are more likely to address a person when we are approaching him or her than when we are looking at the person's back.

Of course, in one respect, T-shirt messages are fundamentally different from the leper's bell. Whereas the leper hoped to avoid injury by scaring off his enemies, the modern T-shirt wearer probably hopes to attract people with similar views. The T-shirts are also a lot quieter than bells.

living—police investigators; judges; psychiatrists; and polygraphers . . . are highly prone to error" (p. 222).

Most studies of operant discrimination use one of three training procedures. Let's look at those now.

Query: In operant discrimination training, the stimulus that indicates the more reinforcing consequence of a behavior is designated _____.

Successive, Simultaneous, and MTS Procedures

In **successive discrimination training,** the S^+ and S^- alternate, usually randomly. When the S+ appears, the behavior is reinforced; when the S^- appears, the behavior is on extinction. For example, a rat may be placed in an experimental chamber with two lightbulbs, one red and one green, over a lever. Whenever the red light is on, lever pressing produces food; whenever the green light is on, lever pressing has no effect.

In **simultaneous discrimination training,** the discriminative stimuli are presented at the same time. For example, our rat may find itself in a chamber in which the red and green lights are on, with each light placed above its own lever. Pressing the lever under the red light results in food; pressing the lever under the green light does not. In a variation of this procedure, Karl Lashley (1930) trained rats to jump from a stand to a platform on which they would find food. To reach the platform, they had to jump through a door. The rats had a choice of two doors, one with vertical lines, the other with horizontal lines; only one door would open. If the animals jumped toward the correct door, the door flew open and the rat passed through to the food; if they chose the wrong door, the door did not open and they fell to a net below and got no food. The rats soon learned to jump toward the proper door.

In a procedure called **matching to sample (MTS),** the task is to select from two or more alternatives (called comparison stimuli) the stimulus that matches a standard (the sample). The comparison stimuli include the S^+—the stimulus that matches the sample—and one or more S^-s. For example, a sample disk on one wall of an experimental chamber may be illuminated by either a red or a green light. On some trials the disk will be red, on some trials green. After a short time the sample disk goes dark, and two comparison disks, one red and one green, are illuminated. The S^+ is the disk of the same color as the sample. If a pigeon pecks the comparison disk that matches the sample, it receives food; if it pecks the other disk, it receives nothing. To obtain reinforcement, the bird must successfully discriminate between the disk that matches the sample (the S^+) and the one that does not (the S^-).

The example of MTS just given is very simple, but the procedure can be far more complicated. For example, the bird may be required to peck a disk that is *different from* the sample, a variation of MTS called **oddity matching** or **mismatching.** The MTS procedure also may be complicated by increasing the number of variations in the sample and/or the comparison disks. For example, the sample may alternate among red, green, and blue, and the comparison disks may be red, green, blue, and yellow.

Errorless Discrimination Training

In the procedures just described, the organism undergoing training inevitably makes a number of mistakes. When discriminative stimuli are very similar, the organism at first behaves at about the same rate to both S⁺ and S⁻, but since performing in the presence of S⁻ is not reinforced, it tends to die out. A discrimination typically takes some time to develop, and dozens of errors may be made along the way. Errors tend to be demoralizing (they punish making an effort), so it is usually desirable to reduce the number of errors that arise during training.

Herbert Terrace (1963a, 1963b, 1964, 1972) found that many of the errors that occur in discrimination training could be avoided through a procedure called **errorless discrimination training.** He presented the S⁺ and reinforced appropriate behavior; but instead of presenting the S⁻ in the usual manner, he presented it in very weak form and for very short periods. For example, in training a pigeon to discriminate between a red disk (the S⁺) and a green disk (the S⁻), Terrace (1963a) presented the red disk at full strength for 3 minutes at a time. Instead of presenting a green disk for 3 minutes, he presented an unlit disk for 5 seconds. Pigeons are less likely to peck a dark disk than a bright one, and the shorter the time the disk is available, the less likely they are to peck it. The result was that the S⁻ was seldom pecked. Gradually, Terrace increased the duration and strength of the S⁻ (beginning with a very dark green disk) while reinforcing pecking at the S⁺. Finally, Terrace was able to present the green disk without the bird pecking it.

Query: In errorless discrimination training, the _____ is

presented in very weak form and gradually "faded in."

In another study, Terrace (1963b) first established a red-green discrimination and then used the errorless procedure to establish a discrimination between a vertical line (the S⁺) and a horizontal line (the S⁻). He did this by fading in a vertical line on the red disk and fading in the horizontal line on the green disk. As the vertical and horizontal lines were faded in, the colors were faded *out* until the birds were pecking a colorless disk with a vertical line and ignoring a colorless disk with a horizontal line.

With the Terrace procedure, a discrimination can be developed with few errors. This is important, since errors tend to arouse undesirable emotional reactions. Birds trained in the traditional manner, for example, often stamp their feet or flap their wings when presented with the S⁻.

Birds trained with the errorless procedure, however, merely watch the disk calmly until the S⁺ reappears.

Errorless discrimination training has been put to good use outside the laboratory, particularly in teaching young children. Richard Powers and his colleagues (1970) found, for instance, that preschoolers learned a subtle color discrimination more quickly and with fewer errors when trained with the Terrace procedure than when trained in the traditional manner. Children trained in the usual way also became emotionally upset during the S⁻ periods: They banged hard on the lever and wandered around the room. In contrast, those who learned through the errorless procedure sat quietly when the S⁻ was present, patiently waiting for the S⁺ to appear.

Errorless discrimination training can greatly reduce the number of errors made during training. Another way to improve the rate of learning is to make use of differential outcomes.

Differential Outcomes Effect

In discrimination training, the behavior required for reinforcement is often the same from trial to trial. A pigeon may receive food if it pecks a disk when the disk is red, for example, but not when it is green. The behavior is the same in either case, but the circumstances under which performing the act is reinforced varies. However, in some forms of discrimination training, two or more behaviors may pay off. For example, a rat may have access to two levers, one on either side of a light. When the light is red, pressing the lever to the right of the light produces food; when a green light is on, pressing the lever to the left of the light pays off. The color of the light indicates that a particular behavior will be reinforced.

The question arises: What would happen if the reinforcer varied systematically with the behavior? Suppose, for example, that appropriate presses of the right lever resulted in food, but appropriate presses of the left lever resulted in water. Would the difference in outcomes affect performance?

It turns out that it does. M. A. Trapold (1970) conducted an experiment like the one just proposed and found that rats learned to make the appropriate discrimination more quickly and achieved a higher level of accuracy than when the two behaviors produced the same consequence. This finding—improved performance in discrimination training as a result of different consequences for different behaviors—is called the **differential outcomes effect** or **DOE** (Peterson & Trapold, 1980; for an excellent review, see Goeters et al., 1992).

In an experiment using a form of successive discrimination training, J. G. Carlson and R. M. Wielkiewicz (1976) presented either a steady tone or a clicking sound. When the tone sounded, pressing the right lever produced reinforcement; when the clicker sounded, pressing the left lever produced reinforcement. For one group of rats, the reinforcer varied consistently with the behavior: Correct presses of one lever always produced one food pellet; correct presses of the other lever always produced five pellets. In a control group, correct presses sometimes produced one food pellet, sometimes five pellets, regardless of which lever was pressed. Errors went unreinforced for both groups. The result was that consistent differences in outcome for each behavior resulted in faster discrimination and fewer errors.

Query: The DOE implies that discrimination training can be

improved by providing different _____ for

different _____ .

In a similar experiment with thoroughbred horses, Yukako Miyashita and colleagues (2000) trained horses to press one of two levers, depending on the color of a center panel. If the panel were blue, a horse was to press the left lever; if the panel were yellow, it was to press the right lever.[7] Reinforcers were bits of carrot and food pellets. The researchers found that performance was best when correct presses on one lever always earned the horse bits of carrot, and correct presses of the other lever produced food pellets. Results were weaker when pressing either lever produced the same food, or when carrots and pellets appeared randomly at one lever or the other.

Normally, training is more effective when it includes immediate reinforcement than when it includes delayed reinforcement. But what if we provide immediate reinforcement for one correct behavior and delayed reinforcement for another correct behavior? Will the DOE still hold?

Carlson and Wielkiewicz (1972) performed just such an experiment and found that the DOE *did* hold. Animals receiving immediate reinforcement for one behavior and delayed reinforcement for the other learned the discrimination faster than animals receiving immediate reinforcement for both behaviors.

The DOE has proved to be a robust phenomenon, found in a wide range of organisms, including pigeons, rats, dogs, chickens, and retarded and autistic children, and with a variety of consequences. The DOE may

---

[7]Apparently, horses do not see the color yellow (Macuda & Timney, 1999). However, as Miyashita and coworkers (2000) note, "Whether the horses saw these colors as we do is not crucial for the purposes of our study."

have important implications for discrimination training with people. For example, efforts to teach children to distinguish among various fruits may be more effective if correct actions produce different kinds or amounts of reinforcement.

The problem of why differential outcomes improve training results is a matter for some debate. One theory suggests that different outcomes result in different expectations (Peterson, 1984). The trouble with the differential expectations theory is that we then have to explain where the expectations came from. The answer inevitably involves identifying elements in the learning history. Once this is done, the expectations are likely to contribute little to our understanding of the problem. Susan Goeters and her colleagues (1992) propose that the DOE (and presumably, any expectations that may arise) can be accounted for in terms of a combination of Pavlovian and operant learning. Unfortunately, their theory requires more space than is available here.

After discrimination training—with or without differential outcomes—the organism responds to certain stimuli but not to other, similar stimuli. At this point, we can say that the discriminative stimuli exert a certain amount of control over the organism's behavior.

REVIEW   When an organism performs an act in the presence of one stimulus but not in the presence of another, we say the organism discriminates. The procedure for establishing a discrimination is called discrimination training. Discrimination training may take different forms, including successive, simultaneous, and matching to sample. Errorless discrimination training establishes a discrimination with a minimum of errors, and differential outcomes speed learning.

Stimulus Control

Consider a rat that has learned to press a lever when a light is on, but not when the light is off. The environment clearly influences the rat's behavior: When the light goes on, the rat presses at a high rate; when the light goes off, lever pressing declines. When discrimination training brings behavior under the influence of discriminative stimuli, the behavior is said to be under **stimulus control** (for a review, see Thomas, 1991).

Rats are not the only creatures, of course, that come under stimulus control. While you are driving, if you approach an intersection and the traffic light turns red, you move your foot to the brake pedal. Your behavior has, as the result of discrimination training, come under the influence of the traffic signal. Similarly, you tend to enter stores that have signs that say "Open" and walk past stores that are marked "Closed." People respond to signs that say "Sale," "Reduced Prices," "Clearance," "Going Out of Business," and the like. Retailers know the influence exerted by such signs and use them to attract shoppers.

Sometimes stimulus control is exerted not by a single stimulus but by a complex array of stimuli that, collectively, influence behavior. We behave differently at a formal ball than we do at a square dance, and behavior that would be acceptable at a beach party is unacceptable at a dinner party. The differential control exerted by such situations probably has to do with a number of stimuli including attire, furniture, food, and the behavior of other people present. When a youngster misbehaves, he often defends his actions by saying, "Well, everyone else was doing it!" This explanation is an appeal to the stimulus control exerted by the behavior of one's peers.

Students often object to the concept of stimulus control, at least as it applies to people. This is partly because the word *control* has negative connotations. (Remember Staats and Staats!) And stimulus control does sometimes work against our best interests. We may find ourselves eating food we don't need, or particularly want, merely because it is available. The food exerts a kind of control over us, like the sign on a restaurant that says "Eat," or the photographs of delicious foods in a menu. Studies have shown that the mere presence of a weapon increases the likelihood of a violent act (Berkowitz, 1964; Berkowitz & LePage, 1967). Leonard Berkowitz (1968) warns that while the finger pulls the trigger of a gun, the trigger also pulls the finger. He is talking about stimulus control.

But there is another way of looking at stimulus control. Discriminative stimuli give us a kind of power. Consider the rat that learns to press a lever when a light is on, but not when it is off. The light is said to control the rat's behavior, but the rat has also gained control: It no longer wastes time and energy pressing a lever when doing so is useless. Similarly, the behavior of motorists comes under the control of traffic lights and signs. But it is this stimulus control that permits us to travel more or less safely and efficiently. Without stimulus control, traffic jams would be routine and our highways would be dangerous gauntlets. In fact, many traffic accidents are attributed to inattentive driving—and what is inattentive driving but a failure of driving behaviors to be under the control of relevant stimuli?

An understanding of the control exerted by stimuli can also give us the power to change our environment appropriately. Dieters who learn that the mere presence of certain foods can affect how much they eat can avoid situations in which those foods are present. People who want to

Stimulus Control and Adaptation

The fact that we come to behave in a given way in certain environments and not in other environments is definitely a good thing. The tendency to generalize is a blessing bestowed on us by evolution because it has survival value. Conditioned taste aversion (see Chapter 4) offers a powerful illustration of this fact: Animals and people made sick by a particular kind of food then refuse to eat not only that food but other foods that resemble it.

We can see the same sort of benefit from the generalization of food gathering skills. In hunter-gatherer societies, young boys practice the skills of the hunt by shooting arrows at leaves. The survival of the group depends not on the boy's ability to shoot a leaf but on his ability to shoot a bird. The mastery of archery skills in the training situation must, and fortunately does, generalize to other similar situations.

Academic education also would be of little value if what we learned did not generalize. School children do not write essays about their summer vacations because they will one day be required to write about those experiences; they write so they will be able to write about other experiences. Similarly, they do not solve the problems in an algebra textbook so they will be able to solve those same problems later on; they solve them so they will be able to solve other problems.

As with generalization, discrimination plays an important role in survival. The blue jay that learns not to eat Monarch butterflies is not helped if it avoids eating all kinds of butterflies. In fact, the blue jay that has been made sick by a Monarch tends also to avoid Viceroys, a harmless butterfly that closely resembles the Monarch. The bird's failure to discriminate between Monarch and Viceroy butterflies handicaps it in its search for food.

In hunter-gatherer societies, girls learn to collect fruits and vegetables for food. They must be able to tell the difference between an edible plant and a

smoke less and who know that they are more likely to smoke when they see other people smoking can reduce their tendency to light up by avoiding areas where smokers congregate.

Researchers have explored ways in which stimulus control can be turned to advantage. G. Alan Marlatt and his colleagues (Marlatt & Gordon, 1985; see also Hickis & Thomas, 1991) have postulated that one reason drug abusers so often relapse after treatment is because they return to an environment in which drug use was reinforced in the past. There are lots of cues (S⁺s) for using drugs. They see the drug peddlers who once sold them drugs, they see friends and neighbors "shooting up," they walk the

poisonous one. They also learn to collect medicinal plants, and again discriminating is important: While some plants heal, others kill.

Discrimination is also important in industrialized societies. The motorist who does not respond differently to red and green traffic signals is unlikely to survive for long on our streets. Similarly, the doctor who does not discriminate accurately between the symptoms of appendicitis and those of indigestion is also in serious trouble—and so is her patient.

Organisms also sometimes benefit from the inability of other organisms to make discriminations. The angler fish waves a fleshy protuberance about in its gaping mouth, and its victims swim after what looks like a tasty morsel. The fish profits from the inability of its prey to discriminate between the fish's lure and the real thing. Some biologists theorize that the rattlesnake's rattle may also provide a kind of lure, citing as evidence the failure of frogs to discriminate between insects and the rattler's tail (Schuett et al., 1984). As the frog lunges for what it takes to be a meal, it instead falls victim to the snake. Similarly, human hunters often use decoys to attract prey within reach of their weapons.

Camouflage may be viewed as an adaptive technique based on the principle of generalization. The chameleon escapes its enemies by changing its color to resemble that of its background. The more it resembles the surface on which it stands, the less likely it is to be eaten. The walking stick, a kind of insect, goes unmolested because it resembles a twig. Human hunters wear uniforms that blend in with their surroundings so as to escape detection by their prey. Such animal and human disguises are effective survival mechanisms because others fail to discriminate between the organism and its surroundings.

We see, then, that for both humans and animals, generalization and discrimination play major roles in adaptation. These phenomena greatly enhance—and complicate—the role of learning in survival.

same streets where they walked when they were high on drugs.[8] In such an environment, it is difficult indeed to continue a life of drug abstinence. The implication is that drug treatment must include learning to avoid or cope with the control exerted by the addict's home environment.

Our environment exerts control over our behavior. Paradoxically, that can increase the control we have over our lives.

---

[8] The situation is analogous to the man who works in a bakery and becomes overweight as a result of snacking on pastries. He can go to a spa and lose weight, but if he returns to work in the bakery he is likely to regain the pounds. He must either find another line of work or learn skills for resisting the temptations before him every day.

Query: Marlatt's work suggests that drug abuse is partly due to

_____.

REVIEW   When a discrimination has been established, the behavior is said to be under stimulus control. Stimulus control can work for or against us, depending on the desirability of the behavior involved.

Theories of Generalization and Discrimination

Three theories of generalization, discrimination, and stimulus control have dominated the field: those of Pavlov, Spence, and Lashley and Wade.

Pavlov's Theory

Pavlov's theory is physiological. He speculated that discrimination training produces physiological changes in the brain. Specifically, it establishes an area of excitation associated with the CS+, and an area of inhibition associated with the CS–. If a novel stimulus is similar to the CS+, it will excite an area of the brain near the CS+ area. The excitation will irradiate to the CS+ area and elicit the CR. Similarly, if a novel stimulus resembles the CS–, it will excite an area of the brain near the CS– area. The excitation of this area will irradiate to the CS– area and inhibit the CR. A similar explanation could be applied to generalization and discrimination following operant learning.

Pavlov's theory provides an intuitively appealing explanation and, wrapped as it is in physiology, it has the smell of science. Unfortunately, the physiological events are merely inferred from observed behavior. Pavlov never saw or measured brain activity in association with conditioning. He presumed that irradiation of excitation occurred because generalization occurred, but there is no independent validation of its happening. The theory therefore suffers from circularity and is for this reason not popular with psychologists. Pavlov's ideas have been modified by other theorists, however, most notably Kenneth Spence.

Query: How is Pavlov's explanation of generalization and

discrimination circular?

Spence's Theory

Pavlov's theory deals with hypothetical physiological events. What Pavlov actually observed, however, was not what went on in the brain but how an animal responded to different stimuli. Kenneth Spence (1936,

1937, 1960) put Pavlov's physiology aside but kept the notions of excitation and inhibition.

Pairing a CS+ with a US results in an increased tendency to respond to the CS+ and to stimuli resembling the CS+. Similarly, reinforcement for responding in the presence of an S⁺ results in an increased tendency to respond not only to the S⁺ but to similar stimuli. The generalization gradient that results is called an **excitatory gradient**. In the same way, presenting a CS– without the US results in a *decreased* tendency to respond to the CS– and to stimuli resembling the CS–. Likewise, withholding reinforcement when responses occur in the presence of an S⁻ results in a decreased tendency to respond to that stimulus and to similar stimuli. The generalization gradient that results is called an **inhibitory gradient**.

Spence proposed that the tendency to respond to any given stimulus was the result of the interaction of the increased and decreased tendencies to respond, as reflected in gradients of excitation and inhibition. Consider a dog that is trained to salivate to the sound of a high-pitched tone, and another that is trained not to salivate to the sound of a low-pitched tone. The first dog will show generalization of excitation around CS+; the second will show generalization of inhibition around CS–. We can plot the excitatory and inhibitory gradients that result and place them next to one another, as depicted in Figure 9-5. Notice that the two curves overlap.

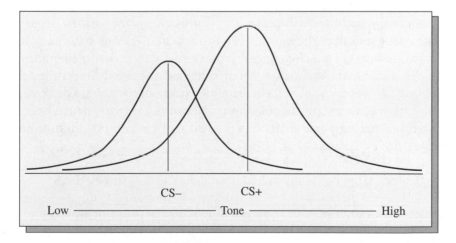

Figure 9-5 *Spence's theory of generalization and discrimination. CS+ training produces a gradient of excitation; CS– training produces a gradient of inhibition. The tendency to respond to a stimulus near the CS+ is reduced to the extent that it resembles the CS–. The tendency not to respond to a stimulus near the CS– is reduced to the extent that it resembles the CS+.*

Discrimination training produces much the same effect within a given organism. That is, the increased tendency to respond to stimuli resembling CS+ (or S+) overlaps with the decreased tendency to respond to stimuli resembling CS– (or S–). What Spence proposed was that the tendency to respond to a novel stimulus following discrimination training would be equal to the net difference between the excitatory and inhibitory tendencies. In other words, the tendency *to* respond to a novel stimulus will be reduced by the tendency *not* to respond to that stimulus.

Consider a hypothetical experiment in which a pigeon is trained to peck an orange disk but not a red one. After training, we give the bird the opportunity to peck the disk when it is a variety of colors, from pale yellow to deep red. What color disk will it peck most often? We know that if the bird had merely received food for pecking the orange disk, it would peck that same color most often. But discrimination training, according to Spence, should result in inhibition of the tendency to peck stimuli resembling the S–. Spence's theory therefore predicts that the peak of responding will not occur at the S+ but at a stimulus further away from the S–. In other words, the peak of responding will not be on the orange disk, but on one that is even less reddish (less like the S–).

This prediction, made in the 1930s, was actually confirmed in the 1950s in an experiment much like that just described. H. M. Hanson (1959) trained pigeons to peck a yellowish-green disk (550 nm, or nanometers, a measure of wavelength) and not to peck a slightly more yellowish (560 nm) disk. A control group of birds did not undergo discrimination training but did receive food for pecking the yellowish-green disk. After training, Hanson let the birds peck disks of various colors, from yellow to green. The control group showed a peak of responding to the discriminative stimulus. Birds that had received discrimination training, however, showed a shift away from the S–; their peak of responding was to a stimulus of about 540 nm (see Figure 9-6). This phenomenon, called **peak shift**, has proved to be a robust phenomenon (Purtle, 1973; Thomas et al., 1991).

Query: Suppose Hanson had used a disk of 530 nm as the S–.

Where would the peak of responding have occurred? (Consider

Figure 9-6.)

The ability of Spence's theory to predict the peak shift phenomenon is impressive. The Lashley-Wade theory also has had its successes.

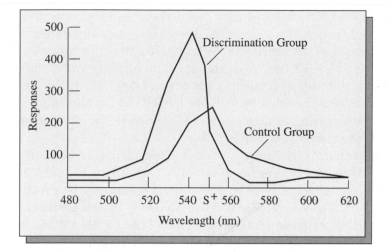

Figure 9-6 *Peak shift. Pigeons trained to discriminate between an S⁺ (550 nm) and an S⁻ (560 nm) responded more often to a 540 nm stimulus than to the S⁺. Birds that had been trained only on the S⁺ did not show this peak shift. (After Hanson, 1959.)*

The Lashley-Wade Theory

Karl Lashley and M. Wade (1946) proposed an approach to generalization and discrimination that differs from those of Pavlov and Spence. These researchers argued that generalization gradients depend on prior experience with stimuli similar to those used in testing. Discrimination training increases the steepness of the generalization gradient because it teaches the animal to tell the difference between the S⁺ and other stimuli. But the generalization gradient is not usually flat even in the absence of training. Why is this so if the gradient depends on training? The answer Lashley and Wade give is that the animal has undergone a kind of discrimination training in the course of its everyday life. A pigeon, for example, learns to discriminate colors long before the psychologist trains it to peck a red disk. The more experience a pigeon has had with colors, especially those resembling the S⁺, the steeper its generalization gradient will be; the less experience the bird has had, the flatter the gradient will be.

The theory implies that if an animal is prevented from having any experience with a certain kind of stimulus, such as color, its behavior following training will be affected. If such a color-naive animal is trained to respond in the presence of a red disk, for example, it will later respond just as frequently to a green disk. In other words, its gradient of generalization will be flat.

Several researchers have attempted to test this hypothesis. In the typical experiment, animals are reared from birth in the dark in order to deprive them of experiences with color. Then they are trained to respond to a stimulus such as a green disk. After this, the animals are tested for generalization by presenting them with disks of other colors and noting the extent to which they discriminate. The results can be compared to those obtained from animals that have been reared normally. If the gradients of the color-deprived animals are flatter, the Lashley-Wade theory is supported; if rearing in the dark makes no difference in the shape of the gradient, the theory is unsupported.

Unfortunately, the results of such experiments have been ambiguous, with one study tending to support the theory and another study tending to undermine it. Moreover, interpretation of the results is subject to argument. When there is no difference in the gradients of deprived and normally reared animals, proponents of the Lashley-Wade theory argue that the rearing procedure did not entirely preclude experience with the relevant stimuli. When deprivation produces a flat gradient, opponents of the theory argue that the deprivation procedure damaged the eyes of the animals so that their physical capacity for discriminating colors has been limited. The Lashley-Wade theory needs a stronger test than deprivation studies can provide.

If the theory is valid, one argument holds that depriving an animal of all experience with a stimulus should not be necessary; merely restricting its experience with the stimulus during training should be sufficient to support the theory. To test this idea, Herbert Jenkins and Robert Harrison (1960) trained pigeons to peck a disk. Some pigeons heard a tone periodically; pecking was reinforced in the presence of the tone but not during periods of quiet. Other pigeons heard the same tone without interruption. In both cases, then, disk pecking was reinforced in the presence of a tone; but in one case, there were periods of silence during which pecking was not reinforced. Next, the experimenters tested all the pigeons for generalization to other tones and to periods of silence. They found that those pigeons that had been exposed to periodic tone were much *less* likely to peck the disk during periods of silence than when the tone sounded. The other pigeons, however, pecked the disk just as much when the tone was on as when it was off. This much is to be expected, since the birds that heard the tone constantly had no opportunity to discriminate, whereas those that heard the tone periodically did. But what would happen when the pigeons were exposed to different tones, sounds that neither group had heard before? The pigeons that had learned to discriminate between periods of tone and periods of silence also discriminated between the original tone and other tones. Pigeons that had received reinforcement during constant sound did not discriminate between tones (see Figure 9-7). These results are just what the Lashley-Wade theory would predict.

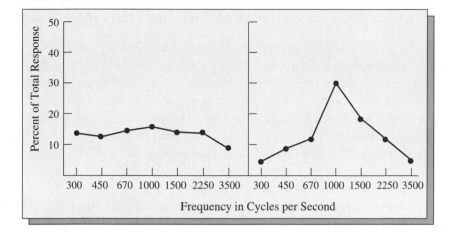

Figure 9-7 *Discrimination training and generalization. Representative performance of two birds that received food for pecking a disk. The record on the left is from a bird that received food for disk pecking during a continuous tone of 1000 cps. The record on the right is from a bird that received food for disk pecking when the tone sounded, but not during periods of silence. (After Jenkins and Harrison, 1960.)*

Not all tests of the Lashley-Wade theory have yielded positive results, but it is now generally acknowledged that the steepness of a generalization gradient depends to some extent on the experience the participant has had with the relevant stimuli before training.

No theory of discrimination and generalization has won universal support, but they have all spurred basic research. Some of this research has provided insights into problems of theoretical and practical importance.

REVIEW   Various theories have been proposed to account for generalization and discrimination. Pavlov explained the phenomena in terms of the irradiation of excitation. In his view, generalization occurs because a stimulus has excited an area of the brain near the part of the brain affected by the CS+. Spence believed that the net difference between gradients of excitation and inhibition predicts the response to novel stimuli. His theory accurately predicted the peak shift phenomenon. The Lashley-Wade theory maintains that generalization occurs because the organism has had too little experience with the stimuli involved to be able to discriminate among them.

Applications of Generalization and Discrimination

Concept Formation

The word **concept** usually refers to any class the members of which share one or more defining features. The defining feature allows us to discriminate the members of one class from the members of another class. For example, all spiders have eight legs; this distinguishes them from other animals, including insects, that have fewer than or more than eight legs. All ice creams have in common that they are sweet, cold, and soft, and it is these features that allow us to distinguish ice cream from, say, popsicles, which are sweet and cold but hard.

Understanding a concept means discriminating between stimuli that fall *within* the concept class and those that fall *outside* the concept class. We do not say that a child understands the concept "car" just because she calls the family car by that name. The child understands "car" only if she regularly calls certain kinds of vehicles by that name but not others.

One way such discriminations—or concepts—are learned is through discrimination training. Richard Herrnstein and his colleagues performed a series of brilliant experiments in which they used discrimination training to teach various concepts to pigeons. In one study, Herrnstein (1979) projected photographic slides on one wall of an experimental chamber. Some of the slides included one or more trees or parts of trees; the others did not. The birds received food if they pecked a disk, but only if the picture currently on their wall included a tree. Herrnstein was amazed at how rapidly the birds learned to discriminate between photographs with trees and those without them. Moreover, when Herrnstein tested the birds with slides they had never seen before, they performed correctly. Thus, the birds appear to have learned the concept "tree."

In another study (Herrnstein et al., 1976), the researchers taught pigeons the concept "human being." The researchers again projected slides on the wall of the pigeon's chamber. This time some of the slides contained images of people; others did not. The birds received food for pecking a disk, but only when the current slide included people. This was no easy task: Sometimes the people depicted appeared alone, sometimes in groups; they were of different sizes, shapes, ages, and sexes; they wore different kinds of clothing, and sometimes no clothing; they were sometimes in full view, other times partially hidden by objects. Nevertheless, the pigeons learned to peck only when human beings were depicted.

Some people have been skeptical about pigeons grasping concepts. S. L. Greene (1983) suggested that the pigeons might simply memorize the figures associated with reinforcement. But if this were the case, the birds would tend not to discriminate accurately when tested on pictures they had not seen before. But C. A. Edwards and W. K. Honig (1987) showed that birds did discriminate when tested on novel stimuli. The birds apparently respond to a feature that defines the category.

An experiment by Robert Allan (1990; see also Allan, 1993) adds support to the idea that pigeons are reacting to a conceptual feature. Allan trained birds to peck a panel on which photographs could be projected, and he provided equipment to record the segment of the panel the bird pecked. His reasoning was that if birds were discriminating on the basis of a conceptual feature, they would peck at the part of the photograph that contained the conceptual item. He projected 40 slides, 20 of which included pictures of humans, the concept to be learned. Birds received food periodically if they pecked while a human figure was displayed. The result was that the birds not only learned to make the appropriate discrimination, but they tended also to peck *the part of the slide in which human figures appeared* (see Figure 9-8). Allan writes that "as the position of the human form changes from one segment to another, the

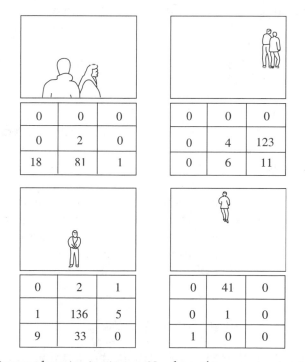

Figure 9-8 *Concept learning in pigeons. Numbers of responses occurring in each of nine equal-area segments of a slide as measured by an infrared touch device. The diagrams immediately above each accumulation set indicate the relative position of the human form in that particular slide. (From "Control of Pecking Response Topography by Stimulus-Reinforcer and Response-Reinforcer Contingencies," by R. W. Allan, 1993, in H. P. Zeigler and H. Bischof,* Vision, Brain, and Behavior in Birds, *p. 291, Figure 16.3. Copyright © 1993 The MIT Press. Reprinted with permission.)*

pigeons track this movement by pecking in the same segment." In a sense, the bird points to the object in the concept category. In considering this finding, it is important to consider that reinforcement was not contingent on pecking the part of the panel in which human figures appeared.

Some concepts differ from the examples given in that they express relationships between two or more items: taller, cheapest, biggest, and so on. We say that one desk is bigger than another, or that it is the biggest of three desks. We say that one job is easier than another or that it is the easiest job in a plant. These relational concepts appear, however, to be learned through the same discrimination process.

In one study, Kenneth Spence (1937) trained chimpanzees to find food under one of two white, metal covers that differed only in size. One chimp got a choice between covers that were 160 and 100 square centimeters. Whenever it chose the larger cover, it found food; whenever it chose the smaller cover, it found nothing. After the chimp had learned to choose the larger cover reliably, Spence presented it with new covers, identical to the first set except that the choice was now between covers that were 320 and 200 square cm. We might expect that the chimp would select the 200 square cm cover, since that one more closely resembled the cover that previously hid food. Instead, the chimp chose the larger cover. It apparently had learned the relational concept "larger than."

In a similar experiment, Wolfgang Kohler (1939) trained chickens to select the lighter of two gray squares. After training, he tested them with the light gray square that had always led to food and with a still lighter gray square they had never seen before. Again, we might expect the animals to select the original gray stimulus, since that had previously led to food. In fact, the birds chose the new, lighter square. Kohler called this phenomenon transposition, since it seemed analogous to musical transposition, in which a composition is played in a key different from the original. But the behavior of the animals also fits our criterion for concept learning.

Query: Transposition involves a _____ concept.

Richard and M. Kay Malott (1970) used discrimination to teach pigeons the concept of sameness. In this study, two halves of a key were illuminated independently and could therefore have different colors. When both halves were the same color (either all red or all violet), pecking the key produced food; when the two halves were different colors (one half red, the other violet), pecking did not produce food. After this discrimination was learned, the birds were tested on four new patterns: blue-blue, yellow-yellow, blue-yellow, and yellow-blue. Three out of the four pigeons pecked more often when the key halves were the same color than when they were different.

K. Fujita has used a similar procedure to study the acquisition of the sameness concept in monkeys. In one experiment, Fujita (reported in Pisacreta et al., 1984) trained monkeys to press a lever when two disks were the same color (either red or purple) and not to press the lever when the disks did not match (red and purple). When the animals mastered this discrimination, Fujita found that the behavior generalized to novel stimuli. When presented with two yellow or two green disks, for example, the monkeys pressed the lever; when presented with one yellow and one green disk, they did not press the lever.

Children, of course, learn relational concepts quite readily. Elizabeth Alberts and David Ehrenfreund (1951) trained children, ages 3 to 5, to find a gumdrop by opening the correct door on a box. The doors differed only in size, and the smaller door always provided the gumdrop. After the children reached a criterion of 9 out of 10 correct, the researchers tested them on a number of new boxes. The doors on these new boxes differed in size from those on the training box, but the smaller door always produced the gumdrop. The children continued to choose the smaller doors. That is, they behaved on the basis of the relative sizes of the doors rather than their similarity to the training doors.

Researchers have demonstrated that pigeons and monkeys, to say nothing of humans, can master the concepts *fish, cats, flowers, ships, oak leaves, cars, letters,* and *chairs,* among others. Teaching more abstract concepts (such as *up* and *down, right* and *left, horizontal* and *vertical, attractive* and *unattractive*) is more difficult. Yet it is surprising what can be accomplished, even with animals, and discrimination training does seem to provide an explanation of concept formation in the natural environment.

Mental Rotation

Roger Shepard is a psychologist who has studied what he calls "mental rotation." In a typical experiment (Cooper & Shepard, 1973), people were shown letters that had been rotated by varying degrees from their normal, upright position and were asked whether the letters were backward (that is, mirror images of the original) or not. The result was that the greater the rotation, the longer it took people to answer. Shepard concludes from such data that people mentally rotate an "internal representation" or image of the letter until it is in its normal, upright position, and then decide whether it is backward.

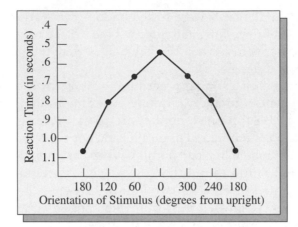

Figure 9-9   *Mental rotation as generalization. Mean reaction time to a familiar stimulus is a function of the orientation of the stimulus. The shortest reaction times occurred when the stimulus was in its normal position (0 degrees from upright). The less the stimulus resembled the normal position, the longer the reaction time. (Compiled from data in Cooper and Shepard, 1973.) (Note: Subjects were tested only once at 180 degrees; the point is plotted twice to show the symetrical natue of the gradient.)*

Although Shepard refers to the rotation of images, his data consist of the time it takes to react to rotated figures. It is interesting that when these data are plotted graphically, the resulting curve looks remarkably like a generalization gradient (Figure 9-9). Participants respond most quickly to the "training stimulus" (the letter they were trained in school to recognize); the less the stimulus resembles the training stimulus, the slower is the response.

In one experiment, Donna Reit and Brady Phelps (Reit & Phelps, 1996) used a computer program to train college students to discriminate between geometric shapes that did and did not match a sample. The items were rotated from the sample position by 0, 60, 120, 180, 240, or 300 degrees. The students received feedback after each trial. When the researchers plotted the data for reaction times, the results formed a fairly typical generalization gradient (see Figure 9-10).

In a second experiment, Phelps and Reit (1997) got nearly identical results, except that with continued training the generalization gradients flattened. This is probably because students continued to receive feedback during testing and therefore improved their reaction times to rotated items. (They could not improve their performance on unrotated items much because they were already reacting to those items quite

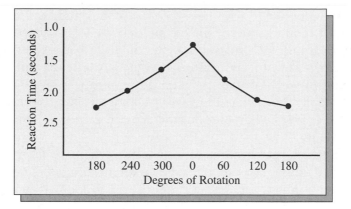

Figure 9-10 *Mental rotation as generalization. Average reaction times to a figure in its normal, upright position (0 rotation) and to varying degrees of rotation. (Adapted from "Mental Rotation Reconceptualized as Stimulus Generalization," by D. J. Reit and B. J. Phelps, Figure 1. Paper presented at the 22nd annual convention of the Association for Behavior Analysis, San Francisco, CA, May 1996. Reprinted by permission of the authors.)*

quickly.) In any case, these data clearly suggest that "mental rotation" data are generalization data.

Phelps and Reit note that most of their students, like Shepard's, reported that they solved the problems by "mentally rotating" the test stimuli. As Phelps and Reit point out, however, the subjective experience of mental rotation does not explain the differences in reaction times. A scientific explanation must point to physical features of the situation and to the learning history of the participant. The expression "mental rotation" at best identifies the covert behavior involved; it does not explain the participant's performance.

Smoking Relapse

Mark Twain, a lifelong cigar smoker, once quipped: "It's easy to quit smoking. I've done it hundreds of times." It is not hard to understand why people who have become addicted to nicotine continue to smoke. By some estimates, cigarette smoking is reinforced 73,000 times a year in a pack-a-day smoker (Lyons, 1991). The act of puffing on a cigarette has therefore been reinforced 730,000 times in a moderate smoker who has used cigarettes for 10 years. For a heavy smoker (two packs a day or more), the number of reinforcements for that period is about one-and-a-half *million*. If each reinforcement increases the resistance of a behavior to change, then it is hardly surprising that people find it difficult to quit smoking.

But why do people who have given up smoking, and who are no longer under the influence of the physiological effects of nicotine, so often resume smoking? Quitting may be difficult because of the physiological effects of not maintaining the nicotine level, but taking up smoking again weeks or months after going through withdrawal seems to many people clear evidence of weak character. But, as we have seen, concepts like weak character do not explain puzzling behavior; they merely label it.

Smoking relapses become less puzzling when we realize that the physiological effects of smoking and of withdrawal are not the only factors in maintaining this habit. In 1988, then Surgeon General C. Everett Koop concluded that "environmental factors, including drug-associated stimuli and social pressure, are important influences of initiation, patterns of use, quitting, and relapse to use of opioids, alcohol, nicotine, and other addicting drugs" (U.S. Department of Health and Human Services, 1988, p. 15). "Drug-associated stimuli" include environmental events that, because they have been paired with tobacco use in the past, have acquired some degree of stimulus control over tobacco use.

Ask smokers when they are most likely to smoke and you are likely to be told on arising from bed in the morning; while having coffee; after eating; during work breaks (including the interval between classes); during or after stress (such as an exam or city driving); after physical exertion; when socializing with friends; after sex, and so on (Buckalew & Gibson, 1984; Smith & Delprato, 1976). Because the use of tobacco and the reinforcing effects of nicotine have frequently occurred together in these situations, they have become discriminative stimuli for lighting a cigarette. And since smokers typically smoke throughout the day, many different situations become discriminative stimuli for smoking. Charles Lyons (1991) writes that "few other activities are so consistently and powerfully strengthened in such a wide range of temporal, situational, and physical settings" (p. 218).

Most people have witnessed stimulus control in smokers, although they may not have realized it at the time. Imagine a moderate smoker who has just joined a group of people in casual conversation. A member of the group lights a cigarette, and this act is a discriminative stimulus for smoking by others. Even if our hypothetical smoker has recently smoked a cigarette, he may light up after seeing someone else do so. The smoker may explain this behavior by saying, "When I see someone else smoke, it makes me think of smoking, and then I have to have a cigarette." Sometimes smokers report that cues that "remind them" of cigarettes also induce feelings of physiological deprivation or "craving." But these feelings do not explain the behavior of smoking any better than a lack of willpower does. The tendency for certain kinds of events to elicit smoking is explained by the history of reinforcement for smoking in the presence of those events.

Smoking in situations previously associated with smoking seems particularly likely to lead to an abrupt return to regular smoking. T. H. Brandon and colleagues (reported in Lyons, 1991) studied people who had quit smoking and who then had a single cigarette in a situation previously associated with smoking. Ninety-one percent of them soon became regular smokers again, nearly half within a day of the single cigarette. In another study, R. E. Bliss and colleagues (1989) found the presence of other people smoking commonly led to relapse.

The research on the role of stimulus control in smoking has important implications for those who would quit for good. It would appear that there are two basic approaches to preventing relapse. The former smoker can avoid situations in which he or she often smoked in the past, thereby avoiding the ability of these situations to elicit smoking. Or the smoker can undergo training to reduce the control these situations have over his behavior. It is extremely difficult, if not impossible, for a smoker to avoid all situations in which he or she has smoked; therefore, the best bet may be to undergo training that will undermine the power of those situations. This might be done, for example, by gradually exposing the smoker to those situations while preventing him or her from smoking. For example, a smoker who typically lights up after drinking coffee may have coffee in a therapist's office without smoking. When this situation no longer arouses the urge to smoke, the same training might be repeated in the nonsmoking section of a restaurant. The training might continue with having a meal in the restaurant, with the therapist (or other supportive person) along to ensure that the smoker does not light up. And so on. The person who would quit smoking may need to be exposed to each situation in which he or she has often smoked in the past. Giving up smoking for good is not a matter of exerting willpower; it is a matter of breaking free of a controlling environment.

Experimental Neuroses

As noted earlier, errors made during discrimination training tend to arouse negative emotional reactions. During a difficult discrimination, these emotional reactions are sometimes quite pronounced. N. R. Shenger-Krestovnikova (in Pavlov, 1927), working in Pavlov's laboratory, trained a dog to salivate at the sight of a circle flashed on a screen and not to salivate at the sight of an oval (see Figure 9-11a). Next, the researcher modified the oval so that it more closely resembled the circle, and then resumed training (see Figure 9-11b). When the animal discriminated between the

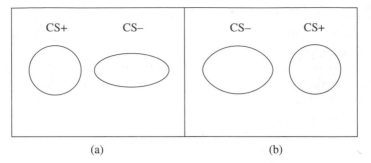

Figure 9-11 *Discrimination and experimental neurosis. A dog learned to salivate at the sight of a circle, but not at an oval (a). As training proceeded, the discrimination became progressively more difficult, with the oval becoming more and more like the circle (b). Eventually, the dog could not discriminate and became "emotionally disturbed."*

two figures, Shenger-Krestovnikova modified the oval again, making it still more like the circle, and resumed training. He repeated this procedure again and again. Finally, when the two forms were nearly identical, progress stopped. Not only did the animal fail to discriminate between the two forms, but, as Pavlov (1927) wrote:

> The whole behavior of the animal underwent an abrupt change. The hitherto quiet dog began to squeal in its stand, kept wriggling about, tore off with its teeth the apparatus for mechanical stimulation of the skin, and bit through the tubes connecting the animal's room with the observer, a behavior which never happened before. (p. 291)

Pavlov called the dog's bizarre behavior an **experimental neurosis** because it seemed to him that the behavior resembled that sometimes seen in people who had had "nervous breakdowns." Analogous findings have been obtained during operant discrimination training (Brown, 1942; see Kazdin, 1978).

We must be careful in using experimental neuroses in animals as an analog for human neuroses. Yet people do sometimes find themselves in situations that require subtle discriminations, and such situations do seem to be stressful. Teenagers, for example, sometimes are praised by their parents for "accepting responsibility," but on other occasions they are criticized for not "knowing their place." The discriminations the adults require of their children are often nearly as subtle as those Shenger-Krestovnikova required of his dog, and often the results are similar. Whether the "nervous breakdowns" that sometimes result in hospitalization are ever the result of this sort of discrimination training is uncertain, but the possibility cannot be ignored.

Query: Is there a lesson for parents in the Shenger-

Krestovnikova experiment?

REVIEW The study of generalization and discrimination has led to an improved understanding of other phenomena, including concept learning, mental rotation, smoking, and possibly some emotional disorders.

RECOMMENDED READING

1. Harlow, H. F. (1949). The formation of learning sets. *Psychological Review, 56,* 51–65.

   Harlow showed that through discrimination training, animals and people could "learn to learn." That is, they could become better at learning new things.

2. Skinner, B. F. (1953). *Science and human behavior.* New York: Free Press.

   See especially Chapter 7, "Operant Discrimination," and Chapter 8, "The Controlling Environment."

3. Staats, A. W., Staats, C. K., & Heard, W. G. (1959). Language conditioning of meaning using semantic generalization paradigm. *Journal of Experimental Psychology, 57,* 187–192.

   An early, but still important study of semantic generalization.

4. Thomas, D. R. (1991). Stimulus control: Principles and procedures. In W. Ishaq (Ed.), *Human behavior in today's world* (pp. 191–203). New York: Praeger.

   An overview of generalization, discrimination, and stimulus control. Thomas discusses many of the topics covered elsewhere in this text (e.g., overshadowing, state-dependent learning) under the heading of stimulus control.

5. Tumlinson, J. H., Lewis, W. J., & Vet, L. E. M. (1993, March). How parasitic wasps find their hosts. *Scientific American,* 100–106.

   An interesting study of the interaction of innate tendencies and discrimination learning in the natural environment.

REVIEW QUESTIONS

1. Define the following terms:

concept	inhibitory gradient
differential outcomes effect (DOE)	matching to sample (MTS)
	mismatching
discrimination	peak shift
discriminative stimulus	S^+
discrimination training	S^-
errorless discrimination training	semantic generalization
	stimulus control
excitatory gradient	simultaneous discrimination training
experimental neurosis	
generalization	successive discrimination training
generalization gradient	

2. Describe the relationship between generalization and discrimination.

3. How is semantic generalization different from other examples of generalization?

4. A student learns to draw human figures. How could you determine whether this learning had improved the student's ability to draw animal figures? What phenomenon would you be studying?

5. There is a saying that goes, "He who has been bitten by a snake fears a rope." What phenomenon does this proverb implicitly recognize?

6. Mark Twain once said that a cat that gets burned on a hot stove thereafter avoids cold stoves as well as hot ones. How could you change the behavior of a cat that fits this description?

7. B. F. Skinner (1951) once taught pigeons to "read." They would peck a disk when a sign read "Peck," and would not peck when a sign read "Don't peck." Describe how Skinner might have accomplished this.

8. Thorndike (1911) wrote that "by taking a certain well-defined position in front of [a monkey's] cage and feeding him whenever he did scratch himself I got him to always scratch himself within a few seconds after I took that position" (p. 236). Explain what sort of training is going on here. Try to identify the S^+, the S^-, the behavior being learned, and the reinforcer.

9. Diane says that in the experiment described in question 8, it is not the monkey that is undergoing discrimination training, but Thorndike. Why might she say this?

10. Why is generalization important to the teacher?

11. How would you test the hypothesis "Experimental neurosis can be avoided through errorless discrimination training"?

12. How might you use discrimination training to make someone capable of recognizing, from facial features and other "body language," when people were lying?

13. What might be the role of discrimination training in racial prejudice?

14. Some people object to the practice of using the pronoun *he* to refer to people in traditional male roles (e.g., scientists) while using *she* to refer to people in traditional female roles (e.g., nurses). Are they right to object?

15. How does Spence's theory differ from Pavlov's?

16. A music teacher has trained students to recognize middle C on the piano. She then tests for generalization by playing other keys. Draw a hypothetical generalization gradient of the results.

17. How could you teach a fellow student the concept of generalization?

18. What implications does research on errorless discrimination training have for the construction of educational software?

19. Explain why a stimulus that becomes an S^+ also becomes a secondary reinforcer.

20. Explain why a person who is red-green color blind (that is, red and green objects look gray) is at a disadvantage compared to his or her peers.

PRACTICE QUIZ

1. One of the first reports of generalization came from _____ in 1898.

2. Arthur Bachrach and others got generalization of therapy in a young woman who would not _____.

3. Gregory Razran found greater generalization in response to words with similar _____ than to words with similar sounds.

4. Richard Herrnstein used discrimination training to teach the concepts "tree" and "human being" to _____.

5. The peak shift phenomenon supports the theory of generalization and discrimination proposed by _____.

6. A smoker always lights a cigarette after a meal. Lighting a cigarette is under _____.

7. Through discrimination training, we can learn to discriminate between _____ and skinheads.

8. When generalization data are plotted on a curve, the result is a generalization _____.

9. One kind of discrimination training procedure is abbreviated MTS. This stands for _____.

10. Requiring an animal or person to discriminate between stimuli that are more and more alike may produce an _____.

QUERY ANSWERS

Page 306. A generalization gradient shows the tendency for a behavior to occur in situations that differ systematically from *the training situation/stimulus*.

Page 308. A building that is on fire presents a very different situation from a building that is not on fire.

Page 310. The Razran study involved the kind of training procedure called *Pavlovian/classical conditioning*.

Page 311. Racial prejudice probably involves *semantic* generalization.

Page 317. In operant discrimination training, the stimulus that indicates the more reinforcing consequence of a behavior is designated S^+.

Page 319. In errorless discrimination training, the S^- is presented in very weak form and gradually "faded in."

Page 321. The DOE implies that discrimination training can be improved by providing different *outcomes* for different *behaviors*.

Page 326. Marlatt's work suggests that drug abuse is partly due to *stimulus control*.

Page 326. Pavlov infers the physiological events from observations about generalization and discrimination and then explains generalization and discrimination by pointing to the supposed physiological events. This is like saying, "Evil spirits cause disease," and then citing illness as proof that evil spirits exist.

Page 328. It would have shifted in the opposite direction, possibly to around 560 nm.

Page 334. Transposition involves a *relational* concept.

Page 341. Parents might have less neurotic children if they made very clear the conditions under which certain behavior was and was not acceptable. (Making it clear means consistently providing appropriate consequences for the behavior in those situations.)

CHAPTER

10

Schedules of Reinforcement

The tendencies to respond eventually correspond to the probabilities of reinforcement.

B. F. Skinner

Most people use the term *learning* to refer to the acquisition of new behavior: A pigeon that never turned in counterclockwise circles now does so reliably and efficiently. A child who could not ride a bicycle at all now rides with skill and ease. A college student for whom the equation F = ma previously meant nothing now uses the formula to solve physics problems.

But we have seen that learning also includes changes in which no new behavior appears. One such change is an increase in the rate of behavior. A pigeon that turns in counterclockwise circles at the rate of three or four a minute may learn to make 10 or 15 turns a minute. A child who previously rode a bicycle once a week now does so every day. A physics student who used to solve textbook problems involving force and mass at the rate of one every 10 minutes now solves two or three of the same kinds of problems in 5 minutes.

Learning can also mean a reduction in the rate of a behavior. A bird that turns counterclockwise 10 times a minute can learn to make one turn a minute. The child who used to ride a bike several times a day may not touch it for weeks. The student who whips through physics problems can learn to take the time to check her work.

Learning can mean a change in the pattern of performance as well as the rate. If a pan of cookies must bake for 10 minutes, it is pointless to check the cookies during the first 5 minutes or so, but it is essential to check on them after an interval of about 8 or 9 minutes. The cook learns to avoid opening the oven in the first few minutes but to check on the cookies more and more often during the last few minutes of baking time.

We can see the same phenomenon in the workplace. Consider a factory worker who is employed at two factories. In one plant he is paid an hourly wage for spray-painting lawn chairs; in the other, he is paid so much per chair for the same work. Very likely the employee will work more steadily and turn out more lawn chairs each day when paid so much per chair.

Just as acquisition of new behavior is partly the product of reinforcement contingencies, so changes in the rate and pattern of performance are partly due to changes in reinforcement contingencies. The changes in the cook's behavior reflect the fact that reinforcement (seeing cookies that are done or nearly done) is available near the end of baking time but not earlier. Similarly, the factory worker on piecework paints more chairs because his earnings reflect the number of chairs painted. For him, each chair painted is a secondary reinforcer. This is not the case when he works on an hourly wage.

The rule describing the delivery of reinforcement is called a **schedule of reinforcement**. We shall see that a particular kind of reinforcement schedule tends to produce a particular pattern and rate of performance, and these **schedule effects** are remarkably reliable. When a given schedule is in force for some time, the organism behaves in a very predictable way. If the organism is removed from the schedule environment for a time and then returned to it, it typically resumes its previous behavior. Moreover, if different schedules are in force for different kinds of behavior, the rates and patterns of behavior will reflect the different schedules. And if an organism is behaving at a steady rate and the reinforcement schedule changes, the behavior will change in predictable ways.

> **Query:**   The term *schedule* _____ refers to the
>
> pattern and rate of performance produced by a particular rein-
>
> forcement schedule.

Such schedule effects are often attributed to character traits, such as laziness or ambitiousness. But the factory worker does not work at different rates in two plants because he is lazy in one factory and ambitious in the other. The differences in behavior merely reflect the different reinforcement schedules in force.

There are, of course, schedules of punishment as well as reinforcement, and behavior can be followed by both reinforcing and punishing events simultaneously. However, in this chapter we will concentrate on reinforcement schedules and their effects on operant behavior.

REVIEW   Learning is a change in behavior, and that includes changes in the rate and pattern of a behavior over time. Behavior rates and patterns are functions of the schedule of reinforcement in effect. There are several kinds of reinforcement schedules, each of which has distinctive effects on behavior.

Simple Schedules

Continuous Reinforcement

The simplest of simple schedules is called **continuous reinforcement**, or **CRF**. In continuous reinforcement, a behavior is reinforced every time it occurs. If, for example, a rat receives food every time it presses a lever, then lever pressing is on a continuous reinforcement schedule, as is the disk pecking of a pigeon if it receives a bit of grain each time it pecks a disk. Likewise, a child's behavior is on CRF if she is praised every time she hangs up her coat, and your behavior is on CRF when you operate a vending machine if, each time you insert the requisite amount of money, you receive the item selected. The opposite of CRF is extinction, which can be thought of as a schedule of *non*reinforcement.

Each reinforcement strengthens behavior, so continuous reinforcement leads to very rapid increases in the rate of behavior. It is especially useful, then, when the task is to shape up some new behavior or behavior chain. You can see that it would be much easier to teach a pigeon to make counterclockwise turns by reinforcing each successive approximation of the desired behavior than it would be if one were to reinforce successive approximations only occasionally.

Although continuous reinforcement typically leads to the most rapid learning of new behavior, it is not the most common schedule in the natural environment. Most behavior is reinforced on some occasions, but not on others. A parent is not able to praise a child every time she hangs up her coat, and vending machines sometimes take our money and give us nothing in return. When reinforcement occurs on some occasions but not others, the behavior is said to be on an **intermittent schedule**. There are many kinds of intermittent schedules (see Ferster & Skinner, 1957), but the most important ones fall into four groups. We begin with those called fixed ratio schedules.

Fixed Ratio Schedules

In a **fixed ratio**, or **FR**, **schedule**, a behavior is reinforced when it has occurred a fixed number of times. For instance, a rat may be trained to press a lever for food. After shaping the behavior, the experimenter may switch to a schedule in which every third lever press is reinforced. In other words, there is a ratio of three lever presses to each reinforcement. The schedule is usually indicated by the letters FR, followed by the number of times the behavior must occur for each reinforcement. The lever pressing of our hypothetical rat, for example, is on an FR 3 schedule. (Continuous reinforcement is actually a kind of fixed ratio schedule, then, and may be designated FR 1.)

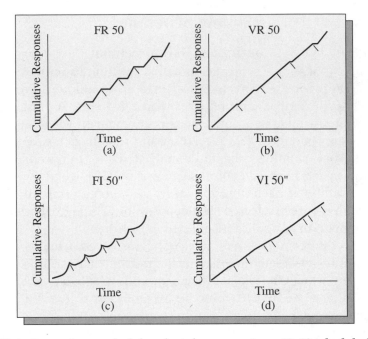

Figure 10-1 *Intermittent schedules of reinforcement. In an FR 50 schedule (a), every 50th response is reinforced; in a VR 50 schedule (b), an average of 50 responses is required for each reinforcement; in an FI 50" schedule (c), a response is reinforced when it occurs after a 50-second interval; in a VI 50" schedule (d), a response is reinforced after an average interval of 50 seconds. Short diagonal lines indicate delivery of a reinforcer. (Hypothetical data.)*

Animals on fixed ratio schedules perform at a high rate, often punctuated by short pauses after reinforcement. A rat that lever presses on an FR schedule for food will press the lever quickly and steadily until food drops into the tray. It will then eat the food, pause for a short time, and then return to work at the lever. The pauses that follow reinforcement are called **post-reinforcement pauses**, and they have generated considerable interest among researchers (see Figure 10-1a).

It is tempting to dismiss post-reinforcement pauses as the result of fatigue. The animal performs a behavior a number of times and then pauses to "catch its breath" before returning to work. But animals on other types of schedules often work even harder without pauses, so fatigue does not seem to be the whole answer.

One variable that seems to be important is the ratio of responses to reinforcement. The more work required for each reinforcement, the longer the post-reinforcement pause (Baron & Derenne, 2000; Ferster & Skinner, 1957). Thus, pauses are longer in an FR 100 schedule than in an FR 20 schedule. The length of post-reinforcement pauses also varies with the size of the reinforcer (Perone & Courtney, 1992), and with other variables.

Variables that affect post-reinforcement pauses do not ordinarily affect **run rate**—the rate at which the organism performs once it has resumed work after reinforcement. Thus, increasing the ratio of lever presses to reinforcers from, say, 5:1 to 10:1 (i.e., from FR 5 to FR 10) does not change how rapidly a rat presses once it has resumed lever pressing. What it does is increase the length of the "breaks" the rat takes after each reinforcement. However, anything that increases the length of post-reinforcement pauses will necessarily reduce the overall rate of performance—i.e., the total number of lever presses per minute or hour.

Fixed ratio schedules are fairly common outside the laboratory. Many games make use of fixed ratio schedules. Perhaps the best examples of FR schedules involve work. Some employees are paid on a fixed ratio schedule, though it is usually called piecework. The garment worker, for instance, is paid so much for each shirt sewn; the field hand is paid so much per basket of apples picked.

Query: The rate at which a behavior occurs once it has begun

is called the _____ rate.

Variable Ratio Schedules

Instead of providing a reinforcer when a behavior has occurred a fixed number of times, it is possible to vary the requirement around some average. For example, instead of reinforcing every fifth lever press, we might reinforce after the second, then after the eighth, then the sixth, the fourth, and so on. On such **variable ratio** or **VR schedules**, the number of lever presses required for reinforcement varies around an average. In a VR 5 schedule, reinforcement may occur after two to ten lever presses, but the overall average will be one reinforcement for every five presses.

Variable ratio schedules typically produce steady performance at run rates similar to comparable FR schedules (see Figure 10-1b). If post-reinforcement pauses occur, they usually appear less often and are for shorter periods than in a comparable FR schedule. In VR schedules, post-reinforcement pauses are strongly influenced by the size of the *average* ratio and by the *lowest* ratio (Blakely & Schlinger, 1988; Schlinger et al., 1990). In a VR 50 schedule, for example, the number of lever presses required for reinforcement on any one run might vary from 10 to 100, or it might vary from 40 to 60. The schedule that requires a minimum of 40 lever presses per reinforcement will produce longer pauses than the schedule that requires a minimum of 10.

> ## VR Harassment
>
> An example of the power of VR schedules to maintain behavior at a high rate may be seen in the case of a man accused of making harassing phone calls ("30,000 Obscene Calls Traced," 1991). Apparently the man would call a woman and tell her he was holding members of her family hostage and would kill them if she did not stand naked outside her home. The ruse worked an average of about once in every 100 attempts, a VR 100 schedule. Such a schedule could be expected to produce a high rate of behavior. Apparently it did: The man made some 30,000 calls. On one day alone he called 130 women.
>
> Not to be outdone, a woman spurned by her former lover called him more than 1,000 times a day for three years ("Woman Pesters Ex-Lover with 1,000 Calls a Day," 2000). To escape the harassment, the man changed jobs and his phone and pager numbers, but the woman discovered the new numbers and resumed the calls—and added 500 faxes a day.
>
> We cannot conclude, of course, that these episodes are due to reinforcement schedules. However, animal studies suggest that people can become very persistent if reinforced intermittently.

Because VR schedules typically produce fewer and shorter post-reinforcement pauses than FR schedules, a VR schedule usually produces more behavior in an hour than a comparable FR schedule. This is so even though the actual payoff is the same. That is, the animal on an FR 50 schedule earns as much food for its 50 lever presses as the animal on a VR 50 schedule does (on average) for its 50.

Variable ratio schedules are common in natural environments. As fast as the cheetah is, it does not bring down a victim every time it gives chase, nor can it depend on being successful on the second, third, or fourth try. There is no predicting which particular effort will be successful. It may be successful on two succeeding attempts, and then it may fail on the next 10 tries. All that can be said is that, on average, one in every so many attempts will be reinforced.

Probably most predatory behavior is reinforced on VR schedules, although the exact schedule varies depending on many factors. For instance, if the elk in a particular area are heavily infested by parasites, they will be easier for wolves to bring down. The average ratio of attacks to reinforcement will be low. As the wolves remove the sicker animals from the herd, however, the remaining elk will be harder to catch and kill and the ratio of attempts to reinforcement will be higher.

Variable ratio schedules are important in human society as well. The classic human example of a VR schedule is the salesperson working on commission: The salesperson is paid for each sale, but not every effort to sell something is successful. One reinforcer for attempting to sell a product is the pay the salesperson receives if successful. But since the salesperson is probably not paid at the moment of the sale, the immediate reinforcer may be the sale receipt, since this signals that a commission will be forthcoming. Another example of the VR schedule among humans is gambling, particularly casino gambling.

Fixed Interval Schedules

Reinforcement need not be based on the number of times a behavior occurs. In interval schedules, reinforcement is dispensed following a behavior, but only when the behavior occurs after a given period of time. In **fixed interval**, or **FI, schedules**, the behavior under study is reinforced the first time it occurs after a constant interval. For example, a pigeon that has learned to peck a disk may be put on an FI 5" (read, FI 5-second) schedule. The first time the bird pecks the disk, food is delivered into its food tray, but for the next 5 seconds, disk pecking produces no reinforcement. Then, at the end of the 5-second interval, the very next disk peck is reinforced. Note that the reinforcer is not delivered merely because a given period of time has elapsed; a disk peck is still required.

Like fixed ratio schedules, fixed interval schedules produce post-reinforcement pauses. Typically, the bird on an FI schedule seldom pecks immediately after reinforcement, and then steadily increases the rate of pecking. By the time the interval has elapsed, the pecking rate is quite high. Thus, FI schedules produce a scalloped-shaped cumulative record (see Figure 10-1c).

Why should FI schedules produce a scalloped-shaped curve while FR schedules produce a steady run rate between pauses? Possibly it is because the FR schedule reinforces steady performance whereas the FI schedule does not. Consider first the case of a rat pressing a lever on an FR 50 schedule. The animal has a lot of work to do before it receives its next reinforcement, and any pause delays the reinforcer's arrival. Now consider the rat on an FI 50" schedule. No lever presses will produce reinforcement until 50 seconds have passed, so pressing during this period is pointless. Gradually the rat increases its rate of lever pressing until, near the end of the interval, it is pressing rapidly and steadily.

We might expect that after some experience with this schedule, the rat would become more efficient, delaying until, say, 40 seconds had elapsed. Surprisingly, this does not happen. No matter how long an animal is on an FI schedule, it begins pressing the lever long before doing so pays off, producing the familiar scalloped-shaped curve.

Good examples of FI schedules in the natural environment are hard to come by. In many animal species, the females become sexually receptive at fairly regular intervals, and attempts by males to mate with them at other times are seldom reinforced. This therefore looks like an FI schedule. But estrus (sexual receptivity) is indicated by specific odors and other discriminative stimuli, and male sexual behavior is more likely to be under the control of these stimuli than under the control of the schedule.

Examples of FI schedules in humans are easier to think of, perhaps because we more often live by the clock. Your behavior is on an FI schedule when you bake bread in an oven, since checking the bread will be reinforced only when it occurs after a specified period. The first time you bake bread, you may open the oven door repeatedly "to see how it's doing." But with experience you learn to wait until the required baking time has nearly elapsed before peeking inside the oven. The closer you get to the end of the required cooking time, the more often you open the oven door.

Edward Crossman (1991) suggests that waiting for a bus meets the criterion for an FI schedule. Suppose you approach a bus stop just as the bus leaves. The buses on this route are normally 15 minutes apart, so you have about 15 minutes to wait. Seeing your bus approach is likely to be reinforcing, but looking in the direction from which the bus will come is unlikely to be reinforced for several minutes. Thus, the behavior of looking for a bus is likely to occur infrequently in the early part of the 15-minute interval and much more frequently as the interval nears its end. When 15 minutes have elapsed, you are likely to be staring fairly steadily in the direction of the bus. Plot this behavior on a cumulative record, and the result will be a scalloped curve.

Studying may provide another example. Many students show little inclination to study during the early days of the semester but spend increasing amounts of time studying as midterm exams approach. After midterms, their study time falls off sharply until shortly before finals. Plotted on a curve, studying would then show the familiar scalloped curve of FI schedules (but see Michael, 1991).

Variable Interval Schedules

Instead of reinforcing a behavior after a fixed interval, it is possible to vary the interval around some average. For example, instead of always reinforcing disk pecking after an interval of 5 seconds, we might reinforce a peck after 2 seconds, then after 8 seconds, 6 seconds, 4 seconds, and so forth. On such **variable interval**, or **VI**, **schedules**, the length of the interval during which performing is not reinforced varies around some average. In a VI 5" schedule, the average interval between reinforced pecks is

5 seconds. Variable interval schedules produce high, steady run rates, higher than FI schedules, but usually not so high as comparable FR and VR schedules.

We can find VI schedules in natural environments as well as in the lab. Leopards often lie in wait for their prey rather than stalk it. Sometimes the wait may be short, sometimes long, but remaining alert and waiting quietly are eventually reinforced by the appearance of prey. The same sort of thing may be seen in spiders and snakes and in many other species.

Human hunters also lie in wait for game. Deer hunters typically take a position in a tree or other high point and wait for a deer to appear within range. Sometimes they wait for hours; sometimes a deer appears almost immediately. Similarly, the nature photographer is on a VI schedule since he or she must wait varying lengths of time before having the opportunity to get a good picture. Air traffic controllers who watch a radar screen are also on a VI schedule, since the signals for which they watch occur at irregular intervals. We also find ourselves on VI schedules when we must wait in line at the bank or the theater.

Query: In ratio schedules, reinforcement is contingent on

_____ ; in interval schedules, reinforce-

ment is contingent on _____.

Interestingly, animals have preferences among the four basic schedules. It is not surprising that a pigeon or a person will prefer a VR 10 schedule over an FR 100 schedule, because the latter requires 10 times as much work for a given amount of reinforcement. But certain types of schedules are preferred over others even when, in the long run, the rate of reinforcement is the same. For example, pigeons sometimes prefer to work on a VR schedule rather than an FR schedule that pays off just as well. One variable is the length of the interval between reinforcements. If the interval is very short, the birds prefer a VR schedule; if it is long, they prefer FR (Field et al., 1996).[1]

Other Simple Schedules

The reinforcement schedules just described are the bedrock of schedules research: Quite possibly more research has been done involving these schedules than with all other schedules combined. Yet there are other simple schedules that have received considerable attention.

---

[1] The efforts to explain these preferences are interesting but beyond the scope of this text (see Field et al., 1996; Hall-Johnson and Poling, 1984; King et al., 1974).

In a **fixed duration**, or **FD**, **schedule**, reinforcement is contingent on the continuous performance of a behavior for some period of time. A typical example of an FD schedule is the child who is required to practice playing a piano for half an hour. At the end of the practice period, and provided the child has practiced the entire time, he receives a reinforcer. For example, a parent may provide milk and cookies or some other treat after a piano practice.

In a **variable duration**, or **VD**, **schedule**, the required period of performance varies around some average. In the case of a child practicing the piano, any given session might end after 30 minutes, 55 minutes, 20 minutes, or 10 minutes. On average, the student will practice for half an hour before receiving the milk and cookies, but there is no telling when the reinforcers will appear.

Unfortunately, parents using duration schedules often provide no reinforcer. The assumption is that the improvement that comes with practice will reinforce the student's work, but often this "intrinsic" reinforcer is too weak to be effective. Providing some treat at the end of the session should be more effective. The Premack principle (see Chapter 5) suggests that if eating cookies and drinking milk are normally reinforcing, and if this behavior is contingent on practicing the piano continuously for some period, then playing the piano should become more reinforcing itself. And indeed, this does seem to be the case.

In some schedules, reinforcement is contingent on the rate at which a behavior occurs. In one of these (mentioned in Chapter 6 as an alternative to punishment), a behavior is reinforced only if a specified period of time has elapsed since the last performance of that behavior. For instance, a rat might receive food for pressing a lever, but only if 5 seconds have elapsed since the last lever press. This schedule, as you may recall, is called differential reinforcement of low rate, or DRL.

In a DRL schedule, the interval begins each time the behavior is performed. In a DRL 5" schedule, for example, a pigeon that pecks a disk receives reinforcement only if 5 seconds have elapsed since the last disk peck. Each disk peck in essence resets the clock, so that pecking before the interval has elapsed delays reinforcement. The longer the interval required between disk pecks, the lower will be the rate of pecking. A DRL 5" schedule would reinforce a maximum of 12 pecks per minute. Pecking before the prescribed interval ends further reduces the number of reinforcements received per minute, as does pecking after a longer interval than is required. You can see that DRL schedules can produce extremely low rates of behavior.

One peculiarity of DRL schedules is that they sometimes result in the performance of a series of behaviors that are quite irrelevant to reinforcement. For example, consider a rat that receives food for pressing a lever on a DRL 10" schedule. It receives food for pressing the lever, but only if at least 10 seconds have elapsed since the last lever press. Every time the rat presses the lever, it must then wait 10 seconds before pressing it again. Nothing it does during this period produces reinforcement, yet sometimes it engages in a series of acts. It may visit a particular part of the chamber or sniff at the food dish. This behavior may be superstitious. The rat has to do *something* during the 10-second interval, and whatever it does may be coincidentally reinforced by the delivery of food after the lever press. In other words, the reinforced behavior may not be lever pressing, but sniffing a particular corner, then walking to the lever and pressing it.

Query: In a DRL 10" schedule, the effect of pressing a lever

after 8 seconds is to _____.

The logical opposite of the DRL schedule is the **DRH** schedule, short for **differential reinforcement of high rate**. DRH schedules require that a behavior be performed a minimum number of times in a given period. A pigeon might be required, for example, to peck a disk five times in a 10-second period. If it pecks fewer than five times during that period, it receives nothing. DRH schedules can produce extremely high rates of behavior, higher than any other schedule.

DRL and DRH schedules have been put to good use in dealing with behavior problems. DRL schedules have been used to help people reduce the rate of a particular behavior, such as nail biting. Similarly, DRH schedules find use when the goal is to increase the rate of a behavior, as in the case of the student who seldom participates in class discussions.

In all of the schedules discussed thus far, reinforcement is contingent on behavior.[2] If a particular behavior doesn't occur, there is no reinforcement. You may recall from Chapter 6 that it is possible to create a schedule in which reinforcers are delivered independently of behavior. In such noncontingent reinforcement schedules a reinforcer is delivered regardless of what the organism does. The two main kinds of noncontingent reinforcement schedules are fixed time and variable time.[3]

---

[2]Or, one might say, contingent on some aspect of behavior: frequency, duration, intensity, etc.

[3]Strictly speaking, these schedules are not truly noncontingent. They are not contingent on behavior, but they *are* contingent on the passage of time. Perhaps a random time schedule, in which reinforcers would be delivered at random intervals, could be said to be truly noncontingent.

In a **fixed time**, or **FT**, **schedule**, a reinforcer is delivered after a given period of time without regard to behavior. Fixed time schedules resemble fixed interval schedules except that in an FT schedule no behavior is required for reinforcement. In an FI 10" schedule, for instance, a pigeon may receive food after a 10-second interval, but only if it pecks a disk. In an FT 10" schedule, the pigeon receives food every 10 seconds whether it pecks the disk or not.[4]

Fixed time schedules are not common outside the laboratory. Unemployment compensation and welfare payments do not precisely meet the definition of fixed time schedules, but they come close. Although certain behaviors are nominally required (e.g., people receiving unemployment compensation are supposed to look for work), in fact, money is provided more or less independently of what the person does. The only true performance requirements are standing in line for the check and *saying* that one has tried to find work. Social critics who would replace welfare with "workfare" are suggesting that money should be contingent on behavior rather than time.

In **variable time**, or **VT**, **schedules**, reinforcement is delivered periodically at irregular intervals without regard for the organism's behavior. The only difference between VT schedules and FT schedules is that in VT schedules the reinforcer is delivered at intervals that vary about some average.

Some researchers have used VT studies to establish superstitious behavior (Ono, 1987). Certain situations outside the laboratory that seem to resemble VT schedules also appear to produce superstitious behavior. Success in sport fishing is at least partly a matter of luck. Periodically the angler gets lucky, and the use of a particular lure or kind of bait or method of casting is coincidentally reinforced. This may explain why people who fish a lot are apt to disagree enthusiastically about the perfect lure, bait, or casting method. (Dedicated anglers will insist, of course, that there is nothing superstitious about *their* preferences. The issue is empirical but beyond the scope of this text.)

Note that there is an important difference between duration schedules and time schedules. In duration schedules, reinforcement is contingent on the continuous performance of the desired behavior. In time schedules, reinforcement is contingent solely on the passage of time; there is no behavior requirement for reinforcement.

---

[4]However, since the pigeon is necessarily doing *something* when the reinforcer appears, that behavior tends to be reinforced. Often the result is that the bird comes to behave as though this behavior caused the reinforcer to appear. Such behavior is called superstitious (see Chapter 7).

Query: In FT and VT schedules, reinforcement is contingent

on _____ rather than _____.

Stretching the Ratio

Rats will press levers and pigeons will peck disks hundreds of times for a single reinforcer, even if that reinforcer is a small amount of food. People have also been known to work steadily on very "thin" schedules—schedules that require many responses for each reinforcement. How is this possible? Why should a rat, much less a person, press a lever hundreds of times for some trivial amount of reinforcement?

The answer is shaping. An experimenter does not train a rat to press a lever and then put the animal on, say, an FR 100 schedule. The experimenter gradually shapes persistence. The experimenter might start with a CRF schedule and, when the animal is working at a steady rate, increase the ratio to FR 3; when this schedule has been in force a while, the experimenter may go to FR 5, then FR 8, FR 12, FR 20, FR 30, and so on. This procedure is known as **stretching the ratio** (Skinner, 1968).[5] It is essentially the same shaping process used to shape any new behavior: Successive approximations of the desired behavior (in this case, performing in the absence of reinforcement) are reinforced.

Query: The thinner of two schedules, FR 3 and VR 4, is

_____.

Stretching the ratio almost certainly occurs in nature. Earlier we considered the wolves that prey on elk. When parasitic infection weakens the elk herd, hunting is relatively easy; as the wolves remove the sicker animals, hunting requires more effort. The shift from a low ratio schedule to a high ratio schedule (one in which most efforts are not reinforced) is probably a gradual one.

We may see stretching of the ratio among human predators and prey by visiting a gambling establishment. Card sharks and pool hustlers sometimes let their competitors win frequently during the early stages of play and then gradually win more and more of the games. They stretch the ratio gradually because they do not want to "lose their pigeon." Stretching the ratio can be put to more benevolent purposes. Parents, for

---

[5] Stretching the ratio is also referred to as "thinning the schedule."

example, may praise their children each time they see them studying; gradually, however, they may reinforce the behavior less often.

Query: Could you stretch the ratio when a behavior is on an

interval schedule?

Stretching the ratio is an important feature of training programs in applied settings. In treating a psychiatric patient who talks very little in groups, for example, the therapist might use DRH to increase the rate of talking. However, if the initial requirement for reinforcement were talking as much as others in the group, the patient might never obtain reinforcement. The therapist may require talking at a slightly higher rate than is usual. When this rate has been reinforced a number of times, the therapist may increase the requirement for reinforcement slightly. When this rate has been reinforced several times, the therapist may increase the rate slightly again, and so on, until the patient is speaking at a normal rate.

Stretching the ratio must be done with some care; stretch too rapidly or too far and the tendency to perform will break down, a phenomenon called **ratio strain**.[6] Workers who grumble about being "overworked and underpaid" and who shirk their responsibilities may be suffering from ratio strain.

Extinction

One way in which reinforcement schedules differ is in the density of reinforcement. At one extreme we find continuous reinforcement, an FR schedule in which every single occurrence of a behavior is reinforced. At the other extreme we find extinction, a schedule in which a behavior is never reinforced.

We discussed the effects of operant extinction in Chapter 5. They include the extinction burst; the appearance of emotional behavior, especially aggression; an increase in the variability of behavior; the fairly steady decline in the strength of the behavior; spontaneous recovery of the behavior when the extinction procedure is interrupted; and resurgence, the reappearance of previously reinforced behaviors.

It was also pointed out in Chapter 5 that the rate at which extinction proceeds is affected by a number of variables, including the number of times the behavior was reinforced prior to extinction, the effort the be-

---

[6] However, Skinner (1953) noted that it is possible to stretch the ratio to the point at which an animal expends more energy than it receives. Christopher (1988) demonstrated this in his study of gambling pigeons (see discussion of gambling, this chapter).

havior requires, and the schedule of reinforcement prior to extinction. Research on this last variable revealed a fascinating problem, to which we now turn.

REVIEW Simple schedules include continuous reinforcement, in which a behavior is reinforced each time it occurs; extinction, in which a behavior is never reinforced; and various kinds of intermittent schedules, in which the behavior is reinforced on some occasions and not on others. Intermittent schedules include FR, VR, FI, VI, FT, VT, FD, VD, DRL, and DRH. A rich schedule can be "thinned" by stretching the ratio.

Intermittent Reinforcement and the PRE

One peculiar schedule effect is the tendency of behavior that has been maintained on an intermittent schedule to be more resistant to extinction than behavior that has been on continuous reinforcement. This phenomenon is known as the **partial reinforcement effect**, or **PRE**.

The PRE was clearly demonstrated in a classic experiment by O. Hobart Mowrer and Helen Jones (1945). These researchers first trained rats to press a lever for food. After this preliminary training, Mowrer and Jones randomly assigned the rats to one of five groups, four of which are of interest to us. In each group, lever pressing was on a different reinforcement schedule: CRF, FR 2, FR 3, and FR 4. After this the rats had a training session each day that lasted until lever pressing had been reinforced 20 times. After 7 days and a total of 140 reinforcements, the researchers put lever pressing on extinction. The total number of presses during extinction showed a clear, counterintuitive pattern: The thinner the reinforcement schedule *before* extinction, the greater the number of lever presses *during* extinction (see Figure 10-2).

Human beings also sometimes show remarkable resistance to extinction following intermittent reinforcement. In one study, Harlan Lane and Paul Shinkman (1963) put a college student's behavior on extinction after reinforcing it on a VI 100" schedule. Although other variables besides the reinforcement schedule may have affected the student's behavior, it is interesting that the student worked for 11 hours and performed the behavior over 8,000 times without reinforcement!

PRE has been put to practical use in applied settings (e.g., Hanley et al., 2001). Once a behavior is well established, the therapist may begin thinning the reinforcement schedule (stretching the ratio). This makes the behavior more resistant to extinction and therefore more likely to persist outside the therapeutic setting. Teachers can also make good use

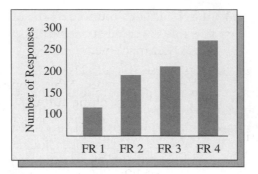

Figure 10-2 *Partial reinforcement effect. Average number of lever presses by rats during extinction following four fixed ratio schedules of reinforcement. The thinner the schedule, the greater the number of responses during nonreinforcement. (Compiled from data in Mowrer and Jones, 1945.)*

of the PRE by first establishing a behavior and then stretching the ratio of reinforcement.

The PRE, which has been demonstrated many times, is paradoxical, since the law of effect implies that the unreinforced lever presses that occur during an intermittent schedule should *weaken* the tendency to press, not make it stronger. Because of this paradox, researchers have devoted considerable time and effort to accounting for the effect. We will consider four hypotheses for explaining the phenomenon.

Discrimination Hypothesis

The **discrimination hypothesis** says that extinction takes longer after intermittent reinforcement because it is harder to discriminate between extinction and an intermittent schedule than between extinction and continuous reinforcement (Mowrer & Jones, 1945).

Imagine that you are vacationing in Las Vegas, and you decide to try your luck at the slot machines. As it happens, the machine you approach is defective. Some gizmo in its works has gone temporarily awry so that it always pays off. You approach the machine, put in a quarter, and push the button. (It's one of the newer machines that uses buttons rather than handles.) You win a dollar. You put in another quarter and win a few more dollars. Each time you put in a quarter and push the button, you win. After you deposit perhaps 100 quarters, and win 200 dollars, the machine suffers another breakdown, and now the machine never pays off. (Of course, you have no way of knowing this.) You put in a quarter, press the button, and much to your surprise, you win nothing. You put in another quarter, then another, and another, and so on, but you never receive anything. You can see that if you were in this situation, it would probably not be long before you would stop gambling at that machine.

You move on to try another machine. As in the first example, the slot machine you try is defective, but this time it does not pay off every time. Instead, it pays off on every 30th attempt. When you have inserted 100 coins—and won 200 dollars—the machine suffers another breakdown that prevents it from ever paying off. You are unaware of the defect and continue inserting coins. Now, how many coins must you insert before you can tell that the reinforcement schedule has changed? The answer is 30 coins. In other words, there is nothing amiss about putting in 29 quarters without winning. You will eventually stop throwing quarters away, but you will probably persist longer than you did at the machine that switched from continuous reinforcement to extinction. The reason, according to the discrimination hypothesis, is that it takes longer to discriminate between extinction and an FR 30 schedule than it does to discriminate between extinction and an FR 1 schedule.

You can probably see that it would take even longer to make the discrimination between extinction and an FR 100 schedule. Discriminating between extinction and a VR 100 schedule would take still longer, since a behavior may occur 150 or more times before producing reinforcement.

Thus, the discrimination explanation of the PRE proposes that behavior extinguishes more slowly after intermittent reinforcement than after continuous reinforcement because the difference between CRF and extinction is greater than the difference between an intermittent schedule and extinction.

As appealing as the discrimination hypothesis is, it has not proved entirely satisfactory at predicting behavior (Jenkins, 1962). Other explanations have attempted to build on the discrimination hypothesis in one way or another. One of these theories is the frustration hypothesis.

Frustration Hypothesis

Abram Amsel (1958, 1962) has proposed the **frustration hypothesis** to explain the PRE. Amsel argues that nonreinforcement of previously reinforced behavior is frustrating. Frustration is an aversive emotional state, Amsel says, so anything that reduces frustration will be reinforcing. In continuous reinforcement, there is no frustration because there is no nonreinforcement. But when the behavior is placed on extinction, there is plenty of frustration. With each nonreinforced act, frustration builds. (Anyone who has repeatedly lost coins in a pay phone or a vending machine is familiar with the aversive state created by nonreinforcement of a behavior that is normally reinforced.) Any behavior that reduces an aversive state is likely to be negatively reinforced, so during extinction, frustration may be reduced by not performing the behavior on extinction. (In the same way, you will quickly abandon a pay phone that cheats you, thereby reducing your annoyance.) Two behaviors then compete with one another during extinction: lever-pressing (previously reinforced by food) and lever-avoiding (currently reinforced by the reduction of frustration).

But when behavior is reinforced intermittently, there are periods of nonreinforcement—and frustration. The organism continues to perform during these periods of frustration and eventually receives reinforcement. Thus, lever pressing *while frustrated* is reinforced. Put another way, the emotional state called frustration becomes an S⁺ (see Chapter 9) for pressing the lever. Now when the behavior is placed on extinction, the organism becomes frustrated, but the frustration is an S⁺ for lever pressing, which causes frustration, which is an S⁺ for lever pressing, and so on.

The thinner the reinforcement schedule during training, the higher is the level of frustration when the rat finally receives food. For the rat on a thin schedule, then, high-level frustration becomes a cue for lever pressing. With continued responding during extinction, the organism becomes increasingly frustrated. But since high-level frustration is an S⁺ for lever pressing (the more frustrated the rat gets, the closer it gets to food), extinction proceeds slowly.

Frustration is one way of accounting for the PRE; E. J. Capaldi offers another.

Sequential Hypothesis

Capaldi's (1966, 1967) **sequential hypothesis** attributes the PRE to differences in the sequence of cues during training. He notes that during training, each performance of a behavior is followed by one of two events: reinforcement or nonreinforcement. In continuous reinforcement, all lever presses are reinforced, which means that reinforcement is an S⁺ for lever pressing. During extinction, no lever presses are reinforced, so an important cue for lever pressing (the presence of reinforcement) is absent. Therefore, extinction proceeds rapidly after continuous reinforcement because an important cue for performing is missing.

During intermittent reinforcement, some lever presses are followed by reinforcement, some by nonreinforcement. The sequence of reinforcement and nonreinforcement becomes important in that it becomes an S⁺ for pressing. A rat on an FR 10 schedule, for example, must press nine times without reinforcement before it presses the tenth time and receives reinforcement. The nine nonreinforced lever presses are a kind of S⁺ for lever pressing. The thinner the reinforcement schedule, the more resistant the rat will be to extinction, since a long stretch of nonreinforced lever pressing has become the cue for continued pressing. In other words, the rat performs in the absence of reinforcement because, in the past, long strings of nonreinforced presses have reliably preceded reinforcement.

The frustration and sequential hypotheses have much in common. Both assume that extinction is an active learning process, and both assume that it involves a kind of discrimination learning. Both Amsel and Capaldi also assume that stimuli present during training become S^+s for behavior. The chief difference seems to be that Amsel finds the S^+ inside the organism (the physiological reaction called frustration) whereas Capaldi finds the S^+ in the organism's external environment (the sequence of reinforcement and nonreinforcement). We now consider a very different approach to the PRE.

Query: The frustration and sequential hypotheses are both

variations of the _____ hypothesis.

Response Unit Hypothesis

Mowrer and Jones (1945) offer another explanation for the PRE called the **response unit hypothesis**. This approach says that to understand the PRE we must think differently about the behavior on intermittent reinforcement.

In lever pressing studies, for example, the lever pressing is usually thought of as one depression of the lever sufficient to produce some measurable effect on the environment, such as activating a recording device. But, say Mowrer and Jones, lever pressing can also be defined in terms of what produces reinforcement.

In the case of a CRF schedule, the two definitions coincide exactly: Each time the rat presses the lever far enough to activate the recorder, it receives a bit of food. But consider what happens if we switch to an FR 2 schedule: One lever press produces nothing, but two presses produce food. If an animal receives food only after pressing the lever two times, "we should not think of this as press-failure, press-reward," write Mowrer and Jones (1945), "but rather as press-press-reward" (p. 301). In other words, if lever pressing is on an FR 2 schedule, then the unit of behavior being reinforced is *two* lever presses; if the schedule is FR 3, then the behavior (or response unit) is *three* lever presses; and so on. VR schedules are more complicated because the response unit is defined not only by the average number of acts required for reinforcement but also by the range of units. In a VR 4 schedule, for instance, producing reinforcement may sometimes require only one lever press and sometimes eight

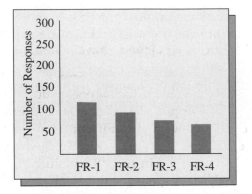

Figure 10-3 *Partial reinforcement effect? Average number of responses by rats during extinction following four fixed ratio schedules of reinforcement. In this case, a response is defined as the number of lever presses required for reinforcement. The thinner the reinforcement schedule, the fewer responses during extinction. (Cf. Figure 10-2.) (Compiled from data in Mowrer and Jones, 1945.)*

lever presses. Nevertheless, the idea that the behavior is defined by the number of times it must occur to produce reinforcement still applies.

Now consider again the Mowrer and Jones experiment described earlier. In the CRF group, the response unit was one lever press; rats in this group produced an average of 128 response units (lever presses) during extinction. In the FR 2 group, the response unit was two lever presses; rats in this group produced an average of 94 responses (188 lever presses divided by 2). In the FR 3 group, the response unit was three lever presses and the rats produced 71.8 responses (215.5 ÷ 3). In the FR 4 group, the response unit was four presses and the rats produced 68.1 responses (272.3 ÷ 4). Notice that when responses are defined in terms of the units required for reinforcement, the total number of responses during extinction *declines* as the reinforcement schedule gets thinner (see Figure 10-3).

Mowrer and Jones note that when we define responses in terms of the units required for reinforcement, we find that "the apparent advantage of so-called intermittent reinforcement disappears" (p. 301). In other words, the PRE is an illusion. Behavior on intermittent reinforcement only *seems* to be more resistant to extinction because we have failed to take into account the response units required for reinforcement. Recent research on behavioral momentum also seems to support the response unit hypothesis. John Nevin (1988) found, for example, that the slope of the extinction curve is steeper (indicating more rapid extinction) following intermittent reinforcement than following CRF. This suggests that CRF makes behavior more resistant to extinction.

Of the four main explanations of the PRE, the response unit hypothesis is easily the most elegant, but the PRE is a very complex problem, and no theory about it can yet claim to have won the day.

REVIEW　The number of times a behavior occurs during extinction varies with the schedule in effect prior to extinction. A behavior typically occurs many more times following intermittent reinforcement than following continuous reinforcement. This is known as the partial reinforcement effect. Attempts to explain the PRE include the discrimination, frustration, sequential, and response unit hypotheses.

We have considered the most common simple schedules. It is now time to turn to the most common complex schedules.

Complex Schedules

Complex schedules consist of various combinations of simple schedules. We will consider only a few of the more important complex schedules.

In a **multiple schedule**, a behavior is under the influence of two or more simple schedules, each associated with a particular stimulus. A pigeon that has learned to peck a disk for grain may be put on a multiple schedule in which pecking is reinforced on an FI 10" schedule when a red light is on, but on a VR 10 schedule when a yellow light is on. The two reinforcement schedules alternate, with the changes indicated by changes in the color of the light. The experimenter refers to this as a MULT FI 10" VR 10 schedule. The bird's cumulative record shows the familiar scalloped curve of FI schedules when the red light is on, followed by the rapid, steady behavior associated with VR schedules when the yellow light is on (see Figure 10-4).

A **mixed schedule** is the same as a multiple schedule except that there are no stimuli (such as red and yellow lights) associated with the change in reinforcement contingencies. In a MIX FI 10" VR 10 schedule, disk pecking might be reinforced on an FI 10" schedule for, say, 30 seconds and then on a VR 10 schedule for 60 seconds, but there is no clear indication that the schedule has changed.

Query:　The difference between multiple and mixed schedules

is that in _____ schedules there is a signal that

the schedule has changed.

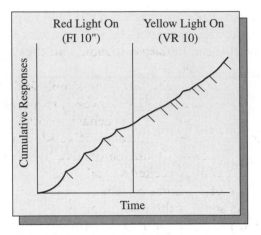

Figure 10-4   *Multiple schedule. A pigeon's rate and pattern of responding change when a stimulus indicates a change in the reinforcement schedule in force. (Hypothetical data.)*

In a **chain schedule**, reinforcement is delivered only on completion of the last in a series of schedules. Consider a pigeon on a CHAIN FR 10 FI 15" VR 20 schedule: The bird pecks a red disk; after the tenth peck the disk changes from red to yellow. The yellow disk signals that an FI 15" schedule is in effect; after 15 seconds, pecking the disk changes it from yellow to green. Working at the green disk results, after an average of 20 pecks, in food. The disk also becomes red again, indicating that the FR 10 schedule is once again in force. Note that the bird receives food only after completing the requirement of the last schedule. Despite this, the bird typically behaves as though food were provided on each of the separate schedules. When it is on the FI 15" schedule, for example, the cumulative record shows the typical scalloped curve associated with FI schedules.

A **tandem schedule** is identical to a chain schedule except that there is no distinctive event (e.g., a light or buzzer) that signals the end of one schedule and the beginning of the next.

Chain and tandem schedules give rise to an interesting question: What reinforces the behavior during the schedules that don't produce food? In the case of chain schedules, discriminative stimuli, such as the disk colors, indicate not only that a new schedule is in force but that the organism is one step closer to reinforcement. These discriminative stimuli may therefore act as secondary reinforcers. But what is the reinforcer in the case of the tandem schedule, where discriminative stimuli are not provided? In this case, it may be that the changes in schedules themselves serve as discriminative stimuli, since they do in fact signal that reinforcement is closer.

The schedules described thus far, both simple and complex, involve an individual organism. It is possible, however, to arrange schedules that make reinforcement dependent on the behavior of two or more individuals. Such arrangements are called **cooperative schedules**. For instance, we might arrange for two pigeons to receive food by pecking a disk when the two of them have pecked a total of 20 times. One might peck the disk at the rate of 10 times a minute while the other pecks at 40 times a minute. As soon as the total number of pecks reaches 20, they each receive a few pieces of grain. Or we might arrange the schedule so that both birds receive food following a total of 20 pecks, but only if each of them has pecked 10 times. In a cooperative schedule, the reinforcement that one subject gets is partly dependent on the behavior of the other subject.

Cooperative schedules involving two individuals are the easiest to manage, but it is possible to arrange cooperative schedules with larger groups. For instance, a group of five birds might receive food when the group as a whole produces 100 disk pecks, provided that each bird pecks the disk at least 10 times.

Cooperative schedules are often used with people, though typically in an inefficient manner. For example, a group of students may be required to work together on a project. Each student in the group receives the same grade for the project, regardless of what each contributes. The students are supposed to share the work equally. However, reinforcement is not contingent on how the work is shared but on what the group as a whole produces. A common result is that some members of the group do more than their fair share while others do less. We can often see the same phenomenon in the workplace when employees are asked to work as a group on some project. This inequality of labor might be avoided or reduced by altering the cooperative schedule so that individual contributions are reinforced as well as the group effort.

In the schedules discussed thus far, only one schedule is available at any given moment. In **concurrent schedules**, two or more schedules are available at once. A pigeon may have the option of pecking a red disk on a VR 50 schedule, or pecking a yellow disk on a VR 20 schedule. In other words, the concurrent schedule involves a choice. In the example just given, the animal would soon choose the yellow disk and the VR 20 schedule.

REVIEW Two or more simple schedules can be combined to form various kinds of complex schedules. When the schedules alternate and each is identified by a particular stimulus, a multiple schedule is said to be in force. When the schedules alternate but there is no signal, a mixed schedule is in force. In a chain schedule, reinforcement occurs only on completion of the last in a series of reinforcement schedules, with each schedule change signaled by a change in stimulus. Tandem schedules resemble chain schedules except that there is no signal. A cooperative schedule makes reinforcement contingent on the behavior of two or more individuals. In concurrent schedules, two or more schedules are available simultaneously, so that the organism must choose among them. Since a great deal of behavior can be thought of as involving choices, we will consider this problem in greater detail.

Choice and the Matching Law

As just noted, a concurrent schedule represents a kind of choice. The pigeon on such a schedule may, for example, peck a red disk or a yellow disk, but it cannot do both simultaneously. In recent years, researchers have become increasingly interested in the study of behavior in such situations.

Making a choice may involve a great deal of thought. Human beings faced with a choice often verbalize silently, and sometimes aloud, about the relative merits of the various options. (We say that we are "weighing the alternatives.") It is possible that some other animals engage in analogous behavior when faced with a choice. However, our interest is not in these cogitations but in the effect that the reinforcement schedules have on the choices made.[7] The task is to be able to predict, from the reinforcement schedules in force, how the person or animal will behave in a choice situation.

Sometimes this is easily done. Imagine a rat in a T-maze arranged so that if the rat enters the arm on the right, it will receive food, but if it enters the arm on the left, it will receive nothing. We have no difficulty in predicting that after a few trials, the rat will regularly turn right rather than left. A choice situation in which behavior A is always reinforced and behavior B is never reinforced quickly results in the reliable performance of behavior A.

---

[7]To say that an organism chooses means that it does one thing rather than another. It may, prior to the behavior, engage in various kinds of covert behavior. People sometimes "agonize" over choices, but the agonizing doesn't account for the choice made. This cogitating is part of the behavior of choosing, and behavior cannot explain itself.

Prediction becomes more difficult, however, when both alternatives are reinforced and the only difference is in the relative frequency of reinforcement. Consider the case of a pigeon given a choice between pecking either of two disks: one red, the other yellow. Pecking the red disk is reinforced on an FR 50 schedule, and pecking the yellow disk is reinforced on an FR 75 schedule. What will the pigeon do? Perhaps it will go back and forth repeatedly between the two disks. Or perhaps it will work steadily at one disk, but the disk will be selected at random, so that one pigeon will peck at yellow, another at red.

In fact, what happens is that the pigeon initially spends some time at each disk, moving back and forth between them, but eventually settles on the disk associated with the richer reinforcement schedule. In fact, some animals have an uncanny knack for selecting the "better-paying" work. Humans have the same ability to discriminate between similar reinforcement schedules (Pierce & Epling, 1983).

Richard Herrnstein (1961, 1970; Herrnstein & Mazur, 1987) led the way in the study of choice and showed that the effort devoted to each of two reinforcement schedules can be expressed by the formula

$$\frac{B_1}{B_2} = \frac{r_1}{r_2}$$

This formula means that given two behaviors, B_1 and B_2, each on its own reinforcement schedule, r_1 and r_2, respectively, the relative frequency of each behavior equals the relative frequency of reinforcement available.[8] This statement is called the **matching law** because the distribution of behaviors matches the availability of reinforcement (Herrnstein, 1961, 1970; see Davison & McCarthy, 1988; Pierce & Epling, 1983, for reviews).

You can see that a choice situation involving different schedules of reinforcement can be viewed as a kind of discrimination task (see Chapter 9). In the case of two ratio schedules, such as FR 30 and FR 40, the subject samples each and then settles on the denser schedule. In concurrent ratio schedules, it makes sense to identify the more reinforcing schedule as quickly as possible and remain loyal to it. Switching back and forth between two ratio schedules is pointless. In the same way, if you can pick beans for Farmer Able for $5 a bushel, or for Farmer Baker for $4 a bushel, it makes little sense to switch back and forth. Other things being equal, your behavior will follow the matching law: You will pick steadily for Farmer Able.

---

[8]I have changed Herrnstein's notation slightly. I have replaced his R_1 and R_2 with B_1 and B_2 so that B refers to behavior, and r to reinforcement. I hope that this will make the formula less confusing to students.

Query: State the matching law in your own words.

Switching makes more sense when concurrent interval schedules are involved. Consider the case of a rat lever pressing on a concurrent FI 10" FI 30" schedule. Clearly, the payoff is better on the FI 10" schedule, so it makes sense for the animal to spend most of its time working on that lever. But even on that schedule, there are periods during which lever pressing is useless. Some of this time could be spent pressing the lever on the FI 30" schedule. And the longer the animal works on the FI 10" schedule, the more likely it is that a behavior on the FI 30" schedule will be reinforced. It therefore makes sense for the animal to devote most of its effort to the FI 10" schedule but occasionally press the lever on the FI 30" schedule. In fact, this is exactly what it does.

What about concurrent VI schedules? Suppose a rat has a choice between VI 10" and VI 30" schedules. Once again it makes sense for the animal to devote most of its time to the VI 10" schedule, but occasional lever presses on the VI 30" schedule are also likely to be reinforced. This is so even though delivery of reinforcement is variable and therefore unpredictable. Once again, animals behave in the most sensible manner: They focus on the VI 10" schedule but periodically abandon this schedule to work on the VI 30" schedule. In this way, they receive more reinforcements than they would if they worked solely on the better paying VI 10" schedule. Even when the differences in schedules are fairly subtle, animals usually behave in a manner that is in their best interests.

We have seen that, given a choice between two interval schedules, an animal will alternate between them. Is it possible to predict, on the basis of the schedules in force, how much an animal will work on each schedule? Herrnstein (1961, 1970) has found that it is indeed possible. He reports that in a two-choice situation, the choice may be predicted according to the mathematical expression

$$\frac{B_A}{B_A + B_B} = \frac{r_A}{r_A + r_B}$$

where B_A and B_B represent two behaviors, behavior A and behavior B, and r_A and r_B represent the reinforcement rates for behaviors A and B, respectively.[9] This equation is merely a reformulation of the matching law.

Take the case of a rat trained to press a lever for food. Presses on lever A are reinforced on a VI 10" schedule; presses on lever B are reinforced on a VI 30" schedule. If the rat were to work solely on the VI 10" schedule, it

---

[9]Again, I have replaced R with B for ease of understanding. See note 8.

would receive a maximum of 6 reinforcers per minute. If it occasionally works on the VI 30" schedule, it could obtain a maximum of two more reinforcers. Thus, of the total reinforcers obtainable, 75% (6 out of 8) are available on the VI 10" schedule and 25% are available on the VI 30" schedule. The value of r_A is therefore about .75; that of r_B is about .25. The formula predicts that the rat will devote approximately three-fourths of its effort to schedule A (the VI 10" schedule), and one-fourth to schedule B (VI 30"). Experimental tests show that such predictions are surprisingly accurate.

Herrnstein has extended the matching law beyond the two-choice situation, suggesting that every situation represents a kind of choice. Consider the pigeon that receives food when it pecks a disk. There are many things the pigeon can do besides peck the disk. The bird may, for instance, groom itself, wander around the cage, peck at objects on the floor or on the walls, or sleep. In pecking the disk, it is therefore choosing to engage in that behavior rather than various others. Indeed, even when the pigeon pecks the disk at a high rate, it continues to engage in other kinds of behavior, such as bobbing its head and turning to the left and right. Theoretically, it is possible to identify all of these actions and the reinforcers that maintain them and to predict the relative frequency of any one of them. This idea can be expressed by the formula

$$\frac{B_A}{B_A + B_O} = \frac{r_A}{r_A + r_O}$$

where B_A represents the particular behavior we are studying, B_O represents all *other* behaviors, r_A represents the reinforcers available for B_A, and r_O represents the reinforcers available for all other behaviors (Herrnstein, 1970). This formula has less predictive value than the formula for the two-choice situation, because it is not possible to specify all the behaviors that may occur, nor all the reinforcers those acts may produce. Some behaviors may, for example, be reinforced by events not readily subject to observation, as in the case of the reinforcement a rat receives when it scratches an itch. Still, the formula reminds us that behavior is a function of the reinforcers available for any behavior that might occur, not merely the reinforcers available for the behavior that interests us at the moment.

William Baum (1974) provides evidence that the matching law describes the foraging of free-ranging pigeons. He set up an apparatus for studying disk pecking in an attic space accessible to wild pigeons. Baum had no control over which birds pecked at a disk, but the apparatus was arranged so that only one bird could work at a time. After the birds had learned to receive food by pecking a disk, Baum gave them a choice

Ghetto Choice

A police officer in a small town arrested a suspected drug dealer (Rivera, 1997). In the 10-minute ride to the police station, the suspect's beeper went off at least 7 times, each time displaying only codes. In a single night's work, a dealer that busy probably makes $5000 in drug sales. What are the dealer's alternatives? What other levers can he press? Typically, the only alternative available to the drug dealer is some sort of unskilled work paying something near minimum wage. As the arresting officer said, "How then can the system expect to rehabilitate him, put him back on the street and have him flip burgers for $5.50 an hour?" (Rivera, 1997, p. B3). Good question.

between two disks. Pecking now paid off on VI schedules, with the disk on the right always providing food more frequently than the one on the left. Because the birds were wild and could come and go as they pleased, it is impossible to say just how many birds "participated" in the experiment, but Baum estimates the number at between 10 and 20 birds. The result for the group as a whole was an almost perfect correspondence with the matching law, with pecks distributed between the disks in proportion to the reinforcement available from each (but see Baum & Kraft, 1998).

Humans likewise benefit from the ability to match behaviors to reinforcement (Kraft & Baum, 2001). No doubt for most of human existence, people have made good use of the ability to apportion behaviors appropriately among the hunting and foraging areas available (but see "Ghetto Choice"). Today, a farmer may do this by devoting most available farmland to a crop that produces a nice profit under typical weather conditions, and planting a smaller area in a less profitable crop that does well under adverse weather conditions. (This is known as hedging one's bet.) The rest of us do the same thing when we spend more time at a high-paying job than at a low-paying one. College students obey the matching law when they devote more time to a five-credit course than to a one-credit course, since a high grade in the former pays better (contributes more to grade point average) than a high grade in the latter. We follow the same principle when we spend more time with someone whose company we enjoy than with someone we find somewhat tiresome.

The matching law has been found to be a robust phenomenon. It holds for a wide variety of species, behaviors, reinforcers, and reinforcement schedules (see deVilliers, 1977, for a review). It holds, for example, whether we are considering different rates of reinforcement (Herrnstein, 1970), different amounts of reinforcement (Todorov et al., 1984), or different reinforcement delays (Catania, 1966). And it holds for punishment schedules as well as reinforcement schedules (Baum, 1975). The matching law is the subject of considerable debate, some of it quite rancorous (Binmore, 1991; Herrnstein, 1990, 1991; Staddon, 1991). It has, however, proved its worth as a stimulus to research.

REVIEW   People and animals have a remarkable ability to discriminate between more and less reinforcing schedules. The tendency to work in proportion to the reinforcement available is so reliable it is called the matching law. In the case of a choice among ratio schedules, the matching law correctly predicts choosing the schedule with the highest reinforcement frequency. In the case of a choice among interval schedules, the matching law predicts working on each schedule in proportion to the amount of reinforcers available on each.

Research on schedules has provided helpful insights in a number of areas, including certain applied problems. We will consider a few of these now.

Applications of Schedules

Compulsive Gambling

Slot machines, roulette wheels, and other forms of casino gambling are designed so that most of the time, most people lose. The average return on $1 "invested" in a slot machine, for example, is usually about 90%. That means that for every $1 gambled, the person wins $.90. Why would anyone agree to give someone $1 in exchange for $.90?

Gamblers themselves often say that they gamble for the fun of winning. But this explanation is unsatisfactory because, in fact, gamblers nearly always lose. Most people look for an explanation of gambling, especially compulsive gambling, in the gamblers themselves: They are morally weak, stupid, have a "gambling gene," are depressed or anxious, or have masochistic impulses. One way or another, the theory goes, there is something about *them* that makes them behave as they do.[10]

---

[10]People often confuse differences with causes. Compulsive gamblers may be more anxious and depressed than other people. A person who, because of gambling, has lost his job, spouse, friends, house, and car, and is in debt to loan sharks, has good reason to be anxious and depressed. Indeed, it is more likely that his anxiety and depression are the results of gambling rather than its causes.

Another possibility is that the source of the problem is not in the gambler but in the gambler's experience, in particular the schedule of reinforcement provided by games of chance (Skinner, 1953). The payoff in most games of chance resembles variable ratio schedules of reinforcement, and such schedules can produce high rates of behavior that are highly resistant to change.

But many people gamble without getting hooked. Why do some become compulsive gamblers while others do not? The most likely explanation is the momentary variations in schedules. The fact that a slot machine pays off on a given schedule, for example, does not mean that everyone playing it has precisely the same experience. One person may have a series of three or four wins in his first 20 tries, while another may win nothing. Or one person may hit a small jackpot of $50 on his tenth bet, while the other never wins more than $1. If both gamblers persist for a prolonged period, their fates are likely to be similar: They will lose money. Yet the variations in the schedule, especially early on, may produce differences in the tendency to continue gambling.

In an experiment with pigeons, Alan Christopher (1988) tested the effects of early wins on willingness to gamble. First, he trained two pigeons to obtain their daily food by pecking at an illuminated disk. Pecking at the disk paid off at a steady rate: 50 pecks earned three seconds at a food tray. This schedule allowed the birds to maintain normal body weight by working only about a half hour a day.

Next Christopher gave the birds a choice between working and gambling. He illuminated a disk that, like a slot machine, paid off in an unpredictable way. But Christopher arranged things so that novice gamblers got "lucky": During the first three days, the pigeons could earn far more food by gambling than they could by working. And Christopher made sure that now and then the birds had a big win—up to 15 seconds at the food tray. After the third day, however, the birds were better off working than gambling. The question was, would they go back to work, or were they hooked on gambling?

They were hooked. The birds pounded relentlessly at the less rewarding gambling disk, so much so that they began to lose weight. Christopher prevented them from gambling for fear that they would starve themselves. Unable to gamble, the birds went back to work and began gaining weight. Christopher provided the gambling disk again to see if the birds had learned their lesson.

They had not. Once again they banged away at the gambler's disk and began losing weight, so Christopher ended the experiment.

In a group design experiment, Jeffrey Kassinove and Mitchell Schare (2000) looked at the effects of "near misses" and big wins on gambling persistence in college students. In their study, students gambled at a computerized version of a four-wheel slot machine. During the first 50 trials, the slot machine had a win rate of 10% (on average, one in 10 trials paid off) and a 90% return (overall, the player lost 10 cents on each dollar gambled). In addition, there were additional near misses when the wheels turned up with all but the last having the same number (e.g., 3337). Half of the students also had a big win ($10) on trial 8. After the first 50 trials, gambling went on an extinction schedule: no wins and a zero rate of return. The question was, Would the differences in near misses and big wins affect how long students continued to gamble during extinction?

Near misses made a substantial difference. Students who had near misses on 30% of the first 50 trials gambled much more during the extinction phase than those who had near misses on only 15% of trials.[11] In contrast to the Christopher study, however, a big win made no difference in the gambling of college students. (It may be that the big win was not big enough: Many of the students in this study came from rather wealthy families.)

Other research also provides evidence that compulsive gambling can be accounted for by the history of reinforcement (Lyons & Ghezzi, 1991; Reid, 1986; Strickland & Grote, 1967). It is also interesting to note that pool hustlers and card sharks regularly let their "pigeons" win several games early on. It may be that a little good luck at the wrong time can turn anyone into a pigeon.[12]

Query: The Kassinove and Schare study suggests that "near

misses" can serve as _____ .

Experimental Economics

Some psychologists and economists have drawn a parallel between research on reinforcement schedules and economics and have made them the foundation of a new field called **experimental** (or **behavioral**) **economics**.

---

[11]From the standpoint of building persistent gambling, having a great many near misses is ineffective. Students who had near misses on 45% of the first 50 trials gambled *less* than those who had near misses on 30% of trials. This might be because near misses have to be associated with wins in order to maintain their value as reinforcers.

[12]The younger a person is when "hooked" on gambling, the more those who profit from gambling stand to make. Slot machines are now showing up in arcades ("Slot Machines for Children Promote Gambling, Critics Say," 1998). The machines closely resemble those used by adults, but pay off in tokens (which can be redeemed for prizes) rather than cash. The situation is analogous to cigarette smoking: The tobacco industry went to great lengths to get children smoking because they typically went on to become lifelong smokers (DiFranza, 1995; DiFranza & Aisquith, 1995; DiFranza & McAfee, 1992; DiFranza et al., 1991).

Certain economic principles have been found to hold in animal experiments. For instance, economists know that when the price of a luxury item rises, the consumption of that item declines. But when the price of an essential item, such as food, rises, there is little change in consumption. The same phenomenon has been demonstrated in rats. Rats will work for psychoactive drugs (a luxury), but increases in the price of a drug (the number of lever presses required for a dose) usually result in decreased consumption; yet large increases in the price of food (an essential) do not lower consumption substantially (Hursh, 1980, 1984).

Other studies have examined economic principles experimentally in human groups. In one study, Ray Battalio and John Kagel (reported in Alexander, 1980) studied the behavior of female patients on the psychiatric ward of a state hospital. The patients could earn tokens for performing various tasks and exchange them for cigarettes, candy, and other items. This can be construed as a choice between activities (making one's bed, doing laundry) for which tokens are available, and activities (watching television, sleeping) for which other reinforcers are available. The situation resembles the society outside the hospital, where people generally have a choice between working for pay or participating in various leisure activities.

One thing the researchers were interested in was how the reinforcers would be distributed among the patients. That is, would each person accumulate about the same number of tokens or would some people end up with far more than others, as is the case for the United States population as a whole? The results revealed that those in the top 20% held a total of 41% of all tokens, while those in the bottom 20% held only 7%. This distribution of wealth closely approximated that of the general population at the time. It appears from such research that schedules research may turn economics into a true experimental science.

Malingering

The experience of pain is primarily a set of reflexive reactions to certain events in the body, but pain also involves other behaviors, including the use of analgesics, complaining about pain, reducing mobility, and avoiding work (Frederiksen et al., 1978). There is no mystery in any of these reactions to pain: All are instrumental in reducing the amount of pain experienced, but the behaviors sometimes continue long after the pain has subsided. Sometimes the patient is malingering: pretending to be in pain in order to avoid unpleasant duties. Most schoolchildren have probably feigned illness in order to avoid going to school, and workers who are injured on the job have been known to take more days of sick leave than they required. Thus, some pain-related behaviors, particularly the avoidance of work, could be maintained by reinforcers other than the reduction of pain (Fordyce, 1976). But feigning pain has a price. If a person can work, but doesn't, the workmen's compensation received may be lower than the usual paycheck. When workmen's compensation runs out, the shirker may have to live on his spouse's income or welfare. He also has to play the part consistently, which means avoiding physical activities that he enjoys: He cannot claim on Friday that his pain prevents him from working on the loading dock, and then spend the weekend rock climbing. Will people really avoid work they can do, even if the result is a reduced income and unnecessarily restricted activities?

Stephen Goldberg and Carl Cheney (1984) tested the idea that operant behavior associated with chronic pain may be maintained by reinforcement after the pain has ceased. In particular, they wanted to see whether shirking would continue. They attempted to create a laboratory analog of this situation using rats as their subjects. They began by training rats to lever press for food and then maintained this behavior on an FR 45 schedule. They then switched to a cooperative schedule in which each rat pressed the lever a minimum of five times, and together they pressed the levers a total of 50 times. The schedule was cooperative because both had to contribute; if one of the rats pressed 100 times and the other rat did nothing, neither received food. Yet this cooperative schedule meant that one of the rats could do far less work, provided that its partner did more work. During a baseline period, both rats in each of three pairs did a good deal of work, but then one of the rats was exposed to a mild electric shock delivered continuously through the grid floor. Thus, the situation was analogous to a person with chronic mild pain. The result was an abrupt reduction in the amount of work done by the rat in pain. These rats continued to press the lever, but at a much lower rate than during baseline.

In the next stage of the experiment, the researchers terminated the shock. Would the rats that had been in pain go back to working at their former rate? The results showed that the rats continued to work at a lower pace, only gradually increasing their share of the workload. This is particularly interesting because the slower rate of work reduced the amount of food both rats received. Although the partner rat could take up the slack, it necessarily took longer to reach the 50 lever presses required for reinforcement when one rat did little work.

This experiment involved rats, not people. Nevertheless, it suggests that there is good reason to believe that people may malinger if others (such as spouses and co-workers) are willing to "press the lever" more often to make up for someone who appears to be hurting. It is important to note that malingering may occur even though everyone, *including the malingerer,* loses by it.

There are, of course, other applications of schedules research, and new uses for schedules are being explored all the time.

REVIEW The study of reinforcement schedules has led to new insights into behavior previously attributed to character and other vague constructs. These insights suggest new ways of dealing with problems such as gambling, malingering, and consumer behavior. In light of the apparent relevance of reinforcement schedules to everyday human behavior, there would seem to be no doubt about the value of research in this area. However, the importance of reinforcement schedules has been questioned.

The Importance of Schedules Research

A great deal of research has been done on schedules of reinforcement and their differential effects, but some psychologists have raised doubts about the significance of this research (see, for example, Schwartz et al., 1978).

Some critics argue that the schedules of reinforcement studied in the laboratory are artificial constructions not found in the real world. It is true that schedules found outside the laboratory are seldom as simple as those created by researchers. But this is true of all laboratory science: Researchers take a problem into the lab precisely because the lab allows them to simplify it. Thus, a psychologist studies a rat's behavior on a concurrent VR 10 VR 15 schedule not because this schedule is particularly representative of the rat's natural environment, but because it is a convenient way of determining the animal's ability to discriminate between similar schedules. The goal is to discover rules that describe the way the environment affects behavior. It is difficult if not impossible to discover such rules unless the experimenter simplifies the environment.

Others complain that schedules research generally produces trivial findings. But it is not trivial to note that personality (i.e., the characteristic behavior of a given individual) is a function of the individual's history of reinforcement. Traditional explanations attribute personality differences to qualities of mind: John is said to smoke because he "lacks willpower"; Mary is a compulsive gambler because of "masochistic urges"; Bill is persistent in his efforts to break the school track record because he "has stick-to-itiveness"; Harry gives up easily because he "lacks stick-to-itiveness"; Phyllis comes up with novel ideas because she "has a lot of imagination." The trouble with all such "explanations" is that they merely name the behavior to be explained. Harry's tendency to give up is called a lack of stick-to-itiveness; Phyllis's high rate of original ideas is called imagination. Identifying the kinds of reinforcement schedules that produce these behaviors is a considerable advance.

Schedules research also allows us to answer questions that might be difficult to answer otherwise. For example, which is more important in affecting behavior—the frequency of reinforcement, or the amount of reinforcement? Is it more effective to deliver large amounts of a reinforcer on a few occasions, or small amounts on many occasions? One way to answer such questions is to compare the performance of rats on concurrent schedules, with one schedule providing frequent, small reinforcers, and the other providing infrequent, large reinforcers. Research of this sort has supported the conclusion that frequency of reinforcement is more important than quantity of reinforcement (Schneider, 1973; Todorov et al., 1984). The use of concurrent schedules has allowed other researchers to test the popular (but essentially inaccurate) notion that extrinsic rewards undermine motivation (Skaggs et al., 1992).

The study of reinforcement schedules gives us a more scientific way of accounting for differences in behavior. If Harry gives up at the first sign of failure, perhaps it is because his reinforcement history has not included reinforcement for persisting in the face of failure. Harry need not have had considerable failure: A steady diet of easy success (otherwise known as continuous reinforcement) makes one especially likely to quit trying when success is not forthcoming (otherwise known as extinction) (Nation et al., 1979).

Some critics charge that reinforcement schedules reveal considerably more about rats and pigeons than they do about people. Studies with humans do sometimes reveal patterns of behavior that differ from those obtained with animals on the same schedules. A rat placed on an FI 15" schedule soon produces the familiar scalloped-shaped cumulative curve; a person on the same schedule may perform at a steady rate. Typically, such differences result because human subjects often receive instructions about what they are to do. Instead of shaping the behavior through continuous reinforcement and then switching to an FI schedule (the usual procedure with animal subjects), researchers often give human participants instructions. "Just press this bar like so," they may be told, "and every once in a while a coin will drop into this tray." Such instructions often have a more powerful effect on human behavior than the reinforcement contingencies. People who have been instructed to press a bar or push a button will often do so at a steady rate, even though the reinforcement schedule does not support this behavior. (People, unlike other creatures, usually have long histories of reinforcement for doing as they are told, even when doing so seems pointless.) However, human schedule behavior shows remarkable similarity to animal behavior when

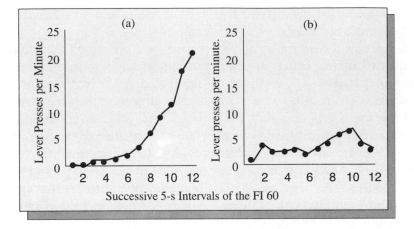

Figure 10-5   *Cocaine effects revealed in schedule performance. Lever pressing reinforced on an FI schedule showed the familiar scallop pattern (a). Cocaine administration had a pronounced effect on performance (b). (Adapted from an unpublished figure provided by T. Belke based on data from Belke and Dunbar, 2001.)*

---

both are shaped by reinforcement contingencies rather than instructions (Lowe et al., 1983; Matthews et al., 1977; Weiner, 1983). Indeed, as psychologist John Malone (1990) puts it, "Those who feel that an unfathomable gulf exists between human and beast are well advised to watch a pigeon pecking for food delivered according to a VR schedule and then go to a video arcade" (p. 245).

Schedule performance also provides a very good way of testing the effects of variables on behavior. For instance, Terry Belke and M. J. Dunbar (2001) trained rats to press a lever to get access to an exercise wheel. The reinforcement schedule was FI 60 seconds, and the reinforcer was 60 seconds in the exercise wheel. This schedule produced a low rate of behavior, usually fewer than six lever presses a minute. Nevertheless, the familiar FI scallop pattern appeared (see Figure 10-5a). At this point the researchers administered cocaine in varying amounts 10 minutes prior to running the rats. The cocaine had no detectable influence on the pattern of behavior until the researchers reached a dosage of 16 milligrams per kilogram of body weight. At this level, the scalloped pattern began to deteriorate (see Figure 10-5b). In much the same way, researchers used schedules as a basis for comparing the effects of alcohol and cocaine on human performance (Higgins et al., 1992). Schedule performance can provide a baseline for evaluating the effects of toxins, diet, sleep deprivation, exercise, brain stimulation, and many other variables.

Reinforcement schedules have been called the "sleeping giant" of behavioral research (Zeiler, 1984). Whether important new insights and useful techniques remain to be discovered from schedules research is unclear, but there can be no doubt that past research in this area has been of great value.

REVIEW   Not everyone believes that schedules research is worthwhile. Critics claim that the work is artificial, and the findings are trivial and don't apply to people. Defenders of schedules research reply that the artificiality is part and parcel of scientific rigor, that the findings have provided new insights into complex behavior, that the findings with humans often parallel those with rats and pigeons when similar procedures are followed, and that schedules provide an extremely useful way of studying a wide variety of problems, such as the effects of drugs on behavior.

RECOMMENDED READING

1. Ferster, C. B., & Skinner, B. F. (1957). *Schedules of reinforcement.* New York: Appleton-Century-Croft.

   The classic work on reinforcement schedules. It describes the basic kinds of reinforcement schedules and provides many graphs illustrating the rates and patterns of behavior associated with each.

2. Hursh, S. R. (1984). Behavioral economics. *Journal of the Experimental Analysis of Behavior, 42*, 435–452.

   A discussion of economics in terms of reinforcement schedules.

3. Lattal, K. A. (1991). Scheduling positive reinforcers. In I. H. Iversen & K. A. Lattal (Eds.), *Experimental analysis of behavior* (pp.87–134). Amsterdam: Elsevier.

   A review of schedules and their distinctive effects.

4. Nevin, J. (1988). Behavioral momentum and the partial reinforcement effect. *Psychological Bulletin, 103*, 44–56.

   Nevin points out the contradiction between behavioral momentum (which suggests that resistance to extinction should be greatest following continuous reinforcement) and the partial reinforcement effect.

5. Rachlin, H. (1989). *Judgment, decision and choice: A cognitive/behavioral synthesis.* New York: W. H. Freeman.

In this short book, Rachlin attempts to show that choice and schedules can account for both overt behavior and rational thought. For serious students only.

REVIEW QUESTIONS

1. Define the following terms:

chain schedule	multiple schedule
concurrent schedule	partial reinforcement effect
cooperative schedule	post-reinforcement pause
CRF	ratio strain
discrimination hypothesis	response unit hypothesis
DRH	run rate
experimental economics	schedule effects
fixed duration schedule	schedule of reinforcement
fixed interval schedule	sequential hypothesis
fixed ratio schedule	stretching the ratio
fixed time schedule	tandem schedule
frustration hypothesis	variable duration schedule
intermittent schedule	variable interval schedule
matching law	variable ratio schedule
mixed schedule	variable time schedule

2. Give an example (not provided by the text) of a decrease in behavior that indicates learning has occurred.

3. John wants to teach Cindy, age 5, the alphabet. He plans to reinforce correct performances with praise and small pieces of candy. What sort of schedule should he use?

4. Mary complains that her dog jumps up on her when she gets home from school. You explain that she reinforces this behavior by petting and talking to the dog when it jumps up, but Mary replies that you must be wrong, since she "hardly ever" does this. How would you respond to Mary's comment?

5. Five-year-old David gives up easily in the face of frustration. How could you develop his persistence?

6. Joyce is annoyed because some of her employees fail to take the periodic rest breaks required by the union and the state's safety regula-

tions. Why do you suppose this happens, and what can Joyce do to correct the problem?

7. Every Saturday at noon, the local fire department tests the fire signal. Is this a reinforcement schedule and, if so, what sort of schedule is it?

8. Many people regularly check the coin return after using a public telephone even though their call went through. Explain this behavior.

9. Mr. Smith and Ms. Jones both give their students new spelling words on Friday. Mr. Smith always tests his students on the following Friday. Ms. Jones also tests her students once a week, but the day varies, and she does not announce the test day in advance. Whose students are more likely to study on Tuesday nights?

10. How might casino operators increase their income by "stretching the ratio"?

11. Concurrent schedules are said to represent a choice situation. Why is a multiple schedule not said to represent a choice?

12. Describe the similarities and differences between multiple and chain schedules.

13. Rat X's lever pressing is put on a concurrent FR 10 FR 20 schedule. Rat Y's behavior is put on a concurrent VR 10 VR 20 schedule. Which rat will select the more reinforcing schedule first?

14. How might you use what you know about reinforcement schedules to study the effects of the presence of observers on human performance?

15. Someone says to you, "George is a nasty fellow. It's just his nature." How could you account for George's personality in a more scientific way?

16. A student tells you that studying reinforcement schedules is a waste of time. Give arguments for the opposing view.

17. A teacher reinforces longer and longer periods of quiet behavior in her students. How can she avoid creating ratio strain?

18. This chapter describes schedules of reinforcement. How would schedules of punishment work? Use, as an example, a VR 10 punishment schedule.

19. Pretend you are a behavioral economist who wishes to know the effect of inflation on purchasing. Describe an experiment that will shed light on the problem.

20. How might an understanding of schedules of reinforcement help account for the poor economic performance of communist countries?

PRACTICE QUIZ

1. In CRF, the ratio of responses to reinforcement is
   _____ to _____.

2. After a reinforcement, the rate of the reinforced behavior may fall to or near zero before increasing again. The period during which the behavior occurs infrequently is called a _____.

3. One difference between FT and FI schedules is that in the _____ schedule, reinforcement is not contingent on a behavior.

4. An excellent schedule for increasing the rate of a behavior is called differential reinforcement of _____.

5. Stretching the ratio too rapidly or too far can produce _____.

6. Of the four explanations of the PRE, the one that essentially says there is no such thing is the _____ hypothesis.

7. If reinforcement is contingent on the behavior of more than one organism, a _____ schedule is in effect.

8. Choice involves _____ schedules.

9. Compulsive gambling may be the product of a _____ schedule of reinforcement.

10. Schedule effects are sometimes very different in people than in rats and pigeons. The difference is often due to the influence of _____.

QUERY ANSWERS

Page 348. The term *schedule effects* refers to the pattern and rate of performance produced by a particular reinforcement schedule.

Page 351. The rate at which a behavior occurs once it has begun is called the *run* rate.

Page 355. In ratio schedules, reinforcement is contingent on *the number of times the behavior occurs;* in interval schedules, reinforcement is contingent on *the behavior occurring after a given interval.*

Page 357. In a DRL 10" schedule, the effect of pressing a lever after 8 seconds is to *"reset the clock"*/delay reinforcement.

Page 359. In FT and VT schedules, reinforcement is contingent on *time* rather than *behavior.*

Page 359. The thinner of two schedules, FR 3 and VR 4, is *VR 4.*

Page 360. You could do something analogous to stretching the ratio by "stretching the interval."

Page 365. The frustration and sequential hypotheses are both variations of the *discrimination* hypothesis.

Page 367. The difference between multiple and mixed schedules is that in *multiple* schedules there is a signal that the schedule has changed.

Page 372. Your answer should be something like this: The rate of behavior matches (or is proportional to) the rate of reinforcement.

Page 377. The Kassinove and Schare study suggests that near misses can serve as *reinforcers.*

CHAPTER 11

Forgetting

Memory is often spoken of as if it involved the actual persistence of the past. . . . This is mere mythology.

Bertrand Russell

The history of memory is a story of metaphors. In ancient times, experiences were impressed on the mind like marks on a wax tablet. To remember an experience, one had only to look on one's mental tablet. In the Renaissance, experience wrote on a blank slate, which could be read so long as the message was not wiped off. In the Industrial Age, the blank slate gave way to memos and snapshots stored in mental filing cabinets. Experiences were "filed away" and retrieved by searching through the appropriate file when the need arose. In the 20th century, memories were once again recorded in wax, but this time the wax was Thomas A. Edison's recording cylinder. Experiences could be replayed so long as one could set the needle at the right place on the cylinder. As magnetic tapes replaced records, memories became magnetic and lasted a long time if not erased or recorded over. The development of high-speed computers provided the current metaphor for memory. Today, by a curious coincidence, experiences are measured in bytes and stored in memory banks.

But while the metaphors have changed, the concept of memory has not. It is still viewed as an "internal record or representation" (as one of many texts puts it) of past experience. Plato would have no trouble recognizing that view of memory: It was his own.

Of course, few psychologists today believe that memories are veridical replicas of experience. Even in ages past, memories were referred to as *"faint* copies" of experience, not exact duplicates. Our tendency to get things wrong (to remember a blue hat as green, to recall the date 1863 as 1836, etc.) argues compellingly against memories as exact copies of the past. But people still believe that experiences are represented in some form within us.

One of B. F. Skinner's most important (and least understood) contributions may have been to offer an entirely different view. To Skinner, experiences are not stored away and retrieved for later use like photographs in an album; rather, experiences change the organism's tendency to behave in certain ways. A dog that had little or no tendency to jump through hoops has, as a result of certain experiences, a greater tendency to do so. A child who could not name two letters now recites the entire alphabet flawlessly. If these changes in behavior do not persist following training, then we say forgetting has occurred.

This approach focuses on the behaving organism and its relation to events in its past and current environments. There is no need to compare the organism to a wax tablet, a computer, or some other device. Memory requires a metaphor; living organisms do not. Our concern is not with metaphors, then, but with understanding why the effects of experience fade with time. Since our focus is on forgetting, we had better start with a definition.

Defining Forgetting

Learning is a marvelous invention of natural selection, but it is far from perfect. The changes in behavior that we call learning are often lost, at least partially, after the learning experiences end. It is this loss to which we refer when we speak of forgetting. Thus, **forgetting** can be defined as deterioration in learned behavior following a period without practice.

Not all deterioration in learned behavior following a period without practice is attributed to forgetting. If a dog is trained to jump through hoops when it is one year old, and is retested following 12 years without practice, the deterioration in performance may have more to do with arthritic joints than with forgetting. Similarly, a person who learns to recite the alphabet may lose that ability as a result of a stroke. For our purposes, then, forgetting refers to changes in behavior that are not due to aging, injury, or disease.[1]

> **Query:**   Forgetting is the deterioration in performance following
>
> _____.

In considering forgetting, it is important to realize that we are concerned here with deterioration in behavior, not the deterioration of a neurological record of experience. As noted in Chapter 2, learning experiences presumably produce some sort of physical (anatomical and/or chemical) change in the organism. Presumably forgetting is accompa-

---

[1] This limitation is arbitrary, of course. One could argue that the inability to perform some previously learned behavior is the essence of forgetting, regardless of why this occurs. The reason for our narrow focus is to leave physiology to the physiologists and concentrate on how experience affects behavior.

nied by physical changes as well. But the nature of the physical changes associated with learning and forgetting are the province of physiology and neuroscience, not learning.[2] Our subject matter is the effects of experience on *behavior*. When we ask whether an individual has forgotten something, then, we are asking whether the changes in behavior produced by experience persist. "Have you forgotten how to ride a bicycle?" is another way of saying, "Can you still ride a bicycle?" "Do you remember the algebra you learned in high school?" is a way of asking, "Can you solve the algebra problems you could solve in high school?" "Do you remember where you parked the car?" means, "Can you find the car?" or, "Can you direct me to the car?" "Do you remember your high school graduation?" means, "Can you describe your high school graduation?"[3]

These particular examples imply that forgetting means a decline in the probability of some behavior, but this is not always the case. For example, a rat that has learned to press a lever for food may, as a result of discrimination training, learn not to press the lever when a light is on. If we remove the rat from the cage and return it a month later, we may find that it presses the lever whether the light is on or not. If so, the rat has forgotten the discrimination learned earlier. Similarly, a stimulus associated with an aversive event will suppress ongoing behavior, a phenomenon called conditioned suppression (see Chapter 4). If, after the training ends, conditioned suppression no longer occurs, or is less pronounced, then forgetting has occurred (Hammond & Maser, 1970). In these instances, forgetting means the reappearance of a behavior.

REVIEW   Forgetting is the deterioration of learned behavior after training ends. Forgetting usually involves a decrease in the strength of a behavior, but under certain circumstances, it can mean an increase in strength. Forgetting is typically incomplete. An organism may fail to perform in exactly the same way it did at the conclusion of training, yet some evidence of learning may linger. Thus, there are degrees of forgetting. There are several ways that the degree of forgetting can be measured, and we consider some of them now.

---

[2]Some cognitive psychologists define forgetting as changes in "cognitive structure." But, again, we will leave that topic to the cognitive psychologists.

[3]Or, perhaps, "Can you visualize a scene from your high school graduation?" The trouble with this interpretation is that it is impossible to measure (at least directly) what a person visualizes. We can, however, ask a person to describe a scene.

Measuring Forgetting

Forgetting, like learning, occurs in time. In measuring forgetting, researchers usually observe behavior after a period during which the learned behavior is not performed. After this period, usually called a **retention interval**, they test in various ways for evidence that the learned behavior is still intact.[4]

In **free recall**, the organism is given the opportunity to perform a previously learned behavior following a retention interval. An example is the student who is required to learn a poem by heart and then is asked to recite it again after a period of time. Or you might have someone learn a finger maze (a small maze that is "run" with a finger or stylus) and then have him run the maze after a period without practice. Forgetting is the deterioration in performance over the retention interval.[5]

The free recall method can also be used to study animal forgetting. A pigeon may learn to peck a disk for food. After training, the bird is removed from the experimental chamber and returned to its home cage. A month passes, during which time the bird has no opportunity to obtain food by pecking on a disk. After the retention interval, the bird is returned to the training cage. If it behaves as it did in the last training session, no forgetting has occurred.

The ability of animals to retain what they learn is often impressive. In one study, John Donahoe and David Marrs (1982) trained a pigeon to peck a disk when it was green, but not when it was red. They found that the bird continued to discriminate correctly after a retention interval of 12 years.

Although free recall is what most of us think of when we think of measuring forgetting, it is sometimes a rather crude yardstick. The student who cannot recall a French word he studied earlier has not necessarily forgotten everything about the missing word. He may be able to say that the word has three syllables, that the emphasis is on the middle syllable, that the word starts with the letter *f*, that it means window. Clearly the effects of the learning experience have not been entirely lost, but the free recall method does not recognize this fact.

A variation of the free recall technique is sometimes used to get at these more subtle remnants of learning. Known as **prompted** or **cued recall**, it consists of presenting hints, or prompts, to increase the likelihood that the behavior will be produced. A person who has studied a list of

---

[4]So-called because the object is to determine how much has been "retained"—i.e., not forgotten.

[5]Occasionally, performance is better after the retention interval than before, a phenomenon called reminiscence. See the box *Reminiscence and the State of Learning.*

French words, for example, may be given a list of anagrams of the words; the participant's task would then be to unscramble the letters. Failure to do so indicates forgetting. It's also possible to provide a series of prompts and measure the degree of forgetting by the number of prompts required to produce the behavior. You might, for instance, give a person the first letter of a French word learned earlier. If she does not answer correctly, you provide the second letter. If that does not prompt the correct word, you provide the third letter, and so on until the word is recalled.

Animal forgetting can also be studied with prompted recall. A chimp will learn to get fruit from a vending machine by inserting tokens into a slot (Cowles, 1937). If it fails to do so after a retention interval, we might prompt the behavior by offering the chimp a token. If the animal uses it correctly, then the effects of the previous learning experience have not been completely lost.

Forgetting can be measured by reinstating the original training procedure. This **relearning method** assumes that the less training required to reach the previous level of performance, the less forgetting has occurred. There is usually a savings compared to the original training program, so this technique is also called the **savings method**. Hermann Ebbinghaus (1885), the German psychologist who conducted the world's first experiments on forgetting, used the relearning method. He memorized lists of nonsense syllables, such as ZAK, KYL, and BOF, until he could produce the list twice without error. Then, after a retention interval, he relearned the list. If it took fewer trials to learn the list the second time, this savings provided a measure of forgetting. The greater the savings, the less the forgetting.

Relearning can be used to study forgetting in animals. If a rat takes 30 trials to learn to run a maze without errors, and if it takes the rat 20 trials to reach that same criterion after a retention interval, then there has been a savings of 10 trials. If another rat has a savings of 15 trials, this second rat has forgotten less.

Query: The relearning method is also called the

_____ method.

Another way of measuring forgetting is called **recognition**. In this case, the participant has only to identify the material previously learned. Typically this is done by presenting the participant with the original learning materials as well as some new material. The person might be shown a list of French words and be asked to say which ones were on a list learned earlier.

The Myth of Permanent Memory

Most people apparently believe that everything they learn is permanently stored away (Loftus & Loftus, 1980). They may not be able to retrieve a memory, the theory goes, but it is there, stored in the brain, ready to be brought to consciousness. While this view of learning is probably ancient, I believe its current popularity may be attributed largely to the work of two people: Sigmund Freud and Wilder Penfield.

Freud (1914) believed that nothing is ever really forgotten. Experiences, he theorized, are permanently recorded in the "mental apparatus." (Freud was never entirely clear about whether "mental apparatus" referred to the brain or to an immaterial mind.) According to this view, if recalling an experience arouses anxiety, it might be repressed—i.e., consigned to the unconscious. However, repressed memories might be brought into consciousness through hypnosis, free association, or, in disguised form, in dreams. Freud did not do experimental research on memory; his evidence was the anecdote and the case study.

Wilder Penfield (1955, 1975) was a neurosurgeon who did pioneer work in the surgical treatment of epilepsy. In order to identify the tissues involved in seizures, Penfield would apply a weak electric current to the surface of the brain. The patient, who was necessarily conscious at this stage, would relate whatever sensations this stimulation triggered. In the course of this work, Penfield found that people often seemed to relive past experiences. For instance, stimulation of an area of the cortex caused one young man to say that he was sitting at a baseball game in a small town and watching a little boy crawl under the fence to watch the game. Another patient was in a concert hall

Another kind of recognition procedure is often used to study forgetting in animals, particularly pigeons. The procedure is called **delayed matching to sample**, or **DMTS** (Blough, 1959). DMTS is similar to the matching to sample procedure introduced in Chapter 9, except that the animal is prevented from performing following presentation of the sample—the stimulus to be "matched." In a typical experiment, a pigeon is presented with a row of three disks. The middle disk is illuminated for a brief period by either a yellow or a blue light. After this, the two disks on either side are illuminated, one with a yellow light, the other with a blue one. If the bird pecks the disk that matches the sample (the middle disk), it receives food. Once the bird has learned to match the sample, the experimenter introduces a delay between the offset of the sample and

listening to an orchestra. Still another heard a mother calling her child. Penfield found that stimulation of a specific area reliably produced a specific experience. In one case, Penfield stimulated the same point 30 times; each time he did so the patient heard a melody being played. "All these were unimportant events," Penfield (1975) would later write, "but recalled with complete detail" (p. 22).

Freud's anecdotal and case study evidence suggested to him that experiences are permanently recorded. Penfield's work seemed to provide proof for Freud's theory: Experiences were stored in the brain where they might be reactivated by the proper stimulation. The idea that a permanent record of experiences is stored away predates Freud and Penfield, but I believe it was their work that convinced the general public that the idea was an established fact.

It is *not* an established fact. Penfield's work, fascinating though it is, does not offer strong support for the permanence of memory. For one thing, very few of Penfield's patients reported experiencing events when stimulated. Another problem is that the stimulated experiences included events that *had never occurred*, and therefore could not have been memories. On reviewing Penfield's work, Ulric Neisser, a prominent cognitive psychologist, concluded that "Penfield's work tells us nothing new about memory" (Neisser, 1967: quoted in Loftus, 1980, p. 53).

Experiences are not recorded and then played back later, like the messages on a telephone answering machine. Rather, experience changes us, so that we behave differently. The durability of those changes in behavior depends on a number of variables, but none can be said to be literally permanent.

the illumination of the two alternative disks. The bird is asked to recognize the training stimulus; failure to do so indicates forgetting. DMTS can, of course, be used to measure forgetting in humans, but it is more often used in animal research.

Another measure of forgetting that is often used with animals is the **extinction method**. Two rats might be trained to press a lever, after which the behavior is put on extinction. In one case there is no delay between training and extinction; in the other case, the rat is removed from the chamber for a time, and then returned to the training chamber for the extinction procedure. How fast does the behavior extinguish in these two situations? If extinction proceeds more rapidly after the retention interval, forgetting has occurred.

Forgetting may also be measured as a flattening of a generalization gradient, a method sometimes called **gradient degradation**. To the extent that training establishes stimulus control, any decline in the steepness of the generalization gradient indicates forgetting. For example, a pigeon may be trained to peck a disk that is a medium yellow. If, immediately after training, the bird is tested with disks that vary from dark yellow to very pale yellow, we would expect to see a steep generalization gradient, with the highest rate of pecking at the disk when it is medium yellow. If the animal is again tested a month later, it might have a greater tendency to peck disks that are lighter or darker than the training disk. This will yield a flatter generalization gradient. This degradation of the gradient provides a measure of forgetting (Thomas, 1981).

It is sometimes suggested that forgetting can be measured without measuring performance. According to this argument, if we ask someone, "Do you remember how to ski?" the person does not need to ski in order to convince us that he remembers something about skiing; he can describe how one skis. This is true enough, but the argument confuses two different skills. One skill is skiing; the other skill is talking about skiing. A person may be able to describe what one does in skiing, yet be unable to ski. Similarly, a person who spent years skiing may be able to ski, yet be unable to describe the process any better than a novice. The only way deterioration in skiing can be measured is to observe skiing. The only way to evaluate the deterioration of talking about skiing is to observe talking about skiing. In each case, forgetting is measured by observing performance.

REVIEW Forgetting may be measured in various ways, including free recall, prompted recall, recognition (including delayed matching to sample), relearning (or savings), and the extinction method. There are other ways of measuring forgetting, mainly variations on the methods just described. Together these methods have allowed researchers to tackle the problem of forgetting. Their research has provided considerable insight into why we forget.

Variables in Forgetting

A famous musician once said that if he went without practicing the piano for one day, only he knew it; if he skipped two days, only he and his tutor knew it; if he skipped three days, everyone knew it. He was talking about forgetting. He recognized that even after mastering a skill at a very high level, that mastery deteriorates if the skill is neglected. But why?

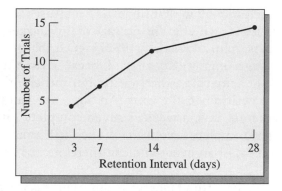

Figure 11-1 *Retention interval and forgetting. Average number of trials required to relearn a response increased with the length of the retention interval. (After Gagné, 1941.)*

Very likely the musician believed that the passage of time since his last "training session" accounted for forgetting. This was the prevailing view of forgetting in his day, and it remains the dominant explanation outside the researcher's laboratory. This view assumes that learning means storing up records of experience, and remembering means activating those records. With the passage of time, the theory goes, the record decays and we forget.

There is a strong relationship between the length of the retention interval and forgetting. Ebbinghaus (1885) found, for instance, that it took him longer to relearn lists of nonsense syllables after a long retention interval than after a short one. More carefully designed research with animals has shown much the same thing. R. M. Gagné (1941) trained rats to run down an alley to find food. After the training, Gagné tested the rats, using the relearning method. Some rats relearned after an interval of 3 days, others after 7 days, 14 days, and 28 days. The results showed clearly that the longer the interval between training and relearning, the greater the deterioration in performance (see Figure 11-1).

In another study, Henry Gleitman and J. W. Bernheim (1963) trained rats to press a lever on an FI schedule and then removed the animals from the training cage for either 24 hours or 24 days. The cumulative records from these sessions showed that there was less of the scalloping associated with FI schedules (see Chapter 10) after the longer interval. After a period of 24 hours, rats were likely to pause following reinforcement; after a period of 24 days, they continued to press the lever. This failure to pause after reinforcement indicated greater forgetting with the longer retention interval.

Such studies clearly show that forgetting increases with the passage of time. The question is whether the passage of time *accounts for* the forgetting that occurs. John McGeoch (1932) argued that it did not. Time cannot explain forgetting, McGeoch said, because time itself is not an event. Time is not something that occurs but rather an invention for talking about the occurrence of events. An hour, for example, is 1/24 of earth's rotation on its axis; a week is seven complete rotations of the earth; a year is one complete revolution of the earth around the sun, and so on. Time itself is not an event and can therefore not be said to cause other events.

Thus, the image on a film fades with time, but it is the action of sunlight, not time, that causes the fading. People develop illnesses over time, but it is bacteria and viruses and toxins that cause disease, not time. Learning occurs in time, but it is certain kinds of experiences, and not time, that produce learning. Likewise, forgetting occurs in time, but it is not time that causes forgetting. "Time, in and of itself," wrote McGeoch, "does nothing" (p. 359).

To explain forgetting, then, we must identify the events that account for its occurrence.[6] Some of those events have been identified, and we may now turn our attention to them.

Degree of Learning

The better something is learned, the less likely it is to be forgotten.[7] Ebbinghaus (1885) demonstrated this long ago. He found a systematic correlation between the number of learning trials and the amount of forgetting. When he practiced a list eight times, for example, the next day he could recall very little; when he practiced a list 64 times, the next day his recall was nearly perfect.

Ebbinghaus demonstrated that learning apparently continues even after we seem to have achieved mastery. William Krueger (1929) performed a famous study that showed just how powerful such **overlearning** can be. He asked adults to learn three lists of words, with each list containing 12 one-syllable nouns. He presented the words one at a time at the rate of

---

[6]As noted earlier, forgetting is probably accompanied by some deterioration of the anatomical and/or chemical changes in the nervous system. But these changes are not explained by the passage of time any more than are the changes in behavior.

[7]Please note that the degree of learning is not necessarily indicated by the degree of confidence a person has in his or her recall. During the United States Senate investigations of the Watergate scandal of the 1970s, a key witness was Nixon's legal adviser, John Dean. Dean provided hours of detailed testimony about conversations that he seemed to recall with photographic memory. But a comparison of Dean's testimony with recorded conversations shows that Dean's recollections were far from accurate: Though apparently confident in his recollections, he "remembered" things that never happened and forgot things that had (Belli et al., 1997).

one word every 2 seconds. After going through the list the first time, the participant's task was to say each word before it was presented.

Training differed for each of the three lists. The participants worked at one list until they produced all 12 words correctly and then stopped. On another list, they continued working beyond this level; this time they went through the list half again as many times as it took to reach one errorless trial. On the third list, the participants went through twice as many trials as it took to learn the list. Suppose, for example, that a given participant took 14 trials to get all 12 words correct on each of the three lists. On one of the lists, he would be allowed to quit (zero overlearning); on another he would be asked to do seven more trials (50% overlearning); and on the third he would be asked to do another 14 trials (100% overlearning). After this initial training, Krueger had his participants relearn the lists. Some participants relearned after an interval of only 1 day; others relearned after 2, 4, 7, 14, or 28 days.

The results clearly showed that the participants recalled more words from the lists they had overlearned. Moreover, the greater the amount of overlearning, the less they forgot. One hundred percent overlearning paid higher dividends than 50% overlearning, but the difference was not as great as that between no overlearning and 50% overlearning. This suggests that there is a point of diminishing returns in overlearning (for more on this, see Underwood, 1957).

Ebbinghaus and Krueger measured the degree of learning in terms of the number of trials required for accurate performance. In recent years, some researchers have measured degree of learning in terms of the number of correct responses per minute. This measure is referred to as *fluency* (Binder et al., 1990; see also Chapter 2).

Suppose that two students are learning the English synonyms for a list of German words. They might do this by going through a series of flash cards, turning each card over as they go to see whether each answer is correct. Suppose that after 10 trials, both students can go through a stack of 20 cards without error in 1 minute. This is their degree of fluency. One student stops at this point, while the other continues practicing until she can go through those 20 cards in 30 seconds without error. Her rate of fluency is now twice that of her classmate. There is evidence that higher rates of fluency produce lower rates of forgetting (Johnson & Layng, 1992).

The benefits of overlearning may endure well beyond the final exam. Harry Bahrick (1984) found that a good indication of how well a person remembered the Spanish he or she studied 20, 30, or even 50 years earlier was how thoroughly he or she had learned Spanish. People who had studied Spanish for only a year and earned a grade of C remembered little of what they once knew. Those who had studied Spanish for 3 years and earned A's did very well when tested, even 50 years later. The difference was not due to differences in the opportunity to practice the language over the years, but to how well the language was learned originally. Findings of this sort have obvious implications for students who want to retain what they learn after the graduation ceremony.

Prior Learning

Forgetting occurs rapidly when we learn unrelated words, random digits, and nonsense syllables. More meaningful material is, however, easier to hold onto.

K. Anders Ericsson and John Karat (reported in Ericsson & Chase, 1982) demonstrated this with sentences from stories by John Steinbeck. They read the words in these sentences, one word per second, as though they were reading digits or nonsense syllables. Sometimes the words were in their correct order, sometimes the words were presented randomly. Not surprisingly, the original sentences were recalled far better than the same words in scrambled order. Most people could recall only about six words correctly when the words were in scrambled order. But people could recall complete sentences of 12 or 14 words when presented in their Steinbeckian splendor. Two of the 20 participants could even recall this 28-word sentence: "She brushed a cloud of hair out of her eyes with the back of her glove and left a smudge of earth on her cheek in doing it."

To say that the rate of forgetting varies with the meaningfulness of the material learned raises a question: What determines whether something is meaningful? We may get an idea by asking ourselves what would happen if we repeated the Ericsson and Karat study with people who did not speak a word of English. It is likely that in this case there would be little difference in recall between the original sentences and a random arrangement of words. Thus, when people speak of the meaningfulness of what is learned, they are really talking about the importance of prior learning.

We can see the benefit of previous learning in studies of forgetting and expertise. In one study, A. de Groot (1966) arranged pieces on a chess board as though a game were in progress. He allowed chess players to study the boards for 5 seconds and then asked them to reproduce the arrangement of pieces on a cleared board. Some of de Groot's participants were chess masters while others were members of a chess club. When he compared the two kinds of players, he found that the chess masters were right 90% of the time; club players were right only 40% of the time.

De Groot's data argue for the influence of previous learning on forgetting. But there is another possibility: Perhaps chess masters simply forget less than other people. To test this hypothesis, William Chase and Herbert Simon (1973) arranged chess pieces on the board in a random fashion and then showed it to chess masters and ordinary players. If the chess masters had fantastic ability to recall, the arrangement of pieces would make no difference; the experts would still come out on top. But Chase and Simon found that the chess masters' superb recall disappeared. In fact, under these conditions, they could recall no better than ordinary players. Their spectacular memories, it turns out, apply only when the chess pieces are placed on the board in "patterns that have become familiar with years of practice" (Ericsson & Chase, 1982, p. 608). Other studies show that past learning plays an important role in recall for contract bridge (Charness, 1979), circuit diagrams (Egan & Schwartz, 1979), and architectural drawings (Akin, 1983).

It is clear, then, that previous learning can reduce forgetting. Under some circumstances, however, old learning can interfere with recall, a phenomenon called **proactive interference**.[8]

Proactive interference is often studied in people by means of **paired associate learning**, a technique invented by Mary Calkins near the end of the 19th century (Calkins, 1894, 1896; see Madigan & O'Hara, 1992). Typically, the object is for the person to learn a list of word pairs, such as *hungry-beautiful,* so that when given the first word (*hungry*), the participant produces the second (*beautiful*). Usually, the list is taught by repeatedly presenting the participant with the first word in each pair, asking for the word that goes with it, and then presenting the correct word.

Query: What sort of learning procedure (Pavlovian, operant,

observational) is paired associate learning?

Typically in these studies all participants learn an A-C list (e.g., hungry-beautiful), but some participants first learn an A-B list (e.g., hungry-fortunate). Then, after a period of time without practice, all participants try to recall the A-C list. Any difference between the two groups in recall can be attributed to learning the A-B list. These studies reliably show that learning the A-B list interferes with recall of items later learned on the A-C list. Moreover, the more lists one learns before the test (A-C) list, the more interference there will be (Underwood, 1957; see Figure 11-2).

---

[8]Also sometimes referred to as proactive inhibition.

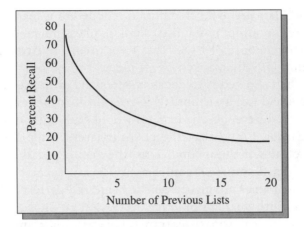

Figure 11-2 *Interference and forgetting. Underwood plotted data from a number of studies and found that forgetting increased with the number of previously learned lists. (After Underwood, 1957.)*

Interference from previous learning accounts for forgetting in more complicated situations. Consider, for example, the findings of a classic study by the famous British psychologist, Sir Frederick Bartlett. Bartlett (1932) had people read a Native American folktale called *The War of the Ghosts*. Although the story runs well under 400 words, it is, by contemporary Western standards, disjointed and confusing. Bartlett had people read the story through twice and then, 15 minutes later, reproduce the story as accurately as they could. Bartlett also had the participants recall the story on other occasions over the coming weeks and months "as opportunity offered." When Bartlett examined the successive recollections, he found that the story became simpler, more coherent, and more modern. This finding can be understood partly in terms of proactive interference: Previous learning about how stories are constructed interfered with recalling a different sort of story.

Social psychologists Jerome Levine and Gardner Murphy (1943) studied the effects of proactive interference in a different way. They had college students read a passage and then, 15 minutes later, reproduce it as accurately as possible. The students then read a second passage and, 15 minutes later, tried to reproduce it. The students read and attempted to reproduce the two passages each week for 4 weeks. Both passages were on what was then a very controversial topic: communism. One of the passages expressed anti-communist sentiments; the other was favorable to communism. Some of the students were strongly disposed toward communism while others were strongly opposed to it. The researchers were interested in whether these personal inclinations would affect recollection.

They did. The results clearly showed that students who were pro-communist forgot more of the anti-communist passage, while students who were anti-communist forgot more of the pro-communist passage.

Such findings are usually interpreted in terms of the effects of attitude or belief on forgetting. But since no one is born with particular inclinations concerning communism (or capitalism, fascism, democracy, homosexuality, or other topics), we have to assume that such views are learned. Thus, studies showing that attitudes affect recall are really studies of proactive interference.

Prior learning can have a profound effect on recall; so, we shall now see, can subsequent learning.

Subsequent Learning

In a classic study by John Jenkins and Karl Dallenbach (1924), two college students learned lists of 10 nonsense syllables. The researchers tested the students for forgetting after 1, 2, 4, or 8 hours of either sleep or wakefulness. The results showed that they forgot less after a period of sleep than after a similar interval of activity. Indeed, after two hours of sleep, additional time had no effect on recall (see Figure 11-3).

Other studies showed that periods of inactivity produce less forgetting than comparable periods of greater activity. In one study, immobilized cockroaches forgot less than those allowed to move about (Minami & Dallenbach, 1946).

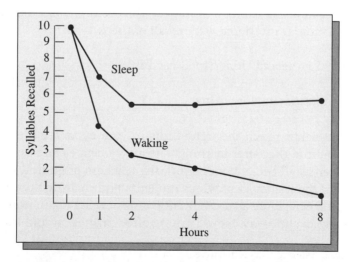

Figure 11-3 *Forgetting and sleep. Average number of syllables recalled by one student after intervals of sleep and waking. (After Jenkins and Dallenbach, 1924.)*

These and similar studies suggest that forgetting is partly due to learning. As Jenkins and Dallenbach (1924) put it, forgetting is "a matter of interference, inhibition, or obliteration of the old by the new" (p. 612). Or, as another psychologist phrases it, "We forget because we keep on learning" (Gleitman, 1971, p. 20).

When what we learn interferes with our ability to recall earlier learning, the phenomenon is called **retroactive interference**.[9] New learning reaches into the past, as it were, to interfere with earlier learning.

Like proactive interference, retroactive interference is often studied by having people learn two or more lists of paired associates. First, the A-B list is learned to a given criterion or for a given number of trials. Then, the A-C list is learned. Finally, the participant's ability to recall the A-B list is measured. Evidence of forgetting on the A-B list can be attributed to interference from learning the A-C list. If, for example, a person forgets the A-B pair, *hungry-beautiful*, this may be because of having learned the A-C pair, *hungry-virtuous*.

Benton Underwood and his colleagues did a number of experiments with paired associates to study the interference effects of learning. In one experiment, he and Leland Thune (Thune & Underwood, 1943) had college students learn lists of 10 paired associates made up of adjectives. Each participant learned an A-B list, then relearned the list after a 20-minute delay. During the delay period, some students just rested, while others had from 2 to 20 trials on an A-C list. Notice that the time lapse was the same for all participants; the difference was in the learning that took place during the retention interval. The results showed that learning the A-C list interfered with recall of the A-B list. Moreover, the better the A-C list had been learned, the more it interfered with recall of the A-B list.

Query: Thune and Underwood used the _____

method of studying forgetting.

You experience much the same thing in your everyday life when, for example, you find that after learning your new license plate number, you can no longer recall the old one. Similarly, teachers often find it difficult to remember the names of previous students after learning the names of new students. And when an accountant learns new tax regulations, the old regulations may slip away. New learning often pushes out old learning.[10]

---

[9]Also sometimes referred to as retroactive inhibition.

[10]Merely imagining an event is sometimes enough to convince a person that the event took place, a phenomenon called *imagination inflation* (Garry & Polaschek, 2000; Garry et al., 1996). Because an experience in the present interferes with recollections about the past, imagination inflation would seem to be an example of retroactive interference.

Interference from subsequent and prior learning is an important factor in forgetting. A related factor is the context in which learning and recall occur.

Context

McGeoch (1932) suggested that another important variable in forgetting was the context in which learning occurred. The idea is that learning inevitably occurs within a particular context—that is, in the presence of a given pattern of stimuli. These stimuli then act as cues that serve to evoke behavior. If, later on, these cues are absent, performance suffers. This is sometimes called **cue-dependent forgetting.**[11]

Consider the case of a person who learns a list of words in the morning and then is tested on those words in the afternoon. Both sessions occur in a research cubicle with a chair, two tables, and a window; the walls are painted a uniform off-white and there are no decorations. The two environments seem identical, but wait: In the morning the window looked out on a foggy landscape, but by afternoon the sun was shining; the researcher was rather abrupt and sour in the morning, but by afternoon he was all smiles; in the morning, the heating system blew warm air on the participant from a heat vent; by afternoon it was warm enough that the heat was off. Can such insignificant differences in the two situations affect forgetting?

A number of experiments suggest that they can. In one study, Charles Perkins and Robert Weyant (1958) trained rats to run a maze. Some rats learned to run a black maze; others learned to run a white maze. The mazes were in all other respects identical. After a retention interval of only 1 minute, the experimenters put the rats back into the mazes. This time, however, there was a difference. Some of the rats that had learned in a white maze were tested in a black one, and some of those that had learned in a black maze were tested in a white one. There was little evidence of forgetting when the animals ran the same maze they had been trained in, but performance suffered when the maze was a different color from the maze used during training.

The same sorts of effects have been demonstrated with people. Joel Greenspoon and R. Ranyard (1957) had students learn lists of words under two different conditions, standing up or sitting down. After this, the students recalled the lists as well as they could. Some tried remembering while standing up, others while sitting down. The results showed that

---

[11]The phenomenon can be likened to stimulus control: A behavior occurs in the presence of certain stimuli, but not in their absence. In cue-dependent forgetting, the cues that were present during training are absent at a later time. In demonstrations of stimulus control, the interval between the two situations (S⁺ and S⁻) is typically extremely short; in demonstrations of cue-dependent forgetting, the interval is typically much longer.

Reminiscence and the State of Learning

Forgetting is usually assumed to occur at a decelerating rate, with the greatest amount of deterioration in performance occurring soon after training ends, and with less and less deterioration occurring as time passes. In general, this is the case. However, performance sometimes improves with the passage of time, a phenomenon called **reminiscence**.

The first study of reminiscence was probably done by Leon Kamin (1957). He gave rats avoidance training, but discontinued training before the skill was thoroughly mastered. He tested the rats immediately after training and at various subsequent intervals. The results showed that the rats were at their best immediately after training—as expected—after which their performance declined. Surprisingly, however, Kamin discovered that the rats' performance improved again, matching their previous best performance 24 hours after training ended.

Why should performance deteriorate, then improve? And why should the improvement occur, as it often does, 24 hours after training ends?

We have seen that performance after training varies depending on the degree to which the testing situation resembles the training situation. In other words, one result of training is inevitably that the stimuli present during training acquire a certain degree of stimulus control over the behavior. But in the experiments showing reminiscence, testing is done under the same conditions. What cues could be available 24 hours after training that are not available, say, 12 hours after training?

The most likely explanation seems to be the physiological state of the organism. Physiological conditions, such as those associated with hunger, fatigue, and alertness, vary in a rhythmic fashion over the course of a day. An hour after training, hormone levels, for example, may be measurably different from levels present immediately after training. Twelve hours after training those

students performed better when tested under conditions similar to those under which they had learned. Those who had learned the lists standing up remembered them best when standing up; those who had learned the lists while sitting down remembered them best while sitting down.

Duncan Godden and Alan Baddeley (1975) performed another imaginative study on the effects of context. In this study, adults learned a list of words. Some of them learned the list on dry land; others learned the list while under water! After training, the participants tried to recall the list. The experimenters tested some participants under the same condi-

levels may be very different. After a 24-hour period, however, the animal's physiology has come full circle. Reminiscence occurs, then, when the physiological conditions present during testing resemble those during training. Apparently, the behavior is under the stimulus control of the learner's physiological state.

This idea is supported by experimental research. In one study, Donald Overton (1964) gave rats a tranquilizing drug and then taught them to run a simple T-maze. Later, when the effects of the drug had worn off, Overton tested the rats and found that they appeared to have forgotten their earlier learning. There is nothing very startling about this; we might easily believe that the drug interfered in some way with the brain's functioning. But Overton took one more step. He tranquilized the rats again and put them back into the maze. This time they performed well! The earlier forgetting was due to a change in the animal's internal state. Thus, behavior that is learned during a particular physiological state is lost when that state passes, a phenomenon now called **state-dependent learning** (see also Girden & Culler, 1937; see Ho et al., 1978, for a review).

Anecdotes abound of people who show state dependent learning as the result of alcoholic intoxication. A person hides his car keys while sober and then cannot find them after drinking; when he sobers up, he knows right where to look. Another person stashes several bottles of whisky in various hiding places while drunk. Then when he is sober and wants a drink, he cannot recall where the bottles are. If he manages to get drunk, he suddenly remembers where the bottles are hidden.

It appears, then, that the context for learning includes the state of the learner, as well as the state of the learner's surroundings.

tions under which they learned, but they tested others under the opposite conditions. For example, some students who learned words on dry land tried to recall those words under water. The results showed that recall suffered when the testing situation was different from the training situation.

The influence of context on recall can be illustrated from everyday experience. For instance, you may know the name of the person who sits next to you in history class, yet find you are unable to think of it when you run into him in a shopping mall. You may learn a speech to perfection at home, only to stumble over it when in front of an audience. And most of us have had the experience of studying until we have the material "down cold," and then "blank out" in the classroom. Such anecdotes are consistent with studies showing that changes in context contribute to forgetting. Even subtle differences in the environment can have important effects on recall.

REVIEW   Forgetting increases with the length of the retention interval, but the passage of time is not itself a cause of forgetting. The rate of forgetting is determined by the amount of training, retroactive interference, proactive interference, and changes in context (including the internal state of the organism). Other variables, such as the amount of material to be learned (Ebbinghaus, 1885), the nature of the recall test (Loftus, 1975; Postman & Rau, 1957), and instructions (Epstein, 1972) also affect forgetting. Understanding forgetting and why it occurs has interested learning researchers partly because of its practical applications.

Applied Research on Forgetting

Foraging

We have seen again and again that learning has tremendous survival value. Like camouflage, flying, and razor-sharp fangs, learning ability evolved because it helped individuals survive and reproduce. Since all organisms must eat to survive, let us examine the role of forgetting—or of *not* forgetting—in the search for food.

In the wild, the availability of food is variable. In particular, food crops tend to be abundant at certain times and scarce at others. One way around the problem is to eat as much as possible when food is plentiful, and then hibernate or sleep a great deal when food is in short supply. Another approach is to migrate when food supplies dwindle to areas where food is more plentiful. A third tactic that works well for a species, although it lacks appeal for the individual, is to have a short life cycle. Many insects are born in the spring, when food becomes available, and die in the fall, when the weather turns cold and food supplies dry up. Many animals, including humans, have taken a fourth course: They reduce the disparity in food supply by storing up excess food when it is plentiful and drawing on these caches when food runs short.

Obviously, people can remember where they cached food for later consumption. Can other animals do so? The popular belief seems to be that most animals, including birds and mammals, forget rapidly. In some circumstances they do. Certain laboratory studies have shown, for example, that pigeons can recall a brief sequence of key pecks only a matter of seconds (Parker, 1984; Shimp, 1976). However, foraging studies suggest that the forgetting curve may be far less steep when what is learned is important to survival.

The Clark's nutcracker, a year-long resident of the American Rocky Mountains, is a case in point (Kamil & Balda, 1985, 1990a, 1990b). It feeds, not on nuts, but on pine seeds. Each bird needs about 10,000 seeds to see it through the winter, so it must set aside seeds and retrieve them later. The birds can store more than 30,000 seeds in over 6,000 caches. But how do they find the 2,000 caches they must locate to make it through the winter?

Kamil and Russell Balda (1990b) conducted an experiment in which nutcrackers stored seeds and were then allowed to recover them 1 week, 3 months, and 6 months later. There was some decline in the ability to find caches after prolonged periods, but even after 6 months the birds found seeds with a level of success that could not be attributed to chance. Kamil and Balda estimate that if nutcrackers relied on luck, their "hit rate" (the proportion of successful probes to all probes) would be only about 10%. In fact, their hit rate is several times that level.

Further evidence supports the notion that learning accounts for the nutcracker's ability to find caches. In one study, Stephen Vander Wall (1982) allowed two Clark's nutcrackers to store seeds in an aviary and later retrieve them. Each bird found many of its own caches, but seldom found caches of the other bird. This suggests that the birds did not find seeds simply by searching likely cache sites or by "sniffing out" the seeds.

Other studies show similar evidence of the ability of animals to retrieve caches after prolonged periods, including chipmunks (Vander Wall, 1991), gray squirrels (Jacobs & Liman, 1991), kangaroo rats (Jacobs, 1992), and monkeys (Menzel, 1991).

Eyewitness Testimony

Elizabeth Loftus has conducted a number of studies illustrating the malleability of memory or, to be more precise, the modifiability of performance after training. In her best-known work, Loftus and her colleagues would show college students short films of traffic accidents and then ask them questions about what they had witnessed. In a classic study (Loftus & Zanni, 1975), students watched a film in which a car makes a right-hand turn into a stream of traffic. The oncoming cars stop suddenly, and there is a five-car collision. After viewing the film, the students filled out a questionnaire about what they had seen. One question asked about a broken headlight. For some students, the question was, "Did you see the broken headlight?" For other students, the question was, "Did you see a broken headlight?" The only difference in the question was the article *the* or *a.*

The definite article *the* implies that the item was present whereas the indefinite article *a* implies only that the item might have been present. If I say to you, "Did you see the spaceship?" the implication is that there was a spaceship to be seen. If I say, "Did you see a spaceship?" the implication is that there might or might not have been a spaceship.

Loftus found that the answers she got depended on the way questions were phrased. Students were twice as likely to answer yes when the question included the definite article than when it included the indefinite article. There was no broken headlight in the film, yet students were far more likely to recall seeing it if they were asked about *the* broken headlight than if asked about *a* broken headlight.

In another of Loftus's classic studies (Loftus & Palmer, 1974), students watched films of traffic accidents and then answered questions about what they saw. One question asked the students to estimate how fast the cars were traveling, but again the question was phrased in different ways for different students. Some students were asked, "About how fast were the cars going when they hit each other?" For other students, the researchers replaced the word *hit* with *smashed, collided, bumped,* or *contacted.* The estimated speeds varied with the word used in the question, with *contacted* resulting in the lowest speeds and *smashed* producing the highest.

Loftus had the students return a week later. Without viewing the film again, they answered more questions about it. The critical question asked whether the students remembered seeing broken glass. In fact, the film showed no broken glass, but students who had been asked earlier about cars smashing together were now twice as likely to report seeing broken glass as were those who had been asked about cars hitting one another.

Query: Loftus found that use of the word _____

resulted in higher estimates of car speed than use of the word *hit.*

Police officers, although trained to observe potential crime scenes carefully, are apparently no better at recalling such events than are other people (Stanny & Johnson, 2000).

One thing that might help explain such findings is the participant's reinforcement history. For example, when you are asked, "Do you remember seeing the hat?" the definite article *the* indicates that there was a hat, and therefore that you might have seen it. (This means that reporting that you saw a hat might be reinforced.) On the other hand, if you are asked, "Do you remember seeing a hat?" the indefinite article *a* makes the existence of a hat less certain. Words such as *the* and *a* affect our behavior (our recall) because of our previous experiences with those words. A similar analysis can be applied to the differential effects of words such as *hit* and *smashed*. *Hit* is used when a relatively mild collision occurs, and *smashed* is used when a more severe collision occurs. Presumably this differential learning history means that the words are likely to produce different reports about observed events.

Research on the effects of hypnosis on recall offers support for this approach. In one study, Bill Putnam (reported in Loftus, 1980) showed people a videotape of an accident between a car and a bicycle. After viewing the tape, Putnam told some participants they would be hypnotized, and that this would enable them to see the accident again just as it had happened. Both groups of participants answered questions concerning the event, but those who were hypnotized did not do better. On the contrary, hypnotized participants made more mistakes and were more likely to be influenced by leading questions than those who were not hypnotized. Those who were hypnotized were more likely, for example, to report seeing a license plate if it was suggested that they saw it. No license plate was visible in the tape, yet one person not only "recalled" seeing it, but identified it as a California plate beginning with a "W" or "V." Studies of so-called hypnotic regression also reveal the plasticity of our efforts to recall events (Orne, 1951).

Research on eyewitness reports shows the impact of environmental events on the accuracy of reports about witnessed events. How accurately a person describes a witnessed event depends in part on how we ask about the event. This finding has obvious implications for juries and others weighing the merits of eyewitness testimony (Loftus, 1979).

REVIEW Learning plays a vital role in survival. Studies of foraging and the retrieval of food caches indicate that animals often have a remarkable talent for retaining learned behavior when the behavior is important to survival. The frailty of learning is indicated by studies of eyewitness testimony. Most people would like to reduce their tendency to forget. Let us consider that problem now.

Learning to Remember

History is replete with examples of people performing extraordinary feats of memory—which is to say, extraordinary feats of learning. Tradition has it that Homer was blind and earned his living by reciting the *Iliad* and *Odyssey*, which he had learned by heart. Cicero and other great poets of ancient times learned many long poems and recited them at banquets and other public functions. And it is said that Dame Judith Anderson, the actress, once performed *Hamlet*—*all* of *Hamlet*, not just one role.

How do they do it? There are, no doubt, genetic differences that affect recall. But it is increasingly clear that the ability to remember is to some extent a learned skill.

Animals have helped to prove this point. In one study, Michael D'Amato (1973) trained monkeys in a delayed matching to sample task. At first, the animals were successful only after very short delays, but they improved with practice. A monkey named Roscoe could respond correctly after an interval of only about 9 seconds at first, but after several years of practice he was able to answer correctly about 70% of the time after a delay of 9 minutes—a 6,000% improvement!

Ericsson and Chase (1982) demonstrated that ordinary humans can show similar improvement in recall. Their first participant was an average college student they called SF. SF showed no special skill at remembering but was eager to participate in the study. He worked with the researchers an hour at a time, 3 to 5 days a week, for almost 2 years, putting in a total of 230 hours. Training consisted of presenting SF with series of digits, one per second, which he then tried to reproduce. The experimenters gave no instruction or suggestions as to how SF was to learn the lists, and at first there was no improvement. He could reliably recall seven digits, but that was all. But after a time his "memory span" seemed to stretch. He could recall 9 digits, 12 digits, 15 digits. The previous record was 18 digits, a feat performed by a German mathematician named Ruckle. SF broke through that barrier and went on to set a new record of 82 digits![12]

Can we improve our ability to remember more useful kinds of things, such as mathematical formulas, French verbs, historical names and dates, lines of poetry, and where we parked our car? The answer is yes, but not without effort. There is, unfortunately, no way to exercise some "memory muscle" in the brain so that, ever after, we can easily recall anything we experience. But there are things we can do to reduce forgetting. Most of these "memory strategies" are really ways of improving learning. Let us consider a few of the more important of these.

---

[12]Ericsson and Chase (1982) replicated these results with another college student, called DD, who had reached a level of 75 digits as of the publication of their article.

Say All Fast Minute Each Day Shuffle

Almost everyone considers flash cards a bit old-fashioned today, but Ogden Lindsley believes that, old-fashioned or not, flash cards work—if they are used properly. The problem is that many students do not use them properly. How should they be used? Lindsley answers with an acronym to help you remember: SAFMEDS.

Say the answer before you turn a flash card over. Go through All of the cards, or as many as you can, as Fast as you can, in one Minute. Do this Each Day. After you go through the cards, Shuffle them.

This use of flash cards is very different from what most students do, and the differences are important. In particular, Lindsley puts great emphasis on the rate at which the student goes through the cards. Often students stare at a card for several seconds or even minutes, trying to recall the correct response. The one-minute time limit puts pressure on the student to work quickly. It also provides a convenient measure of fluency. Each time you make an error, you toss that card aside. At the end of a minute, you count the number of cards you got right. At first, you may get only 10 or 15 correct answers in a minute. But with practice you may get 40, 50, 60, or even more correct answers in a minute. This means you can easily assess your degree of learning, and the likelihood that you will forget.

Students are inclined to cram before exams, and this leads to rapid forgetting. Lindsley advises students to distribute their practice by using the cards at least once each day.

Finally, the sequence of cards can provide clues about the answers. The student may go through the cards without error but find he does not know the answers in a different context, such as a test. For this reason, it is important to shuffle the cards after each use.

Flash cards are out of favor with some educational experts these days, and have been for many years. Fortunately, this does not keep them from working!

Overlearn

We saw earlier that there is a strong, inverse relationship between the degree of learning and the rate of forgetting. The implication is clear: To forget less, study more.

Do not merely go through those German flash cards until you get all the words correct one time; keep at it until you reach a rate of fluency of, say, 30 cards a minute (see "Say All Fast Minute Each Day Shuffle"). To give a good speech, continue practicing even after you are satisfied with your performance. To play a sonata brilliantly at the concert, continue practicing after you get through it without errors. To do a good job in the play, go to all the rehearsals and spend extra time practicing your lines.

It should be noted that there is a point of diminishing returns from overlearning, with each additional trial resulting in a smaller improvement in recall later on. Nevertheless, overlearning does reduce forgetting.

Use Mnemonics

A **mnemonic** is any device for aiding recall. Typically, these devices involve learning cues that will later prompt the behavior to be recalled.

One common mnemonic is rhyme. Perhaps the best-known example is the little ditty we all memorize to help us remember the spelling of certain words: "Use i before e, except after c, and in sounding like a, as in *neighbor* and *weigh*." Another is the rhyme that reminds us how many days are in each month: "Thirty days hath September, April, June, and November . . ." In the film *My Fair Lady*, Professor Higgins has Eliza Doolittle learn pronunciation and enunciation by repeating the line "The rain in Spain falls mainly in the plain." If the plains of Spain *do* get most of the country's rain, this bit of rhyme would help us remember that fact.

Sometimes a mnemonic combines rhyme with a code in which, for example, the first letter of each word to be learned is the first letter of a word in the rhyme. Medical students learn the names of the 12 cranial nerves by memorizing the following doggerel:

> On Old Olympus's towering top,
> a Finn and German
> vault and hop.

The first letter of each word provides the first letter of each cranial nerve (optic, otolaryngeal, etc.), and this hint helps prompt the wanted terms.

Sometimes we can get by with a sentence that does not rhyme. To recall the names of the planets in our solar system in their relation to the sun (Mercury, Venus, Earth, Mars, Jupiter, Saturn, Uranus, Neptune, Pluto), we have only to remember that "Many very early maps just show us nine planets."

A similar mnemonic is the acronym, a set of letters, often forming a pronounceable set, each of which provides the first letter of a word. The North Atlantic Treaty Organization, for example, is NATO. The colors of the prism in their right order are remembered as Roy G. Biv, for red, orange, yellow, green, blue, indigo, and violet. And it is relatively easy to recall the names of the Great Lakes (Huron, Ontario, Michigan, Erie, and Superior) once you have learned that they spell HOMES.

Try a Mnemonic System

Books that offer to improve memory typically devote considerable space to what are called **mnemonic systems**. Professional entertainers who do "impossible" memory feats, such as learning the names of 30 or 40 people in an audience, typically use a mnemonic system.

One popular system is the **method of loci**. This system dates back to the times of the ancient Greeks. Legend has it that a roof collapsed during a party, killing everyone inside and disfiguring many of the revelers so badly that they could not be recognized. A poet named Simonides, who had left the building just before the roof fell in, was able to identify the bodies by recalling where each person had been sitting. Thus, the method of loci fixes each fact to be recalled to a particular location. Later, when it is necessary to recall that fact, we simply "go to" the location and "see" what is there.

Typically the locations used are familiar places. You might, for example, use the house in which you grew up, or a park where you regularly jog. Any place will do as long as it is sufficiently large to hold a number of items, and as long as you can "see" it fairly clearly when you close your eyes.

Here is how the method of loci works: Suppose you must remember to buy several items at the grocery store: bread, milk, eggs, radishes, lettuce, paper towels, and toothpaste. And suppose the locus that you use is a park you frequently visit. You begin an imaginary walk through the park. Along the path there are various landmarks, and at each landmark you place one of the things to be remembered. You come to a park bench and put the loaf of bread on the bench, perhaps enlarging the loaf so that it takes up the entire bench. You continue your walk and come to the second landmark, a huge oak tree with a cavity where a branch has long since fallen off. You put a carton of milk in the cavity, but extending out of it so that you will see it later on when you pass by. Just as you move on, you see that the carton is leaking, and milk is spilling down the side of the tree and onto the path. Next, you come to a small pond, where a family of ducks is often to be seen. You see a duck in harness pulling a barge laden with a carton of eggs. The rest of the items are distributed along the path in the same way.

When you arrive at the grocery store, you can recall the items on the list by walking through the park. As you approach the park bench, you see someone is taking a nap. When you get closer, you see that it is not a person at all, but a huge loaf of bread. You walk on and come to the huge oak. The walk is covered with some sort of white liquid. You look up and see a leaky milk carton in the tree's cavity. Farther along the trail you come to the pond . . . and so on.

Another popular mnemonic system is called the **peg word system**. In this approach, one memorizes a list of "pegs" on which items can later be hung, much as you hang a hat on a peg. The pegs are numbered and made easy to remember by making them rhyme with their numbers. For instance, the peg word for number one is usually the word *bun*; two is *shoe*; three is *tree*; four is *door*; five is *hive*; and so on.

Just about anything can be used as a peg, as long as it is a concrete object that can easily be imagined. (Abstract concepts such as beauty and truth do not work well as pegs because we cannot "see" them.) Now, if you want to learn a grocery list, you fasten each item to a peg. One is a bun. Let us imagine that it is a hot dog bun. You put the loaf of bread into the bun as you would a hot dog. Two is a shoe. It is an old fashioned shoe, the type in which Mother Hubbard lived. You put a carton of milk in the shoe. Three is a tree. You hang eggs from the tree like Christmas ornaments. And so on. To recall the list, you run through the numbers and look at the pegs.

Do such mnemonic systems really work? Yes, they do—if they are used regularly. The trouble is, people tend not to use them, at least not for long. Even memory researchers do not use them (Parks et al., 1986). The systems are not difficult to learn, but they probably have limited utility for most people. Memorizing a list of items to buy at the store is relatively easy, but it takes something of an expert to use the method of loci or the peg word system to recall the anatomical parts of a bird. It is even more difficult to use such a system to memorize abstract ideas, such as the tenets of Arthur Schopenhauer's philosophy.

Use Context Cues

We saw earlier that we remember better when cues present during learning are present during recall. It follows that we can improve performance by identifying cues that will be present during recall, and then learning in the presence of those cues.

Students typically do exactly the opposite: They study in their room, often while lying on a bed and eating some sort of snack. Or, if the weather is pleasant, they sit under a large tree or on a park bench. Often friends stop by and chat, and studying gets mixed up with socializing. When they take a test on what they have studied, they are typically in a classroom, seated in a rather uncomfortable chair, typically in the presence of a number of other students with whom they cannot converse. The two situations, learning and testing, are very different, and these differences in context no doubt account for some forgetting. Students find themselves unable to recall facts that they "knew cold" before they walked into the classroom.

The clear implication is that students should study under conditions that closely resemble the conditions under which testing will take place. A student studying for a paper and pencil exam might even do well to spend some time studying in the classroom where the test will take place.

A less obvious implication of the work on context is that if we want to remember what we learn well after the final exam, we should study in a variety of situations. Why? Because what we learn is apt to be needed in a wide variety of situations. If you are to be an engineer, the mathematics you study today may be needed at a construction site, on a factory floor, or in an executive's office. If you are to be a historian, the history you study today may be needed not only in classrooms, but at historical sites, in libraries, and at meetings of historical societies. Or, to take an example of more immediate relevance, if you are trying to learn principles of learning that will reduce forgetting, then you should keep in mind that you will need to recall those principles not only where you usually study, but anywhere that you are likely to learn. Because what we learn is apt to be needed in many different situations, the best practice may be to study in many different situations: at home, on the bus, in classrooms and coffee shops, while walking across campus or relaxing on the beach—any place and every place is a good place to learn.

Use Prompts

A prompt is an S^+ (see Chapter 9) that can be used to evoke behavior. One sort of prompt is the memorandum. To remember what groceries to buy, we make a list. To ensure that we do not forget an important meeting, we make a note on the calendar. Memoranda are obviously very useful memory aids. Even pigeons have been known to use a kind of memorandum (Epstein & Skinner, 1981). Some people would argue that memoranda do not aid recall but rather remove the need for recall. But a memorandum usually provides no more than a hint, a reminder, of the behavior to be produced. A note to "Call Jim about Mary" would be meaningless to anyone except the person who wrote it.

Parents used to tie a string around a child's finger as a reminder to ask the teacher when the costumes are needed for the school play, to buy bread on the way home, or to turn the oven off at 4 P.M. The child sees or feels the string during the course of the day and this prompts him to take the appropriate action. (Or someone else may see the string and ask what it is for, which has the same effect.) One problem with string is that it does not necessarily prompt the desired behavior at the right time. The string has given way to the electronic watch. Beep! It is time to take your medicine. Beep! It is time to call Margaret. Beep! It is time to turn off the oven.

But even an electronic watch can prompt a behavior only if we program it to do so in advance, and that is not always possible. Suppose the weather report predicts rain. The report prompts the comment (or thought), "I should take my umbrella." But it is not time to leave, and walking around the house with an umbrella is a nuisance. On the other hand, when you are ready to leave, you may forget the umbrella. What we need to do in situations like this is ensure that a prompt will occur when it is needed. You cannot be sure just when you will leave, so an alarm watch is not helpful. But you can put the umbrella where you will see it when you are about to depart. So, Skinner (1983c) suggests, when rain is predicted put the umbrella on the door handle. As long as you leave by that door, you will see the umbrella and it will provide the necessary prompt.[13]

In the same way, we can use prompts to induce ourselves to produce weak behaviors. Consider the problem of trying to recall someone's name. At one time you knew the person's name but find you are now unable to say it. You may be able to induce yourself to produce the name by using various kinds of prompts. For example, you might recall things about the person other than his name, such as the circumstances under which you met, the nature of conversations you have had with him, his occupation, and where he works. You may also recall things about the name itself that will prove helpful: that it is Anglo-Saxon, two syllables, with hard consonants. Recalling such things may, in turn, evoke the person's name.

You might also go through the alphabet, trying to recognize the first letter or sound of the name. If this is successful, you may use the beginning of the name as a prompt for the rest of the name by trying out various names that start with that sound: "I think it starts with 'Ba.' Ba . . . Barns, Barnaby, Baker, Bantry, Battry. Aha! It's *Batman!*"

We can also try to prompt a forgotten name by practicing an introduction covertly (that is, to ourselves): "This is Mr. . . . ," "I'd like you to meet . . ." In doing so we create an unpleasant situation from which we can escape only by producing the person's name. We may be able to do the same sort of thing to recall the name of the sea captain who defeated the Spanish armada. We simply imagine introducing him to Queen Elizabeth I: "Your Majesty, it is a great honor to introduce to you the hero of the Atlantic, conqueror of the Spanish invaders, Sir . . . Francis Drake."

As you know, any stimulus that is present during learning can later be used as a prompt for the behavior so learned. If, during a paper-and-pencil test on computer keyboard commands, you are unable to recall the command to begin an electronic search of a document, try putting your hands on the keyboard and typing the command. The keys may prompt the ap-

---

[13]Of course, if you leave by some other exit, you'll probably get wet.

The Man Who Couldn't Forget

One day, around 1920, a young man named S. V. Shereshevski walked into the office of the now famous Russian neuropsychologist, Aleksandr Luria. He had come to have his memory tested.

Testing a person's memory is ordinarily one of the easier tasks a neuropsychologist performs. But in the case of S, as Luria called him, it was quite difficult. Luria read off long strings of words or numbers only to have S recite them with ease, as though reading over Luria's shoulder. Even lists of 70 items caused no problem, and S would repeat them without error as presented or, if Luria wished, in reverse order. And S could still repeat what he had learned a day later, a week later, a month later, a year later, even, it turned out, 15 or more years later—the man never seemed to forget.

Luria tried to discover how S accomplished his amazing feats. He found that S used a combination of mnemonic techniques, including the method of loci. But he also experienced synesthesia, a synthesis of different senses. A sound, for example, may produce an experience of light, color, taste, odor, and touch. For S, a rainbow was not merely an array of colors, it was a shower of sensations. These experiences evidently helped make every experience memorable.

Students who hear of S's talent are sure to envy him. For him, there was no need to spend hours struggling to learn formulas, historical dates and events, passages of poetry, the periodic table, or the principles of learning. All such material could be learned with ease and recalled years later as if by reading from an invisible book.

Yet the story of S is a rather sad one. It is sad, not in spite of his extraordinary talent, but in large measure because of it. You see, S's talent so preoccupied him that it interfered with his ability to do ordinary things. Sometimes he would get so engrossed in the sensory qualities of a person's voice that he could not follow what the person was saying. Sometimes S would interrupt a story Luria was telling. "This is too much," he would say. "Each word calls up images; they collide with one another, and the result is chaos. I can't make anything out of this" (Luria, 1968, p. 65).

The least little thing could trigger a whole series of experiences, along with all sorts of sensations. Most people struggle to remember, but S never stopped remembering. For him, the problem was not how to remember, but how to forget.

propriate action. If a keyboard is not available, it may suffice to pretend that you are at the keyboard. Arrange your hands as you would if the keyboard were present, and try typing the wanted command.

> **Query:**   Name four skills for reducing forgetting.

REVIEW   To some extent, people can improve their ability to retain what they learn, mainly by using strategies to improve the initial level of learning. These strategies include overlearning, using mnemonics and mnemonic systems, learning in an appropriate setting, and using prompts.

A Final Word on Forgetting

All the techniques just reviewed—mnemonics, overlearning, and so on— are proven ways to reduce forgetting. Yet, even when these techniques are used, we forget. We may remember the rhyme about a Finn and German vaulting and hopping on Olympus's towering top yet be unable to remember any of the cranial nerves that rhyme is supposed to call up.

Sometimes the alacrity with which we forget is demoralizing. A comic (whose name I cannot recall!) suggests that what the typical college student remembers from a year of course work in American history is, "North wore blue; South wore gray." That is an exaggeration, of course, but it is an exaggeration that reveals a basic truth. We *do* forget a great deal of what we learn. So why bother learning? In particular, why spend years in school learning if much of that learning is bound to slip away from us?

Perhaps the answer is to be found in the realization that to learn is to change. We are, in a very real sense, different people each time we learn something. The white, middle-class student who reads *The Autobiography of Malcolm X* may recall little about the book, or about Malcolm X, years later. But despite all the student has forgotten, she may behave differently toward African Americans. And if you one day forget most of what you now know about learning, you may still view behavior somewhat differently from the way you would have had you not taken the course. Learning means a change in behavior due to experience; it does not necessarily mean that we recall the experience that produces the change.

We are bound to forget, but even the experiences we have forgotten leave their mark on us.

RECOMMENDED READING

1. Bartlett, F. C. (1932). *Remembering: A study in experimental and social psychology.* London: Cambridge University Press.

In this classic study of forgetting, Bartlett was among the first to cast doubt on the "recorder" theory of memory.

2. Ebbinghaus, H. (1885/1964). *Memory* (H. A. Ruger & C. E. Bussenius, Trans.). New York: Dover.

   Probably the first true experimental research on forgetting, this is the origin of the nonsense syllable and the famous "forgetting curve."

3. Ericsson, K. A., & Chase, W. G. (1982). Exceptional memory. *American Scientist, 70,* 607–615.

   The authors review cases of extraordinary memory and then argue that such feats are well within the range of ordinary people.

4. Loftus, E. (1980). *Memory: Surprising new insights into how we remember and why we forget.* Reading, MA: Addison-Wesley.

   This is an excellent and highly readable summary of memory research by one of the leaders in the field.

5. Luria, A. *The mind of a mnemonist.* (1968). New York: Avon.

   Luria offers a fascinating look at someone whose compulsive use of mnemonics prevented him from forgetting even trivial events and interfered with his ability to enjoy life.

REVIEW QUESTIONS

1. Define the following terms:

cue-dependent forgetting	paired associate learning
delayed matching to sample	peg word system
extinction method	proactive interference
fluency	prompted recall
forgetting	recognition
free recall	relearning method
gradient degradation	reminiscence
method of loci	retention interval
mnemonic	retroactive interference
mnemonic systems	savings method
overlearning	state-dependent learning

2. Why do some teachers ask their students to take the same seat at each class meeting, particularly at the beginning of the year?

3. John was determined to do well on the final exam in biology, so he studied from 10:00 P.M. to 2:00 A.M. each night for the two weeks

before the test. To keep from falling asleep, he drank strong coffee. The night before the 8:00 A.M. exam, he made sure he got a good night's sleep, but he did not do nearly as well on the test as he thought he should. What explanation can you offer? Describe how you could test the accuracy of your explanation.

4. How could you use fluency to measure forgetting?

5. Freud believed that nothing we experience is ever truly forgotten. How could you prove or disprove this statement?

6. Hilda and Ethel work together to train a rat to press a lever. When they are satisfied that the behavior has been well learned, Hilda suggests that they remove the lever from the cage for a while and then reinstall it to see what happens. Ethel proposes that they leave the lever in place but disconnect the feeding mechanism. Then they begin to wonder whether they would be studying different phenomena or the same thing. What do you think?

7. In paired associate learning, what is the reinforcer?

8. The amount of forgetting varies directly with the length of the retention interval. Why, then, is time not a cause of forgetting?

9. What is wrong with defining forgetting as the loss of behavior?

10. What is the defining difference between free recall and prompted recall?

11. Which measure of learning discussed in the text is likely to detect the most subtle degrees of forgetting? How could you prove you are right?

12. What is the implication of research on overlearning for your study practices?

13. Which is more likely to be a factor in forgetting what you have learned from this course: retroactive interference or proactive interference?

14. What is the practical significance of the study by Greenspoon and Ranyard (1957)?

15. Some psychologists maintain that spontaneous recovery is a form of forgetting. Explain this.

16. Mary went through a bad divorce and later found that the whole experience seemed a blank; she could remember almost nothing that

happened. When she went through a second divorce some years later, she found herself remembering all sorts of things about her first divorce. Explain why.

17. Give an example of both retroactive and proactive interference from your own experience.

18. Humans forget a great deal. Why have they not evolved a better ability to retain what they learn?

19. What sorts of prompts (or self-probes) could you use to remember the name of the sea captain in *Moby Dick*?

20. Some people say that what happened in Nazi Germany in the 1930s and 1940s could never happen here. What have you learned about forgetting that would make you doubt the truth of this statement?

PRACTICE QUIZ

1. The period between training and testing for forgetting is called the _____ interval.

2. In his studies of nonsense syllables, Ebbinghaus used the _____ method.

3. DMTS stands for _____.

4. John McGeoch argued that _____ does not cause forgetting.

5. Practicing a skill even after it is performed without errors is called _____.

6. When experiences after training interfere with performance, the effect is called _____ interference.

7. The tendency for performance to *improve* after training ends is called _____.

8. The research of Elizabeth Loftus and her colleagues raises doubts about the trustworthiness of _____ testimony.

9. _____ is known for his study of the man who could not forget.

10. _____ and _____ believed that experiences are permanently stored in the mind or brain.

QUERY ANSWERS

Page 390. Forgetting is the deterioration in performance following *a period without practice.*

Page 393. The relearning method is also called the *savings* method.

Page 401. Paired associate learning is probably best viewed as an operant procedure. A behavior is followed by either a reinforcing or punishing consequence (the correct word).

Page 404. Thune and Underwood used the *relearning/savings* method of studying forgetting.

Page 410. Loftus found that use of the word *smashed* resulted in higher estimates of car speed than use of the word *hit.*

Page 420. Answers should include four of the following: overlearn; use mnemonics; use a mnemonic system; make use of context cues; use prompts.

The Limits of Learning

We cannot command nature except by obeying her.

Francis Bacon

I n the preceding chapters, we saw that learning plays a vital role in the
behavior of animals and humans. It is clear, then, that to understand
human nature—or the nature of chimpanzees, monkeys, giraffes, rats,
pigeons, and many other animals—we must understand how behavior is
changed by experience: We must understand learning.

But we must also understand the limits of learning. For while learning contributes to the differences in behavior that distinguish a person
from a chimpanzee, and one person from another person, there are limits
to what people and chimpanzees can learn. In this chapter, we will discuss some of these limitations.

Physical Characteristics

Fish can't jump rope, humans can't breathe under water, cows can't coil
up like snakes. The very structure of an organism's body makes certain
kinds of behavior possible and other kinds of behavior impossible. What
an organism can learn to do is therefore limited by what it is physically
capable of doing. This is such an obvious fact that one might think it
goes without saying. Indeed, it is seldom, if ever, mentioned in learning
texts. But obvious generalizations are sometimes worth making because
the particulars that lead to the generalization are not always so obvious.

For instance, a dog's keen sense of smell enables it to find objects hidden from sight. Similarly, a hawk's superb vision allows it to distinguish
between heads and tails on a quarter at a great distance, whereas a person
would be unable to see the coin at all. Under certain circumstances, then,
dogs and hawks would learn faster than people. All sorts of physical characteristics set limits on what organisms can learn (see Figure 12-1).

Some years ago, various attempts were made to teach chimpanzees to
talk (Hayes, 1951; Kellogg, 1968). These efforts were almost wholly unsuccessful and convinced many people that chimpanzees could not acquire
language. It seemed that language was the one difference that set us off
from furrier creatures. But then Allen and Beatrice Gardner (1969) began
teaching Washoe, a young female chimpanzee, the sign language of the
deaf. In less than 2 years, Washoe had a vocabulary of over 30 signs, and by
the time she was 7, her vocabulary approached 200 signs. Since the
Gardners' first efforts, a number of other researchers have taught sign lan-

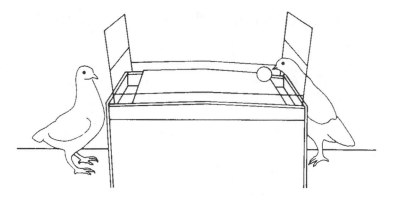

Figure 12-1 *Physical characteristics and learning. Pigeons cannot learn to play Ping-Pong in the usual manner, but these two have learned to play a variation of the game. (From "Two Synthetic Social Relations," by B. F. Skinner, 1962,* Journal of the Experimental Analysis of Behavior, *5, p. 531. Copyright © 1962 by the Society for the Experimental Analysis of Behavior, Inc. Reprinted by permission.*

guage to chimps. Researchers have also attempted to teach sign language to a gorilla (Patterson, 1978; Patterson et al., 1987) and to an orangutan (Shapiro, 1982). Whether any of these animals has really learned to communicate in the human sense is subject to debate (see, for example, Petitto & Seidenberg, 1979; Terrace, 1979). The point, however, is not that chimps and other animals are as adept as humans at learning language, but rather that their difficulty in learning to *speak* is due at least partly to inadequate anatomical structures. People would also have a difficult time learning to speak if they had the kind of vocal structures that chimps have.

> **Query:** Gardner and Gardner showed that the failure of chim-
>
> panzees to learn to speak may be due more to differences in
>
> _____ than in learning ability.

REVIEW An understanding of learning is essential to an understanding of behavior, especially human behavior, but there are limits on what learning can accomplish. The physical structure of an organism sets limits on what it can learn. Chimpanzees, for example, are apparently incapable of learning to speak because of the nature of their vocal equipment. Physical characteristics set important, but not always obvious, limits on what an organism can learn.

Nonheritability of Learned Behavior

Another obvious limitation of learning is that learned behavior is not inherited. Reflexes and fixed action patterns are passed on from generation to generation, but behavior that is acquired through learning dies with the individual. This places a serious limitation on the ability of a species to benefit from experience because it means that every individual is as ignorant at birth as its parents were when they were born. The lion cub must learn to stalk antelope just as its parents did; the rat must learn to avoid poisonous water; the child must learn to look for traffic before crossing streets.

The idea that learned behavior is not inherited was not always obvious. In fact, it was not so long ago that many people, including a number of scientists, believed that learning experiences might somehow benefit an organism's offspring. The idea grew out of the work of a French naturalist named Jean de Lamarck.

Lamarck tried to account for the peculiarly adaptive physical features of many animals. The crane, for example, finds food by wading in shallow waters. How is it that the crane has such conveniently long legs, legs that ideally suit the bird to its habitat? Or take the giraffe, an animal that lives on the African plains where it feeds on the leaves of trees; were it not for its long neck, the giraffe would not be able to reach the highest leaves. How did the giraffe come by so sensible a physique?

Lamarck, writing in the early 1800s, theorized that these and other physical characteristics were acquired adaptations that were passed on from generation to generation. Consider the giraffe. Suppose the food supply is scarce, so that the giraffe has to stretch its neck in an effort to reach higher leaves. If the animal had to do this day after day, it might, Lamarck speculated, make a slight difference in the length of the giraffe's neck. If this slight change were inherited by the giraffe's offspring, then over the course of several hundred generations, the giraffe's neck might get longer and longer until it reached its present, very adaptive length. For Lamarck, evolution was the result of a given species' adaptations to its environment. (For an interesting new wrinkle on this idea, see Landman, 1993.)

Query: The theories of Lamarck and Darwin both assume

that organisms evolve as a result of the influence of the

_____.

The Lamarckian theory of evolution was replaced by Darwin's theory of natural selection. But some scientists, most notably the eminent psychologist William McDougall, adopted a Lamarckian view of learned behavior. They argued that when experience modifies the behavior of an organism, it also modifies its genes in some way. This did not mean that if a person learned to read Latin, his or her offspring would be born knowing how to read Virgil. But McDougall and others did imply that, other things being equal, the offspring might have a slightly easier time mastering Latin than had the parent. And if each successive generation learned Latin, then each child would find the task easier than his parents had.

McDougall was no armchair psychologist, and he spent years performing experiments to test his theory. In a typical experiment, McDougall (1927, 1938) would train rats to avoid electric shocks. Then he would train the offspring of these rats on the same task, and then their offspring, and so on for several generations. The idea was that each generation should inherit more and more skill until, after many generations, the offspring would learn to avoid shock much more easily than their progenitors had. McDougall's research convinced him that his hypothesis held true.

Other scientists, although they respected McDougall's integrity, doubted his data. They ran similar experiments with better controls than McDougall had used and found no evidence that succeeding generations of animals learned a task any more readily than their forebears (see, for example, Agar et al., 1954).

The nonheritability of learning would seem to be the severest of all limitations on learning. Certainly, anyone who has had a difficult time mastering parallel parking or memorizing the forms of the French verb *être* will agree that being able to benefit from the learning experiences of one's parents would be helpful.

It is possible, however, that if we did inherit learned behavior, we would not be entirely happy with the results. Had our ancestors been born expert hunters and gatherers, for example, they might never have invented agriculture, probably the most important development in human history. In the past 50 years, there have been dramatic changes in the social roles of men and women in Western societies. It seems unlikely that such changes would have occurred if, over the past million years, men and women had inherited the roles of their parents. Inherited learning might also have slowed the advance of science. Had Copernicus been born *knowing* that the sun revolved about the earth, he might not have developed the view that the earth revolves about the sun.

The value of learning is that it enables us to adapt to changes in our environment. If we inherited learned behavior that was no longer adaptive, learning might be more of a hindrance than a help. Yet we must admit that the nonheritability of learning places severe limitations on what any individual can learn in a lifetime.

REVIEW   Learned behavior is not passed on to future generations, which means that each individual must learn many of the same skills acquired by its parents. This limits what any one individual can learn in its lifetime.

Heredity and Learning Ability

There is nothing about the gross anatomy of the chimpanzee (e.g., the way its arms and legs are put together) that keeps it from learning calculus. Yet it seems extremely unlikely that anyone will ever succeed in training a chimpanzee, or any other animal, to perform so sophisticated a skill.

Apparently, the principal reason that some people can master calculus while no chimpanzee can has to do with inherited differences in learning ability. It is also clear that there are pronounced differences in the learning abilities of individuals within a given species, and these differences are also partly due to heredity. Alas, it appears that few of us are born with the learning ability of Albert Einstein.

While the role of heredity in learning ability is controversial, there can be no doubt that it plays a part. Robert Tryon (1940) demonstrated this in animals many years ago. He ran a large number of rats through a maze and recorded the number of errors each rat made on a series of trials. There was a great deal of variability among the rats in the total number of errors made, with some rats making over 20 times as many errors as others. Tryon then bred those rats that had made the fewest errors with each other, and those that had made the greatest number of errors with each other. Next, Tryon tested the offspring of these rats on the maze and again bred the brightest of the bright with each other and the dullest of the dull with each other. He continued this procedure for 18 generations, all the while keeping the environments of the two strains as much alike as possible. The average number of errors in maze running for the two groups got farther and farther apart with each generation (see Figure 12-2), thus suggesting that heredity was having an important impact on learning.

In a more recent study, Harry and Martha Frank (1982) compared the problem-solving abilities of wolves and dogs. They placed wolf pups on one side of a barrier from which they could see but not reach food. To get

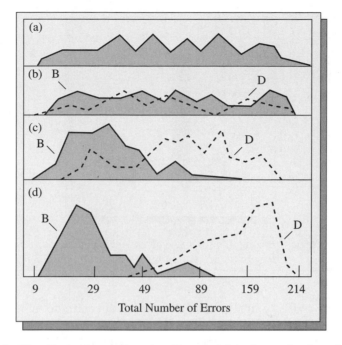

Figure 12-2   *Heredity and maze learning. Tryon's original sample of rats (a) showed wide variation in maze learning. The first generation of selectively bred rats (b) showed considerable overlap between maze bright (B) and maze dull (D) rats, but the second generation (c) showed clear differences in maze-learning ability. By the seventh generation (d) there was a substantial difference in the average number of errors made by the two groups. (From "Genetic Differences in Maze-Learning Ability in Rats," by R. Tryon, 1940,* Thirty-Ninth Yearbook of the National Society for the Study of Education, Intelligence: Its Nature and Nurture, Part I: Comparative and Critical Exposition, *G. M. Whipple [Ed.], p. 113. Copyright © 1940 by the National Society for the Study of Education. Reprinted by permission of the publisher.)*

the food, they had to go around the barrier. The Franks counted the number of errors the wolf pups made and compared these data with similar data obtained by other researchers with dog pups. On three different tests, the wolves did far better than the dogs (see Figure 12-3). Dogs and wolves are genetically almost identical, yet they performed differently. The Franks suggest that domestication has relieved pressure toward intelligence in the dog. In other words, because of dogs' association with humans, they are no longer naturally selected for intelligence whereas wolves must live by their wits or die.

There is also evidence that heredity plays an important role in human learning abilities. Studies of identical twins separated at or soon after birth

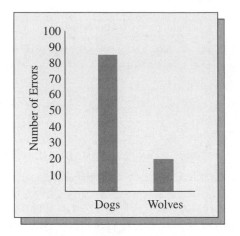

Figure 12-3 *Barrier learning in dogs and wolves. Average number of daily errors in wolves and dogs on three problems. (Compiled from data in Frank and Frank, 1982.)*

find that the twins typically have similar IQs, despite being reared in different environments (Newman et al., 1937). And adopted children are more likely to resemble their biological parents in intelligence than their adoptive parents (Skodak & Skeels, 1949). This is not to say that environment is unimportant in determining learning ability, but genes do play a role in what we learn.

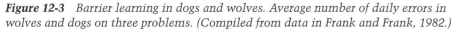

REVIEW The role of heredity in learning is controversial, but there is strong evidence that genes contribute to differences within, as well as between, species.

Neurological Damage and Learning

The biological equipment with which we learn is not determined solely by heredity. The environment may limit learning ability, and therefore what we learn, by damaging the nervous system.

Prenatal exposure to alcohol and other drugs can interfere with neurological development, resulting in limited learning ability (Hawkins, 1983). Often the damage is not apparent at birth and may be revealed only when the child goes to school. It is even possible that children judged to be perfectly normal have somewhat less learning ability than would have been the case had they never been exposed prenatally to drugs.

Neurotoxins, substances that damage nerve tissues, are also a threat to learning ability after birth, particularly in infancy and early childhood.

Recipe for Genius

Many of the world's geniuses have had unusually enriched early environments (Albert, 1980; Simonton, 1987). In fact, the childhoods of eminent figures such as Ludwig van Beethoven and Francis Galton are seldom ordinary. Could it be that we could create more geniuses by providing certain kinds of experiences in childhood? No one has performed an experiment that would answer this question with certainty. However, there is some very intriguing evidence to support the idea.

The nineteenth-century British philosopher and historian James Mill could be said to have performed a kind of enrichment experiment with his first-born son, John Stuart Mill. The boy's father began tutoring him when he was still in the cradle. John was reading by age 3 and routinely answered questions from his father about what he had read. By the time John was 8 years old, he had already read most of the Greek classics (in Greek, incidentally), and as an adult, he went on to outdistance his father as a philosopher. James Mill was unable to devote the same effort to educating his other children, and none of them matched the achievements of their elder brother.

A more recent effort to improve ability by providing an enriched environment came from a man named Aaron Stern (1971). Too ill to work, Stern decided that he would devote his time toward the education of his daughter. When Edith was still an infant, Stern played classical music for her, showed her cards with numbers on them, read to her, and made a point of speaking to her slowly and in complete sentences. When she was 18 months old, Stern taught Edith math with an abacus, showed her words on cards, and taught her to read street signs. By age 2, Edith was reading books intended for children of 6 and 8; by age 4, she was reading *The New York Times* and playing chess; by age 5, she had read much of the *Encyclopaedia Britannica*; by age 6, she was reading Dostoevsky and Tolstoy; and by age 15, Edith had graduated from college and begun graduate work at Michigan State University.

Of course, it is possible that the remarkable achievements of John Stuart Mill and Edith Stern had little to do with the special environments in which they were reared. Nevertheless, these and other cases leave open the possibility that a rich intellectual environment in early childhood can have important effects on the ability to learn.

One of the most pervasive neurotoxins is lead, commonly found in old paint and drinking water. Poor children often live in buildings with peeling paint, which they eat. The damage is not usually immediately obvious, but it is cumulative; over a period of months, it may make an important difference in the individual's ability to learn.

Query: Substances that damage neural tissues are called

_____.

Head injury can also diminish learning ability (Chance, 1986). This may seem an insignificant factor, but child abuse is fairly widespread and often involves blows to the head or shaking of the child. The "punch drunk" boxer provides anecdotal evidence of the cumulative effects of repeated closed head injuries. Violently shaking a child causes the brain to bounce back and forth within the skull and can cause serious damage.

Disease and malnutrition, especially during fetal development, infancy, and early childhood, can also prevent normal neurological development and result in reduced learning.

REVIEW   Neurological damage due to disease, malnutrition, head trauma, and exposure to neurotoxins can have a profound effect on learning. Unfortunately, anything that damages the brain is likely to reduce the ability to benefit from experience.

Critical Periods

Sometimes, organisms are especially likely to learn a particular kind of behavior at one point in their lives; these stages for optimum learning are referred to as **critical periods**.

For example, many animals are especially likely to form an attachment to their mothers during a critical period soon after birth. If the mother is unavailable, the youngster will become attached to any moving object that happens to pass by, whether another animal of the same species, a mechanical object, or a human being. Konrad Lorenz (1952) was one of the first to study this phenomenon, which he called **imprinting**. He discovered that if you remove a newly hatched goose chick from an incubator, you will have inadvertently become a parent; the chick will follow you about and ignore its mother. "If one quickly places such an orphan amongst a brood which is following its parents in the normal way," writes Lorenz,

> the gosling shows not the slightest tendency to regard the old birds as members of its own species. Peeping loudly, it runs away and,

should a human being happen to pass, it immediately follows this person; it simply looks upon human beings as its parents. (quoted in Thorpe, 1963, p. 405)

Imprinting has been demonstrated in coots, moorhens, turkeys, ravens, partridges, ducks, chickens, deer, sheep, buffalo, zebras, guinea pigs, baboons, and other animals. Young animals have been imprinted to species different from themselves, including humans, and to objects such as wooden decoys and electric trains. All that is necessary for imprinting to take place is that the young animal be able to view the "mother" and that the mother-object move.[1]

Imprinting is not the only evidence for critical periods. John Paul Scott (1958) has shown that social behavior in the dog depends on its experiences during certain critical periods. He points out, for example, that if a puppy is to become a good house pet, it must have contact with people when it is between 3 and 12 weeks old. Dogs completely deprived of human contact during this period behave like wild animals, ever fearful of humans.

Maternal behavior also may have to be learned during critical periods. Scott (1962) once bottle-fed a lamb for the first 10 days of its life and then put the lamb in with a flock of sheep. The lamb cared little for the sheep, preferring to be with people. And when this lamb gave birth, it was a poor mother: It allowed its offspring to nurse, but took no particular interest in other motherly activities.

Harry and Margaret Harlow (Harlow, 1958; Harlow & Harlow, 1962a, 1962b) obtained similar results when they reared rhesus monkeys in isolation. In the Harlows' experiments, young monkeys were fed by a surrogate mother, a terry cloth-covered object that did nothing but provide food and warmth. The infants became very attached to these cloth mothers and would cling to them for hours. If a monkey were exploring about the cage and became frightened, it would run to "mother" for protection. Later, when these monkeys were placed in cages with normally reared monkeys, they were terrified. They would run to a corner of the cage and roll up into a ball, sometimes sucking on a finger. As adults, these monkeys did not play or mate or rear young the way normally reared monkeys do. Although it was possible for these animals to acquire some social skills as adults, they always seemed to be socially retarded. Apparently, the early part of their lives, when they ordinarily would have interacted with their mothers and young monkeys, was a critical period for acquiring social skills.

---

[1] There is some evidence, however, that reinforcement may be involved in imprinting (Hoffman & Ratner, 1973; Suzuki & Moriyama, 1999).

It is not clear whether there are critical periods for learning in humans. It is possible that there is a critical period in infancy or early childhood for learning to care about others (David et al., 1988). And there is evidence that the first 12 years of life may be a critical period for learning language (Harley & Wang, 1997; Patkowski, 1994). But the evidence for critical periods in people is generally far weaker than the evidence for such periods in animals.[2]

REVIEW   Organisms may be prepared to learn certain things at certain stages in their development. Such critical periods appear to play an important role in imprinting and other forms of social behavior. It is not clear whether there are critical periods for learning in human development. When critical periods do occur, they place severe limits on learning. Certain opportunities for learning may occur but once in a lifetime.

Preparedness and Learning

In the 1960s, researchers began to notice that the ease with which learning occurs varies not only across time, as the work on critical periods shows, but also across situations. Whereas a given animal might learn quite readily in one situation, it might seem downright stupid in a slightly different situation.

Keller and Marion Breland (1961) were among the first to report this phenomenon. They used operant procedures to train hundreds of animals to perform in TV commercials and films and in shopping center promotions. For example, "Priscilla the Pig" turned on a radio, ate breakfast at a table, picked up dirty clothes and put them in a hamper, ran a vacuum cleaner, and chose the sponsor's brand of animal feed. The Brelands were expert animal trainers, yet they sometimes had great difficulty getting an animal to perform what seemed to be a simple task. In a classic article entitled "The Misbehavior of Organisms," they describe some of the peculiar problems they encountered in their work.

For instance, the Brelands wanted to train a raccoon to pick up some coins and put them in a metal box that served as a bank. The raccoon quickly learned to pick up a coin and carry it to the box, but the animal "seemed to have a great deal of trouble letting go of the coin. He would

---

[2]Feierman and Feierman (2000) note that the paraphilias resemble imprinted behavior in that they are difficult to change. It is conceivable that sexual orientation is also the result of imprinting that occurs early in life. This would account for both the fact that homosexuals feel that they were "born that way" and the fact that sexual orientation is very resistant to change. But this is pure speculation.

rub it up against the inside of the container, pull it back out, and clutch it firmly for several seconds" (p. 682). When the Brelands tried to teach the animal to pick up two coins and put them in the box, the raccoon became even more of a dunce. Instead of dropping the coins into the box, it would rub them together "in a most miserly fashion" (p. 682) and dip them in and out of the box. None of this behavior was reinforced by trainers.

It might seem reasonable to conclude that the task was simply too difficult for the raccoon to master. But the raccoons had no trouble learning other, equally complex tasks.

Time and again, the Brelands had trouble getting animals to perform acts that should have been easy. In some cases, the Brelands managed to teach an animal to perform the desired behavior, only to find that the act later broke down. For example, they taught a pig to make bank deposits in a manner similar to that of the raccoon. But after a time, the pig began to behave oddly. Instead of picking up the large wooden coin and carrying it to the bank, the pig would drop the coin to the ground, push at it with its snout, throw it up into the air, and nudge it again with its snout. None of this behavior had been reinforced by the Brelands. In fact, the animal's errant behavior delayed reinforcement.

Why did such "misbehavior" occur? The Brelands theorized that innate tendencies interfered with learning. In the wild, raccoons dip their prey into the water and then rub it between their paws, as if washing it. Some biologists speculate that this serves to break away the outer shell of the crayfish that often forms an important part of the raccoon's diet. In any case, it appears that this behavior interfered with teaching the raccoon to drop coins into a bank. Similarly, pigs dig their snouts into the ground to uncover edible roots, and this rooting behavior interfered with their learning to carry coins.

Query: The Brelands showed that _____ might

facilitate learning in one situation and inhibit it in another.

The tendency of an animal to revert to a fixed action pattern, a phenomenon called **instinctive drift**, sets limits on learning. If a particular act conflicts with a fixed action pattern, the animal will have trouble learning it. After the Brelands' discoveries, other researchers began to report evidence that animals show peculiar talents for learning some things but are peculiarly resistant toward learning others. The limitations that the latter oddities place on learning were nicely illustrated in a study of taste aversion in rats.

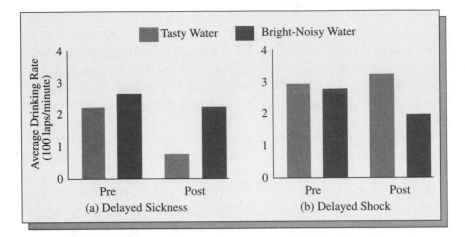

Figure 12-4 *Preparedness and taste aversion. Rats were given the opportunity to drink bright-noisy and tasty water before and after conditioning. When drinking preceded sickness, rats later tended to avoid tasty water (a); when drinking preceded shock, the rats learned to avoid bright-noisy water (b). ("Relation of Cue to Consequence in Avoidance Learning," by John Garcia and Robert Koelling, 1966, Psychonomic Science, 4, p. 124, Figure 1. Copyright 1966 by the Psychonomic Society. Reprinted by permission of the publisher and authors.)*

John Garcia and Robert Koelling (1966) set up four classical conditioning experiments in which they paired water with aversive stimuli. The water was flavored, and a light and a clicking noise came on whenever the rat drank. Thus, in one experiment, rats drank water that was bright, noisy, and tasty, and later they became sick from exposure to X-radiation. In another experiment, rats drank water that was bright, noisy, and tasty, and later they received an electric shock. After training, the experimenters gave the rats a choice between bright-noisy water and water that was tasty. The researchers found that rats that had been made sick were more likely to avoid the *tasty* water; those that had been shocked were more likely to avoid the *bright-noisy* water (see Figure 12-4). The rats had an apparently innate bias toward learning one thing rather than another.

The facility with which animals learn certain behaviors is illustrated by a classic experiment conducted by Paul Brown and Herbert Jenkins (1968). These researchers put pigeons into experimental chambers rigged so that periodically a disk would be illuminated. The disk remained lit for a few seconds, and when the light went off a food tray provided the pigeon with grain. The birds did not have to do anything to receive food, yet all the birds began pecking the disk.

Robert Epstein and Skinner (1980; see also Skinner, 1983a) got similar results with a slightly different procedure. They shone a spot of light

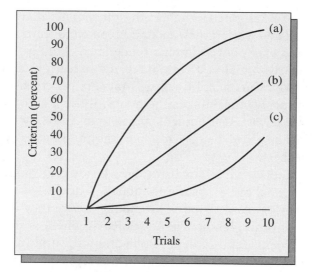

Figure 12-5   *Preparedness and learning. Hypothetical learning curves for a task an organism is prepared to learn (a), unprepared to learn (b), and contraprepared to learn (c).*

on a screen and made it move. When it reached the edge of the screen, the bird received some food. The bird did not have to do anything to receive food, nor did anything it did speed up delivery of the food. Nevertheless, the bird began pecking at the moving spot of light, as if driving it across the screen. This phenomenon, now often called **sign tracking**, has proved to be robust and has been demonstrated in several species, including humans.[3]

These and other studies show that animals have an inclination to behave in certain ways, and this means they will learn some things with great ease while learning other things only with the greatest difficulty. Martin Seligman (1970) proposed that such tendencies can be characterized as a **continuum of preparedness**: An organism comes to a learning situation genetically prepared to learn (in which case learning proceeds quickly), unprepared (in which case learning proceeds steadily but more slowly), or contraprepared (in which case the course of learning is slow and irregular; see Figure 12-5).

---

[3] Sign tracking is also referred to as autoshaping. Various explanations for sign tracking have been offered. An early theory attributed it to coincidental reinforcement (Brown & Jenkins, 1968). The procedure does resemble Skinner's superstition experiment, but this theory has been criticized. Another theory relies on Pavlovian conditioning (e.g., Schwartz & Gamzu, 1977).The idea is that pecking is a UR to grain, so if a lighted disk is repeatedly paired with food, the bird will peck the disk just as it does the grain that follows.

According to Seligman's theory, the raccoon's innate tendency to pick up its food and wash it may make it prepared to learn to pick up and carry coins to a bank, but its innate tendency to hold on to food it has dipped into a stream makes it contraprepared to learn to drop coins into a bank. Similarly, Garcia and Koelling's rats are genetically prepared to learn to avoid water that makes them sick if the water has a distinct taste, but not if it has a distinct look and sound. And Brown and Jenkins' pigeons pecked a lighted disk because pigeons are genetically prepared to peck bright objects.

In the chapter on vicarious learning, we saw that monkeys can acquire a fear of snakes by observing models who feared them. Fear of snakes has obvious survival value for monkeys. Are they as adept at acquiring fears of other, less dangerous objects? There is some evidence that monkeys can acquire a fear of objects not found in their natural habitat through observation (Stevenson, reported in Mineka & Cook, 1988). However, monkeys seem to be particularly adept at acquiring modeled fear of snakes. In one experiment, Michael Cook and Susan Mineka (1990) had rhesus monkeys watch videotapes of monkeys reacting fearfully either to snakes or to flowers. The observers acquired a fear of snakes but not of flowers.

The durability of learning also seems to reflect preparedness. The rate of forgetting can vary greatly depending on whether what is learned has survival value. You may recall (from Chapter 11) that birds can retrieve food that they cached months before.

Are people genetically prepared to learn some things more readily than others? Some people think so. Psycholinguist Eric Lenneberg (1967, 1969) points out that language development follows a regular, predictable pattern around the world, which might suggest that people are prepared to learn language in a certain way. In addition, Lenneberg notes that the language skills of retarded children freeze at a primitive stage of development. They learn language in the same way as more intelligent people, though they cannot learn to the same level of complexity.

Seligman (1970, 1971) has proposed that phobias provide additional evidence of human preparedness (see also Ost & Hugdahl, 1985). Certain objects, he points out, are far more likely than others to become phobic stimuli. He adds that "the great majority of phobias are about objects of natural importance to the survival of the species" (p. 320). People are far more likely to fear sharks, spiders, snakes, and dogs than they are lambs, trees, houses, and cars. Seligman and Joanne Hager (1972b) tell the story of a 7-year-old girl who saw a snake while playing in the park. Some time later, the girl accidentally slammed a car door on her hand, after which she developed a fear of snakes. Obviously, the snake did not hurt her

Learning and Humanity

A common misconception about evolution is that it is a form of progress, as though each species were aimed at a distant goal and evolution were its means of reaching it. In fact, there is no evolutionary goal. Certain characteristics arise merely because those individuals that possess them tend to survive and pass on their genes.

Learning, as we have seen, is a kind of individual evolution: New behavior appears and either "survives" or "dies out." And like evolution, it has no ultimate goal. What we learn depends on the experiences we have, not on some scheme of nature.

We forget this. We tend to speak of learning as if it were necessarily a good thing, and use the term almost as a synonym for improvement. It is true that love, compassion, tenderness, cooperativeness, sharing, musical composition, and great literature are largely the products of learning. But so are the most despicable acts of which we are capable. Consider this report of one survivor of the concentration camp in Dachau, Germany:

> It was common practice to remove the skin from dead prisoners. . . .
> It was chemically treated and placed in the sun to dry. After that it was
> cut into various sizes for use as saddles, riding breeches, gloves,
> house slippers and ladies' handbags. Tattooed skin was especially valued by SS men. (Blaha, 1946; in Carey, 1988, pp. 557f)

This excerpt reveals that learning does not always mean progress. You may also see the undesirable effects of learning in your own reaction to the passage above. There was a time, not so very long ago, when reading such material would have made some students physically ill. Today's students have viewed so much brutality on television, and sometimes in the streets, that many can read Blaha's account without discomfort.

Learning defines our humanity. For better, and for worse.

hand. The implication is that people are biologically prepared to acquire a fear of snakes but not a fear of cars, yet in this case, a car phobia would have made more sense.

The idea that people have an innate disposition to fear certain kinds of stimuli is supported by research showing that when people are shown an array of images and are asked to find the spider or the snake, they are faster at doing so than when asked to find less hazardous items (Öhman et al., 2001).

There is also some evidence from twin studies supporting the preparedness concept. K. S. Kendler and colleagues (1992) studied female twins and found that various social phobias (such as a fear of meeting people) and agoraphobia (fear of open places) have a genetic basis. While not born with such phobias, some people may be genetically prepared to acquire them.

Seligman (1970) also observes that people are far more likely to form strong attachments to some objects than to others. As he notes, the cartoon character Linus carries a security blanket, not a security shoe.

But the case for preparedness in humans is not clear-cut. Joseph Wolpe (in Wolpe & Plaud, 1997) points out that objects that are seldom feared, such as flowers, are those to which we have been exposed many times without adverse effects. In other words, flowers are normally paired with positive or neutral stimuli. Work on latent inhibition allows us to predict that such pre-exposure should make it difficult to establish flowers as a CS for fear. On the other hand, commonly feared objects such as snakes are encountered less frequently and are more likely to be paired with unpleasant stimuli, such as a person shouting a warning.[4]

REVIEW   It seems clear that in most animals, learning depends partly on whether the organism is genetically prepared, unprepared, or contraprepared to learn the task in question. Such genetic preparation sets limits on what is learned from a given experience.

Conclusion

We have concluded our introduction to the study of learning and behavior by examining the limits on learning. Those limits make learning appear to be a feeble weapon with which to battle the problems that threaten civilization. The world is faced with war, famine, pollution, crime, disease, unemployment, drug abuse, child abuse, and the grandfather of all problems, overpopulation. What good is a science of learning and behavior in overcoming problems of such magnitude?

The answer becomes obvious once we realize that most of the serious problems confronting us are fundamentally behavior problems. War is a form of conflict. Famine is less the result of bad weather than of mismanaged resources. Pollution is the improper disposal of wastes. Crime is the performance of socially prohibited acts. Most diseases are at least partly the product of unhealthy behavior. And so on.

---

[4]For a review of preparedness and phobias, see McNally (1987).

Once we recognize that the great problems facing society are essentially behavioral, not technological or natural, we realize that we can prevent, solve, or at least ameliorate them *by changing behavior.* A science of behavior change, of learning, then becomes critically important and suggests certain solutions.

Consider, as an example, the problem of teen pregnancy in this country. Each year, thousands of babies are born to young teenage girls. These mothers have a tendency to produce low birth weight babies, and such babies have a tendency to have health problems and learning difficulties. In addition, most teen mothers are ill-equipped to take on the burden of rearing children. Many of them neglect their children and some become abusive parents. Their children tend also to produce children at an early age, so the cycle continues.

Most people probably will agree that it would be a good idea if babies were born to women 18 or older. To reach that goal, we must change the behavior of the people involved, the girls who are getting pregnant and the males who are impregnating them. But how do we change their behavior? So far, we have attempted to change teenage sexual practices primarily with slogans and lectures. The study of learning and behavior suggests that other methods might be more effective.

Early pregnancy is primarily a problem among the poor. For poor teens, producing children may win both the father and mother the admiration of their peers and adults. It may also be a way to escape an unpleasant home environment, since the girl may be able to move out and receive government assistance. A kind of trap is probably involved, since for many poor teens the positive consequences of becoming pregnant are immediate, whereas the negative consequences are more remote.[5] Learning research suggests that if we change the consequences of the teen's behavior, the behavior will change. One way to do this would be to provide cash payment to poor teenage girls each year that they do not have a baby. Each successive year without a baby would result in a larger cash prize.

There is no way to know *a priori* whether such a change in consequences would substantially reduce the incidence of teen pregnancy. But there is, as you have seen, good reason to believe that it might. And, of course, there are many other ways of applying what we know about behavior change to this problem.

To suggest that we can draw on learning research in dealing with societal problems docs not mean that the problems will be easily solved. Human behavior is extremely complicated, and solutions to social problems

---

[5]For more on traps of this sort, see Platt (1973).

are apt to come slowly. But there is good reason to hope that through the application of scientific method, solutions will come.

Indeed, it may be our only hope.

RECOMMENDED READING

1. Breland, K., & Breland, M. (1961). The misbehavior of organisms. *American Psychologist, 16,* 681–684.

   A classic paper on instinctive drift and individual differences among species in learning.

2. Hayes, C. (1951). *The ape in our house.* New York: Harper & Row.

   The Hayeses brought an infant chimpanzee into their home to see what it could accomplish if reared as a human.

3. Lamal, P. A. (Ed.). (1997). *Cultural contingencies.* New York: Praeger.

   Analysis of the cultural practices (including preventive medicine, the role of women, and welfare) in three countries.

4. Seligman, M. E. P., & Hager, J. L. (Eds.). (1972). *Biological boundaries of learning.* New York: Appleton-Century-Crofts.

   One of the classic works on the limits of learning.

5. Wilson, E. O. (1975). *Sociobiology: The new synthesis.* Cambridge, MA: Harvard University Press.

   Wilson stirred considerable controversy with this treatise on the role of evolution and heredity in human affairs.

REVIEW QUESTIONS

1. Define the following terms:

continuum of preparedness	instinctive drift
critical period	preparedness
imprinting	sign tracking

2. Sally buys a high-frequency whistle at a discount store. She attempts to train her dog to come on command using the whistle as a signal. She follows the correct training procedures but is unsuccessful. What is the likely cause of the failure?

3. Explain why it is sometimes difficult to assess the intelligence of people who suffer from infantile paralysis and similar disorders.

4. Suppose that, because of its superior vision, a falcon can learn a discrimination task faster than a person. Mary believes this means the bird is smarter than the person. What reasons might she have for this idea?

5. Design an experiment that would determine whether there are genetic differences in the learning abilities of men and women.

6. How might preparedness to learn be nonadaptive?

7. Explain the role of evolution in the findings of Garcia and Koelling.

8. In what sense might it be said that autoshaping represents preparedness to acquire a superstition?

9. Some people believe that it is important for a human infant to have intimate contact with the mother during the first few hours after birth (rather than being hurried off to a nursery). How could you determine whether there is a critical period for the formation of an adult-infant bond?

10. Design a study to determine the effects of prenatal exposure to tobacco on subsequent learning ability.

11. Could variability in learning ability be useful to the survival of our species?

12. Suppose you had inherited everything your parents and grandparents knew. How would you be different?

13. Identify a social problem and explain how it might be dealt with through the application of learning principles you have learned in this text.

14. How would you go about creating a genius?

15. A visitor to New York complained about the noise of the city. Her host replied, "Oh, you get used to it." Does this demonstrate that learning is helpful or harmful?

16. How could you determine whether humans are biologically prepared to learn language?

17. Roger McIntire (1973) recommends that people be required to undergo training in child rearing before being allowed to have children. What support for his position can you provide?

18. What would it take to make our judicial system an effective instrument for reducing crime?

19. Explain why it would be desirable to have political leaders who understand basic learning principles.

20. What protection could the public have against the abuse of learning principles by political leaders?

PRACTICE QUIZ

1. An example of the role of physical characteristics in learning is provided by the difficulty apes had in learning _____.

2. Harry and Martha Frank found that _____ solved certain problems better than dogs.

3. William _____ mistakenly believed that learned behavior could be inherited.

4. Substances that damage neural tissues are called
   _____.

5. A _____ is a stage in development during which an organism is particularly likely to learn a particular behavior.

6. Soon after hatching, ducklings become _____ on an object that moves, usually their mother.

7. _____ drift is the tendency of an animal to revert to innate patterns of behavior.

8. Garcia and Koelling found that when rats became sick after drinking water that was tasty and noisy, they were more likely to drink water that was _____ than water that was
   _____.

9. According to Martin Seligman, all behavior falls along a continuum of _____.

10. Rhesus monkeys can acquire a fear by observing a fearful model, but Cook and Mineka found that they are more likely to acquire a fear of snakes than of _____.

QUERY ANSWERS

Page 427. Gardner and Gardner showed that the failure of chimpanzees to learn to speak may be due more to differences in *anatomy* than in learning ability.

Page 428. The theories of Lamarck and Darwin both assume that organisms evolve as a result of the influence of the *environment*.

Page 434. Substances that damage neural tissues are called *neurotoxins*.

Page 437. The Brelands showed that *heredity/genetic factors* might facilitate learning in one situation and inhibit it in another.

Glossary

Note: The number at the end of each entry indicates the page on which the glossary term is first used.

ABA reversal design A type of within-subject experiment in which behavior is observed before (A) and after (B) an experimental manipulation. The original (A) condition is restored, sometimes followed again by the experimental (B) condition. 53

Anecdotal evidence First- or secondhand reports of personal experience. 47

Attentional processes In Bandura's theory of vicarious learning, any activity by an observer that aids in the observation of relevant aspects of a model's behavior and its consequences. 288

Autoshaping *See* sign tracking.

Aversion therapy A form of counterconditioning in which a CS is paired with an aversive US, often nausea-inducing drugs. 119

Aversive (n.) Any stimulus the removal of which is reinforcing; (adj.) characterizing an event that is likely to be avoided. 17

Backward chaining A chaining procedure in which training begins with the last link in the chain and adds preceding links in reverse order. 158

Backward conditioning A Pavlovian conditioning procedure in which the US precedes the CS. (*Cf.* forward chaining.) 80

Baseline period In a within-subject experiment, a period of observation (often designated "A") during which no attempt is made to modify the behavior under study. 52

Behavior Anything a person or animal does that can be measured. In practice, the term usually refers to publicly observable overt behavior. However, behavior that is available only to the person performing it (such as thinking) may be included if it can be reliably measured. 37

Behavior chain A series of related behaviors, the last of which produces reinforcement. 156

Behavioral economics *See* experimental economics.

Between-subjects experiment An experimental design in which the independent variable is made to vary across two or more groups of subjects. Also called between-treatment or group experiment. 50

Blocking Failure of a stimulus to become a CS when it is part of a compound stimulus that includes an effective CS. The effective CS is said to block the formation of a new CS. (*Cf.* overshadowing.) 86

Case study Detailed study and description of a single case. Usually used in clinical settings. 48

CER *See* conditioned emotional response.

Chaining In operant training, the procedure of establishing a behavior chain. (*See* behavior chain; forward chaining; backward chaining.) 156

Chain schedule A complex reinforcement schedule that consists of a series of simple schedules, each of which is associated with a particular stimulus, with reinforcement delivered only on completion of the last schedule in the series. (*Cf.* tandem schedule.) 368

Classical conditioning *See* Pavlovian conditioning.

Compound stimulus Two or more stimuli presented simultaneously, often as a CS. 84

Concept Any class (i.e., group, category) the members of which share one or more defining features. 332

Concurrent schedule A complex reinforcement schedule in which two or more simple schedules are available at the same time. 369

Conditional reflex A reflex acquired through Pavlovian conditioning and consisting of a conditional stimulus and a conditional response. (*Cf.* unconditional reflex.) 70

Conditional response The response part of a conditional reflex; the response elicited by a conditional stimulus. Often called *conditioned response.* Abbreviated CR. 71

Conditional stimulus The stimulus part of a conditional reflex; the stimulus that elicits a conditional response. Often called *conditioned stimulus.* Abbreviated CS. 71

Conditioned emotional response An emotional response to a stimulus that is acquired through Pavlovian conditioning. Abbreviated CER. 107

Conditioned reinforcer *See* secondary reinforcer.

Conditioned suppression A reduction in the rate of responding due to the noncontingent presentation of an aversive CS. 111

Conditioned taste aversion An aversion, acquired through Pavlovian conditioning, to foods with a particular flavor. 122

Contiguity Nearness of events in time (temporal contiguity) or space (spatial contiguity). 82

Contingency A dependency between events. An event may be stimulus-contingent (dependent on the appearance of a stimulus) or response-contingent (dependent on the appearance of a behavior). 81

Continuous reinforcement A reinforcement schedule in which a behavior is reinforced each time it occurs. Abbreviated CRF. (*Cf.* intermittent schedule.) 349

Continuum of preparedness The idea that organisms are genetically disposed to learn some things and not others. 439

Control group In a between-subjects experiment, those subjects not exposed to the independent variable. 50

Cooperative schedule A complex reinforcement schedule in which reinforcement is contingent on the behavior of two or more individuals. 369

Counterconditioning The use of Pavlovian conditioning to reverse the unwanted effects of prior conditioning. 109

CR *See* conditional response.

CRF *See* continuous reinforcement.

Critical period A period in the development of an organism during which it is especially likely to learn a particular kind of behavior. 434

CS *See* conditional stimulus.

CS+ In Pavlovian discrimination training, the stimulus that is regularly paired with a US. (*Cf.* CS–.) 313

CS– In Pavlovian discrimination training, the stimulus that regularly appears in the absence of the US. (*Cf.* CS+.) 313

Cue-dependent forgetting Forgetting that results from the absence of cues that were present during training. 405

Cued recall *See* prompted recall.

Cumulative record A graphic record of behavior, each point of which reflects the total number of times a behavior has been performed as of that time. (*Cf.* cumulative recorder.) 45

Cumulative recorder An apparatus (or software) that records every occurrence of a behavior, thereby producing a cumulative record. (*Cf.* cumulative record.) 45

Delayed conditioning A Pavlovian conditioning procedure in which the CS starts before, and then overlaps with, the US. 74

Delayed matching to sample A method of measuring forgetting in which the opportunity to match a sample follows a retention interval. Abbreviated DMTS. (*Cf.* matching to sample.) 394

Dependent variable The variable by which the outcome of an experiment is measured. It is expected to vary with (to depend on) the independent variable. 50

Descriptive study A study in which the researcher attempts to describe a group by obtaining data from its members. 49

Differential outcomes effect The finding that discrimination training proceeds more rapidly when different behaviors produce different reinforcers. Abbreviated DOE. 320

Differential reinforcement Any operant training procedure in which certain kinds of behavior are systematically reinforced and others are not. 211

Differential reinforcement of alternative behavior A form of differential reinforcement in which a behavior that is different from an undesired behavior is systematically reinforced. (The procedure provides an alternative way of obtaining reinforcers.) Abbreviated DRA. 213

Differential reinforcement of high rate A form of differential reinforcement in which a behavior is reinforced only if it occurs at least a specified number of times in a given period. Abbreviated DRH. (*Cf.* differential reinforcement of low rate.) 357

Differential reinforcement of incompatible behavior A form of differential reinforcement in which a behavior that is incompatible with an unwanted behavior is systematically reinforced. Abbreviated DRI. 212

Differential reinforcement of low rate A form of differential reinforcement in which a behavior is reinforced only if it occurs no more than a specified number of times in a given period. Abbreviated DRL. (*Cf.* differential reinforcement of high rate.) 211

Differential reinforcement of zero responding A form of differential reinforcement in which reinforcement is contingent on the complete absence of a behavior for a period of time. Also called differential reinforcement of other behavior, since some other behavior is necessarily reinforced. Both terms are abbreviated DRO. 212

Discrete trials procedure An operant training procedure in which performance of a behavior defines the end of a trial. (*Cf.* free operant procedure.) 144

Discrimination The tendency for a behavior to occur in the presence of certain stimuli, but not in their absence. (*Cf.* generalization.) 313

Discrimination hypothesis The proposal that the PRE occurs because it is harder to discriminate between intermittent reinforcement and extinction than between continuous reinforcement and extinction. 362

Discrimination training Any procedure for establishing a discrimination. Pavlovian discrimination training consists of present-ing one stimulus (the CS+) with the US and presenting another stimulus (the CS–) without the US. Operant discrimination training normally consists of reinforcing a behavior when it occurs in the presence of one stimulus (the S^+ or S^D), but not when it occurs in the presence of another stimulus (the S^- or S^Δ). *See* errorless discrimination training; matching to sample; simultaneous discrimination training; successive discrimination training. 313

Discriminative stimulus In operant discrimination training, any stimulus that signals either that a behavior will be reinforced (an S^+ or S^D) or will not be reinforced (an S^- or S^Δ). 314

DMTS *See* delayed matching to sample.

DOE *See* differential outcomes effect.

DRA *See* differential reinforcement of alternative behavior.

DRH *See* differential reinforcement of high rate.

DRI *See* differential reinforcement of incompatible behavior.

Drive In Hull's theory of reinforcement, a motivational state (such as hunger) caused by a period of deprivation (as of food). 172

Drive-reduction theory The theory of reinforcement that attributes a reinforcer's effectiveness to the reduction of a drive. 173

DRL *See* differential reinforcement of low rate.

Equilibrium theory *See* response deprivation theory

Errorless discrimination training A form of discrimination training in which the S^- is introduced in very weak form and gradually strengthened. The usual result is that discrimination is achieved with few or no errors. Also called the Terrace procedure. 319

Escape-avoidance learning A form of negative reinforcement in which the subject first learns to escape, and then to avoid, an aversive. 178

Escape training *See* negative reinforcement.

Excitatory gradient In Spence's theory of generalization and discrimination, a generalization gradient showing an increased tendency to respond to the S^+ or CS+ and stimuli resembling them. (*Cf.* inhibitory gradient.) 327

Experiment A research design in which the researcher measures the effects of one or more independent variables on one or more dependent variables. 50

Experimental economics The use of reinforcement schedules, among other techniques, to study economic principles. Also called behavioral economics. 377

Experimental group In a between-subjects experiment, those subjects exposed to the independent variable. 50

Experimental neurosis Any bizarre or neurotic-like behavior induced through an experimental procedure such as discrimination training. 340

Extinction (1) In Pavlovian conditioning, the procedure of repeatedly presenting a CS without the US. (2) In operant training, the procedure of withholding the reinforcers that maintain a behavior. (*Cf.* forgetting.) 91, 167

Extinction burst A sudden increase in the rate of behavior during the early stages of extinction. 167

Extinction method A method of measuring forgetting by comparing the rate of extinction after a retention interval with the rate of extinction immediately after training. 395

FD schedule *See* fixed duration schedule.

FI schedule *See* fixed interval schedule.

Fixed action pattern Any largely inherited series of interrelated acts, usually elicited by a particular stimulus (the releaser). Formerly called instinct. Abbreviated FAP. (*Cf.* general behavior trait.) 12

Fixed duration schedule A reinforcement schedule in which reinforcement is contingent on the continuous performance of a behavior for a fixed period of time. Abbreviated FD. (*Cf.* variable duration schedule.) 356

Fixed interval schedule A reinforcement schedule in which a behavior is reinforced the first time it occurs following a specified interval since the last reinforcement. Abbreviated FI. (*Cf.* variable interval schedule.) 353

Fixed ratio schedule A reinforcement schedule in which every nth performance of a behavior is reinforced. Abbreviated FR. (*Cf.* variable ratio schedule.) 349

Fixed time schedule A reinforcement schedule in which reinforcement is delivered independently of behavior at fixed intervals. Abbreviated FT. (*Cf.* variable time schedule.) 358

Forgetting Deterioration in learned behavior following a period without practice. (*Cf.* extinction; reminiscence.) 390

Forward chaining A chaining procedure in which training begins with the first link in the chain and adds subsequent links in order. (*Cf.* backward chaining.) 157

Free operant procedure An operant training procedure in which a behavior may be repeated any number of times. (*Cf.* discrete trials procedure.) 145

Free recall A method of measuring forgetting that consists of providing the opportunity to perform the learned behavior. (*Cf.* prompted recall.) 392

FR schedule *See* fixed ratio schedule.

Frustration hypothesis The proposal that the PRE occurs because nonreinforcement is frustrating and during intermittent reinforcement frustration becomes an S$^+$ for responding. 363

FT schedule *See* fixed time schedule.

General behavior trait Any general behavioral tendency that is strongly influenced by genes. Examples include introversion and general anxiety. (*Cf.* fixed action pattern.) 17

Generalization The tendency for a learned behavior to occur in the presence of stimuli that were not present during training. (*Cf.* discrimination.) 304

Generalization gradient Any graphic representation of generalization data. 306

Generalized imitation The tendency to imitate modeled behavior even though the imitative behavior is not reinforced. 280

Generalized reinforcer Any secondary reinforcer that has been paired with several different reinforcers. 151

Gradient degradation A method of measuring forgetting in which a behavior is tested for generalization before and after a retention interval. A flattening of the generalization gradient indicates forgetting. 396

Group experiment *See* between-subjects experiment.

Habituation A decrease in the intensity or probability of a reflex response resulting from repeated exposure to a stimulus that elicits that response. (*Cf.* sensitization.) 11

Higher-order conditioning A variation of Pavlovian conditioning in which a stimulus is paired, not with a US, but with a well-established CS. 75

Imprinting The tendency of some animals, particularly birds, to follow the first moving object they see after birth, usually (but not necessarily) their mother. 434

Independent variable In an experiment, the variable that the researcher controls. The independent variable is usually expected to affect the dependent variable. 50

Inhibitory gradient In Spence's theory of generalization and discrimination, a gradient showing a decreased tendency to respond to the S⁻ or CS− and stimuli resembling them. (*Cf.* excitatory gradient.) 327

Instinct *See* fixed action pattern.

Instinctive drift The tendency for behavior to "drift toward" a fixed action pattern. 437

Instrumental learning *See* operant learning.

Intermittent schedule Any of several reinforcement schedules in which a behavior is sometimes reinforced. Also called partial reinforcement. (*Cf.* continuous reinforcement.) 349

Intertrial interval The interval separating the trials of a discrete trial procedure. 89

Latent inhibition In Pavlovian conditioning the failure of a CR to appear as a result of prior presentation of the CS in the absence of the US. 86

Law of effect The statement that behavior is a function of its consequences. So called because the strength of a behavior depends on its past *effects* on the environment. Implicit in the law is the notion that operant learning is an active process, since it is usually the behavior of the organism that, directly or indirectly, produces the effect. 137

Learned helplessness The failure to escape an aversive following exposure to an inescapable aversive. 250

Learning A change in behavior due to experience. 24

Matched sampling A procedure for reducing extraneous differences among subjects in between-subjects experiments by matching those in the experimental and control groups on specified characteristics, such as age, sex, and weight. 51

Matching law The principle that, given the opportunity to respond on two or more reinforcement schedules, the rate of responding on each schedule will match the reinforcement available on each schedule. 371

Matching to sample A discrimination training procedure in which the task is to select from two or more comparison stimuli the one that matches a sample. Abbreviated MTS. 318

Method of loci A mnemonic system in which each item to be recalled is "placed" in a distinctive spot in an imagined scene, such as a walking path. 415

Mismatching A variation of matching to sample in which reinforcement is available for selecting the comparison stimulus that is different from the sample. Also called oddity matching. 318

Mixed schedule A complex reinforcement schedule in which two or more simple schedules, neither associated with a particular stimulus, alternate. (*Cf.* multiple schedule.) 367

Mnemonic Any technique for aiding recall. 414

Mnemonic system Any of several systems for aiding recall, including the method of loci and the peg word system. 415

Motivational processes In Bandura's theory of vicarious learning, the expectation that a modeled behavior will be reinforced. 288

Motor reproductive processes In Bandura's theory of vicarious learning, the skills required to perform modeled behavior. 288

MTS *See* matching to sample.

Multiple schedule A complex reinforcement schedule in which two or more simple schedules alternate, with each schedule associated with a particular stimulus. (*Cf.* mixed schedule.) 367

Mutation Any change in a gene. When the modified gene occurs in a reproductive cell, the mutation may be passed on to offspring. 7

Natural selection The tendency for characteristics that contribute to the survival of a species to persist, and for those that do not to disappear. 4

Negative punishment A punishment procedure in which a behavior is followed by the removal of, or a decrease in the intensity of, a stimulus. Also called type 2 punishment or penalty training. (*Cf.* positive punishment.) 191

Negative reinforcement A reinforcement procedure in which a behavior is followed by the removal of, or a decrease in the intensity of, a stimulus. Sometimes called escape training (*Cf.* positive reinforcement; punishment.) 142

Negative reinforcer Any stimulus which, when removed following a behavior, increases or maintains the strength of that behavior. 142

Noncontingent reinforcement The procedure of providing reinforcers independently of behavior. Abbreviated NCR. 213

Observational learning *See* vicarious learning.

Oddity matching *See* mismatching.

One-process theory The view that avoidance and punishment involve only one procedure—operant learning. (*Cf.* two-process theory.) 182

Operant learning Any procedure in which a behavior becomes stronger or weaker (eg., more or less likely to occur), depending on its consequences. Also called instrumental learning. *See* law of effect. 138

Operational definition A definition that specifies the operation (procedure) by which a term will be measured. 38

Overlearning The continuation of training beyond the point required to produce one errorless performance. 398

Overshadowing Failure of a stimulus that is part of a compound stimulus to become a CS. The stimulus is said to be overshadowed by the stimulus that does become a CS. (*Cf.* blocking.) 84

Paired associate learning A learning task involving pairs of words or other stimuli in which the subject is presented with the first item of a pair and is expected to produce the second item. 401

Partial reinforcement effect The tendency of a behavior to be more resistant to extinction following partial reinforcement than following continuous reinforcement. Abbreviated PRE. (Also often referred to as the partial reinforcement extinction effect, or PREE.) 361

Participant modeling A procedure in which a trainer first models a behavior and then assists the observer to perform it. 296

Pavlovian conditioning The procedure of pairing a neutral stimulus (typically referred to as the CS) with a US. Also called classical or respondent conditioning. 72

Peak shift The tendency following discrimination training for the peak of responding in a generalization gradient to shift away from the CS– or S–. 328

Peg word system A mnemonic system in which each of the first n integers is associated with a particular image (a "peg"), and each item to be recalled is "placed" on a peg. 416

Penalty training *See* negative punishment.

Positive punishment A punishment procedure in which a behavior is followed by the presentation of, or an increase in the intensity of, a stimulus. Also called type 1 punishment. (*Cf.* negative punishment.) 191

Positive reinforcement A reinforcement procedure in which a behavior is followed by the presentation of, or an increase in the intensity of, a stimulus. Sometimes called reward training, although the term *reward* is problematic. (*Cf.* negative reinforcement.) 142

Positive reinforcer Any stimulus which, when presented following a behavior, increases or maintains the strength of that behavior. 142

Post-reinforcement pause A pause in responding following reinforcement; associated primarily with FI and FR schedules. 350

PRE *See* partial reinforcement effect.

Premack principle The observation that high-probability behavior reinforces low-probability behavior. 175

Preparatory response theory Theory of Pavlovian conditioning that proposes that the CR prepares the organism for the occurrence of the US. 97

Preparedness *See* continuum of preparedness.

Primary reinforcer Any reinforcer that is not dependent on another reinforcer for its reinforcing properties. (*Cf.* secondary reinforcer.) 149

Proactive interference Forgetting caused by learning that occurred prior to the behavior in question. (*Cf.* retroactive interference.) 401

Prompted recall A method of measuring forgetting in which hints (prompts) about the behavior to be performed are provided. Also called cued recall. (*Cf.* free recall.) 392

Pseudoconditioning The tendency of a neutral stimulus to elicit a CR when presented after a US has elicited a reflex response. Apparently due to sensitization. 77

Punisher Any consequence of a behavior that decreases the strength of that behavior. (*Cf.* reinforcer.) 190

Punishment The procedure of providing consequences for a behavior that reduce the strength of that behavior. (*See* positive punishment and negative punishment; *Cf.* reinforcement.) 190

Ratio strain Disruption of the pattern of responding due to stretching the ratio of reinforcement too abruptly or too far. 360

Recognition A method of measuring forgetting in which the subject is required to identify stimuli experienced earlier. 393

Reflex A relationship between a specific event and a simple, involuntary response to that event. The term usually refers to an unconditional reflex. (*See* unconditional reflex; *Cf.* conditional reflex.) 8

Reinforcement The procedure of providing consequences for a behavior that increase or maintain the strength of that behavior. (*See* positive reinforcement and negative reinforcement; *cf.* punishment.) 141

Relative value theory Theory of reinforcement that considers reinforcers to be behaviors rather than stimuli and that attributes a reinforcer's effectiveness to its probability relative to other behaviors. 174

Relearning method A method of measuring forgetting in which a behavior is learned to criterion before and after a retention interval. Also called the savings method. 393

Releaser Any stimulus that reliably elicits a fixed action pattern. 13

Reminiscence Improvement in performance following a retention interval. (*Cf.* forgetting.) 406

Respondent conditioning *See* Pavlovian conditioning.

Response deprivation theory The theory of reinforcement that says a behavior is reinforcing to the extent that the organism has been deprived (relative to its baseline frequency) of performing that behavior. Also called equilibrium theory. 176

Response prevention The procedure of altering the environment to prevent unwanted behavior from occurring. 209

Response unit hypothesis The proposal that the PRE is due to differences in the definition of a behavior during intermittent and continuous reinforcement. 365

Resurgence The reappearance during extinction of a previously reinforced behavior. 169

Retention interval The time between training and testing for forgetting. 392

Retentional processes In Bandura's theory of vicarious learning, any activity by an observer that aids recall of modeled behavior. 288

Retroactive interference Forgetting caused by learning that occurred subsequent to the behavior in question. (*Cf.* proactive interference.) 404

Reward training *See* positive reinforcement.

Run rate The rate at which a behavior occurs once it has resumed following reinforcement. 351

S⁺ A stimulus in the presence of which a behavior will be reinforced. Also called S^D, pronounced *ess-dee*. (*Cf.* S–.) 314

S⁻ A stimulus in the presence of which a behavior will not be reinforced. Also called S^Δ, pronounced *ess-delta*. (*Cf.* S⁺.) 314

Savings method *See* relearning method.

Schedule effects The distinctive rate and pattern of responding associated with a particular reinforcement schedule. 348

Schedule of reinforcement A rule describing the delivery of reinforcers for a behavior. 348

Secondary reinforcer Any reinforcer that has acquired its reinforcing properties through its association with other reinforcers. Also called conditioned reinforcer. (*Cf.* primary reinforcer.) 149

Semantic generalization Generalization based on an abstract (as opposed to a physical) property of a stimulus. 308

Sensitization An increase in the intensity or probability of a reflex response resulting from earlier exposure to a stimulus that elicits that response. (*Cf.* habituation.) 10

Sensory preconditioning A procedure in which two neutral stimuli are paired, after which one is repeatedly paired with a US. If the other stimulus is then presented alone, it may elicit a CR even though it was never paired with the US. 88

Sequential hypothesis The proposal that the PRE occurs because the sequence of reinforced and nonreinforced behaviors during intermittent reinforcement becomes an S⁺ for responding during extinction. 364

Shaping In operant training, the procedure of reinforcing successive approximations of a desired behavior. 152

Sidman avoidance procedure An escape-avoidance training procedure in which no stimulus regularly precedes the aversive stimulus. Also called unsignaled avoidance. 181

Sign tracking A procedure in which a stimulus is followed by a reinforcer regardless of what the organism does. The procedure often results in the "shaping" of behavior without reinforcement. Also called autoshaping. 439

Simultaneous conditioning A Pavlovian conditioning procedure in which the CS and US occur together in time. 80

Simultaneous discrimination training A discrimination training procedure in which the S⁺ and S⁻ are presented at the same time. 318

Single-case experiment *See* within-subject experiment.

Single-subject experiment *See* within-subject experiment.

Spontaneous recovery The sudden reappearance of a behavior following its extinction. 92

State-dependent learning Learning that occurs during a particular physiological state (such as alcoholic intoxication) and is lost when that physiological state passes. 407

Stimulus Any event that affects, or is capable of affecting, behavior. 40

Stimulus control The tendency for a behavior to occur in the presence of an S⁺ but not in the presence of an S⁻. (*Cf.* discrimination.) 322

Stimulus substitution theory In Pavlovian conditioning, the theory that the CS substitutes for the US. Assumes that the CR is essentially the same as the UR. 96

Stretching the ratio The procedure of gradually increasing the number of responses required for reinforcement. 359

Successive discrimination training A discrimination training procedure in which the S⁺ and S⁻ are presented one after the other in random sequence. 318

Superstitious behavior Any increase in the strength of behavior that is due to coincidental reinforcement. 244

Tandem schedule A complex reinforcement schedule that consists of a series of simple schedules, with reinforcement delivered only on completion of the last schedule in the series. The simple schedules are not associated with different stimuli. (*Cf.* chain schedule.) 368

Task analysis The procedure of identifying the component elements of a behavior chain. 157

Test trial In Pavlovian conditioning, the procedure of presenting the CS on some occasions without the US to determine whether learning has occurred. 77

Trace conditioning A Pavlovian conditioning procedure in which the CS begins and ends before the US is presented. 79

Two-process theory The view that avoidance and punishment involve two procedures—Pavlovian and operant learning. (*Cf.* one-process theory.) 179

Type 1 punishment *See* positive punishment.

Type 2 punishment *See* negative punishment.

Unconditional reflex A synonym for reflex. An unconditional reflex consists of an unconditional stimulus and an unconditional response. (*See* reflex; *Cf.* conditional reflex.) 70

Unconditional response The response elicited by an unconditional stimulus. Often called an unconditioned response. Abbreviated UR. (*Cf.* conditional response.) 71

Unconditional stimulus The stimulus that elicits an unconditional response. Often called an unconditioned stimulus. Abbreviated US. (*Cf.* conditional stimulus.) 71

Unsignaled avoidance *See* Sidman avoidance procedure.

UR *See* unconditional response.

US *See* unconditional stimulus.

Variable duration schedule A reinforcement schedule in which reinforcement is contingent on the continuous performance of a behavior for a period of time, with the length of the time varying around an average. Abbreviated VD. (*Cf.* fixed duration schedule.) 356

Variable interval schedule A reinforcement schedule in which a behavior is reinforced the first time it occurs following an interval since the last reinforcement, with the interval varying around a specified average. Abbreviated VI. (*Cf.* fixed interval schedule.) 354

Variable ratio schedule A reinforcement schedule in which, on average, every *n*th performance of a behavior is reinforced. Abbreviated VR. (*Cf.* fixed ratio schedule.) 351

Variable time schedule A reinforcement schedule in which reinforcement is delivered at varying intervals regardless of what the organism does. Abbreviated VT. (*Cf.* fixed time schedule.) 358

VD schedule *See* variable duration schedule.

VI schedule *See* variable interval schedule.

Vicarious learning. Any procedure in which an organism learns by observing the behavior of another organism. Also called observational learning. 266

VR schedule *See* variable ratio schedule.

VT schedule *See* variable time schedule.

Within-subject experiment A research design in which the independent variable is made to vary at different times for the same subject. (Thus, each subject serves as both an experimental and control subject.) Also called single-subject or single-case experiment. 52

References

Abramowitz, A. J., & O'Leary, S. G. (1990). Effectiveness of delayed punishment in an applied setting. *Behavior Therapy, 21,* 231–239.

Adams-Curtiss, L., & Fragaszy, D. M. (1995). Influence of a skilled model on the behavior of conspecific observers in tufted capuchin monkeys (Cebus apella). *American Journal of Primatology, 37,* 65–71.

Ader, R., & Cohen, N. (1975). Behaviorally conditioned immunosuppression. *Psychosomatic Medicine, 37,* 333–340.

Ader, R., & Cohen, N. (1993). Psychoneuroimmunology: Conditioning and stress. *Annual Review of Psychology, 33,* 53–86.

Agar, W. E., Drummond, F. H., Tiegs, O. W., & Gunson, M. M. (1954). Fourth (final) report on a test of McDougall's Lamarckian experiment on the training of rats. *Journal of Experimental Biology, 31,* 307–321.

Agras, S., Sylvestor, D., & Oliveau, D. (1969). The epidemiology of common fears and phobias. *Comprehensive Psychiatry, 10,* 151–156.

Akin, O. (1983). *The psychology of architectural design.* London: Pion.

Albert, R. S. (1980). Family positions and the attainment of eminence. *Gifted Child Quarterly, 24,* 87–95.

Alberts, E., & Ehrenfreund, D. (1951). Transposition in children as a function of age. *Journal of Experimental Psychology, 41,* 30–38.

Alexander, T. (1980, December 1). Economics according to the rats. *Fortune,* 127–130, 132.

Alford, B. A. (1986). Behavioral treatment of schizophrenic delusions: A single-case experimental analysis. *Behavior Therapy, 17,* 637–644.

Allan, R. W. (1990). *Concept learning and peck location in the pigeon.* Paper presented at the 16th annual convention of the Association for Behavior Analysis, Nashville, TN.

Allan, R. W. (1993). Control of pecking response topography by stimulus-reinforcer and response-reinforcer contingencies. In H. Philip Zeigler & Hans-Joachim Bischof (Eds.), *Vision, brain, and behavior in birds.* Cambridge, MA: MIT Press.

Allan, R. W. (1998). Operant-respondent interactions. In W. T. O'Donohue (Ed.), *Learning and behavior therapy.* Boston, MA: Allyn & Bacon.

Allen, C. T., & Janiszewski, C. A. (1989). Assessing the role of contingency awareness in attitudinal conditioning with implications for advertising research. *Journal of Marketing Research, 26,* 30–43.

Allen, C. T., & Madden, T. J. (1985). A closer look at classical conditioning. *Journal of Consumer Research, 12,* 301–315.

Alloway, T., Wilson, G., Graham, J., & Krames, L. (2000). *Sniffy the virtual rat: Pro version.* Belmont, CA: Wadsworth.

Amabile, T. M. (1982). Children's artistic creativity: Detrimental effects of competition in a field setting. *Personality and Social Psychology Bulletin, 8,* 573–578.

Amabile, T. M. (1983). *The social psychology of creativity.* New York: Springer-Verlag.

American Psychiatric Association. (1973). *Behavior therapy in psychiatry.* New York: Aronson.

American Psychological Association Ethics Committee. (1992). Ethical principles of psychologists and code of conduct. *American Psychologist, 47,* 1597–1611.

Amsel, A. (1958). The role of frustrative nonreward in noncontinuous reward situations. *Psychological Bulletin, 55,* 102–119.

Amsel, A. (1962). Frustrative nonreward in partial reinforcement and discrimination learning: Some recent history and theoretical extension. *Psychological Review, 69,* 306–328.

Anderson, P., Rothbaum, B. O., & Hodges, L. F. (2000). *Social phobia: Virtual reality exposure therapy for fear of public speaking.* Paper presented at the annual meeting of the American Psychological Association, Washington, DC.

Anger, D. (1963). The role of temporal discrimination in the reinforcement of Sidman avoidance behavior. *Journal of the Experimental Analysis of Behavior, 6,* 477–506.

Anrep, G. V. (1920). Pitch discrimination in the dog. *Journal of Physiology, 53,* 367–385.

Austad, C. S., Sininger, R., Daugherty, J., Geary, D., & Strange, J. (1984). Studies of imitative learning and vicarious reinforcement. *Psychological Reports, 55,* 279–289.

Axelrod, S. (1983). Introduction. In S. Axelrod & J. Apsche (Eds.), *The effects of punishment on human behavior.* New York: Academic Press.

Ayllon, T., & Haughton, E. (1962). Control of the behavior of schizophrenic patients by food. *Journal of the Experimental Analysis of Behavior, 5,* 343–352.

Azerrad, J., & Chance, P. (2001, September). Why our kids are out of control. *Psychology Today,* 42–48.

Azrin, N. H., & Holz, W. C. (1961). Punishment during fixed-interval reinforcement. *Journal of the Experimental Analysis of Behavior, 4,* 343–347.

Azrin, N. H., & Holz, W. C. (1966). Punishment. In W. K. Honig (Ed.), *Operant behavior: Areas of research and application.* New York: Appleton-Century-Crofts.

Azrin, N. H., Holz, W. C., & Hake, D. F. (1963). Fixed-ratio punishment. *Journal of the Experimental Analysis of Behavior, 6,* 141–148.

Azrin, N. H., Hutchinson, R. R., & Hake, D. F. (1966). Extinction-induced aggression. *Journal of the Experimental Analysis of Behavior, 9,* 191–204.

Azrin, N. H., Hutchinson, R. R., & McLaughlin, R. (1965). The opportunity for aggression as an operant reinforcer during aversive stimulation. *Journal of the Experimental Analysis of Behavior, 8,* 171–180.

Azzi, R., Fix, D. S. R., Keller, F. S., & Rocha, M. I. (1964). Exteroceptive control of response under delayed reinforcement. *Journal of the Experimental Analysis of Behavior, 7,* 159–162.

Bachrach, A. J., Erwin, W. J., & Mohr, J. P. (1965). The control of eating behavior in an anorexic by operant conditioning techniques. In L. P. Ullmann & L. Krasner (Eds.), *Case studies in behavior modification.* New York: Holt, Rinehart & Winston.

Baer, D. M., & Deguchi, H. (1985). Generalized imitation from a radical-behavioral viewpoint. In S. Reiss & R. R. Bootzin (Eds.), *Theoretical issues in behavior therapy.* Orlando, FL: Academic Press.

Baer, D. M., Peterson, R. F., & Sherman, J. A. (1967). The development of imitation by reinforcing behavioral similarity to a model. *Journal of the Experimental Analysis of Behavior, 10,* 405–416.

Baer, D. M., & Sherman, J. A. (1964). Reinforcement control of generalized imitation in young children. *Journal of Experimental Child Psychology, 1,* 37–49.

Bahrick, H. P. (1984). Semantic memory content in permastore: Fifty years of memory for Spanish learned in school. *Journal of Experimental Psychology: General, 113,* 1–29.

Bailey, J. M., & Benishay, D. S. (1993). Familial aggregation of female sexual orientation. *American Journal of Psychiatry, 150,* 272–277.

Bailey, J. M., & Pillard, R. C. (1995). Genetics of human sexual orientation. *Annual Review of Sex Research, 6,* 126–150.

Baker, B. L. (1969). Symptom treatment and symptom substitution in enuresis. *Journal of Abnormal Psychology, 74*(1), 42–49.

Bales, J. (1984, November). Rozin Talk "Disgusts" Crowd. *APA Monitor,* 26.

Balster, R., et al. (1992, December). In defense of animal research. *APA Monitor,* 3.

Bandura, A. (1965). Vicarious processes: A case of no-trial learning. In L. Berkowitz (Ed.), *Advances in experimental social psychology* (Vol. 2). New York: Academic Press.

Bandura, A. (1971a). Analysis of modeling processes. In A. Bandura (Ed.), *Psychological modeling: Conflicting theories.* Chicago: Aldine-Atherton.

Bandura, A. (Ed.). (1971b). *Psychological modeling: Conflicting theories.* Chicago: Aldine-Atherton.

Bandura, A. (1971c). *Social learning theory.* New York: General Learning Press.

Bandura, A. (1973). *Aggression: A social learning analysis.* Englewood Cliffs, NJ: Prentice-Hall.

Bandura, A. (1977). *Social learning theory.* Englewood Cliffs, NJ: Prentice-Hall.

Bandura, A. (1986). *Social foundations of thought and action.* Englewood Cliffs, NJ: Prentice-Hall.

Bandura, A., Blanchard, E. B., & Ritter, B. (1969). Relative efficacy of desensitization and modeling approaches for inducing behavioral, affective and attitudinal changes. *Journal of Personality and Social Psychology, 13,* 173–199.

Bandura, A., & McDonald, F. J. (1963). Influence of social reinforcement and the behavior of models in shaping children's moral judgments. *Journal of Abnormal and Social Psychology, 67,* 274–281.

Bandura, A., & Menlove, F. L. (1968). Factors determining vicarious extinction of avoidance behavior through symbolic modeling. *Journal of Personality and Social Psychology, 8,* 99–108.

Bandura, A., & Mischel, W. (1965). Modification of self-imposed delay of reward through exposure to live and symbolic models, *Journal of Personality and Social Psychology, 2,* 698–705.

Bandura, A., Ross, D., & Ross, S. A. (1963). Vicarious reinforcement and imitative learning. *Journal of Abnormal and Social Psychology, 67,* 601–607.

Bandura, A., & Walters, R. H. (1959). *Adolescent aggression.* New York: Ronald Press.

Barash, D., & Lipton, J. (2001). *The myth of monogamy.* San Francisco: Freeman.

Barnett, P. E., & Benedetti, D. T. (1960, May). *A study in "vicarious conditioning."* Paper presented at the Rocky Mountain Psychological Association, Glenwood Springs, CO.

Baron, A., & Derenne, A. (2000). Progressive-ratio schedules: Effects of later schedule requirements on earlier performances. *Journal of the Experimental Analysis of Behavior, 73,* 291–304.

Bartlett, B. (1992, March). Mistaken identity. *Teacher Magazine,* 12–13.

Bartlett, F. C. (1932). *Remembering: A study in experimental social psychology.* New York: Macmillan.

Batsell, W. R. (2000). Augmentation: Synergistic conditioning in taste-aversion learning. *Current Directions in Psychological Science, 9*(5), 164–168.

Batson, J. D., & Batsell, W. R. (2000). Augmentation, not blocking, in an A+/AX+ flavor-conditioning procedure. *Psychonomic Bulletin & Review, 7*(3), 466–471.

Baum, W. M. (1974). Choice in free-ranging wild pigeons. *Science, 185,* 78–79.

Baum, W. M. (1975). Time allocation in human vigilance. *Journal of the Experimental Analysis of Behavior, 23,* 43–53.

Baum, W. M., & Kraft, J. R. (1998). Group choice: Competition, travel, and the ideal free distribution. *Journal of the Experimental Analysis of Behavior, 69,* 227–245.

Belke, T. W., & Dunbar, M. J. (2001). Effects of cocaine on fixed interval responding reinforced by the opportunity to run. *Journal of the Experimental Analysis of Behavior, 75,* 77–91.

Belli, R. F., Schuman, A., & Jackson, B. (1997). Autobiographical misremembering: John Dean is not alone. *Applied Cognitive Psychology, 11*(3), 187–209.

Berger, S. M. (1962). Conditioning through vicarious instigation. *Psychological Review, 69,* 450–466.

Berger, S. M. (1971). Observer perseverance as related to a model's success: A social comparison analysis. *Journal of Personality and Social Psychology, 19,* 341–350.

Berkowitz, L. (1964). Aggressive cues in aggressive behavior and hostility catharsis. *Psychological Review, 71,* 104–122.

Berkowitz, L. (1968, September). Impulse, aggression and the gun. *Psychology Today,* 18–22.

Berkowitz, L. (1983). Aversively stimulated aggression: Some parallels and differences in research with animals and humans. *American Psychologist, 38,* 1135–1144.

Berkowitz, L., & Donnerstein, E. (1982). External validity is more than skin deep: Some answers to criticisms of laboratory experiments. *American Psychologist, 37,* 245–257.

Berkowitz, L., & LePage, A. (1967). Weapons as aggression-eliciting stimuli. *Journal of Personality and Social Psychology, 7,* 202–207.

Bernal, G., & Berger, S. M. (1976). *Journal of Personality and Social Psychology, 34,* 62–68.

Bernstein, I. L. (1978). Learned taste aversion in children receiving chemotherapy. *Science, 200,* 1302–1303.

Bertelsen, A., Harvald, B., & Hauge, M. (1977). A Danish twin study of manic-depressive disorders. *British Journal of Psychiatry, 130,* 330–351.

Binder, C. V., Haughton, E., & Van Eyk, D. (1990). Increasing endurance by building fluency: Precision teaching attention span. *Teaching Exceptional Children, 22,* 24–27.

Binmore, K. (1991). Rational choice theory: Necessary but not sufficient. *American Psychologist, 46,* 797–799.

Bitterman, M. E. (1964). Classical conditioning in the goldfish as a function of the CS-US interval. *Journal of Comparative and Physiological Psychology, 58,* 359–366.

Blaha, F. (1946). In trial of the major German war criminals. *Proceedings of the International Military Tribunal at Nuremberg,* HMSO. Reprinted in J. Carey (Ed.), *Eyewitness to history.* Cambridge, MA: Harvard University Press.

Blakely, E., & Schlinger, H. (1988). Determinants of pausing under variable-ratio schedules: Reinforcer magnitude, ratio size, and schedule configuration. *Journal of the Experimental Analysis of Behavior, 50,* 65–73.

Bliss, R. E., Garvey, A. J., Heinold, J. W., & Hitchcock, J. L. (1989). The influence of situation and coping on relapse crisis outcomes after smoking cessation. *Journal of Consulting and Clinical Psychology, 57,* 443–449.

Blough, D. S. (1959). Delayed matching in the pigeon. *Journal of the Experimental Analysis of Behavior, 2,* 151–160.

Boe, E. E., & Church, R. M. (1967). Permanent effects of punishment during extinction. *Journal of Comparative and Physiological Psychology, 63,* 486–492.

Bouchard, T. J. (1997, September/October). Whenever the twain shall meet. *The Sciences,* 52–57.

Bouton, M. E., & Swartzentruber, D. (1991). Source of relapse after extinction in Pavlovian and instrumental learning. *Clinical Psychology Review, 11,* 123–140.

Bovbjerg, D. H., Redd, W. H., Maier, L. A., Holland, J. C., Lesko, L. M., Niedzwiecki, D., Rubin, S. C., & Hakes, R. B. (1990). Anticipatory immune suppression and nausea in women receiving cyclic chemotherapy for ovarian cancer. *Journal of Consulting and Clinical Psychology, 58,* 153–157.

Boyle, M. E., & Greer, R. D. (1983). Operant procedures and the comatose patient. *Journal of Applied Behavior Analysis, 16,* 3–12.

Braun, H. W., & Geiselhart, R. (1959). Age differences in the acquisition and extinction of the conditioned eyelid response. *Journal of Experimental Psychology, 57,* 386–388.

Breland, K., & Breland, M. (1961). The misbehavior of organisms. *American Psychologist, 16,* 681–684.

Bridger, W. H. (1961). Sensory habituation and discrimination in the human neonate. *American Journal of Psychiatry, 117,* 991–996.

Brogden, W. J. (1939). Sensory pre-conditioning. *Journal of Experimental Psychology, 25,* 323–332.

Brower, L. P. (1971). Prey coloration and predator behavior. In V. Dethier (Ed.), *Topics in animal behavior, topics in the study of life: The BIO source book, part 6.* New York: Harper & Row.

Brown, J. F., & Hendy, S. (2001). A step towards ending the isolation of behavior analysis: A common language with evolutionary science. *The Behavior Analyst, 24,* 163–171.

Brown, J. S. (1942). Factors determining conflict reactions in different discriminations. *Journal of Experimental Psychology, 31,* 272–292.

Brown, P. L., & Jenkins, H. M. (1968). Autoshaping of the pigeon's key-peck. *Journal of the Experimental Analysis of Behavior, 11,* 1–8.

Bruner, A., & Revusky, S. H. (1961). Collateral behavior in humans. *Journal of the Experimental Analysis of Behavior, 4,* 349–350.

Bruner, J. S. (1983). *In search of mind: Essays in autobiography.* New York: Harper/Collins.

Bryan, W. L., & Harter, N. (1899). Studies on the telegraphic language. The acquisition of a hierarchy of habits. *Psychological Review, 6*, 345–375.

Buckalew, L. W., & Gibson, G. S. (1984). Antecedent and attendant stimuli in smoking: Implications for behavioral maintenance and modification. *Journal of Clinical Psychology, 40*, 1101–1106.

Burdick, A. (1991, November/December). Spin doctors. *The Sciences*, 54.

Burish, T. G., & Carey, M. P. (1986). Conditioned aversive response in cancer chemotherapy patients: Theoretical and developmental analysis. *Journal of Consulting and Clinical Psychology, 54*, 593–600.

Buss, D. M. (2000). Natural selection. In A. Kazdin (Ed.), *Encyclopedia of psychology* (Vol. 2, pp. 398–402). Washington, DC: American Psychological Association and Oxford University Press.

Cahoon, D. D. (1968). Symptom substitution and the behavior therapies: A reappraisal. *Psychological Bulletin, 69*(3), 149–156.

Calkins, M. W. (1894). Association: I. *Psychological Review, 1*, 476–483.

Calkins, M. W. (1896). Association: II. *Psychological Review, 3*, 32–49.

Camp, D. S., Raymond, G. A., & Church, R. M. (1967). Temporal relationship between response and punishment. *Journal of Experimental Psychology, 74*, 114–123.

Campos, J. J. (1984). Johannes Ludvicus Vives on the principles of conditioning. *Journal of the Experimental Analysis of Behavior, 41*, 16.

Capaldi, E. J. (1966). Partial reinforcement: A hypothesis of sequential effects. *Psychological Review, 73*, 459–477.

Capaldi, E. J. (1967). A sequential hypothesis of instrumental learning. In K. W. Spence & J. T. Spence (Eds.), *The psychology of learning and motivation* (Vol. 1). New York: Academic.

Capehart, J., Viney, W., & Hulicka, I. M. (1958). The effect of effort upon extinction. *Journal of Consulting and Clinical Psychology, 51*, 505–507.

Carey, J. (Ed.). (1988). *Eyewitness to history.* Cambridge, MA: Harvard University Press.

Carlin, A. S., Hoffman, H. G., & Weghorst, S. (1997). Virtual reality and tactile augmentation in the treatment of spider phobia: A case study. *Behavior Research and Therapy, 35*, 153–158.

Carlson, J. G., & Wielkiewicz, R. M. (1972). Delay of reinforcement in instrumental discrimination learning of rats. *Journal of Comparative and Physiological Psychology, 81*, 365–370.

Carlson, J. G., & Wielkiewicz, R. M. (1976). Mediators of the effects of magnitude of reinforcement. *Learning and Motivation, 7*, 184–196.

Carr, A. (1967). Adaptive aspects of the scheduled travel of Chelonia. In R. M. Storm (Ed.), *Animal orientation and navigation.* Corvallis: Oregon State University Press.

Carr, E. G. (1985). Behavioral approaches to language and communication. In E. Schopler & G. Mesibov (Eds.), *Current issues in autism: Vol. 3. Communication problems in autism.* New York: Plenum.

Carr, E. G. (1988). Functional equivalence as a mechanism of response generalization. In R. H. Horner, R. L. Koegel, & G. Dunlap (Eds.), *Generalization and maintenance: Lifestyle changes in applied settings.* Baltimore: Brookes.

Carr, E. G., & Durand, V. M. (1985). Reducing behavior problems through functional communication training. *Journal of Applied Behavior Analysis, 18*, 111–126.

Carr, E. G., & Kemp, D. C. (1989). Functional equivalence of autistic leading and communicative pointing: Analysis and treatment. *Journal of Autism and Developmental Disorders, 19*, 561–578.

Carr, E. G., & McDowell, J. J. (1980). Social control of self-injurious behavior of organic etiology. *Behavior Therapy, 11*, 402–409.

Carr, E. G., & Newsom, C. (1985). Demand-related tantrums: Conceptualizations and treatment. *Behavior Modification, 9*, 403–426.

Carr, E. G., Newsom, D. D., & Binkoff, J. A. (1976). Stimulus control of self-destructive behavior in a psychotic child. *Journal of Abnormal Child Psychology, 4*, 139–153.

Carr, E. G., Robinson, S., & Palumbo, L. W. (1990a). The wrong issue: Aversive versus nonaversive treatment. The right issue: Functional versus nonfunctional treatment. In A. Rapp & N. Singh (Eds.), *Perspectives on the use of nonaversive and aversive interventions for persons with developmental disabilities.* Sycamore, IL: Sycamore Press.

Carr, E. G., Robinson, S., Taylor, J. C., & Carlson, J. I. (1990b). Positive approaches to the treatment of severe behavior problems in persons with developmental disabilities: A review and analysis of reinforcement and stimulus-based procedures. *Monograph of the Association for Persons with Severe Handicaps,* No. 4.

Carr, J. E., Coriaty, S., Wilder, D. A., Gaunt, B. T., Dozier, C. L., Britton, L. N., Avina, C., & Reed, C. L. (2000). A review of "noncontingent" reinforcement as treatment for the aberrant behavior of individuals with developmental disabilities. *Research in Developmental Disabilities, 21*(5), 377–391.

Carter, H. D. (1933). Twin similarities in personality traits. *Journal of Genetic Psychology, 43,* 312–321.

Catania, A. C. (1966). Concurrent operants. In W. K. Honig (Ed.), *Operant behavior: Areas of research and application.* New York: Appleton-Century-Crofts.

Catania, A. C. (1998). *Learning* (4th ed.). Upper Saddle River, NJ: Prentice-Hall.

Cautela, J. R. (1966). Treatment of compulsive behavior by covert sensitization. *Psychological Record, 16,* 33–41.

Chall, J. S. (1995). *Learning to read: The great debate.* New York: Harcourt Brace.

Chambers, K., Goldman, L., & Kovesdy, P. (1977). Effects of positive reinforcement on creativity. *Perceptual and Motor Skills, 44,* 322.

Chance, P. (1974, January). After you hit a child, you can't just get up and leave him; you are hooked to that kid: An interview with Ivar Lovaas. *Psychology Today,* 76–84.

Chance, P. (1975, December). Facts that liberated the gay community: An interview with Evelyn Hooker. *Psychology Today,* 52–55, 101.

Chance, P. (1986, October). Life after head injury. *Psychology Today,* 62–69.

Chance, P. (1997). Speaking of differences. *Phi Delta Kappan, 78*(7), 506–507.

Chance, P. (1999). Thorndike's puzzle boxes and the origins of the experimental analysis of behavior. *Journal of the Experimental Analysis of Behavior, 72*(3), 433–440.

Charness, N. (1979). Components of skill in bridge. *Canadian Journal of Psychology, 33,* 1–50.

Chase, W. G., & Simon, H. A. (1973). Perception in chess. *Cognitive Psychology, 4,* 55–81.

Chickens of the sea. (1992, May). *Harper's Magazine,* 35.

Christopher, A. B. (1988). *Predisposition versus experiential models of compulsive gambling: An experimental analysis using pigeons.* Unpublished Ph. D. dissertation, West Virginia University, Morgantown.

Coates, B., & Hartup, W. (1969). Age and verbalization in observational learning. *Developmental Psychology, 1,* 556–562.

Cobb, P. (2000). Constructivism. In A. Kazdin (Ed.), *Encyclopedia of psychology.* (Vol. 2, pp. 277–279). Washington, DC: American Psychological Association and Oxford University Press.

Cook, M., & Mineka, S. (1990). Selective associations in the observational conditioning of fear in rhesus monkeys. *Journal of Experimental Psychology: Animal Behavior Processes, 16,* 372–389.

Cooley, C. H. (1902). *Human nature and the social order.* New York: Charles Scribner's Sons.

Cooper, L. A., & Shepard, R. N. (1973). Chronometric studies of the rotation of mental images. In W. G. Chase (Ed.), *Visual information processing.* New York: Academic.

Cordoba, O. A., & Chapel, J. L. (1983). Medroxyproesterone acetate antiandrogen treatment of hypersexuality in a pedophiliac sex offender. *American Journal of Psychiatry, 140*(8), 1036–1039.

Cotton, J. W. (1953). Running time as a function of amount of food deprivation. *Journal of Experimental Psychology, 46,* 188–198.

Cowles, J. T. (1937). Food-tokens as incentives for learning by chimpanzees. *Comparative Psychology Monographs 14* (No. 5).

Cronk, L. (1992, January/February). On human nature: Old dogs, old tricks. *The Sciences,* 13–15.

Crossman, E. K. (1991). Schedules of reinforcement. In W. Ishaq (Ed.), *Human behavior in today's world.* New York: Praeger.

Cuny, H. (1962). *Ivan Pavlov: The man and his theories* (P. Evans, Trans.). Greenwich, CN: Fawcett World Library.

D'Amato, M. R. (1973). Delayed matching to sample and short-term memory in monkeys. In G. H. Bower (Ed.), *The psychology of learning and motivation: Advances in research and theory* (Vol. 7). New York: Academic.

Daniels, A. (1994). *Bringing out the best in people.* San Francisco: McGraw-Hill.

Darwin, C. (1859). *On the origin of species.* London: J. Murray.

Darwin, C. (1874). *The descent of man* (2nd ed.). New York: Thomas Y. Crowell & Co. (Original work published 1871)

Da Silva, S., & Lattal, K. A. (2001, May 25–29). *Effects of reinforcement history on response resurgence.* Poster presented at the annual meeting of the Association for Behavior Analysis, New Orleans.

David, H. P., Dytrych, Z., Matejcek, Z., & Schuller, V. (Eds.). (1988). *Born unwanted: Developmental effects of denied abortion.* New York: Springer.

Davis, H., & Hurwitz, H. M. (Eds.). (1977). *Operant-Pavlovian interactions.* Hillsdale, NJ: Erlbaum.

Davis, W. M., & Smith, S. G. (1976). Role of conditioned reinforcers in the initiation, maintenance and extinction of drug-seeking behavior. *Pavlovian Journal of Biological Science, 11,* 222–236.

Davison, M., & McCarthy, D. (1988). *The matching law: A research review.* Hillsdale, NJ: Erlbaum.

Dawkins, R. (1986). *The blind watchmaker.* New York: Norton.

Dawkins, R. (1995a, November). God's utility function. *Scientific American,* 80–86.

Dawkins, R. (1995b). *River out of Eden.* New York: Basic.

DeAngelis, T. (1992, May). Senate seeking answers to rising tide of violence. *APA Monitor,* 11.

Deci, E. L., & Ryan, R. M. (1985). *Intrinsic motivation and self-determination in human behavior.* New York: Plenum.

DeGrandpre, R. J. (1999, March/April). Just cause? *The Sciences,* 14–18.

de Groot, A. D. (1966). Perception and memory versus thought: Some old ideas and recent findings. In B. Kleinmuntz (Ed.), *Problem solving: Research, method and theory.* New York: Wiley.

Delprato, D. J. (2001). Comparisons of discrete-trial and normalized behavioral language intervention for young children with autism. *Journal of Autism and Developmental Disorders, 31*(3), 315–326.

Deran, R., & Whitaker, K. (1980). *Fear of flying: Impact on the U. S. air travel industry.* Boeing Company Document #BCS-00009-RO/OM.

Dethier, V. G., Solomon, R. L., & Turner, L. H. (1965). Sensory input and central excitation and inhibition in the blowfly. *Journal of Comparative and Physiological Psychology, 60,* 303–313.

deVilliers, P. A. (1977). Choice in concurrent schedules and a quantitative formulation of the law of effect. In W. K. Honig & J. E. R. Staddon (Eds.), *Handbook of operant behavior.* Englewood Cliffs, NJ: Prentice-Hall.

Dews, P. B. (1959). Some observations on an operant in the octopus. *Journal of the Experimental Analysis of Behavior, 2,* 57–63.

Dickinson, A., Watt, A., & Griffiths, W. J. H. (1992). Free-operant acquisition with delayed reinforcement. *Quarterly Journal of Experimental Psychology, 45B,* 241–258.

DiFranza, J. R. (1995). The effects of tobacco advertising on children. In K. Slama (Ed.), *Tobacco and health* (pp. 87–90). New York: Plenum.

DiFranza, J. R., & Aisquith, B. F. (1995). Does the Joe Camel campaign preferentially reach 18 to 24 year old adults? *Tobacco Control, 4*(4), 367–371.

DiFranza, J. R., & McAfee, T. (1992). The tobacco institute: Helping youth say "yes" to tobacco. *Journal of Family Practice, 34*(6), 694–696.

DiFranza, J. R., Richards, J. W., Paulman, P. M., Wolf-Gillespie, N., Fletcher, C., Jaffe, R. D., & Murray, D. (1991). RJR Nabisco's cartoon camel promotes Camel cigarettes to children. *Journal of the American Medical Association, 266*(22), 3149–3153.

Dinsmoor, J. A. (1954). Punishment: I: The avoidance hypothesis. *Psychological Review, 61,* 34–46.

Dinsmoor, J. A. (1955). Punishment: II: An interpretation of empirical findings. *Psychological Review, 62,* 96–105.

Dinsmoor, J. A. (2001). Stimuli inevitably generated by behavior that avoids electric shock are inherently reinforcing. *Journal of the Experimental Analysis of Behavior, 75,* 311–333.

Diven, K. (1937). Certain determinants in the conditioning of anxiety reactions. *Journal of Psychology, 3,* 291–308.

Donahoe, J. W. (1999). Edward L. Thorndike: The selectionist connectionist. *Journal of the Experimental Analysis of Behavior, 72,* 451–454.

Donahoe, J. W., & Marrs, D. P. (1982). Twelve-year retention of stimulus and schedule control. *Bulletin of the Psychonomic Society, 19*(3), 184–186.

Donahoe, J. W., & Palmer, D. C. (1994). *Learning and complex behavior.* Boston, MA: Allyn & Bacon.

Ducharme, D. E., & Holborn, S. W. (1997). Programmed generalization of social skills in preschool children with hearing impairments. *Journal of Applied Behavior Analysis, 30*(4), 639–651.

Durant, W. (1926/1927). *The story of philosophy.* Garden City, NY: Garden City Publishing.

Durlach, P. J. (1982). Pavlovian learning and performance when CS and US are uncorrelated. In M. L. Commons, R. J. Herrnstein, & A. R. Wagner (Eds.), *Quantitative analysis of behavior: Vol.3. Acquisition.* Cambridge, MA: Ballinger.

Dweck, C. S., & Repucci, N. D. (1973). Learned helplessness and reinforcement responsibility in children. *Journal of Personality and Social Psychology, 25,* 109–116.

Dworkin, B. R., & Miller, N. E. (1986). Failure to replicate visceral learning in the acute curarized rat preparation. *Behavioral Neuroscience, 100,* 299–314.

Dyson, F. J. (1999, March/April). Miracles of rare device. *The Sciences,* 32–37.

Eaton, G. G. (1976). The social order of Japanese macaques. *Scientific American, 234,* 96–106.

Ebbinghaus, H. (1885). *Memory, a contribution to experimental psychology* (H. A. Ruger, Trans., 1913). New York: Columbia University Press.

Edwards, C. A., & Honig, W. K. (1987). Memorization and "feature selection" in the acquisition of natural concepts in pigeons. *Learning and Motivation, 18,* 235–260.

Egan, D. E., & Schwartz, B. J. (1979). Chunking in recall of symbolic drawings. *Memory and Cognition, 7,* 149–158.

Eikelboom, R., & Stewart, J. (1982). Conditioning of drug-induced physiological responses. *Psychological Review, 89,* 507–528.

Eisenberger, R. (1992). Learned industriousness. *Psychological Review, 99*(2), 248–267.

Eisenberger, R., & Armeli, S. (1997). Can salient rewards increase creative performance without reducing intrinsic creative interest? *Journal of Personality and Social Psychology, 72,* 652–663.

Eisenberger, R., Armeli, S., & Pretz, J. (1998). Can the promise of reward increase creativity? *Journal of Personality and Social Psychology, 74,* 704–714.

Eisenberger, R., & Cameron, J. (1996). Detrimental effects of reward: Reality or myth? *American Psychologist, 51,* 115–166.

Eisenberger, R., & Cameron, J. (1998). Reward, intrinsic interest, and creativity: New findings. *American Psychologist, 53,* 676–679.

Eisenberger, R., Karpman, M., & Trattner, J. (1967). What is the necessary and sufficient condition in the contingency situation? *Journal of Experimental Psychology, 74,* 342–350.

Eisenberger, R., Masterson, F. A., & McDermott, M. (1982). Effects of task variety on generalized effort. *Journal of Educational Psychology, 74*(4), 499–505.

Eisenberger, R., & Rhoades, L. (2001). Incremental effects of reward on creativity. *Journal of Personality and Social Psychology, 81*(4), 728–741.

Eisenberger, R., & Selbst, M. (1994). Does reward increase or decrease creativity? *Journal of Personality and Social Psychology, 66,* 1116–1127.

Ekman, P., & Patterson, J. (1992). *The day America told the truth.* New York: Prentice-Hall.

Elliott, M. H. (1928). The effect of change of reward on the maze performance of rats. *University of California Publications in Psychology, 4,* 19–30.

English, H. B., & English, A. C. (1958). *A comprehensive dictionary of psychological and psychoanalytic terms.* New York: McKay.

Epstein, R. (1981). On pigeons and people: A preliminary look at the Columban simulation project. *The Behavior Analyst, 4,* 43–55.

Epstein, R. (1983). Resurgence of previously reinforced behavior during extinction. *The Behavior Analyst Letters, 3,* 391–397.

Epstein, R. (1984). Simulation research in the analysis of behavior. *Behaviorism, 12,* 41–59.

Epstein, R. (1985). Extinction-induced resurgence: Preliminary investigation and possible application. *Psychological Record, 35,* 143–153.

Epstein, R. (1996). *Self-help without the hype.* Tucker, GA: Performance Management Publications.

Epstein, R. (1997). Skinner as self-manager. *Journal of Applied Behavior Analysis, 30,* 545–568.

Epstein, R. (1999). Generativity theory. In M. Runco (Ed.), *Encyclopedia of creativity.* New York: Academic.

Epstein, R., Kirshnit, C., Lanza, R., & Rubin, L. (1984). Insight in the pigeon: Antecedents and determinants of an intelligent performance. *Nature, 308,* 61–62.

Epstein, R., Lanza, R. P., & Skinner, B. F. (1981). "Self-awareness" in the pigeon. *Science, 212,* 695–696.

Epstein, R., & Skinner, B. F. (1980). Resurgence of responding after the cessation of response-independent reinforcement. *Proceedings of the National Academy of Sciences, 77,* 6251–6253.

Epstein, R., & Skinner, B. F. (1981). The spontaneous use of memoranda by pigeons. *Behavior Analysis Letters, 1,* 241–246.

Epstein, W. (1972). Mechanisms of directed forgetting. In G. H. Bower (Ed.), *The psychology of learning and motivation* (Vol. 6). New York: Academic.

Ericsson, K. A., & Chase, W. G. (1982). Exceptional memory. *American Scientist, 70,* 607–615.

Ericsson, K. A., & Simon, H. A. (1993). *Protocol analysis* (rev.ed.). Cambridge, MA: MIT Press.

Estes, W. K. (1944). An experimental study of punishment. *Psychological Monographs, 57* (whole no. 263).

Estes, W. K., & Skinner, B. F. (1941). Some quantitative properties of anxiety. *Journal of Experimental Psychology, 29,* 390–400.

Eysenck, H. J. (1952). The effects of psychotherapy: An evaluation. *Journal of Consulting Psychology, 16,* 319–324.

Eysenck, H. J. (1960). *Behavior therapy and the neuroses.* New York: Pergamon.

Eysenck, H. J. (1976). *Sex and personality.* Austin: University of Texas Press.

Farber, S. (1981). *Identical twins reared apart: A reanalysis.* New York: Basic.

Feierman, J. R., & Feierman, L. A. (2000). Paraphilias. In L. T. Szuchman & F. Muscarella (Eds.), *Psychological perspectives on human sexuality* (pp. 480–518). New York: Wiley.

Ferster, C. B., & Culbertson, S. (1982). *Behavior principles* (3rd ed.). Englewood Cliffs, NJ: Prentice-Hall.

Ferster, C. B., & Skinner, B. F. (1957). *Schedules of reinforcement.* New York: Appleton-Century-Crofts.

Field, D. P., Tonneau, F., Ahearn, W., & Hineline, P. N. (1996). Preference between variable-ratio schedules: Local and extended relations. *Journal of the Experimental Analysis of Behavior, 66,* 283–295.

Fiorito, G., & Scotto, P. (1992). Observational learning in *Octopus vulgaris. Science, 256,* 545–547.

Fisher, J. L., & Harris, M. B. (1976). The effects of three model characteristics on imitation and learning. *Journal of Social Psychology, 98,* 183–199.

Fisher, J. L., & Hinde, R. A. (1949). The opening of milk bottles by birds. *British Birds, 42,* 347–357.

Fordyce, W. E. (1976). *Behavioral methods for chronic pain and illness.* St. Louis, MO: Mosby.

Forthman, D. L., & Nicolaus, L. K. *Conditioned taste aversion: Another tool in primate conservation* (unpublished ms).

Fowler, B. P. (1986). Emotional crisis imitating television. *Lancet, 1*(8488), 1036–1037.

Fox, M. (1999, November 22). Constant barking must be halted. (Wilmington, DE) *Sunday News Journal,* p. G11.

Foxx, R. M. (2001, March 8). *Behavioral treatment of aggression, self-injury, and other severe behaviors: Methods, strategies, and skill building interventions.* Address given at the annual meeting of the Association for Science in Autism Treatment, San Diego, CA.

Frank, H., & Frank, M. G. (1982). Comparison of problem-solving performance in six-week-old wolves and dogs. *Animal Behavior, 30,* 95–98.

Frederiksen, L. W., Lynd, R. S., & Ross, J. (1978). Methodology in the measurement of pain. *Behavior Therapy, 9,* 486–488.

Freud, S. (1913) *Totem and taboo* (A. A. Brill, Trans.). New York: Moffat Yard.

Freud, S. (1914). *The psychopathology of everyday life.* New York: Macmillan.

Fuller, J. L., & Scott, J. P. (1954). Heredity and learning ability in infrahuman mammals. *Eugenics Quarterly, 1,* 28–43.

Furedy, J. J., & Kristjansson, M. (1996). Human Pavlovian autonomic conditioning and its relation to awareness of the CS/US contingency: Focus on the phenomenon and some forgotten facts. *Behavioral and Brain Sciences, 19,* 555–556, 558.

Gagné, R. M. (1941). The retention of a conditioned operant response. *Journal of Experimental Psychology, 29,* 296–305.

Gallup, A. M., & Elam, S. M. (1988). The 20th annual Gallup Poll of the public's attitude toward the public schools. *Phi Delta Kappan, 70,* 33–46.

Gallup, G. G. (1970). Chimpanzees: Self-recognition. *Science, 167,* 86–87.

Gallup, G. G. (1979). Self-awareness in primates. *American Scientist, 67,* 417–421.

Gantt, W. H. (1941). Introduction. In I. P. Pavlov, *Lectures on conditioned reflexes and psychiatry* (Vol. 2) (W. H. Gantt, Trans.). New York: International Publishers.

Gantt, W. H. (1966). Conditional or conditioned, reflex or response. *Conditioned Reflex, 1,* 69–74.

Garcia, J. (1981). Tilting at the paper mills of academe. *American Psychologist, 36,* 149–158.

Garcia, J., Kimeldorf, D. J., & Koelling, R. A. (1955). A conditioned aversion towards saccharin resulting from exposure to gamma radiation. *Science, 122,* 157–158.

Garcia, J., & Koelling, R. A. (1966). Relation of cue to consequence in avoidance learning. *Psychonomic Science, 4,* 123–124.

Gardner, R. A., & Gardner, B. T. (1969). Teaching sign language to a chimpanzee. *Science, 165,* 664–672.

Garry, M., Manning, C. G., Loftus, E. F., & Sherman, S. J. (1996). Imagination inflation: Imagining a childhood event inflates confidence that it occurred. *Psychonomic Bulletin & Review, 3,* 208–214.

Garry, M., & Polaschek, D. L. L. (2000). Imagination and memory. *Current Directions in Psychological Science, 9*(1), 6–10.

Gaudet, C. L., & Fenton, M. B. (1984). Observational learning in three species of insectivorous bats (chiroptera). *Animal Behavior, 32,* 385–388.

Gewirtz, J. L. (1997). The R-S contingency. *The Behavior Analyst, 26,* 121–128.

Girden, E., & Culler, E. A. (1937). Conditioned responses in curarized striate muscle in dogs. *Journal of Comparative Psychology, 23,* 261–274.

Gleeson, S., Lattal, K. A., & Williams, K. S. (1989). Superstitious conditioning: A replication and extension of Neuringer (1970). *Psychological Record, 39,* 563–571.

Gleitman, H. (1971). Forgetting of long-term memories in animals. In W. K. Honig & P. H. R. James (Eds.), *Animal memory.* New York: Academic Press.

Gleitman, H., & Bernheim, J. W. (1963). Retention of fixed-interval performance in rats. *Journal of Comparative and Physiological Psychology, 56,* 839–841.

Glover, J., & Gary, A. L. (1976). Procedures to increase some aspects of creativity. *Journal of Applied Behavior Analysis, 9,* 79–84.

Godden, D. B., & Baddeley, A. D. (1975). Context-dependent memory in two natural environments: On land and under water. *British Journal of Psychology, 66,* 325–331.

Goeters, S., Blakely, E., & Poling, A. (1992). The differential outcomes effect. *Psychological Record, 42,* 389–411.

Goetz, E. M. (1982). A review of functional analysis of preschool children's creative behavior. *Education and Treatment of Children, 5,* 157–177.

Goetz, E. M., & Baer, D. M. (1973). Social control of form diversity and the emergence of new forms in children's block-building. *Journal of Applied Behavior Analysis, 6,* 209–217.

Goldberg, S. G., & Cheney, C. D. (1984). Effects of chronic shock on cooperation: A potential model of learned chronic pain behavior. *Psychological Reports, 55,* 899–906.

Goldberg, S. R., Spealman, R. D., & Goldberg, D. M. (1981). Persistent behavior at high rates maintained by intravenous self-administration of nicotine. *Science, 214,* 573–575.

Goldiamond, I. (1965). Self control procedures in personal behavior problems. *Psychological Reports, 17,* 851–868.

Goldiamond, I. (1975a). A constructional approach to self-control. In A. Schwartz & I. Goldiamond (Eds.), *Social casework: A behavioral approach.* New York: Columbia University Press.

Goldiamond, I. (1975b). Insider-outsider problems: A constructional approach. *Rehabilitation Psychology, 22,* 103–116.

Goldschmidt, T. (1996). *Darwin's dreampond: Drama in Lake Victoria.* Cambridge, MA: MIT Press.

Goodman, B. (2001). Acronym acrimony. *Scientific American, 285*(5), 21.

Gormezano, I. (2000). Learning: Conditioning approach. In A. Kazdin (Ed.), *Encyclopedia of psychology* (Vol. 5, pp. 5–8). Washington, DC: American Psychological Association and Oxford University Press.

Gormezano, I., & Moore, J. W. (1969). Classical conditioning. In M. H. Marx (Ed.), *Learning: Processes.* London: MacMillan.

Gorn, G. J. (1982). The effects of music in advertising on choice behavior: A classical conditioning approach. *Journal of Marketing, 46,* 94–101.

Gottesman, I., McGuffin, P., & Farmer, A. E. (1987). Clinical genetics as clues to the "real" genetics of schizophrenia. *Schizophrenia Bulletin, 13*(1), 23–47.

Gould, S. J. (1999). *Rocks of Ages: Science and Religion in the Fullness of Life.* New York: Ballantine.

Graham, J. M., & Desjardins, C. (1980). Classical conditioning: Induction of luteinizing hormone and testosterone secretion in anticipation of sexual activity. *Science, 210,* 1039–1041.

Grant, B. S. (2002). Sour grapes of wrath. *Science, 297,* 940–941.

Greene, S. L. (1983). Feature memorization in pigeon concept formation. In M. L. Commons, R. J. Herrnstein, & A. R. Wagner (Eds.), *Quantitative analysis of behavior: Vol. 4. Discrimination processes.* Cambridge, MA: Ballinger.

Greenspoon, J. (1955). The reinforcing effect of two spoken sounds on the frequency of two responses. *American Journal of Psychology, 68,* 409–416.

Greenspoon, J., & Ranyard, R. (1957). Stimulus conditions and retroactive inhibition. *Journal of Experimental Psychology, 53,* 55–59.

Greenwood, C. R. (1991). A longitudinal analysis of time, engagement, and achievement in at-risk versus non-risk students. *Exceptional Children, 57,* 521–535.

Grether, W. H. (1938). Pseudo-conditioning without paired stimulation encountered in attempted backward conditioning. *Journal of Comparative Psychology, 25,* 141–158.

Grossman, R. P., & Till, B. D. (1998). The persistence of classically conditioned brand attitudes. *Journal of Advertising, 27*(1), 23–32.

Gursky, D. (1992, March). The writing life. *Teacher Magazine,* 10–11.

Gustavson, C. R., Garcia, J., Hankins, W. G., & Rusiniak, K. W. (1974). Coyote predation control by aversive conditioning. *Science, 184,* 581–583.

Gustavson, C. R., & Gustavson, J. C. (1985). Predation control using conditioned food aversion methodology: Theory, practice, and implications. *Annals of the New York Academy of Sciences, 443,* 348–356.

Gustavson, C. R., Jowsey, J. R., & Milligan, D. N. (1982). A three-year evaluation of taste aversion coyote control in Saskatchewan. *Journal of Range Management, 35,* 57–59.

Gustavson, C. R., Kelly, D. J., Sweeney, M., & Garcia, J. (1976). Prey-lithium aversions: I. Coyotes and wolves. *Behavioral Biology, 17,* 61–72.

Guthrie, E. R. (1960). *The psychology of learning* (rev. ed.). Gloucester, MA: Smith. (Original work published 1935)

Guttman, N. (1963). Laws of behavior and facts of perception. In S. Koch (Ed.), *Psychology: A study of a science* (Vol. 5). New York: McGraw-Hill.

Guttman, N., & Kalish, H. I. (1956). Discriminability and stimulus generalization. *Journal of Experimental Psychology, 51,* 79–88.

Hall, C. S. (1937). Emotional behavior in the rat. *Journal of Comparative Psychology, 24,* 369–375.

Hall, C. S. (1951). The genetics of behavior. In S. S. Stevens (Ed.), *Handbook of Experimental Psychology* (pp. 304–329). New York: Wiley.

Hall, J. F. (1984). Backward conditioning in Pavlovian-type studies: Reevaluation and present status. *Pavlovian Journal of Biological Sciences, 19,* 163–168.

Hall-Johnson, E., & Poling, A. (1984). Preference in pigeons given a choice between sequences of fixed-ratio schedules: Effects of ratio values and duration of food delivery. *Journal of the Experimental Analysis of Behavior, 42,* 127–135.

Hammond, L. J. (1980). The effect of contingency upon the appetitive conditioning of free-operant behavior. *Journal of the Experimental Analysis of Behavior, 34*(3), 297–304.

Hammond, L. J., & Maser, J. (1970). Forgetting and conditioned suppression: Role of a temporal discrimination. *Journal of the Experimental Analysis of Behavior, 13,* 333–338.

Haner, C. F., & Whitney, E. R. (1960). Empathic conditioning and its relation to anxiety level. *American Psychologist, 15,* 493.

Hanley, G. P., Iwata, B. A., & Thompson, R. H. (2001). Reinforcement schedule thinning following treatment with functional communication training. *Journal of Applied Behavior Analysis, 34,* 17–38.

Hanson, H. M. (1959). Effects of discrimination training on stimulus generalization. *Journal of Experimental Psychology, 58,* 321–334.

Harley, B., & Wang, W. (1997). The critical period hypothesis: Where are we now? In A. M. E. deGroot & J. F. Kroll (Eds.), *Tutorials in bilingualism: Psycholinguistic perspective.* Mahwah, NJ: Erlbaum.

Harlow, H. F. (1949). The formation of learning sets. *Psychological Review, 56,* 51–65.

Harlow, H. F. (1958). The nature of love. *American Psychologist, 13,* 673–685.

Harlow, H. F., & Harlow, M. K. (1962a). The effect of rearing conditions on behavior. *Bulletin of the Menninger Clinic, 26,* 213–224.

Harlow, H. F., & Harlow, M. K. (1962b) Social deprivation in monkeys. *Scientific American, 207,* 136–146.

Harris, B. (1979). Whatever happened to Little Albert? *American Psychologist, 34,* 151–160.

Hart, B. M., Allen, K. E., Buell, J. S., Harris, F. R., & Wolf, M. M. (1964). Effects of social reinforcement on operant crying. *Journal of Experimental Child Psychology, 1,* 145–153.

Hart, B., & Risley, T. R. (1995). *Meaningful differences in the everyday experience of young American children.* Baltimore: Paul H. Brookes.

Hawkins, D. F. (Ed.). (1983). *Drugs and pregnancy.* Edinburgh: Churchill Livingston.

Hayes, C. (1951). *The ape in our house.* New York: Harper & Row.

Hayes, K. J., & Hayes, C. (1952). Imitation in a home-raised chimpanzee. *Journal of Comparative and Physiological Psychology, 45,* 450–459.

Haynes, S. N., & Geddy, P. (1973). Suppression of psychotic hallucinations through time-out. *Behavior Therapy, 4,* 123–127.

Hennessey, B., & Amabile, T. (1988). The conditions of creativity. In R. J. Sternberg (Ed.), *The nature of creativity* (pp. 11–38). Cambridge, England: Cambridge University Press.

Hennessey, B., & Amabile, T. (1998). Reward, intrinsic motivation, and creativity. *American Psychologist, 53,* 674–675.

Hepper, P. G. (1995). The behavior of the fetus as an indicator of neural functioning. In J.-P. Lecanuet, W. P. Fifer, N. A. Krasnegor, & W. P. Smotherman (Eds.), *Fetal development: A psychobiological perspective* (pp. 405–417). Hillsdale, NJ: Erlbaum.

Herbert, M. J., & Harsh, C. M. (1944). Observational learning by cats. *Journal of Comparative Psychology, 37,* 81–95.

Herman, R. L., & Azrin, N. H. (1964). Punishment by noise in an alternative response situation. *Journal of the Experimental Analysis of Behavior, 7,* 185–188.

Herrnstein, R. J. (1961). Relative and absolute strength of response as a function of frequency of reinforcement. *Journal of the Experimental Analysis of Behavior, 4,* 267–272.

Herrnstein, R. J. (1966). Superstition: A corollary of the principle of operant conditioning. In W. K. Honig (Ed.), *Operant behavior: Areas of research and application.* New York: Appleton-Century-Crofts.

Herrnstein, R. J. (1969). Method and theory in the study of avoidance. *Psychological Review, 76,* 49–69.

Herrnstein, R. J. (1970). On the law of effect. *Journal of the Experimental Analysis of Behavior, 13,* 243–266.

Herrnstein, R. J. (1979). Acquisition, generalization, and discrimination reversal of a natural concept. *Journal of Experimental Psychology: Animal Behavior Processes, 5,* 116–129.

Herrnstein, R. J. (1990). Rational choice theory: Necessary but not sufficient. *American Psychologist, 45,* 356–367.

Herrnstein, R. J. (1991). Reply to Binmore and Staddon. *American Psychologist, 46,* 799–801.

Herrnstein, R. J., & Hineline, P. N. (1966). Negative reinforcement as shock-frequency reduction. *Journal of the Experimental Analysis of Behavior, 9,* 421–430.

Herrnstein, R. J., Loveland, D. H., & Cable, C. (1976). Natural concepts in pigeons. *Journal of Experimental Psychology: Animal Behavior Processes, 2,* 285–311.

Herrnstein, R. J., & Mazur, J. E. (1987, November/December). Making up our minds. *The Sciences,* 40–47.

Heth, C. D. (1976). Simultaneous and backward fear conditioning as a function of number of CS-US pairings. *Journal of Experimental Psychology: Animal Behavior Processes, 2,* 117–129.

Hickis, C., & Thomas, D. R. (1991). Application: Substance abuse and dependency. In W. Ishaq (Ed.), *Human behavior in today's world.* New York: Praeger.

Higgins, S. T., Morris, E. K., & Johnson, L. M. (1989). Social transmission of superstitious behavior in preschool children. *Psychological Record, 39,* 307–323.

Higgins, S. T., Rush, C. R., Hughes, J. R., Bickel, W. K., Lynn, M., & Capeless, M. A. (1992). Effects of cocaine and alcohol, alone and in combination, on human learning and performance. *Journal of the Experimental Analysis of Behavior, 58,* 87–105.

Hilgard, E. R. (1936). The nature of the conditioned response: I. The case for and against stimulus substitution. *Psychological Review, 43,* 366–385.

Hilgard, E. R., & Marquis, D. G. (1935). Acquisition, extinction and retention of conditioned lid responses to light in dogs. *Journal of Comparative Psychology, 19,* 29–58.

Hinde, R. A., & Fisher, J. (1972). Some comments on the re-publication of two papers on the opening of milk bottles in birds. In P. H. Klopfer & J. P. Hailman (Eds.), *Function and evolution of behavior.* Reading, MA: Addison-Wesley.

Hirakawa, T., & Nakazawa, J. (1977). Observational learning in children: Effects of vicarious reinforcement on discrimination shift behaviors in simple and complex tasks. *Japanese Journal of Educational Psychology, 25,* 254–257.

Hirata, S., & Morimura, N. (2000). Naive chaimpanzees' (Pan troglogytes) observation of experienced conspecifics in a tool-using task. *Journal of Comparative Psychology, 114*(3), 291–296.

Hiroto, D. S. (1974). Locus of control and learned helplessness. *Journal of Experimental Psychology, 102,* 187–193.

Hiroto, D. S., & Seligman, M. E. P. (1974). Generality of learned helplessness in man. *Journal of Personality and Social Psychology, 102,* 187–193.

Ho, B. T., Richards, D. W., & Chute, D. L., (Eds.). (1978). *Drug discrimination and state dependent learning.* New York: Academic Press.

Hoffman, H. S., & Ratner, A. M. (1973). A reinforcement model of imprinting. *Psychological Review, 80,* 527–544.

Holland, J. G. (1978). Behaviorism: Part of the problem or part of the solution? *Journal of Applied Behavior Analysis, 11,* 163–174.

Hollis, K. L. (1997). Contemporary research on Pavlovian conditioning: A "new" functional analysis. *American Psychologist, 52,* 956–965.

Holquin-Acosta, J. (1997). The neurology of dyslexia. *Revista Neurologia, 25,* 739–743.

Honig, W. K., & Slivka, R. M. (1964). Stimulus generalization of the effects of punishment. *Journal of the Experimental Analysis of Behavior, 7,* 21–25.

Honig, W. K., & Urcuioli, P. J. (1981). The legacy of Guttman and Kalish (1956): Twenty-five years of research on stimulus generalization. *Journal of the Experimental Analysis of Behavior, 36,* 405–445.

Hooper, J. (2002). *Of moths and men: The untold story of science and the peppered moth.* New York: Norton.

Hopkins, B. L., & Conard, R. J. (1975). Putting it all together: Superschool. In N. G. Haring & R. L. Schiefelbusch (Eds.), *Teaching special children* (pp. 342–385). New York: McGraw-Hill.

Horn, J. C. (1985, October). Fan violence: Fighting the justice of it all. *Psychology Today,* 30–31.

Horner, R. H. (1994). Functional assessment: Contributions and future directions. *Journal of Applied Behavior Analysis, 27,* 401–404.

Horowitz, E. L. (1936). The development of attitude toward the Negro. *Archives of Psychology, 28,* 510–511.

Horridge, G. A. (1962). Learning of leg position by headless insects. *Nature, 193,* 697–698.

Hovland, C. I. (1937a). The generalization of conditioned responses: I. The sensory generalization of conditioned responses with varying frequencies of tone. *Journal of General Psychology, 17,* 125–148.

Hovland, C. I. (1937b). The generalization of conditioned responses: IV. The effects of varying amounts of reinforcement upon the degree of generalization of conditioned responses. *Journal of Experimental Psychology, 21,* 261–276.

Huesmann, L. R., & Miller, L. S. (1994). Long-term effects of repeated exposure to media violence in childhood. In L. R. Huesmann (Ed.), *Aggressive behavior: Current perspectives.* New York: Plenum.

Hugdahl, K. (1995/2001). *Psychophysiology: The mind-body perspective.* Cambridge, MA: Harvard University Press.

Hull, C. L. (1943). *Principles of behavior.* New York: Appleton-Century-Crofts.

Hull, C. L. (1951). *Essentials of behavior.* New Haven, CT: Yale University Press.

Hull, C. L. (1952). *A behavior system.* New Haven, CT: Yale University Press.

Hummel, J. H., Abercrombie, C., & Koepsel, P. (1991). Teaching students to analyze examples of classical conditioning. *The Behavior Analyst, 14,* 241–246.

Hunter, W. S. (1913). The delayed reaction in animals and children. *Behavior Monographs, 2,* 1–86 (whole no. 1).

Hursh, S. R. (1980). Economic concepts for the analysis of behavior. *Journal of the Experimental Analysis of Behavior, 34,* 219–238.

Hursh, S. R. (1984). Behavioral economics. *Journal of the Experimental Analysis of Behavior, 42,* 435–452.

Ito, M., & Nakamura, K. (1998). Humans' choice in a self-control choice situation: Sensitivity to reinforcer amount, reinforcer delay, and overall reinforcement density. *Journal of the Experimental Analysis of Behavior, 69,* 87–102.

Iwata, B. A., Pace, G. M., Dorsey, M. F., Zarcone, J. F., et al. (1994). The functions of self-injurious behavior: An experimental-epidemioloigcal analysis. *Journal of Applied Behavior Analysis, 27,* 215–240.

Jacobs, L. F. (1992). Memory for cache locations in Merriam's kangaroo rats. *Animal Behavior, 43,* 585–593.

Jacobs, L. F., & Liman, E. R. (1991). Grey squirrels remember the locations of buried nuts. *Animal Behavior,* 103–110.

Jankowski, C. (1994). Foreword. In G. Wilkes, *A behavior sampler.* North Bend, WA: Sunshine Books.

Jenkins, H. M. (1962). Resistance to extinction when partial reinforcement is followed by regular reinforcement. *Journal of Experimental Psychology, 64,* 441–450.

Jenkins, H. M., & Harrison, R. H. (1960). Effect of discrimination training on auditory generalization. *Journal of Experimental Psychology, 59,* 246–253.

Jenkins, J. C., & Dallenbach, K. M. (1924). Obliviscence during sleep and waking. *American Journal of Psychology, 35,* 605–612.

John, E. R., Chesler, P., Bartlett, F., & Victor, I. (1968). Observational learning in cats. *Science, 159,* 1489–1491.

Johnson, K. R., & Layng, T. V. J. (1992). Breaking the structuralist barrier: Literacy and numeracy with fluency. *American Psychologist, 47,* 1475–1490.

Joncich, G. (1968). *The sane positivist: A biography of Edward L. Thorndike.* Middleton, CN: Wesleyan University Press.

Jones, M. C. (1924a). The elimination of children's fears. *Journal of Experimental Psychology, 7,* 382–390.

Jones, M. C. (1924b). A laboratory study of fear: The case of Peter. *Pedagogical Seminary, 31,* 308–315.

Justice, T. C., & Looney, T. A. (1990). Another look at "superstitions" in pigeons. *Bulletin of the Psychonomic Society, 28*(1), 64–66.

Kamil, A. C., & Balda, R. P. (1985). Cache recovery and spatial memory in Clark's nutcrackers. *Journal of Experimental Psychology: Animal Behavior Processes, 11,* 95–111.

Kamil, A. C., & Balda, R. P. (1990a). Spatial memory in seed-caching corvids. In G. H. Bower (Ed.), *Psychology of learning and motivation* (Vol. 26). New York: Academic.

Kamil, A. C., & Balda, R. P. (1990b). Differential memory for cache cites in Clark's nutcrackers. *Journal of Experimental Psychology: Animal Behavior Processes, 16,* 162–168.

Kamin, L. J. (1957). The retention of an incompletely learned avoidance response. *Journal of Comparative and Physiological Psychology, 50,* 457–460.

Kamin, L. J. (1969). Predictability, surprise, attention and conditioning. In B. A. Campbell & R. M. Church (Eds.), *Punishment and aversive behavior.* New York: Appleton-Century-Crofts.

Kamin, L. J., Brimer, C. J., & Black, A. H. (1963). Conditioned suppression as a monitor of fear of the CS in the course of avoidance training. *Journal of Comparative and Physiological Psychology, 56,* 497–501.

Kanfer, F. H., & Marston, A. R. (1963). Human reinforcement: Vicarious and direct. *Journal of Experimental Psychology, 65,* 292–296.

Kassin, S. M. (1997). The psychology of confession evidence. *American Psychologist, 52*(3), 221–233.

Kassinove, J. I., & Schare, M. L. (2001). Effects of the "near miss" and the "big win" on persistence at slot machine gambling. *Psychology of Addictive Behavior, 15*(2), 155–158.

Kawamura, S. (1963). The process of subcultural propagation among Japanese macaques. In C. H. Southwick (Ed.), *Primate social behavior.* New York: Van Nostrand.

Kazdin, A. E. (1978). *History of behavior modification: Experimental foundations of contemporary research.* Baltimore: University Park Press.

Keen, S. (1986). *Faces of the enemy.* New York: Harper & Row.

Keith-Lucas, T., & Guttman, N. (1975). Robust single-trial delayed backward conditioning. *Journal of Comparative and Physiological Psychology, 88,* 468–476.

Keller, F. S., & Schoenfeld, W. N. (1950). *Principles of psychology.* New York: Appleton-Century-Crofts.

Kellogg, W. N. (1968). Communication and language in the home-raised chimpanzee. *Science, 162,* 423–427.

Keltner, D., & Anderson, C. (2000). Saving face for Darwin: The functions and uses of embarrassment. *Current Directions in Psychological Science, 9*(6), 187–192.

Kendler, K. S., Neale, M. C., Kessler, R. C., & Heath, A. C. (1992). Generalized anxiety disorder in women: A population-based twin study. *Archives of General Psychiatry, 49,* 267–272.

Kerr, S. (1975). On the folly of rewarding A, while hoping for B. *Academy of Management Journal, 18,* 769–783.

Kettlewell, H. B. D. (1959). Darwin's missing evidence. *Scientific American, 200,* 48–53.

Killeen, P. R., & Hall, S. S. (2001). The principal components of response strength. *Journal of the Experimental Analysis of Behavior, 75,* 111–134.

Kimble, G. A. (1947). Conditioning as a function of the time between conditioned and unconditioned stimuli. *Journal of Experimental Psychology, 37,* 1–15.

Kimble, G. A. (1993). A modest proposal for a minor revolution in the language of psychology. *Psychological Science, 4,* 253–255.

King, G. D., Schaeffer, R. W., & Pierson, S. C. (1974). Reinforcement schedule preference of a raccoon (Procyon lotor). *Bulletin of the Psychonomic Society, 4,* 97–99.

Kingsley, H. L., & Garry, B. (1962). *The nature and conditions of learning* (2nd ed.). New York: Prentice-Hall.

Klatt, K. P., & Morris, E. K. (2001). The Premack principle, response deprivation, and establishing operations. *The Behavior Analyst, 24,* 173–180.

Kohler, W. (1939). Simple structural function in the chimpanzee and the chicken. In W. A. Ellis (Ed.), *A sourcebook of Gestalt psychology.* New York: Harcourt Brace.

Kohler, W. (1973). *The mentality of apes* (2nd ed.). New York: Liveright. (Original work published 1927)

Kraft, J. R., & Baum, W. M. (2001). Group choice: The ideal free distribution of human social behavior. *Journal of the Experimental Analysis of Behavior, 76,* 21–42.

Krasner, L. (1958). Studies of the conditioning of verbal behavior. *Psychological Bulletin, 55,* 148–170.

Krech, D., & Crutchfield, R. S. (1961). *Elements of psychology.* New York: Knopf.

Krueger, W. C. F. (1929). The effects of overlearning on retention. *Journal of Experimental Psychology, 12,* 71–78.

Kruglanski, A. W., Friedman, I., & Zeevi, G. (1971). The effects of extrinsic incentive on some qualitative aspects of task performance. *Journal of Personality, 39*, 606–617.

Kuo, Z. Y. (1930). The genesis of the cat's response to the rat. *Journal of Comparative Psychology, 11*, 1–36.

Kuo, Z. Y. (1967). *The dynamics of behavior development: An epigenetic view.* New York: Random House.

Kymissis, E., & Poulson, C. L. (1990). The history of imitation in learning theory: The language acquisition process. *Journal of the Experimental Analysis of Behavior, 54*, 113–127.

Lacey, J. I., Smith, R. L., & Green, A. (1955). Use of conditioned autonomic responses in the study of anxiety. *Psychosomatic Medicine, 17*, 208–217.

Lamal, P. A. (Ed.). (1997). *Cultural contingencies.* New York: Praeger.

Landman, O. E. (1993). Inheritance of acquired characteristics. *Scientific American, 266*, 150.

Lane, H. L., & Shinkman, P. G. (1963). Methods and findings in an analysis of a vocal operant. *Journal of the Experimental Analysis of Behavior, 6*, 179–188.

Lanza, R. P., Starr, J., & Skinner, B. F. (1982). "Lying" in the pigeon. *Journal of the Experimental Analysis of Behavior, 38*(2), 201–203.

Larsen, O. N., Gray, L. N., & Fortis, J. G. (1968). Achieving goals through violence on television. In O. N. Larsen (Ed.), *Violence and the mass media.* New York: Harper & Row.

Larson, J. D., Calamari, J. E., West, J. G., & Frevent, T. A. (1998). Aggression-management with disruptive adolescents in the residential setting: Integration of a cognitive-behavioral component. *Residential Treatment for Children and Youth, 15*, 1–9.

Lashley, K. S. (1930). The mechanism of vision: I. A method of rapid analysis of pattern-vision in the rat. *Journal of Genetic Psychology, 37*, 453–640.

Lashley, K. S., & Wade, M. (1946). The Pavlovian theory of generalization. *Psychological Review, 53*, 72–87.

Latham, G. I. (1994). The power of positive parenting. North Logan, UT: P & T.

Latham, G. I. (1999). Parenting with love: Making a difference in a day. Salt Lake City, UT: Bookcraft.

Lattal, K. A. (1995). Contingency and behavior analysis. *The Behavior Analyst, 18*, 209–224.

Lattal, K. A. (2001). The human side of animal behavior. *The Behavior Analyst, 24*, 147–161.

Lattal, K. A., & Gleeson, S. (1990). Response acquisition with delayed reinforcement. *Journal of Experimental Psychology: Animal Behavior Processes, 16*, 27–39.

Laurenti-Lions, L., Gallego, J., Chambille, B., Vardan, G., & Jacquemin, C. (1985). Control of myoelectrical responses through reinforcement. *Journal of the Experimental Analysis of Behavior, 44*, 185–193.

Lavigna, G. W., & Donnellan, A. M. (1986). *Alternatives to punishment: Solving behavior problems with non-aversive strategies.* New York: Irvington.

Lavin, N. I., Thorpe, J. G., Barker, J. C., Blakemore, C. B., & Conway, C. G. (1961). Behavior therapy in a case of transvestism. *Journal of Nervous and Mental Disorders, 133*, 346–353.

Layng, T. V. J., & Andronis, P. T. (1984). Toward a functional analysis of delusional speech and hallucinatory behavior. *The Behavior Analyst, 7*, 139–156.

Leader, L. R. (1995). The potential value of habituation in the prenate. In J.-P. Lecanuet, W. P. Fifer, N. A. Krasnegor, & W. P. Smotherman (Eds.), *Fetal development: A psychobiological perspective* (pp. 383–404). Hillsdale, NJ: Erlbaum.

Leander, J. D., Lippman, L. G., & Meyer, M. E. (1968). Fixed interval performance as related to subjects' verbalization of the reinforcement contingency. *The Psychological Record, 18*, 469–474.

Lenneberg, E. (1967). *The biological foundations of language.* New York: Wiley.

Lenneberg, E. (1969). On explaining language. *Science, 164*, 635–643.

Lepper, M. R. (1998). A whole much less than the sum of its parts. *American Psychologist, 53*, 675–676.

Lerman, D. C., Iwata, B. A., Shore, B. A., & De Leon, I. G. (1997). Effects of intermittent punishment on self-injurious behavior: An evaluation of schedule thinning. *Journal of Applied Behavior Analysis, 30*, 187–201.

Lett, B. T., Grant, V. L., Koh, M. T., & Smith, J. F. (2001). Wheel running simultaneously produces conditioned taste aversion and conditioned place preference in rats. *Learning and Motivation, 32*(2), 129–136.

Levine, J. M., & Murphy, G. (1943). The learning and forgetting of controversial material. *Journal of Abnormal and Social Psychology, 38,* 507–517.

Levy, E. A., McClinton, B. S., Rabinowitz, F. M., & Wolkin, J. R. (1974). Effects of vicarious consequences on imitation and recall: Some developmental findings. *Journal of Experimental Child Psychology, 17,* 115–132.

Lichstein, K. L., & Schreibman, L. (1976). Employing electric shock in autistic children: A review of the side effects. *Journal of Autism and Childhood Schizophrenia, 6,* 1163–1173.

Lieberman, D. A., McIntosh, D. C., & Thomas, G. V. (1979). Learning when reward is delayed: A marking hypothesis. *Journal of Experimental Psychology: Animal Behavior Processes, 5,* 224–242.

Lightfoot, L. O. (1980). *Behavioral tolerance to low doses of alcohol in social drinkers.* Unpublished Ph.D. dissertation, Waterloo University, Ontario, Canada.

Locke, J. (1975). *An essay concerning human understanding* (P. H. Nidditch, Ed.). Oxford, England: Clarendon Press. (Original work published 1690)

Loftus, E. F. (1975). Leading questions and the eyewitness report. *Cognitive Psychology, 7,* 560–572.

Loftus, E. F. (1979). *Eyewitness testimony.* Cambridge, MA: Harvard University Press.

Loftus, E. F. (1980). *Memory: Surprising new insights into how we remember and why we forget.* Reading, MA: Addison-Wesley.

Loftus, E. F., & Loftus, G. R. (1980). On the permanence of stored information in the human brain. *American Psychologist, 35,* 409–420.

Loftus, E. F., & Palmer, J. C. (1974). Reconstruction of automobile destruction: An examination of the interaction between language and memory. *Journal of Verbal Learning and Verbal Behavior, 13,* 585–589.

Loftus, E. F., & Zanni, G. (1975). Eyewitness testimony: The influence of the wording of a question. *Bulletin of the Psychonomic Society, 5,* 86–88.

Logue, A. W. (1998). Self-control. In W. T. O'Donohue (Ed.), *Learning and behavior therapy.* Boston, MA: Allyn & Bacon.

Logue, A. W., Logue, K. R., & Strauss, K. E. (1983). The acquisition of taste aversion in humans with eating and drinking disorders. *Behavior Research and Therapy, 21,* 275–289.

Lorenz, K. (1952). *King Solomon's ring.* New York: Crowell.

Lovaas, O. I. (1987). Behavioral treatment and normal educational and intellectual functioning in young autistic children. *Journal of Consulting and Clinical Psychology, 55,* 3–9.

Lovaas, O. I. (1993). The development of a treatment-research project for developmentally disabled and autistic children. *Journal of Applied Behavior Analysis, 26,* 617–630.

Lovaas, O. I., Berberich, J. P., Perloff, B. F., & Schaeffer, B. (1966). Acquisition of imitative speech by schizophrenic children. *Science, 151,* 705–707.

Lovaas, O. I., & Simmons, J. Q. (1969). Manipulation of self-destruction in three retarded children. *Journal of Applied Behavior Analysis, 2,* 143–157.

Lowe, C. F., Beasty, A., & Bentall, R. P. (1983). The role of verbal behavior. *Journal of the Experimental Analysis of Behavior, 39,* 157–164.

Lubow, R. E. (1965). Latent inhibition: Effects of frequency of nonreinforced preexposure of the CS. *Journal of Comparative and Physiological Psychology, 60,* 454–457.

Lubow, R. E., & Moore, A. V. (1959). Latent inhibition: The effect of nonreinforced pre-exposure to the conditional stimulus. *Journal of Consulting and Clinical Psychology, 52,* 415–419.

Luria, A. R. (1968). *The mind of a mnemonist: A little book about a vast memory* (L. Solotaroff, Trans.). New York: Basic.

Lykken, D. T., McGue, M., Tellegen, A., & Bouchard, T. J., Jr. (1992). Emergenesis: Genetic traits that may not run in families. *American Psychologist, 47,* 1565–1577.

Lyons, C. (1991). Application: Smoking. In Waris Ishaq (Ed.), *Human behavior in today's world.* New York: Praeger.

Lyons, C. A., & Ghezzi, P. M. (1991). Manipulation of wagering on a large scale: Adjustments in the Oregon lottery. *Behaviorological Commentaries, 1,* 14–17.

Mace, F. C., Lalli, J. S., Shea, M. C., & Nevin, J. A. (1992). Behavioral momentum in college basketball. *Journal of Applied Behavior Analysis, 25,* 657–663.

Mace, F. C., Mauro, B. C., Boyojian, A. E., & Eckert, T. L. (1997). Effects of reinforcer quality on behavioral momentum: Coordinated applied and basic research. *Journal of Applied Behavior Analysis, 30,* 1–20.

Mackintosh, N. J. (1974). *The psychology of animal learning.* New York: Academic.

Macuda, T., & Timney, B. (1999). Luminance and chromatic discrimination in the horse (Equus caballos). *Behavioral Processes, 44*(3), 301–307.

Madigan, S., & O'Hara, R. (1992). Short-term memory at the turn of the century. *American Psychologist, 47*(2), 170–174.

Madison, L. S., Madison, J. K., and Adubato, S. A. (1986). Infant behavior and development in relation to fetal movement and habituation. *Child Development, 57,* 1475–1482.

Madler, G., & Kaplan, W. K. (1956). Subjective evaluation and reinforcing effect of a verbal stimulus. *Science, 124,* 582–583.

Madsen, T., Shine, R., Loman, J., & Hakansson, T. (1992). Why do female adders copulate so frequently? *Nature, 355,* 440–441.

Maier, S. F., Albin, R. W., & Testa, T. J. (1973). Failure to learn to escape in rats previously exposed to inescapable shock depends on the nature of the escape response. *Journal of Comparative and Physiological Psychology, 85,* 581–592.

Maletzky, B. M. (1980). Assisted covert sensitization. In D. J. Cox & R. J. Daitzman (Eds.), *Exhibitionism: Description, assessment, and treatment.* New York: Garland.

Malone, J. C. (1990). *Theories of learning: A historical approach.* Belmont, CA: Wadsworth.

Malott, R. W., & Malott, M. K. (1970). Perception and stimulus generalization. In W. C. Stebbins (Ed.), *Animal psychophysics: The design and conduct of sensory experiments.* New York: Appleton-Century-Crofts.

Mansfield, R. J. W., & Rachlin, H. C. (1970). The effect of punishment, extinction, and satiation on response chains. *Learning and Motivation, 1,* 27–36.

Markowitz, H. (1982). *Behavioral enrichment in the zoo.* New York: Van Nostrand Reinhold.

Marlatt, G. A., & Gordon, J. R. (Eds.). (1985). *Relapse prevention: Maintenance strategies in the treatment of addictive behaviors.* New York: Guilford Press.

Marschall, L. A. (1992, January/February). Books in brief. *The Sciences,* 52.

Marschall, L. A. (1993, March/April). Books in brief. *The Sciences,* 45.

Martin, G. L., & Osborne, J. G. (1989). *Psychological adjustment to everyday living.* Englewood Cliffs, NJ: Prentice-Hall.

Masia, C. L., & Chase, P. N. (1997). Vicarious learning revisited: A contemporary behavior analytic interpretation. *Journal of Behavior Therapy & Experimental Psychiatry, 28,* 41–51.

Masserman, J. H. (1943). *Behavior and neurosis: An experimental-psychoanalytic approach to psychobiologic principles.* New York: Hafner.

Masserman, J. H. (1946). *Principles of dynamic psychiatry.* Philadelphia: Saunders.

Matthews, B. A., Shimoff, E., Catania, A. C., & Sagvolden, T. (1977). Uninstructed human responding: Sensitivity to ratio and interval contingencies. *Journal of the Experimental Analysis of Behavior, 27,* 453–467.

Max, L. W. (1935). An experimental study of the motor theory of consciousness: III. Action—Current responses in deaf-mutes during sleep, sensory stimulation, and dreams. *Journal of Comparative Psychology, 19,* 469–486.

Mayr, E. (2000, July). Darwin's influence on modern thought. *Scientific American,* 79–83.

Mazur, J. E. (1975). The matching law and quantifications related to Premack's principle. *Journal of Experimental Psychology: Animal Behavior Processes, 1,* 374–386.

McCarty, R. (1998, November). Making the case for animal research. *APA Monitor,* 18.

McDougall, W. (1908). *An introduction to social psychology.* London: Methuen.

McDougall, W. (1927). An experiment for the testing of the hypothesis of Lamarck. *British Journal of Psychology, 17,* 267–304.

McDougall, W. (1938). Fourth report on a Lamarckian experiment. *British Journal of Psychology, 28*, 321–345.

McGeoch, J. A. (1932). Forgetting and the law of disuse. *Psychological Review, 39*, 352–370.

McIntire, R. W. (1973). Parenthood training or mandatory birth control: Take your choice. *Psychology Today, 34*, 36–38, 132–133, 143.

McNally, R. J. (1987). Preparedness and phobias: A review. *Psychological Bulletin, 101*, 283–303.

McPhee, J. E., Rauhut, A. S., & Ayres, J. J. B. (2001). Evidence for learning-deficit vs. performance-deficit theories of latent inhibition in Pavlovian fear conditioning. *Learning and Motivation, 32*, 1–32.

Mead, G. H. (1934). *Mind, self and society.* Chicago: University of Chicago Press.

Menzel, C. R. (1991). Cognitive aspects of foraging in Japanese monkeys. *Animal Behavior, 41*, 397–402.

Michael, J. (1975). Positive and negative reinforcement: A distinction that is no longer necessary; or, a better way to talk about bad things. *Behaviorism, 3*, 33–44.

Michael, J. (1991). A behavorial perspective on college teaching. *The Behavior Analyst, 14*, 229–239.

Midgley, B. D. (1987). Instincts—Who needs them? *The Behavior Analyst, 10*, 313–314.

Miller, N. E. (1948). Studies of fear as an acquired drive: I. Fear as a motivation and fear-reduction as reinforcement in learning of new responses. *Journal of Experimental Psychology, 38*, 89–101.

Miller, N. E. (1960). Learning resistance to pain and fear: Effects of overlearning, exposure, and rewarded exposure in context. *Journal of Experimental Psychology, 60*, 137–145.

Miller, N. E. (1978). Biofeedback and visceral learning. *Annual Review of Psychology, 29*, 373–404.

Miller, N. E. (1985). The value of behavioral research on animals. *American Psychologist, 40*, 423–440.

Miller, N. E., & DiCara, L. (1967). Instrumental learning of heart rate changes in curarized rats: Shaping and specificity to discriminative stimulus. *Journal of Comparative and Physiological Psychology, 63*, 12–19.

Miller, N. E., & Dollard, J. (1941). *Social learning and imitation.* New Haven, CN: Yale University Press.

Miller, S. J., & Sloane, H. N. (1976). The generalization effects of parent training across stimulus settings. *Journal of Applied Behavior Analysis, 9*, 355–370.

Minami, H., & Dallenbach, K. M. (1946). The effect of activity upon learning and retention in the cockroach (Periplaneta americana). *American Journal of Psychology, 59*, 1–58.

Mineka, S., & Cook, M. (1988). Social learning and the acquisition of snake fear in monkeys. In T. R. Zentall, & B. G. Galef, Jr. (Eds.), *Social learning: Psychological and biological perspectives.* Hillsdale, NJ: Erlbaum.

Mineka, S., Davidson, M., Cook, M., & Keir, R. (1984). Observational conditioning of snake fear in rhesus monkeys. *Journal of Abnormal Psychology, 93*, 355–372.

Miyashita, Y., Nakajima, S., & Imada, H. (2000). Differential outcome effect in the horse. *Journal of the Experimental Analysis of Behavior, 74*, 245–253.

Monany, V. (2000). *Animal experimentation: A guide to the issues.* New York: Cambridge University Press.

Moore, D. S. (2001). *The dependent gene: The fallacy of nature vs. nurture.* New York: W. H. Freeman

Morange, M. (2001). *The misunderstood gene.* Cambridge, MA: Harvard University Press.

Morris, E. K. (2001). B. F. Skinner. In B. J. Zimmerman & D. H. Schunk (Eds.), *Psychology: A century of contributions.* Hillsdale, NJ: Erlbaum.

Morris, E. K., Baer, D. M., Favell, J. E., Glenn, S. S., Hineline, P. N., Malott, M. E., & Michael, J. (2001). Some reflections on 25 years of the Association for Behavior Analysis: Past, present, and future. *The Behavior Analyst, 24*(2), 125–146.

Morrow, G. R., & Dobkin, P. L. (1988). Anticipatory nausea and vomiting in cancer patients undergoing chemotherapy: Prevalence, etiology, and behavioral interventions. *Clinical Psychology Review, 8*, 517–556.

Morse, W. H. (1966). Intermittent reinforcement. In W. H. Honig (Ed.), *Operant behavior.* New York: Appleton-Century-Crofts.

Mowrer, O. H. (1940). An experimental analysis of "regression" with incidental observations on "reaction-formation." *Journal of Abnormal and Social Psychology, 35,* 56–87.

Mowrer, O. H. (1947). On the dual nature of learning: A reinterpretation of "conditioning" and "problem solving." *Harvard Educational Review, 17,* 102–150.

Mowrer, O. H., & Jones, H. (1945). Habit strength as a function of the pattern of reinforcement. *Journal of Experimental Psychology, 35,* 293–311.

Myers, L. L., & Thyer, B. A. (1994). Behavioral therapy: Popular misconceptions. *Scandinavian Journal of Behavior Therapy, 23*(2), 99–107.

Myowa-Yamakoshi, M., & Matsuzawa, T. (2000). Imitation of intentional manipulatory actions in chimpanzees (Pan troglodytes). *Journal of Comparative Psychology, 114*(4), 381–391.

Nation, J. R., Cooney, J. B., & Gartrell, K. E. (1979). Durability and generalizability of persistence training. *Journal of Abnormal Psychology, 88,* 121–136.

Neuringer, A. J. (1970). Superstitious keypecking after three peck-produced reinforcements. *Journal of the Experimental Analysis of Behavior, 13,* 127–134.

Neuringer, A. J. (1986). Can people behave "randomly"? The role of feedback. *Journal of Experimental Psychology: General, 115,* 62–75.

Neuringer, A., Kornell, N., & Olufs, M. (2001). Stability and variability in extinction. *Journal of Experimental Psychology: Animal Behavior Processes, 27*(1), 79–94.

Nevin, J. A. (1988). Behavioral momentum and the partial reinforcement effect. *Psychological Bulletin, 103,* 44–56.

Nevin, J. A. (1992). An integrative model for the study of behavioral momentum. *Journal of the Experimental Analysis of Behavior, 57*(3), 301–316.

Nevin, J. A. (1999). Analyzing Thorndike's law of effect: The question of stimulus-response bonds. *Journal of the Experimental Analysis of Behavior, 72,* 447–450.

Newman, H., Freeman, F. N., & Holzinger, K. J. (1937). *Twins: A study of heredity and environment.* Chicago, IL: University of Chicago Press.

Newsom, C., Flavall, J. E., & Rincover, A. (1983). Side effects of punishment. In S. Axelrod & J. Apsche (Eds.), *The effects of punishment on human behavior.* New York: Academic.

Nichols, J. R., & Hsiao, S. (1967). Addiction liability of albino rats: Breeding for quantitative differences in morphine drinking. *Science, 157,* 561–563.

Nisbett, R. E. (1990). The anticreativity letters: Advice from a senior tempter to a junior tempter. *American Psychologist, 45,* 1078–1082.

O'Donnell, J. (2001). The discriminative stimulus for punishment or S^{Dp}. *The Behavior Analyst, 24,* 261–262.

O'Donnell, J., & Crosbie, J. (1998). Punishment gradients with humans. *Psychological Record, 48*(2), 211–233.

Öhman, A., Flykt, A., & Esteves, F. (2001). Emotion drives attention: Detecting the snake in the grass. *Journal of Experimental Psychology: General, 130*(3), 466–478.

Öhman, A., Fredrikson, M., Hugdahl, K., & Rimmo, P. A. (1976). The premise of equipotentiality in human classical conditioning: Conditioned electrodermal responses to potentially phobic stimuli. *Journal of Experimental Psychology: General, 103,* 313–337.

O'Leary, K. D., & Becker, W. C. (1968–1969). The effects of the intensity of a teacher's reprimands on children's behavior. *Journal of School Psychology, 7,* 8–11.

O'Leary, K. D., Kaufman, K. F., Kass, R. E., & Drabman, R. S. (1970). The effects of loud and soft reprimands on disruptive students. *Exceptional Children, 37,* 145–155.

Ono, K. (1987). Superstitious behavior in humans. *Journal of the Experimental Analysis of Behavior, 47,* 261–271.

Orne, M. T. (1951). The mechanisms of hypnotic age regression: An experimental study. *Journal of Abnormal and Social Psychology, 46,* 213–225.

Ost, L., & Hugdahl, K. (1985). Acquisition of blood and dental phobia and anxiety response patterns in clinical patients. *Behavior Research and Therapy, 23,* 27–34.

Overmier, J. B., & Seligman, M. E. P. (1967). Effects of inescapable shock upon subsequent escape and avoidance learning. *Journal of Comparative and Physiological Psychology, 63,* 23–33.

Overton, D. A. (1964). State-dependent or "dissociated" learning produced by pentobarbital. *Journal of Comparative and Physiological Psychology, 57,* 3–12.

Padilla, A. M. (2000). Vives, Juan Luis (1492–1540). In A. Kazdin (Ed.), *Encyclopedia of psychology* (Vol. 8, pp. 209–210). Washington, DC: American Psychological Association and Oxford University Press.

Padilla, A. M., Padilla, C., Ketterer, T., & Giacalone, D. (1970). Inescapable shocks and subsequent avoidance conditioning in goldfish (Carrasius auratus). *Psychonomic Science, 20,* 295–296.

Page, S., & Neuringer, A. (1985). Variability is an operant. *Journal of Experimental Psychology: Animal Behavior Processes, 11,* 429–452.

Papini, M. R., & Bitterman, M. E. (1990). The role of contingency in classical conditioning. *Psychological Review, 97,* 396–403.

Papka, M., Ivry, R. B., & Woodruff-Pak, D. S. (1997). Eyeblink classical conditioning and awareness revisited. *Psychological Science, 8,* 404–408.

Parker, B. K. (1984). Reproduction memory of two-event sequences in pigeons. *Journal of the Experimental Analysis of Behavior, 41,* 135–141.

Parks, D., Cavanaugh, J., & Smith, A. (1986). *Metamemory 2: Memory researchers' knowledge of their own memory abilities.* Washington, DC: American Psychological Association.

Parsons, M. B., & Reid, D. H. (1990). Assessing food preferences among persons with profound mental retardation. *Journal of Applied Behavior Analysis, 23,* 183–195.

Patkowski, M. S. (1994). The critical age hypothesis and interlanguage phonology. In M. S. Yavas (Ed.), *First and second language phonology.* San Diego, CA: Singular Publications Group.

Patterson, C. J., & Mischel, W. (1976). Effects of temptation-inhibiting and task-facilitating plans on self-control. *Journal of Personality and Social Psychology, 33,* 209–217.

Patterson, F. P. (1978). The gesture of a gorilla: Language acquisition in another pongid. *Brain and Language, 5,* 72–97.

Patterson, F. P., Patterson, C. H., & Brentari, D. K. (1987). Language in child, chimp and gorilla. *American Psychologist, 42,* 270–272.

Pavlov, I. P. (1906). The scientific investigation of the psychical faculties or processes in the higher animals. *Science, 24,* 613–619.

Pavlov, I. P. (1927). *Conditioned reflexes* (G. V. Anrep, Ed. and Trans.). London: Oxford University Press.

Pavlov, I. P. (1941). *Lectures on conditioned reflexes*: Vol. 2. *Conditioned reflexes and psychiatry* (W. H. Gantt, Ed. and Trans.). New York: International Publishers.

Pear, J. J. & Chan, W. S. (2001, May 25–29). Video tracking of male Siamese fighting fish *(Betta splendens).* Poster presented at the annual meeting of the Association for Behavior Analysis, New Orleans.

Pear, J. J., & Eldridge, G. D. (1984). The operant-respondent distinction: Future directions. *Journal of the Experimental Analysis of Behavior, 42,* 453–467.

Peckstein, L. A., & Brown, F. D. (1939). An experimental analysis of the alleged criteria of insightful learning. *Journal of Educational Psychology, 30,* 38–52.

Pedersen, N. L., Plomin, R., McClearn, G. E., & Friverg, L. (1988). Neuroticism, extraversion, and related traits in adult twins reared apart and reared together. *Journal of Personality and Social Psychology, 55,* 950–957.

Penfield, W. (1955). The permanent record of the stream of consciousness. *Acta Psychologica, 11,* 47–69.

Penfield, W. (1975). *The mystery of the mind.* Princeton, NJ: Princeton University Press.

Perkins, C. C., Jr., & Weyant, R. G. (1958). The interval between training and test trials as determiner of the slope of generalization gradients. *Journal of Comparative and Physiological Psychology, 51,* 596–600.

Perone, M., & Courtney, K. (1992). Fixed-ratio pausing: Joint effects of past reinforcer magnitude and stimuli correlated with upcoming magnitude. *Journal of the Experimental Analysis of Behavior, 57,* 33–46.

Peterson, G. B. (1984). How expectancies guide behavior. In H. L. Roitblat, T. G. Bever, & H. S. Terrace (Eds.), *Animal cognition.* Hillsdale, NJ: Erlbaum.

Peterson, G. B., & Trapold, M. A. (1980). Effects of altering outcome expectancies on pigeons' delayed conditional discrimination performance. *Learning and Motivation, 11,* 267–288.

Petitto, L. A., & Seidenberg, M. S. (1979). On the evidence for linguistic abilities in signing apes. *Brain and Language, 8,* 162–183.

Phelps, B. J., & Reit, D. J. (1997). *The steepening of generalization gradients from "mentally rotated" stimuli.* Paper presented at the 23rd annual convention of the Association for Behavior Analysis, Chicago, IL.

Pierce, W. D., & Epling, W. F. (1983). Choice, matching, and human behavior: A review of the literature. *The Behavior Analyst, 6,* 57–76.

Pipitone, A. (1985, April 23). Jury to decide if sex obsession pushed man over edge. *The (Baltimore) Evening Sun,* pp. D1–D2.

Pisacreta, R., Redwood, E., & Witt, K. (1984). Transfer of matching-to-sample figure samples in the pigeon. *Journal of the Experimental Analysis of Behavior, 42,* 223–237.

Platt, J. (1973). Social traps. *American Psychologist, 28,* 641–651.

Polenchar, B. E., Romano, A. G., Steinmetz, J. E., & Patterson, M. M. (1984). Effects of US parameters on classical conditioning of cat hindlimb flexion. *Animal Learning and Behavior, 12,* 69–72.

Pontieri, F. E., Monnazzi, P., Scontrini, A., Buttarelli, F. R., & Patacchioh, F. R. (2001). Behavioral sensitization to WIN 55212.2 in rats pretreated with heroin. *Brain Research, 898*(1), 178–180.

Porter, D., & Neuringer, A. (1984). Music discrimination by pigeons. *Journal of Experimental Psychology: Animal Behavior Processes, 10,* 138–148.

Postman, L., & Rau, L. (1957). Retention as a function of the method of measurement. *University of California Publications in Psychology, 8,* 217–270.

Powell, K. R., & Holtzman, S. G. (2001). Parametric evaluation of the development of sensitization to the effects of morphine on locomotor activity. *Drug and Alcohol Dependence, 62*(1), 83–90.

Powers, R. B., Cheney, C. D., & Agostino, N. R. (1970). Errorless training of a visual discrimination in preschool children. *Psychological Record, 20,* 45–50.

Premack, D. (1959). Toward empirical behavioral laws: I. Positive reinforcement. *Psychological Review, 66,* 219–233.

Premack, D. (1962). Reversibility of the reinforcement relation. *Science, 136,* 255–257.

Premack, D. (1965). Reinforcement theory. In D. Levine (Ed.), *Nebraska Symposium on Motivation* (Vol. 13). Lincoln: University of Nebraska Press.

Premack, D. (1971). Catching up with common sense or two sides of a generalization: Reinforcement and punishment. In R. Glaser (Ed.), *The nature of reinforcement.* New York: Academic.

Presley, W. J., & Riopelle, A. J. (1959). Observational learning of an avoidance response. *Journal of Genetic Psychology, 95,* 251–254.

Prokasy, W. F., & Whaley, F. L. (1963). Intertrial interval range shift in classical eyelid conditioning. *Psychological Reports, 12,* 55–88.

Pryor, K. (1991). *Lads before the wind* (2nd ed.). North Bend, WA: Sunshine Books. (Original work published 1975)

Pryor, K. (1996). Clicker training aids shelter adoption rates. *Don't shoot the dog! News, 1*(2), 2.

Pryor, K., Haag, R., & O'Reilly, J. (1969). The creative porpoise: Training for novel behavior. *Journal of the Experimental Analysis of Behavior, 12,* 653–661.

Purkis, H. M., & Lipp, O. V. (2001). Does affective learning exist in the absence of contingency awareness? *Learning and Motivation, 32*(1), 84–99.

Purtle, R. B. (1973). Peak shift: A review. *Psychological Bulletin, 80,* 408–421.

Quay, H. C. (1959). The effect of verbal reinforcement on the recall of early memories. *Journal of Abnormal and Social Psychology, 59,* 254–257.

Rachlin, H. (1976). *Behavior and learning.* San Francisco: W. H. Freeman.

Rachlin, H. (1990). Why do people gamble and keep gambling despite heavy losses? *Psychological Science, 1*(5), 294–297.

Rachlin, H. (2000). *The science of self control.* Cambridge, MA: Harvard University Press.

Rachlin, H., & Herrnstein, R. L. (1969). Hedonism revisited: On the negative law of effect. In B. A. Campbell & R. M. Church

(Eds.), *Punishment and aversive behavior.* New York: Appleton-Century-Crofts.

Rachman, S. (1977). The conditioning theory of fear acquisition: A critical examination. *Behaviour Research and Therapy, 15,* 375–387.

Raine, A., & Dunkin, J. J. (1990). The genetic and psychophysiological basis of antisocial behavior: Implications for counseling and therapy. *Journal of Counseling and Development, 68,* 637–644.

Razran, G. (1939). A quantitative study of meaning by a conditioned salivary technique (semantic conditioning). *Science, 90,* 89–90.

Razran, G. (1956). Extinction re-examined and re-analyzed: A new theory. *Psychological Review, 63,* 39–52.

Reber, A. S. (1995). *Penguin dictionary of psychology.* New York: Penguin.

Redd, W. H., & Andresen, G. V. (1981). Conditioned aversion in cancer patients. *The Behavior Therapist, 4,* 3–4.

Redmon, W. K., & Dickinson, A. M. (1990). *Promoting excellence through performance management.* New York: Haworth Press.

Reed, P. (1991). Multiple determinants of the effects of reinforcement magnitude on free-operant response rates. *Journal of the Experimental Analysis of Behavior, 55,* 109–123.

Reed, P., & Yoshino, T. (2001). The effect of response-dependent tones on the acquisition of concurrent behavior in rats. *Learning & Motivation* (electronic edition published 3/20/01).

Reed, T. (1980). Challenging some "common wisdom" on drug abuse. *International Journal of Addiction, 15,* 359.

Reese, H. W. (2001). Some recurrent issues in the history of behavioral sciences. *The Behavior Analyst, 24,* 227–239.

Reid, R. L. (1986). The psychology of the near miss. *Journal of Gambling Behavior, 2,* 32–39.

Reit, D. J., & Phelps, B. J. (1996, May 24–28). *Mental rotation reconceptualized as stimulus generalization.* Paper presented at the 22nd annual convention of the Association for Behavior Analysis, San Francisco.

Rescorla, R. A. (1967). Pavlovian conditioning and its proper control procedures. *Psychological Review, 74,* 71–80.

Rescorla, R. A. (1968). Probability of shock in the presence and absence of CS in fear conditioning. *Journal of Comparative and Physiological Psychology, 66,* 1–5.

Rescorla, R. A. (1972). "Configural" conditioning in discrete-trial bar pressing. *Journal of Comparative & Physiological Psychology, 79,* 307–317.

Rescorla, R. A. (1973). Evidence of "unique stimulus" account of configural conditioning. *Journal of Comparative and Physiological Psychology, 85,* 331–338.

Rescorla, R. A. (1988). Pavlovian conditioning: It's not what you think it is. *American Psychologist, 43,* 151–160.

Rescorla, R. A., & Wagner, A. R. (1972). A theory of Pavlovian conditioning: Variations in the effectiveness of reinforcement and nonreinforcement. In A. H. Black & W. F. Prokasy (Eds.), *Classical conditioning, II: Current research and theory.* New York: Appleton-Century-Crofts.

Revusky, S. H., & Garcia, J. (1970). Learned associations over long delays. In G. H. Bower & J. T. Spence (Eds.), *The psychology of learning and motivation* (Vol. 4). New York: Academic Press.

Reynolds, W. F., & Pavlik, W. B. (1960). Running speed as a function of deprivation period and reward magnitude. *Journal of Comparative and Physiological Psychology, 53,* 615–618.

Richman, S., & Gholson, B. (1978). Strategy modeling, age, and information-processing efficiency. *Journal of Experimental Child Psychology, 26,* 58–70.

Rilling, M., & Caplan, H. J. (1973). Extinction-induced aggression during errorless discrimination learning. *Journal of the Experimental Analysis of Behavior, 20,* 85–91.

Ritter, B. (1968). The group desensitization of children's snake phobia using vicarious and contact desensitization procedures. *Behavior Research & Therapy, 6,* 1–6.

Roane, H. S., Fisher, W. W., & Sgro, G. M. (2001). Effects of a fixed time schedule on aberrant and adaptive behavior. *Journal of Applied Behavior Analysis, 34,* 333–336.

Robert, M. (1990). Observational learning in fish, birds, and mammals: A classified bibliography spanning over 100 years of research. *The Psychological Record, 40,* 289–311.

Robinson, B., & Bradley, L. J. (1998). Adaptation to transition: Implications for working with cult members. *Journal of Humanistic Counseling, Education, and Development, 36*(4), 212–222.

Robinson, G. (2001). *By order of the President: FDR and the internment of Japanese Americans.* Cambridge, MA: Harvard University Press.

Roediger, H. L. (1990). Implicit memory: Retention without remembering. *American Psychologist, 45*(9), 1043–1056.

Rosenhan, D. L. (1973). On being sane in insane places. *Science, 179,* 250–258.

Rosekrans, M. A., & Hartup, W. W. (1967). Imitative influences of consistent and inconsistent response consequences to a model on aggressive behavior in children. *Journal of Personality and Social Psychology, 7,* 429–434.

Rosenzweig, M. R., Krech, D., Bennett, E. L., & Diamond, M. C. (1968). Modifying brain chemistry and anatomy by enrichment or impoverishment of experience. In G. Newton & S. Levine (Eds.), *Early experience and behavior: The psycho-biology of development* (pp. 258–298). Springfield, IL: Thomas.

Rothbaum, B. O., Hodges, L. F., Kooper, R., Opdyke, D., Williford, J. S., & North, M. (1995). Virtual reality graded exposure in the treatment of acrophobia: A case report. *Behavior Therapy, 26,* 547–554.

Rothbaum, B. O., Hodges, L., Ready, D., Graap, K., & Alarcon, R. (2001). Virtual reality exposure therapy for Vietnam veterans with posttraumatic stress disorder. *Journal of Clinical Psychiatry, 62,* 617–622.

Rothbaum, B. O., Hodges, L. F., Smith, S., Lee, J. H., & Price, L. (2000). *A controlled study of virtual reality exposure therapy for the fear of flying.* Paper presented at the annual meeting of the American Psychological Association, Washington, DC.

Roylance, F. D. (1986, September 17). Atmosphere of hate in nation described. (Baltimore) *Evening Sun*, p. A10.

Rundquist, E. A. (1933). Inheritance of spontaneous activity in rats. *Journal of Comparative Psychology, 16,* 415–438.

Ruppell, G. (1975). *Bird flight.* New York: van Nostrand Reinhold.

Russell, D. E. H. (1986). *The secret trauma: Incest in the lives of girls and women.* New York: Basic.

Russell, M., Dark, K. A., Cummins, R. W., Ellman, G., Callaway, E., & Peeke, H. V. S. (1984). Learned histamine release. *Science, 225,* 733–734.

Rutter, M. L. (1997). Nature-nurture integration: The example of antisocial behavior. *American Psychologist, 52,* 390–398.

Savory, T. (1974). *Introduction to arachnology.* London: Muller.

Schiffman, K., & Furedy, J. J. (1977). The effect of CS-US contingency variation on GSR and on subjective CS-US relational awareness. *Memory and Cognition, 5,* 273–277.

Schlinger, H. D. (1996). How the human got its spots. *Skeptic, 4,* 68–76.

Schlinger, H. D., & Blakely, E. (1994). The effects of delayed reinforcement and a response-produced auditory stimulus on the acquisition of operant behavior in rats. *The Psychological Record, 44,* 391–409.

Schlinger, H. D., Blakely, E., & Kaczor, T. (1990). Pausing under variable-ratio schedules: Interaction of reinforcer magnitude, variable-ratio size, and lowest ratio. *Journal of the Experimental Analysis of Behavior, 53,* 133–139.

Schneider, J. W. (1973). Reinforcer effectiveness as a function of reinforcer rate and magnitude: A comparison of concurrent performance. *Journal of the Experimental Analysis of Behavior, 20,* 461–471.

Schneider, S. (1990). The role of contiguity in free-operant unsignaled delay of positive reinforcement: A brief review. *The Psychological Record, 40,* 239–257.

Schneirla, T. C. (1944). A unique case of circular milling in ants, considered in relation to trail following and the general problem of orientation. *American Museum Novitiates, 1253,* 1–26.

Schreibman, L., Kaneko, W. M., & Koegel, R. L. (1991). Positive affect of parents of autistic children: A comparison across teaching techniques. *Behavior Therapy, 22,* 479–490.

Schuett, G. W., Clark, D. L., & Kraus, F. (1984). Feeding mimicry in the rattlesnake Sistrurus catenatus, with comments on the evolution of the rattle. *Animal Behavior, 32,* 624–629.

Schwartz, B., & Gamzu, E. (1979). Pavlovian control of operant behavior: An analysis of autoshaping and its implication for operant conditioning. In W. K. Honig & J. E. R. Staddon (Eds.), *Handbook of operant behavior*. Englewood Cliffs, NJ: Prentice Hall.

Schwartz, B., & Lacey, H. (1982). *Behaviorism, science, and human nature*. New York: Norton.

Schwartz, B., Schuldenfrei, R., & Lacey, H. (1978). Operant psychology as factor psychology. *Behaviorism, 6*, 229–254.

Scott, J. P. (1958). *Animal behavior*. Chicago: University of Chicago Press.

Scott, J. P. (1962). Critical periods in behavioral development. *Science, 138*, 949–958.

Sears, R. R., Maccoby, E. E., & Levin, H. (1957) *Patterns of child rearing*. Evanston, IL: Row, Peterson.

Seligman, M. E. P. (1970). On the generality of the laws of learning. *Psychological Review, 77*, 406–418.

Seligman, M. E. P. (1971). Phobias and preparedness. *Behavior Therapy, 2*, 307–321.

Seligman, M. E. P. (1975). *Helplessness: On depression, development, and death*. San Francisco: Freeman.

Seligman, M. E. P., & Hager, J. L. (Eds 1972a). *Biological boundaries of learning*. New York: Appleton-Century-Crofts.

Seligman, M. E. P., & Hager, J. L. (1972b, August). Biological boundaries of learning: The sauce-bearnaise syndrome. *Psychology Today*, 59–61, 84–87.

Seligman, M. E. P., & Maier, S. F. (1967). Failure to escape traumatic shock. *Journal of Experimental Psychology, 74*, 1–9.

Servatius, R. J., Brennan, F. X., Beck, K. D., Beldowicz, D., & Coyle-Di Norcia, K. (2001). Stress facilitates acquisition of the classically conditioned eyeblink response at both long and short interstimulus intervals. *Learning and Motivation, 32*(2), 178–192.

Shanks, D. R., & St. Johns, M. F. (1994) Characteristics of dissociable human learning systems. *Behavioral and Brain Sciences, 17*, 367–447.

Shapiro, G. L. (1982). Sign acquisition in a home-reared, free-ranging orangutan: Comparisons with other signing apes *American Journal of Primatology, 3*, 121–129.

Shapiro, K. J. (1991a, July). Rebuttal by Shapiro: Practices must change. *APA Monitor*, 4.

Shapiro, K. J. (1991b, July). Use morality as a basis for animal treatment. *APA Monitor*, 5.

Sharpless, S. K., & Jasper, H. H. (1956). Habituation of the arousal reaction. *Brain, 79*, 655–680.

Sheffield, F. D. (1965). Relation between classical conditioning and instrumental learning. In W. F. Prokasy (Ed.), *Classical conditioning* (pp. 302–322). New York: ACC.

Sheffield, F. D., Roby, T. B., & Campbell, B. A. (1954). Drive reduction versus consummatory behavior as determinants of reinforcement. *Journal of Comparative and Physiological Psychology, 47*, 349–354.

Sheffield, F. D., Wulff, J. J., & Barker, R. (1951). Reward value of copulation without sex drive reduction. *Journal of Comparative and Physiological Psychology, 44*, 3–8.

Shepher, J. (1971). Mate selection among second-generation kibbutz adolescents and adults: Incest avoidance and negative imprinting. *Archives of Sexual Behavior, 1*, 293–307.

Shermer, M. (1997). *Why people believe weird things*. New York: Freeman.

Sherry, D. F., & Galef, B. G., Jr. (1984). Cultural transmission without imitation: Milk bottle opening in birds. *Animal Behavior, 32*, 937–938.

Shiffman, K., & Furedy, J. J. (1977). The effect of CS-US contingency variation on GSR and on subjective CS-US relational awareness. *Memory and Cognition, 5*, 273–277.

Shimp, C. P. (1976). Short-term memory in the pigeon: Relative recency. *Journal of the Experimental Analysis of Behavior, 25*, 55–61.

Sidman, M. (1953). Avoidance conditioning with brief shock and no exteroceptive warning signal. *Science, 118*, 157–158.

Sidman, M. (1960/1988). *Tactics of scientific research*. Boston: Authors Cooperative.

Sidman, M. (1962). Reduction of shock frequency as reinforcement for avoidance behavior. *Journal of the Experimental Analysis of Behavior, 5*, 247–257.

Sidman, M. (1966). Avoidance behavior. In W. K. Honig (Ed.), *Operant behavior.* New York: Appleton-Century-Crofts.

Sidman, M. (1989a). Avoidance at Columbia. *The Behavior Analyst, 12,* 191–195.

Sidman, M. (1989b). *Coercion and its fallout.* Boston, MA: Authors Cooperative.

Siegel, S. (1975). Evidence from rats that morphine tolerance is a learned response. *Journal of Comparative and Physiological Psychology, 89,* 498.

Siegel, S. (1983). Classical conditioning, drug tolerance, and drug dependence. In R. G. Smart, F. B. Glaser, Y. Israel, H. Kalant, R. E. Popham, & W. Schmidt (Eds.), *Research advances in alcohol and drug problems* (Vol. 7). New York: Plenum.

Siegel, S. (1984). Pavlovian conditioning and heroin overdose: Reports by overdose victims. *Bulletin of the Psychonomic Society, 22,* 428–430.

Siegel, S., Hinson, R. E., Krank, M. D., & McCully, J. (1982). Heroin "overdose" death: Contribution of drug-associated environmental cues. *Science, 216,* 436–437.

Simmons, R. (1924). The relative effectiveness of certain incentives in animal learning. *Comparative Psychology Monographs,* No.7.

Simonton, D. K. (1987). Developmental antecedents of achieved eminence. *Annals of Child Development, 5,* 131–169.

Siqueland, E., & Delucia, C. A. (1969). Visual reinforcement on non-nutritive sucking in human infants. *Science, 165,* 1144–1146.

Skaggs, K. J., Dickinson, A. M., & O'Connor, K. A. (1992). The use of concurrent schedules to evaluate the effects of extrinsic rewards on "intrinsic motivation": A replication. *Journal of Organizational Behavior Management, 12,* 45–83.

Skinner, B. F. (1938). *The behavior of organisms: An experimental analysis.* New York: Appleton-Century-Crofts.

Skinner, B. F. (1948). Superstition in the pigeon. *Journal of Experimental Psychology, 38,* 168–172.

Skinner, B. F. (1951). How to teach animals. *Scientific American, 185,* 26–29.

Skinner, B. F. (1953). *Science and human behavior.* New York: Free Press.

Skinner, B. F. (1957). *Verbal behavior.* New York: Appleton-Century-Crofts.

Skinner, B. F. (1962). Two "synthetic" social relations. *Journal of the Experimental Analysis of Behavior, 5,* 531–533.

Skinner, B. F. (1966). The phylogeny and ontogeny of behavior. *Science, 153,* 1205–1213.

Skinner, B. F. (1968) *The technology of teaching.* Englewood Cliffs, NJ: Prentice-Hall.

Skinner, B. F. (1969). *Contingencies of reinforcement: A theoretical analysis.* New York: Appleton-Century-Crofts.

Skinner, B. F. (1977). *The shaping of a behaviorist.* New York: Knopf.

Skinner, B. F. (1981). Selection by consequences. *Science, 213,* 501–504.

Skinner, B. F. (1983a). *A matter of consequences.* New York: Knopf.

Skinner, B. F. (1983b). Can the experimental analysis of behavior rescue psychology? *The Behavior Analyst, 6,* 9–17.

Skinner, B. F. (1983c). Intellectual self-management in old age. *American Psychologist, 38,* 239–244.

Skinner, B. F. (1984). The evolution of behavior. *Journal of the Experimental Analysis of Behavior, 41,* 217–221.

Skinner, B. F. (1987). What is wrong with daily life in the western world? In B. F. Skinner (Ed.), *Upon further reflection* (pp. 15–31). New York: Prentice Hall.

Skodak, M., & Skeels, H. M. (1949). A final follow-up study of one hundred adopted children. *Journal of Genetic Psychology, 75,* 85–125.

Sloane, H. N., Endo, G. T., & Della-Piana, G. (1980). Creative behavior. *The Behavior Analyst, 3,* 11–22.

Slonaker, J. R. (1912). The normal activity of the albino rat from birth to natural death, its rate of growth and the duration of life. *Journal of Animal Behavior, 2*(1), 20–42.

Slot machines for children promote gambling, critics say. (1998, May 26). *The (Wilmington, DE) News Journal,* p. B4.

Smith, G. S., & Delprato, D. J. (1976). Stimulus control of covert behaviors (urges). *The Psychological Record, 26,* 461–466.

Smith, K. (1984). "Drive": In defence of a concept. *Behaviorism, 12,* 71–114.

Smith, P. (1995). *Democracy on trial: The Japanese American evacuation and relo-*

cation in World War II. New York: Simon & Schuster.

Solomon, R. L., & Wynne, L. C. (1953). Traumatic avoidance learning: Acquisition in normal dogs. *Psychological Monographs, 67* (whole no. 354).

Spence, K. W. (1936). The nature of discrimination learning in animals. *Psychological Review, 43,* 427–449.

Spence, K. W. (1937). The differential response in animals to stimuli varying within a single dimension. *Psychological Review, 44,* 430–444.

Spence, K. W. (1953). Learning and performance in eyelid conditioning as a function of intensity of the UCS. *Journal of Experimental Psychology, 45,* 57–63.

Spence, K. W. (1960). *Behavior theory and learning.* Englewood Cliffs, NJ: Prentice-Hall.

Spetch, M. L., Wilkie, D. M., & Pinel, J. P. J. (1981). Backward conditioning: A reevaluation of the empirical evidence. *Psychological Bulletin, 89,* 163–175.

Staats, A. W., & Staats, C. K. (1958). Attitudes established by classical conditioning. *Journal of Abnormal and Social Psychology, 57,* 37–40.

Staats, C. K., & Staats, A. W. (1957). Meaning established by classical conditioning. *Journal of Experimental Psychology, 54,* 74–80.

Stack, S. (1987). Celebrities and suicide: A taxonomy and analysis, 1948–1983. *American Sociological Review, 52*(3), 401–412.

Stack, S. (2000). Media impacts on suicide: A quantitative review of 293 findings. *Social Science Quarterly, 81*(4), 957–971.

Staddon, J. E. R. (1991). Selective choice: A commentary on Herrnstein (1990). *American Psychologist, 46,* 793–797.

Staddon, J. E. R. (2001). *The new behaviorism: Mind, mechanism, and society.* Philadelphia, PA: Psychology Press.

Staddon, J. E. R. (2001). *Adaptive dynamics: The theoretical analysis of behavior.* Cambridge, MA: MIT Press.

Staddon, J. E. R., & Simmelhag, V. L. (1971). The "superstition" experiment: A reexamination of its implications for the principles of adaptive behavior. *Psychological Review, 78,* 3–43.

Stanny, C. J., & Johnson, T. C. (2000). Effects of stress induced by a simulated shooting on recall by police and citizen witnesses. *American Journal of Psychology, 113*(3), 359–386.

Stern, A. (1971, August). *The making of a genius.* Miami: Hurricane House.

Stewart, T., Ernstam, H. T., Farmer-Dougan, V. (2001, May 25–29). *Operant conditioning of reptiles: Conditioning two Galapagos and one African Spurred Tortoises to approach, follow and stand.* Poster presented at the annual convention of the Association for Behavior Analyis, New Orleans.

Strickland, L. H., & Grote, F. W. (1967). Temporal presentation of winning symbols and slot-machine playing. *Journal of Experimental Psychology, 74,* 10–13.

Strum, S. C. (1987). *Almost human: A journey into the world of baboons.* New York: Random House.

Stuart, E. W., Shimp, T. A., & Engle, R. W. (1987). Classical conditioning of consumer attitudes: Four experiments in an advertising context. *Journal of Consumer Research, 14,* 334–349.

Sullivan, M. W., & Calvin, A. D. (1959). Further investigation of verbal conditioning. *Psychological Reports, 5,* 79–82.

Suzuki, T., & Moriyama, T. (1999). Contingency of food reinforcement necessary for maintenance of imprinted responses in chicks. *Japanese Journal of Animal Psychology, 49,* 139–156.

Tarpley, H. D., & Schroeder, S. R. (1979). Comparison of DRO and DRI on rate of suppression of self-injurious behavior. *American Journal of Mental Deficiency, 84,* 188–194.

Taylor, J. A. (1951). The relationship of anxiety to the conditioned eyelid response. *Journal of Experimental Psychology, 41,* 81–92.

Templeman, T. L., & Stinnett, R. D. (1991). Patterns of sexual arousal and history in a "normal" sample of young men. *Archives of Sexual Behavior, 20,* 137–150.

Terrace, H. S. (1963a). Discrimination learning with and without "errors." *Journal of the Experimental Analysis of Behavior, 6,* 1–27.

Terrace, H. S. (1963b). Errorless transfer of a discrimination across two continua. *Journal of the Experimental Analysis of Behavior, 6,* 223–232.

Terrace, H. S. (1964). Wavelength generalization after discrimination learning with and without errors. *Science, 144*, 78–80.

Terrace, H. S. (1972). By-products of discrimination learning. In G. H. Bower (Ed.), *The psychology of learning and motivation* (Vol. 5). New York: Academic Press.

Terrace, H. S. (1979). *Nim*. New York: Knopf.

30,000 obscene calls traced. (1991, July 7). *The (Wilmington, DE) News Journal*, p. A2.

Thomas, D. R. (1981). Studies of long-term memory in the pigeon. In N. E. Spear & R. R. Miller (Eds.), *Information processing in animals: Memory mechanisms*. Hillsdale, NJ: Erlbaum.

Thomas, D. R. (1991). Stimulus control: Principles and procedures. In W. Ishaq (Ed.), *Human behavior in today's world*. New York: Praeger.

Thomas, D. R., Mood, K., Morrison, S., & Wiertelak, E. (1991). Peak shift revisited: A test of alternative interpretations. *Journal of Experimental Psychology: Animal Behavior Processes, 17*, 130–140.

Thompson, R. F. (2000). Habituation. In A. E. Kazdin (Ed.), *Encyclopedia of Psychology* (pp. 47–50). New York: Oxford University Press.

Thorndike, E. L. (1898). Animal intelligence. *Psychological Review Monographs, 2*(8).

Thorndike, E. L. (1901). The mental life of the monkeys. *Psychological Review Monographs, 3*(15).

Thorndike, E. L. (1911). *Animal intelligence: Experimental studies*. New York: Hafner.

Thorndike, E. L. (1927). The law of effect. *American Journal of Psychology, 39*, 212–222.

Thorndike, E. L. (1932). *Fundamentals of learning*. New York: Teachers College Press.

Thorndike, E. L. (1936). Autobiography. In C. Murchison (Ed.), *A history of psychology in autobiography* (Vol. 3). Worcester, MA: Clark University Press.

Thorndike, E. L. (1968). *Human learning*. Cambridge, MA: MIT Press. (Original work published 1931)

Thorpe, W. H. (1963). *Learning and instinct in animals*. London: Methuen.

Thune, L. E., & Underwood, B. J. (1943). Retroactive inhibition as a function of degree of interpolated learning. *Journal of Experimental Psychology, 32*, 185–200.

Timberlake, W. (1980). A molar equilibrium theory of learned performance. In G. H. Bower (Ed.), *The psychology of learning and motivation* (Vol. 14). New York: Academic Press.

Timberlake, W., & Allison, J. (1974). Response deprivation: An empirical approach to instrumental performance. *Psychological Review, 81*, 146–164.

Timberlake, W., & Lucas, G. A. (1985). The basis of superstitious behavior: Chance contingency, stimulus substitution, or appetitive behavior? *Journal of the Experimental Analysis of Behavior, 44*, 279–299.

Tinbergen, N. (1951). *The study of instinct*. Oxford: Clarendon Press.

Todd, D. E., Besko, G. T., & Pear, J. J. (1995, May 26–30). *Human shaping parameters: A 3-dimensional investigation*. Poster presented at the meeting of the Association for Behavior Analysis, San Francisco, CA.

Todd, J. T., & Morris, E. K. (1992). Case histories in the great power of steady misrepresentation. *American Psychologist, 47*, 1441–1453.

Todd, J. T., Morris, E. K., & Fenza, K. M. (1989). Temporal organization of extinction-induced responding in preschool children. *The Psychological Record, 39*, 117–130.

Todorov, J. C., Hanna, E. S., & Bittencourt de Sa, M. C. N. (1984). Frequency versus magnitude of reinforcement: New data with a different procedure. *Journal of the Experimental Analysis of Behavior, 4*, 157–167.

Tolman, E. C., & Honzik, C. H. (1930). Degrees of hunger, reward and non-reward, and maze learning in rats. *University of California Publications in Psychology, 4*(16), 241–256.

Torrey, E. F., & Knable, M. B. (2002). *Surviving manic depression: A manual on bipolar disorder for patients, families, and providers*. New York: Basic.

Tracy, J. A., Ghose, S. S., Stecher, T., McFall, R. M., & Steinmetz, Joseph E. (1999). Classical conditioning in a nonclinical obsessive-compulsive population. *Psychological Science, 10*(1), 9–13.

Trapold, M. A. (1970). Are expectancies based upon different positive reinforcing events discriminably different? *Learning and Motivation, 1*, 129–140.

Treiman, R. (2000). The foundations of literacy. *Current Directions in Psychological Science, 9*(3), 89–92.

Trowbridge, M. H., & Cason, H. (1932). An experimental study of Thorndike's theory of learning. *Journal of General Psychology, 7*, 245–260.

Trut, L. N. (1999). Early canid domestication: The farm-fox experiment. *American Scientist, 87*, 160–169.

Tryon, R. C. (1940). Genetic differences in maze-learning ability in rats. In *Thirty-ninth yearbook of the National Society for the Study of Education. Intelligence: Its nature and nurture, Part I. Comparative and critical exposition.* Bloomington: Public School Publishing Co.

Tune, G. S. (1964). A brief survey of variables that influence random generation. *Perceptual and Motor Skills, 18*, 705–710.

Turkkan, J. S. (1989). Classical conditioning: The new hegemony. *Behavioral and Brain Sciences, 12*, 121–179.

Ulrich, R. E., & Azrin, N. A. (1962). Reflexive fighting in response to aversive stimuli. *Journal of the Experimental Analysis of Behavior, 5*, 511–520.

Ulrich, R. E., Hutchinson, R. R., & Azrin, N. H. (1965). Pain-elicited aggression. *The Psychological Record, 15*, 116–126.

Underwood, B. J. (1957). Interference and forgetting. *Psychological Review, 64*, 49–60.

U. S. Department of Health and Human Services. (1988). *The health consequences of smoking: Nicotine addiction. A report of the Surgeon General* (DHHS Publication No. (CDC) 88–8406). Washington, DC: U. S. Government Printing Office.

Valentine, C. W. (1930). The innate bases of fear. *Journal of Genetic Psychology, 37*, 394–420.

Vander Wall, S. B. (1982). An experimental analysis of cache recovery by Clark's nutcracker. *Animal Behavior, 30*, 80–94.

Vander Wall, S. B. (1991). Mechanisms of cache recovery by yellow pine chipmunks. *Animal Behavior, 41*, 851–863.

Van Houten, R. (1983). Punishment: From the animal laboratory to the applied setting. In S. Axelrod & J. Apsche (Eds.), *The effects of punishment on human behavior.* New York: Academic Press.

Van Tighem, Patricia. (2001). *The bear's embrace: A story of survival.* New York: Pantheon.

Venn, J. R., & Short, J. G. (1973). Vicarious classical conditioning of emotional responses in nursery school children. *Journal of Personality and Social Psychology, 28*, 249–255.

Verplanck, W. S. (1955). The operant, from rat to man: An introduction to some recent experiments on human behavior. *Transactions of the New York Academy of Sciences, 17*, 594–601.

Vollmer, T. R., Marcus, B. A., & Ringdahl, J. E. (1995). Noncontingent escape as treatment for self-injurious behavior maintained by negative reinforcement. *Journal of Applied Behavior Analysis, 28*, 15–26.

Vollmer, T. R., Ringdahl, J. E., Roane, H. S., & Marcus, B. A. (1997). Negative side effects of noncontingent reinforcement. *Journal of Applied Behavior Analysis, 30*, 161–164.

Volpicelli, J. R., Ulm, R. R., Altenor, A., & Seligman, M. E. P. (1983). Learned mastery in the rat. *Learning and Motivation, 14*, 204–222.

Vyse, S. A. (1997). *Believing in magic: The psychology of superstition.* New York: Oxford University Press.

Vyse, S. A., & Heltzer, R. A. (1990). *Intermittent consequences and problem solving: The experimental control of "superstitious" beliefs.* Paper presented at the 98th annual convention, American Psychological Association, Boston, MA.

Wagenaar, W. A. (1971). Serial randomness as a function of duration and monotony of a randomization task. *Acta Psychologica, 35*, 70–87.

Wagner, G. A., & Morris, E. K. (1987). "Superstitious" behavior in children. *The Psychological Record, 37*, 471–488.

Wallace, K. J., & Rosen, J. B. (2000). Predator odor as an unconditional fear stimulus in rats: Elicitation of freezing by Trimethylthiazoline, a component of fox feces. *Behavioral Neuroscience, 114*(5), 912–922.

Wallace, P. (1976). Animal behavior: The puzzle of flavor aversion. *Science, 193*, 989–991.

Walters, R. H., & Brown, M. (1963). Studies of reinforcement of aggression: III. Transfer of responses to an interpersonal situation. *Child Development, 34*, 563–571.

Ward, R., Jensen, P., & Chance, P. (2002, February 3). *Learning history and superstition.* Paper presented at the annual meeting of the California Association for Behavior Analysis, San Francisco.

Warden, C. J., & Aylesworth, M. (1927). The relative value of reward and punishment in the formation of a visual discrimination habit in the white rat. *Journal of Comparative Psychology, 7*, 117–128.

Warden, C. J., Fjeld, H. A., & Koch, A. M. (1940). Imitative behavior in cebus and rhesus monkeys. *Journal of Genetic Psychology, 56*, 311–322.

Warden, C. J., & Jackson, T. A. (1935). Imitative behavior in the rhesus monkey. *Journal of Genetic Psychology, 46*, 103–125.

Wasserman, E. (1989). Pavlovian conditioning: Is temporal contiguity irrelevant? *American Psychologist, 44*, 1550–1551.

Wasserman, I. M. (1984). Imitation and suicide: A reexamination of the Werther Effect. *American Sociological Review, 49*(3), 427–436.

Watanabe, S., Sakamoto, J., & Wakita, M. (1995). Pigeons' discrimination of paintings by Monet and Picasso. *Journal of the Experimental Analysis of Behavior, 63*, 165–174.

Watriss, W. (1982, October). Kinfolk: The people of the ridge. *Science Digest*, 83–88, 103.

Watson, D. L., & Tharp, R. G. (1989). *Self-directed behavior: Self-modification for personal adjustment* (4th ed.). Monterey, CA: Brooks/Cole.

Watson, J. B. (1908). Imitation in monkeys. *Psychological Bulletin, 5*, 169–178.

Watson, J. B. (1930/1970). *Behaviorism.* New York: Norton & Co.

Watson, J. B., & Rayner, R. (1920). Conditioned emotional reactions. *Journal of Experimental Psychology, 3*, 1–4.

Watson, J. B., & Watson, R. R. (1921). Studies in infant psychology. *Scientific Monthly, 13*, 493–515.

Webb, R. C. (1999). *Psychology of the consumer and its development: An introduction.* New York: Kluwer Academic/Plenum.

Weil, J. L. (1984). The effects of delayed reinforcement on free-operant responding. *Journal of the Experimental Analysis of Behavior, 41*, 143–155.

Weiner, H. (1983). Some thoughts on discrepant human-animal performance under schedules of reinforcement. *The Psychological Record, 33*, 521–532.

Weiner, J. (1994) *The beak of the finch: A study of evolution in our time.* New York: Knopf.

Wells, H. K. (1956). *Pavlov and Freud: I. Toward a scientific psychology and psychiatry.* London: Lawrence and Wishart.

Wertheim, M. (1999, March/April). The odd couple. *The Sciences*, 38–43.

Wickramasekera, I. (1976). Aversive behavior rehearsal for sexual exhibitionism. *Behavior Therapy, 7*(2), 167–176.

Widom, C. S. (1989). Does violence beget violence? A critical examination of the literature. *Psychological Bulletin, 106*, 3–28.

Wiehe, V. R. (1992). Abusive and nonabusive parents: How they were parented. *Journal of Social Services Research, 15*, 81–93.

Wilder, D. A., Masuda, A., O'Conner, C., & Baham, M. (2001). Brief functional analysis and treatment of bizarre vocalizations in an adult with schizophrenia. *Journal of Applied Behavior Analysis, 34*, 65–68.

Wilgoren, J. (2001, May 3). Lawsuits touch off debate over paddling in schools. *The New York Times* electronic edition.

Wilkenfield, J., Nickel, M., Blakely, E., & Poling, A. (1992) Acquisition of lever-press responding in rats with delayed reinforcement: A comparison of three procedures. *Journal of the Experimental Analysis of Behavior, 58*, 431–443.

Wilkes, G. (1994). *A behavior sampler.* North Bend, WA: Sunshine Books.

Williams, J. E. (1966). Connotations of racial concepts and color names. *Journal of Personality and Social Psychology, 3*, 531–540.

Williams, J. E., & Edwards, C. D. (1969). An exploratory study of the modification of color concepts and racial attitudes in preschool children. *Child Development, 40*, 737–750.

Williams, S. B. (1938). Resistance to extinction as a function of the number of reinforcements. *Journal of Experimental Psychology, 23*, 506–522.

Wilson, E. O. (1978). *On human nature.* Cambridge, MA: Harvard University Press.

Wilson, E. O. (1984) *Biophilia.* Cambridge, MA: Harvard University Press.

Wilson, K. G., & Blackledge, J. T. (1999). Recent developments in the behavioral analysis of language: Making sense of clinical phenomena. In M. J. Dougher (Ed.), *Clinical behavior analysis.* Reno, NV: Context Press.

Winston, A. S., & Baker, J. E. (1985). Behavior-analytic studies of creativity: A critical review. *The Behavior Analyst, 8,* 191–205.

Wolf, M. M., Birnbrauer, J. S., Williams, T., & Lawler, J. (1965). A note on apparent extinction of the vomiting behavior of a retarded child. In L. P. Ullmann & L. Krasner (Eds.), *Case studies in behavior modification* (pp. 364–366). New York: Holt, Rinehart, & Winston.

Wolf, M. M., Braukmann, C. J., & Ramp, K. A. (1987). Serious delinquent behavior as part of a significantly handicapping condition: Cures and supportive environments. *Journal of Applied Behavior Analysis, 20,* 347–359.

Wolf, M. M., Risley, T., Johnson, M., Harris, F., & Allen, E. (1967). Application of operant conditioning procedures to the behavior problems of an autistic child: A follow-up and extension. *Behavior Research and Therapy, 5,* 103–111.

Wolfe, J. B. (1936). Effectiveness of token-rewards for chimpanzees. *Comparative Psychology Monographs, 12*(5).

Wolfe, J. B. (1936). Effectiveness of token rewards for chimpanzees. *Comparative Psychological Monographs, 12,* No. 60.

Wolpe, J. (1973). *The practice of behavior therapy* (2nd ed.). New York: Pergamon.

Wolpe, J., & Plaud, J. J. (1997). Pavlov's contributions to behavior therapy: The obvious and the not so obvious. *American Psychologist, 52,* 966–972.

Woman pesters ex-lover with 1,000 calls a day. (2000, February 24). Reuters News Service on American Online.

Woodruff-Pak, D., Papka, M., Romano, S., & Li, Y. (1996). Eyeblink classical conditioning in Alzheimer Disease and cerebrovascular dementia. *Neurobiology of Aging, 17*(4), 505–512.

Woods, P. J. (1974). A taxonomy of instrumental conditioning. *American Psychologist, 29*(8), 584–597.

Wyatt, W. J. (2001). TV, films, blamed for child violence. *Behavior Analysis Digest, 13*(2), 7.

Yando, R. M., Seitz, V., & Zigler, E. (1978). *Imitation: A developmental perspective.* Hillsdale, NJ: Erlbaum.

Yates, A. J. (1958). Symptom and symptom substitution. *Psychological Review, 65*(6), 371–374.

Yerkes, R. M., & Morgulis, S. (1909). The method of Pavlov in animal psychology. *Psychological Bulletin, 6,* 257–273.

Zahavi, A., & Zahavi, A. (1999). *The handicap principle: A missing piece of Darwin's puzzle.* New York: Oxford University Press.

Zeiler, M. D. (1984). The sleeping giant: Reinforcement schedules. *Journal of the Experimental Analysis of Behavior, 42,* 485–493.

Zener, K. (1937). The significance of behavior accompanying conditioned salivary secretion for theories of the conditioned response. *American Journal of Psychology, 50,* 384–403.

Zimmerman, D. W. (1957). Durable secondary reinforcement: Method and theory. *Psychological Review, 64,* 373–383.

Author Index

Subject Index

TO THE OWNER OF THIS BOOK:

I hope that you have enjoyed *Learning and Behavior*, 5th edition, as much as I have enjoyed writing it. I'd like to know your thoughts and experiences about the book as a student. In what ways did it help you, and how can I make it better for future readers?

School and address: _____

Department: _____

Instructor's Name: _____

1. What did you like most about *Learning and Behavior*, 5th edition?

_____

_____

2. What did you like least about the book? _____

_____

_____

3. Were all of the chapters of the book assigned for you to read? _____

    If not, which ones weren't? _____

4. Were the in-text queries helpful? _____

5. Were the Practice Quizzes and Review Questions helpful to you?

    Why or why not? _____

_____

_____

6. In the space below, or on paper attached, please let me know any additional reactions that you may have. (For example, did you find any of the chapters particularly difficult?) I'd be delighted to hear from you!

_____

_____

_____

_____

OPTIONAL:

Your name: _____ Date: _____

May Wadsworth quote you, either in promotion for *Learning and Behavior,* 5th edition, or in future publishing ventures?

Yes: _____ No: _____

Sincerely yours,

Paul Chance, Ph.D.

FOLD HERE

BUSINESS REPLY MAIL

FIRST CLASS   PERMIT NO. 358   PACIFIC GROVE, CA

POSTAGE WILL BE PAID BY ADDRESSEE

NO POSTAGE NECESSARY IF MAILED IN THE UNITED STATES

ATTN: *Paul Chance* _____

WADSWORTH PUBLISHING
511 FOREST LODGE ROAD
PACIFIC GROVE, CA 93950-9968

FOLD HERE